# So Dreadfull a Judgment

# So Dreadfull a Judgment

## PURITAN RESPONSES TO KING PHILIP'S WAR 1676–1677

*EDITED BY*
Richard Slotkin
*AND*
James K. Folsom

*Wesleyan University Press*
Published by University Press of New England
Hanover and London

LIBRARY OF CONGRESS CATALOGING IN PUBLICATION DATA

Main entry under title: So dreadfull a judgment.
Bibliography: p.
Includes index.
1. King Philip's war, 1675–1676—Sources.
2. Puritans—New England—Sources 3. New England—History—Colonial period, ca. 1600–1775—Sources
I. Slotkin, Richard, 1942- II. Folsom, James K.
E83.67.S65 973.2'4 77-14847
ISBN 0-8195-5027-2
ISBN 0-8195-6058-8 pbk.

Manufactured in Canada

First edition, 1978

First paperback edition, 1978; second printing, 1988; third printing 1999

Now these *are* the nations which the LORD left, to prove Israel by them, *even* as many of *Israel* as had not known all the wars of Canaan;

Only that the generations of the children of Israel might know to teach them war, at the least such as before knew nothing thereof . . .

And they were to prove Israel by them, to know whether they would hearken unto the commandments of the LORD, which he commanded their fathers by the hand of Moses.

Judges, 3: 1–2, 4.

# *CONTENTS*

# *LIST OF ILLUSTRATIONS*

# So Dreadfull a Judgment

# INTRODUCTION

> God hath denounced it as an heavy Judgment which should come to punish that sin of mens unfaithfulness . . . *I will give them into the hands of their enemies, and into the hand of them that seek their life, and their dead bodies shall be for meat to the fowles of heaven, and to the beasts of the earth.* Now all these things have been verified upon us. Is it nothing that so many have been cut off by a bloody and barbarous Sword? Is it nothing that Widows and Fatherless have been multiplyed among us? that in a small Plantation we have heard of eight widows, and six and twenty fatherless children in one day? And in another of the Villages of our Judah, of seven Widows and about thirty fatherless children all at once: How can we speak of such things without bleeding Lamentation: . . . Alas that New-England should be brought so low in so short a time (for she is come down wonderfully) and that by such vile enemies, by the Heathen, yea the worst of the Heathen . . .
>
> Increase Mather
> *An Ernest Exhortation* (1676)

KING PHILIP'S WAR (1675–76) was the great crisis of the early period of New England history. Although it lasted little more than a year, it pushed the colonies perilously close to the brink of ruin. Half the towns in New England were severely damaged—twelve completely destroyed—and the work of a generation would be required to restore the frontier districts laid waste by the conflict. The war all but wrecked the colonial economy, disrupting the trade in furs and drawing off so much manpower that the fishing fleet and seaborne trade with the West Indies were almost totally inactivated. The colonial treasuries, chronically short of capital in the best of times, spent nearly a hundred thousand pounds on the war, bringing them to the edge of bankruptcy. Beyond the loss in treasure, King Philip's War was (in proportion to population) the costliest in lives of any American war. Out of a total population of some thirty thousand, one in every sixteen men of military age was killed or died as a result of war; and many men, women, and children were killed, were carried to captivity, or died of starvation and exposure as a result of the Indian raids. In a society so relatively small, made up of small towns and hamlets, such extensive losses meant that virtually every community and every family would partake of the common grief. And losses on this scale among the mature male population posed a real threat to, the colony's continued prosperity, perhaps even its survival.[1]

The spiritual and psychological immiseration caused by the war, the trauma to the Puritan colonists in their collective spirit, was as deeply felt as the material and personal losses the colonies suffered. For a community that had conceived of itself as the new chosen people of the Lord, as the bearers of Christian light to heathen darkness, the fulfillers of a divinely inspired "Errand into the Wilderness," the catastrophe of the Indian war threatened their most basic assumptions about their own character and their relationship to God and to their new world. Surely the war was a sign of God's anger toward a people that had degenerated from the days of the colonial patriarchs, who had been so wonderfully protected from just such catastrophes. But was the Lord so angered that he would withdraw his sanction from the Puritan enterprise, or was the war merely a warning of the possible consequences of any further degeneration of virtue?

It was to answer such questions as these that Puritan ministers, historians, and memoirists began to study and investigate the events of King Philip's War. The process of reconstructing and explaining the history of their great calamity forced the Puritans to test the strength and validity of their central dogmas and structuring myths against overwhelming and unprecedented experience. In the process their myths and dogmas underwent transformations that marked the beginning of a new phase in the cultural history of the colonies. The histories, narratives, and sermons collected in this anthology represent the range of Puritan responses to the war; and in them the first stages of the process of transformation can be traced.

## *Myth and History*

Although this compilation reproduces some of the basic documents on which histories of King Philip's War have been based, its purpose is not primarily that of documentation. Rather, the usefulness of these texts lies in their aptness for the study of how events are processed by the consciousness of historians and participant-reporters. The small scale of the events and communities concerned, and the relative thoroughness with which the Puritan society and mind have been analyzed, make it possible for us to compare the real and the written event, and to account for the characteristic distortions that appear in the latter.

Before discussing the specific events and texts, it may be useful to outline some of the theoretical bases of this approach to historiography. The historian—like the poet, novelist, memoirist, journalist—seeks both to explain and to reconstruct some important human experience. In doing so he filters the "unprocessed historical record" through his consciousness, choosing (intuitively or analytically) from among several possible approaches to the definition of a "problem," the selection of "important" (and rejection of "unimportant") data, and the adoption of a mode of narrative or analytical expression.[2] Because the historian or writer is a person socialized in a particular culture, time, and place, the language in which he thinks has certain characteristic biases or emphases that shape the making of each of these decisions. For the Puritans, the historian's problem was to find out the will of God; and for this purpose extraordinary and atypical events were as useful as (or perhaps more useful than) events that reflected the political events or the character of common life, such as interest the modern political or social historian.

Two sorts of language are used to explain historical experience: a language of concepts, ordered analytically or rhetorically, and a language of evocative symbols, ordered as narratives. Using the former, we can extrapolate the ideology of a culture from its attempts to explain itself; using the latter, we can define the mythology of that culture.

As the term is used here, *mythology* signifies a set of structuring narratives and a vocabulary of evocative or value-laden symbols, sanctioned by traditional usage, derived from and related to the historical life of a people, which provide and sanction scenarios of response to social, psychological, and metaphysical crises. A myth is a story that functions in a society as an explanation of historical experience—an explanation that both accounts for the past and offers a model of behavior that will propitiate the gods of history to yield a prosperous future. Myths arise from a coincidence of social and personal anxieties and needs, and historical circumstances. They enter the language as narratives, accounts of experience that possess a special coherence; and because these accounts strike a responsive chord in the minds of people in a given time and place, they are habitually used models of human (and divine) action.

Symbolism develops as a kind of shorthand, in which some key element in the tale becomes a totem evocative of the whole myth—as the display of the cross evokes the myth-narrative of the Christian messiah to an audience of believers. Over time a vocabulary of myths and symbols develops and is communicated as an aspect of language from generation to generation. The symbols and scenarios of myth are thus available in the way that language is available; they appear on the surface of consciousness when the right circumstances evoke them.[3]

Both ideology and mythology are conceptual systems that define a culture's world view and sanction particular social and political structures and behaviors. But the logic of ideological statement is rhetorical or philosophical in form, and offers the pretense at least that it is open to argument and refutation. On the other hand, the logic of myth is the logic of narrative, which is less open to rational criticism or refutation. Ideology postulates that certain causes produce certain effects. The myth-narrative reduces the postulate to a symbol, perhaps a personification, then embodies the cause-effect theory in a pseudofactual sequence of events that proceeds according to a formulaic pattern.

In literate and bourgeois societies, mythology and ideology coexist. The periodic transformations of social order, the great mobility and alienation of populations perpetually undercut the mythologies of traditional communities by transforming or uprooting the communities themselves. The effort to reconcile the contradictions between the ideology of a changing society and the traditional mythology of the previous, vanishing social order, become a major preoccupation of literary enterprise.

In colonial New England, the literary press was controlled by the magistrates and ministers who were likewise preeminent in civil and ecclesiastical government. The writings they authorized for publication were those that served to reinforce the religious and political ideology that provided the sanction for their continued hegemony. To a larger degree than a modern reader might credit, the works they produced (and sold widely) were likely to be abstruse and sophisticated discussions of theology, dealing with the conceptual bases of Puritan society on an explicitly ideological plane. However, the Puritan rulers also believed in the efficacy of the moral fable, the didactic narrative, to inculcate by example the dispositions of heart that mere intellectual conviction could not attain. Moreover, since the whole purpose of historical analysis was, in the Puritan view, ultimately metahistorical—to discover the timeless purpose of God in temporal events—the mythic element in Puritan historiography is especially important.[4]

The formation and active functioning of mythological and ideological systems have been associated with periods of social stress or cultural transformation.[5] Cultures do not need to develop elaborate ideological rationales for their social arrangements until something calls those arrangements into question. But where ideology rationalizes, the narratives of myth define new situations by referring to traditional history; and thus they persuade their audience that the demands of a new epoch can be met without breaking traumatically with the wisdom and world-concepts of the past. The mythic reading of a historical moment typically denies the fact of change or the presence of new and troubling elements. Rather, it represents such events as episodes in an eternal and recurrent cycle, akin to the cycles of nature. As Roland Barthes says, "driven to having either to unveil or liquidate [a] concept, [myth] will naturalize it. We reach here the very principle of myth: it transforms history into nature," the contingent into the absolute and eternally recurring.[6] In the case of the Puritans, the disorienting experience of the Indian war evoked a mythology compounded of Biblical tradition, typological exegesis, theology and philosophy, a revolutionary political and economic ideology, and the peculiar life experiences of individuals and communities. The literary efforts of Puritan ideologists and mythmakers brought all these to bear in an attempt to rationalize and explain the war, buttressing rhetorical argument with typological readings of Biblical myths and with evocative renderings of those moments in the history of their own community that had already become charged with symbolic meaning. Out of their efforts emerged mythology and ideology capable of rationalizing the historical process by which the New World was to be colonized and the deep dilemmas of politics, religion, and the troubled human heart resolved.

## *The Colonial Crisis*

The crisis that came to a head in the 1670s was a complex one, extending beyond the important area of white-Indian relations to touch every aspect of the colonies' experience. The war exploded in a society that was already riven by an internal crisis: at war with itself over Indian policy and over economic, social, political, and religious issues, and divided along lines of class, race, interest, and generation. Cutting across and complicating these internal crises were the political conflicts that set the four colonies of New England against one another in political and commercial rivalry, after two decades of relative harmony under the confederation of the United Colonies. And overriding all these conflicts was the external threat posed by the restoration of the Stuarts and revival of efforts to reassert the primacy of royal government in the colonies.[7]

Puritan writers of the 1670s tended to see New England as having left its best and brightest days behind. The new leadership of the colonies looked back on the early years of the settlements as a heroic or a golden age, in which divinely inspired patriarchs commanded a willing and responsive people in a greater-than-Moses' Exodus, leaving an England in the throes of degeneracy and destruction to accomplish an "Errand into the Wilderness" at Christ's calling. Benjamin Tompson, in his poem on King Philip's War, speaks of a time when Puritan colonists lived simply and abstemiously, in a harmony of classes and generations that prevented the rich from oppressing and the poor from envying and kept the son obedient to the father's will:

> The times wherein old *Pompion* was a Saint,
> When men far'd hardly yet without complaint
> On vilest *Cates;* the dainty *Indian Maize*
> Was eat on *Clamp-shells* out of wooden Trayes
> Under thatched *Hutts* without the cry of *Rent,*
> And the best *Sawce* to every Dish, *Content.*
> . . .
>
> These golden times (too fortunate to hold)
> Were quickly sin'd away for love of gold.

In the praise of the past we are to read a critique of the present, in which Puritan virtues in dress, deportment, economics, and piety have degenerated, and with them the perfection of social and religious form that supposedly characterized the original colony.

That this view of the past constituted a kind of myth needs no argument. However, the social need that required the making of such a myth does require description. The Puritan adult of 1670 had seen the colonies of New England emerge from the hardships and strife of the early years (1620–1640) to a condition of relative ease and prosperity. The scattered villages of refugees from the religious and political strife of Stuart England had succeeded in establishing themselves as permanent colonies, despite (or perhaps because of) the home government's inability to aid or support them. Without outside help they negotiated land settlements with the local Indians and fought a successful war against the only tribe to resist them (the Pequots) in 1637–1638. They had negotiated an uneasy peace with the neighboring Dutch colony in New York and with the more distant French colonies in Acadia and Canada. They had established the authority of their governments against local dissenters and the claims of rival colonizing enterprises.

The New England colonies had also managed to overcome to a degree the religious and political differences that divided them. Although all four colonies were Puritan in their Calvinistic religious affinities, they represented very different sects and tendencies within the Puritan movement. Plymouth had been settled by Separatist Puritans, who favored a break with the Church of England. Massachusetts was settled by non-Separatist Puritans, who adhered to a conservative theology and polity; although opposed to the idea of separating from the Church of England, they were strict Congregationalists and opponents of any form of religious heirarchy, including both the Catholic and Anglican priesthoods and the Presbyterian system favored by the Scottish Calvinists. Connecticut and Rhode Island were formed by groups of religionists who could not fit themselves into the Massachusetts system: in Connecticut Thomas Hooker developed a quasi-Presbyterian polity, while Rhode Island became a refuge for heterodox religious radicals of various kinds—Seekers, Baptists, and Quakers most prominent among them. Although such differences of ideology, theology, and politics remained essentially unreconciled, the four colonies were able to work out a *modus vivendi:* in 1643 they agreed to form a confederation, the United Colonies of New England—an organization that enabled them to better control intercolonial trade and dealings with the Indians and with their Dutch rivals in New York. During the civil wars between the King and Parliament, the confederation enabled them to maintain that uneasy neutrality they felt was essential to their survival.

The end of the civil wars had seen the triumph of Puritanism, albeit in a somewhat imperfect form (as Massachusetts, at least, judged such things); and the New England colonies grew steadily in population, land, and wealth. What had seemed in 1630 a temporary refuge for a visionary experiment in biblical government had become, by 1650, a permanent home for a population that had successfully put its house in order and had begun to think of itself as native.

However, beginning in 1660, symptoms of a reversal in direction began to manifest themselves. Cromwell's government might not have suited the doctrinal preferences of the Massachusetts clergy, but it was infinitely preferable to the restoration of the Stuarts, which occurred in 1660. Following on the heels of his restoration, Charles II initiated efforts to revoke the charters under which the colonies had enjoyed virtual self-government for thirty or forty years. Puritans saw in his efforts a threat to their economic and political freedom to tax themselves and regulate their trade with other countries and colonies; and behind the economic motive, they saw a desire to expunge the last of the hated Puritan jurisdictions from the map. In 1674 Charles had appointed Sir Edmund Andros governor of New York, and given him a charge to unite New York and New England under a single royal governorship. This was followed by the appointment of royal commissioners to review the colonial governments and to take from them the colonial charters that were the basis of colonial liberties. It is worth noting also that after King Philip's War Andros succeeded for a time in governing New England; although he was overthrown by the Puritans in the American version of the Glorious Revolution of 1689, the Protestant King William III carried through the Stuarts' policy on the charters (and even rewarded the deposed Andros with another governorship).

Thus the era of King Philip's War saw the end of the first phase of colonization, in which the colonies had been nearly self-governing, and the beginning of the century of struggle over royal government that would end in the War of Independence.

## *The Internal Crisis of Puritanism*

The external crisis of Puritan affairs was accompanied by an internal crisis; to understand this we need to know something of the character of colonial Puritanism. The founders of the New England colonies had been motivated by powerful religious commitment. They conceived of themselves as the vanguard of the Protestant movement that had begun in Germany a century before, as a new chosen people of the Lord, predestined to provide a government that would serve as a model of Christian piety and polity. They were initially uncertain whether New England was to be their Israel or their Wilderness of Sinai—that is, a permanent dwelling-place for the elect of God, or a temporary refuge in which their religious affections and institutions would be tried, purged, and perfected. Originally, they aimed at the conquest of England, and the world, for their faith; but whether that conquest would require their physical return to England, or only the force of their example as a "Citty on a Hill" was left for later generations to resolve. In general they were convinced that they had a mission, a divinely appointed "Errand into the Wilderness," and that in going to the New World they were fulfilling an evident purpose of God. Success in their worldly endeavor was only one element of their concern, perhaps not the most important; for beyond the vicissitudes of temporal history, the Puritans read the larger "history of Redemption," and in that larger, sacred history, they believed they would play a part. At the height of their fervor, they believed that the history of New England was a sequel to the history that began with Genesis and was transfigured in Revelation. Just as they interpreted the "types" of the Old Testament for previsions of the coming of Christ, so they read events in their own lives in the light of the sacred and apocalyptic symbolism of the New Testament.

Their religion was first an affirmation of what they were, and second a means for conceptualizing and finally controlling the political order they inherited from a moribund feudalism. They were men and women who had risen from relative poverty to relative economic independence on the strength of their own intelligence, skill, and labor. Hence their ideal of human behavior emphasized the importance of labor in one's "calling" as an act of worship; they saw the archetypal story of a human life as the narrative of a transformation of sinner into saint, the base into the glorified. The conversion experience was central to Puritan consciousness: the achievement of such an experience was the test for admission to full membership in the Puritan community. Although theology often explicitly disclaimed any necessary connection between religious conversion and the transformation of the poor man into a wealthy one, such an association was part of the Puritan mythology from the beginning and became most marked in the later stages of Puritanism's history. Yet the achievement of wealth for its own sake was never portrayed as an acceptable goal in colonial New England. Even in prosperity, the Puritan was to adopt the style of poverty, affirming as eternal virtues those forms of self-deprivation that he had necessarily undergone in accumulating wealth from his own labors and contrasting the virtuousness of acquired wealth with the ostentatious consumption of inherited resources by the crown and its aristocracy.

In their political and social application, Puritan doctrine and practice were revolutionary. By asserting the sovereignty of God and the necessity of an individual approach to the central matter of the soul's salvation, the Puritans effectively eliminated the mediating powers that sustained the church and state of a dying feudalism—that is, the Catholic priesthood and the King. They attacked these institutions (and their sustaining ideologies) at the high level of theological and political doctrine and on the more basic level of community organization. In the feudal community, membership in the church (conferred by infant baptism) was virtually automatic—one was born into the religious community. Similarly, traditional forms determined one's position in the community and one's relationship of fealty or obligation to one's lord and king. By insisting that the experience of religious conversion by a morally mature individual (not necessarily a chronological adult) was the precondition for church and community membership (and hence for salvation), the Puritans struck a blow at the organic or traditional character of religious communities—just as their economic and social mobility had already served to weaken or dissolve the secular forms that had held the feudal commune together. Even before they embarked for the New World, Puritans were almost by definitions "voyagers" or "pilgrims": people who had left the security and well-defined social order of traditional society to pursue their "calling" to follow Christ. The solidarity of the traditional commune was behind them; they needed to create new models of order and community to maintain their sense of place.

The central institutions of the Puritans' new order were a new model community and a new model family. The congregation was to be the basic communal unit: not an organic community (at least at first) but a select community of Visible Saints—Puritans who had experienced bona fide conversion, and were deemed to be among the elect. The head of the congregation was to be an educated minister, "called" or elected by the community; the larger community would provide a body of ministers, educated at Harvard College or in England, from which to choose. The minister's role was essentially that of teacher, his sermons called "lectures." He was deemed to be better informed than his parishioners on scriptural evidence and doctrinal theory; yet his access to grace was no greater than theirs, and he was in no sense a mediator between the individual parishioner and the Deity.

This educative model of the relations between minister and congregation was paralleled by familial and political relationships. The male head of a household was expected to be the teacher of the small congregation that was his family, providing moral as well as physical nurture to those dependent on him. The class of dependents included his wife and children, and also any household servants, particularly if these were heathens—that is, African or Indian slaves or bondservants. Similarly, civil officials were to hold a tutelary relationship to the citizens, legislating for the moral benefit of the people by providing for public education and support of ministers and by enforcement of the Sabbath and related "blue laws." The tutelary role was particularly important as a rationale for the colonial Indian policy. The conversion of the heathen and their subjection to English law were tasks enjoined upon the colonial governments both by their charters and by the practical exigencies of political affairs. Both of these tasks could readily be conceived as analogous to the tutelary relations of superiors to dependents sanctioned in the religious and household organization of the society.

Symbolically and actually, the Puritan concern with their children was central to their enterprise. Among the motives cited by Bradford for the removal of the Pilgrims to what they believed was a howling wilderness was his fear for the children:

> For many of their children, that were of best disposition, and gracious Inclinations (haveing learn to bear the yoake in their youth) and willing to bear parte of their parents burden, were (often times) so oppressed with their hevie labours, that though their minds were free and willing, yet their bodies bowed under the weight of the same, and became decrepid in their early youth; the vigor of nature being consumed in the very budd as it were. But that which was more lamentable and of all sorowes most heavie to be borne, was that many of their children, by these occasions, and the great licentiousness of youth in that country, and the manifold temptations of the place, were drawn away by evill examples . . . So that they saw their posteritie would be in danger to degenerate and be corrupted.[8]

Something of the same reasoning lay behind the Puritan emigration of 1630.

But the conditions of life in the colonies did not make for the sort of education that the Puritans had originally conceived. Their idea of the New World had been expressed in essentially negative terms: it was a place that had no plagues, no priests, no kings, no external forces to interfere with religious life such as they had known in England. Physical hardship and the enmity of wild beasts and Indians were not in the same class of opponents as royal Charles and Archbishop Laud. However, American conditions posed threats to the Puritan system that they could not have anticipated. Far from being a purely negative quantity, the presence of the wilderness and the Indian profoundly affected the development of the Puritan community by being both more threatening and less antipathetic than anticipated. The wilderness was not the Desert of Sinai, but a fertile forest well endowed with game, lumber, and arable land; the Indians were not Canaanites or Amalekites, but for the most part amenable (at first) to selling or sharing their land with Englishmen. Thus one of the first threats to the solidarity of each colony and the uncomplicated education of the children was the opportunity for cheap land on the borders. The secular motive, the desire for economic independence—which was included in the Puritan notion of "calling"—thus came up against the communitarian concept on which the congregation/colony was based. One of the recurring themes in the writings of conservative Puritans like the Mathers is the condemnation of the tendency for land-hungry Puritans to desert the "institutions of God" to pursue secular prosperity in the wilderness.[9]

This basic conflict had both a political-economic and a religious side. The successful frontiersmen who lived beyond the reach of minister and magistrate were economic competitors of the established ruling class of the towns—the class of "Men of Note" from whom ministers and magistrates were traditionally drawn. Their communities sought representation in the legislature; and since the establishment of congregations on the borders lagged somewhat behind the pace of settlement, the frontiersmen also constituted a pressure group for the dismantling of the theocratic church-state connection, by which citizenship was restricted to members of congregations. Moreover, the ministers complained that the conditions of border life were such as to distract the people from religious concerns, so that a nonreligious spirit, rather than a religious one, was the result of a wilderness education. After the first generations of American-born children had grown to maturity, these tensions produced a form of class struggle within the Puritan community that threatened to divide it in its struggle with Andros and the Crown.[10]

In the early days of the colonies, when religious feeling was higher, the frontier had also provided refuge for religious and political dissidence. With the cooperation of the Crown and the Indians, Roger Williams was able to establish the heterodox colony of Rhode Island; Antinomian settlers founded New Hampshire; and Thomas Hooker established a distinctly different form of church government in Connecticut. These colonies represented competing sovereignties, sanctuaries for religious "guerrillas" like the Quakers, and thus undermined the Puritan attempt to keep the means of government and manner of education "in conformity with the end wee aim at."

The conditions of life in America forced changes in governmental form and ultimately in religious doctrine as well. The power and importance of the new proprietors of the frontier districts eventually forced the pace of democratization in New England. In church government, the problems of organizing congregations in a wilderness compelled the Congregationalists to organize in a more hierarchical fashion than their theory justified. In Connecticut this took the extreme form of quasi-Presbyterian organization, but even Massachusetts was forced by events to emphasize the power and doctrinal preeminence of the Boston ministry as a counterweight to frontier secularism and heterodoxy. The intense bonds of familial feeling that united these exiles in their isolation and their perilous position eventually forced modification of the standards for admission to the congregation and thus affected the basic structure of the Puritan community.

This last point needs further discussion. Ministers had remarked a decline in church membership, which was attributed to a decline in the religious fervor of the American-born second generation of colonists and a consequent falling off in the number of legitimate conversion experiences. Because of the linkage between church membership and political citizenship in the Puritan colonies, the consequences of this tendency were political and social as well as religious. The respectable children of converted parents (with other well-behaved and useful citizens) were being excluded from participation in the political life of their society, with the result that their sense of affiliation with and loyalty to that society might be weakened. The contradiction between the Puritan ideals of a viable Bible commonwealth and of purely reformed churches had been apparent quite early in colonial history, but by the 1660s the crisis had become acute. A ministerial synod in 1662 recognized the necessity of accepting a Half-Way Covenant, according to which children of converted congregants, if they were of a Christian disposition and well behaved, could be admitted to conditional communion.

The controversy over the Half-Way Covenant revealed some of the complex ways in which the Puritan community divided itself. Orthodox ministers divided on the issue, and the synod worked out elaborate compromises that failed to satisfy everyone. Since the religious doctrine and polity of the colonies differed, they responded differently; there was deep division between congregations and ministers and between those inside and those presently outside the covenant.[11] These last oppositions were in some ways the most crucial, since the laity resisted the change longer than the ministry. At the least, the opposition indicated the presence of a critical attitude toward the ministers. Beyond this, the opposition to extended membership by those already in the congregation suggests the existence of a privileged party within the community—one reluctant to divide its privileges of status and power with newcomers.

It was in the midst of this crisis over church membership and ministerial authority that King Philip's War broke out; and the fear and insecurity produced by the war helped resolve the controversy in favor of the Half-Way Covenant.

In a society organized like that of the Puritan colonies, religious and social conflicts are never entirely unrelated. If the generation gap manifested itself as a decline in religious fervor in church, it manifested itself in daily life as a preoccupation with getting wealthy by acquiring land—chiefly Indian land. Land-hunger turned the minds of the colonists away from spiritual and toward worldly things; it led them to move beyond the reach of established churches and approved ministers. Land-hunger therefore was cited by the ministers as a precipitating cause of the war. Frontiersmen in turn blamed the ministers for "coddling" the Indians in the hope of making converts. In the first year of the war there was a near-riot when a band of the "Commonality" turned from attempting to lynch some Indian prisoners to trying the same thing on two members of the ruling elite: the minister-missionary John Eliot and the magistrate Captain Guggins.[12] Increase Mather and Nathaniel Saltonstall also noted the frequency of internal conflicts among the different classes in the colonial population, especially the growing disrespect and disaffection for figures of authority.[13]

Things never went as far in New England in 1676 as they did at the same time in Virginia, but a comparison of events in the two colonies is useful. In Virginia the ambitions and fears of frontier planters clashed with the desire of the royal governor to maintain a monopoly of trade with the Indians. The rebels, led by a recent immigrant named Nathaniel Bacon, first attacked a band of friendly Indians, precipitating a war; they then used their forces for a march on the capital, which they held temporarily.[14] In New England there was less concern with trade than with the missionary enterprise and with a complex struggle for Indian lands. But in both colonies the ambitions of an entrepreneurial or pioneering class of frontiersmen and would-be proprietors clashed with the need of the authorities to control access to the Indians and to the various forms of wealth they possessed.

Thus in both colonies the Indian war was related directly to the external conflict of Royal and Colonial governments, and the internal conflict of social classes and parties; and in New England, these were related in turn to religious divisions. Thus the Indian war precipitated conflicts inherent in the structure of colonial society and offered the model of a conflict of races as an analogy for the internal and external conflicts of that society.

## *Puritan Indian Policy*

Before examining the symbolism of the Indian war, we need to look at the reality of Puritan Indian policy, not merely to expose the Puritan myths as rationalizations of policy but to show the necessary linkage between reality and functioning historical myth.

The character of Puritan Indian policy and its relation to the causes of the war are a matter of controversy among historians. In giving an account of the background of the war, it is therefore necessary to review briefly some of the major statements in the controversy. In addition to providing some insight into the historical facts of the case, this review is also necessary to an appreciation of the importance of the texts reprinted here, because many of the cultural and historical premises and factional alignments that characterize the present controversy have their roots in the apologetic and hortatory interpretations of the Indian war produced by the Puritans.

Traditional Puritan accounts (as the reader of this anthology will see) were mainly apologetic, seeking to justify Puritan actions toward the Indians and to paint Philip as motivated less by reason or policy than by pure malice—either inspired by the Devil, or by some innate Indian unreasonableness. "Indian spirits need / No grounds but lust to make a Christian bleed," as

Benjamin Tompson put it. Nineteenth-century historians modified this polemic in two ways. Proponents of manifest destiny saw the Indian's decline as an inevitable consequence of his racial and cultural weakness and the white man's vigor. An alternative school of writers, which romanticized the "Vanishing American," viewed King Philip as an Indian patriot, victimized by the rapacity as much as by the cultural and racial superiority of the whites. Although modern historians have attempted a more systematic analysis of the conflict, the pro- and anti-Indian schools persist. Douglas Leach's excellent history of the war, *Flintlock and Tomahawk,* tries to balance the views of the competing schools of thought. Leach concludes that the land-hunger of the whites and their rising power and population were the environing causes of the war, and that Philip's personal resentment of his tribe's declining power was the precipitating element. Alden Vaughan (in *New England Frontier*) delves more deeply into the prewar Indian policies of the English, and reaches conclusions more favorable to the Puritans.

Vaughan notes that Puritan frontiersmen did not push the Indian off his land (as later frontiersmen are said to have done). Rather, the Puritan government maintained careful controls over the taking-up of Indian land from first to last and sought to regulate white-Indian economic contacts fairly (according to their lights). Abuses occurred, but in a context that was procedurally fair, according to Vaughan. Nor were the Indians, Vaughan states, faced with depleted land and game resources as a result of Puritan purchases and development of land; rather, he asserts that game remained ample, that the land they sold was surplus (that is, not needed to supply food for the villages), and that the trade in furs was a source of prosperity. Nor did the Puritans exterminate the Indians in battle, although particular engagements might have had the character of massacres (such as the fight at the Pequot Fort in 1637 and the Swamp Fight of 1675). Vaughan also minimizes the cultural disorganization that, according to the anti-Puritan school, was inflicted by the whites on the Indians through their economic, political, and religious intrusions into Indian life. Vaughan admits that "under certain circumstances [the Indian] was the victim of discrimination. But for the seventeenth century, these were unusually mild proscriptions on a people that was not only an ethnic minority but a religious and political minority as well. And in each instance of discriminatory legislation, the motive was security, not social or religious bias."[15]

Vaughan is certainly correct in contrasting the organized, official process of land acquisition under Puritan governments with those that characterized certain phases of eighteenth- and nineteenth-century Indian policy, and in this he provides a necessary correction to Leach. However, he shares with the Puritan apologists a certain degree of ethnocentricity. It is important that Puritan attitudes be distinguished from current notions of race prejudice, but such distinctions cannot have affected the responses of seventeenth-century Indians to discrimination. Vaughan misses the significance of his own remark that the discriminated-against Indian was a religious and political minority within an ethnic minority (since the objects of discrimination were Indians who had not converted to Christianity). From the perspective of Indian culture, this minority status was a symptom of a sudden and precipitous decline in tribal power and solidarity: within a few generations the native ethnic majority had become a minority, internally divided into pro-Puritan and "pagan" or loyalist factions and sects. The objects of discrimination were those who remained true to the traditional ways of their culture. But for Vaughan, the resistance of the proponents of the older culture was simply irrational:

> While there is fascination in studying primitive cultures, there is no reason to expect the participants in those cultures to remain stagnant in the face of better alternatives. No society of any appreciable magnitude has ever chosen to reject "westernization," nor has western civilization itself remained static. Adaptation, amalgamation, and integration have been the hallmarks of human progress, not only in the material realm but in human rights and social justice. There is no reason why the Indians should not have shared in this almost universal trend if they so chose. There is some evidence that the far greater number of them would have thrown off the shackles of the Stone Age if their sachems had not been so reluctant to jeopardize their own power and wealth.[16]

Here Vaughan's characterization of the basis of conflict and the nature of white-Indian interaction is fairly close to that expressed a decade earlier by Samuel Eliot Morison in his introduction to Leach's book (although Vaughan's language is more temperate and his view of the Indians less crudely ethnocentric). Morison begins by paralleling King Philip's War with struggles of our own time, suggesting the use of the colonial struggle as a symbol or paradigm for modern wars of national liberation: "In view of our recent experiences of warfare, and of the many instances today of backward peoples getting enlarged notions of nationalism and turning ferociously on Europeans who have attempted to civilize them, this early conflict of the same nature cannot help but be of interest." The sarcasm implicit in Morison's image of the backward peoples' "enlarged" or excessive pretensions to nationhood suggests that the function of the parallel is to denigrate modern anticolonial wars by equating them with an Indian war. But Morison next suggests that such wars are of ultimate seriousness, despite the absurdity of the rebels' pretensions—in fact, it is the existence of a race that seems to be at stake: King Philip's War "was an intensely dramatic struggle, decisive for the survival of the English race in New England, and the eventual disappearance of the Algonkian Indians." He goes on to note that such wars have been characteristic of human history in general, suggesting that wherever advanced and backward races meet conflict seems inevitable, and the dispossession and extermination of the more backward race becomes inevitable:

> Behind King Philip's War was the clash of a relatively advanced race with savages, an occurrence not uncommon in history. The conquering race (and this is as true of the Moslems and Hindus as of Christians) always feels duty-bound to impose its culture upon the native; the native in the process of absorbing it acquires the conqueror's vices and diseases as well, and in the end is either absorbed or annihilated, the only compromise being a miserable existence on a "reservation." . . . The New England colonists tried hard to be fair and just to the natives; but their best was not good enough to absorb them without conflict.[17]

There are several obvious things wrong with Morison's analysis, deriving from his lumping various cultural, national, and ethnic entities under the term *race.* Behind this confusion lies a racialist view of the historical conflict and development of cultures and nations that derives from the racialist historians of the late nineteenth and the early twentieth centuries—Theodore Roosevelt, T. L. Stoddard, Madison Grant, and Brooks Adams. Racialist historiography, so characteristic of the Progressive Era and the start of America's imperial adventures in Asia and Latin America, conceived of historical progress as the result of conflict between superior and inferior races in which the processes of struggle served to perfect the dominant virtues of the superior group, so that the struggle for dominance ultimately produced higher forms of civilization rather than mere sequences of conquest. Part of the purpose of this anthology is to show the earliest phase of the development of that racialist historiography.

Vaughan's view is certainly preferable to Morison's. However, Vaughan's cultural biases are similar: westernization is synonomous with progress and liberty; to resist its course is therefore to choose poverty over well-being, stagnation over progress, and injustice over justice. He holds at one moment that no culture of any significance has ever *chosen* to resist westernization; yet the only recognizable symptom of such choice—the fact of resistance—he dismisses as the product either of irrational behavior or of the manipulation of the people by corrupt leaders and priests. Ethnocentric bias of this kind, while it is far from being equivalent to racism, does blind the historian to alternative interpretations of events. For example, Vaughan's characterization of Philip and the Indian shamans as a political and economic elite manipulating apathetic or politically disengaged followers is inaccurate as a portrayal of Indian political systems and behavior. To the extent that the chiefs had become more wealthy than their followers and the shamans had become the manipulators of an alienated tribal religious consciousness, their status and behavior were symptoms of that very cultural disintegration that Vaughan is at pains to deny: only through participation in the English trade nexus did Indian sachems become dominant men of property in the English sense. The English demanded stable leadership systems in their Indian allies and dependents, because they could understand no other basis for arriving at political and economic accommodations than that of agreement to contracts, covenants, or treaties by parties legally qualified to act in the name of their households or societies. This pattern of behavior fostered the development of Indian "governors" even when the

Puritans did not (as they occasionally did) intervene directly to create "sachems" favorable to their policies. Only if one shares the colonizing power's assumption of the universal validity and applicability of its peculiar political, social, and economic forms can one see the colonizers' self-protective laws and rationalizations as "reasonable" and native resentment and resistance as "irrational."

An alternative approach to the problem of Puritan Indian policy before King Philip's War is taken by Francis Jennings in *The Invasion of America: Indians, Colonialism, and the Cant of Conquest.* Jennings takes a fresh look at the primary evidence available on colonial Indian policies in French and Spanish as well as in English colonies and couples these white accounts with a reading of historical and anthropological studies of Indian responses to colonialization. In his account of King Philip's War he tries to set aside both the apologetic historical accounts on which Vaughan often relies and the ethnocentric bias of Vaughan and Morison; he attempts instead to reconstruct a plausible Indian interpretation of the events leading up to the outbreak of war.[18] Jennings has his own, anti-Puritan, bias, which he candidly admits; it leads him at times to force his evidence in directions that will yield maximum discredit to the Puritans. However, the major premises of his study do provide a view of the overall shape and tendency of Puritan policy that is persuasive and accounts for both the fact of the outbreak of war and the peculiar form of the struggle in ways that older interpretations do not.

Jennings accepts Vaughan's distinction between the entrepreneurial land-acquisition policies of later frontiers and the state-controlled policies of seventeenth-century New England. Cultural and religious factors, especially the Puritan desire to keep a tight moral and political rein on the frontier-going citizenry, partly explain this pattern of control. But the peculiar legal situation of the colonies was perhaps a more potent factor. The four colonies were allowed to hold their land and govern their citizenry because they possessed corporate charters, granted by the King, in whose name all the English lands of America were held. The royal title was deemed to have been derived from the consent of Indian kings to vassalage or subjection to the English monarch. But the charters of the four colonies were by no means simple or unencumbered titles. Plymouth was a colony settled because of an error in navigation and never had a completely valid charter. Rhode Island obtained its charter only after years of litigation against the Massachusetts interests and, even after obtaining it, faced a recurrent challenge from its neighbors. Connecticut was likewise an offshoot of Massachusetts; Hartford and New Haven for a while had separate charters. By 1660 even Massachusetts held its charter under sufferance and might have had it recalled by the Crown if its terms had not been fully observed. To shore up shaky titles, the Puritan colonies attempted to gain the fealty or clientage of particular tribes or clans of Indians: enjoyment of a protectorate over such an Indian entity would associate the colonial government with those deemed to possess the soil by primitive right; this might be of some help in litigation with other colonies or with the Crown itself, since the Crown's original possession was by purchases from the Indians.[19]

Before 1660 the motives for creating Indian clients were chiefly economic and only secondarily legal and political. Each colony sought to obtain the subjection of a particular tribe in order to have a monopoly of the right to purchase Indian lands. Such a monopoly not only was a source of profit to individuals but also created a legal basis for claims expanding the territory of the colony in question into Indian lands nominally controlled by a rival colony. In 1660 the restoration of the Stuarts led directly to a royal movement to invalidate or recall the charters; this effort was given force by the arrival in the colonies of royal commissioners, empowered to inspect and judge the colonies' execution of their charter obligations and to repossess the charters if possible. This move overthrew the precarious balance of power among the colonies themselves and between the colonies and the Indians. If the charters and jurisdictions of the colonies were to be redefined and if continued political existence as well as economic profit was at stake, then rivalry over disputed boundaries was bound to intensify.

In these circumstances the vigorous economic and agrarian expansion of the colonies became simultaneously a source of strength and of weakness. To acquire new lands from the Indians, to acquire new Indian clients, was essential both to prosperity and to the prospects for continued political survival. Yet the process of acquisition was bound to intensify intercolonial conflict, while the nature of the clientage system would also foster greater hostility among the Indian clients of rival colonies and between those rival clients and competing groups of white colonists.[20] For example, according to Jennings, Plymouth "continued to rely heavily for legality upon its protectorate over the Wampanoag Indians" of King Philip, for "so long as the Wampanoags dealt in land affairs exclusively with Plymouth, the protectorate served to convert Indian rights into colony rights." In this setting, the attempts of Rhode Island and Massachusetts to purchase land from the Wampanoags threatened not only Plymouth's economic future, but its political existence. For Rhode Island a similar case prevailed: religiously opposed to the other colonies, she depended for her economic and political survival on her control of the powerful Narragansett tribe as "client," while Connecticut and Massachusetts, if they could obtain the sanction of the Narragansetts, could expand into the borderland where the three colonies came together.[21]

The struggle for land and clients focused at two points: the Plymouth–Rhode Island border, where the two weakest colonies struggled for political and economic survival and competed for control of the Wampanoag client, and the Narragansett country on the Rhode Island–Connecticut–Massachusetts border, where the two most powerful colonies competed with each other and with the heterodox Rhode Islanders for control. In these circumstances the Indians possessed certain advantages as clients. Since their allegiance was being bid for, they had a chance to make good bargains for themselves, at least in theory. In practice, such "bargains" amounted to the right to sell their land to one colony or another or to place themselves under the protection (and the rule) of one colony or another; while short-term advantages could be achieved, the long-term advantages were few.

In the royal commissioners, the Indians had a potential defender of their rights and powers: "No colony hath any just right to dispose of any lands conquered from the natives, unless both the cause of the conquest be just and the land lie within the bounds which the king by his charter hath given it, nor yet to exercize any authority beyond those bounds." They followed this statement by voiding all grants made by "the usurped authority called the United Colonyes" and abrogating Massachusetts's discriminatory land-tenure law that gave "superior rights" to Christians as against non-Christians.[22] Here (as in the contest over the charters) the choice confronting the New England governments clearly linked continued control of Indian affairs with the maintenance of political autonomy.

The Indians, however, were unaware of their opportunity, engaged as they were in the problems of client politics, opposing the clients of rival protectors and bidding for the favor of their own. The fifteen years from the Restoration to King Philip's War are therefore marked by mutual hostilities and recriminations between the Wampanoags and the Narragansetts, each tribe seeking to ingratiate itself with the colonies at the other's expense while maintaining as far as possible its own tribal autonomy and the integrity of its remaining lands. Against this element creating rivalry between the two most powerful tribes in southern New England was the single common factor: both tribes were under pressure to sell their land and to commit themselves more firmly to subjection or vassalage to their respective protectors. The period from 1650 to 1675 saw the major Indian aggregations move from a rivalry of each against each to a limited unity that was both less than a pan-Indian movement and greater than any previous combination of tribes or clans.

The demands that the English made on their Indian clients seemed to them entirely fair and reasonable; how the Indians perceived them is another matter. Before the English came to dominate the scene, the Indians of New England lived in autonomous bands or clans, traditionally, but from an anthropological view not accurately, called "tribes." The groups shared a common Algonkian language base and had similar political structures and religious rituals. The bands of particular areas were associated by close ties of kinship and acknowledged occasional paramount chiefs; these loose aggregations were the "tribes" with which the colonies had to deal—the Wampanoags, Narragansetts, Pequots, Mohegans, and Nipmucks, to name the most important. Although each aggregation controlled an identifiable hunting/farming/fishing territory and engaged in rivalry for control with its neighbors, ties of kinship did apparently bind aggregation to aggregation. This factor, along with the Indians' lack of a definitive conception of private property, served to limit the intensity of intertribal conflict. To the New England Indians, the "sale" of land did not involve the relinquishment or conferral of exclusive possession in perpetuity but rather signified the admission of a neighbor (and potential kinsman) to the right of participation in the use of the available land. Such arrangements had obvious utility in minimizing the intensity of intertribal conflict and establishing a formula for the accommodation of rival territorial claims short of war.[23]

The English, on the other hand, did believe passionately in private property, likening it to the right of the individual to take care of his own religious conscience. Land sold to the English was land from which the Indian was to be forever excluded. Similarly, the political relations of Indian client to colonial government involved exclusive possession by the colony of the right to make deals with the Indians: like the land, the Indian's political power was to be permanently alienated. Moreover, an Indian band that placed itself under the dominion of an English colony thereby acquired a political obligation radically different from, and inconsistent with, the traditional ties of interband kinship.[24]

The work of English missionaries extended and compounded the difficulty. According to both Vaughan and Jennings, the sponsorship of Indian missions by the colonies represented an effort to acculturate the Indians to English ways as well as to convert them; Jennings sees certain aspects of Massachusetts missionary system as designed to reinforce the clientage system. Whatever the proportion of missionary fervor to *realpolitik* in the motivation behind the missions, they constituted an incursion into the very heart of tribal or band organization.[25] Just as the English governments insisted on exclusive monopolies of the land-selling power, the English church insisted that the convert to Christianity belong exclusively to his new church: he must abandon his village for a "Praying Town" and his Indian life style and language for those of the English, and he must set at naught the ties of kinship—even those that bound parents and children, husband and wife, and siblings. Thus the great missionary John Eliot chided Indians seeking conversion if they displayed a disposition to be overly lenient in disciplining their children or too passionate in mourning for their dead relatives, since to do so seemed to Eliot to be a questioning of God's judgment. And Eliot's pupil answered:

> Christ saith, he that loveth father, or mother, or wife, or Child, better than me, is not worthy of me. Christ saith, I

> must correct my Child, if I should refuse to do that, I should not love Christ . . . I am greatly grieved about these things, and now God tryeth me whether I love Christ or my Child best.[26]

Under any circumstances the success of such missionary work—however limited in numbers the converts might be—would have been perceived as a threat to the fundamental social bonds of Indian society: the ties of kinship and the unity of political and religious thought and behavior that characterize tribal societies. When to the progress of the missions is added the fact that the work of Eliot and his fellows was backed by several legislative acts designed to coerce Indians into accepting missionaries and their message, the causes for alarm among Indian chiefs and shamans become obvious.

Despite the history of clientage relationships between the English and the New England Indians, despite the traditional rivalries that pitted tribe against tribe, by 1670 it had become apparent to a number of Indian groups that they had perhaps more in common in their vulnerability to English pressure and dominance than they had to divide them. The English did not compete in the Indian manner: they played for keeps, not for shares, whether the area of rivalry was land acquisition, political control, or religious and cultural identification. Their modes and motives for warfare were also different in the same way: where ties of kinship and a disposition to limit the casualties in warfare (plus inefficient weaponry) had made precolonization Indian warfare only minimally bloody, the wars of the English against the Indians—exemplified by the Pequot War of 1637–1638—were characterized by indiscriminate massacre of men, women, and children. The Mohegan allies of the English in that war were appalled when the English, having taken the Pequot fort, proceeded to murder as many Indians as they could catch, burning many alive in the fort when they destroyed it. Nineteenth-century historians like Francis Parkman established as a given the premise that the warfare of Indian savages was originally a war of extermination. However, the best available evidence shows that the indiscriminate massacre was far more typical of European than of Indian warfare before the coming of the whites (and was in fact sanctioned, under certain circumstances, by the European laws of war). Only when Europeans had established precedents and offered bounties for such attacks, only when they supplied both efficient weaponry and an economic motive (dominance of the fur trade) for exterminating rather than merely warning off rivals, did wars of extermination become part of Indian-Indian warfare.[27]

The success of clientage politics in white-Indian relations before 1662 had been based on English exploitation of existing rivalries between the different tribal and clan groups of southern New England. After 1662 a number of tendencies in colonial politics and Indian policy impelled the different tribes and factions toward a kind of common understanding and sense of their relation to the English. The increase of English population and power—coupled with the exclusiveness of English land laws and discriminatory legislation—began to be felt as a potential threat to remaining Indian lands and to the political independence of each tribe or clan entity. More aggressive pursuit of direct land purchases, coupled with a more intrusive insistence by the colonial governments on the right to police land sales, made this demographic/economic threat palpable in political terms. The Pequot War had showed the Indians that "the English way of war had no limit of scruple or mercy" and that English weapons were greatly superior to those of the natives. And the clientage struggles sponsored by the English showed them to be unscrupulous in their pursuit of *realpolitik*. In addition, the work of missionaries like Eliot, especially when backed by the coercive and cooptative powers of the state, appeared to intrude directly into the cultural life of Indian communities, attacking the religious and familial bonds that were the social cement of such communities and coupling the work of a "fifth column" to the direct aggressions of the magistrates against Indian sovereignty. These factors, working separately and in combination on different communities of Indians, created the sense of common interest on which the so-called conspiracy of King Philip was based.[28]

Whether or not they were reached by Philip's emissaries, the Indians of New England—including large numbers of nominal converts—came over to the side of the hostiles. Included in the number were Indians like the Narragansetts, who had been Philip's chief rivals in the 1660s when as clients of Plymouth and Rhode Island, the Wampanoags and Narragansetts had jockeyed for influence and patronage. The only Indians who remained consistently loyal were the Pequots and Mohegans of Eastern Connecticut, whose role as Connecticut's clients coincided perfectly (in this instance) with their traditional hostility to the Narragansetts.

## *King Philip's War*

Metacom or "King Philip" was the paramount chief of the Wampanoags, who inhabited the islands of Narragansett Bay and the Mount Hope Peninsula, and whose kinship structures bound them closely to Indians of the southern Massachusetts coast out to the western half of Cape Cod.[29] Philip was the second of two sachems who succeeded the old friend of the Pilgrims, Massasoit; Philip's brother Wamsutta (or "Alexander") was the first. The Wampanoags and their sachems thus had a history of friendship for the English, attested by their being given English names; yet they remained "free sachems," whose oaths of obedience were given to the distant King rather than to any colonial jurisdiction. Their most independent action in their years of contact with the English was the division of their loyalties between Plymouth and Rhode Island colonies—that is, they sold land to both colonies rather than permitting either to monopolize and control their power to alienate their own land. Both Plymouth and Rhode Island had questionable charters, the former colony having been planted in error, and the latter having been established in despite of Massachusetts by Cromwell's government. Both colonies needed to establish a protectorate over the Wampanoags to control their land and to possess the primitive land-tenure that could establish their claim to a valid charter.

In 1664 Major Winslow of Plymouth seized Wamsutta by force to compel him to sell his land to Plymouth rather than to the weaker (and friendlier) colony of Rhode Island. In the course of his captivity to Winslow, Wamsutta fell ill and died, and Philip succeeded to the sachemship. Almost immediately, Philip was haled to Plymouth and accused of plotting rebellion; in the face of the military force (and the will to use it displayed in the seizure of Wamsutta), Philip swore his innocence and promised never to sell his lands without the consent of the Plymouth government. Thus fortified, Plymouth took up the legal challenge of

Rhode Island's charter, seeking both to destroy that colony's jurisdiction and to confirm its own.[30] Between 1665 and 1671 Plymouth used its advantageous settlement with Philip to expand its holdings at the neck of Mount Hope Peninsula. When the Indians objected to this settlement and menaced some settlers, Philip was summoned to Taunton and fined; he was additionally compelled to make a retroactive declaration that his people had always been subject to Plymouth colony as well as to the English King (which had manifestly not been the case before 1664).

Hoping to turn intercolonial rivalry to his advantage, Philip appealed from Plymouth to Boston, perhaps hoping that Massachusetts (like Rhode Island) would see in the retroactive submission to Plymouth a threat to Massachusetts lands bought privately of Philip's predecessors without the consent of Plymouth. But Massachusetts was not as vulnerable as Rhode Island, and Philip's appeal merely served to bind Plymouth more firmly to its northern neighbor; the two colonies combined to force Philip to sign a somewhat revised version of the Taunton agreement that left the Wampanoags subject to Plymouth.[31] Stung by the insulting and contemptuous manner of the English, directly threatened as chief by their intrusions upon his power and on the integrity of his territory, Philip began covertly to articulate Indian discontent, while maintaining outward friendship to the English. Whether or not he determined on war and how (or if) he planned to attack the English, are debated questions. He evidently attempted to gather his nearest neighbors into a kind of allegiance, but the alacrity with which outlying bands joined the war is testimony more to the ubiquitous effects of English encroachment than to the power of Philip as a conspirator. His designs were revealed to the English by the Sogkonate Squaw-sachem Awashonks, who told them to her good friend Benjamin Church, and by the murder of John Sassamon or Sausamon, a Praying Indian who was Philip's secretary and supposedly a spy for the English.

Philip led the first attack, on Swansea, Massachusetts, June 20, 1675—a Sabbath day, with the townsfolk in church. Troops from Massachusetts, Plymouth, and Rhode Island assembled at Miles' Garrison opposite Mount Hope Neck, Philip's home base; after a series of skirmishes, they attempted to "sweep" the neck on June 30. This ineptly executed retaliatory strike succeeded only in driving Philip from the neck and into closer contact with the Pocasset Indians, his allies. In a brief interlude of uneasy peace, the colonial governments attempted a diplomatic offensive, directed toward containing the war by overawing two powerful potential enemies, the Narragansetts of western Rhode Island and the Nipmucks of eastern and central Massachusetts – the latter a tribe that had been hitherto friendly to the English and that contained many villages of converts. Although the Narragansetts were kept temporarily neutral, the embassy to the Nipmucks failed, to the outraged astonishment of Massachusetts. By the middle of August hostilities had spread northward to the Nipmuck country and the upper Connecticut Valley, where Captains Thomas Wheeler and Edward Hutchinson were besieged at Brookfield by Nipmucks they had come to treat with. Although Philip fled northward from the Pocasset country to join the Nipmucks, English military efforts in this period of the war were ineptly conducted, marked by imperfect organization and general ignorance of the techniques of Indian warfare.

In the middle of August the Indians launched a series of concerted raids on the most exposed Massachusetts settlements. Lancaster, where Mary Rowlandson was later captured, was unsuccessfully attacked on August 19; Hadley, on September 1; and Northfield, which had to be abandoned, on September 2. English reaction was quick: the New England Confederation declared war against King Philip on September 9 and levied an army of one thousand to prosecute hostilities. But the skill to organize and apply such a force was still lacking. The two months that followed the declaration of war saw hostilities spread further to the north and east, saw the abandonment of Deerfield and the ambush of the retreating soldiers at Bloody Brook, and saw, finally, the breakdown of the peace arrangements with the powerful Narragansetts. Early in November the commissioners of the United Colonies, meeting in Boston, determined to send a force of a thousand men under Plymouth's General (and Governor) Winslow to attack the Narragansetts (still nominally at peace with the English) in their winter stronghold in the swamps of central Rhode Island. Marshaled at Wickford, R.I., this force marched on December 18 and attacked the palisaded village of the Narragansetts on the nineteenth. In the Swamp Fight that followed, approximately eighty English (including many officers) and six hundred Indians—men, women, and children—were killed. The English troops, enraged by the difficulties of the march and their losses in battle, apparently lost control and perpetrated something of a massacre, one consequence of which was the burning of the Indian village and with it the only available shelter for the army's wounded. Captain Benjamin Church, who had become something of an expert in Indian warfare and diplomacy, argued in vain against the destruction. Crippled by their losses from wounds and exposure and by a lack of provisions, the English were unable to pursue the fleeing Indians, who took refuge with the Nipmucks. This had the unfortunate result, which became apparent later, of isolating a revengeful enemy from its only available source of supply without having significantly crippled its retaliatory power.

During the winter Philip took many of his people to the Mohawk country in New York, seeking allies, arms, and ammunition. According to some accounts he attempted to embroil the Mohawks with the English, but his designs were penetrated; in any case, the Mohawks rebuffed him, attacked his camps, and inflicted a signal defeat on Philip.

Philip's return to New England coincided with the beginning of a great Indian offensive. Indian forces attacked frontier towns all along the Massachusetts border and deep in Plymouth territory. Among the towns they attacked was Lancaster, which they besieged for the second time on February 10, 1676. The Rowlandson garrison was successfully stormed and its defenders killed or taken prisoner, among them Mary Rowlandson—who, because of her husband's ministerial position, was (in the eyes of the Massachusetts government) the most notable of the war's captives. Although Rowlandson's was the only garrison captured of the six in the town, the threat of further siege caused the settlers to abandon Lancaster, which the Indians subsequently burned.

The Indians now pressed closer to Boston through the encircling belt of frontier towns, striking to within ten miles of Boston itself. To the south, Plymouth Town (capital of the colony) was attacked, and Captain Pierce's company was wiped out in an ambush on the Pawtucket River near Rehoboth on March 26; Providence was destroyed on March 29. Colonial authorities, fearing that towns would be deserted by their inhabitants, forbade settlers to leave their towns without official permission. To the north and east, settlers were attacked in the upper Connecticut Valley. In April an epidemic ravaged the New England towns, carrying off many colonists including former Governor John Winthrop; and the Indians gathered for a grand assault on Sudbury, seventeen miles from Boston.

This was the Indians' high water mark. In a day-long battle the attackers of Sudbury were defeated. Both sides suffered heavy losses; but the Indians were not able to replace their lost men, while the English were. On May 18–19 an English force under Captain Turner surprised and defeated a large Indian force at the Falls of the Connecticut near Deerfield; then he and about a quarter of his 150 soldiers were killed in an Indian counterattack. Although technically an Indian victory, this battle cost the Indians so many warriors and so great a quantity of their supplies that it constituted a major defeat. Pressing their advantage, the English launched other retaliatory raids against the Indians, who were both culturally and logistically unable to mount a long war of attrition. In June, Major Talcott led the English to a series of victories in the Hadley area; then in July he conducted an offensive sweep through the Narragansett country, inflicting two major defeats on the Indians. At the same time, the loss of leading chiefs like the Narragansett Canonchet, and the defection of allied Indians like the Sogkonates—wooed from Philip by Benjamin Church—took both heart and substance from Indian resistance.

With his allies surrendering in ever larger groups, Philip fled to his old home grounds about Mount Hope Neck. There he was isolated and hunted down by a party of rangers led by Benjamin Church, and was killed on August 12, 1676. Many of the surviving Visible Saints took grim pleasure in that final demonstration of the wonderful providence of God which delivered the widow and nine-year-old son of Philip—who had captured so many English women and children—into English hands and subsequent slavery in the West Indies.

With the surrender of the last sizeable band of Indian warriors on August 28 the war was to all intents and purposes finished. The Indian confederacy had been dealt a blow from which it never recovered, and Indian resistance to the whites in southern New England was finally at an end. Most of the Indian "rebels" who escaped execution were, with their wives and children, sold into slavery in the West Indies. Those who remained suffered the expropriation of lands and penal servitude on local plantations. The inroads of disease and cultural dissolution reduced most of the tribes and clans—both hostiles and friendlies—to the vanishing point before 1830.

The narratives reprinted here illustrate the centrality of the Indian rebel in the ideo-mythology by which Puritans came to terms with their social, ethnic, and generational conflicts. In the mythologized history of the war (as Puritans told it) the defeat and exile (or extermination) of the Indians potentially constituted a symbolic purging of evils from the whole body politic and spiritual community. However, this myth of exorcism and purgation was not invented for the occasion. Rather, it represented a development of patterns of associated images and narrative structures already in existence.

## *The Symbolic Role of the Indian*

For the Puritan, as for other settlers, the Indian was seen as the human expression of the peculiar character of American nature. Elizabethan explorers had painted the Indians as Arcadian innocents, living in a pre-Christian golden age—a concept suited to their desire to promote colonization, and one which they rarely stayed long enough to test out. The Puritans, however, designed a permanent establishment in the wilderness and had therefore to take the Indians and the land more seriously. The first Puritan settlers, the Pilgrims of Plymouth, had few expectations about the Indians; and those they had were not flattering. William Bradford speaks of the Pilgrims' fear of Indian cruelty and cannibalism, but he considers the Indians as no more significant than "the wild beasts" of the country. The lands of America, he says, are essentially "unpeopled," a blank slate on which the design of a new order could be freely inscribed. Remnants of this idea can be seen in the frequent wartime allusion to the Indians as "them that are not a people"—a reference to the Biblical prophecy that Israel should be punished for its sins through the attacks of tribes so primitive as not to have true political organization as a "nation" or a "people." [32]

By the time of the Massachusetts settlement of 1630, such illusions had been partly dispelled. While not very numerous or densely settled, the Indians of New England were a power to be reckoned with—and not merely in military or economic terms. The Indians possessed a distinctive culture with an animistic religion, an essentially democratic political structure, a communal idea of property, and sexual mores that struck the Puritans as wildly permissive (although they were in fact governed by rather strict taboos, of a kind radically different from those recognized by English morality). Although there were periods of hostility, the Indians were basically hospitable. They taught the English the techniques of survival in the wilderness, showed them how to adapt agricultural techniques to the local crops and climatic conditions, aided them in starving times, showed them how to live and clothe themselves by using the products of the land. The English were both grateful and suspicious of their intentions; they were also anxious about the effects of Indian adaptation on their English character. For the Puritans, as for most immigrant communities, transplantation to a New World required some acculturation. Any such process threatens the immigrants with the loss of the only cultural identity they have known. For the Puritans, more than for most subsequent immigrants, cultural identity and religious character were different aspects of the same thing. One sees this in Bradford's account of the Pilgrims' departure from Holland: they feared that their children would forget how to speak English and how to be good Christians—the two concepts went together.[33]

As we have seen, one of the basic conflicts in the Puritan colonies was between those who sought to make independent lives and fortunes in new territories and those who sought to maintain social and religious discipline by limiting the ability of individuals to move far beyond the reach of ministers and magistrates or to make private deals with the Indians. A favorite rhetorical device used for discrediting the emigrant was that of accusing him of "Indianizing"; this device could be extended symbolically to those who left the community in spirit while remaining physically within it. "How many that although they are Christians in name, are no better than *Heathens* in heart . . . [living] like *profane Indians*,"[34] wrote Increase Mather in 1676—and the anathema applied equally to those who had moved beyond the reach of instituted church worship and to those nearer at hand who remained unconverted or unregenerate.

The Indian missionaries had a role to play in the development of this rhetoric and its symbol system that paralleled their importance in the politics of clientage. In the 1650s the missionaries published many tracts on their work, which had the primary aim of justifying the Puritan colonies to the Cromwellian and later the Restoration governments. The conversion of the Indians was among the chief premises on which the colony had been granted its charter; therefore, some progress at that work had to be shown to still criticism. However, such tracts could also serve the purposes of propaganda within New England (and English) society as well. One of the typical features of these missionary tracts was their contrasting the supposed progress of the work of conversion among the base Indian heathens to the symptoms of unregeneracy and spiritual recalcitrance among white Christians. There was little reality to these accusations, since the progress of Indian conversions was slight. However, such a contrast might serve to shame a New English congregation to emulation. At the least it would provide a supplement to condemnations of white "Indianization" like that of Mather quoted above. In England, moreover, (where the tracts were published) the contrast served to refer English critics of New England to the critics' failure to do as well in converting the heterodox population of England as the Puritan colonists had supposedly done in America.

Beyond these immediate concerns, the conversion of the Indians was seen by the Puritans as one of the steps necessary to the achievement of the Millennium. Their typological interpretation of the Indian missions will be more thoroughly discussed in the introductions to the works of Mather and Nowell; at this point it is sufficient to note that, despite differences about organization and funding, and the interpretations of certain events, the Puritan clergy generally saw the Indian missions as central to the sacred mission, as well as to the secular success, of their colonies.

Although the contrast of white and Indian conversions is a rhetorical device, its aptness as a symbol should not be ignored. The role of the missionary among the Indians was in every way analogous to that of the minister in a congregation of unconverted or half-converted whites, or to that of the patriarch among the unlettered children and servants of his household. There was of course an implicit contradiction in suggesting that heathen Indians and unregenerate whites were in the same spiritual state, while at the same time using the progress of the Indian to shame the white man, since such shame has as its premise the idea that the Indian is intrinsically inferior in spiritual or cultural endowment. However, it is important to see that the missionary literature *contains* that contradiction without apparent strain. If there is racialism implicit in the use of the Indian as a symbol by the missionaries, there is also a suggestion that the Indians may be equal to white men in spiritual and cultural potential. It was the war itself that accelerated and exaggerated the racialist direction of white-Indian relationships in New England.

The outbreak of King Philip's War precipitated a new mythology of Indian-Puritan relationships in which war and exorcism replaced tutelage and conversion. This can be seen clearly in the writings of Increase Mather. Since the Indian was the human symbol of the New World itself, there emerged a new mythological definition of the white man's role in America. Under pressure of the need to define and account for the extraordinary calamities they suffered, Puritans began to interpret earlier ideas and images of the New World more intensively. Symbolic associations that had developed unconsciously in the process of colonial development now were taken up and worked into a larger system, a more comprehensive vision of American history. The formulaic association of Indians and unconverted or backsliding whites took on new relevance and meaning when the failure of the missionary enterprise became so dramatically clear. Perhaps the "rebellion" of the Indians was simply a more violent symbolic expression of the spirit of recalcitrance that prevented the propagation of the religious ferver of the Puritan fathers among the younger generation. If that were so, then the war could be accounted for as a warning from God to a people that had grown complacent and lost the keen edge of their faith. If the Half-Way Covenant and the rushing of settlers to the farther frontier could be understood as aspects of the "Indianization" of the American-born Puritans, then perhaps the antiorthodox tide of events could be reversed by a revulsion of colonial feeling; a return to racial, cultural, and religious affiliation; and a restoration of solidarity between the conflicting classes, sects, and jurisdictions that had divided New England. Used as a device for interpreting their cultural and political crisis, the Indian war became a symbolic drama of compelling force—a myth. The Puritans came to understand the chaotic history of events as a scenario of guilt and purgation, in which the destruction of the Indians—representing in their character all of the sinful nature of Man in general, and of New England in particular—was equated with the casting-out of collective and personal guilt, and they came to see the mythology of race and race-war as a metaphor that allowed them to interpret and hold in abeyance the class and generational struggles that divided their society.

## *The King Philip's War Narratives*

King Philip's War was thus the precipitant of a whole complex of internal and external political, religious, economic, and psychological crises in New England affairs. Coming at a time when Puritan institutions were beleaguered both by England and by internal struggles with heterodoxy and secularism, it appeared to the Puritans as a particular rebuke from God for their failures. It was in the nature of Puritanism that, among their responses to the crisis, the literary element should be most prominent. The Puritans were preeminently "the people of the Book." Their religious doctrine required literacy so that the individual could understand the word of God appearing in Scripture. Puritan sermons likewise demanded a literate audience, for despite the effort to achieve a "plain style," the Puritan "teacher" did not soften the rigor and difficulty of theological argument for his hearers. Thus the colonists had developed an extensive system of public education which made their population probably the most thoroughly literate in the world. As a consequence of this, they were able also to augment the Bible and the oral sermon by the publication and mass distribution of tractarian literature—an activity of such importance that a printing press was the next thing that the colony financed after the creation of Harvard College for educating ministers. They wished to be as self-sufficient as possible both in ministerial education and in the production of educational literature for their people.[35]

The Puritans were thus the originators of American popular literature—the first to produce literature designed for mass distribution to an American audience, on American presses. Puritan intellectuality and addiction to symbolism played a dual role here, stimulating the original desire for a popular printing/bookselling trade and enriching the literature it produced with complex ideas, symbols, and myths. The unique character of their culture can perhaps be appreciated when we contrast their reaction to Philip's war with the contemporary reaction to the Indian war and Bacon's Rebellion in Virginia. The Virginia situation was in many respects similar: there was division between colonial authorities and the ambitions frontiersmen, culminating in attempted revolution rather than mere riotings; moreover, the political crisis was associated with Indian hostilities on the border. However, the literature of Bacon's Rebellion was scanty and published mainly in England, since the low rate of literacy in Virginia made a local printing/bookselling trade economically unfeasible. Hence the literature of Bacon's Rebellion did not become part of a developing popular culture, while the narratives of King Philip's War became the seeds out of which a new literary mythology of America developed.

The works collected in this anthology illustrate the processes and stages by which this mythology developed. They are meant also to suggest the variety of ways in which the Puritans responded to the war—for not all responses were consistent with the orthodox mythology propounded by the ministry, and not all of the orthodox drew the same political conclusions from the official myths. The texts are drawn from works published in the colonies during the war, or published afterwards by those who participated directly in the war; histories written well after the war by nonparticipants are often interesting in their own right, but do not directly reveal the mind of the generation that confronted Philip. Contemporary works published abroad and unpublished manuscripts have also been excluded, in order to focus more precisely on defining an American public understanding of the events: all the pieces collected here were produced for, and consumed by, the reading public in New England.

Although unfamiliar to most modern readers, these works were not without their influence. Three of them—the works by Mather, Hubbard, and Nowell—are significant documents in the development of Puritan political ideology, as T. H. Breen has argued in *The Character of the Good Ruler.* All the texts, as part of the public literary domain, became basic sources for the later mythologizers of American history and the frontier: from Cotton Mather to Francis Parkman, from Charles Brockden Brown to Cooper, Melville, and Hawthorne, and the scores of lesser writers who exploited the New England past and the Indian wars.[36] But their interest as literary and political source material is not their only significance. Rather, they should also be read as participant-stories—for even the minister-historians lived through the events they chronicled. They provide an account of people attempting to comprehend and control an overwhelming historical experience while it is occurring, through both physical and intellectual action, through the development of new policies and institutions and the generation of new ideologies and mythologies.

The texts are presented (with one exception) in chronological order, according to their date of first American publication. The literature of the war falls into several different genres, only one of which is not represented here: this is the "newsletter" type of pamphlets, essentially bulletins from the battlefront, which were printed in England all during the war. These are of slight literary interest, contain no information not found in the texts reprinted here, and have in any case been reprinted elsewhere; hence their omission.

The first text, Increase Mather's *Brief History,* was composed while the war was still in progress and published shortly thereafter. It is thus a kind of "instant history," an attempt to describe the events of the war and provide an orthodox Puritan framework of interpretation in which they might be understood. The introduction to this text develops in greater depth the discussion of Puritan literary and historical theories begun in this General Introduction.

The second document is Benjamin Tompson's epic poem on the war—the first of its genre to be published in the New World and based on American history. Tompson's view of the war is essentially ministerial, but his medium requires him to amplify and emphasize imagery at the expense of ideology. His poem is therefore rich in images essential to the development of American mythology.

Samuel Nowell's sermon, *Abraham in Arms,* stands somewhere between the ministerial histories and the accounts of actual combatants which follow. Nowell was both a military chaplain with battlefield experience and an associate of Increase Mather. His sermon—with its emphasis on militarism and its vision of New England as an Israel battling in a world-wide Armageddon—is curiously similar in tone and content to the speeches of later exponents of manifest destiny and imperialism; and it illustrates the common understanding of the war's meaning and significance for New England's future guidance.

The narratives of Thomas Wheeler, Mary Rowlandson, and Benjamin Church are accounts of actual participants, not ministers or high officials. They differ radically as representations of "heroism"—of the possible roles that human beings can play in the making of history. Wheeler's account of the siege of Brookfield, in addition to being a vivid piece of narrative writing, speaks for the Puritan notion of heroism—one in which the power of God, not man, is emphasized and credited with the victory, and in which piety, rather than prowess, is the sign of heroic virtue. Mary Rowlandson's narrative of her captivity is perhaps the most significant and influential of these texts. Her narrative became the model for the "captivity narrative" genre, one of the most popular versions of the frontier mythology from Puritan times down to the present. For the Puritans, the tale of captivity became the American myth par excellence—the story that, for them, summed up their experience in the New World. Told in naive, straightforward language, the narrative is also a powerfully evocative revelation of a human character undergoing the most searching of ordeals. The last narrative, Benjamin Church's *Entertaining Passages,* was not published until long after the war. It is the humorous and boastful account of the adventures of a frontier hero, a prototype of Daniel Boone and Leatherstocking, whose values (both personal and literary) were antithetical to those of his Puritan contemporaries. Church's book illustrates the division between frontiersman and orthodox minister in the interpretation of the war; and his book indicates that the direction of cultural change favored the decline of the orthodox and the rise of the "Americanized" view.

One major school of literature that derives from King Philip's War is not represented here. Long after Philip was safely dead and the Indians driven out of New England (or into a peculiar form of semiassimilation that rendered them nearly invisible), the descendents of the Puritans came to view the vanished red Americans as part of their lost heroic age. In the revival of the concept of the Indian as Noble Savage, Philip reappeared as a primitive patriot whose opposition to the Puritans was stimulated by the admirable traits of loyalty to his nation and his gods, as well as by opposition to that commercial civilization from which his Romantic panegyrists also felt alienated. John Augustus Stone in *Metamora: Or the Last of the Wampanoags*, one of the most popular plays of the 1820s, portrayed Philip with sympathy, as did Washington Irving in his essays "Traits of Indian Character" and "Philip of Pokanoket" (written in 1814 and later published in the famous *Sketch Book*), and B. B. Thatcher in his *Indian Biography . . .* of 1834. Canonchet, another of the Indian leaders, had a leading and not unsympathetic role in Cooper's *The Wept of Wish-ton-wish* (1829), in which Philip and Benjamin Church also had "walk-on" parts. In G. H. Hollister's *Mount Hope; or, Philip, King of the Wampanoags: An Historical Romance* (1851) Philip is represented as an Indian aristocrat, graceful and athletic in body, and with a face that "bore more of the marks of intellect, forecast, and a firm, immoveable purpose, than of the characteristics commonly attributed to savages. . . . He seemed formed alike for thought or action—a stern lawgiver or a swift avenger—but in either capacity a king." Church appears as a middling to lower class frontiersman of the Leatherstocking type, more active than intellectual, but expert in Indian warfare: "An Indian is like a fox: you must take him as he runs." He thinks of the Indian as a clever and dangerous beast, and believes warfare between the races to be inevitable—a position closer to Leatherstocking's than to that of the historical Church.[37]

In addition to these fictional representations, the years from 1820 to 1840 also saw a revival of interest in the primary literature of the colonial wars, much of which was edited and reprinted by Samuel G. Drake.[38] While all of this literature is highly interesting in its own right, it lies outside the scope of this anthology, which centers on the Puritan response to King Philip's War in the seventeenth and early eighteenth centuries.

# NOTES

1. Douglas Edward Leach, *Flintlock and Tomahawk: New England in King Philip's War,* pp. 243–44.

2. Hayden White, *Metahistory: The Historical Imagination in Nineteenth Century Europe,* pp. ix–xii, 1–42. Although derived explicitly from nineteenth-century sources, White's theoretical discussion of historical writing is applicable to earlier historians as well.

3. For a fuller discussion of the theory of myth used here, see Richard Slotkin, *Regeneration through Violence: The Mythology of the American Frontier, 1600–1860,* chap. 1.

4. Sacvan Bercovitch, *The Puritan Origins of the American Self,* esp. chaps. 2 and 4; Perry Miller and Thomas H. Johnson, eds., *The Puritans,* pp. 545–52; Kenneth Silverman, *Colonial American Poetry,* pp. 31–45.

5. Clifford Geertz, "Ideology as a Cultural System," in *Ideology and Discontent,* ed. David E. Apter, pp. 47–76.

6. Roland Barthes, "Myth Today," in *Mythologies,* trans. Annette Lavers, p. 129. In this connection see the discussion of typology below, pp. 58–60, 260–61, 264–65.

7. The literature on Puritanism is extensive. The discussion which follows is based largely on the following: Bercovitch, *Puritan Origins of the American Self;* T. H. Breen, *The Character of the Good Ruler;* Perry Miller, *Errand into the Wilderness;* Perry Miller, *The New England Mind: The Seventeenth Century;* Miller and Johnson, *The Puritans;* Edmund S. Morgan, *The Puritan Family: Religion and Domestic Relations in Seventeenth Century New England;* Richard H. Tawney, *Religion and the Rise of Capitalism;* Michael Walzer, *Revolution of the Saints: A Study in the Origin of Radical Politics;* Owen C. Watkins, *The Puritan Experience: Studies in Spiritual Autobiography;* Max Weber, *The Protestant Ethic and the Spirit of Capitalism;* A. W. Plumstead, ed., *The Wall and the Garden: Selected Massachusetts Election Sermons, 1670–1775.*

8. William Bradford, *Of Plymouth Plantation,* ed. Samuel Eliot Morison, pp. 25–26.

9. Slotkin, *Regeneration through Violence,* pp. 84–87, 99–100.

10. Breen, *Character of the Good Ruler,* pp. 142–47.

11. The standard interpretations of the Half-Way Covenant developed by Perry Miller in *The New England Mind* have been extensively revised by recent scholarship. See Robert G. Pope, *The Half-Way Covenant: Church Membership in Puritan New England,* esp. chap. 10; and David D. Hall, *The Faithful Shepherd: A History of the New England Ministry in the Seventeenth Century,* pp. 200–217.

12. N[athaniel] S[altonstall], *The Present State of New England with Respect to the Indian War,* reprinted in *Narratives of the Indian Wars,* ed. Charles H. Lincoln, pp. 40–41; *A Farther Brief and True Narration,* ibid., p. 3.

13. N[athaniel] S[altonstall], *A Continuation of the State of New England* ibid., pp. 51–74.

14. See Wilcomb E. Washburn, *The Governor and the Rebel: A History of Bacon's Rebellion in Virginia.*

15. Alden T. Vaughan, *New England Frontier: Puritans and Indians 1620–1675,* pp. 322–38.

16. Ibid., p. 326.

17. Samuel Eliot Morison, "Preface," in Leach, *Flintlock and Tomahawk,* pp. lx-x.

18. Francis Jennings, *The Invasion of America: Indians, Colonialism, and the Cant of Conquest,* pp. 11–12, 180–81.

19. Ibid., pp. 110, 178–79, 205–6, 226–27.

20. Ibid., pp. 282–83.

21. Ibid., pp. 228, 288.

22. Ibid., pp. 285–86.

23. Slotkin, *Regeneration through Violence,* pp. 43–45.

24. Jennings, *Invasion of America,* p. 115.

25. Ibid., pp. 231–32, 239–40, 250–51, 286–87.

26. John Eliot, *A Late and Further Manifestation of the Progress of the Gospel among the Indians . . .,* reprinted in *Collections of the Massachusetts Historical Society,* series 3, vol. 4, p. 274. See also Slotkin, *Regeneration through Violence,* pp. 194–98.

27. Patrick M. Malone, "Changing Military Technology among the Indians of Southern New England, 1600–1677," *American Quarterly* 25:1 (March, 1973), 60–61; George T. Hunt, *The Wars of the Iroquois: A Study in Intertribal Trade Relations,* pp. 7–9, 18–19; Jennings, *Invasion of America,* pp. 220–27.

28. Jennings, *Invasion of America,* p. 227.

29. The historical account which follows is derived from Leach, *Flintlock and Tomahawk,* except where other sources are cited.

30. Jennings, *Invasion of America,* p. 291.

31. Ibid., pp. 293–94.

32. Bradford, *Of Plymouth Plantation,* p. 25.

33. Bradford, *Of Plymouth Plantation,* pp. 25–26.

34. Increase Mather, *An Earnest Exhortation,* pp. 174–75.

35. See Kenneth A. Lockridge, *Literacy in Colonial New England: An Enquiry into the Social Context of Literacy in the Early Modern West.*

36. Slotkin, *Regeneration through Violence,* chaps. 11–14.

37. G. H. Hollister, *Mount Hope: An Historical Romance,* pp. 7–8, 17–18.

38. Slotkin, *Regeneration through Violence,* pp. 358–59, 444–45.

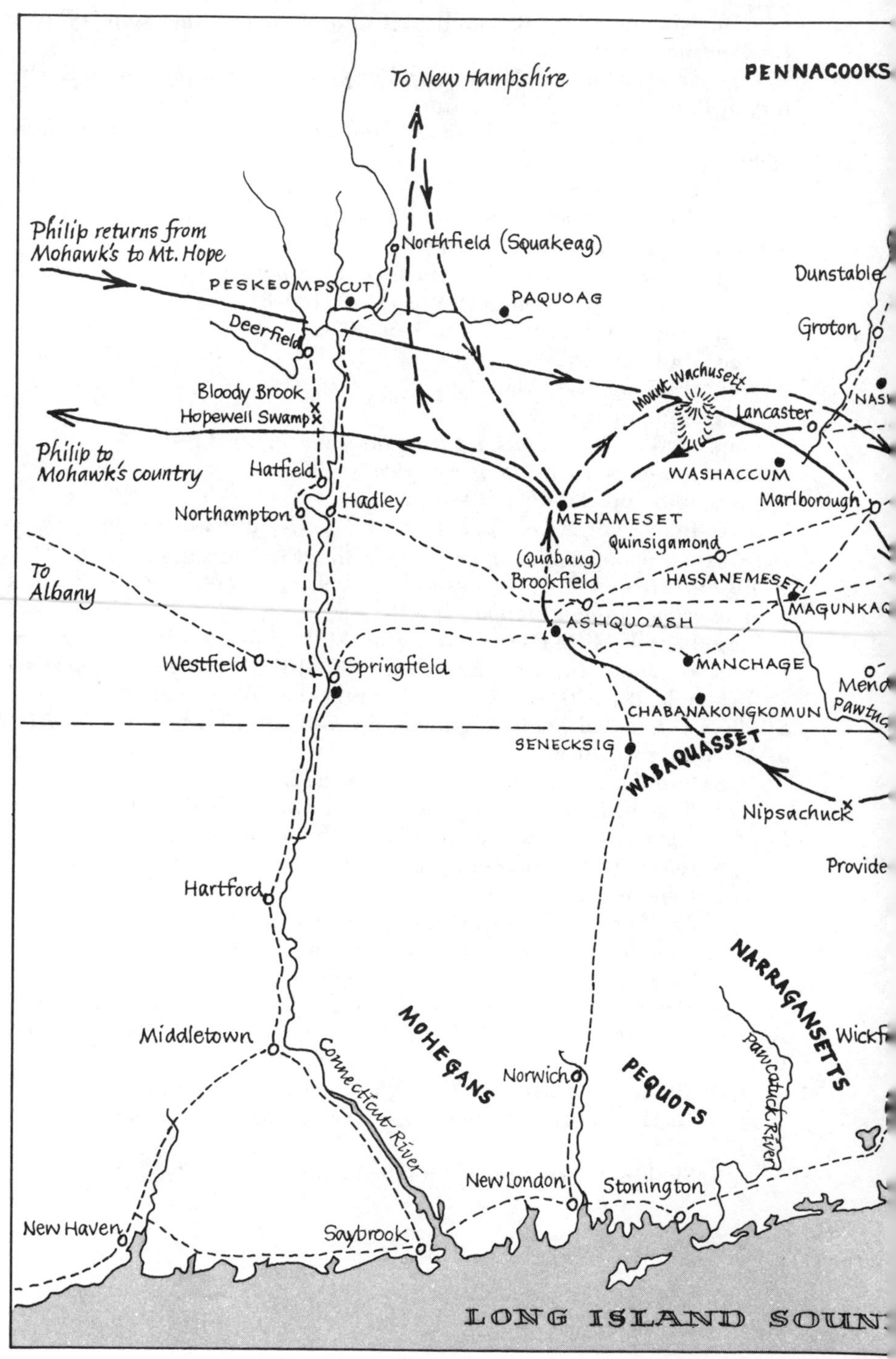
To New Hampshire
PENNACOOKS
Philip returns from Mohawk's to Mt. Hope
Northfield (Squakeag)
PESKEOMPSCUT
PAQUOAG
Dunstable
Groton
Deerfield
Bloody Brook
Hopewell Swamp
Mount Wachusett
Lancaster
Philip to Mohawk's country
Hatfield
WASHACCUM
Hadley
Marlborough
Northampton
MENAMESET
Quinsigamond
(Quabaug)
To Albany
Brookfield
HASSANEMESET
MAGUNKAG
ASHQUOASH
Westfield
Springfield
MANCHAGE
CHABANAKONGKOMUN
SENECKSIG
WABAQUASSET
Nipsachuck
Hartford
NARRAGANSETTS
MOHEGANS
Middletown
Connecticut River
Norwich
PEQUOTS
Pawcatuck River
New London
Stonington
New Haven
Saybrook
LONG ISLAND SOUN

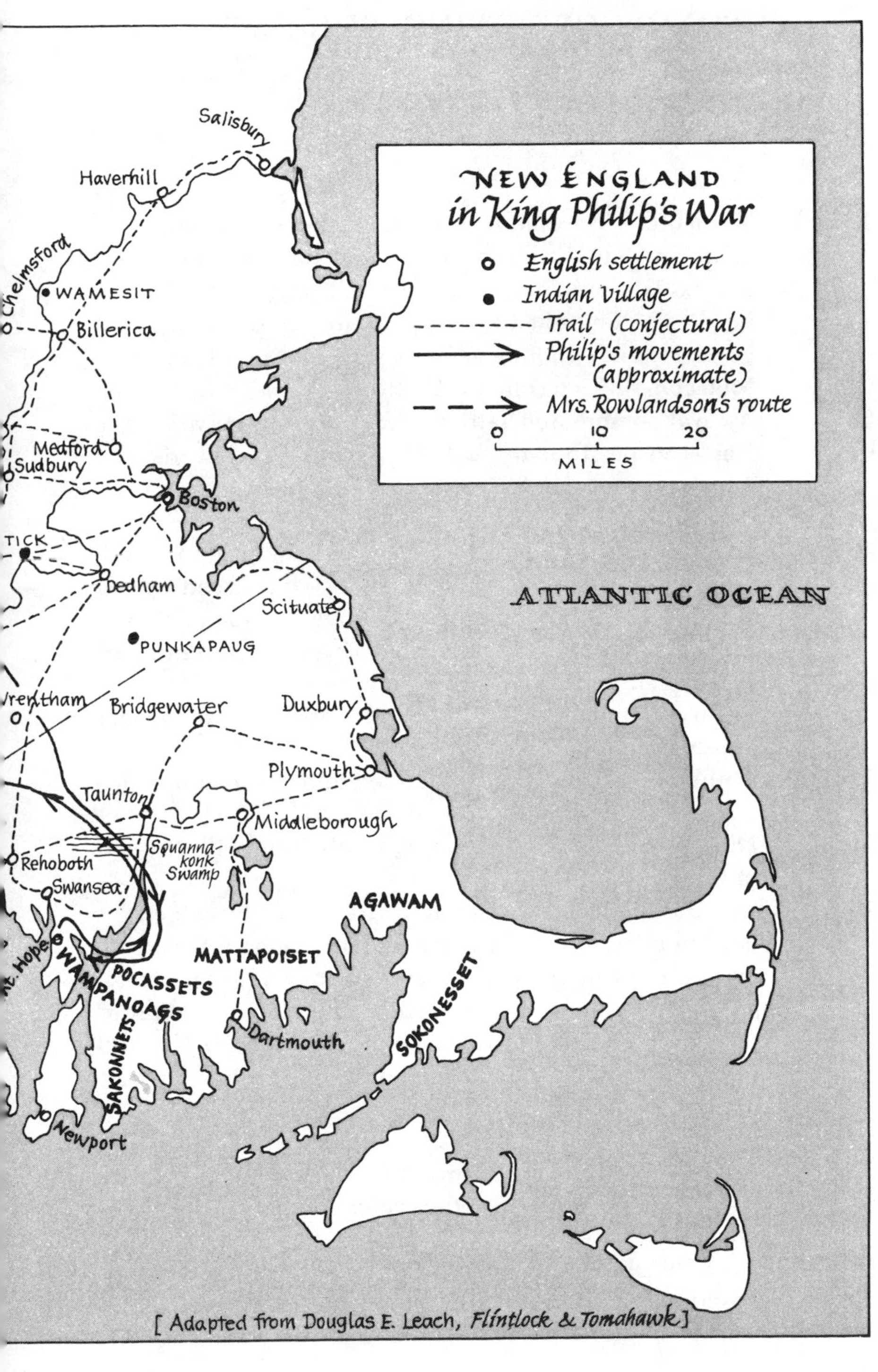
NEW ENGLAND
in King Philip's War
English settlement
Indian village
Trail (conjectural)
Philip's movements
(approximate)
Mrs. Rowlandson's route
0
10
20
MILES
ATLANTIC OCEAN
Salisbury
Haverhill
Chelmsford
WAMESIT
Billerica
Medford
Sudbury
Boston
TICK
Dedham
Scituate
PUNKAPAUG
Wrentham
Bridgewater
Duxbury
Plymouth
Taunton
Middleborough
Squannakonk Swamp
Rehoboth
Swansea
AGAWAM
Mt. Hope
WAMPANOAGS
POCASSETS
MATTAPOISET
SOKONESSET
Dartmouth
SAKONNETS
Newport
[ Adapted from Douglas E. Leach, Flintlock & Tomahawk ]

## CHRONOLOGY OF KING PHILIP'S WAR

Dates are given in New Style.

1662: Wamsutta ("Alexander"), chief of the Wampanoags, is summoned to Duxbury, Mass., to answer accusations that he is plotting war; after submitting to questioning, he dies of fever at the home of Josiah Winslow, later governor of Plymouth, and is succeeded by his brother, Metacom or Metacomet ("Philip").

1665: A royal commission settles a land dispute between the Narragansett Indians and Massachusetts, but the arrangement merely focuses a growing hostility between the parties.

1666: Philip warns the English of New York of an impending raid by the Narragansetts and is himself accused by the chief of that tribe, Ninigret. Although the incident suggests the strength of intertribal rivalries, it reinforces English suspicions of Indian intentions.

1667: Philip is summoned by Plymouth authorities to answer an accusation of "plotting."

1668–69: Philip is involved in an extended and acrimonious litigation over land in the Wrentham area.

1669: Ninigret is accused of plotting a rebellion with the aid of the French.

1671: *April* Philip signs the Taunton agreement, by which he is compelled to acknowledge and apologize for plotting against the English and to agree to surrender his arms.

*September 24–29* Philip is tried in Plymouth for failure to live up to Taunton agreement; he is fined £100 and required to submit to the colonial government in all matters involving war or the sale of Indian lands.

1671–75: Philip presumably builds a conspiracy against the English, partly overcoming the rivalry with the Narragansetts and engaging the cooperation of the Nipmucks.

1675: *January 29* John Sassamon, Philip's secretary and a supposed informer, is murdered; some days earlier he warned authorities of an impending war.

*June 1–8* Sassamon's murderers tried and executed; Sassamon's information is formally published.

*11* Wampanoags are reported arming near Swansea and Plymouth.

*14–15* Benjamin Church visits Awashonks, Squaw-sachem of the Sogkonates, and is warned of Philip's plans for war.

*16* Church warns Governor Winslow of Plymouth, who notifies Governor Leverett of Massachusetts.

*17* Wampanoags seize, then release, a party of horse-hunters; this suggests that Philip had chosen his moment of attack.

*20* Wampanoags attack Swansea.

*21–23* Massachusetts, Plymouth, and Rhode Island mobilize troops; Massachusetts begins a "diplomatic offensive" among the Wampanoags, Nipmucks, and Narragansetts.

*24* Plymouth declares a Fast Day; Wampanoags attack Swansea in force.

*25* A special administrative committee for financing and conducting the war is established in Boston.

*28* Connecticut is asked to cooperate in a united effort. Troops of Massachusetts, Plymouth, and Rhode Island are concentrated at Miles's (Myles's) Garrison; Church leads militia in skirmish at the bridge.

*29* Attacks on settlers in Rehoboth-Taunton area begin.

*30* Colonial army "sweeps" Mount Hope Neck, while Philip escapes to Pocasset country; he joins forces with Weetamoo, the Squaw-sachem, on July 5.

*July 1* Connecticut agrees to send troops.

Defensive policy is adopted in Mount Hope area, which allows Philip freedom of movement.

*5* Philip arrives at Weetamoo's village.

*5–15* Captain Edward Hutchinson marches the Massachusetts troops from Mount Hope to the Narragansett country to negotiate for that tribe's neutrality; the rest of the army is therefore immobilized.

*8* Governor Andros of New York attempts to seize Saybrook, Conn., but is forced to retreat.

Church's Pease-field Fight occurs.

Middleborough and Dartmouth, Plym., are attacked.

*14* Nipmucks attack Mendon, Mass.

*15* Hutchinson compels Narragansetts to sign a treaty, which proves impossible to enforce.

*16–24* Captain Curtis tries to negotiate with the Nipmucks.

*19* Battle of Pocasset Swamp convinces the English commanders they cannot "fight the wild beast in his Den": they commit their greatest blunder of the war, abandoning offensive operations and building a fort to "besiege" Philip in the swamp.

*28* Captain Hutchinson, escorted by Captain Thomas Wheeler's troop of cavalry, marches to contact the Nipmuck sachems near Brookfield.

*29* Philip escapes from Pocasset swamp, crosses Taunton River and heads northeastward for the Nipmuck country.

*31* Captain Henchman, with Mohegan allies and English troops, overtakes and attacks Philip at Nipsachuck, but he fails to press his attack and allows Philip to escape with small losses.

*August 2–4* Hutchinson and Wheeler are besieged at Brookfield.

*4–24* Philip himself is lost to view, but the war spreads to the upper Connecticut Valley, the Merrimac Valley, and Maine.

*24–25* Battle of Hopewell Swamp is fought south of Deerfield, Mass.; retreating Indians beat off English pursuit.

*30* Captain Samuel Moseley arrests a group of Praying Indians at Marlborough; they are nearly lynched that night.

*September 3* Captain Beers is ambushed while evacuating Squakeag, northeast of Deerfield.

*12* Deerfield, Squakeag, and Brookfield are evacuated.

*17* Day of Public Humiliation is proclaimed in Boston.

*18* Captain Lathrop, escorting evacuees from

Deerfield, is ambushed and defeated at Bloody Brook.

*22* Narragansett sachems confer with colonial representatives at Wickford, R.I.

*October 4–5* Springfield, Mass., is attacked and partly burned; Major Appleton replaces Major Pynchon in Connecticut Valley command.

*7* Day of Public Humiliation is held in Boston.

*13–18* Appleton skirmishes in Northampton area.

*18* Indians attack Hatfield and are repulsed.
Narragansetts sign new treaty in Boston.

*19* Connecticut and Massachusetts embargo trade in provisions—a symptom both of hard times and of intercolonial hostilities.

*November 2–12* Commissioners of the United Colonies decide to attack the Narragansetts with an army of a thousand men.

*December 2* A Day of Prayer is held in Boston, for the sake of the army.

*8* Forces for Narragansett Expedition, to be commanded by Governor Winslow of Plymouth, muster at Dedham, Mass., Taunton, Plym., and New London, Conn.

*12–18* Winslow's force unites at Wickford, R.I. Lack of provisions compels an early advance.

*16* Bull's Garrison, an alternative base for the army, is destroyed by Indians.

*18* Winslow's army marches into the Narragansett swamp.

*19* The Great Swamp Fight occurs; eighty English and about six hundred Narragansetts (half of them women and children) are killed.

*20* Winslow's battered army retreats to Wickford.

1676: *January* During the winter Philip goes to the Mohawk country in New York seeking allies and provisions; he is rebuffed and attacked by the Mohawks and returns to New England in February or March.

Winslow's army is immobilized by losses and lack of provisions for a month after the Swamp Fight.

*27* Indians raid Pawtuxet, R.I.

Winslow, reinforced and partly reprovisioned, attempts an offensive, but his troops are plagued by hunger and desertion, and the march is a failure.

*February 5* The "Hungry March" ends; Winslow's army disbands.

*10* Lancaster, Mass. is attacked and Mary Rowlandson captured. An Indian offensive begins.

*21* Medfield, twenty miles from Boston, is attacked and burned, despite the presence of a large militia force.

*23* On a Day of Public Humiliation, Indian attacks come within ten miles of Boston.

*March* During the first week of March Philip is in the Northampton area, unsuccessfully pursued by Major Savage's cavalry.

*12* Clark's Garrison, Plym., is destroyed.

*13* Groton, Mass., is attacked and abandoned.

*14* Philip attacks Northampton. Massachusetts authorities plan a palisade to enclose the Boston area, leaving the country towns outside.

During this period the Praying Indians are persecuted and are removed to Deer Island.

*26* Worshipers on their way to church are massacred at Longmeadow, Mass.

Marlborough is partially destroyed; English pursuers defeat Indian rearguard.

Simsbury, Conn., is deserted and burned.

Captain Pierce's company of English and Indian allies are ambushed and wiped out on Pawtucket River near Rehoboth, Mass.

*27* A battle is fought near Sudbury, Mass.

*28* Indians attack Rehoboth.

Commissioners launch a diplomatic offensive, aimed at dividing Indians or at least ransoming the captives.

*29* Providence, R.I., is destroyed.

*April 9* Canonchet, the Narragansett sachem, is captured and executed by Connecticut forces in western Rhode Island.

*mid-April* By this time the outer ring of settlements west of Boston has been largely abandoned, and an epidemic begins which will carry off many colonists, including former governor Winthrop and many senior military officers.

*20* A Day of Public Humiliation is held in Boston.

*21* Indians attack Sudbury, seventeen miles from Boston. Militia from Boston and nearby towns gather, pursue the Indians, and fight a day-long battle in which both sides suffer heavily. This is the Indians' high water mark.

*27* Captain Henchman resumes the offensive in eastern Massachusetts.

*May 1* Wachusett Council: colonists meet with Indian representatives to set ransoms for captives.

*2–3* Mary Rowlandson is ransomed and returned. Connecticut passes new laws designed to avert God's wrath by correcting public morals.

*6* Henchman's troops win several skirmishes.

Bridgewater is attacked; an Indian offensive begins in Plymouth Colony, perhaps signaling Philip's movement southward.

*11* Plymouth Town is attacked.

*18–19* Captain Turner surprises an Indian encampment at the Falls of the Connecticut above Deerfield and routs the Indians; but an Indian attack on the retreating troops leads to a rout of Turner's command, with the death of Turner and a quarter of his 150 men. This is in fact a Pyrrhic victory for the Indians.

*24* Captain Brattle surprises and defeats Indians on Pawtucket River.

*June 2* Major Talcott of Connecticut leads a combined force against Philip in western Massachusetts.

*3–10* Benjamin Church returns to the war, is authorized to recruit both white and Indian soldiers; returning from Plymouth, he meets with some Sogkonates, establishes connections with Awashonks, and negotiates the detachment of her people from Philip's cause.

*12* Hadley, Mass., is attacked.

*15–20* Major Talcott arrives at Hadley and campaigns in the area.

*19* Massachusetts offers amnesty to Indians who surrender.

*29* A Day of Public Thanksgiving is celebrated in Boston.

*30* Awashonks meets with the Plymouth army under Bradford and fulfills her promise to Church by formally changing sides.

*July 2–3* Talcott moves against the Narragansetts and inflicts major defeats on them at Nipsachuck and Warwick.

In Maine, Wannalancet and Major Waldron sign a treaty ending hostilities.

*6–16* Major Bradford pursues and nearly catches Philip's party.

*11* Taunton is attacked.

Church wins two skirmishes at Middleborough and Monponsett.

*17–22* Church skirmishes and recruits among Philip's followers near Taunton.

*24* Church receives a new commission granting him broad discretionary powers.

*25* Pomham, an important sachem, is captured.

*27–30* One hundred eighty Nipmucks surrender at Boston.

*30* Church begins his pursuit of Philip.

*31* Church's troops kill Philip's uncle.

*August 1* Church captures Philip's wife and son; Philip escapes.

*3* Church temporarily halts pursuit.

Talcott pursues and defeats Indians fleeing westward to Housatonic River.

*6* Weetamoo is defeated near Taunton and drowns while fleeing.

*9* Church captures "Sam Barrow."

*10–12* Church pursues and ambushes Philip, who is shot by an Indian named Alderman. The war is effectively ended.

*September-October* Minor skirmishes are fought, and Church captures Annawon. Many captured Indians are executed, enslaved, or deported to the West Indies.

## A NOTE ON FORMAT

The texts used in this book are taken from copies of first editions. Except where noted, the original spelling and punctuation have generally been left as found, although some corrections are interpolated in square brackets for the sake of clarity. Difficult or abstruse passages, as well as the occasional Latin, Greek, or Hebrew phrase, arc translated in the notes.

The notes also refer the reader to other primary and secondary materials relevant to the texts themselves or to the introductory essays. Full bibliographic entries and additional sources are listed in the Selected Bibliography.

## ONE

# *INCREASE MATHER*
## Puritan Mythologist

A COMPLETE study of the career of Increase Mather would require, in effect, a complete analysis of the intellectual history of Puritan New England during Massachusetts's transition from theocratic state to imperial province. With his son Cotton, Increase Mather shaped the political program, as well as the philosophic-theological theory, of the Puritan conservatives through the crises of King Philip's War, the Half-Way Covenant, the first French and Indian Wars, and the struggles with the Crown over Massachusetts's charter and government. His writings and speeches cover virtually the entire spectrum of Puritan concerns, including predestinarian theology, historical theory, educational theory, politics (both civil and ecclesiastical), and scientific speculation. Although a brief overview of his career and concerns can be given here, the main purpose of this essay is to show the effect of King Philip's War on Mather's thought and the consequences of Mather's response to the war for Puritan culture.[1]

Increase Mather was born in Dorchester, Mass., in 1639. He was educated in Boston, at Harvard, and later at Trinity College in Dublin. A brilliant scholar and theologian, Mather was offered a faculty position at Trinity but he declined it, taking up instead an offer to preach to and lead a congregation in England. The fall of the Cromwellian Protectorate led him finally to abandon England and return to Boston in 1661—after having refused substantial inducements from the Anglican prelacy to abandon Congregational Puritanism. In Boston he married the daughter of John Cotton, one of the leading figures in the founding generation of Puritans; that same year he became a leader in opposing the Half-Way Covenant movement, which sought to ease the requirement for church membership by setting aside the requirement that would-be congregants undergo a "conversion experience." Unlike some of his associates, Mather gradually altered his opposition to the Half-Way Covenant and by 1675 was a partial defender of it, largely on the pragmatic ground that by opening the doors of the church wider the covenant made possible a wider dissemination of the gospel preached from the ministerial pulpit. In 1674 he became one of the licensers of the press (in effect a censor) and a member of Harvard's governing board; in 1681 he became the president of Harvard but refused to give up his pulpit in Boston's Second Church.

From 1680 to 1692 Increase Mather and his son Cotton were preeminent both in theological debate and in colony politics. Increase Mather was a leader of the so-called theocratic resistance to the government of Andros, and after the revocation of the charter served as Massachusetts's ambassador to the courts of James II and William III. Disagreement over the political and religious compromise worked out by Mather, coupled with his support of the inept governor Sir William Phipps and his association with the witchcraft persecutions of 1692, undercut Mather's political position. In 1701 he was removed as president of Harvard, and he spent his remaining years in scientific and theological pamphlet-wars.

Mather's attitudes toward the expansion of the settlements and the pragmatic religious and political adjustments they necessitated were ambivalent. On the one hand, the expansion was widening the scope and increasing the potential power of the Puritan experiment; devices like the Half-Way Covenant similarly expanded the population over which Puritan teachers could exercise their influence. Yet Mather feared that the consequence of uncontrolled geographic or congregational expansion would so weaken the core of Puritan doctrine and discipline as to defeat the colony's ultimate aims. What theory commanded him to oppose, pragmatism required him to accept. The problem was not his alone but was endemic to the Puritan colonies.

The center of Mather's mythology was his linkage of adherence to orthodox doctrine with loyalty to the personalities of the founding generation—his own father and father-in-law being prominent examplars of the type. Loyalty to the fathers is the central value in Mather's universe and is expressed socially and politically as well as personally and religiously. It implies the filial obedience of sons to parents, of servants to masters, of parishioners to teachers, of citizens to magistrates, of the "worser classes" to their "betters." Since such loyalty was, for Mather, the symbol of adherence to orthodox doctrine, he was amenable to compromises that permitted the classes who inherited and embodied the afflatus of the fathers to maintain their rule of the colony. However, such compromise must not involve any compromise of the central doctrines themselves on the level of theory; nor must the keepers of the tradition abandon their efforts to achieve the wholesale conversion of their Half-Way Covenanted parishioners. Let a liberalized doctrine bring the people to the church; but let the minister remember that the enlarged audience is not the end of his striving, but merely the means to a wider propagation of the gospel. Let the minister also remember that he is the teacher of his congregation, and not its pupil. Doctrine proceeds from a sovereign God; while the minister is not God's vicar, he is the interpreter of that authoritative word for the masses. Indeed, the aim of his scholarship is to make his interpretation of the Word "authoritative," valid by every measure of philosophic and scientific analysis.

King Philip's War precipitated the crisis of seventeenth-century Puritanism just at the time (1674–1675) that Increase Mather was coming into his own as a theological and political leader. He perceived the war both as divine punishment for New England's sins and as a double-edged testing of the colonists' valor and virtue and of God's disposition toward New England. The events of the war had to be read comprehensively, for their significance would have bearing on matters ranging from the microcosmic polity of the family to the organization of the cosmos under God. The war therefore evoked the full range of Mather's learning and intelligence, his theology, his basic assumptions, and his personal mythology.

In histories, tracts, and sermons, Mather sought to convert the raw material of an ongoing historical experience—the Indian war—into a coherent myth in which these dilemmas would be resolved. Each event would be seen as an act of divine pedagogy, a dramatic "lecture" on the nature of God and his universe and man's place therein. Specific lessons would be drawn and utilized for the reform of the outward behavior of the colonists in manners, economics, and politics. But more significantly, the war's history, while events were fresh and vivid in memory, would be used to recreate the world view of orthodox Calvinism among a generation that had forgotten how a Puritan was supposed to perceive the world around him.

Mather published two histories of the war, appending a sermon to each in which the theological analysis of the historical experience was systematically carried forward. While the later work, *A Relation of the Troubles Which Have Hapened in New-England* . . . (1677), is more reflective and systematic, the first book is perhaps the more interesting. *A Brief History of the War with the Indians in New-England* (1676) appeared just after Philip's death, while the war was still in progress, and it shows Mather's mind at work on his materials.

For Mather and the Puritans all literature had to serve the requirement of propagating the true gospel and maintaining the solidarity and religious commitment of the Puritan community of Visible Saints.[2] To do this, all writing had ultimately to begin with the divine Word expressed in the Bible. The Puritans, and the Mathers in particular, favored typological schemes for connecting Biblical events and prophecies to temporal history. Typological exegesis and historiography are complex techniques, with roots in the earliest scholarship and theology of the Christian era; it would be impossible to reproduce here the complex and subtle analysis of Puritan typology developed by Sacvan Bercovitch in his *Puritan Origins of the American Self*. It is sufficient for our purposes to note that Mather's typological historiography interprets temporal history according to an archetype derived from a combination of Old Testament history and prophecy and the myth of Christ in the New Testament. Since the coming of Christ was an event determined at the beginning of time, typological readings of the Old Testament find in the collective experience of the Hebrews and in the lives of individual heroes, saints, and prophets prefigurations of the first coming of Christ. Similarly, the historical record of the New Testament is seen as containing a prefigurative model for the history of mankind's future redemption: just as the Old Testament prefigures Christ's coming and martyrdom, the New predicts the pattern of the Second Coming, Apocalypse, and Millennium. The purpose of Mather's historical writing was to "impose a sacred *telos* on secular events" by correlating them to prophecies or events in the New Testament (most particularly in the book of Revelation).

It is possible to see this approach as fundamentally antihistorical in its pressuring of actual events to fit the mold of a preestablished archetype. Certainly it goes against the theory of secular and empirical historiography, although it is questionable whether any historical method is entirely free from dependence on unvalidated and perhaps unprovable assumptions. However, from Mather's viewpoint the approach is anything *but* antihistorical. Where the empirical historian perceives events that are varied and complexly developed through time, Mather sees in temporal history only endlessly (perhaps absurdly) recurring cycles. Men are born and die, civilizations rise and fall, power and wealth wax and wane, to what end? Only the paradigmatic history of redemption (typologically deduced from scripture) can provide meaning by showing the direction of history and offering a scale against which particular events can be seen as pointing toward the fulfillment or the obstruction of God's plan, the establishment or the persecution of God's church. The "apocalyptic timetable" (as Bercovitch terms it) gives direction and meaning to the otherwise incoherent and contradictory flow of events, providences, catastrophes, and triumphs.[3]

Typology provided the interpretive mode and sermon form provided the rhetorical structure for Mather's history. This seems natural enough for a historian who was primarily a preacher; but the sermon structure is worth some notice for the insight it gives into the Puritans' way of processing ideas and experiences. The logic and rhetoric of the Puritan sermon were central to their religious discipline and their world view. There were four primary sections: text, doctrine, reasons, and uses or application. The *text* was a passage from the Bible, which was presumed to "contain" the meanings and imperatives that the sermon exfoliated. All that the minister said was interpretation of the divine Word, and his ideal was to say neither less nor more than the passage and its Author required. The *doctrine* was a brief exposition of the interpreter's essential thesis, designed to prepare the audience for the argumentation to follow by warning it in advance of what the conclusion would be. The *reasons* constituted the justification of the doctrine, argued in a carefully articulated sequence of numbered paragraphs and subparagraphs. The *uses* section applied the moral argument directly and explicitly to particular sins prevalent in the community and pointed the way to reform. The whole of the argument was to be couched in a "Plain Style," avoiding scholastic jargon, "Latin quotations or glittering phrases that might distract attention from content to form."[4]

In that time and place, the Puritan sermon was perhaps the most effective medium for disseminating to a mass audience the information and philosophic method necessary for a comprehension of a difficult and often abstruse theology.

> The testimony of visitors, travelers, and memoirs agrees that during the Puritan age in New England the common man, the farmer and merchant, was amazingly versed in systematic divinity. A gathering of yeomen and "hired help" around the kitchen fire of an evening produced long and unbelievably technical discussions of predestination, infant damnation, and the distinction between faith and works.[5]

The development of the book trade in New England was a corollary of this, an extension of the sermon by means of print into a portable and more permanent record, for use in private meditation and family discussion. Literacy in New England was a widespread fact, underwritten by a clergy concerned that people read and understand the Bible and the sermon, and this literate audience provided the economic basis for the first mass literature produced in the New World.

As minister and censor, and now as historian, Mather was determined that narrative literature would complement and reinforce, not play against, the sermon. Just as the preacher's task in composing his sermon is to seek the meaning of the scriptural passage, the historian's task is to seek the Word of God in the more confused Book of Events. Similarly, the scientist will read the Book of Nature in order to interpret the meanings placed there by God and not to find explanations that deny or avoid the fact of divinity. Indeed, as Mather states in his preface, his real concern with keeping a record of historical events was not that of a historian but that of a preacher: "the thing which I mainly designed, was the subsequent *Exhortation* which is annexed herewith wherein I have desired to approve myself as in the sight of God, speaking what I believe God would have me to speak, without respect to any person in this world." In effect the history part of the book is an extended *reasons* section for the purposed sermon.

The history begins with an account of the circumstances under which the book was written: the felt need for a systematic and orthodox response to the crisis that could "order" it and the political need for a Puritan response to the critical accounts published by Quakers from Rhode Island, which weakened the colony's position in England. To these general concerns, Mather adds a long defense of the Indian missions against those in New England who have neglected, denigrated, and more latterly assaulted the work and the workmen. Mather states that this is "one thing . . . concerning which I could wish I had said more," and he frames his remarks as an interpretation of a sermon by his father-in-law, John Cotton, in which Cotton was said to have argued that the conversion of the Indians would not succeed until after the prophesied "conversion of the Jews." Mather takes Cotton as a symbol of the virtues and doctrines of the colony's founding patriarchs and avers that one of the chief originating purposes of the colony was the desire to convert the Indians.

> But it was never intended that the Assertion [of Cotton's] should be improved, so as to discourage from the prosecution of that which was the professed, pious, and main design of the *Fathers* of this *Colony, vic. To propagate* the Gospel and Kingdome of Christ, among these Indians, who in former Ages had not heard of his fame and Glory.

This misinterpretation of the word of Cotton, of the mandate of the Founding Fathers, is symptomatic of a larger disease—the backsliding or degeneration of the sons from their fathers' wisdom and piety and the consequent misinterpretation of the Word of God. Such misinterpretation is no trivial matter. Cotton's sermon had to do with the symbolism of the vials in Revelation, the book richest in detailed prophecies of the Second Coming. Using the often obscure symbolism of Revelation, typological analysis could correlate current events and the apocalyptic timetable. Behind Cotton's argument lies the further controversy over the origins of the American Indians: specifically the question raised by John Eliot (and others) over whether the Indians were the Lost Tribes of Israel. If they were, then the conversion of the Jews could not be completed until the Indians were Christianized, and a theological controversy existed as to whether the conversion of the heathen were to be expected before or after the conversion of the Jews. Conversion of both the heathens and the Jews, in some proper sequence, was a precondition for the Second Coming. Mather seeks to avoid the dilemma by arguing that whether the Indians are heathen or Jews, and whether (therefore) their conversion may be expected early or late, it is clear that the conversion of the Indians is necessary to the Millennium and the work must be carried on. To fail to do so not only will produce dire secular consequences such as the war; it may delay the coming of the Millennium itself.[6]

The use of the Indian missions as a test of Puritan piety poses some difficulties for Mather, since in the history that follows he is obliged to represent the Indians as fiendish sons of Satan and to defend their displacement as tenants of the land by the English. The distinction between "praying" and "heathen" Indians is helpful, since the former supposedly accepted their being displaced and ruled by the English, implictly acknowledging the justice of the English cause; and Mather does defend the activity of the Praying Indians during the war. But it was undeniably the case that many Praying Indians reverted to their tribes on the outbreak of war, some after being abused by the English, others out of a renascent sense of tribal loyalty. It was equally true that some of the most effective allies of the English were the unconverted Indians—Mohawks and Sogkonates among them—who fought against Philip. Nor was Mather blind to the fact that whites had given even heathen Indians just cause for complaint.

The opening paragraph of the history states its "doctrine": first, "That the Heathen People amongst whom we live, and whose Land the Lord God of our Fathers hath given to us for a rightful possession, have at sundry times been plotting mischievous devices against . . . the English *Israel*"; and second, that the unleashing of the Indian attack is a divine judgment, withheld "untill *the Body of the first Generation* was removed" but now sent thundering on the heads of the second generation, "which hath not so pursued, as ought to have been, the blessed design of their Fathers, in following the Lord into this Wilderness, when it was a land not sown." Here the "design" referred to is more general than the specific design of converting the Indians that Mather cites in his preface.

By generalizing the "failure" of the second generation to adhere to the "design of their Fathers," Mather gets around the problem of sympathy for the Indians. The war is to be seen as the consequence of the Puritan sons' failures, but their crime (failure to pursue the design) does not invalidate the design itself. In fact, since the war is a rebuke from God for their failure, the war validates the original program of the colony.

In Mather's real priorities, the conversion of the heathen Indians is less significant than the conversion of the unconverted colonists. Indian missions are valued not so much for their effects on Indians as for their moralizing effect on the population that engages in and supports such missions. The conquest of New England by Christianity is God's purpose, and Philip is wicked to oppose it. But that opposition, and its temporary successes, are predetermined by the will of God and sent as warnings to New England to mend its ways.

It is vital to note that Mather's support of the concept of Indian missions has more to do with theology than with secular policy—that is, it is important for the moral health of the citizens that they support such good works, and it is vital for the fulfillment of the prophecies that the work be done. However, if the survival of the holy experiment of New England seems to recognize the extermination of the Indians, Mather is willing to accept that outcome (preferably coupled with the conversion of as many as possible along the way). Indeed, in his later works he subtly shifts the biblical and typological framework in which he places the Indians, converting them into "Amalekites"—the people whose extermination God demanded, punishing the King of Israel who took tribute instead of fulfilling the commandment of genocide. This shift in Mather's response to the Indians reflects the transformation of basic values induced by the war.

The larger failures of the colonists are suggested in the account of the massacre of "Old Wakely" and his family by Indians in Maine. "Him with his Wife, Son and Daughter in law (who was greate with Childe) and two Grand-children, they cruelly Murdered, and took three Children alive, and led them into Captivity." Wakely's offense, for which God sent Indians to destroy him, was that he had left his original congregation to take up land on the frontier, moving beyond the bounds of church and law for the sake of worldly gain:

> This old *Wakely* was esteemed a godly Man. He would sometimes say with tears, that he believed God was angry with him, because although he came into *New-England* for the Gospels sake, yet he had left another place in this Coun-

> try, where there was a Church of Christ, which he once was in Communion with, and had lived many years in a Plantation where was no *Church, nor Instituted Worship.*

Because he had broken the filial ties of congregant to partriarch-minister, citizen to magistrate, his own family is destroyed and dispersed, carried into captivity by fiends. If such is the fate of a godly and repentant man, what must be in store for those whose departure for the woods was attended by no such heart-burnings as Wakely endured?

The unfolding events of the war become, in Mather's book, a series of "experiments," in which the shifting intentions and dispositions of Jehovah toward his backsliding chosen people are carefully measured. Mather counterpoints two categories of events—incidents of the battlefield and accounts of public fast-days, humiliation-days, and special prayer-offerings. In the sort of history modern readers are used to, a similar counterpoint would be established between battlefield incidents and political or strategic decisions taken by the government. Certainly there was such a counterpoint in fact: war policy was discussed and developed by political and military leaders and was responsive to both battlefield conditions and the political requirements of the allied colonies. A secular history or memoir like that of Benjamin Church shows that the interaction between field commanders and the colonial governments was a crucial factor in organizing and adjusting the strategic response to Philip's assaults. But to Mather, the essential war is not that between Indians and English troops but that between Christ and Satan. Therefore, the high strategy is not the political decision to conclude an alliance with, say, the Sogkonates; rather, it is the decision by the ministry to pursue a more intensive program of prayer, fasting, and public exhortation. The ministers, not the generals, are the true commanders, and the only politics that is relevant concerns the relationship between the supplicant parishioners and their sovereign Jehovah.

Mather's rejection of the secular is not simply an ideological stance but is organic, built into the structure of the narrative. He treats such basic components of historical writing as chronology and the narrative of physical actions and movements in ways very different from the methods of modern historical writing. For example, he makes no attempt to account for the movements of the Indians, nor any but the most perfunctory attempt to trace the movements of Philip and the other chiefs whom he supposes to be the movers behind the rebellion; for the English, however, he provides a rational account of political and military decisions and movements. The effect of this different treatment is to present the Indian war effort as random and undirected, save by the malice of individuals and tribes, while the English seem rational and orderly in their responses. But while they have no central directing intelligence, the Indians are nonetheless ubiquitous. Their malice seems to erupt here, there, and everywhere at once—because Mather does not recount Indian campaigns as sustained, continuing patterns of movement. This reinforces Mather's thesis that the Indians are less political and cultural rivals of the English than symbolic representatives of Satanic malice and racial insanity.

Mather's distortion of chronology is a still more significant part of his method. Mather most frequently dates events not according to the time of their occurrence but according to the time that news of them was received by the pious rulers and ministers in Boston. This method tends to make the perspective of Mather himself—as symbol of the ministry—the point about which all events organize themselves. From a secular military or historical point of view, it is important to know when and where a given body of Indians was met with, because such information sheds light on Indian movements and the course of the temporal war. But from Mather's viewpoint, the interaction between the prayerful congregation and its God is the crucial dialectic of the war, and hence the vital correlations are those between events in Church—prayers, fasts, humiliations—and communications from the battlefield. Such communications, arriving during official religious ceremonies, are read as responses to prayer. No matter if the news contained in the dispatch is some days old—the fact of its arrival during a period of prayer gives it status as a message from God reflecting his shifting disposition toward his errant children.

This total setting-aside of secular politics and strategic analysis, this effectual obliteration of the secular element from history, constitutes Mather's chief accomplishments as a historian (and his great liability as a political leader). His purpose is to restore the orthodox world view, in which a generation of true believers actually perceives, in experiential or "experimentall" terms, that all events proceed directly from the sovereign will of God. Here he recounts the history of an overwhelming current event without effective reference to secular power. History is seen simply as the unfolding and gradual discovery of divine purpose.

The war begins with an Indian attack on a congregation observing a day of humiliation proclaimed by a ministry concerned with the deterioration of Indian relations. The people in their congregation council approach the throne of their sovereign to beseech mercy and learn his will; he expresses it in a rebuke, sending the servants of Satan to punish his recalcitrant children. "The Providence of God is deeply to be observed, that the Sword should be first drawn upon a day of Humiliation, the Lord thereby declaring from heaven that he expects something else from his People besides fasting and prayer." (Periodically throughout the war the General Council or particular churchmen call for similar services of humiliation, public supplication, and fasting. Each such occasion provides a test of the shifting state of divine intention.) The next news received is a bulletin directly from Jehovah. A great council meeting is held in Boston on September 17, 1675, which attempts to regain the favor of the Almighty by calling for public reforms, rebuking New England for

> ill entertainment of the Ministry of the precious Gospel of peace: leaving our first love, dealing falsely in the Covenant of the Lord our God: the Apostasy of many from the inordinate Affection, and sinful Conformity to this present evil vain World: and (beside many horrid and scandalous sins breaking forth among us, for which we have cause to be greatly humbled before the Lord) our great unsensibleness of the Displeasure of the Lord, in suffering these abominations to be perpetuated; together with our carnal Security, and unquietness under the judgement of God upon us . . .

This call to reform and the declaration of a day of humiliation are not regarded as sufficient. The next news brings tidings of Indian victory "that very day when this Fast was kept."

Mather's account of the planning and execution of the expedition against the Narragansetts, which terminated in the Swamp Fight, is a model of his methods. After analyzing Puritan reasons for suspecting treachery on the part of the nominally neutral Narragansetts, he briefly notes one bit of secular planning—the discussion of the choice of a commanding general. The gathering of the army takes a sentence, the strategy consists of an intention to "execute the vengeance of the Lord upon the perfidious and bloudy Heathen." Then the serious moment arrives: before the army marches, "the Churches were all upon their knees before the Lord." As they pray, God signifies his intention by allowing the Indians to burn down the settlement at Quonsickamuck. This sufficiently prophesies the ultimate fate of the expedition, which is decimated after defeating the Narragansetts and burning their village. The extent of Mather's misunderstanding of both the manner and the significance of the battle and its aftermath can only be gauged by setting his account beside that of a participant like Benjamin Church. But such misunderstanding from the secular viewpoint is essential to the concept of history Mather employs and advocates.

In a war conceived in these terms, small incidents involving one or two individuals may yield intelligence more significant than either that brought in by spies or experts in Indian affairs or that revealed in major confrontations. Since it is Jehovah whose wrath has allowed the Indians to triumph, not any strategic genius in Philip and his chieftains, the only intelligence that matters is that which reflects God's intentions. Thus providential deaths and rescues, incidents in which peculiar ironies and coincidences are prominent, become central to the narrative. The case of Wakely is such an instance, as is that of the captivity and eventual ransoming of Mary Rowlandson, taken while her minister-husband was away in Boston. These incidents are so numerous as not to require particular discussion here. But their cumulative effect, from the viewpoint of secular history, is distorting, since their use tends to equate politically and strategically insignificant incidents with major battles and policy decisions. This distortion of course suits Mather's intention, which is to restore a religious world view, a God-centered consciousness of historical process, and a sense of man's powerlessness and absolute dependence on the will of an angry God.

Using divinity as a standard of measurement, Mather assigns gradation of value to different "providences." Small incidents following major fast- and humiliation-days or meetings of the council are of high significance, since they represent immediate responses to major supplications. Major battles like the Swamp Fight are of sufficient size and weight to impress Mather, but such human events are given no greater weight than substantial natural disasters—providential thaws that cripple or save the army, visitations by epidemic, the death of Governor Winthrop, the appearance of prodigious omens like the apparition of a gigantic "Indian Bow" in the sky, or monstrous births.

For Mather, the recounting of such prodigies was central to historical analysis and indeed constituted the application of "scientific" methods. He took such phenomena as physical manifestations of divinity within the temporal frame; and he had the authority of the Bible (as well as the writings of generations of pagan and Christian omen-spotters) for this belief. Using the biblical instances of the appearance of "prodigies" as precedents or models, Mather believed he was scientifically verifying some crucial points in his presentation of the war—his belief that God was directly concerned in it, that he intended the war as a warning to New England, and (consequently) that he still considered the Puritans as the New Israel, the new chosen people.[7]

Behind the various incidents Mather recounts, one central theme gradually emerges to consciousness, carrying with it the revelation of the true meaning of the war and the way to turn aside God's wrath. At the war's outset, the English find themselves struggling blindly in a jungle that is both of the world and of the spirit. At the beginning of the war a group of English soldiers pursuing Philip is ambushed in a swamp, which is "so Boggy and thick of Bushes" that "It could not there be discerned who were *English* and who the *Indians.*" As a result, the English find themselves killing their own men instead of the enemy. This confusion in the swamp expresses quite concisely the spiritual crisis to which Mather addresses himself. The English have become like Indians, whoring after strange gods, emigrating to forest plantations without instituted worship, indulging the pleasures of the flesh, reveling in a merely carnal sense of security and complacency. The war is therefore not so much an instance of Indians murdering whites as it is a case of self-murder; since the sins of the English are responsible for God's wrath, therefore the guilty English are responsible for their own murder, captivity, misery, and impoverishment. When the guilt of the nation is purged, the war will cease. The symbolic Indian, the Indian as metaphor for the guilt of the English, must be purged; the fate of his worldly avatar is important, but not equally so.

The sign that the war approaches a successful conclusion comes when Philip is killed by one of his own people. Like the English at the war's start, the Indians now begin to kill one another.

According to the narrative of Benjamin Church, whose recruitment of Indians from Philip's forces in fact led directly to the sachem's destruction, it is Church's expert diplomacy and carefully learned Indian-fighting technique that make the destruction of Philip's alliance (and Philip's death) possible. Mather notes Church's successes but attributes them not so much to the hero's expertise and courage as to the fact that before his climactic expedition the citizens of Bridgewater experience a religious revival, undergoing great spiritual exercises and anxieties, and renewing their "Covenant." This actual signing of the congregational roll signifies their sense that they have been unregenerate, unconverted, merely formal in their church membership, but have now experienced true conversion. God responds immediately to this act of renewal by giving the Bridgewater troops a victory over Philip. Earlier the entire colony of Plymouth did the same thing. This for Mather is the turning point of the war, the moment at which the successful strategy is discovered:

> So that there is of a late such a strange *turn of providence* (especially in *Plimouth* Colony, since the Churches in that Colony being thereunto provoked by the godly advice and Recommendation of the civil authority in that Jurisdiction) did solemnly *renew their Covenant with God and one another*) as the like hath rarely been heard of in any age.

The result is striking: "Whereas formerly almost every week did conclude with sad tydings, now the Lord sends us good news weekly." The assurance of victory is clear, although hostilities persist as the book goes to press.

Having completed his narrative and demonstrated the way in which God uses history to speak to his people, Mather proceeds to the sermon that will sum up the experience and systematize its lessons. The people are to learn to read in such events God's displeasure with their sinfulness, their failure to heed the Scriptures and respect their ministers. Above all, New England is to heed the particularity of the divine warning by examining carefully the nature of his chosen instruments. God's use of Indians to rebuke the English suggests that the English have become heathens in his sight:

> 4. *Consider how this Judgment is circumstanced,* If we mind where it began and by what Instruments, we may well think that God is greatly offended with the *Heathenisme* of the English People. How many that although they are *Christians* in name, are no better than *Heathens* in heart, and in Conversation? How many Families that live like *profane Indians* without any *Family prayer?* Yea there have been whole Plantations that have lived from year to year, without any publick Invocation of the Name of God, and without his Word. And in most places Instituted Worship (whereby *Christians* are distinguished from *Heathen*) hath been too much neglected.

Neglect of the injunction to fulfill the intention of the founding fathers is the major cause of God's paternal chastisement; a chief symptom is the decline of religious fervor, the rise of a "Formality of Religion" symptomatized by the decline in religious conversions. To this traditional rebuke of New England backsliding, Mather brings the force of a new myth, built on the analogy between the Indian war and the war between sin and grace in the individual soul. The Indians are merely concretions of our internal dispositions to evil; hence each sin Indianizes the Englishman, leagues him with those who have murdered, captured, and burned the congregant's friends, relatives, and immediate family.

The frontiersmen in particular are rebuked for departing from the restraint of the "First Generation" in regard to worldly wealth:

> [Whereas] the first Planters that they might keep themselves together were satisfied with one Acre for each person, as his propriety, and after that with twenty Acres for a Family, how have men since coveted after the earth that many hundreds, nay thousands of Acres, have been engrossed by one man, and they that profess themselves Christians have forsaken Churches, and Ordinances, and all for land and elbow-room.

More than a century and a half before Daniel Boone made the phrase legendary, the quest for "elbowroom" is associated by Mather with the antisocial, anti-institutional aspects of the individual quest for prosperity through expansion of the frontier.

From this perspective, the English victory in the war appears almost as dangerous to Puritanism as defeat might have been. The land-hungry frontiersmen may grow insolent in their pride of victory, and the weakening of the Indians may stimulate their greed further; Mather pejoratively links this frontier temperament with the boastful reaction of New England's Indians:

> "Many of those Heathen that have of late submitted themselves, are treacherous and bloudy, And the Indians that have been helpfull in this War, will be apt to grow insolent upon conceiting, that we could not have subdued our enemyes if it has not been for them; and it will be a great mercy if rude ungoverned English do not ere long scandalize and exasperate them."

Mather's charge is more general than a critique of frontiersmen and Indian policy. He is also criticizing the worldly spirit of a whole class of Puritans, many of the "rising generation," for whom the New World has become primarily a place in which to achieve wealth and status and for whom the preservation of orthodox purity is less important than political and social compromises that would ensure them protection of life and property against the taxation of the Crown and the vexation of the Indians. In an important sense, Mather's sermon is a rebuke to that very spirit of capitalism that later historians have seen as nearly synonymous with the rise of Puritanism.

Mather confronts directly the contradiction between the secular and religious aspects of Puritanism. While Puritan doctrine encouraged the pursuit of one's calling and prosperity was taken for a sign of divine favor, to pursue one's calling primarily to accumulate wealth was to violate the spirit of the Puritan ethic. Such pursuit caused first of all a degeneration of religious consciousness, of "experimental" piety. Then it promoted the division of a congregation of fellow saints into classes of rich and poor, employers and employed, each contending for economic and political power. Mather's contemporary, the poet-minister Benjamin Tompson, was just then mourning the passing of a golden age of Puritanism when men had been brothers in piety and poverty. They had greeted each other as equals without either obsequiousness in the poor or vaunting pride in the rich, and the air was not charged with the perpetual "cry of Rent."

But although Mather rebukes the rich for oppressing the poor, his severest rebukes are reserved for the lower classes. In part, he sees their poverty as a sign of a lack of diligence in their callings, of personal impiety or incontinence, or of divine disfavor. But perhaps their chief sin is their ambition to rise, to imitate the style and hope to acquire the wealth of their social betters. Condemning drunkenness and the delight in such "whorish" fashions as the wearing of expensive "perriwigs," Mather declares that there are "none more guilty then the poorer sort of people, who will need go in their Silks and Bravery as if they were the Best in the Land." These sins are directly rebuked by the fate of the frontier captives (mainly of the poorer sort, although with some notables like Mary Rowlandson among them). Love of fashion is rebuked when the captive is stripped naked; and the essentially "heathen" character of the victim's sin is revealed when the skin, "exposed to the burning heat of the sun, [is] burnt and tauned thereby until they become of an hue like unto these Indians."

The minister addressing his congregation becomes, by analogy, a white missionary addressing a mob of unregenerate and recalcitrant heathen who, like the Indians, have refused to show the ministry due respect, who have failed to achieve conversion, and who in effect insult and injure the messenger of Christ's Word. "And what though some [Praying Indians] may be hypocrites," Mather declares, "Are not some *Praying English* as perfidious?" To Mather—who was educated and came to manhood in England, now serving among people from whom he had been long separated—the analogy had real force.

Thus, Mather makes a complex association between general sinfulness, the particular sins of the ambitious lower classes (particularly on the frontier), and Indians. This effectively associates the aspirations of the lower classes and frontiersmen with racial degeneration or Indianization. By implication, despite Mather's critique of Puritan capitalism, it enlists Puritan mythology on the side of already established wealth and social status.

Taken as a whole, all these sins and punishments feed the

general thesis that New England's grief is the consequence of filial impiety, the failure of the sons to fulfill the mission laid down by the fathers: "The breach of the *fifth Commandment* is one of the great and *National sins,* which the Indians are guilty of: their Children have no regard nor reverence towards their Fathers. If we learn the way of the Heathen, and become like them, God will punish us by them." So long as the first generation survived, there was little to fear for New England. God acknowledged the piety of the fathers in his holding the Indians in fear of the English. The first generation removed, there is much to be feared. The history provides numerous instances of families wiped out root and branch, exterminated utterly from patriarch to child in the womb. If New England heeds the call, then God will fulfill his evident intention to destroy the Indians, and it will appear that his unleashing them was a providential means for accomplishing (and simultaneously justifying) their extermination by disease, internal warfare, and English muskets. But if this is to come to pass, New England must *"Remember the Errand that our Fathers came into this Wilderness for."* The ministry must be respected and heeded, the magistrates must enforce the laws more strictly, fathers must take care of their children's spiritual welfare, and Indian missions must be supported. No new settlements should be begun without a minister and church being provided at the outset, which is to say that individual pioneering must be discouraged. Should New England fail to reform, the wrath of God may again be poured out. Yet the sense of humiliation before and dependence on God ought not to lead to despair: God's evident intention in giving the English victory is to maintain the realm so recently gained for Christ.

The *Brief History* and *Earnest Exhortation* establish the groundwork for the mythology in which Increase Mather and his son Cotton seek to encase and preserve the ideology of orthodox Calvinism. Increase Mather would extend and elaborate the mythology and ideology of these works in his second history of the war and the sermon on "The Prevalency of Prayer." In the latter, the theory of history implicit in the early narrative of events is made explicit: each event of the war is seen to be a direct consequence of prayers offered up in church: "How often have we prayed that the Lord would take those Enemies into his own avenging Hand, . . . This Prayer hath been heard; . . . Yea the Indians themselves have testified, that more amongst them have ben cut off by the Sword of the Lord . . . then by the Sword of the English." [8]

It is difficult to know how his audience might have responded to so tendentious an argument, but it is not too much to say that the effectiveness of the sermon depends for its force on the audience's prior acceptance of the world view implicit in the *Brief History*. Narrative and myth establish the association of fact with idea with emotional force, and so prepare the audience to accept as given the most basic premises of the ideologist. The effectiveness of Mather's myth-making is suggested in part by the success of Mary Rowlandson's narrative, in which a vivid account of personal suffering and redemption, of alienation and reconciliation, is built on the same mythic pattern: the interaction between sovereign God and the individual soul, the association of the outer Indian with "Indian" traits of spirit in the Christian, the salvationary exorcism of both Indians by means of providential rescue, and the final renewing of the covenant between individual and God, citizen and society.

This myth is central to American responses to the Indian and the wilderness, and it would require an extended study to detail its development after 1677, only part of which can be fleshed out in this anthology. Its importance within the framework of Puritan history can be seen in the merging of the Matherian myth with the common language of Puritan religious discourse. To take one prominent example, Jonathan Edwards's "Sinners in the Hands of an Angry God" owes much of its force to the invocation of images from the mythology of the Indian wars and captivities. His text is that applied by Mather to the death of King Philip, and his depictions of the perilous state of sinners are laden with references to "unseen arrows" and ambushes.[9]

The most prolific interpreter of Increase Mather's version of the war was his son Cotton, who borrowed liberally from his father's histories in composing his account of the Indian wars in that most ambitious theodicy/history, the *Magnalia Christi Americana*. In Cotton Mather the ideological implications and typological interpretation of the original version are extended and exaggerated.[10] Increase Mather depicted the Indians as aggressors, but was also concerned for Indian missions; for Cotton Mather the missions are part of a vanished glory, and the Indians are "rabid animals" fit only for extermination. Like his father, he condemned the land hunger that led to a too-rapid expansion to the frontier. But his condemnation of the settlers is far more thoroughgoing and rigorous, since he was more clearly embroiled with them as a political entity. According to him, among the causes of King Philip's War was that "a great part of the English . . . grew too like the Indians, among whom they lived in their *unchristian* way of living; and . . . neither christianized the *pagans*, nor . . . take a due course to preserve themselves from losing of *christianity* in *Paganism*." Even more pointed, and like his father's, was his condemnation of the younger generation, among whose degeneracies and backslidings wilderness-going was counted.

Thus in his *Short History of New-England* (1694) he wrote:

> Observe *Goings out* as well as *Breakings in*, if you would see where the *Hedge* [i.e. protective wall of the Christian community] is deficient . . . Ah! Lord! Is there no way for us to hinder our Sons, from *Going Out* at our *Wall*, that they may be among, I know not what Cursed *Crues*, *Offer* themselves a *Burnt Offering* unto the *Devil?* . . . Do our *Old* People, any of them, Go out from the Institutions of God, Swarming into New Settlements, where they and their Untaught Families are like to Perish for Lack of Vision?[11]

It was useful for Cotton Mather to use his father's myth of King Philip's War as a key for interpreting the confusing struggles of the 1680s and 1690s, which pitted the New England rulers against both Anglo-Catholic and Protestant kings, royal governors and Puritan dissidents, and French-and-Indians all together. Cotton Mather extends the logic of his father's allegorization of history to read the events of the *Decennium Luctuosum* (or woeful decade, as he called it) as proof that the conflicts are but signs of the metaphysical combat of good and evil. Thus he sees the supposed outbreak of witchcraft in Salem in 1692 as simply another phase of the strategy of Satan for ruining the Puritan experiment:

> The Story of the Prodigious War, made by the Spirits of the Invisible World upon the People of New England, in the year, 1692, . . . [has] made me often think, that this inexplicable War might have some of its Original among the

> Indians, whose Chief Sagamores are well known unto some of our Captives, to have been horrid Sorcerers, and hellish Conjurors such as conversed with daemons.[12]

Mather also wrote a narrative of an attempt to exorcise a demon from one Mercy Short, a former Indian captive. Here he attempts to prove his thesis by invoking the mythology of Indian captivity, and by heightening and intensifying its symbolism (for which see the chapter on Mary Rowlandson). The girl's devil is a "Black Man," but of a "Tawney" or "Indian" blackness. Among her visions is one of a devil's sabbath attended by French priests and Indian "sagamores"—a dream perfectly understandable in secular terms as a nightmare rendering of the girl's captivity, but one which Mather will read only as revelation.[13]

The mythology that provided such vivid language for Matherian attempts at religious revival also served a political turn. The association of frontiersman and Indians made possible the condemnation of religious dissidents like the Reverend George Burroughs and political enemies like Governor Andros:

> Libells . . . were carried up and down against the Govern't and those in Authority,—how the Governour had confederated with the freemen [French bushrangers], Mohoques and other Indians to destroy the Colony and cut off the People . . . that the Governour had drawn all the Youth of the Country to the Eastward [i.e. the Maine frontier], on purpose to destroy them . . . That the Indian war was but a sham, for hee design'd noe evil to the Indians, but the destruction of the Country. That he admitted the Squaws dayly to him; or else he went out and lodged with them; that noe Soldier durst kill an Indian because the Governour had given positive orders to the Contrary . . .[14]

The problem with the mythology was that it provided only one method of dealing with the problems posed by settlement in the wilderness—the method of scapegoating, in which the Indian was substituted for the sins of the white man and exorcized like a demon. Its obsession with demonic and divine explanations for events prevented an effective response to the real conditions of the frontier. The Andros matter is a case in point, since the issue that provoked the "Libells" cited above was Andros's attempt to reinforce the Maine frontier with Bay Colony militia. Sending troops into that "boggy Swamp" was, from the Matherian viewpoint, an attempt to place white men where only Indians should be. There they would be separated from spiritual authority, exposed to temptation, perhaps involved with the Indians as Andros was supposed to be. The overthrow of Andros and withdrawal of the troops exposed the frontier to the Indian raids that decimated the settlements in 1688, yet the Matherian mythology forbade the drawing of policy lessons favorably reflecting on the Indian-demon-loving Andros.

The success of the American settlements required another sort of approach, that represented here by the narrative of Benjamin Church. Yet the Matherian mythology did not entirely fall to the ground, like the deacon's one-horse shay, when orthodox Calvinism entered its decadence. The pattern of associations that linked the Indians and the devil, the Indians and the suppressed aspects of white consciousness, the Indians and social dissidence, remained as a basic component of the American mythology of race and class.

## NOTES

1. Biographies of Mather are: Mason I. Lowance, *Increase Mather;* Robert Middlekauf, *The Mathers: Three Generations of Puritan Intellectuals;* Kenneth B. Murdock, *Increase Mather: The Foremost American Puritan.* For analyses of Mather as an intellectual and historian, see Sacvan Bercovitch, *The Puritan Origins of the American Self;* T. H. Breen, *The Character of the Good Ruler,* pp. 97–110.

2. Bercovitch, *Puritan Origins of the American Self,* pp. 52–57.

3. Ibid., pp. 42–43.

4. Perry Miller and Thomas H. Johnson, *The Puritans,* pp. 64–79, 665–69.

5. Ibid., p. 14.

6. Bercovitch, *Puritan Origins of the American Self,* pp. 54–55; Christopher Hill, *Antichrist in Seventeenth-Century England,* pp. 71, 183–84; J. F. Maclear, "New England and the Fifth Monarchy: The Quest for the Millennium in Early American Literature," *William and Mary Quarterly* 32:223–60.

7. Bercovitch, *Puritan Origins of the American Self,* pp. 54–55.

8. Increase Mather, *Historical Discourse Concerning the Prevalency of Prayer . . . ,* pp. 256–57.

9. Richard Slotkin, *Regeneration through Violence*, pp. 103–6, 109, 111.

10. Bercovitch, *Puritan Origins of the American Self*, discusses Cotton Mather at some length; see esp. pp. 49, 64–65.

11. Cotton Mather, *Magnalia Christi Americana*, 2:499; *The Short History of New-England*, pp. 42–43.

12. Cotton Mather, *Decennium Luctuosum*, in *Narratives of the Indian Wars*, Charles Lincoln, ed., pp. 242–47.

13. Cotton Mather, "A Brand Pluck'd Out of the Burning," in *Narratives of the Witchcraft Cases*, ed. G. L. Burr, pp. 257–87.

14. Robert Ratcliffe, *A Particular Account of the Late Revolution at Boston*, in *Narratives of the Insurrections*, ed. C. M. Andrews, p. 197.

A

# BRIEF HISTORY OF THE VVARR

## With the *INDIANS* in NEVV-ENGLAND,

(From *June* 24, 1675. when the first English-man was murdered by the Indians, to *August* 12. 1676. when *Philip*, alias *Metacomet*, the principal Author and Beginner of the Warr, was slain.)

Wherein the Grounds, Beginning, and Progress of the Warr, is summarily expressed.

TOGETHER WITH A SERIOUS

## EXHORTATION

to the Inhabitants of that Land,

By *INCREASE MATHER*, Teacher of a Church of Christ, in *Boston* in *New-England*.

Levit. 26 25. *I will bring a Sword upon you, that shall avenge the quarrel of the Covenant.*

Psal. 107 43 *Whoso is wise and will observe these things, even they shall understand the Loving-kindness of the Lord.*

Jer. 22.15 *Did not thy Father doe Judgment and Justice and it was well with him.*

Segnius irritant animos demissa per aures,<br>
Quàm quæ sunt oculis commissa fidelibus. *Horat.*<br>
Lege Historiam ne fias Historia. *Cic.*

*BOSTON*, Printed and Sold by *John Foster* over against the Sign of the *Dove*. 1676.

## *TO THE READER*[1]

Although I was not altogether negligent, in noting down such occurrences, respecting the present *Warr* with the Heathen in *New-England*, as came to my knowledge, in the time of them; yet what I did that way was meerly for my own private use; nor had I the least thought of publishing any of my *Observations*, until such time as I read a *Narrative* of this *Warr*, said to be written by a Merchant in *Boston*, which it seems met with an *Imprimatur* at *London* in December last:[2] the abounding mistakes therein caused me to think it necessary, that a true *History* of this affair should be published. Wherefore I resolved (σὺτ Θεῷ)[3] to *methodize* such scattered *Observations* as I had by me, so were the *Horae subsecivae*[4] of a few dayes improved. Whilst I was doing this, there came to my hands another *Narrative* of this Warr, written by a *Quaker* in *Road-Island*, who pretends to know the Truth of things;[5] but that Narrative being fraught with worse things then *meer Mistakes*, I was thereby quickned to expedite what I had in hand. I moved that some other might have done it, but none presenting, I thought of his Saying. *Ab alio quovis hoc fieri mallem quam a me, sed a me tamen potius quam a nemine.*[6] And I hope that in one thing, (though it may be in little else) I have performed the part of an *Historian*, viz. in endeavouring to relate things truly and impartially, and doing the best I could that I might not lead the *Reader* into a Mistake. *History* is indeed in itself a profitable Study. Learned men know that *Polybius*, and the great Philosopher call it, ἀλη Θιγωτάτην παιζείαν καὶ κρησίμην γυμνασίαν.[7] And there is holy Scripture to encourage in a work of this nature, for what was the *Book of the Warrs of the Lord.* Num. 21.14.? And that Book of *Jasher* which we read of in *Joshuah* and in *Samuel*? Yea and the Book of the *Cronicles*, mentioned in the Book of Kings (for we find not some of those things referred unto in the *Canonical* Book of *Cronicles*)[.] What were these Books, but the faithfull *Records* of the providentiall Dispensations of God, in the dayes of old? Yea and it is proper for the Ministers of God to ingage themselves in Services of this nature; Witness the *History*, or *Commentary* מדרש *of the Prophet Iddo*, 2. Cron. 13.22. Whether my defective manner of management in this History renders it unprofitable, I know not. Considering the other employments that are alwayes upon me, together with my personal inabilityes, I have cause to suspect it may be so, in a great measure. If anyone shall hereby be incited to do better, I hope I shall rather thank then envy him. πλεόνων ἔργον ἄνεΛνον.[10] And I earnestly wish that some effectual course may be taken (before it be too late) that a just *History of New-England* be written and published to the world. That is a thing that hath been often spoken of, but was never done to this day, and yet the longer it is deferred, the more difficulty will there be in effecting of it.

Moreover, the thing which I mainly designed, was the subsequent *Exhortation* which is annexed herewith, wherein I have desired to approve my self as in the sight of God, speaking what I believe God would have me to speak, without respect to any person in this world: And there is one thing insisted on therein, concerning which I could wish that I had said more, I mean that which doth respect endeavours for the *Conversion* of the *Heathen* unto *Christ*. There are some that make a wronge use of a Notion of Mr. *Cottons* touching this matter, alleadging that he taught that a general *Conversion* of *Indians* is not to be expected before the seven Vials are poured forth upon the Antichristian slate, nor before the conversion of the Jewish nation. It is far from my purpose to contradict that *Great Author*, unto whose dust (in respect of near *Affinity* as well as on the account of his eminency in Grace and spiritual Gifts) I owe a sacred Reverence; & it is known that I have my self asserted the same notion both in Sermons, and in a printed *Discourse concerning the Salvation of the tribes of Israel.*[11] But it was never intended that that Assertion should be improved, so as to discourage from the prosecution of that which was the professed pious, and a main design of the *Fathers* of this *Colony*, viz. *To propagate the Gospel and Kingdome of Christ among these Indians, who in former Ages had not heard of his fame and Glory.* It is indeed true, that although a *Fullness of the Gentiles* in respect of *Apostasy*, shall be accomplished (so must they *fulfill their Times*) before the calling of the Jews, yet the fullness of the Gentiles in respect of *Conversion*, will not come in before that. Nevertheless a glorious Sprinkling, and great Success of the Gospel, may be in particular places at present, even amongst Heathen.[12] And the Salvation of a few immortal Souls is worth the labour of many, all their lives. And happy experience hath confirmed this; for here in *New-*

*England,* six Churches have been constituted amongst the Indians. And the labours of *Robert Junius* forty years since amongst the East-Indians in *Formosa,* were wonderfully successfull, For (*as Caspar Sibellius* Pastor of the Church in *Daventry* in *Holland* writing the *History* of that affair, doth relate) there were no less than *five thousand & nine hundred Indians* that became professedly subject to the Gospel, & were all, together with their children, baptized into the Name of *Jesus Christ.*[13] *Junius* having learned the *Indian* Language, and being a Man of exemplary Piety in his conversation, and one also that excelled in Wisdome and Spiritual Abilities, God was with him, and made him an happy Instrument of winning Souls. He translated some part of the Scripture, and wrote Catechismes, and other profitable Books in their Language. He caused Schools to be erected among those blind *Barbarians,* so as that *Six hundred* of them were able to read, and write, and about *fifty* who excelled in Knowledge, and were of approved godliness, became *Instructors* of others in the Principles of the true Christian Religion: yea in *three and twenty Towns,* there were *Indian* Christian *Churches Planted.* And learned Men were sent out of *Holland,* in order to a further propagation of the interest of the Gospel in those remote parts of the World. Also *Justus Heurnius,* who was at first a *Physitian,* being inflamed with a singular zeal after Gods glory, and the Salvation of Souls of men, left his practising in *Medicinal Cures,* and betook himself wholy to the study of *Divinity;* after which he engaged in a Voyage towards the *East-Indians,* designing their *Conversion,* and having learned their *Language,* spent fourteen years amongst them: and as the great *Voetius*[14] (in his Disputation, *de vocatione Gentium*) testifieth, was instrumental to the *Conversion* of many of those *Indians,* so as to erect *Churches* of them in divers places, yea, and took care for the *learned Education* of divers young-men, even amongst the *Indians* themselves, so as that they were able to instruct the several Churches, which by the blessing of God upon his Labours had been lately formed. It is great pity then, that we in *New-England,* who do not come behind others in Profession, and Pretences to Religion, should fall short in real endeavours, for the promotion, and propagation of Religion, & Christianity amongst those that have been for ages that are past, *without God, and without Christ, and Strangers to the Common-wealth of Israel.* It troubleth me, when

I read how the *Papists* glory in that they have converted so many of the East and West *Indians* to the Christian Faith, and reproach *Protestants* because they have been no more industrious in a work of that nature. Though I know they have little cause to Glory, if the whole truth were known. For as for many of *their Converts,* inasmuch as they are become *Vassals,* not only to the Heresies, but to the Persons of those who have Proselyted them,[15] they are as Christ said concerning the Proselytes of the Scribes and Pharisees, *twofold more the Children of Hell,* then they were before;[16] and many of them know little of *Christianity* besides the *Name.* Witness the celebrated Story of that *Franciscan,* who wrote a Letter to a Friend of his in *Europe,* wherein he glorieth that having lived six and twenty years amongst the *Indians,* he had converted many thousands of them to the Faith, and he desired his Friend to send him a Book called the *Bible,* for he heard there was such a Book in *Europe* which might be of some use to him. Surely, *Francis* himself did not excel this *Franciscan,* in profound Ignorance.[17] It is also true, that the *Hollanders* have formerly (as was in part intimated but now) done something towards the *Conversion* of those *Indians* where they have Plantations settled. For they have caused some part of the Scripture to be translated into the *Indian* Language, and have out of their publick Treasuries maintained some learned and meet persons, on purpose, that they might become *Preachers to the Indians:* Nevertheless, *Voetius* in his dissertation *de plantatoribus Ecclesiarum,*[18] greatly bewaileth it that no more care hath been taken about that concern of the Gospel and Kingdome of Christ, and declareth what were the unhappy obstructions, hindring the *Belgick* Churches, from attaining a further progress in a work so desirable; but (as he there speaketh) *infanda illa nihil attinet hic referre.*[19] And I know not, but that the Lords Holy design in the *War* which he hath brought upon us, may (in part) be to punish us for our too great neglect in this matter. I would not detract from what hath been done that way, but rather with my Soul bless God for it. It is well known, that sundry of the Lords Servants in this Land, have laboured in that work: Especially Reverend Mr. *Eliot* hath taken most indefatigable pains, having Translated the whole Bible into the *Indian Language,* in which respect *New-England* (let Christ alone have the praise of it) hath out-done all other places, so far as I have heard or read.[20] But it cannot be long, before that faithful, and now aged Servant of the Lord rest from his Labours: sad will it be for the Succeeding Generation, if they shall suffer the work of Christ amongst the *Indians* to dye with him who began it. *Sed meliora speramus.*[21]

I shall add no more, but leave the success of this undertaking to him who alone can give it. And I earnestly desire the Prayers of every Godly Reader,

*Increase Mather.*

That the Heathen People amongst whom we live, and whose Land the Lord God of our Fathers hath given to us for a rightfull Possession, have at sundry times been plotting mischievous devices against that part of the English Israel which is seated in these goings down of the Sun, no man that is an Inhabitant of any considerable standing, can be ignorant. Especially that there have been *(nec injuria)*[22] jealousies concerning the *Narragansets* and *Wompanoags,* is notoriously known to all men. And whereas they have been quiet untill the last year, that must be ascribed to the wonderfull Providence of God, who did (as with Jacob of old, and after that with the Children of Israel) lay the fear of the *English,* and the dread of them upon all the *Indians.* The terror of God was upon them round about. Nor indeed had they such advantages in former years as now they have, in respect of Arms and Ammunition, their bows and arrows not being comparably such weapons of death and destruction, as our guns and swords are, with which they have been unhappily furnished.[23] Nor were our sins ripe for so dreadfull a judgment, untill *the Body of the first Generation* was removed, and another Generation risen up which hath not so pursued, as ought to have been, the blessed design of their Fathers, in following the Lord into this Wilderness, whilst it was a land not sown.

As for the Grounds, justness, and necessity of the present *War* with these barbarous Creatures which have set upon us,* my

* *Read the Postscript at the end of this History.*

design is not to *inlarge* upon that Argument, but to leav that to others whom it mostly concerns, only in brief this. The irruption of this flame at this time was occasioned as followeth.

In the latter end of the year 1674, *An Indian* called *John Sausaman,* who had submitted himself unto, and was taken under the protection of the *English* perceiving that the *profane Indians* were hatching mischief against the English, he faithfully acquainted the Governour of *Plimouth,* with what he knew, and also what his fears were together with the grounds thereof, withall declaring, that he doubted such and such Indians belonging to *Philip* the Sachem of *Pokanoket* or *Mount-hope,* would murder him; which quickly hapned accordingly: for soon after this, *John Sausaman* was barbarously murthered by an Indian called *Tobias* (one of *Phillip's* chief Captains and Counsellors) and by his son, and another Indian, who knocked him on the head and then left him on the Ice on a great Pond. Divine providence which useth to bring murther to light, so ordered as that an Indian unseen by those three that killed *Sausaman,* beheld all that they did to him, and spake of it, so as that a *Praying* (and as there is cause to hope) a godly *Indian, William Nahauton* by name, heard of it, and he forthwith revealed what he knew to the English. Whereupon the three Indians who had committed the murther were apprehended, and the other Indian testified to their faces that he saw them killing *Sausaman.* They had a fair tryall for their lives, and that no appearance of wrong might be, *Indians* as well as English sate upon the *Jury,* and all agreed to the condemnation of those Murtherers, who were accordingly executed in the beginning of the 6th Month called *June* Anno 1675. They stoutly denied the fact, only at last *Tobias's* son confessed that his father and the other Indian killed *Sausaman,* but that himself had no hand in it, only stood by and saw them doe it.

No doubt but one reason why the Indians murthered *John Sausaman,* was out of hatred against him for his Religion, for he was Christianized and baptiz'd, and was a Preacher amongst the Indians, being of very excellent parts, he translated some part of the bible into the Indian language, and was wont to curb those Indians that knew not God on the account of their debaucheryes;[24] but the main ground why they murthered him seems to be, because he discovered their subtle and malicious designs, which they were complotting against the English. *Philip* perceiving that the Court of *Plimouth* had condemned and executed one of his Counsellors, being (as is upon strong grounds supposed) conscious to the murther committed upon *John Sausaman,* must needs think that ere long they would do to him (who had no less deserved it) as they had done to his Counsellour: wherefore he contrary to his Covenant and Faith engaged to *Plimouth* Colony, yea and contrary to his promise unto some in this Colony (for about five years agoe *Philip* made a disturbance in Plimouth Colony, but was quieted by the prudent interposition of some in our Colony, when he ingaged, that if at any time hereafter he should think the English among whome he lived did him wronge he would not cause any disquietments before such time as he had acquainted the English of *Mattachusets,* but contrary to these solemn ingagements he) doth call his men together and *Arme* them, and refused to come when sent for by the authority of Plimouth, unto whose government he had subjected himself.[25]

Hereupon the English in *Plimouth* Jurisdiction sent a small *Army* to those towns next *Mount-Hope* in order to reducing *Philip* to his obedience, and for the security of those places which were in great danger and in no less fear by reason of the insolency of the Heathen.[26]

*June.* 24 (Midsummer-day) was appointed and attended as a day of solemn Humiliation throughout that Colony, by fasting and prayer, to intreat the Lord to give success to the present expedition respecting the Enemy. At the conclusion of that day of Humiliation, as soon as ever the people in *Swanzy* were come from the place where they had been praying together, the Indians discharged a volly of shot whereby they killed one man & wounded others. Two men were sent to call a Surgeon for the relief of the wounded, but the Indians killed them by the way: and in another part of the town six men were killed, so that there were nine english men murthered this day.
Thus did the *War* begin, this being the first english blood which was spilt by the Indians in an hostile way.[27] The Providence of God is deeply to be observed, that the sword should be first drawn upon a day of Humiliation, the Lord thereby declaring from heaven that he expects something else from his People besides fasting and prayer.

*Plimouth* being thus suddenly involved in trouble, send to the other united Colonyes for aid, and their desires were with all readiness complyed with.

Souldiers marched out of Boston toward *Mount-Hope, June. 26th.* and continued marching that night, when there hapned a great Eclipse of the Moon, which was totally darkned above an hour. Only it must be remembred that some dayes before any Souldiers went out of *Boston* Commissioners were sent to treat with *Philip,* that so if possible ingaging in a War might be prevented. But when the Commissioners came near to *Mount-Hope,* they found diverse english men on the ground weltring in their own blood having been newly murthered by the Indians, so that they could not proceed further.[28] Yea the Indians killed a man of this Colony as he was travelling in the roade before such time as we took up arms: in which respect no man can doubt of the *justness* of our cause, since the enemy did shed the blood of some of ours who never did them (our enemyes themselves being judges) the least wrong before we did at all offend them, or attempt any act of hostility towards them.[29]

*June 29th.* was a day of publick *Humiliation* in this Colony appointed by the Council[30] in respect of the *war* which is now begun.

This morning our army would have ingaged with the enemy, The Indians shot the Pilot who was directing our Souldiers in their way to *Philips* Countrey, and wounded several of our men, and ran into Swamps, rainy weather hindred a further pursuit of the Enemy.[31] An awfull Providence happened at this time: for a souldier (a stout man) who was sent from *Watertown,* seing the English *Guide* slain, and hearing many profane oathes among some of our Souldiers (namely those Privateers, who were also Volunteers) and considering the unseasonableness of the weather was such, as that nothing could be done against the Enemy; this man was possessed with a strong conceit that God was against the english, whereupon he immediately ran distracted,[32] and so was returned home a lamentable Spectacle.

In the beginning of *July* there was another Skirmish with the Enemy, wherein several of the Indians were killed, amongst whome were *Philips* chief Captain, and one of his Counsellors.[33]

Now it appears that *Squaw-Sachem* of *Pocasset* her men were conjoyned with the *Womponoags* (that is Philips men) in this Rebellion.[34]

About this time they killed several English at *Taunton,* and burnt diverse houses there. Also at *Swanzy* they caused about half the Town to be consumed with merciless Flames. Likewise

*Middlebury* and *Dartmouth* in *Plimouth* Colony did they burn with Fire, and barbarously murthered both men and women in those places, stripping the slain whether men or women, and leaving them in the open field as naked as in the day wherein they were born.[35] Such also is their inhumanity as that they flay of [f] the skin from their faces and heads of those they get into their hands, and go away with the hairy Scalp of their enemyes.

*July* 19. Our Army pursued *Philip* who fled unto a dismal Swamp for refuge: the *English Souldiers* followed him, and killed many of his Men, also about fifteen of the *English* were then slain.[36] The Swamp was so Boggy and thick of Bushes, as that it was judged to proceed further therein would be but to throw away Mens lives. It could not there be descerned who were *English* and who the *Indians.* Our Men when in that hideous place if they did but see a Bush stir would fire presently, whereby 'tis verily feared, that they did sometimes unhappily shoot *English men* instead of *Indians.* Wherefore a *Retreat* was Sounded, and night coming on, the *Army* withdrew from that place. This was because the desperate Distress which the Enemy was in was unknown to us: for the *Indians* have since said, that if the *English* had continued at the Swamp all night, nay, if they had but followed them but one half hour longer, *Philip* had come and yielded up himself. But God saw that we were not yet fit for Deliverance, nor could Health be restored unto us except a great deal more Blood be first taken from us: and other places as well as *Plimouth* stood in need of such a course to be taken with them.[37] It might rationally be conjectured that the unsuccessfulness of this Expedition against *Philip* would embolden the *Heathen* in other parts to do as he had done, and so it came to pass. For *July* 14, the *Nipnep* (or *Nipmuck*) *Indians* began their mischief at a Town called *Mendam* (had we amended our ways as we should have done, this Misery might have been prevented) where they committed *Barbarous Murders.* This Day deserves to have a *Remark* set upon it, considering that Blood was never shed in *Massachusets Colony* in a way of Hostility before this day. Moreover the Providence of God herein is the more awful and tremendous, in that this very day the Church in *Dorchester* was before the Lord, humbling themselves by Fasting and Prayer, on account of *the Day of trouble* now begun amongst us.

The news of this Blood-shed came to us at *Boston* the next

day in Lecture time, in the midst of the Sermon, the Scripture then improved being that, *Isai.*42.24. *Who gave Jacob to the spoil, and Israel to the robbers? did not the Lord, He against whom we have sinned?*

As yet *Philip* kept in the Swamp at *Pocasset,* but *August* 1. (being the Lords day) he fled. The *English* hearing that *Philip* was upon flight, pursued him, with a party of *Monhegins,* i. e. *Unkas* (who approved himself faithful to the *English* almost forty years ago in the time of the *Pequod* Wars, and now also in this present War) his *Indians.* They overtook *Philips* Party and killed about thirty of his men, none of ours being at that time cut off.[39] Had the *English* pursued the Enemy they might easily have overtaken the Women and Children that were with *Philip,* yea and himself also, and so have put an end to these tumults: but though Deliverance was according to all Humane probability near, God saw it no good for us as yet. Wherefore *Philip* escaped and went to the *Nipmuck Indians* who had newly (as hath been intimated) done Acts of Hostility against the *English.* But mean while endeavours were used to keep those *Indians* from engaging in this War, and that those persons who had committed the Murder at *Mendam* might be delivered up to Justice. Captain *Hutchinson* with a small party was sent to *Quabaog* where there was a great Rendezvouze of *Nipnep Indians.* They appointed time and place of Treaty to be attended, *August* 2. accordingly Captain *Hutchinson* rode to the Place fixed on to Treat in.[40] But the *Indians* came not thither according to their Agreement, whereupon Captain *Hutchinson* resolved to go further to seek after them elsewhere, and as he was riding along, the Perfidious *Indians* lying in Ambuscado in a Swamp, shot at him and wounded him, of which Wounds he after dyed, and eight men that were with him were struck down dead upon the place. Captain *Wheeler* who was in that Company was shot through the Arm, his dutiful Son alighting to relieve his Father, was himself shot and sorely wounded, willingly hazarding his own life to save the life of his Father. The *English* were not in a capacity to look after their dead, but those dead bodies were left as meat for the Fowls of Heaven, and their Flesh unto the Beasts of the Earth, and there was none to bury them.

Captain *Hutchinson* and the rest that escaped with their lives, hastened to *Quabaog,* and the *Indians* speedily followed, violently set upon the Town, killed divers, burning all the Houses therein down to the ground, except only one unto which the Inhabitants fled for succour, and now also (as since we have understood) did *Philip* with his broken Party come to *Quabaog.* Hundreds of *Indians* beset the House, and took possession of a Barn belonging thereunto, from whence they often shot into the House, and also attempted to fire it six times, but could not prevail, at last they took a Cart full of Flax and other combustible matter, and brought it near the House, intending to set it on fire; and then there was no appearing possibility, but all the *English* there, Men and Women, and Children must have perished, either by unmerciful flames, or more unmerciful hands of wicked Men whose tender Mercies are cruelties, so that all hope that they should be saved was then taken away: but behold in this Mount of Difficulty and Extremity ( יהוה יראה ) *the Lord is seen.*[41]

For in the very nick of opportunity God sent that worthy Major *Willard,* who with forty and eight men set upon the *Indians* and caused them to turn their backs, so that poor People who were given up for dead, had their lives given them for a prey.[42] Surely this was a token for good, that however we may be diminished and brought low through Oppression, Affliction, and Sorrow, yet our God will have compassion on us, and this his People shall not utterly perish. And this Salvation is the more remarkable, for that albeit the *Indians* had ordered Scouts to lye in the way, and to give notice by firing three Guns, if any *English* came to the relief of the Distressed; yet although the Scouts fired when Major *Willard* and his Souldiers were past them, the *Indians* were so busie and made such a noise about the House, that they heard not the report of those Guns; which if they had heard, in all probability not only the People then living at *Quabaog,* but those also that came to succour them had been cut off.

Things being brought to this state, the Tumult of those that are risen up increaseth continually: For *August* 22. being the Lords Day, the *Indians* about *Lancaster* killed a Man and his Wife and two Children in the afternoon exercise.[43] And we hear that *Philip* and the *Quabaog Indians* are gone more Westward, not far from *North-hampton, Hadly, Deer-field, &c.* whereupon Forces are sent from hence, under the command of Captain *Lathrop,* Captain *Beers,* and (after that) Captain *Mosely* to relieve those distressed Towns and pursue the Enemy. Also our Brethren at *Connecticut* afforded their Assistance, Major *Treat* being sent to *Hadly* with a party of *English,* and some of *Unkas* his Men. The *Indians* inhabiting about *Connecticut River* pretended great fidelity to the *English,* and that they would fight against *Philip,* who it seems had been tampering with them in the Spring before the War broke out, endeavoring by money (*i. e. Wampampeag* which is the *Indians* Money) to engage them in His bloody design against the *English.*[44]

At first they were so far credited as to be *Armed* by the *English,* hoping they might do good service as the *Monhegins* and *Natick Indians* had done. But within a while their Treachery was justly suspected. Whereupon Souldiers were sent (on or about *August* 25.) to demand their Arms. They were then gone out of their Forts, our Men searching after them, they suddenly shot out of a Swamp, and after that an hot dispute continued for some hours.[45] How many *Indians* were slain we know not, but nine English fell that Day, wherein this Providence is observable, that those *nine men* which were killed at that time belonged to *nine several Towns,* as if the Lord should say, that he hath a controversie with every Plantation, and therefore all had need to repent and reform their ways.

Now the *English* have a multitude of open Enemies more then when this trouble began, so that greater desolations are now expected.

Wherefore *September* 1. the *Indians* set upon *Deerfield,* (alias *Pacomptuck*) and killed one man, and laid most of the Houses in that new hopeful Plantation in ruinous heaps. That which addeth solemnity and awfulness to that Desolation, is, that it happened on the very day when one of the Churches in *Boston* were seeking the face of God by Fasting and Prayer before him. Also that very day the Church in *Hadly* was before the Lord in the same way, but were driven from the Holy Service they were attending by a most sudden and violent *Alarm,* which routed them the whole day after. So that we may humbly complain, as sometimes the Church did *how long hast thou smoaked* עָשַׁנְתָּ *against the Prayers of thy People.*[46] Not long after this, Captain *Beers* with a considerable part of his men fell before the Enemy.[47] Concerning the state of those parts at this time until *September* 15. I received information from a good hand, whilst things were fresh in memory, which I shall here insert, as containing a brief *History* of the Transactions which happened within the time mentioned, those parts being then the Seat of the War: the Letter which I intend is that which followeth.

*Reverend and dear Brother;*[48]

"I received yours, wherein among other things you desire an account of the passages of our War with the *Indians:* I shall in answer to your desire relate the most remarkable passages: the people here having many causes of jealousie, of the unfaithfulness of our *Indians* presented the same before the Committees of the Militia, whereupon it was thought meet to desire of them the surrendry of their Arms, and by perswasion obtained about nine and twenty: But about three dayes after they being desirous to go forth with some Forces from *Harford,* both *Indians* and *English,* and some from the *Bay* in pursuit of *Philip,* their Arms were delivered to them again: but a while after their return, jealousies still increasing, there was a general desire in the People of these three Towns, that they should be again disarmed, and such things as these were presented to the Council here, as inducing thereunto: 1. That when they heard of the Massacre at *Quabaog,* they made in the Fort eleven Acclamations of joy, according to the number of our men that were slain. 2. A *French-man* that was going to *Boston* gave Testimony that he met three *Indians* that told him they were coming to perswade *North-Hampton Indians* to fight with *Philip,* and that at his return he askt our *Indians* whether they would fight, they said they could not tell. 3. One of their *Sachims* owned that there were several among them false to the *English,* but would not tell who they were. 4. A Woman of ours was warned by a *Squaw* to remove with her Children into the middle of the Town: told her withal, she durst not tell News, for if she did the *Indians* would cut off her head. 5. Some of theirs gave out very suspicious Expressions: one upbraided the English, that *Coy* was dead already, and *Eyer* and *Pritchet* were dead already: said further that the *Indians* went out to find *Philip* with the *English,* that when *Philip* was fighting with them in the front, they might fall on them in the rear: another said the reason why he went not out with the Army was that he might help to destroy the *English* at home: another threatned a maid of our town to knock her on the head. 6. when they were out with our Army, they shewed much unwillingness to fight, alleadging they must not fight against their mothers and brothers and cousins (for *Quabaog* Indians are related unto them) 7. Unkas his son,[49] who went out the same time complained that our Indians had almost spoiled his, and that the English were blind and could not see the falshood of these Indians. 8. They shot bullets five several times at our men in diverse places. Other things too many to numerate were presented, and the Councill saw cause to demand their arms[.] Aug 24. They made some objections, but were fully answered: The Sachem left the Councill to try whether he could perswade the Indians, promising however to bring in his own. In the after-noon the Councill sent to the Fort for their answer: they told the Messenger that some Indians were abroad in the Meadows, and they were not willing to deliver up their arms without their consent: but in the morning they should have their answer. The Messenger was desired to go again to them, in the evening, to conferre with them, to try whether he could perswade them, and coming to the other side of the River, wisht some of them to come over, they bid him come over to them, and bid him kiss— —Whereupon Captain *Lathrop* & *Beers*, with whom the thing was left, intended to take their arms by force, and at mid-night sent over to our officers, to draw as nigh the Fort as they could without being perceived, and they would do the like on *Hatfield* side, and so at break of day come upon them[;] but before they came the Indians were fled, having killed an old *Sachem* that was not willing to go with them. The Captains resolved to follow them, and pursued a great pace after them, with about an hundred men, having sent back a part of ours for a Guard of the Town. A little before they overtook the Indians, they heard two strange claps of Thunder, like two volleys of shot; at length they saw a single Indian, but shot not at him, though they might have killed him, because they intended to parly with them, but on a sudden the Indians let fly about forty gunns at them, and was soon answered by a volley from our men['s] about forty ran down into the Swamp after them, poured in shot upon them, made them throw down much of their luggage, and after a while our men after the Indian manner got behind trees, and watcht their opportunities to make shotts at them; the Fight continued about three hours, we lost six men upon the ground, though one was shot in the back by our own men, a seventh dyed of his wound coming home, and two dyed the next night, nine in all, of nine several towns, everyone of these towns lost a man: Of the Indians as we hear since by a Squaw that was taken, and by three Children that came to our town from them the day after, there were slain twenty six: the same day there was an Indian that lodged in our town the night before, taken by our men, and a *Squaw* that belonged to our Fort that was coming from *Spring-field*, they both owne that our Indians received Wompam from *Philip* in the Spring, to ingage them in the War. The fellow also owns that there were seven of our Indians that went to *Quabaog*, where they heard that they intended to fight. After this fight we heard no more of them till the first of September, when they shot down a Garison Souldier of *Pacomptuck*, that was looking after his horse, and ran violently up into the town, many people having scarcely time enough to get into the Garisons. That day they burnt most of their houses and barns, the Garisons not being strong enough to sally out upon them, but killed two of their men from the Forts. The next day they set upon several men that were gone out of the Fort at *Squakheag*, they slew eight of our men, not above one of them being slain that we know of, but made no attempt upon the Fort. The next day (this Onset being unknown) Capt, *Beers* set forth with about thirty six men and some Carts to fetch of the garison at *Squakheag*, and coming within three miles of the place, the next morning were set upon by a great number of Indians from the side of a Swamp, where was an hot Dispute for some time:* they having lost their *Captain* and some others, resolved at last to fly, & going to take horse lost several men more, I think about twelve: the most that escaped got to *Hadly* that evening: next morning another came in, and at night another that had been taken by the Indians, and loosed from his bonds by a *Natick* Indian, he tells the Indians were all drunk that night, that they mourned much for the loss of a great Captain, that the English had killed twenty five of their men. Six dayes after another Souldier came in, who had been lost ever since the fight, and was almost famished, and so lost his understanding, that he knew not what day the fight was on.

"On the 5*th* of *September* Major *Treat* set forth for *Squak-*

---

* *It seems Capt* Beers *and those* 36 *men that were with him, fought courageously till their Powder and shot was spent; then the Indians prevailed over them so as to kill above* 20 *of them only* 13 *escapted with their lives, at which time a Cart, with some Ammunition fell into the hands of the enemy.*

*heag* with above an hundred men, next day coming nigh *Squakheag,* his men were much daunted to see the heads of Captain *Beers* Souldiers upon poles by the way side; but after they were come to *Squaukheag,* some partyes of them went into the Meadow, but hearing some gunns about the Fort, they ran up to see what the matter was, but by the way were fired upon by about fourteen Indians as they judg, out of the bushes; one or two Indians were slain, Major *Treat* was struck upon the thigh, the bullet pierced his cloaths, but had lost its force, and did him no harm: coming to the Fort he called his Councill together, and concluded forthwith to bring off the garison: so they came away the same night, leaving the Cattel there, and the dead bodyes unburied: since which seventeen of their Cattel came a great part of the way themselves, and have since been fetcht into *Hadly.*

Upon the 12*th*: of this month the Indians made an assault upon twenty two men of *Pocomptuck,* that were going from one garison to the other to *Meeting* in the afternoon: made a great volley of shot at them, but killed not one man, they escaped to the Garison whither they were going, only one man running to the other garison was taken alive: The Indians took up their rendezvouze on an hill in the meadow, burnt two more house, kil'd many horses, carryed away horse-loads of beef and pork to the hill: they sent the same night for more aid, but partly through the strictness of the Commission of our Garison souldiers, or at least their interpretation of it, and partly through the wetness of the weather, there was nothing done that night: the next day we perswaded some of our Inhabitants to go Volunteers, and sent to *Hadly* to doe the like, who going up with some of Captain *Louthrops*[50] souldiers, joyned themselves to the garison at *Pocomptuck,* and on Tuesday very early went out to assault the Indians, but they were all fled. Last night Captain *Mosely* with his men came into *Hadly,* and this night we expect more Forces from *Hartford.*

"If the Lord give not some sudden Check to these Indians, it is to be feared that Most of the Indians in the Countrey will rise.

"I desire you would speak to the *Governour,* that there may be some thorough care for a *Reformation,* I am sensible there are many difficulties therein: many sins are grown so in fashion, that it becomes a question whether they be sins or no. I desire you would especially mention, *Oppression,* that intollerable Pride in cloathes and hair: the tolleration of so many *Taverns,* especially in *Boston,* and suffering home-dwellers to lye tipling in them. Let me hear soon from you: the Lord bless you and your Labours, forget us not at the throne of Grace: It would be a dreadfull Token of the Displeasure of God, if these afflictions pass away without much spiritual advantage: I thought to have written somewhat more large with respect to *Reformation,* but I hope I need not, you will I presume be forward of your self therein.["][51]

Not many dayes after this Letter was written, the English received a sadder rebuke of Providence, then anything that hitherto had been. For *September* 18. Captain *Lothrop* (a godly and courагious Commander) with above seventy men were sent to be as a Guard to some that were coming from *Deer-field* with Carts loaden with Goods and Provision, to be removed to *Hadly,* for security: But as they were coming, the Indians, whose cruel Habitations are the dark corners of the Earth, lurked in the Swamps, and multitudes of them made a sudden and frightful assault. They seized upon the Carts and Goods (many of the Souldiers having been so foolish and secure, as to put their Arms in the Carts, and step aside to gather *Grapes,* which proved dear and deadly Grapes to them) killed Captain *Lothrop,* and above threescore of his men, stripped them of their clothes, and so left them to lye weltring in their own Blood.[52] Captain *Mosely* who was gone out to range the Woods, hearing the Guns, hasted to their help, but before he could come, the other Captain, and his men were slain, as hath been expressed. Nevertheless he gave the Indians Battle: they were in such numbers as that he and his company were in extream danger, the Indians endeavouring (according to their mode of fighting) to encompass the English round, and then to press in upon them with great numbers, so to knock them down with their Hatchets. In the nick of time Major *Treat,* with above an hundred men, and threescore of *Unkas* his Indians came in to succour those that were so beset with the Enemy, whereupon the Enemy presently retreated, and night coming on, there was no pursuing of them. In this fight, but few of Captain *Mosely's* men were slain: How many *Indians* were killed is unknown, it being their manner to draw away their dead men as fast as they are killed, if possibly they can do it: yea, they will venture their own lives for that end, which they do out of policy, that so their Enemies may think that few or none of them are killed, when nevertheless they have lost many. I am informed that some of the *Indians* have reported that they lost ninety six men that day, and that they had above forty wounded, many of which dyed afterwards.[53] However, this was a black and fatal day, wherein there were eight persons made Widows and six and twenty Children made Fatherless, all in one little Plantation, and in one day; and above sixty Persons buried in one dreadful Grave. And this was the state of the *Western* parts in respect of the War with the Heathen.

We must now take a step backwards, and a little consider the *Eastern Plantations.*[54] For in the Month of *September,* did the flame break out there. Some who had their hearts exercised in discerning things of that nature, were from the beginning of the War, not without sad Apprehensions concerning the Inhabitants in those parts of the Country, in that they were a scattered people, and such as had many of them Scandalized the Heathen, and lived themselves too like unto the Heathen, without any *Instituted Ordinances,* also the Indians thereabouts were more numerous then in some other places. They began their Outrages, at the House of one Mr. *Purchase,* who had been a great Trader with the Indians. After that they came to the House of an old Man in *Casco-bay,* whose name was *Wakely.* Him with his Wife, Son and Daughter in law (who was great with Childe) and two Grandchildren, they cruelly Murdered, and took three Children alive, and led them into Captivity.

This old *Wakely* was esteemed a godly Man. He would sometimes say with tears, that he believed God was angry with him, because although he came into *New-England* for the Gospels sake, yet he had left another place in this Country, where there was a Church of Christ, which he once was in Communion with, and had lived many years in a Plantation where was no *Church, nor Instituted Worship.* If a Faithful Minister of Christ happened to Preach in *Casco,* he would with much affection entertain him, saying *Blessed is he that cometh in the Name of the Lord.* After this good man was murthered by the Indians, they quickly did more mischief: so that in *Falmouth* there were five Houses burnt, four Men, two Women, and two Children killed, and three Children carried away Captive. After this they set upon

*Sacoe,* where they slew thirteen Men, and at last burnt the Town. A principle Actor in the destruction of *Sacoe* was a strange *Enthusiastical Sagamore,* called *Squando,* who some years before pretended that God appeared to him, in the form of a tall Man, in black Cloaths, declaring to him that he was God, and commanded him to leave his Drinking of Strong Liquors, and to pray, and to keep Sabbaths; and to go to hear the Word Preached, all which things the *Indian* did for some years, with great seeming Devotion and Conscience observe. But the God which appeared to him, said nothing to him about Jesus Christ; and therefore it is not to be marvelled at, that at last he discovered himself to be no other wise then a Childe of him, that was a Murtherer and a Lyar from the beginning.[55] Also these inraged *Barbarians,* being annimated with their success at *Falmouth* and *Sacoe,* they went to *Black-Point* and there killed six Men and a Woman, and burnt two and twenty dwelling Houses. In the mean time, the *English* at *Kenebeck* endeavoured that the Indians in those parts might be kept from joyning in this *Insurrection,* whereto they were tempted and sollicited by their neighbours. The prudent endeavours of the English proved happily successful, insomuch as the *Sachems* there, brought Presents with great Protestations of Amity and Fidelity, and desired that no more Liquors might be sold to the *Indians,* professing that that was a principle cause of the mischiefs that had been done, and that they were not able to keep their men in subjection, when once they were become mad with drink.

After these things, the *Indians* killed two men at *Kittery,* and stripped them. Lieutenant *Playster* with twenty two English went out to fetch off the dead bodies, and to bury them; as they were putting one of them into the Cart, suddenly a small party of *Indians* shot out of a Swamp. And the greatest part of the English did unworthily forsake their *Leader* in that hazard, only seven remained with him. He thinking his men had been near at hand, faced the Enemy, killed and wounded many of them, but the *Indians* perceiving that all but seven of the *English* were fled, took courage and killed Mr. *Plaister* (who was a good and useful man) and one of his Sons, and another man: the other four seeing that, ran for their lives, and so escaped until they came safe into a *Garrison,* which was not far off.

Behold how great a matter a little fire kindleth. This fire

which in *June* was but a little spark, in three months time is become a great flame, that from East to West the whole Country is involved in great trouble, and the Lord himself seemeth to be against us, to cast us off, and to put us to shame, *and goeth not forth with our Armies.* Wherefore the Magistrates of this Jurisdiction, earnestly called upon the Inhabitants thereof, to humble themselves before the Lord, and to confess and turn from transgression. Inasmuch as the expressions contained in that paper, which was at this time published by the Councils order, for a day of publick Humiliation, to be observed through this Jurisdiction, are most serious, and gracious, and greatly expressive of the sinful *Degenerate Estate* of the *present Generation in New-England,* and that Declaration will turn for a Testimony to our faithful Rulers, both now and hereafter; considering also, that it is in but few hands, I shall therefore here insert, and republish it. 'Tis that which followeth.[56]

AT A
COUNCIL
Held at *Boston*, *Sept.* 17. 1675.

*It having pleased the Holy God (all whose works are Truth, and his Wayes Judgement) for our sins whereby he hath been provoked, in special by the undervaluation of our pleasant things; great unthankfullness for, and manifold abuses of our wonderfull peace, and the blessings of it in this good land which the Lord hath given us, ill entertainment of the Ministry of the precious Gospel of peace: leaving our first love, dealing falsely in the Covenant of the Lord our God: the Apostacy of many from the Truth unto Heresies, and pernicious Errors: great Formality, inordinate Affection, and sinful Conformity to this present evil vain World: and (beside many horrid and scandalous sins breaking forth among us, for which we have cause to be greatly humbled before the Lord) our great unsensibleness of the Displeasure of the Lord, in suffering these abominations to be perpetuated; together with our carnal Security, and unquietness under the judgements of God upon us, our abiding very much unreformed, notwithstanding all Warnings, and Chastisements, whereby the Lord hath been, and is still debating with us, we having greatly incensed him to stir up many Adversaries against us, not only abroad, but also at our own Doors (causing the Heathen in this Wilderness to be as Thorns in our sides, who have formerly been, and might still be a wall unto us therein; and others also to become a Scourge unto us) the Lord himself also more immediately afflicting us by Diseases, whereof so many Children in some of our Towns have died this Summer. His not going forth with our Armies as in former times, but giving up many of our Brethren to the mouth of the devouring Sword, yea, shewing himself angry with the Prayers of his People: threatning us also with scarcity of Provision, and other Calamities, especially if this present War, with the Barbarous Heathen should continue; and that the Lord of Hosts withdraw not the Commission he hath given to the Sword, and other Judgements to prevail against us;*

The Governour and Council of this Jurisdiction therefore (being under the sense of these evils; and also of the distressed state of the rest of the Colonies confederate with our selves, and of the Churches of Christ in other parts of the Christian World, in this day of Trouble, Rebukes, and Blasphemy: and fearing the sad issue thereof, unless the Lord help us with our whole heart, and not feignedly, to turn unto himself) Do Appoint and Order the seventh day of the next Month, to be a Day of publick Humiliation, with Fasting and Prayer, throughout this whole Colony; that we may set ourselves sincerely to seek the Lord, rending our hearts, and not our garments before him, and pursue the same with a thorough Reformation of what ever hath been, or is an Image of jealousie before the Lord to offend the eyes of his Glory; if so be, the Lord may turn from his fierce anger, that we perish not: we do therefore require all the Inhabitants of this Jurisdiction to forbear servile labour upon that day, and that they apply themselves respectively to observe the same, as is appointed.

By the Council, *Edward Rawson* Secr't.

*Octob* the *7th.* This day of Humiliation appointed by the Council, was solemnly observed: yet attended with awfull testemonyes of divine displeasure. The very next day after this Fast was agreed upon by those in civill Authority, was that dismal and fatal blow, when Captain *Lothrop* and his company (in all near upon fourscore souls) were slaughtered, whereby the Heathen were wonderfully animated, some of them triumphing and saying, that so great slaughter was never known: and indeed in their Warrs one with another, the like hath rarely been heard of. And that very day when this Fast was kept, three Persons were killed by the Indians near *Dover*, one of them going from the publick Worship. Also that very day at the close of it, the sad tidings of *Springfields* Calamity came to us here in *Boston*. And inasmuch as this news came at the conclusion of a day of Humiliation, surely the *solemn voice of God to New-England* is still as formerly, *Praying* without *Reforming* will not do. And now is the day come wherein the Lord is fulfilling the word which himself hath spoken, saying, I will send wild Beasts among you, which shall rob you of your Children, and destroy your Cattle, and make you few in number, *and if you will not be reform'd by these things, I will bring your Sanctuaryes to Desolation, and I will not smell the sweet Savor of your Odours.*[57] The Providence of God is never to be forgotten, in that *Churches have been signally spared for so long a time.* Although some Plantations wherein Churches have been settled were in most eminent danger, and the Enemy might easily have swallowed them up, yet God so ordered that they received little or no detriment, when other places were laid utterly waste; the Lord manifesting how loth he was to disgrace the Throne of his Glory, but now he begins with the Sanctuary. As for *Springfields* misery, it thus came to pass: Whereas there was a body of *Indians* that lived in a *Fort* near to that *Town of Springfield,* and professed nothing but Friendship towards the *English,* they treacherously brake in upon the Town, when a party of our Souldiers who had been there, were newly gone to *Hadly.* They killed several, amongst others their Lieutenant *Cooper* was most perfideously Murthered by them, without the least occasion or Provocation given. They burnt down to the ground above thirty dwelling houses, and above twenty out-houses: amongst others, Mr. *Pelatiah Glover* Teacher of the Church there, is a great sufferer, his House, and Goods and Books, and Writings being all consumed in one hour. Nevertheless there was a great mixture of mercy in this dark and dismal dispensation. For God so ordered, as that an *Indian* who knew what was designed the next day, ran away in the night, and acquainted the *English* therewith, whence they had time and opportunity to escape to an house that was Fortified, otherwise in probability the Inhabitants had surely had their lives as well as their dwelling places cut off.

*October* 13. The *General Court* sat in *Boston,* during this Session, a *Committee* was with the concurrance of both Houses appointed in order to a *Reformation* of those Evils which have provoked the Lord to bring the Sword upon us, and to withdraw from our *Armies* from time to time. The Assistance of the *Teaching Elders* in the Churches was desired, as in a case of that nature, it was proper for them to advise and help according to God.

There was a gracious presence of God with them in their consultations, all that were there with one voice agreeing in many particulars, in respect whereof *Reformation* should be, and must be: *e. g.* 'That some effectual course should be taken for the Suppression of those proud Excesses in Apparrel, hair, &c: which many (yea and the poorer sort as well as others) are shamfully guilty of. That a due testimony should be borne against such as are false Worshippers, especially Idolatrous *Quakers,* who set up Altars against the Lords Altar, yea who set up a Christ whom the Scriptures know not. That whereas excess in drinking is become a common Sin, meanes should be used to prevent an unnecessary multiplication of Ordinaries, and to keep Town dwellers from frequenting Taverns: and that whereas Swearing hath been frequently heard, they that hear another Swear profanely and do not complain of it to Authority, shall be punished for that concealment. Also that some further care should be taken, that the fourth and fifth Commandments be better observed then formerly, and that there may be no more such Oppression, either by Merchants or day-Labourers as heretofore hath been, and that the Indian Trading-houses, whereby the Heathen have been debauched and scandalized against Religion, be suppressed; and that more care should be taken respecting the *Rising Generation,* then formerly hath been, that they might be brought under the discipline of Christ &c.['][58] These things were unanimously consented to.

*October* 19. The Conclusions of the Committee, respecting *Reformation* of provoking evils were signed, and delivered in to the General Court, who voted acceptance thereof, and appointed another Committee to draw up Laws in order to the establishment of the things agreed on. Now as I remember that famous Martyrologist Mr. *Fox* (in *Acts & Monuments,* vol. 2. pag.

669) observes, with respect to the *Reformation* in K. *Edward* the 6*th* his dayes, that that very day and hour when the Act for *Reformation* was put in execution at *London,* God gave the *English* a signal victory against the *Scots* at *Muscleburrough;* so it was proportionably with us. For that day when there was a vote passed for the Suppression and Reformation of those manifest evils, whereby the eyes of Gods Glory are provoked amongst us, the Lord gave success to our Forces, who that day encountred with the *Indians* at *Hatfield.*[59] The *English* lost but one man in the fight (albeit some that were sent forth as Scouts were killed or Captivated) the Enemy fled before them, and ran into the River, many of them being seen to fall, but night coming on, it was in vain to follow them further. And after that day, the *Western Plantations* had little or no disturbance by them, but lived in quietness all the Winter. All this notwithstanding, we may say as sometimes the Lords People of old, *the Harvest is past, the Summer is ended, and we are not saved.*[60] The Sword having marched *Eastward, & Westward,* and *Northward,* now beginneth to face toward the *South* again. The *Narragansets,* who were the greatest body of *Indians* in *New-England;* there being no less then six Sachims amongst them, having not as yet appeared in open Hostility. Nevertheless *Philips and Squaw-Sachims* men,[61] when routed by the *English* Forces, were harboured amongst the *Narragansets.* When the Commissioners of the united Colonies sat at *Boston,* in the latter end of *September,* one of the *Narraganset Sachims,* and Messengers from other Sachims there, made their appearance in *Boston;*[62] they pretended nothing but good-will to the *English,* and promised that those Enemies of ours, who had burnt so many houses, and committed so many Murders, and had fled to them for refuge, should be delivered up by the latter end of *October.* But when the time prefixed for the surrendry of the *Wompanoags* and *Squaw-Sachems Indians* was lapsed, they pretended they could not do as they had ingaged at present, but after winter they would do it. In the meanwhile, when the English had any ingagement with the Indians, wounded Indians came home to the *Narragansets,* especially after the fight at *Hatfield,* Octob. 19*th,* about fourty wounded men were seen crossing the woods towards the *Narragansets;* also some (at least two Indians) from amongst themselves, came to the English, and told them that the *Narragansets* were resolved (if they could) to destroy the

English: but they were loth to begin to fall upon them before winter, but in the Spring when they should have the leaves of trees and *Swamps* to befriend them, they would doe it: wherefore it was judged necessary to send out Forces against them, and preparations were made accordingly.[63]

There was some agitation amongst those whom it did concern, where a person suitable for so great a trust might be found as *General;* and that worthy Gentleman *Josiah Winslow Esq,* who succeeds his Father (of blessed memory) as Governour of *Plimouth,* was pitched upon for this Service.

Under his conduct therefore, an Army consisting of at first a thousand, and at last about fifteen hundred men, were sent forth to execute the vengeance of the Lord upon the perfidious and bloudy Heathen. But before they set out, the Churches were all upon their knees before the Lord, the God of Armyes, entreating his favour and gracious success in that undertaking, wherein the welfare of his people was so greatly concerned. This day of Prayer and Humiliation was observed *Decemb. 2d.* when also something hapned intimating as if the Lord were still angry with our Prayers, for this day all the houses in *Quonsickamuck* were burnt by the Indians.[64]

*Decemb. 8th.* The Army set out from Boston. Whilst they were upon this march, an *Indian* whose name was *Peter,* having received some disgust among his Country-men, came to the English, and discovered the plotts of the Indians, told where they were, and promised to conduct the Army to them. They were no sooner arrived in the Narraganset Country, but they killed and took captive above fourty Indians.[65] Being come to Mr. *Smith's* house, they waited some dayes for *Connecticut* Forces. In the mean while a party of the enemy did treacherously get into the house of *Jerem. Bull* (where was a Garison) burned the house, and slew about fourteen persons.[66]

*Decemb.* 18. *Connecticut* Forces being come, a March toward the enemy was resolved upon: *Peter* Indian having informed that the *Body of Indians* (only *Ninnigret* being one of their old crafty *Sachems,* had with some of his men withdrawn himself from the rest, professing that he would not ingage in a *War* with the English, therefore did he goe into a place more remote) was in a Fort about eighteen miles distant from the place where our Army now was. The next day, although it were the

Sabbath, yet, provisions being a[l]most spent by our Souldiers, waiting so long for Connecticut Forces, the Councill of War resolved to give Battle to the enemy. The English Souldiers played the men wonderfully; the Indians also fought stoutly, but were at last beat out of their Fort, which was taken by the English, There were hundreds of *Wigwams* (or Indian houses) within the Fort, which our Souldiers set on fire, in the which men, women and Children (no man knoweth how many hundreds of them) were burnt to death. Night coming on, a Retreat was sounded.[67]

Concerning the number of Indians slain in this Battle, we are uncertain: only some Indians which afterwards were taken prisoners (as also a wretched English man that apostatized to the Heathen, and fought with them against his own Country-men, but was at last taken and executed) confessed that the next day they found three hundred of their fighting men dead in their Fort, and that many men, women and children were burned in their *Wigwams*, but they neither knew, nor could conjecture how many: it is supposed that not less then a thousand Indian Souls perished at that time. *Ninnigret* whose men buried the slain, affirmeth that they found twenty & two Indian Captains among the dead bodyes. Of the English there were killed and wounded about two hundred and thirty, whereof only eighty and five persons are dead. But there was a solemn rebuke of Providence at this time, in that six of our Captains were slain, viz. Captain *Johnson* of Roxbury, Captain *Gardner* of Salem, Captain *Davenport* of Boston (son to that Captain *Davenport* who did great Service in the expedition against the Indians in the *Pequod* war, Anno 1637) Captain *Gallop* of New-London, Captain *Marshal* of Windsor, Captain *Siely* of Stratford, who dyed of his wounds some dayes after the fight was over. The three Captains first mentioned, belonged to *Mattachusets* Colony, the three last to *Connecticut*, of *Plimouth* Colony Captain *Bradford* (one of their faithfull Magistrates, and son of him that was many years Governour there) was sorely wounded, but God had mercy on him, and on his people in him, so as to spare his life, and to restore him to some measure of health, albeit the bullet shot into him is still in his body. Also Captain *Goram* of *Barnstable* in Plimouth Colony fel sick of a feaver whereof he dyed.

Thus did the Lord take away seven Captains out of that Army. Also four *Leiutenants* were wounded in that *Fort fight*, so that although the English had the better of it, yet not without solemn and humbling Rebukes of Providence. At night as the army returned to their Quarters, a great Snow fell, also part of the army missed their way, among whom was the *General* himself with his Life-guard. Had the enemy known their advantage, and pursued our Souldiers (and we have since heard that some of the *Indians* did earnestly move, that it might be so, but others of them through the overruling hand of Providence would not consent) when upon their retreat, they might easily have cut off the whole Army: But God would be more gracious to us. Here then was not only a *Victory*, but also a signal *Preservation*, for which let the Father of mercyes have eternal Glory.[68]

After this God seemed to withdraw from the English, and take part with the enemy. The next day the Indians finding but few English men dead in the Fort amongst their three hundred Indians that were slain, were much troubled and amazed, supposing that no more of ours had been killed; this blow did greatly astonish them, and had the English immediately pursued the Victory begun, in all likelyhood there had been an end of our troubles: but God saw that neither yet were we fit for deliverance[.] Wherefore *Connecticut* Forces withdrew to *Stonington*, and there being so many killed and wounded amongst those that remained in the *Narraganset* Country, also bread for the Souldiers being wanting, by reason the extremity of the weather was such, as that the Vessels loaden with provision could not reach them, therefore the army lay still some weeks.

In this interval of time, the town of *Mendam* (which before that had been forsaken of its Inhabitants) was burnt down by the Indians.

Now doth the Lord Jesus begin solemnly to fulfill his word, in *removing Candlesticks* out of their places, because of *Contentions*, and loss of first Love.[69] Surely when those places are destroyed where Churches have been planted, Candlesticks are removed out of their places. But to proceed, When the Army was just upon the Resolve to return home, because provisions were spent, God so ordered, as that a Vessel loaden with Victuals arrived, whereupon it was determined (σὺν Θεῷ)[70] to pursue the enemy. Only it was thought necessary to desist from this pursuit untill *Connecticut* Forces could return and joyn with ours. In the *interim*, a strange sudden *Thaw* hapned in the midst of *January* (when in New-England the season is wont to be extream cold) that the snow melted away in a little time: the like weather hath rarely been known in this Land at that time of the year, albeit some of the first Planters say it was so above fifty years agoe: However this made wonderfully for the Indians advantage, for now they fled out of the *Narraganset* Country, and whereas they had been sorely straightned and distressed for victuals, now the snow being wasted, they lived upon Ground-nuts.

In fine, the Army pursued them several dayes, overtook some of them, killed and took about seventy persons, were in sight of the main Body of them, and could they have held out to have pursued them but one day longer probably this unhappy War had then been ended: but the Souldiers were tired with eight dayes March, and (having spent much of their provision whilst waiting for our *Connecticut* Brethren) their bread faild, so as that they were forced to kill horses and feed upon them.[71]

We have often carried it before the Lord as if we would *Reform* our wayes, and yet when it hath come to, we have done nothing: So hath the Lord carried toward us, as if he would deliver us, and yet hath deferred our *Salvation*, as we our selves have delayed *Reformation*.

So then *February* 5. The Army returned to *Boston*, not having obtained the end of their going forth. It was easie to conjecture that the *Narraganset*, and *Nipmuck*, and *Quabaog*, and *River Indians*,[72] being all come together, and the *Army* returned, they would speedily fall upon the *Frontier Towns*. And some of the Praying *Indians* who had been sent out as Spies, and had been with the *Indians* beyond *Quabaog*, brought intelligence, that a *French Man* that came from *Canady* had been amongst them, animating them against the *English*, promising a supply of *Ammunition*, & that they would come next summer and assist them: also the Indian Spies declared, that there was a designe, within such a time to burn Lancaster, which came to pass both as to the time and manner accordingly.[73]

For upon the 10*th* day of *February* some hundreds of the *Indians* fell upon *Lancaster*, burnt many of the Houses, killed and took Captive above forty persons. Mr. *Rowlandson* (the faithful Pastor of the Church there) had his House, Goods, Books, all burned; his Wife, and all his Children led away Captive before the Enemy. Himself (as God would have it) was not at home, whence his own person was delivered, which otherwise (without a Miracle) would have been endangered. Eight men lost their lives, and were stripped naked by the *Indians,* because they ventured their lives to save Mrs. *Rowlandson.*

As this good Man returned home (having been at *Boston* to intercede with the Council that something might be done for the safety of that place) he saw his *Lancaster* in flames, and his own house burnt down, not having heard of it till his eyes beheld it, and knew not what was become of the Wife of his bosome, and Children of his Bowels. This was a most awful Providence, and hath made me often think on those words, *though Noah, Job and Daniel were in it, they should deliver but their own Souls, they should deliver neither Sons nor Daughters, they only shall be delivered, but the Land shall be desolate.*[74] And this desolation is the more tremendous, in that this very day the Churches *Westward* were humbling themselves before the Lord. Within a few dayes after this, certain *Indians* did some mischiefs at *Malbery,*[75] *Sudbery, Chelmsford.*

*February* 21. The *Indians* assaulted *Medfield,* and although there were two or three hundred Souldiers there, they burnt half the Town, killed several Men, Women, and Children (about eighteen in all) amongst others their Lieutenant *Adams* was slain. And soon after he was killed, his Wife was casually[76] slain by an *English-man,* whose Gun discharged before he was aware, and the Bullet therein passed through the Boards overhead, and mortally wounded Lieutenant *Adam's* wife, It is a sign God is angry, when he turns our Weapons against our selves.

*February* 23. A day of Humiliation was attended in the old Meeting-house in *Boston,* but not without much Distraction, because of an Alarm, by reason of rumors, as if the *Indians* were doing mischief within ten miles of *Boston.*

*February* 25. This night the *Indians* fired [e]leven Houses and Barns in *Weymouth.*

In the beginning of *March,* another small Army was sent out from *Boston,* under the conduct of that expert Souldier and Commander Major *Savage,* to seek out the Enemy, Connecticut Forces met with ours at *Quabaog,* and they marched together, but not following the direction of the *(Natick) Praying Indians,* who were sent as Pilots, the Army missed their way, and was bewildred in the Woods. On a sudden when they thought on no such thing, a party of *Indians* fired upon them, and killed one man, and wounded Mr. *Gershom Bulkly,* who is Pastor of the Church in *Wethersfield;* whereupon those *Indians* were immediately pursued, who hastened towards *North-Hampton.* The Army following them thither, missed of the main Body of *Indians.* Nevertheless, there was a singular providence of God ordering this matter, for the relief of those *Western Plantations,* which otherwise, in probability had been cut off.

For upon the fourteenth of *March* a multitude of *Indians* fell upon *North-Hampton,* broke through their Fortification in three places, burned five houses, and five barns, and killed four Men, and one Woman: but the Town being full of Souldiers, the Enemy was quickly repulsed, with the loss of many of their lives.

March the 10*th.* Mischief was done, and several lives cut off by the *Indians* this day, at *Groton* and at *Sudbury.* An humbling Providence, inasmuch as many Churches were this day Fasting and Praying.

*March* 12. This Sabbath eleven *Indians* assaulted Mr. *William Clarks* House in *Plimouth,* killed his Wife, who was the Daughter of a godly Father and Mother that came to *New-England* on the account of Religion, (See *July* 6.) and she herself also a pious and prudent Woman; they also killed her sucking Childe, and knocked another Childe (who was about eight years old) in the head, supposing they had killed him, but afterwards he came to himself again. And whereas there was another Family besides his own, entertained in Mr. *Clarks* house, the *Indians* destroyed them all, root and branch, the Father, and Mother, and all the Children. So that eleven persons were murdered that day, and under one roof; after which they set the house on fire. The Leader of these *Indians* was one *Totoson,* a fellow who was well acquainted with that house, and had received many kindnesses there, it being the manner of those bruitish men, who are only skilful to destroy, to deal worst with those who have done most for them.

*March* 13. The Indians assaulted *Groton,* and left but few houses standing. So that this day also another Candlestick was removed out of its place. One of the first houses that the Enemy destroyed in this place, was the *House of God, h.e.*[77] which was built, and set apart for the celebration of the publick Worship of God.

When they had done that, they scoffed and blasphemed, and came to Mr. *Willard* (the worthy Pastor of the Church there) his house (which being Fortified, they attempted not to destroy it) and tauntingly, said, *What will you do for a house to pray in now we have burnt your Meeting-house?* Thus hath the Enemy done wickedly in the Sanctuary, they have burnt up the Synagogues of God in the Land; they have cast fire into the Sanctuary; they have cast down the dwelling place of his name to the Ground. *O God, how long shall the Adversary reproach? Shall the Enemy Blaspheme thy Name for ever? why withdrawest thou thine hand, even thy right hand? pluck it out of thy bosome.*[78]

*March.* 17. This day the *Indians* fell upon *Warwick,* and burnt it down to the ground, all but one house.

*March.* 20. Some of them returned into the *Narraganset* Country,[79] and burnt down the remaining English houses there.

We are now come to the conclusion of the year 1675. which hath been the most troublesome year that ever poor *New-England* saw. What ending the present year shall have, is with God, but it hath a most dolefull beginning.[80]

For *March* 26. 1676. being the *Sabbath-day,* the Indians assaulted *Mal*bery, and consumed a great part of the town: after which the inhabitants apprehended themselves under a necessity of deserting that place which was done accordingly; so that here is another Candlestick removed out of his place. This day also, Captain *Pierce* of *Scituate* with a party of about fifty *English* and twenty *Indians,* who were Friends to the *English,* pursued a small number of the Enemy, who in desperate subtilty ran away from them, and they went limping to make the *English* believe they were lame, till they had led them into a snare: for suddenly a vast body of *Indians* did encompass them round, so that Captain *Pierce* was slain, and forty and nine *English* with him, and eight (or more) *Indians* who did assist the *English,* and fought bravely in that engagement.[81]

How many of the Enemy fell we know not certainly, only we hear that some *Indians,* which have since been taken by the *English,* confess that Captain *Pierce,* and those with him killed an hundred and forty of them before they lost their own lives.

Upon this Lords-day another sad thing likewise hapned, for near *Springfield,* there were eighteen *English-men* riding to the Town, to attend the solemn Worship of God on his Holy day.

And although they were Armed, there were seven or eight *Indians,* who lying in Ambuscado, were so bold as to shoot at them. They killed a Man and a Maid that rode behind him, the English being surprised with fear, rode away to save their lives: in the mean while the Indians seized upon two women and Children, and took them away alive, so that here we have cause to think of Joshuahs words, who said, *O Lord What shall I say when Israel turns their backs before their Enemies?*[82] What shall be said when eighteen English-men well arm'd, fly before seven Indians? This seems to argue something of a divine forsaking, and displeasure in heaven against us. The next day those Indians were pursued, but when the *English* came in sight those barbarous wretches hasted to run away, but before that they knocked the two Children on the head, as they were sucking their mothers breasts, and then knocked their Mothers on the head: Nevertheless one of them was alive when the souldiers came to her, and able to give an account of what the Indians had told her. Amongst other particulars, they did affirm to her that there was a Body of about three thousand Indians (no doubt but in that they did hyperbolize) near to *Deerfield,* and that they had newly received a great supply of powder from the Dutch at *Albany:* men that worship *Mammon,* notwithstanding all prohibitions to the contrary, will expose their own and other mens lives unto danger, if they may but gain a little of this worlds good.[83]

*March.* 27. Some of the inhabitants of *Sudbury,* being alarumed by what the Indians did yesterday to their neighbours in *Malbury,* apprehending they might come upon the enemy unawares, in case they should march after them in the night time, they resolved to try what might be done, and that not altogether without success. For towards the morning whilst it was yet dark, they discerned where the Indians lay by their Fires. And such was their boldness, as that about three hundred of them lay all night, within half a mile of one of the garison houses in that town where they had done such mischief the day before. Albeit the darkness was such as an English man could not be discerned from an Indian, yet ours being forty in number, discharged several times upon the enemy, and (as Indians taken since that time do confess) God so disposed of the bullets that were shot at that time, that no less then thirty Indians were wounded, of whom there were fourteen that dyed several of which had been principal actors in the late bloudy Tragedyes. They fired hard upon the

English, but neither killed nor wounded so much as one man in the Skirmish.

*March* 28. The Indians burnt about thirty Barns, and near upon fourty dwelling Houses in *Rehoboth,* so that thereby the dissiyation[84] and desolation of that Church is greatly threatned.

The next day they burnt about thirty houses at the town called *Providence.*

In the beginning of *April* they did some mischief at *Chelmsford* and *Andover,* where a small party of them put the town into a great fright, caused all the people to fly into Garison-houses, killed one man, and burnt one house. And to shew, what barbarous creatures they are, they exercised cruelty toward dumb creatures. They took a Cow, knocked off one of her horns, cut out her tongue, and so left the poor creature in great misery. They put an horse, ox &c. into an hovil, and then set it on fire, only to shew how they are delighted in exercising cruelty.[85]

*April.* 9*th.* This day being the Lords day, there was an alarum at *Charlestown, Cambridge,* and other towns, by reason that sundry of the enemy were seen at *Billerica,* and (it seemeth) had shot a man there. This week we hear from *Connecticut,* that a party of their Souldiers went with many of the *Pequods,* and *Monhegins,* and some of *Ninnegrets* Indians, to seek after the enemy, and they killed and took captive forty and four Indians without the loss of any of ours: amongst whom were several of their *Chief Captains,* and their great Sachem called *Quanonchet,* who was a principal Ring-leader in the *Narraganset* War, and had as great an interest and influence, as can be said of any among the Indians. This great Sachem was pursued into a River by one of *Ninnegret* his men, and there taken. Being apprehended he was carried away to *Stonington,* where the English caused the *Pequods* and *Monhegins,* and *Ninnegrets* Indians, to joyn together in shooting *Quanonchet,* and cutting off his head, which was sent to *Hartford.* And herein the English dealt wisely, for by this meanes, those three Indian Nations are become abominable to the other Indians, and it is now their interest to be faithful to the English, since their own Country-men will never forgive them, on account of their taking and killing the Sachem mentioned: So that there was a gracious smile of providence in this thing, yet not without matter of humbling to us, in that the Sachem was apprehended not by English but by Indian hands.

*April.* 19. The Indians killed a man at *Weymouth,* and another at *Hingham.* And they burnt down the remaining deserted houses at *Malbery.*

*April* 20*th.* A day of Humiliation was observed in *Boston.* The next day sad tidings came to us. For the enemy set upon *Sudbury,* and burnt a great part of the town. And whereas Capt. *Wadsworth* (a prudent & faithfull man) was sent out for their relief, with about seventy armed men, a great body of Indians surrounded them, so as that above fifty of ours were slain that day, amongst whom was Capt. *Wadsworth* and his Leiutenant *Sharp.* Also Captain *Brattlebanck* (a godly and choise spirited man) was killed at the same time. Also they took five or six of the English and carried them away alive, but that night killed them in such a manner as none but *Salvages* would have done. For they stripped them naked, and caused them to run the Gauntlet, whipping them after a cruel and bloudy manner, and then threw hot ashes upon them, cut out the flesh of their legs, and put fire into their wounds, delighting to see the miserable torments of wretched creatures. Thus are they the perfect children of the Devill. What numbers the Indians lost in this fight, we know not, onely a Captive since escaped out of their hands, affirms that the Indians said one to another, that they had an hundred and twenty fighting men kill'd this day.

The same day (as is judged fifty) Indians burnt nineteen houses and barns at *Scituate* in *Plimouth* Colony, but were notably encountered and repelled from doing further mischief by the valor of a few of the inhabitants.

*Apr.* 24*th,* Skulking Indians did some mischief in *Braintry,* but the inhabitants received not any considerable damage by them.[86]

*April.* 27. A small number of them near *Woodcocks* who keeps the *Ordinary* in the roade to *Rehoboth,* watched their opportunity and killed his son, and another man, and greatly wounded another of his sons, and shot himself through the arm, and then burnt[87] his sons house.

At *Boston* there is a Press[88] in order to sending forth another Army to pursue the enemy; for we hear there is a great body of them near *Malbury,* (as tis ayprehended) of many hundreds.

About this time, in *Connecticut-Colony,* Capt. *Dennison* with sixty six Volunteers, & an hundred and twelve *Pequod-Indians,* pursuing the common enemy, took and slew seventy and six Indians. Amongst the slain was the Sachem *Pomham* his Grandchild, who was also a Sachem, and another *Sachem* called *Chickon,* and one great Counsellour. They took and spoiled an hundred and sixty bushels of the Indians corn. None of ours either English or Indians that did ingage with and for the English, were lost when this exploit was done.

In the moneth of *April,* many of the Eastern Indians[89] having been sorely distressed, and fain to wonder up and down for meat, so as that they lived for some time upon no other food then the skins of wild creatures, which they soaked in water till they became soft and eatable; notwithstanding the outrages and murthers (for they have shed the blood of about forty seven persons) by them committed, they did in confidence of favour from the English come and submit themselves, alleadging that the injuryes done by them were grounded upon a mistake. For when a party of English came in a Warlike posture upon some of their *Webbs* (as they call them) *i.e. Women* as they were gathering corn, an Indian seing it, ran to the other Indians and told them that the English had (though it were not at all so) killed all those Indian women, and therefore they took up arms to revenge that supposed injury. Also they plead for themselves, that a Fisherman told one of them, that the English would destroy all the Indians, and when inquiry was made of another English man (thought to be more discreet then the former) he confirmed what the other had said, and that some rude English did purposely overset a *Canoo* wherein was an Indian Lad; and that although a *Squaw* dived to the bottome of the River and fetched him up alive, yet that the Lad never came to himself again. It is greatly to be lamented that the heathen should have any ground for such allegations, or that they should be scandalized by men that call themselves Christians.[90]

*May* 3d. Was the day of *Election* for Governour and Magistrates in the *Mattachusets Colony.* This day the Lord by a wonderfull hand of providence, wrought Salvation for *Mrs. Rowlandson* & returned her to *Boston,* after she had been eleven weeks in Captivity amongst the heathen. This is a Token for good, being a great answer of Prayer. For by reason of her near relation to a *Man of God,* much prayer had been particularly made before the Lord on her behalf. Nevertheless did the Lord manifest his holy displeasure, inasmuch as at *Haveril* and *Bradford,* a small company of Indians killed two men and carryed away a man and a woman, & five Children alive.

*May. 6th.* Our Forces which is abroad met with a party of Indians, and killed about thirteen of them, and had probably destroyed many more of them, had not an English-man unhappily sounded a trumpet, whereby the enemy had notice to escape. The *Praying Indians* did good Service at that time, insomuch as many who had hard thoughts of them all, begin to blame themselves, and to have a good opinion of those *Praying Indians* who have been so universally decryed.[91]

*May* 8. About seventeen Houses and Barns did the *Indians* fire and destroy at *Bridge-water.* About this time they killed four men at *Taunton,* as they were at work in the field, by whose death about thirty Children were made fatherless. But the Lord in the nick of time, sent Thunder and Rain, which caused the Enemy to turn back.

*May,* 9. A day of Humiliation by Fasting and Prayer, was attended in the Town-house at *Boston,* by the Magistrates, and Deputies of the General Court, with Assistance to so many Teaching Elders as could be obtained. Although many such solemn occasions have at times been attended in former years, yet it hath been observed by some, that God did alwayes signally own his Servants, upon their being before him in such a way and manner: And so it was now; for the very next day after this, a Letter came from *Connecticut* to *Boston,* informing that God had let loose the *Mohawks* upon our Enemies, and that they were sick of Fluxes, and Fevers, which proved mortal to multitudes of them. And whereas a special request left before the Lord this day, was, that he would (as a token for good) cause our poor Captives to be returned to us again, and particularly those that were taken from Haveril the last week, God gave a gracious and speedy Answer, bringing home those very Captives in particular, and many other, yea at least sixteen of our poor sighing Prisoners, who were appointed to death, did the Lord loose and return unto us, within eight weeks after this day, and divers of them within three dayes after this solemn day of Prayer. There are who have dated the turn of Providence towards us in this Colony, and against the Enemy in a wonderful manner, from this day forward: yet some lesser and more inconsiderable devastations happened soon after in Plimouth Colony. For,

*May* 11. A company of *Indians* assaulted the Town of *Plimouth,* burnt eleven Houses and five Barns therein: ten *English-men* were going to seek after the Enemy, and having an *Indian* with them, who was true to the *English,* he spied a party of *Indians* lying in Ambush, who in probability had otherwise cut off many of them, but the *English* having the opportunity of the first shot, struck down several *Indians,* one of which had on a great Peag Belt. But he and the other that fell were dragged away, and the Indians *fled,* when they saw themselves pursued, though but by a few. Nevertheless two dayes after this, they burnt seven Houses and two Barns more in *Plimouth,* and the remaining Houses in *Namasket.*

*May.* 18. This day that happened which is worthy to be remembred. For at *North-hampton, Hadly,* and the Towns thereabouts, two *English* Captives escaping from the Enemy, informed that a considerable body of *Indians,* had seated themselves not far from *Pacomptuck,* and that they were very secure: so that should Forces be sent forth against them, many of the Enemy would (in probability) be cut off, without any difficulty. Hereupon the Spirits of Men in those Towns were raised with an earnest desire to see and try what might be done. They sent to their neighbours in *Connecticut* for a supply of Men, but none coming, they raised about an hundred and four score out of their own Towns, who arrived at the *Indian Wigwams* betimes in the morning, finding them secure indeed, yea all asleep without having any Scouts abroad; so that our Souldiers came and put their Guns into their Wigwams, before the *Indians* were aware of them, and made a great and notable slaughter amongst them. Some of the Souldiers affirm, that they numbred above one hundred that lay dead upon the ground, and besides those, others told about an hundred and thirty, who were driven into the River, and there perished, being carried down the Falls, *The River Kishon swept them away, that ancient River, the river Kishon, O my soul thou hast troden down strength.*[92] And all this while but one *Englishman* killed, and two wounded, But God saw that if things had ended thus; another and not Christ would have had the Glory of this Victory, and therefore in his wise providence, he so disposed, as that there was at last somewhat a tragical issue of this Expedition. For an *English* Captive Lad, who was found in the Wigwams, spake as if *Philip* were coming with a thousand *In-*

*dians:* which false report being famed *(Famâ bella stant)*[93] among the Souldiers, a pannick terror fell upon many of them, and they hasted homewards in a confused rout: πολλὰ κενὰ τοῦ πολεμοῦ.[94] In the meanwhile a party of Indians from an Island (whose coming on shore might easily have been prevented, and the Souldiers before they set out from *Hadly* were earnestly admonished to take care about that matter) assaulted our men; yea, to the great dishonour of the English, a few Indians pursued our Souldiers four or five miles, who were in number near twice as many as the Enemy. In this *Disorder,* he that was at this time the chief Captain, whose name was *Turner,* lost his life, he was pursued through a River, received his Fatal stroke as he passed through that which is called the *Green River,* & as he came out of the *water* he fell into the hands of the *Uncircumcised,* who stripped him, (as some who say they saw it affirm) and rode away upon his horse; and between thirty and forty more were lost in this Retreat.

Within a few dayes after this, Capt. *Turners* dead Corps was found a small distance from the River; it appeared that he had been shot through his thigh and back, of which its judged he dyed speedily without any great torture from the enemy. However it were, it is evident that the English obtained a victory at this time, yet if it be as some Indians have since related, the Victory was not so great as at first was apprehended: For sundry of them who were at several times taken after this slaughter, affirm that many of the Indians that were driven down the Falls, got safe on shore again, and that they lost not above threescore men in the fight: also that they killed thirty and eight English men which indeed is just the number missing. There is not much heed to be given to Indian Testimony, yet when circumstances and Artificial arguments confirm what they say, it becometh an impartial *Historian* to take notice thereof, nor is it to be doubted but the loss of the enemy was greater than those Captives taken by our Forces abroad did acknowledge. Some other Indians said that they lost several hundreds at this time, amongst whom there was one Sachem. I am informed that diverse Indians who were in that battell, but since come in to the English at *Norwich,* say that there were three hundred killed at that time, which is also confirmed by an Indian called *Pomham,* who saith that of that three hundred there were an hundred and seventy fighting men.[95] Whatever the victory or success of that ingagement might be, it was the Lords doing, and let him alone have all the Glory.

*May.* 23. Some of our Troopers fell upon a party of Indians (about fifty in number) not far from *Rehoboth,* and slew ten or twelve of them, with the loss of onely one English-man. The Indians betook themselves to a River, and had not some Foot-Souldiers on the other side of the River, too suddenly discovered themselves, probably there had been a greater slaughter of the enemy, who hasted out of the river again, and fled into a Swamp where there was no pursuing of them.

*May* 30*th.* The enemy appeared at *Hatfield,* fired about twelve houses and barns without the Fortification, killed many of their Cattle, drave away almost all their sheep, spread themselves in the meadow between *Hatfield* & *Hadly.* Whereupon twenty five active and resolute men went from *Hadly* to relieve their distressed Brethren. The Indians shot at them ere they could get out of the Boat, & wounded one of them. Ours nevertheless charged on the enemy, shot down five or six at the first volley near the River. Then they made hast toward the town fighting with a great number of the enemy, many falling before them. And though encompassed with a numerous swarm of Indians, who also lay in Ambush behind almost every Tree, and place of advantage, yet the English lost not one man, till within about an hundred Rod of the Town, when five of ours were slain; among whom was a precious young man, whose name was *Smith,* that place having lost many in losing that one man. It speaketh sadly to the rising Generation when such are taken away, After this the Enemy fled, having lost five and twenty in this fight.

In these two last months of *May & April,* besides the *Sword of War,* in respect of the Heathen, the *Sword of the Lord* hath been drawn against this Land, in respect of Epidemical Diseases, which sin hath brought upon us; Sore and (doubtless) *Malignant Colds* prevailing every where. I cannot hear of one Family in *New-England* that hath wholly escaped the Distemper, but there have been many Families wherein every one in the House was sick and ill-disposed. So as that there have been many sick and weak, and some are fallen asleep, yea some eminent and useful Instruments hath the Lord removed, and made breaches thereby upon divers of the Colonies of *New-England.*

*Connecticut* is deprived of their Worthy and publick-spirited Governour *Winthrop*. This Colony of *Mattachusets* hath been bereaved of two (*viz.* Major *Willard*, and Mr. *Russel*) who for many years had approved themselves faithful in the magistracy. And the death of a few such is as much as if thousands had fallen: yet many other righteous and useful ones are gone, leaving us behind in the storm. And amongst the common people, not a few have been carried to their Graves in these two last months. We have heard of no less than eight in one small Plantation, buried in one week, wherein also twenty persons died this Spring. And in another little Town nineteen persons have died within a few weeks. We in *Boston* have seen (a sad and solemn spectacle) Coffins meeting one another, and three or four put into their Graves in one day. In the month of *May* about fifty persons are deceased in this Town. By which things, God from Heaven speaks to us and would give us to understand, that if the Sword will not reform us, he hath other Judgements in store, whereby he can suddenly and easily bring us down. The Lord help us to apply our hearts unto Wisdome, and make us thankful, in that he hath been entreated graciously and wonderfully to restore Health unto us again.

In the latter end of *May*, and beginning of *June*, the *Indians* have been less active in the pursuit of their mischievous designes against the *English*. One reason whereof hath been, in that it was now their Planting and Fishing time: for at this time of the year, they supply themselves with fish out of the Ponds and Rivers, wherewith this good Land doth abound, and dry it against the sun, so as they can lay up in store, for to serve them the year about. But it would have been no wisdome for the English to suffer them so to do. Wherefore about four or five hundred Souldiers were sent out of this Colony, and as many (*English* and *Indians* together) of *Connecticut*, to seek out and disrest the Enemy.

*June* 7. Our Forces now abroad came upon a party of Indians, not far from *Lancaster*, and killed seven of them, and took nine and twenty of them Captive: some of which not long since had English Captives under them. Thus did they that had led into Captivity, go into Captivity; and they that killed with the Sword were themselves killed with the Sword.[96]

Also *Connecticut* Forces, whilst upon their march, killed and took above fifty *Indians:* and not long after that, a small party of *Connecticut* Souldiers with the Assistance of a few of those *Indians* who have been friends to the *English,* slew and took forty and four of the Enemy in the *Narraganset* Country; all these exploits being performed without the loss of any of ours.

*June* 12. The Enemy assaulted *Hadly,* in the morning, Sun an hour high, three Souldiers going out of the Town without their Arms, were disswaded therefrom by a Serjeant, who stood at the Gate, but they alleadging that they intended not to go far, were suffered to pass, within a while the Serjeant apprehended, that he heard some men running, and looking over the Fortification he saw *twenty Indians* pursuing those three men, who were so terrified, that they could not cry out; two of them were at last killed, and the other so mortally wounded, as that he lived not above two or three dayes[;] wherefore the Serjeant gave the *Alarme.* God in great mercy to those *Western Plantations* had so ordered by his providence, as that *Connecticut* Army was come thither before this onset from the enemy. Besides English, there were near upon two hundred Indians in *Hadly,* who came to fight with and for the English, against the common enemy, who was quickly driven off at the *South end* of the Town; whilst our men were pursuing of them there, on a sudden a great Swarm of Indians issued out of the bushes, and made their main assault at the *North end* of the Town, they fired a Barn which was without the Fortifications, and went into an house, where the inhabitants discharged a great Gun upon them, whereupon about fifty Indians were seen running out of the house in great haste, being terribly frighted with the Report and slaughter made amongst them by the great 'Gun.[97] Ours followed the enemy (whom they judged to be about five hundred, and by Indian report since, it seems they were seven hundred) near upon two miles, and would fain have pursued them further, but they had no Order so to do. Some in those parts think, that as great an opportunity and advantage as hath been since the war began, was lost at this time; the Lord having brought the enemy to them, and there being English and Indians enough to pursue them: But others supposing that then they should impede the design of coming upon them at the *Falls,* nothing was done untill it was too late, only the Towns in those places were eminently saved, and but few of ours that lost their lives in this Skirmish, nor is it as yet known how many the enemy lost in this fight.[98] The English could find but three dead Indians: yet some of them who have been taken Captive, confess that they had thirty men kill'd this day. And since we have been informed by Indians, of that which is much to be observed, *viz,* that while the Indian men were thus fighting against *Hadley,* the hand of the Lord so disposed, as that the *Mohawks* came upon their Head Quarters, and smote their women and Children with a great Slaughter, and then returned with much plunder. If indeed it was so (and the Indians are under no temptation to report a falshood of this nature) it is a very memorable passage.

*June* 15. This day was seen at *Plimouth* the perfect form of an *Indian Bow* appearing in the aire, which the Inhabitants of that place (at least some of them) look upon, as a *Prodigious Apparition.* The like was taken notice of, a little before the Fort Fight in the *Narraganset* Countrey. Who knoweth but that it may be an *Omen* of ruine to the enemy, and that the Lord will break the bow and spear asunder, and make warrs to cease unto the ends of the earth?[99] Nor is this (may I here take occasion a little to *digress,* in order to the inserting of some things, hitherto not so much observed, as it may be they ought to be) the first *Prodigy* that hath been taken notice of in *New-England.* It is a common observation, verifyed by the experience of many Ages, that *great and publick Calamityes seldome come upon any place without Prodigious Warnings to forerun and signify what is to be expected.* I am slow to believe Rumors of this nature, nevertheless some things I have had certain Information of.[100]

It is certain, that before this Warr brake out; viz. on Sept. 10.1674. In *Hadley, Northampton,* and other Towns thereabouts, was heard the report of a great piece of Ordinance, with a shaking of the earth, and a considerable Echo, whenas there was no ordinance really discharged at or near any of those Towns at that time. Yea no less then seven years before this warr there were plain prodigious *Notices* of it. For,

Anno 1667. There were fears on the spirits of many of the English, concerning *Philip* and his Indians, and that year, Novemb. 30. about 9, or 10 *ho.*[101] A.M. being a very clear, still, Sunshine morning, there were diverse Persons in *Maldon,* who heard in the air on the South-east of them, a great Gun go off, and as soon as that was past, they heard the report of small Guns like musket shott discharging very thick, as if it had been at a general Training; but that which did most of all amaze them was the flying of the Bullets which came singing over their heads, and seemed to be very near them, after this they heard drums passing by them & going Westward. The same day, at *Scituate*, (and in other places) in *Plimouth* Colony, they heard as it were the running of troops of horses.

I would not have mentioned this relation, had I not received it from serious, faithfull, and Judicious hands, even of those who were ear witnesses of these things.

And now that I am upon this *Digression*, let me add, that the monstrous births which have at sundry times hapned, are speaking, solemn providences. Especially that which was at *Woburn*, Febru.23.1670. When the wife of *Joseph Wright* was delivered of a Creature, the form whereof was as followeth. ["]The head, neck and arms in true Form and shape of a child, but it had no breast bone nor any back bone, the belly was of an extraordinary bigness, both the sides and back being like a belly, the thighs were very small without any thigh bones; It had no buttocks, the *Membrum virile*[102] was a meer bone, it had no passage for nature in any part below,[103] the feet turned directly outward, the heels turned up, and like a bone, It being opened, there were found two great lumps of flesh on the sides of the seeming belly; the bowels did lye on the upper part of the breast by the Vitalls." This was testified before the Deputy Governour Mr. *Willohghby* on the 2*d.* of March following, by Mrs. *Johnson* Midwife, *Mary Kendal, Ruth Bloghead, Lydia Kendall.* Seen also by Capt. *Edward Johnson, Leiut. John Carter, Henry Brook, James Thomson, Isaac Cole.*

There are judicious persons, who upon the consideration of some relative circumstances, in that monstrous birth, have concluded, that God did thereby bear witness against the *Disorders* of some in that place. As in the dayes of our Fathers, it was apprehended that God did testifie from heaven against the monstrous Familitical Opinions that were then stirring, by that direfall Monster which was brought forth by the wife of *William Dyer* Octo. 17, 1637 a description whereof may be seen in Mr. *Welds* his History of the Rise and Ruine of Antinomianisme. p.43, 44. and in Mr. *Clarks Examples* vol. 1.p. 249.[104]

Certainly God would have such providences to be observed

and recorded; He doth not send such things for nothing, or that no notice should be taken of them, And therefore was I willing to give a true account thereof, hoping that thereby mistakes and false Reports may be prevented.

To goe on then with our History.

*June.* 16. Our Forces marched towards the Falls, ours on the *East* and *Connecticut* on the *West* side of the river. When they were about three miles out of the Towns, a vehement storm of rain, with thunder and lightening overtook them, yet continuing but a while, they passed on til they came to the *Falls,* but the enemy was then gone. The next day it rained again, and continued a cold *Euroclidon,*[105] or, *North-East* storm all that day and night, so that our Souldiers received much damage in their arms, ammunition and provision; and the next day (being Lords day) returned to the Towns, weary and discouraged, the Lord having seemed to fight against them by the storm mentioned. Thus doth the Lord in Wisdome and Faithfulness mix his Dispensations toward us.

*June* 19. A party of Indians set upon *Swanzy* and burnt down the remaining houses there, except five houses whereof four were Garisons.

*June* 20. *Connecticut* Forces returned home in order to a recruit, intending to meet with ours the next week at *Quabaog.*

*June.* 21. was kept as a day of solemn *Humiliation* in one of the Churches in *Boston,* so was the next day in all the Churches throughout the Colony of *Plimouth.* After which we have not received such sad tidings, as usually such dayes have been attended with, ever since this *warr* began (as the precedent *History* doth make to appear) but rather such Intelligence from diverse parts of the Countrey as doth administer ground of hope, and of rejoycing, the Lord seeming to return with mercy to his people, and to bring the enemy into greater distresses then formerly.

*June.* 28. About thirty of ours adventured to go up the River towards the Falls at *Deerfield,* to see what Indians they could espy thereabouts, but coming they found none. They went to an Island where they found an hundred *Wigwams,* and some English plundered Goods, which they took, and burnt the *Wigwams.* Also they marched up to a Fort which the Indians had built there, and destroyed it. Digging here and there they found several Indian Barns, where was an abundance of Fish, which they took and spoiled, as also thirty of their *Canoos*, so that it appears that the Heathen are distressed and scattered, being no more able to continue together in such great Bodyes as formerly.

*June* 29. Was observed as a day of publick *Thanksgiving* to celebrate the praises of that God, who hath begun to answer Prayer. And although there is cause for Humiliation before the Lord, inasmuch as the Sword is still drawn against us, nevertheless we are under deep engagement to make his praise glorious; considering how wonderfully he hath restrained and checked the insolency of the Heathen. That Victory which God gave to our Army, *December* 19. and again *May* 18. is never to be forgotten: also in that divers *Indian Sachims* (especially their great Sachim *Quanonchet*) have fallen before the Lord, and before his Servants. And in that things have been no worse with us, since the year of trouble hath been upon us, that no more Indians have been let loose upon us, but many of them have been our friends; that no more *Plantations* have been made *desolate*, which nothing but the restraining gracious providence of God hath prevented, for the Enemy might easily have destroyed ten times as many Towns as they have done, had not he that sets bounds to the raging of the Sea, restrained them; yea, *one whole Colony* hath been in a manner untouched, saving that one small deserted Plantation therein was burnt by the Indians;[106] also sundry Towns that have been fiercely assaulted by the Enemy, having obtained help from God, do continue to this day, as brands plucked out of the fire, and as monuments of the sparing mercy of God, although they have been in the fire they are not consumed.[107] And God hath returned many of our *Captives*, having given them to find compassion before them who led them Captive, and caused the Enemy to entreat them well, in the time of affliction, and in the time of evil, and by strange wayes at last delivered them. He hath also sent in a supply of Corn[108] from beyond Sea, this Spring, and before winter, without which we could not easily have sent out such Armies (however small and not worthy of the name of *Armies* in other parts of the World, yet with us they are Armies) as have been pursuing the Enemy. Its wonderful to consider, how that the Lord hath visited his People in giving them Bread, when a Famine was expected. And this Summer, God hath caused the showre to come down in its season, there have been showres of Blessing when some beginnings of a Drought were upon the Land. And some Diseases hath the Lord rebuked; whereas the *small Pox* and other *Malignant* and *Contagious Distempers* have been amongst us since this *War* began, God hath been entreated to have compassion on us, and to restore health unto his people. Moreover, we are still under the enjoyment of our *Liberties,* both Civil and Spiritual:[109] for such causes as these, the day mentioned was observed (by order of the Council) as a day of publick Thanksgiving throughout this Colony: And behold, when we began to sing and to praise the Lord whose mercy endureth for ever, he hath as it were set Ambushments against the Enemy, and they were smitten, yea they have since that been smiting and betraying one another.

There are two things here observable:

1. Whereas this very day of the Month (*viz. June* 29.) was kept as a day of publick *Humiliation* the last year, being the first *Fast* that was observed in this Colony on the account of the present *War,* God hath so ordered, as that the same day of the month was in the year after set apart to magnifie his Name on the account of mercies received, being the first publick day of Thanksgiving, which hath been attended throughout this Colony since the *War* began.[110]

2. The Lord from Heaven smiled upon us at this time; for the day before this *Thanks-giving,* as also the day after, he gave us to hear of more of our Captives returned: particularly Mr. *Rowlandsons* Children are now brought in as answers of Prayer. It is not a small mercy, that the mother and children (only one childe was killed when the other were taken) should all of them be saved alive, and carried through the Jaws of so many deaths, and at last brought home in peace, that so they and all that ever shall hear of it, might see and know, that the Lord Jehovah, is a God that heareth prayer. Also the night after this *Thanks-giving,* intelligence came to *Boston,* that a chief *Narraganset Sachim,* is now suing to the English for peace, and that an Indian was come in to the English near *Rehoboth,* who informed that *Philip* was not far off, and that he had but thirty men (besides Women and Children) with him; and promised to conduct the English to the place where *Philip* was lurking, and might probably be taken; Morever, the Indian affirmed, that those Indians who are known by the name of *Mauquawogs* (or Mohawks) i.e. Man eaters) had lately fallen upon *Philip,* and killed fifty of his men. And if the

variance between *Philip* & the *Mauquawogs* came to pass, as is commonly reported & apprehended, there was a marvellous finger of God in it. For we hear that *Philip* being this winter entertained in the *Mohawks* Country, Made it his design to breed a quarrel between the English & them, to effect which divers of our returned Captives do report that he resolved to kill some scattering *Mohawks*, & then to say that the English had done it: but one of those whom he thought to have killed, was only wounded, and got away to his Country men, giving them to understand, that not the English but *Philip* had killed the Men that were Murdered, so that instead of bringing the *Mohawks* upon the English, he brought them upon himself. Thus hath he conceived mischief and brought forth falshood, he made a pit and digged it, and is fallen into the ditch which he hath made, his mischief shall return upon his own head, and his violent dealing shall come down upon his own pate. The Heathen are sunk down into the pit that they made, in the net which they had hid, is their own foot taken; the Lord is known by the Judgment which he executeth, the wicked is snared in the work of his own hands. *Higgaion*. Selah.[111]

*June* 30. This day Souldiers marched out of *Boston* towards the place, where *Philip* was supposed to be. But when they came thither, they found that he was newly gone. We hear that he is returned to *Mount-hope*, and that a considerable body of Indians are gathered to that place, where the *War* began, and where (it may be) way must be made towards an end of these troubles. Yet who knoweth how cruelly a dying *Beast* may bite before his expiration? Also *Plimouth* Companies being abroad under the conduct of Major *Bradford*, the Lord went forth with them, this day causing the enemy to fall before them. They were in danger of being cut off by a party of Indians who lay in Ambush for that end, but some of the *Cape-Indians*, who have been faithful to the English, discovered the *Stratagems* of the Adversary, whereby their intended mischief was happily prevented. Divers of them were killed and taken, without the loss of so much as one of ours. And whereas, three Messengers from *Squaw-Sachem* of *Sakonet*, were gone to the *Governour* of *Plimouth*, offering to submit themselves, and engaging Fidelity to the English for the future, if they might but have a promise of life, and liberty, before the Messengers returned from their treaty, that *Squaw-Sachem* with about *ninety* persons, hearing that *Plimouth* Forces were approaching to them, came and tendred themselves to Major *Bradford,* wholly submitting to mercy, so that this day were killed, taken, and brought in no less then *an hundred and ten Indians.* And the providence of God herein is the more observable, in that the very day before this, the Lords People in *Plimouth* did unanimously consent to renew their Covenant with God, and one another, and a day of Humiliation was appointed for that end, that so a work so sacred and awful might be attended with the more solemnity: also in the week before these signal smiles from Heaven upon that *Colony,* most of the Churches there, had *renewed their Covenant,* viz. on the day of *Humiliation* which was last attended throughout that Jurisdiction. God then saith unto us, that if we will indeed hearken unto his voice, the haters of the Lord shall soon submit themselves.[112]

*July* 8. Whereas the Council at *Boston* had lately emitted a Declaration, signifying, that such Indians as did within fourteen dayes come in to the English, might hope for mercy, divers of them did this day return from among the *Nipmucks.* Amongst others, *James* an Indian, who could not only reade, and write, but had learned the Art of Printing, notwithstanding his Apostasie, did venture himself upon the mercy and truth of the English Declaration which he had seen and read, promising for the future to venture his life against the common Enemy. He and the other now come in, affirm that very many of the Indians are dead since this *War* began; and that more have dyed by the hand of God, in respect of Diseases, Fluxes, and Feavers, which have been amongst them, then have been killed with the Sword.

*July* 2. This day *Connecticut* Forces being in the *Narraganset* Country met with a party of Indians, pursued them into a Swamp, killed and took *an hundred and fourscore* of them (amongst whom was the old *Squaw-Sachem* of *Narraganset*) without the loss of one English-man. Only an Indian or two that fought for the English, was killed in this engagement. The English would gladly have gone further, and have joyned with *Boston* and *Plimouth* Companies to pursue *Philip* at *Mount-hope,* but the *Connecticut* Indians would by no means be perswaded thereunto, until such time as they had returned home with the booty they had taken. And as they were on their march homeward, they took and slaughtered *threescore* more *Indians.* In the mean while the other Colonyes are sending out souldiers toward *Mount-Hope,* where *Philip* with a multitude of Indians lately flocked thither is reported to be, designing speedily to fall upon the neighbouring Towns.

*July* 6. Five or six Indian *Sachems* did make peace with the English in the Eastern parts of this Colony.[113] They have brought in with them three hundred men besides women and Children. One of the *Sachims* did earnestly desire, that the English would promise that no more *liquors* should be sold or given to the *Indians,* that so they might not be in a Capacity of making themselves drunk, having found by wofull experience, that that hath been a ruining evill to many of them. This week also about *two hundred Indians* more came & submitted themselves to mercy, in *Plimouth Colony,* being partly necessitated thereunto by the distresses which God in his holy providence hath brought them into, and partly encouraged by a promise from the Government there, that all such Indians as would come in, and lay down their armes should have life and liberty granted to them, excepting only such as had been active in any of the murthers which have been committed. When these Indians were in the hands of the English, a certain *Squaw* amongst them, perceiving that it would be pleasing to the English, if the murderers were discovered, she presently told of one who had had a bloudy hand in the murthers which were done in Mr. *Clarks* house *March* the twelfth, the Indian immediately confessed the Fact, only said that there was another who had as great an hand therein as he, which other Indian being examined, confessed, the thing also, and he revealed a third Indian Murderer, who upon Examination owned the thing, whereupon they were all three forthwith executed, thus did God bring upon them the innocent blood which they had shed. Also the Indians who had surrendred themselves, informed that a bloody Indian called *Tuckpoo* (who the last summer murdered a Man of *Boston* at *Namasket*) with about *twenty Indians* more, was at a place within 16 miles of *Plimouth,* and manifested willingness to go and fetch him in, whereupon eight English with fourteen Indians marched out in the night, and seized upon them all, none of ours receiving any hurt at this time. Justice was speedily executed upon the Indian, who had been a Murderer, the other having their lives granted them.

*July* 7. A small party of our Indians having some English

with them, took and killed seven of the Enemy in the Woods beyond *Dedham*, whereof one was a petty *Sachem*. The two Indians which were then taken Prisoners, say that many of their men who were sent to *Albany* for a supply of Powder, were set upon in the way by the *Mohawks*, and killed. It is certain that about this time some of those *Indians* who are in *Hostility* against the English (amongst whom the *Sachim* of *Springfield* Indians, was one) came to *Albany*, to buy Powder, and that they might effect their designe, they lyed and said, that now they had made peace with the English, and desired Powder only to go an hunting in the Woods: we hear, that the other Indians were very desirous to have slain them, but the Governour of *New-York* secured them;[114] and gave notice to the Council at *Hartford:* since that we have Intelligence that many of our enemies, yea and such as have been notorious Murderers, are fled for refuge to those about *Albany*.

*July* 11. A Party of Indians (tis conjectured that there were about two hundred of them) assaulted *Taunton*. And in probability, that Town had at this time been brought under the same desolation other places have experienced, had not the Lord in his gracious providence so ordered, that a Captive *Negro*, the week before escaped from *Philip* and informed of his purpose speedily to destroy *Taunton*, whereupon Souldiers were forthwith sent thither, so that the enemy was in a little time repulsed, and fled, after they had fired two Houses: but not one English Life was lost in this Ingagement. What loss the enemy sustained is as yet unknown to us. There was a special providence in that *Negroes* escape, for he having lived many years near to the *Indians*, understood their Language, and having heard them tell one another what their designs were, he acquainted the English therewith, and how *Philip* had ordered his men to lye in *Ambuscadoes* in such and such places, to cut off the English, who by meanes of this intelligence escaped that danger, which otherwise had attended them.

About this time we hear that there are three hundred *Mohaugs*, who have armed themselves, as being desirous to be revenged upon those Indians who have done so much harm to *New-England* (if they receive no discouragement as to their designed Expedition) And that they purpose to *color* their heads and make them *yellow*, that so they may not upon their approach to any of our Plantations, be mistaken for other *Indians*.[115]

There is another thing which though it doe not concern the Warr, yet hapning this week, it may not be amiss here to take notice of it. At *Saconesset* in *Plymouth* Colony, a female Child was born with two heads, perfectly distinct each from other, so that it had four eyes, and four ears, and two mouthes and tongues, &c.[116]

*July* 22. Some of our Companies returned from *Mount-hope* to *Boston*. And albeit they have not attained that which was the main end proposed in their going forth, *sc.* the Apprehension of *Philip*, nevertheless God was in a gracious measure present with them; for they killed and took about an hundred and fifty *Indians* in this expedition, with the loss of but one *English-man*. One night they lodged very near unto *Philip*, but he kept himself private and still in a *Swamp*, ours not imagining that he had been so near, as afterwards (by *Indian* Captives) they perceived he was; after this an *Indian* that was taken Prisoner engaged that if they would spare his life, he would forthwith bring them to *Philip*, but our Souldiers were not able to go the nearest way towards him, yet in about two hours space, they came whither the Indian conducted them, and found that a great many Indians were newly fled, having for hast left their *Kettles* boyling over their fires, and their Belts, and Baskets of *Wampampeag*, yea and their dead unburied. At that time did the English take and kill about seventy persons: since an Indian that came into *Rhode-Island*, informeth, that *Philip* is gone to a Swamp near *Dartmouth:* and that when our Forces were pursuing of him, he with a few hid himself in *Squanakunk* Swamp, till our Souldiers were past, and then with one Indian in a *Canoo* crost the river to *Pocasset*. It seems the body of the Indians belonging to him went over on two Rafts, in which passage they lost several Guns, and wet much of their Ammunition. The reason why *Philip fled* to this place, was because if he went *Northward*, the *Mohawks* would be upon him, if *Southward* he was in danger of the *Monhegins*, and he dirst not hide himself any longer about *Metapoisit*, because the Woods thereabouts were filled with Souldiers.[117] This week also, Captain *Church* of *Plimouth*, with a small party consisting of about eighteen English, and two and twenty Indians had four several engagements with the Enemy, and killed and took Captive seventy nine Indians, without the loss of so much as one of ours, it having been his manner, when he taketh any Indians by a promise of favour to them, in case they acquit themselves well, to set them an hunting after more of these Wolves, whereby the worst of them, sometimes do singular good service in finding out the rest of their bloody fellows. In one of these skirmishes, *Tiashq Philips* chief Captain ran away leaving his Gun behind him, and his *Squaw,* who was taken. They came within two miles of the place where *Philip* hideth himself, and discerned at a distance about fifty Indians with Guns, thought to be *Philips* Hunters for Provision, and were desirous to have engaged with them, but being loaden with Captives and Plunder, they could not then attend it.[118] Also a *Sachim* of *Pocasset* hath submitted himself with fourty Indians more, to the Governour of *Plymouth.* So that there is of late such a strange *turn of providence* (especially in *Plimouth* Colony, since the Churches in that Colony (being thereunto provoked by the godly advice and Recommendation of the civil Authority in that Jurisdiction) did solemnly *renew their Covenant with God and one another*) as the like hath rarely been heard of in any age. Whereas formerly almost every week did conclude with sad tydings, now the Lord sends us good news weekly. Without doubt, there are in the World who have been praying for us, and God hath heard them. If our poor prayers may be a means to obtain mercy for them also, who have prayed for us, how shall we rejoyce, when we meet together before Jesus Christ at the last and great day?

*July* 25. Thirty and six English-men who went out of *Medfield* and *Dedham,* having nine of the *Praying Indians* with them, pursued and overtook a party of the Enemy, killed and took alive fifty of them, without the loss of any of ours: The nine Indians stored themselves with plunder when this exploit was done: For besides Kettles, there was about half a Bushel of *Wampampeag,* which the Enemy lost, and twelve pound of Powder, which the Captives say they had received from *Albany,* but two dayes before. At this time, another of the *Narraganset Sachims* was killed, whose name was *Pomham,* and his Son was taken alive, and brought Prisoner to *Boston.* This *Pomham* after he was wounded so as that he could not stand upon his legs, and was thought to have been dead, made a shift (as the Souldiers were pursuing others) to crawl a little out of the way, but was found again, and when an *English-man* drew near to him, though he could not stand, he did (like a dying Beast) in rage and revenge, get hold on that Souldiers head, and had like to have killed him, had not another come in to his help, and rescued him out of the inraged dying hands of that bloody *Barbarian,* who had been a great promoter of the *Narraganset War.*

*July* 27. One of the *Nipmuck Sachims* (called Sagamore *John*) came to Boston, and submitted himself to the mercy of the *English,* bringing in about *an hundred and fourscore Indians* with him. And that so he might ingratiate himself with the *English,* he apprehended *Matoonas* and his Son, and brought them with him to *Boston,* which *Matoonas* was the beginner of the *War* in this Colony of *Massachusets;* for it was he that committed the murders which were done at *Mendam, July* 14. 1675. Being thus taken and examined before the Council, he had little to plead for himself, and therefore was condemned to immediate death. Sagamore *John* was desirous that he and his men might be the Executioners; wherefore *Matoonas* was carried out into the Common at Boston, and there being tied to a Tree, the *Sachim* who had now submitted himself, with several of his men, shot him to death. Thus did the Lord (a year after) retaliate upon him the innocent blood which he had shed, as he had done so God hath requited him: And inasmuch as *Matoonas* who began the War and Mischiefs which have followed thereon, in this Colony of *Massachusets* is taken and Justice glorified upon him, it seems to be a good *Omen,* that ere long *Philip* who began the *War* in the other Colony, shall likewise be delivered up unto Justice. In due time his foot shall slide, and the things which shall come upon him seem to make haste.[119]

*July* 31. A small party of Souldiers, whose hearts God had touched, marched out of Bridgewater in order to pursuing the Enemy. And (about $3^h$ *p.m.*) not far from *Tetignot River,* they unexpectedly to themselves and undiscerned by the Enemy, came upon a company of Indians, amongst whom *Philip* himself was, though his being there was not known to our men, until the engagement was over. They shot down ten Indians, they were well armed, and at first snapped their Guns at the English, but not one of them took fire, wherefore, the terrour of God fell upon the Indians, that fifteen of them threw down their Guns, and submitted themselves to the English, the rest fled: *Philip* himself escaped very narrowly with his life. He threw away his stock of Powder into the Bushes, that he might hasten his escape, albeit some of his men the next day found it again. Our Souldiers took about twenty pound of Bullets and Lead, and seven Guns, five of which were loaden and primed: yea they took the chief of *Philips Treasure*, not being able to carry away all their Plunder that day, for they found much English goods which *Philip* had stolen. *Philip* made his escape with three men, one of which was killed. And although he himself got clear, yet his Uncle whose name was *Uncompoen*, being one of his chief Councellors was slain, and *Philips* own sister was taken Prisoner: not so much as one English-man received any hurt at this time. Thus did God own *Bridgewater*, after the People therein had subscribed with their hands, and solemnly renewed their holy Covenant with God, and one another, that they would reform those evils which were amongst them, and endeavour for the future, to walk more according to the will of God in Jesus Christ.

*August* 1. Captain *Church* with thirty *English-men*, and twenty *Indians* following *Philip* and those with him, by their track, took twenty and three Indians. The next morning they came upon *Philips* head quarters, killed and took about an hundred and thirty Indians, with the loss of but one English-man. In probability many of the English-Souldiers had been cut off at this time, but that an Indian called *Matthias*, who fought for the English, when they were come very near the Enemy, called to them in their own Language with much vehemency, telling them they were all dead men if they did but fire a Gun, which did so amuse and amaze the Indians that they lost a great advantage against the English. *Philip* hardly escaped with his life this day also. He fled and left his *Peag* behind him, also his *Squaw and his Son were taken Captives*, and are now Prisoners in *Plimouth*. Thus hath God brought that grand Enemy into great misery before he quite destroy him. It must needs be bitter as death to him, to loose his Wife and only Son (for the Indians are marvellous fond and affectionate towards their Children) besides other Relations, and almost all his Subjects and Country too.[120]

*August* 3. This day the Lord smiled upon this Land by signal fauour, in another respect which concerns not the present War. For whereas in the month of *July*, there had been a sore Drought, which did greatly threaten the Indian Harvest, God opened the bottles of Heaven and caused it to rain all this night, and the day after, so as that the Indian corn is recovered to admiration, the English Harvest being already gathered in, and more plentifull then in some former years, insomuch that this which was expected to be a year of Famine, is turned to be a year of plenty as to provision.[121]

Whilst I am writing this, good information is brought to me, that in some parts of *Connecticut* Colony, the Drought was sorer then in this Colony, inasmuch as the Trees began to languish, and the Indians to despair of an harvest, wherefore *Unkas* (for although he be a friend to the English, yet he and all his men continue *Pagans* still) set his *Powaws* on work to see if they could by powawing (i.e. conjuring) procure rain, but all in vain, He therefore sent Westward to a noted *Powaw*, to try his skill, but neither could that Wizzard by all his hideous and diabolical howlings, obtain Showers. Whereupon he (i.e. *Uncas*) applyed himself to Mr. *Fitch* (the faithfull and able Teacher of the Church in *Norwich*) desiring that he would pray to God for rain. Mr. *Fitch* replyed to him that if he should do so, and God should hear him, as long as their *Powaws* were at work, they would ascribe the rain to them, and think that the Devill whome the Indians worship, and not God had sent that rain, and therefore he would not set himself to pray for it, untill they had done with their vanities and witcheries. *Uncas* and his son *Oweneco*[122] declared that they had left off *Powawing*, despairing to obtain what they desired. Mr. *Fitch* therefore called his Church together, and they set themselves by Fasting and Prayer, to ask of the Lord Rain in the time of the latter Rain, and behold! that very night, and the next day, He that saith to the small rain, and to the great rain of his Strength be thou upon the earth, gave most Plentifull Showers, inasmuch as the Heathen were affected therewith, acknowledging that the God whom we serve is a great God, and there is none like unto him.[123]

*August* 6. An Indian that deserted his Fellows, informed the inhabitants of *Taunton* that a party of Indians who might be easily surprised, were not very far off, and promised to conduct any that had a mind to apprehend those Indians, in the right way towards them, whereupon about twenty Souldiers marched out of *Taunton*, and they took all those Indians, being in number thirty and six, only the *Squaw-Sachem* of *Pocasset*, who was next unto

*Philip* in respect of the mischief that hath been done, and the blood that hath been shed in this Warr, escaped alone; but not long after some of *Taunton* finding an Indian Squaw in *Metapoiset* newly dead, cut off her head, and it hapned to be *Weetamoo*, i.e. *Squaw-Sachem* her *head.* When it was set upon a pole in *Taunton,* the Indians who were prisoners there, knew it presently, and made a most horrid and diabolical Lamentation, crying out it was their Queens head. Now here it is to be observed, that God himself by his own hand, brought this enemy to destruction. For in that place, where the last year, she furnished *Philip* with Canooes for his men, she her self could not meet with a Canoo, but venturing over the River upon a Raft, that brake under her, so that she was drowned, just before the English found her. Surely *Philips* turn will be next.

*August* 10. Whereas *Potock* a chief Counsellor to the old Squaw-Sachem of *Narraganset,* was by some of Road-Island brought into *Boston,* and found guilty of promoting the War against the English, he was this day shot to death in the Common at *Boston.* As he was going to his execution, some told him that now he must dy, he had as good speak the truth, and say how many Indians were killed at the Fort-Fight last winter. He replyed, that the English did that day kill above seven hundred fighti[n]g men, and that three hundred who were wounded, dyed quickly after, and that as to old men, women and Children, they had lost no body could tell how many, and that there were above three thousand Indians in the Fort, when our Forces assaulted them, and made that notable slaughter amongst them.

*August* 12. This is the memorable day wherein *Philip,* the perfidious and bloudy Author of the War and wofull miseryes that have thence ensued, was taken and slain. And God brought it to pass, chiefly by Indians themselves. For one of *Philips* men (being disgusted at him, for killing an Indian who had propounded an expedient for peace with the English) ran away from him and coming to Road-Island, informed that *Philip* was now returned again to *Mount-Hope,* and undertook to bring them to the Swamp where he hid himself. Divine Providence so disposed, as that Capt. *Church* of *Plymouth* was then in Road-Island, in order to recruiting his Souldiers, who had been wearied with a tedious march that week, But immediately upon this Intelligence, he set forth again, with a small company of English and Indians. It seemeth that night *Philip* (like the man in the Host of *Midian*) dreamed that he was fallen into the hands of the English, and just as he was saying to those that were with him, that they must fly for their lives that day, lest the Indian that was gone from him should discover where he was, Our Souldiers came upon him, and surrounded the *Swamp* (where he with seven of his men absconded)[.] Thereupon he betook himself to flight, but as he was coming out of the Swamp, an English-man and an Indian endeavoured to fire at him, the English-man missed of his aime, but the Indian shot him through the heart, so as that he fell down dead. The Indian who thus killed *Philip,* did formerly belong to Squaw-Sachim of *Pocasset,* being known by the name of *Alderman.* In the beginning of the war, he came to the Governour of *Plymouth,* manifesting his desire to be at peace with the English, and immediately withdrew to an Island not having ingaged against the English nor for them, before this time. Thus when *Philip* had made an end to deal treacherously, his own Subjects dealt treacherously with him. This Wo was brought upon him that spoyled when he was not spoyled. And in that very place where he first contrived and began his mischief, was he taken and destroyed, and there was he (Like as Agag was hewed in pieces before the Lord)[124] cut into four quarters, and is now hanged up as a monument of revenging Justice, his head being cut off and carried away to Plymouth, his Hands were brought to *Boston. So let all thine Enemies perish, O Lord!* When *Philip* was thus slain, five of his men were killed with him, one of which was his chief Captains son, being (as the Indians testified) that very Indian, who shot the first gun at the English, when the War began. So that we may hope that the War in those parts will dye with *Philip.*

A little before this, the Authority in that Colony had appointed the seventeenth of this instant to be observed as a day of *publick Thanksgiving* throughout that Jurisdiction, on the account of wonderful success against the Enemy, which the Lord hath blessed them with, *ever since they renewed their Covenant* with him, and that so they might have hearts raised and enlarged in ascribing praises to God, he delivered *Philip* into their hands a few dayes before their intended Thanksgiving. Thus did God break the head of that Leviathan, and gave it to be meat to the people inhabiting the wilderness,[125] and brought it to the Town of *Plimouth* the very day of their solemn Festival: yet this also is to be added and considered, that the Lord (so great is the divine faithfulness) to prevent us from being lifted up with our successes, and that we might not become secure, so ordered as that not an *English-man* but an *Indian* (though under *Churches* influence) must have the honour of killing *Philip*. And the day before this, was attended with a doleful Tragedy in the Eastern parts of this Country, *viz.* at *Falmouth* in *Casco-bay,* where some of those treacherous and bloody Indians who had lately submitted themselves, and promised Fidelity to the English, killed and took Captive above thirty Souls. The chief Author of this mischief, was an Indian called *Simon,* who was once in the hands of the English, and then known to have been active in former Murders, having bragged and boasted of the mischief and murders done by him: we may fear that God, who so awfully threatned *Ahab,* when he had let go out of his hand a Blasphemous, Murderous Heathen, whom the Lord had devoted to destruction, was not well pleased with the English for concluding this, and other bloody Murders, in the late Eastern peace,[126] What the issue of this new flame thus breaking forth, shall be, or how far it shall proceed is with him whose wisdome is infinite; and who doth all things well: inasmuch as it is too evident that a *French* Coal hath kindled this unhappy fire (blood and fire being the Elements which they delight to swim in) it is not like to be extinguished in one day. But we must leave it to God and time, fully to discover what hath been, and what shall be.

Thus have we a brief, plain, and true Story of the *War* with the Indians in *New-England,* how it began, and how it hath made its progress, and what present hopes there are of a comfortable closure and conclusion of this trouble; which hath been continued for a whole year and more. Designing only a *Breviary of the History of this war;* I have not enlarged upon the circumstances of things, but shall leave that to others, who have advantages and leasure to go on with such an undertaking.

*Magna dabit, qui magna potest, mihi parva potenti,*
*Parvaq*[*ue*], *poscenti, parva dedisse sat est,*[127]

There is one thing admirable to consider; I mean the providence of God in keeping one of these three *United Colonies,* in a manner untouched all this while: For *Connecticut Colony* hath not been assaulted by this Enemy, only a few houses in one deserted Plantation were burnt: and it is possible that one Indian alone might do that. Whether God intends another tryal for them, or for what reason he hath hitherto spared them, no one may as yet determine. Christ said unto *Peter, What I do thou Knowest not now, but thou shalt know hereafter:*[128] even so, although we do not at present fully perceive the meaning of this providence, yet hereafter it will be manifest. And albeit the same sins and provocations have been found with them that are to be charged upon others, nevertheless, it must needs be acknowledged (for why should not that which is praise-worthy in Brethren be owned, that so God may have the glory of his grace towards and in his Servants?) they have in the management of this affair, acquitted themselves like men and like Christians. It was prudently done of them, not to make the *Indians* who lived amongst them their Enemies, and the Lord hath made them to be as a Wall to them, and also made use of them to do great service against the common Enemies of the English. The Churches there have also given proof of their charity and Christianity, by a liberal Contribution towards the necessity of the Saints impoverished by this *War* in the other two Colonies, having collected and transported above a thousand Bushels of Corn, for the relief and comfort of those that have lost all through the Calamity of War; God will remember and reward that pleasant fruit. Nor have some of the Churches in this Colony (especially in *Boston,* which the Grace of Christ hath alwayes made exemplary, in works of that nature) been unwilling to consider their poor Brethren according to their Ability.

To *Conclude* this *History,* it is evident by the things which have been expressed, that our deliverance is not as yet perfected; for the *Nipmuck* Indians are not yet wholly subdued: Moreover, it will be a difficult thing, either to subdue or to come at the *River Indians,* who have many of them withdrawn themselves, and are gone far westward, and whilst they and others that have been in hostility against us, remain unconquered, we cannot enjoy such perfect peace as in the years which are past. And there seems to be a dark Cloud rising from the East in respect of Indians in those parts, yea a Cloud which streameth forth blood. But that which is the saddest thought of all, is that of late some unhappy scandals have been, which are enough to stop the current of mercy, which hath been flowing in upon us, and to provoke the Lord to let loose more Enemies upon us, so as that the second error shall be worse then the first. Only God doth deliver for his own Names sake: the Lord will not forsake his people for his great Names sake; because it hath pleased the Lord to make us his people. And we have reason to conclude that *Salvation is begun*, and in a gracious measure carried on towards us. For since last *March* there are two or 3000. *Indians* who have been either killed, or taken, or submitted themselves to the English. And those *Indians* which have been taken Captive, (& others also[)], inform that the *Narragansets* are in a manner ruined, there being (as they say) not above an hundred men left of them who the last year were the greatest body of Indians in *New-England*, and the most formidable Enemy which hath appeared against us. But God hath consumed them by the Sword & by Famine and by Sickness, it being no unusual thing for those that traverse the woods to find dead Indians up and down, whom either Famine, or sickness hath caused to dy, and there hath been none to bury them. And *Philip* who was the *Sheba*, that began & headed the Rebellion, his head is thrown over the wall, therefore have we good reason to hope that this *Day of Trouble* is near to an end, if our sins doe not undoe all that hath been wrought for us.[129] And indeed there is one sad consideration which may cause humble tremblings to think of it, namely in that the *Reformation* which God expects from us is not so hearty and so perfect as ought, to be. Divines observe, that whereas upon *Samuels Exhortations*, the people did make but imperfect work of it, as to the *Reformation* of provoking evills, therefore God did only begin their deliverance by *Samuel*, but left scattered *Philistines* unsubdued, who afterwards made head and proved a sore scourge to the Children of Israel, untill *Davids* time, in whose Reign there was a full Reformation, and then did the Lord give unto his people full deliverance.[130] Nevertheless a sad *Catastrophe* will attend those that shall magnifie themselves against the people of the Lord of Hosts. It hath been observed by many, that never any (whether Indians or Others) did set themselves to do hurt to *New-England*, but they have come to lamentable ends at last. *New-England* hath been a burthensome stone, all that have burthened themselves with it, have been cut in pieces. The experience of the present day, doth greatly confirm that observation, and give us ground to hope, that as for remaining enemies, they shall fare as others that have gone before them, have done. Yet this further must needs be acknowledged, that as to Victoryes obtained, we have no cause to glory in anything that we have done, but rather to be ashamed and confounded for our own wayes. The Lord hath thus far been our Saviour for his Names sake, that it might not be profaned among the Heathen whither he hath brought us. And God hath let us see that he could easily have destroyed us, by such a contemptible enemy as the Indians have been in our eyes, yea he hath convinced us that we our selves could not subdue them. They have advantages that we have not, knowing where to find us, but we know not where to find them, who nevertheless are alwayes at home, and have in a manner nothing but their lives and souls (which they think not of) to loose; every Swamp is a Castle to them, and they can live comfortably on that which would starve English-men. So that *we have no cause to glory,* for it is God which hath thus saved us, and not we our selves. If we consider the time when the enemy hath fallen, we must needs own that the Lord hath done it. For we expected (and could in reason expect no other) that when the Summer was come on, and the bushes and leaves of trees come forth, the enemy would do ten times more mischief then in the winter season, whenas since that the Lord hath appeared against them that they have done but little hurt comparatively. Had there not been, Θεὸω ἀπὸ μηχανῆς a divine hand beyond all expectation manifested, we had been in a state most miserable this day. Also if we keep in mind the means and way whereby our deliverance hath thus been accomplished, we must needs own the Lord in all. For it hath not been brought to pass by our numbers, or skill, or valour, *we have not got the Land in possession by our own Sword, neither did our own arm save us.*[132] But God hath wasted the Heathen, by sending the destroying Angell amongst them, since this War began, and (which should alwayes be an humbling consideration unto us) much hath been done towards the subduing of the enemy, by the Indians who have fought for us, sometimes more than by the English. And no doubt but that a great reason why many of them have, of late been desirous to submit themselves to the English, hath been, because they were afraid of the *Mohawgs* who have a long time been a Terror to the other Indians. I have received it from one who was returned out of Captivity this Summer, that the Indians where he was would not suffer any fires to be made in the night, for fear lest the *Mohawgs* should thereby discern where they were, and cut them off.

Now, as the Lord, who doth redeem Israel out of all his troubles, hath graciously and gloriously begun our Salvation, so let him perfect it, in such a way as that no honour at all may come unto us, but that great glory may be to his own blessed Name for ever. Let him bring health and cure unto this *Jerusalem,* and reveal the abundance of peace and truth: And it shall be unto him a Name of joy, a Praise and an honour before all the Nations of the earth, which shall hear all the good that he will doe unto us, and they shall fear and tremble for all the goodness, and for all the prosperity that he will procure. If wee hearken to his voice in these his solemn Dispensations, it surely shall be so. *Not unto us O Lord, not unto us, but unto thy Name give Glory for thy mercy and for thy Truths sake.*[133] Amen!

Δόξα ἐν ὑχίστοις θεῷ.[134]

## *POSTSCRIPT*

Since I wrote the preceding Narrative, I hear that there are who make a scruple of using the word *Army,* when applied to such inconsiderable *Forces,* as those which have been raised and sent forth by us, in the late War. I pretend not to any skill or accuracy of speaking as to modern platforms of *Military Discipline;* but sure I am that of old, a few *Cohorts* being under the command of a chief Captain, though in all there were not above four or five hundred souldiers, this was called *στράτευμα* an *Army,* Acts. 23.27. Yea those three hundred Souldiers who were under *Gideon* as their *General,* are styled an *Army,* Judg.8.6, The Hebrew word there used cometh from צבא , which signifies *turmatim congregari ad militandum,* when Troopes are assembled together, this did the Hebrews call an *Host* or an *Army.* There are small *Armies* as well as great ones, 2 Cron. 24.24. ·חיל which is the word used in that place signifies, *Forces:* that Term have I commonly chosen, though the other being of most frequent use, and aptly enough expressing what is meant by it, I have not wholly declined it. For amongst us

-------- *Sic volet usus*
*Quem penes Arbitrium est et jus et norma loquendi.*[135]

And Reason saith, that those *Forces* may pass for *Armies* in one part of the world, that will not do so in another. But my design in this *Postscript* is not to Criticize or Apologize about the use of a Term. There is another matter of greater importance, sc. *That which doth concern the Grounds of this Warr, and the justness of it on our part:* concerning which I shall here adde a few words. It is known to every one, that the *Warr* began not amongst us in *Mattachusets* Colony; nor do the Indians (so far as I am informed) pretend that we have done them wrong. And therefore the cause on our part is most clear, and unquestionable: For if we should have suffered our Confederates, and those that were ready to be slain, to be drawn to death, & not have endeavoured to deliver them, when they sent unto us for that end, the Lord would have been displeased; nor should we have acted like the Children of Abraham, Gen. 14.14.[136] Yea, all the world would justly have condemned us. And as for our Brethren in that Colony, where these tumults first hapned, It is evident that the Indians did most unrighteously begin a Quarrel, and take up the Sword against them.

I said at the beginning, I would not inlarge upon that Argument, which concerns the *Grounds of the Warr*, neither will I, because that would make the *History* too voluminous, contrary to my design. Nevertheless, inasmuch as some are dissatisfied thereabouts, so as to receive impressions and prejudices in their minds, concerning our Brethren in *Plymouth* Colony (as it is natural for men in trouble to lay blame upon every body but themselves) supposing that they have without just cause, engaged themselves and all these united Colonies in an unhappy *War*. Yea and that the *Indians* were provoked to do what they did, whenas (whatever may be said of some private persons, of whose injurious dealings no complaint was made & proved) it seems very manifest to impartial Judges, that the *Government* in that Colony is *innocent* as to any *wrongs* that have been *done* to the Heathen, by those *where the Warr began.* And therefore for their vindication, and for the satisfaction of those amongst our selves, (or else where) who are cordially desirous to have things cleared, respecting the *Grounds of the Warr,* I shall here subjoyn a Letter, which I received from *Generall Winslow* (whose integrity, and peculiar capacity, (as being *Governour* of *Plymouth* Colony) to give information in this affair is well known) together with a *Narrative of the beginning of these Troubles* as it was presented to the *Commissioners* of the *united Colonyes*, in September last, for the satisfaction of confederate Brethren.

*Reverend Sir,*

['] The many Testimonyes you have given, not only for your good respects to my unworthy self personally, but also to this whole Colony, manifested in your endeavours to vindicate us from undeserved aspersions, that some ignorant or worse then uncharitable persons would lay upon us, respecting the Grounds of these troubles, calls for a greater Retribution then a bare acknowledgment. But sir, my present design is only to give you further trouble, by enabling you to say something more particularly on our behalfe; to that end I have sent you the enclosed Paper which is an exact *Narrative* given in by Mr. *Hinkly* and my self, to the first Sessions of the *Commissioners* of the *Confederate Colonyes*, September last; from which the Commissioners and the *Councill* of your Colony, and afterwards your *General Court*, took full satisfaction, as you see by their subsequent acts and actions. Yet much more we can truly say in our Vindication, (viz) that we have endeavoured to carry it justly and faithfully towards them at all times, and friendly beyond their deserts. I think I can clearly say, that before these present troubles broke out, *the English did not possess one foot of Land in this Colony, but what was fairly obtained by honest purchase of the Indian Proprietors:* Nay, because some of our people are of a covetous disposition, and the Indians are in their Streits easily prevailed with to part with their Lands, we first *made a Law that none should purchase or receive of gift any Land of the Indians, without the knowledge and allowance of our Court,* and penalty of a fine, five pound per Acre, for all that should be so bought or obtained. And lest yet they should be streightned, we ordered that *Mount-Hope, Pocasset* & several other Necks of the best Land in the Colony, (because most suitable and convenient for them) should never be bought out of their hands, or else they would have sold them long since. And our neighbors at *Rehoboth* and *Swanzy;* although they bought their Lands fairly of this *Philip,* and his Father and Brother, yet because of their vicinity, that they might not trespass upon the *Indians,* did at their own cost set up a very substantial fence quite cross that great Neck between the English and the Indians, and *payed due damage if at any time any unruly horse or other beasts broke in and trespassed.* And for diverse years last past (that all occasion of offence in that respect might be prevented) the English agreed with *Philip* and his, for a certain Sum yearly to maintain the said Fence, and secure themselves. And *if at any time they have brought complaints before us, they have had justice impartial* and speedily, so that *our own people* have frequently complained, that *we erred on the other hand in shewing them overmuch favour.* Much more I might mention, but I would not burden your patience; yet we must own that God is just and hath punished us far less then our iniquityes have deserved; yea just in using as a Rod, whose enlightning and Conversion we have not endeavoured as we might & should have done, but on the contrary have taught them new sins that they knew not. The Lord *Humble* us and *Reform* us, that he may also save and deliver us, and in his own time I trust he will. Sir, I have nothing of Intelligence worthy your knowledge. The Colds are very general amongst us and some very afflictive. The Lord rebuke the mortal Distemper that prevailes so much in your Town, and sanctifie all his Visitations to us.

'Thus craving the benefit of your Prayers, in this day of Gods Visitation,

I rest

Your obliged friend to serve you, [']

*Marshfield. May.*I.
1 6 7 6. *Jos. Winslow*

A brief Narrative of the beginning and progress of the present Troubles between us and the Indians, taking rise in the Colony of *New-Plimouth June* 1675. Given by the Commissioners of that Colony, for the satisfaction of their Confederate Brethren, and others.

'Not to look back further than the Troubles that were between the Colony of *New-Plimouth,* and *Philip,* Sachem of *Mount-Hope,* in the Year 1671. It may be remembred, that the settlement and issue of that controversie was obtained and made (principally) by the mediation and interposed advice, and counsel of the other two confederate Colonies, who upon a careful enquiry and search into the grounds of that trouble, found that the said *Sachems,* Pretences of wrongs and injuries from that Colony were groundless and false, and that he (although first in Arms) was the peccant offending party, and that *Plimouth* had just cause to take up Arms against him: and it was then agreed that he should pay that Colony a certain summe of Mony, in part of their Damage and Charge by him occasioned, and he then not only renewed his ancient Covenant, of Friendship with them, but made himself and his People absolute Subjects to our Soveraign Lord King *Charles* the II. and to that his Colony of *New-Plimouth,* since which time, we know not that the English of that, or any other of the Colonies have been injurious to him or his, that might justly provoke them to take up Arms against us: But sometime last winter, the Governour of Plimouth was informed, by *Sausaman* a faithful Indian, that the said *Philip* was undoubtedly endeavouring to raise new troubles, and to engage all the Sachems round about in War against us. Some of the English also that lived near the said Sachem, communicated their fears and jealousies concurrent with what the Indian had informed. About a week after *John Sausaman* had given his Information, he was Barbarously Murdered by some Indians, for his faithfulness (as we have cause to believe) to the Interest of God, and of the English. Sometime after *Sausamans* death, *Philip* having heard that the Governour of Plimouth had received some information against him, and purposed to send to him to appear at the next Court, that they might enquire into those Reports, came down of his own accord to *Plimouth,* a little before the Court, in the beginning of *March* last, at which time the Councill of that Colony, upon a large debate with him, had great reason to believe that the information against him might be in substance true: But not having proof thereof, and hoping that very discovery of it so far would cause him to desist, they dismist him friendly, giving him only to understand, that if they heard further concerning that matter, they might see reason to demand his Arms to be delivered up for their security (which was according to former agreement between him and them) and he engaged on their demand they should be surrendred to them or their order. At that Court we had many Indians in Examination concerning the Murder of *John Sausaman,* but had not then testimony in the case, but not long after an Indian appearing to testifie, we apprehended three by him charged to be the Murderers, and secured them, to a tryal at our next Court holden in *June,* at which time, and a little before the Court, *Philip* began to keep his men in arms about him, and to gather Strangers to him, and to march about in Arms towards the upper end of the Neck in which he lived; and near to the English houses, who began thereby to be something disquieted, but took as yet no further notice, but only to set a Military Watch, in the next Towns of *Swanzy* and *Rehoboth.* Some hints we had that *Indians* were in *Arms,* whilst our Court was sitting, but we hoped it might arise from a guilty fear in Philip, that we would send for him, and bring him to tryal with the other Murderers, and that if he saw the Court broke up, and he not sent for, the cloud might blow over. And indeed our Innocence made us very secure, and confident it would not have broke into a *War.* But no sooner was our Court dissolved, but we had intelligence from Lieut. *John Brown* of *Swanzy* that *Philip* and his men continued constantly in *Arms,* many strange Indians from several places flocked in to him, that they sent away their Wives to *Narraganset,* and were giving our People frequent Alarums by Drums, and Guns in the night, and had guarded the passages towards Plimouth, and that their young Indians were earnest for a War. On the seventh of *June,* Mr. *Benjamin Church* being on Rhode-Island, *Weetamoe* (the *Squaw-Sachim* of *Pocasset*) and some of her chief men told him, that *Philip* intended a War speedily with the English; some of them saying, that they would help him, and that he had already given them leave to kill English-mens Cattle, and rob their Houses.[137] About the 14. and 15*th.* of *June,* Mr. *James Brown* went twice to *Philip* to perswade him to be quiet, but at both times found his Men in Arms, and *Philip* very high and perswadable to peace. On the 14*th* of *June,* our Council writ an amicable, friendly letter to him, shewing our dislike of his practises, and advising him to dismiss the strange *Indians,* and command his own men to fall quietly to their business, that our people might also be quiet, and not to suffer himself to be abused by reports concerning us, who intended no hurt towards him; but Mr. *Brown* could not obtain any Answer from him. On the 17*th* of *June,* Mr. *Pain* of *Rehoboth,* and several English going unarmed to *Mount-hope* to seek their Horses, at *Philips* request; the Indians came and presented their Guns at them, and carried it very insolently, though no way provoked by them. On the 18 or 19*th* of *June Job Winslow's* House, was broke open at *Swanzy,* and rifled by *Philips* men, *June* 20. being Sabbath day, the People of *Swanzy* were Alarmed by the *Indians,* two of our Inhabitants turned out of their Houses, and their Houses rifled, and the Indians were marching up (as they judged) to assault the Town, and therefore intreated speedy help from us. We thereupon, the 21*st.* of *June,* sent up some to relieve that Town, and dispatched more with speed, On Wednesday 23*d.* of *June* twelve more of their Houses at *Swanzy* were rifled. On the 24*th Layton* was slain at the Fall River near Pocasset. On the 25*th* of *June,* divers of our people at *Swanzy* were slain, and many Houses burned: until which time, and for several dayes after, though we had a considerable force there, both of our own, and of the *Massachusets* (to our grief and shame) they took no revenge on the Enemy. Thus slow were we and unwilling to engage our selves and Neighbours in a *War,* having many insolencies, almost intollerable, from them, at whose hands we had deserved better;[']

*Josiah Winslow.*
*Thomas Hinckley.*

At a Meeting of the Commissioners of the United Colonies held at
*Boston September* 9*th.* 1 6 7 5.

['] We having received from the Commissioners of *Plimouth,* a Narrative, shewing the rise and several steps of that Colony, as to the present *War* with the *Indians,* which had its beginning there, and its progress into the *Massachusets,* by their insolencies, and outrages, Murthering many persons, and burning their Houses in sundry Plantations in both Colonies. And having duely considered the same; do Declare, That the said *War* doth appear to be both just and necessary, and its first rise only a *Defensive War.* And therefore we do agree and conclude, that it ought now to be joyntly prosecuted by all the United Colonies, and the charges thereof to be born and paid as is agreed in the Articles of Confederation. [']

*John Winthrop.*
*James Richards.*

*Thomas Danforth.*
*William Stoughton.*
*Josiah Winslow.*
*Thomas Hinckley.*

The above expressed Letter and Narrative will (I hope) tend to remove Prejudices out of the spirits of dissatisfyed persons, touching the grounds of the present *Warr*. Some have thought that if *Philip* (the Ring-leader of all the mischief & misery which hath hapned by this *War*) his solemn ingagement to the English, above four years before these Troubles began, were published, it would farther clear the justice of the Warr on our part, and the more, in that he doth desire, that the Covenant might testifie against him to the world, if ever he should prove unfaithfull therein. I shall therefore here subjoyn what was by him together with his council, subscribed, (in the presence of sundry appertaining to this Jurisdiction) and doth still remain with their Names set to it, in the publick Records of the Colonyes.

It is that which followeth.

*Taunton, Apr.* 10.*th.* 1671

Whereas my Father, my Brother and my self have formerly *submitted our selves and our people unto the Kings Majesty of England, and to this Colony of New-Plymouth,* by solemn Covenant under our Hand; but I having of late through my indiscretion, and the naughtiness of my heart violated and broken this my Covenant with my friends by *taking up Armes,* with evill intent against them, and that *groundlesly;* I being now deeply sensible of my unfaithfulness and folly, do desire at this time solemnly to renew my Covenant with my ancient Friends, and my Fathers friends above mentioned, and doe desire this may testifie to the world against me, if *ever I shall again fail* in my faithfullness towards them *(that I have now and at all times found so kind to me) or any other of the English Colonyes;* and as a reall Pledge of my true Intentions, for the future to be faithfull and friendly, I doe freely ingage to resign up unto the Government of *New-Plymouth,* all my English Armes to be kept by them for their security, so long as they shall see reason. For true performance of the Premises I have hereunto set my hand together with the rest of my Council.

In the Presence of
William Davis.
William Hudson.
Thomas Brattle.

The Mark of P. *Philip*
chief Sachem of *Pocanoket.*
The Mark of V. *Tavoser.*
The Mark of M Capt. *Wisposke*
The Mark of T *WVoonkaponehunt*
The Mark of 8 *Nimrod.*

By all these things it is evident, that we may truly say of *Philip*, and the *Indians*, who have fought to dispossess us, of the Land, which the Lord our God hath given to us, as sometimes *Jephthah*, and the Children of *Israel*, said to the King of *Ammon*, *I have not sinned against thee, but thou dost me wrong to war against me; the Lord the Judge, be Judge this day between the Children of Israel, and the Children of Ammon.* And as *Iehoshaphat* said, when the Heathen in those dayes, combined to destroy the Lords People, *And now behold the Children of Ammon, and Moab and Mount Seir, whom thou wouldest not let Israel invade when they came out of the Land of Egypt, but they turned from them, and destroyed them not, behold how they reward us, to come to cast us out of thy Possession, which thou hast given us to inherit, O our God wilt thou not judge them?*[138] Even so, when *Philip* was in the hands of the *English* in former years, & disarmed by them, they could easily but would not destroy him and his men. The Governours of that Colony have been as careful to prevent injuries to him as unto any others; yea, they kept his Land not *from* him but *for* him, who otherwise would have sold himself out of all, and the Gospel was freely offered to him, and to his Subjects, but they despised it: And now behold how they reward us! will not our God judge them? yea he hath and will do so.

---

FINIS.

---

## ERRATA.

*P*.8.1.3.r. עָשַׁנְתָּ *p*. 13. *l*. 22. *r*. principal. *p*. 18. *l*. 2. *r*. Committee. *p*. 27 *l*. 3. *dele* of. In *p*. 29. That passage relating to the Thunder and Rain, hapning on May 8. hath respect to *Bridgewater*, whenas by an oversight printed, as though it referred to what was done at *Taunton*.[139]

## NOTES

1. Epigraphs on title page: The three Biblical texts provide a miniature statement of the thesis of the *History,* as is typical in a sermon-form narrative. The quotation from Leviticus explains the war as a divine punishment for the people's sins; that from Psalms justifies the writing of secular history as a recounting of divine acts reflecting the disposition of God towards his people; and the passage from Jeremiah points the reader's attention to the wisdom, justice and piety of the elder generation of Puritan founders—Mather's perennial model of Christian belief and behavior. Note the frequency with which quotations from Jeremiah occur in the *History* and the *Earnest Exhortation:* as a prophet concerned with the supposed "degeneration" of the chosen people, the imminence of punishment, and the need for a return to the piety of the Patriarchs, Jeremiah was most congenial to Puritans who shared Mather's theological and social vision—so much so that a subgenre of Puritan sermons in this vein, preached by Mather and his group, has been dubbed "the Jeremiads." *The Character of the Good Ruler,* pp. 97–123 discusses the religious and political vision of the Jeremiads in detail.

The two Latin quotations are from Horace *("Horat.")* and Cicero *("Cic.").* The first is from Horace, *Ars Poetica* 180–81, and may have been quoted by Mather from memory, since the word "*aures*" has been substituted for the correct "*aurem,*" and "*commissa*" for the correct "*subjecta.*" The passage compares the narration of offstage action to onstage action in tragic drama: "What is reported to the ear excites the spirit more sluggishly than what is presented to the trusty eyes." The quotation from Cicero translates: "Read history lest you become history." (I am indebted for these and other translations from Latin and Greek to Professor David Konstan.).

2. Refers to Richard Hutchinson, *The Present State of New-England with Respect to the Indian War* . . . (London, 1675). Hutchinson was a nephew of Anne Hutchinson, but apparently did not join in the Antinomian heresy. His history contains a number of inaccuracies and omissions. Reprinted in Charles H. Lincoln, *Narratives of the Indian Wars,* pp. 19–49.

3. "With God."

4. "Spare hours" or "leisure hours."

5. [Edward Wharton], *New-Englands Present Sufferings* . . . (London, 1675).

6. "I would prefer this to be done by anyone else, rather than by me; but nevertheless by me, rather than by no-one."

7. The quotation is from Polybius 1.1.2: "The study of history is the truest cultivation [and most useful training] for political activity." Mather may again be quoting from memory, since he has added a word ("Κπησίμην") which does not appear in the original; and which, if it did appear, should properly have been "Χπησίμην." The phrase has been

translated as Mather gives it, with the added phrase in square brackets.

8. Numbers, 21:14, and references which follow to Jasher (Joshua, 10:13 and 2 Samuel, 1:18), and the books of Kings and Chronicles are references to canonical and noncanonical works of history concerning the wars of Israel. Their presence in Scripture, either as books or as references to books, is offered as justifications for the writing of secular history, illustrating that works of that kind which are consistent with Scripture and give glory to God may even enjoy Scriptural status.

9. Hebrew. Midrash, commentary. (I am indebted to Prof. Jeremy Zwelling for translations of Hebrew terms.)

10. "a better work (or deed) than most."

11. John Cotton, *The Powring Out of the Seven Vialls* . . . (London, 1642) is an extended interpretation of *Revelation*, especially the sixteenth chapter which was "that on which the eschatological interpretation of New England was most firmly based." (Larzer Ziff, *The Career of John Cotton*, p. 172.) Cotton uses the text to locate and interpret immediate current events as signs pointing towards the imminence of the Second Coming promised in *Revelation*. Mather does something similar in his *A Dissertation Concerning the Future Conversion of the Jewish Nation* . . . (London, 1709), a published work based on the *Discourse Concerning the Salvation of the Tribes of Israel* referred to here. Cotton had been the dominant figure in New England religious and intellectual life from the moment of his arrival in the colony (despite a temporary cloud on his reputation cast by his partial countenancing of the Hutchinsonians and Antinomians). His writings on Church government were read as definitive statements in New England; hence Mather's concern with the interpretation of Cotton's book.

12. The conversion of the Jews was an event promised as one of the final steps before the return of Christ. Some controversialists identified the Indians with the Ten Lost Tribes of Israel, and held that until the Indians were completely converted the conversion of the Jews could not be consummated, and the Second Coming would be delayed. Mather's position is different from this. He identifies the Indians as heathen or Gentiles (*A Dissertation Concerning the Future Conversion* . . ., chapter 8), and questions whether the conversion of the heathen is to be completed before that of the Jews. Mather and Cotton both argue that the conversion of the Jews would have precedence; and this argument had apparently been used to justify the neglect or discontinuation of Indian missions. Mather argues that while the conversion of the heathen will not be completed before that of the Jews, it does not follow that the work of the missionaries to the heathen should not be begun immediately, nor that such missions may not expect some successes along the way.

13. Caspar Sibel or Sibellius (1590–1658) was a Dutch Reformed theologian, and pastor of the church at Deventer ("Daventry") in Holland. The book referred to concerns Dutch missions in their Asian possessions and trading stations. Note that Mather refers to the Formosans

as "Indians"—a clever use of the Columbian confusion of America with the (East) Indies, which permits Mather to associate Dutch work among the East Indians with Puritan missions to the American Indians.

14. Gisbertus Voetius or Gijsbert Voet (1589–1676) was a Dutch Reformed theologian whose political doctrines coincided in important respects with those of the New England Congregationalists. The title of his book translates, "*On the Calling of the Nations* [or *Peoples*]."

15. Note Mather's pointed contrast of the political consequences of particular religious professions: Catholic converts become feudal "vassals" to both the "heresies" and persons of those that convert them; Protestant converts become participants in "the Common-wealth of Israel" as freemen, citizens of a bourgeois society based on a nonfeudal social compact.

16. Matthew, 23:15 and Luke, 20:47.

17. The source of this story is not identified. Mather is here mocking the glorification of Saint Francis' supposed ignorance of Scripture at the time of his conversion, contrasting the "superstition" of Catholic hagiography with the informed theology of the educated Puritan cleric.

18. "*On Religious Plantations.*"

19. "There is no point in reporting those unspeakable things here."

20. See the biography of Eliot in Samuel Eliot Morison, *Builders of the Bay Colony*, pp. 289–319.

21. "But we hope for better things."

22. "Not because of injury (by the English to the Indians)."

23. According to Patrick M. Malone, "Changing Military Technology Among the Indians of Southern New England, 1600–1677," *American Quarterly* 25:1 (March, 1973), pp. 48–63, the Indians had adopted English firearms quite early in the period of colonization, and chose among available weapons those best suited to forest warfare (e.g., expensive flintlocks rather than the cheaper matchlocks favored by the parsimonious colonists when supplying their own militia). They also had craftsmen capable of maintaining their store of firearms.

24. Mather represents Sassamon as virtually an Indian John Eliot. In fact he was a good deal less than that, having been sufficiently disaffected from the English to ingratiate himself with Philip. See Douglas Leach, *Flintlock and Tomahawk*, p. 31, and Francis Jennings, *The Invasion of America*, pp. 295–97.

25. The "solemn ingagements" were Philip's "Covenant" with Plymouth, 1667, and the Taunton agreement of April 1671. Both treaties were made "under the gun."

26. Mather writes wholly from the perspective of Boston, Massachusetts. Thus for him the initial mustering of troops is ordered in response to intelligence or expectation of hostilities. In fact, hostilities had already begun for Plymouth Colony on June 20, and reinforcements for the Swansea garrison arrived on June 21. This sort of inconsistency in dating produced innumerable confusions for later historians, who thought of New England as a single unit (which Mather did not).

27. The beginning of this paragraph is not indented in the original. Mather is correct in stating this date for the first English deaths, since the attack on June 20 resulted only in the burning of a few houses in Swansea. According to John Easton, the first person killed in the war was an Indian shot in a cornfield on June 23, a full day before any English were killed by Indians; but Easton's political opposition to Massachusetts's policy may have motivated him to attempt to put the Bay Colony and Plymouth as much in the wrong as possible. Leach, *Flintlock and Tomahawk*, p. 42.

28. This mission was sent out on June 23, led by Thomas Savage, James Oliver, and Thomas Brattle.

29. See note 27 above. This is a radical oversimplification of the grounds of conflict. Actually, both English and Indians appear to have been preparing for conflict well before war broke out; and the causes went deeper than the single deaths cited by Mather and Easton as *casus belli*.

30. The government of Plymouth is cited by Leach as having proclaimed the Day of Humiliation; perhaps both colonies did. *Flintlock and Tomahawk*, p. 43.

31. This is the initial skirmish at the bridge, referred to by Benjamin Church, pp. 401–2, below.

32. Went mad.

33. This refers to the minor skirmish which followed the bloodless sweep of the Mount Hope peninsula by colonial forces on June 30–July 1. Mather omits reference to the first major offensive of the war, and reports extensively on the misadventure of a single soldier because of its utility as a moral and theological exemplum. This scale of values persists throughout the history.

34. Weetamoo is the Squaw Sachem of Pocasset. Mather fails to draw a connection between the failure of the offensive, the adoption of the defensive posture, and the escape to and reorganization of Philip's forces in Pocasset. Compare Church, pp. 403–4.

35. July 9; Middleborough is the correct spelling.

36. Battle of Pocasset Swamp.

37. The reference here is to the medical practice of bleeding the sick, a "course" of treatment God prescribes for curing the body politic of New England.

38. Mendon. Mather puns on the town's name not only to amuse, but to illustrate God's allegorizing method of making historical events teach moral lessons.

39. This was the first battle of Nipsachuck, in which Captain Henchman commanded. Despite the long-standing friendship between Uncas and the English, Connecticut deemed it prudent to hold Mohegan hostages. Uncas and his Mohegans provide the names (at least) for Cooper's "Mohicans," Chingachgook being presented as a lineal descendent of Uncas.

40. The seige of Brookfield is described at length in Thomas Wheeler's narrative, below.

41. Hebrew. Actually "The Lord will see."

42. Jeremiah, 21:9. The chapter tells of the King of Judah's plea that Jeremiah tell him whether the Lord will permit the Babylonians to triumph in the war. Jeremiah replies that because of their sins, the Lord will fight against the people of Israel, and give them into the hands of the heathen, who will slay them and carry their children into captivity. Then Jeremiah adds that the Lord has provided a choice: since his wrath is directed against the city, those who flee its walls and surrender to the Chaldeans will be spared: "He that abideth in this city shall die by the sword, and by the famine, and by the pestilence: but he that goeth out, and falleth to the Chaldeans that besiege you, he shall live, and his life shall be given unto him for a prey." The last phrase means that his own life will be all the spoil of battle that he will be granted. The reference conveys both the gratitude of the besieged for their providential rescue and also their humbling: they have only their lives for a prey, and have not spoiled their enemies; and they are likened to the survivors of a city condemned for sinfulness. Wheeler uses the same phrase in his account of the battle (see below, pp. 241), which suggests that Mather may have seen Wheeler's book in manuscript.

43. This was the first attack upon Lancaster, where Mary Rowlandson was later taken captive. The "afternoon exercise" is a religious service.

44. Mather interprets the sending of *wampumpeag* as a bribe, equating the beaded belt with cash. In fact the *wampum* served other symbolic purposes, perhaps in this case as a call for bands that had earlier promised aid to redeem their pledges. In any case, the value-equivalents for *wampum* were not expressible in purely monetary terms. See Slotkin, *Regeneration through Violence*, pp. 42–43, 49–50.

45. The soldiers left Hadley on August 24, and fought at Hopewell Swamp on the 25th.

46. Hebrew. "Smoked," or "waxed angry."

47. September 3, 1675.

48. What follows is an account of the events leading up to the Battle of Hopewell Swamp (August 25), and subsequent events to September 12, 1675, including the ambushes of troops evacuating the northern Connecticut Valley towns under Beers (September 3) and Treat (September 5).

49. Son of the Mohican chief, Uncas.

50. Lathrop or Lothrop.

51. Mather's colleague thus appears as one of those who have requested Mather to put himself forward as historian and interpreter of God's will.

52. Battle of Bloody Brook.

53. Mather's estimate of losses is wildly conjectural.

54. Maine and New Hampshire. These were frontier districts with few formally instituted congregations. They were also refuges for heresiarchs like Anne Hutchinson and John Underhill. Hence Mather's special emphasis on God's rebuke to the settlers on this frontier.

55. That is, a child of Satan. Despite Squando's failure to allude to Jesus Christ by name in his account of his vision—an omission that would have discredited the religious profession of any applicant for admission to a Puritan church—it seems likely that Squando intended the speech to be conciliatory, and to signify his willingness to consider seeking guidance from Christian emissaries. For another account of the grounds of Squando's hostility to the English see Slotkin, *Regeneration through Violence*, pp. 118–19.

56. The proclamation bears many marks of Mather's influence on phrasing and content. Note the reference to enemies abroad, whose dangerousness is given priority over the immediate Indian enemy. The allusion is to the struggle between the colonies and the royal government, and the larger Protestant-Catholic struggle of which the Puritan resistance to the Stuart restoration government is a part. So intent on this message are the colonists that they can still express the hope that the Indians may yet be converted into a bulwark of the colony in its struggle with its greatest enemies, including the French in Canada (with whom a war in the near future is expected).

57. Leviticus, 26:31. The phrase "*and if you will not be reformed by this*" is added by Mather, although typographically it appears to be part of the quotation.

58. This paragraph neatly summarizes Mather's program of moral and political reform. Note especially the strictures against Quakers, so prominent in the government of Rhode Island; the attack on the "Oppression" of employers and workers who demand excessive prices or wages; and the condemnation of Indian trading houses, in favor of a monopolization of the channels of white-Indian contact by the official agents of the government and the church.

59. The battle was fought on October 18, the day previous to that cited by Mather. He has taken the date of receiving the news as the basis for his providential coincidence.

60. Jeremiah, 8:20.

61. Weetamoo, not Awashonks, is meant.

62. The Narragansett sachems met the English at Wickford, R.I., on September 22, and in Boston on October 18, 1675.

63. The history of the Narragansett problem is much more complex than Mather indicates. See Leach, *Flintlock and Tomahawk*, pp. 56–57, and pp. 23–26, 29–30, above.

64. Quinsigamond (Worcester), Mass.

65. December 14, 1675.

66. December 16, 1675. Bull's Garrison had been considered as an alternate base for the expedition.

67. The army marched on the 18th, fought the Swamp Fight on the 19th, and retreated on the night of the 19th–20th of December 1675.

68. Leach, *Flintlock and Tomahawk,* pp. 131–33, gives the loss of officers as seven, apart from one who died of disease after the fight. Estimates of Indian losses range from two hundred warriors and an unknown number of women and children, to the one thousand cited by Mather. As in Vietnam, body counts were made by wishful estimate. Compare Mather's account of the retreat with that of Church, p. 416, below: Mather is pleased that the retreat was nearly an utter catastrophe, since the avoidance of an ultimate disaster bespeaks a favoring Providence; Church is infuriated by the blunders that made the retreat so nearly fatal. For an account of Indian fort-building, see Malone, "Changing Military Technology," p. 59.

69. Revelation, 2:5. "Remember therefore from whence thou art fallen, and repent, and do the first works; or else I will come unto thee quickly, and will remove thy candlestick out of his place, except thou repent." Mather is interpreting "candlestick" ingeniously here, because the passage so obviously suits his major thesis.

70. "With God."

71. This was the "Hungry March," January 28, 1676 (N.S.) to February 5, at the end of which the army disbanded.

72. Indians of the upper Connecticut River valley.

73. There is no evidence of any direct role played by the French in Canada, although the Puritans suspected there might be. In fact, the chief suppliers of arms to the Indians were the English themselves, as Mather elsewhere scathingly notes. See Malone, "Changing Military Technology," p. 51.

74. Ezekiel, 14:20. The implication of the passage is that the illustrious ancestors of the present corrupt generation of Israel/New England will not be able to save that generation from divine wrath. This speaks directly to the issue of the Half-Way Covenant, which permitted the children of church members to enter the congregation without themselves having experienced conversion, solely for their parents' sakes.

75. Marlborough.

76. Accidentally.

77. *h. e.* = *i. e. (hoc est).*

78. Psalms, 74: 10–11.

79. Western Rhode Island, along Narragansett Bay and back into the swamp and forest region.

80. In the Old Style calendar, the New Year began March 21.

81. Near Rehoboth.

82. Joshua, 7:8. The men of Ai were permitted to triumph over the Israelites because of Israel's sin "in the accursed thing." Verse 12 gives the rest of the context, which suits Mather's thesis: God tells Joshua, "neither will I be with you any more, except ye destroy the accursed thing from among you."

83. From the context it would seem that the "accursed thing" Mather has in mind is commercial cupidity, or the worship of Mammon. The equation of Mammon with covetousness is made only in the New Testament (Matthew, 6:24 and Luke, 16:9, 11, 13).

84. Typographical error in original. "Dissipation" is meant.

85. Mather has a double standard here, condemning the Indians as barbaric for burning animals in their shelters after having praised the English for doing the same to Indian women and children at the Swamp Fight. Note also the manner of Canonchet's execution, below; and see Benjamin Church, *Entertaining Passages*, n. 23, below.

86. In the first edition the first line of the paragraph below, which begins "About this time . . . ," was erroneously set just after this sentence.

87. Burnt.

88. Press-forced recruitment or conscription. Its institution suggests the extent of Puritan discouragement.

89. I.e., the Indians of Maine.

90. Hostilities in Maine were not actually settled until July 3, 1676.

91. Under Captain Henchman, operating in eastern Massachusetts.

92. Judges, 5:21.

93. "Wars exist by rumor."

94. "Many things in war are vain."

95. By this account it would appear that at least half of the slain were women and children.

96. Battle of Washaccum. Psalms, 68:18, "thou hast led captivity captive."

97. Artillery piece, most likely a small cannon and not the larger "great guns" used for sieges.

98. That is, they feared that a pursuit would cause the Indians to move away from the Falls, where the English planned to strike them. As always in Indian warfare, locating and fixing the enemy was the primary difficulty.

99. Psalms, 46:9. Verse 10 continues the prophecy in a vein congenial to the exponent of Indian missions: "I will be exalted among the heathen, I will be exalted in the earth."

100. This and the passages that follow are instances of Mather's attempt to bring a scientific spirit to his theology and historiography. He is attempting to correlate instances of prodigies or "illustrious providences" with significant historical events, to establish the utility of such providences as predictors—although he permits himself an unconscionably wide time-latitude in correlating events.

101. Hours.

102. Penis.

103. I.e., for voiding excrement.

104. Thomas Weld, or Welde, and Governor John Winthrop published *A Short History of the Rise, Reign, and Ruine of the Antinomians, Familists & Libertines* . . . (London, 1644), an account of the offi-

cial handling of the Antinomian crisis and the trial of Anne Hutchinson. Hutchinson was delivered of a "monstrous birth," which helped to discredit her. The tract is reprinted in David D. Hall, ed., *The Antinomian Controversy, 1636–1638: A Documentary History,* pp. 199–310.

105. Acts, 27:14. Euroclydon is a "tempestuous wind" that wrecks the vessel carrying Paul to Italy; God grants rescue to Paul and his companions, who are saved by placing their faith in their teacher and guide.

106. Connecticut is meant.

107. Zechariah, 3:2. Increase Mather's son Cotton uses the same text as the title of an extremely interesting account of Indian captivity and demonic possession, titled "A Brand Pluck'd Out of the Burning." Reprinted in George L. Burr, ed., *Narratives of the Witchcraft Cases,* pp. 256–87.

108. Wheat is meant; the word for what is now called "corn" was "maize" or "Indian corn."

109. These liberties had been threatened by Andros's ambitions to attach New England to New York, and by the still-active royal commission led by Randolph.

110. Mather here presents the act of the Council as a providential coincidence directed by God—a confusion of divine and human agency that is characteristic of Mather's history, is in this instance somewhat more exaggerated than usual.

111. Psalms, 9:16.

112. Contrast this account, with its emphasis on prayer, the signing of the Covenant, and the role of Major Bradford, with that of Benjamin Church, who negotiated the surrender. *Entertaining Passages,* pp. 422–27, below.

113. Wanalancet's treaty with Major Waldron, July 3, 1676.

114. Edmund Andros.

115. They would dye their hair or paint their heads and faces.

116. Mather is compelled by his theory of "providences" to record this prodigy, although he cannot readily use it as a predictor nor work it into his scheme, since now the disorder of New England's body and spirit is beginning to mend.

117. This pursuit of Philip by troops under Major Bradford of Plymouth took place from July 6–16, 1676. Mather's date is that of the receipt of news at Boston.

118. July 11–22, 1676.

119. Deuteronomy, 32:35. The chapter begins by speaking of the piety of the elder generation of Israel, and of God's protection of them in the wilderness; then threatens punishment to the later generation for its neglect of God in the pursuit of physical comfort. Thus the context of the passage evokes the thesis of Mather's history and sermon. This is the text used by Jonathan Edwards for "Sinners in the Hands of an Angry God."

120. The Puritans were much concerned with altering the affectional quality of Indian family life, to make the parents better dis-

ciplinarians and enforcers of Christian morality. See John Eliot, *A Late and Further Manifestation of the Progress of the Gospel Among the Indians in New-England . . .* reprinted in *Collections of the Massachusetts Historical Society* 3d Series, 4 (1834) p. 274; and Slotkin *Regeneration through Violence,* pp. 196–97.

121. "Indian harvest" refers to the harvest of "Indian corn" or maize planted by the English; "English harvest" is of "English corn" or wheat.

122. Usually spelled "Oneco." An Indian of that name figures as a major character in Catherine M. Sedgwick's novel *Hope Leslie: Or, Early Times in the Massachusetts* (Boston, 1827), in which Oneco marries a white girl who has been taken captive and raised as an Indian.

123. Job, 37:6.

124. 1 Samuel, 15:33. Saul contented himself with spoiling Amalek, and so failed to do the Lord's bidding, which was to utterly exterminate Agag and his people. Thus Saul lost the Lord's favor. Mather's use of this Biblical analogy, with its genocidal implications, is seemingly inconsistent with his support of Indian missions and the concept of the Indian "bulwark"; yet it is not fortuitous, since he uses the same kind of text as the epigraph to his second, more formal history of the war, *A Relation of the Troubles . . .* (Boston, 1677). The inconsistency illustrates the profound ambivalence toward the Indians that existed even among those who were their nominal friends among the English.

125. Psalms, 74:14. The feast of Leviathan was also supposed to accompany the coming of the Messiah. Cotton Mather elaborates this metaphor extensively in *Magnalia Christi Americana,* pp. 500–502; and see Church, *Entertaining Passages,* n. 15, below.

126. 1 Kings, 20:42. Again Mather implies that the extermination of the heathen, rather than their conversion, is commanded. For allowing the King of Syria to go free, Ahab is told, "Thy life shall go for his life, and thy people for his people."

127. "He will give much who can do so; for me, little able and demanding little, it is sufficient to have given little."

128. John, 13:7.

129. Sheba the son of Bichri, a rebel against King David, is meant. 2 Samuel, 20.

130. The idea that the heathen are left unsubdued to test the virtue and valor of Israel is raised in Judges, 3: 1,2. The allusion summarizes the whole of the Books of Samuel, Kings, and Chronicles insofar as these concern the reign of David. See Samuel Nowell, *Abraham in Arms,* pp. 264, 283, below.

131. The Greek for "*Deus ex machina,*" the God from the machine who intervenes to shape and evaluate action in Greek tragedy.

132. Psalms, 44:3. Compare Church's use of the same verse to very different purpose, p. 403, below.

133. Psalms, 96:7.

134. "Glory to God in the highest" *(Gloria in excelcis deo).*

135. "So would usage demand, with which lies the judgment and rule and standard of speaking," Horace, *Ars Poetica,* 71–72.

136. See Samuel Nowell's sermon on this text, below.

137. Winslow and Hinckley have confused the squaw-sachems of Sakonnet (Awashonks, Church's friend) and Pocasset (Weetamoe, Philip's ally).

138. The strife with Ammon is related in Judges, 11. The chapter is rich in formulations useful for rationalizing the conquest and possession of the lands of heathen by a chosen people.

139. Errata: The page numbers in the present edition are 93, 100, 105, 115, and 118.

AN EARNEST

# EXHORTATION

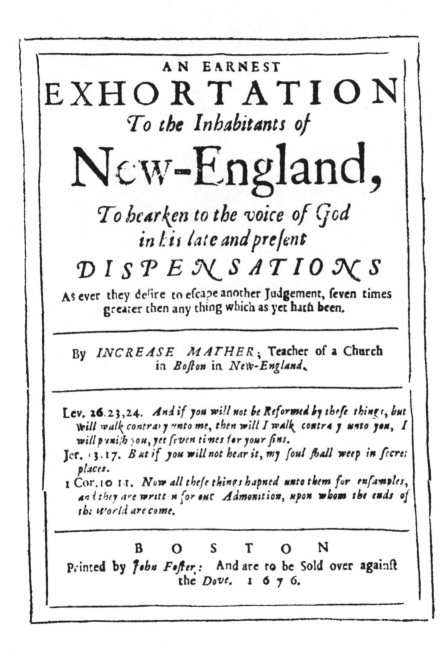

*To the Inhabitants of*

# New-England,

*To hearken to the voice of God in his late and present*

*DISPENSATIONS*

As ever they desire to escape another Judgement, seven times greater then any thing which as yet hath been.

---

By *INCREASE MATHER*; Teacher of a Church in *Boston* in *New-England*.

---

Lev. 26.23,24. *And if you will not be Reformed by these things, but will walk contrary unto me, then will I walk contrary unto you, I will punish you, yet seven times for your sins.*

Jer. 13.17. *But if you will not hear it, my soul shall weep in secret places.*

1 Cor.10 11. *Now all these things hapned unto them for ensamples, and they are written for our Admonition, upon whom the ends of the World are come.*

---

BOSTON

Printed by *John Foster*: And are to be Sold over against the *Dove*. 1676.

## *TO THE READER*

*This following* Exhortation *was written two or three months agoe, since which time the Lord hath given us to see a wonderfull* Turn of Providence, *in a way of signal mercy towards his poor* New-England-People. *Nevertheless I have for weighty Reasons, been willing to let it pass, as it is, the main design of it being to quicken sedulous endeavours towards the* Reformation *of provoking Evills, and there is still cause for urgency in that matter. God forbid that we should act as if we were delivered to do abominations, for then it is certain that the continuance of this affliction would have been a far greater mercy, then deliverance out of it. And I will freely confess, that I am not altogether without fears, that there is yet another Storm hastening upon this Land, if Repentance avert it not. For as yet men aren't convinced of that which I believe is the Lords* Special Controversie *with this Land. Though some doe, yet* the generality of the people *do not see and own those iniquityes, which the righteous God hath been contending for. Nor is there to this day so much done respecting a General Reformation of evills amongst us, as the Lord expects. Nay, there have been such trespasses committed, in the time of our distress, as I am perswaded God will yet visit for. It hath often been so, that if much sin hath been committed, eminent deliverances have been attended with sad after-claps. When the children of Israel were saved from the* Midianites, *the Inhabitants of* Succoth *and* Penuel *did perish after that. And in* Jephthahs *dayes, he had no sooner subdued the common enemy, but intestine troubles arose, so that* there fell of the Ephraimites at that time forty and two thousand.[1] *Let us not then be high-minded*[2] *but fear: especially considering that of late time, the Lord in his providence hath been giving us very* solemn warnings, *The deaths of so many righteous and useful ones, both of the* first generation, *and also a great number of precious ones of the* second generation, *and have bin* taken away this year *by Gods own hand, seems to be portentous of more* evil to come. *And the sudden awfull deaths of some, whom the Lord hath overthrown, as God overthrew Sodom and Gomorrah, look like ominous warnings. And that* Epidemical Disease *that prevailed this Spring, is a very solemn voice from Heaven unto us. We have heard also how terrible the Lord hath been in his doings towards our Country-men and Brethren in other parts of the World. Not to speak of the present state of bleeding* Virginia, *what an awfull providence was that which hapned in* Barbados *in* August *last, when a Plantation there, was* visited with thunder, and with great noise, and with a storm and tempest, and flame of devouring fire, *so that in a few hours a considerable town was brought into ruinous heaps,*[3] *The Lord give unto that* Island *Grace, duly to consider of it, and to sin no more* lest a worse thing come unto them. *And how awfull was the hand of God in* September *last, when a fire brake forth in a famous town in the heart of* England *(*North-Hampton *by name) and in about the space of eight hours, consumed the whole Town, that very few houses were left standing, and the Inhabitants many of them, saved nothing but the cloathes on their backs. Now if we that hear of these things,* fear God and receive instruction, our dwellings shall not be cut off, *but if we be secure and unaffected with the divine Dispensations, how can we think that the worst is past? The Lord can easily punish us by the same Instruments again, if we go onto provoke him. Yea if the power and good providence of God prevent it not, it will be so. Many of those Heathen that have of late submitted themselves, are treacherous and bloudy, And the* Indians *that have been helpfull in this* War, *will be apt to grow insolent upon conceiting, that we could not have subdued our enemyes if it had not been for them; and it will be a great mercy if rude ungoverned* English *do not ere long scandalize and exasperate them.*[4] *Or if none of those things should be, God hath a thousand wayes to punish us, which we cannot think of. Why then should carnal security grow upon us? When some said unto the holy Prophet,* Watchman what of the night? Watchman what of the night? *He replyed,* The morning cometh and also night.[5] *Even so, albeit at present, a comfortable Morning is dawned upon us, it concerns us to improve it well, otherwise we shall have cause to think on the other words also the night. Only it must be remembered that things of this nature, (all promises and threatnings respecting temporal mercies or Judgments are so) are to be understood* conditionally, *according to that which the Lord expresseth, Jer 18:7, 8, 9, 10.* At what instant I shall speak concerning a nation, and concerning a Kingdom to pluck up, to pull down, and to destroy it, if that nation against whom I have pronounced, turn from their evill, I will repent of the evill that I thought to doe unto them. And at what instant I shall speak concerning a nation and concerning a Kingdom to build and to plant it: if it do evill in my sight, that it obey not my voice, then I will repent of the good wherewith I said I would benefit them.[6] *We had need then to pray earnestly, that past and present dispensations may be sanctified to us. If we be indeed bettered thereby, we are like to see happy dayes again in* New-England, *but if otherwise,* New-England hath not yet seen its worst dayes. *Now the Lord Jesus help us to consider it. O that there were such an heart in us, that we would fear him & keep all his Commandments, alwayes, that it may be well with us and with our children forever, Which is the prayer of him who accounts himself happy, if he may do any faithfull Service, for God and for his People.*

*Boston, N. E.*
26. *of* 5m.
*1 6 7 6*

*Increase Mather.*

# AN EXHORTATION *To the inhabitants of* NEW-ENGLAND

God who sometimes said unto *Jerusalem,* be instructed lest my Soul depart from thee, and thou become desolate, a Land not inhabited, doth by his solemn Judgements in like manner call from Heaven upon *New-England,* saying, be thou instructed, lest I depart from thee, and thou become desolate without an *English* Inhabitant.

Wherefore we are to be exhorted (and Oh that we might be perswaded) since we have been brought into such a bleeding state, *to make a right improvement of this dreadful Dispensation.* O let not the Lord complain of *New-England,* as sometimes of *Israel, My People know not the Judgement of the Lord.*[7] But to speak a little more fully and plainly:

1. *Let us be auely and deeply affected with the awful hand of the most High.* Our Friends in other parts of the World, that wish us well, are greatly affected with our miseryes[.] It was said of old, concerning *Egypt* and *Tyre, at the report concerning Egypt, and at the report of Tyre, they shall be sorely payned,*[8] even so the report of Gods dealing thus with his *New-England-People:* the report of poor *New-England's* Calamity, hath caused those that are in Lands afar off to be amazed and troubled; and shall not we our selves be affected with our own doleful state? And shall it be said of thee? O *New-England,* shall it be said of thee, the Lord hath poured on thee the fury of his Anger, and the Strength of Battel, and he hath set thee on fire round about, yet thou knewest not, and it burned thee, yet thou laydst it not to heart. A Sword, a Sword is sharpened, and also fourbished, it is sharpned to make a sore slaughter, it is fourbished that it may glitter, *should we then make mirth.*[9] Dismal things we see are come upon us, It is mentioned in the Scripture as a sad thing, *Ephraim shall bring forth children for the Murderer.*[10] And again the Lord threatneth his people saying, *thou shalt beget sons and daughters but shalt not enjoy them, for they shall go into captivity.*[11] And in another place the Lord saith, *your young men have I*

*slain with the sword, and have taken away your horses, and I have made the stink of your camps to come into your nostrills.*[12] Also God hath denounced it as an heavy Judgment which should come to punish that sin of mens unfaithfulness in respect of promises & ingagements one to another (which hath been very much the sin of many in N.E.) *I will give them into the hand of their enemyes, and into the hand of them that seek their life, and their dead bodies shall be for meat to the fowles of heaven, and to the beasts of the earth.*[13] Now all these things have been verified upon us. Is it nothing that so many have been cut off by a bloody and barbarous Sword? Is it nothing that Widdows and Fatherless have been multiplyed among us? that in a small Plantation we have heard of eight widows, and six and twenty fatherless children in one day? And in another of the Villages of our Judah, of seven Widows and about thirty fatherless children, all at once: How can we speak of such things without bleeding Lamentation! Shall not such solemn strokes at last awaken us? The Inhabitants of the world would not have believed that the enemy should have prevailed so far, and done such things in *New-England;* that so many Plantations should have been brought to utter desolation! How are we spoiled? we are greatly confounded because our dwelling places have cast us out. Alas that *New-England* should be brought so low in so short a time (for she is come down wonderfully) and that by such vile enemyes, by the Heathen, yea *the worst of the Heathen:* that should be an affecting humbling Consideration to us, that our heavenly Father should be provoked to set *vile Indians* upon the backs of his Children to scourge them so severely, because of the provoking of his sons and his daughters, the Lord hath moved us to anger with a foolish Nation, and moved us to jealousie with those which are not a people.[14] As the Lord begins to deliver us, we are apt to forget the fears and sorrows which have been upon us, but that is the ready way to great Calamity.

Verily if we lay not these things to heart, there is cause to fear that those other Judgments (which nothing but wonderfull mercy hath saved us from) even *Famine and Pestilence* are not far off. We have seen the Lord come riding amongst us upon his *Red horse,* if this awaken us not, how can we expect other, but that ere long we shall behold a *Black Horse,* yea and a *Pale Horse,* and his name that shall sit thereon is *Death.*[15]

2. *Let an enquiry be made into the cause of the Lords controversie with us.* We know in general, it is for sin, Mich.1.5. *For the transgression of Jacob is all this, and for the sins of the house of Israel.* God is never wont to forsake his People except they do first forsake him, 2 *Chron.*15.2, *The Lord is with you whilst you be with him, but if you forsake him he will forsake you.* Inasmuch then as God hath seemed to cast us out, and put us to shame, and hath refused to go forth with our *Armies,* he doth by his Providence testifie against us to our faces, that we have forsaken him[.] He would not have given us to the Spoil, and to the Robbers, if we had not sinned against him. But some one will say, *how shall we know what sin it is that the Lord now contends with us for? Answer.* Although that be a most needful Question to be enquired into, yet I shall not say much to it, besides what I have at sundry times expressed, when speaking in the Name of the Lord.

1. *Take we heed how we embrace such notions as will lead us into mistakes about the causes of our misery,* e.g. that imagination which some have, that all this is come upon us, only for tryal, and not for Correction on the account of sins, without doubt it is for both.[16] Why should we suppose that God is not offended with us, when his displeasure is written, in such visible and bloody Characters? and truly before the present Judgement came upon us, it was evident that the glorious Lord was provoked against us: those general and *continued Blastings,* which were upon the fruits of the Earth, spake no less, when the like hand of God was upon the Land of Israel, though but for three years, *David* enquired of the Lord about the cause of his holy displeasure. Interpreters observe, that the first and second year *David* made no inquiry, because he might possibly think it was nothing, but what according to the ordinary Course of Nature might well be expected, but when he saw that drought was upon the Land for three years together, he concluded that it was for some sin that had provoked the Most High.[17] So with us, God by a continued *Series* of Providence for more then three times three years, one after another, hath been blasting the fruits of the earth in a great measure, therefore we may know that God is angry for something.

Again, that notion, that God is provoked for one sin only, or for some secret unknown sin only, tends to lead into mistakes concerning the true cause of our miseries. Not but that there may be *Secret sins which the Lord doth set in the light of his countenance*, and which we ought diligently to search after: but when there are so many evils visible and manifest, it is the subtilty of Satan to perswade men that this judgement cometh for some one secret sin, that so he may keep them from taking notice of that which is indeed the Lords controversie, and from repenting of those evils, which if they be truly repented of, the Judgements which have been upon us will certainly be removed: Also that principle, that whoever suffers in this common Calamity is the cause of it, will surely lead into misapprehensions concerning it.

In the Primitive times, when Plagues and Wars arose, because the Heathen Nations in those times persecuted the Church, some Christians perished (as to their Estates, Bodies, Lives) in the common calamity, albeit it was not for the sake of their sins, but for the sake of unworthy dealings towards them, that those desolating *Plagues* came upon the World: look as wicked men do sometimes escape temporal Judgements, for the sake of the Righteous amongst whom they dwell, so do the Righteous many times suffer great outward Calamity, because of the Wickedness of those they live among: once more, they that suppose this Judgement cometh on account of adherence to any principle alwayes avowed by the *chief of the Fathers* in these Churches, will (I doubt not) mistake in their conclusions. Those Principles which concern the *Purity of Churches*, the *Authority of Elders*, the *Liberty of Brethren*, a due extent of the Grace of *the Covenant*, *zeal for God in matters of the first as well as of the second Table*,[18] were alwayes asserted and pleaded for by the *chief of the Fathers of New-England*, when God did wonderfully own this People, and suffered no Weapon that was formed against them to prosper: but all that did attempt to devour them offended, and evil came upon them, wherefore it will be in vain to Impute our Calamities, unto any of the Principles (or practices according thereunto) which have been mentioned.[19]

2. *Search the Scriptures.* The wayes of God are everlasting; wherefore he brings the same Judgements upon his People now as in the dayes of old, in case there be the same transgressions: if then we would know why Droughts, Blastings, &c. have been upon our Land, let us search the Scriptures, and see for what sins those Judgements have befallen Gods Israel of old. Was it not

because the good Creatures of God were abused, to nourish pride and sensuality? and because Temple-work was neglected, and because men were guilty of robbing God? are the same sins found amongst us? then we may safely conclude, that those Judgements have come in special for those sins: and let us look into the Scripture, and there see what sins have in former ages brought the punishment of the *Sword* upon a professing People: and if those very sins are prevailing amongst us, write upon it, that it is for them, that this Judgment is come upon us.

3. *Hearken to the voice of God in the Ministry of his word,* mind what the Messengers of God speak in his name, *for surely the Lord will do nothing, but he revealeth his secrets to his Servants the Prophets,* Amos. 3.7. If I were to give Counsel to *N. E.* for my life, it should be the same that *Jehosaphat* gave to the people of God in his time, when circumstanced in respect of a Combination of heathen Enemies, against them, as we are this day: 2 *Chron.* 20.20. *Believe in the Lord your God, so shall you be established, believe his Prophets so shall you prosper.* What though in these dayes Ministers are not infallible? yet they are in respect of Office *Watchmen* and *Seers,* and therefore you may expect that God will communicate Light to you by them, yea they told you of these dayes before they came.[20] Do not say that the Ministers of God cannot tell you why this Judgment is come, how then could they give you faithfull warning thereof long enough before it came? I pray you consider this one thing, What were the sins which the Messengers of God declared would certainly bring *A day of Trouble* upon this Land? And hath the Lord confirmed the word of his Servants? then you may without danger conclude, it is for those sins that the Lord is now contending: And truly if we refuse to hearken to the voice of God not only in the *former Prophets,* but also by those who are still speaking in his name, why should we marvel that the Lord doth not incline his ear to our voice when we pray and humble our Souls before him? God cryeth to us by his Messengers, and we will not hear; therefore it is that though we cry to God he will not hear. *Isai.* 65.12. with *Zacha* 7.11,12,13.

4. *Consider how this Judgment is circumstanced,* If we mind where it began and by what Instruments, we may well think that God is greatly offended with the *Heathenisme* of the English People. How many that although they are *Christians* in name,

are no better then *Heathens* in heart, and in Conversation? How many Families that live like *profane Indians* without any *Family prayer?* Yea there have been whole Plantations that have lived from year to year, without any publick Invocation of the Name of God, and without his Word. And in most places Instituted Worship (whereby *Christians* are distinguished from *Heathen*) hath been too much neglected. Now there is no place under heaven where the neglect of *Divine Institutions* will so highly provoke and incense the displeasure of God as in *New-England,* because (as after shall be said) *Religion is our Interist* and that which our Fathers came into this Land for.[21]

3. *Let there be a sincere Reformation of those evills which have provoked the eyes of Gods Glory.* Deliverance will never come in mercy, except we turn to him that smiteth us. It is true that this Judgment may possibly be removed, though there be not Repentance, but then another Judgment will come ere long that will be seven times greater then this. Wofull experience may convince us of the truth of this, for the Providence of God is very observable, in that the Blasting that hath been without Intermission for these many years, hath not been this last year as formerly, but behold another judgment seven times greater is come in the roome of it. Yea moreover, either *Reformation* must be, or else (as long as the 26*th.* chapter of *Leviticus* is Scripture) at the last *Desolation* shall be, *I will make you desolate because of your Sins,* Micah 6.13.[22]

I remember it is storied concerning *Tamerlain* the great, that when he laid Seige against his enemyes, the first day he would set out a *white Flag,* to signifie mercy in case they did submit, and the next day *a red Flag,* to intimate they must now look for the Sword, and the third day *a black Flag,* to signify utter destruction and desolation. Truly the Lord hath been displaying the white Flagg, for many years before us, but it hath been dispised, and now he cometh with his red Flag, if this doe us not good, we have cause to fear that the *Black Flag will come ere long.*[23] How easily can the Lord destroy us: there is not the most contemptible Creature, but he can arm it so as there shall be no standing before it. I have read of a great City that was destroyed by Ants; and of another that was destroyed by Rats, and of whole Countreys that have been depopulated by Frogs, yea by Fleas. Though the Indians are a *Despicable* Enemy, yet the Lord is able to cut us down by a small *Indian axe.* But though I thus speak, I believe that God will reform his people by this Judgment, by this shall the Inquiry of Jacob be purged, and this shall be all the fruit to take away his sin.

*Qu: But what shall be done that so there may be such a Reformation as God will accept of?*

Ans. 1. *Those Evills which have been confessed before the Lord, and which are manifest let them be reformed.* In that *Order* before mentioned respecting a day of publick Humiliation appointed by *Authority* there are many Evills instanced in as matter of Confession and Humiliation before the Lord, let those sins be repented of, and turned from. We shall here take notice of some of them.

1. *Manyfold abuses of Peace and the Blessings of God in this good land.* Alas when we have had peace from enemies, we would not be at peace among our selves. And as the Calamity which is come upon us is General, so *Contention* is a sin which all sorts of men have been too guilty of: and now we see the bitter fruit of it, whilst the Sheep (yea the Shepherds too some of them) have been contending one with another, God hath let loose Wolves upon us all. And how have the Blessings of God been abused to serve *Baal?* The Plenty, which our Peace hath been attended with, hath been abused unto great Sensuality, and many Professors and Church-Members have been shamefully guilty in that respect. How common hath it been with them *to haunt Taverns,* and squander away precious hours, nay dayes in publick houses, which if but half that time had been spent in Meditation, Secret Prayer and Self-Examination, it had been happy for them, and it may be for others for their sakes. When as our Fathers were *Patterns of Sobriety,* they would not drink a cup of wine nor strong drink, more then should suffice nature, and conduce to their health, men of later time could transact no business, nor hardly ingage in any discourses, but it must be over a pint of wine or a pot of beer, yea so as that Drunkenness in the sight of man is become a common Sin, but how much more that which is Drunkenness in the sight of God. And how have the Blessings of God been abused to nourish *pride?* There hath been no small Provocation before the Lord in that thing, yea as to *Pride in respect of Apparel.* People in this Land have not carryed it, as it becometh those that are in a Wilderness, especially when

it is such an humbling time as of late years hath been. And none more guilty then the poorer sort of people, who will needs go in their Silks and Bravery as if they were the best in the Land. Though it be also too true that the rich and honourable have many of them greatly offended by strange Apparel, especially here in *Boston.* A proud Fashion no sooner comes into the Country, but *the haughty Daughters of Zion* in this place are taking it up, and thereby the whole land is at last infected. What shall we say when men are seen in the Streets with monstrous and horrid *Perriwigs,* and Women with their *Borders and False Locks* and such like whorish Fashions, whereby the anger of the Lord is kindled against this sinfull Land! And now behold how dreadfully is God fulfilling the third chapter of Isaiah. *Moreover the Lord saith,* (if the Lord say it who dare slight what is said) *because the Daughters of Zion are haughty, therefore he will discover their Nakedness.* Hath not the Lord fulfilled this threatning, when the *Indians* have taken so many and stripped them naked as in the day that they were born. *And instead of a sweet smell there shall be a Stink,* Is not this verified when poor Creatures are carried away Captive into the Indians filthy and stinking *Wigwams,* yea when so many English are faign to croud together, till it becomes loathsome and unsavoury? *And burning instead of Beauty,* is it not so when poor creatures are exposed to the burning heat of the sun, and burnt and tauned thereby till they become of an hue like unto these Indians? *Thy men shall fall by the Sword, & thy Mighty by the War.* Hath not that word been fulfilled upon us when so many have fallen by the Sword, yea so many Captains in this War, and this is because of the pride of the Daughters of Zion.[24] Oh then let that sin be reformed and repented of.

2. Another sin mentioned by the Council in that Order for a day of publick Humiliation, before hinted at, is, *Ill entertainment of the Ministry of the Gospel of Peace.* It cannot be denied but that the Ministers of God in this Land have for the generality of them, had miserable encouragement from men in the work of Christ. Through the undeserved mercy of God, and love of a dear People amongst whom I live, I am not at present under such personal temptation to speak in this matter as many better then my self are, but therefore I may the more freely speak in the behalf of my Brethren whose sorrows I greatly condole. How many of

the Servants of Christ have there been, that though they have preached the Gospel, have not (as the Scripture saith it should be) lived on the Gospel? but when their whole time and studyes should have been taken up in attending Services for Christ and for his people, they have been constrained (as the Levites in Nehemiah) *even to flee everyone into his Field, and the house of God hath been forsaken.*[25] I doubt it will one day appear, that the coals which have been stolen from Gods Altar, have burnt down many of those Plantations which are now desolate. Worthy Mr. *Davenport*[26] in a Letter which he wrote to me bearing Date 12*th* of 4 *mo.* 1666. thus expresseth himself, *I have* (saith he) *long been of that mind that N. E. is guilty of great unthankfulness for the Gospel, & strait-heartedness, & closehandedness toward the Ministers. Your blessed Father in law Mr.* Cotton, *was sensible of it, as I can shew in his letters to me in answer of mine to him, his conclusion after some other expressions was that the Ministry of the Gospel is the cheapest Commodity in this Land: when I consider these things I see cause of Admiration that the Gospel is yet continued in N. E. & that our Candlesticks are not removed: but it is from Gods pitty to some sucking Children that the Breasts are not yet dryed up.* Thus Mr. *Davenport.*

And verily I cannot believe, that God would have taken away so many of his Ministers out of *New-England* in so short a time, if the People had carried towards God and them, as ought to have been. *Through the wrath of the Lord of Hosts is the Land darkned.*[27] He that holds the Stars in his right hand hath removed many of them, and great darkness hath followed. In about thirteen years space there have been (to my observation) no less then five and thirty Stars that have set in this Horizon, I mean five and thirty Ministers (and some of them Stars of the first magnitude) that have in so short a time dyed in *New-England:* why did we not behold the *War* a coming when we saw the Lord calling home the Ambassadours of peace! I am not without fears lest that most awful passage which blessed Mr. *Shephard* hath (in his *Sound Believer* p. 250.) be prophetical, *Verily I am afraid* (saith he) *such a dismal Night is towards, such sore afflictions of Famine, Wars, Blood, Mortality, Death of Gods precious Servants especially, that the Lord will fill the hearts of all Churches, Families, Christians that shall live in those dayes, with such rendings, tearings, shakings, anguish of Spirit as scarce any were, in the worst dayes of our Fore-fathers, and that this shall continue, until the remnant that escape, shall say, blessed is he that cometh in the Name of the Lord, Blessed be the face and feet of that Minister that shall come unto us in Christs Name.*[28] O then let this sin of ill entertainment of the Ministry be repented of and reformed.

3. Another sin which hath been confessed is, that of *Formality in Religion.* These are perillous times which we now live in, when men are getting their Bread with the peril of their lives, because of the Sword of the Wilderness, when they can scarce look out of doors, but they are in danger of being seized upon by ravening Wolves, who lye in wait to shed blood, when men go not forth into the field, nor walk by the way side, but the Sword of the Enemy, and fear is on every side: surely the times are perillous, and that which brings such times is, the *taking up a form of godliness without the power of it:* and is it not so with us, the *first Generation* which was in this Land, had much of the power of Godliness, but the present *Generation* hath the form, and as to the *body of the Generation,* but little of the power of *Religion.* Alas in our Churches, we have a form of Discipline, but little of the power of it, and how it is in Families, and in Closets God knows, yea and as to our publick and most solemn approaches before the Lord, how slight and formal are the most of men? little or no preparation for them, no brokenness of heart in them, in which respect we have no cause to wonder that sad tydings hath come to us so often on dayes of Fasting and Prayer. Historians observe that *Pompey* seized upon the Temple, when it was the Jews solemn Fasting-day: and after that *Sosius* took *Jerusalem* upon a day of solemn Humiliation.[29] The Jews were then exceedingly degenerated having the form of these duties, but little of the power of them: hath it not been so with us in a sad degree? let us then no more content our selves, with having a name to live, and yet be Dead.

4. Another Evil, which we have confessed before the Lord is, that of *inordinate Affection to the World.* Idolatry brings the Sword, and Covetousness is Idolatry. *Land! Land!* hath been the Idol of many in *New-England:* whereas the first Planters here that they might keep themselves together were satisfied with one Acre for each person, as his propriety, and after that with twenty Acres for a Family, how have Men since coveted after the earth,

that many hundreds nay thousands of Acres, have been engrossed by one man, and they that profess themselves Christians have forsaken Churches, and Ordinances, and all for land and elbow-room enough in the World. Lot would forsake the Land of Canaan, and the Church, which was in *Abrahams* Family, that he might have better wordly accommodations in *Sodome,* and we see what came of it, God fired him out of all; his house and goods were burnt, and he forced to leave his goodly Pastures, which his heart (though otherwise a good man) was too much set upon.[30] Is the interest of *New-England* indeed changed from a Religious to a Wordly Interest? that's a *strange God,* and if it be so, no wonder that there is *War in our Gates:* do men prefer their Farms and Merchandize above the Gospel? here is the reason why Armies are sent forth against us, and our Cities are burnt up. Inordinate love to *this present evil World,* hath been the Fountain of all that misery, that we are bleeding under at this day; Those unhappy *Indian-trading-houses,* whereby the Heathen have been so wofully scandalized, hath not covetousness built them, and continued them for so long a time? and was it not from the same root of all evil, that the Indians have been furnished with Arms, and Amunition? would ever men have sold Guns, and Powder, and Shot, to such faithless and bloody creatures, if a lust of Covetousness had not too far prevailed with them? now then since these evils which have been mentioned (not to insist upon other particulars) have bin confessed, let us be sure to reform them, otherwise in our Confessions we have but dallied with the Almighty, who will never suffer himself to be mocked by any of the Sons of men.

And besides these Iniquities which have been acknowledged, as hath been expressed, there are other evils *manifest,* in respect whereof *Reformation* is necessary, as ever we desire to see good times and happy dayes in this Land. For alas it may be said, that *because of Swearing the Land mourneth;* not only in that Swearing is become a common sin, which even Children in the streets are guilty of, but in other respects which few take notice of. It is well if the *Freemans Oath* be not violated by too many, who are acted more by faction, then by Conscience.[31] Solemn Oaths upon trivial differences are too frequent. The body of the present Generation is guilty of *Sacramental perjury* in the sight of God, by breaking their *Baptismal vow,* and not observing all things whatsoever the Lord Jesus hath commanded them. Also wrath is come upon *New-England,* because the *Sabbath* hath been profaned. Persons under pretence of difference in Judgement about the beginning of the Sabbath (some being for the evening and others for the morning) keep *no night* at all *holy* unto the Lord. And it is to be feared that even since this War began servile works have been attended upon the Lords day, more then any necessity hath called for. And if we look into Families, Churches, or Common-wealth, we shall see such rebellious breaches of the *fifth Commandment,* as may cause horror when we think of it. That Spirit of *Koraisme*[32] which blessed Mr. *Wilson,* when dying did so sadly bewaile, and testifie against, how hath it prevailed? and men will not be convinced of this evil, except God open their eyes by strange Plagues, which are yet behind, and it may be not farr off.

The breach of the *fifth Commandment* is one of the great and *National sins,* which the Indians are guilty of: their Children have no regard nor reverence towards their Fathers.[33] If we learn the way of the Heathen, and become like them, God will punish us by them. And it is to me a sad and solemn thought, that this miserable War, hath been raised and fomented by proud and vain young men. The old Indians were very unwilling to engage in a War with the English, but the young men would do it, whether their Fathers would or no, and did at last precipitate you also into it, to the ruine of both Fathers and Children. I pray the Lord, that ungoverned young men in Families and Societies may not prove the ruine of *New-England:* if Fathers, if *Abners* will say, let the young men now arise and play before us, it may be it will be bitterness in the latter end.[34]

Moreover, what shall be said concerning that sin of *Oppression,* which is a general sin, and yet no man is guilty of it: since *Day-labourers* and *Mechanicks* are so unreasonable in their demands, and *Merchants* (some of them) so excessive in the prizes which they set upon their Goods, it is enough to bring the *Oppressing Sword.* And what a shame is it that ever that odious sin of *Usury* should be pleaded for, or practised in *New-England,* especially by such as should give a better example? Now for the Lords sake let such evils as these are be reformed, and no more heard of amongst us.

And there is another evil, which although it hath not been

confessed so much as should have been, yet it is a *manifest* provocation, and although I touch'd upon it before, yet I can hardly forbear inlarging upon that particular, I mean those *woful Contentions* which have made such a noise as is enough to provoke the Lord to turn us out of his house. This is a sin which doth escape altogether unpunished as to men, but therefore God will punish it, and the rather because his own Children and Servants have been found faulty in respect of a divided heart. No doubt but the *Wars and Fightings* which we have had one with another have brought the Judgements of War upon us, from the Lord. O that God would help those whose hands have been chief in this trespass, sadly to consider of it, lest another evil greater then this overtake us in our security ere long. If we will be pecking at one another, it may be the God of Heaven will send a great Kite, ready to devour us all.

2. In order to Reformation: *Let there be a due execution of wholsome Laws which are founded upon the Word of God.* If there be any Laws amongst us which cannot be warranted from the Word, change them and establish other in their room (I speak of Laws which respect the punishment of transgressors) but if the Scripture will justifie this or that testimony against Transgressors; either of first or second Table, let that and only that be done which shall please God: I have read, that it is a Rule in *Politicks, that a bad Executioner of Laws is worse then a violator of them.* Our defect is not so much in respect of the want of good Laws, as in the non-execution of those Laws that are good. It were better never to make Laws for the suppressing of Evils that are provoking in the sight of God, then not to see them faithfully executed when they are made.

3. *Solemn Renewal of Covenant with God in Jesus Christ, is a great Scripture expedient in order to Reformation:* we finde that the second Generation, of them who came out of Egypt, whilst yet in the Wilderness having also a difficult undertaking before them, being to engage with their Heathen Enemies, and in other respects their state and case to be parallel with ours, they did most solemnly renew their Covenant with God. It seems to be of weighty consideration, that although the Lords People of old did frequently renew their Covenant with him, yet it was never done but a blessed effect followed thereupon, not so much as one Instance to be given in all the Book of God, when his

People did *explicitly* renew the Covenant but a wonderful blessing did ensue. There is the nature of a Vow in this matter. Now Divines are wont to observe, that no instance can be mentioned out of the Scripture, when the Servants of God have vowed as well as prayed, but God hath heard them, we read that *when the Canaanites fought against Israel, and took some of them Prisoners* (just as it is with us) *and Israel vowed a vow unto the Lord, and the Lord hearkened to the voice of Israel, and delivered up the Canaanites,* Numb.21.1,2,3. And in *Hezekiahs* time (to omit other Examples) he considering that there was wrath upon *Jerusalem,* and those that fell by the Sword, and whose Sons, and Daughters, and Wives were in Captivity (all which things may be said of us) *It was in his heart to make a Covenant with the Lord God of Israel, that his fierce wrath may turn away from us,* 2 Cron.29.8.9, 10. If the Lord help these Churches to attend this thing with such seriousness and sincerity, as ought to be, without doubt we shall see good dayes in *New-England.*

And that it may be done the more effectually, it is much to be desired that the *Civil Authority* would (though not impose yet) recommend this matter to the Churches, otherwise it will meet with insuperable obstructions in some places; also that not some only but all the Churches engage herein: and that the special evils prevailing in this or that place, be particularly bewailed, and Reformation of them inserted, and (by the help of Christ) promised, in this *renewed Covenant.* Verily I do believe, the neglect of our duty in this matter hath retarded our deliverance for so long a time, why then should we not make haste, and not delay to keep the Lords Commandments?

4. One thing more I shall add, which if it be hearkned unto, to be sure *Reformation* acceptable to the Lord will be, It is this, *Let every man strive to amend one.* And who amongst us but have cause to think of Reforming? There are none of us so good but we may be better, we may (and should) grow in Grace and make progress in the work of Mortification. And God by the Judgment, which is upon us, doth evidently point at, and call upon all sorts of men to the work of *Reformation.* As for our faithful Magistrates (whom we have great cause to bless the Lord for) it shall be far from me to go about to discover the Nakedness of Fathers,[35] or to say that which may tend to weaken their Authority amongst the people, nevertheless I will be bold to say,

that if the Lord help them by this affliction to be more forward in the work of Reformation, more zealous in looking after the execution of wholesome, good and righteous Laws, more carefull to sanctifie God before the people, that in open Courts they may not (since God was angry with Moses upon that account) discover unseemly Passions, and more carefull to restrain their children that they may not (as Josias were, for which God at last punished them *Zeph.*1.8)[36] either in their attire (or however) be evill examples, and thereby hinder the Reformation of others in that particular; we shall then have cause to magnify the faithfulness of that God, who hath brought such an affliction upon us and sanctifyed it to us. And as for us who are Ministers in the house of God (and some of us amongst the deepest Sufferers in the present Calamity) are there not with us even with us also sins against the Lord our God? Have all of us in every respect been ensamples to the Flock? Have we given our selves to Reading and Meditation, and have we been very much in prayer for our selves and for the dear people of God? Have we been wholly in these things, without concerning our selves in affairs not proper for us to ingage in? when we have been unworthily reflected upon by these or those, have we not been more moved at it, then hath become us to be in our own case, considering that we should shew our selves examples in Patience, and Long-Suffering? Have we abstained from all appearance of evill? Is there no one that hath brought reproach upon the Ministry? Have none of us affected worldly *Gallantry* more then becometh the Ministers of God to doe, who should approve themselves *Patterns of Mortification* to all the world about them? Have we ruled our own houses aright? As for some of us, have not people seen our Relations, our Wives, our Children flaunting of it, and gaudy and Fashionable, whereby others have been scandalized: let us then be humbled and *Reform,* yea let us never leave Fasting and Praying, until the promise of the Father come upon us, and the Lord Jesus pour of his Spirit from on high upon us, in that measure as is needfull for men in that relation which we stand in before the Lord & before his people. And as it is noted of the great *Athanasius,* that by his Prayers and tears, and sweating labours in writing and Preaching, (like the bleeding of a chast vine) he cured much of the Leprosie of that tainted age wherein he lived, so let us endeavour to do the like.[37] It may be, that God intends by the present fiery Dispensations, to purify the Sons of Levi, then shall the offerings of Jerusalem be pleasant unto the Lord, as in the dayes of old, and as in former years.[38] And let not people think to free themselves by charging their *Leaders* with miscarriages. Through the abundant Grace of Christ towards his Servants there is no such cause of complaint, as some have made, whether against Moses, or against Aaron. It was most truly and solemnly affirmed by our famous, and now blessed Mr. *Norton,* in his last *Election-Sermon* speaking concerning the Ministry in *New-England, I may* (said he) *say this much, and pardon my speech, a more yeelding Ministry to the people, I believe is not in the world.*[39] Yea they have many of them stood in the Gap, and have turned away the wrath of God from this people. This Judgment had come sooner if they had not improved their interest in heaven to divert it, and if their counsels and earnest *Exhortations* had been hearkned to, the present misery had never been. And therefore let all the People of the Land turn unto the Lord, and hear this Rod and him that hath appointed it, so will he *soon subdue our enemies and turn his hand* (a Turn of Gods hand will save us) *against our Adversaryes, and the haters of the Lord shall submit themselves,*[40] then God will restore *New-England* to its former state, yea it shall be better with us then at our beginning.

4. *Let us beware of adding new sins to the old score.* When the host goeth forth against their enemies, keep thee from every evill thing. There were provocations enough before this Calamity came upon us, from which we are not cleansed untill this day: But alas! How have we lengthned out our sorrows by fresh bleeding guilt in the sight of God? A Judgment may come upon a people for one sin and be continued for another, it may begin on the account of former Iniquityes, and be continued because of later transgressions, It is possible that those evills which have provoked the Lord to whet his glittering Sword, and his hand to take hold on Judgment, may be seen and acknowledged, and yet he may goe on to smite us because of some evills which the eyes of his glory have been provoked by, since this *War* began.

I will (by the help of Christ) speak faithfully as I shall answer it before him that hath set me a *Watch-man,* another day. No man in the world could have perswaded me, that such a spirit would have been discovered amongst Professors in *New-England,* as hath lately been manifest. What unquietness hath there been under the hand of God, men being like a wild Bull in a net, full of the fury of the Lord, of the rebuke of God? what murmurings have have there been against *Moses* and against *Aaron,* albeit thousands of the Children of Israel lost their lives, because they said, *you Moses and Aaron have killed the Lords People,* yea God was so angry for that sin, that he threatned to consume them in a moment.[41] Nevertheless how many with us have cause to charge themselves, & cry guilty before the Lord in this respect? I remember it is *Pareus* his Observation, *that whereas the Children of Israel were guilty of murmuring eight times whilst in the wilderness, the mercifull God passed it by diverse times, nevertheless when their Murmurings were attended with a malignant mutinous Spirit* (as with us it hath been) *some signal Judgment or other did alwayes follow.*[42] And hath there not been great *Ingratitude* amongst us? Have not men that have deserved well, been recompensed evil for their good Services? Have they not been slanderously reported? Have not some evil spirits fomented false Reports and others too ready to take them up? The Lord lay it not to the Charge of *New-England.* Moreover since this *War* begun, the *Indians* have been scandalized by the *English:* It is well if some English have not the guilt of Indian bloud upon their souls, yea if in their skirts be not found the bloud of the souls of poor innocents. And what could have been done more then hath been done by too many, to prejudice the *Indians* against the *English* interest, yea against the interest of Christ in this Land? what madness and rage hath there been against all Indians whatsoever? Yea what willingness to destroy those that (like the *Gibeonites* of old)[43] are *Proselyted* to the Faith, and have put themselves under the *Protection* of the *English Israel* in this land, though they never did us hurt, but they have jeoparded their lives, and some of them lost their lives in the high places of the Field that so they might save ours. Judicious Authors conceive that the reason why the Lord did so plague his people *Israel,* when *Saul* had slain the *Gibeonites,* was because though Saul did it, yet *the body of the People* approved of it and rejoyced in that bloudy fact when it was done. As also that so the world might see how much the Lord is delighted in the *Conversion of Heathen.* Surely then we have many of us cause to tremble. How sad is it to consider, that an *Indian* should write a Letter to an English man and thus express himself, *When any hurt is done, you say that we have done it though we never did wronge to English-men and hope we never shall. You have driven us from our houses and lands, but that which most of all troubles us, is that whereas we began to know Jesus Christ, you have driven us away from serving God.* Truely when I think of what things have hapned at *Chelmsford* my heart doth ake and bleed within me. *Be mercifull O Lord unto thy people Israel whom thou hast redeemed, and lay not innocent bloud unto the People Israels charge.*[44] Furthermore, how hath the Indian work, I mean the work of Christ among them (which indeed hath been one of the Gloryes of *New-England*) been slighted, scorned, vilified? Albeit it is a sure principle grounded upon Scripture, that God never sends his Gospel to be constantly dispensed to any people, except he hath some elect amongst them, if the *waters of the Sanctuary* come, though it be into the *dead Sea,* there is some Fish to be healed and made alive there: yet how many with us have condemned all *Praying Indians,* crying out, they are all nought, there is not one good amongst them? And what though some of them may be Hypocrites? are not some *Praying English* as perfidious, as hypocritical, in heart as profane as some *Praying Indians?* Shall we therefore condemn all? Is there such a spirit in this Generation, as that they are ready to destroy? (& hath it been an hard matter to keep their hands from shedding bloud?) the righteous with the wicked? cease then to wonder that Desolation is come upon Sanctuaryes, and that the Lord hath been cutting off from us the righteous and the wicked. The Lord Jesus did intimate to the Jews that they *should see many from the East & from the West sitting with Abraham and Isaac & Jacob in the Kingdome of God, when they should see themselves shut out,*[45] So I doe believe, that many English-men that look with a disdainfull eye upon these poor Praying Indians, shall see a number of them sitting down with Abraham, Isaac and Jacob in the Kingdome of God, when I pray God they may not see themselves shut out. And truely, if it were only the profane world, that had been guilty of this Sin, it may be I should not have spoken so much as I have, but Professors and Church-Members have many of them cause to lament before the Lord for this evill. Now from the Lord I *Exhort* and beseech you, whoever you be that have been guilty of murmurings in any respect, or of casting a stumbling Block before the Indians, go to God in secret places, confess your sin before him, pray that it may not be imputed to you or to your Families, or to the Land for your sakes. In the Love of Christ have I thus spoken to you.

5. *Remember the Errand that our Fathers came into this Wilderness for, and pursue that Interest.* In general, it was on the account of *Religion,* that our Fathers followed the Lord into this Wilderness, whilst it was a Land which was not sown. There are other out-goings of our *Nation,* besides these Colonies in *New-England,* but they were not built upon a Foundation or Interest *purely Religious,* as is to be affirmed of these *Plantations.* It was with respect to some worldy accommodation, that other Plantations were erected, but *Religion and not the World* was that which our Fathers came hither for? why did the Children of Israel of old go into the wilderness? was it not that they might serve God? for the very same reason did our Fathers come into this Wilderness, even that so they might worship God according to his Will, and that all things which concern the house of God might be according to the pattern shewed in the Mount. *Pure Worship and Ordinances* without the mixture of humane Inventions, was that which the first Fathers of this Colony designed in their coming hither. We are the Children of the good old *Non-Conformists:*[46] and therefore we are under the deepest engagement, not only to reject *Inventions Humane* in the things of God, but to come up to the practice of *Institutions Divine.* As to our Ecclesiastical constitution, the *Congregational way,* as 'tis distinguished from the rigid extreams of *Presbyterianisme,* and *Brownisme,*[47] is that which we profess. And as to our *Civil Polity,* our Profession hath been, that they that are Rulers should be men that fear God, and that they that choose them should be such also, and that Laws in the Common-wealth should be regulated by the Word of God, that so the Lord Jesus may reign there.

It was worthily spoken by blessed Mr. *Mitchel* in a *Lecture Sermon,* that there is much of the Kingdome of Christ in our Civil Constitution: and it will be sad for those who shall put their hands to alter it. Such dash themselves against that stone, that whoso falls upon it, shall be broken to shivers. Therefore that Man of God solemnly protested, saying, *Wo to that man, be he old or young, Church-member or non-member, Freeman or non-freeman, that shall go about to destroy, or basely betray the liberties of this People; it were better for him, that a Mill-stone were hanged about his neck, and he thrown with it into the midst of the Sea.*[48]

Moreover, it was in a special manner with respect to posterity, that our Fathers came into this Land, that so their Children might not see evil examples, and be in danger of being corrupted thereby, as 'tis in other parts of the world, but that they might be left under the Government and Discipline of Christ in his Church, and be sure to have the great advantage of a Religious Education. And therefore that woful neglect of the *Rising Generation* which hath bin amongst us, is a sad sign that we have in great part forgotten our *Errand* into this Wilderness: and then why should we marvail that God taketh no pleasure in our young men, but they are numbred for the Sword, the present judgement lighting chiefly upon the *Rising Generation.* Yet more, our Fathers came hither to this end, that they might *Propagate the Gospel,* and be instrumental to set up the Kingdome of the Lord Jesus amongst the *Heathen.* And although some of the Lords Servants here have been sent forth (not without gracious success) to labour in that work, yet it is great pity, and I doubt one of the great sins which the English have been guilty of, that no more hath been done in order to the conversion of the Heathen: how great then is their sin, who do wholly despise and decry that work, and those beginnings of the Kingdome of the Lord Jesus, which is to be seen amongst them, our Fathers were of another Spirit. There is a letter printed which was written by my honourned Father (*'ο νὑν̓ εν 'αγίος*)[49] in the year 1652, wherein he declareth what himself (being one of those Elders who was sent to *Natick* formerly, to enquire into that affair) knew concerning the blessed success which the Gospel then had amongst the Indians: and he thus writes;

*There is so much of Gods work amongst them, as that I cannot but count it a great evil, yea a great injury to God and his goodness, for any to make light or nothing of it, to see and to hear Indians opening their mouths and lifting up their hands and their eyes in a solemn Prayer to the living God, calling on him by his Name Jehovah, in the mediation of Jesus Christ, to hear and see them, exhorting one another from the Word of God, confessing the Name of Jesus Christ, and their own sinfulness; this is more then usual, we saw them, and we heard them perform the duties mentioned, with such plenty of Tears trickling down the cheeks of some of them, as did argue to us that they spake with much good Affection and holy Fear of God, that it much affected our hearts.*

He that wrote these lines hath been in Heaven now above seven years, how would he mourn if he were here at this day, to behold the strange degeneracy that is in the spirit of the present Generation, who will neither believe that there is any good work begun amongst the Indians, nor yet desire and pray that it might be so? Believe it, if that holy designe of using means for the Conversion of the *Indians* be not duely prosecuted; the Prayers of our blessed Fathers will rise up in Judgement against us, yea the *Patent* it self will be produced as a Witness against this Generation at the last day, if that work be neglected.[50] For it is pretended (and those Worthies who were the *Patentees* would not have made such a Profession if they had not been real in it) in the *Patent,* that one special ground and end of this Plantation was, that so the Heathen in these parts might be brought to the knowledge of Jesus Christ: The words in the Patent, concerning this matter are,

*That to win and incite the Natives of the Country, to the knowledge and obedience of the only true God and Saviour of Mankind, and the Christian Faith, in the Adventurers free profession is the principal end of this Plantation.*

Yea more, the publick *Seal of the Country* will be a witness against this and succeeding Generations, if that design be not prosecuted[;] for we know the publick Seal of this Colony represents an *Indian* with these words *Come and help us* (as is to be seen in the preceding History, P. 15[51] alluding to that Vision which appeared to the Apostle *Paul,* when there stood a man of *Macedonia,* and prayed him, saying *Come over into Macedonia and help us, whereby the Apostles gathered, that the Lord had called them to Preach the Gospel to the Macedonians:*[52] So did the Fathers of this Country conclude, that the Lord had called them to take an effectual course, that the Gospel might be Preached to the Indians, and therefore it is not to be wondred at that the Lord hath afflicted us by the Indians *since the body of the present Generation hath no more of an heart to endeavour their Conversion and Salvation.* The Histories of our own Nation Declare, that whereas there were famous Christian Churches amongst the ancient *Brittains,* yet when in process of time, they scandalized the *Heathen Saxons,* who lived amongst them, *and neglected to use means for their Conversion unto Christ.* God was displeased with those Churches, so as to dissipate and drive them out of their Land by those very Heathen Nations, whose conversion they should have but did not endeavour, let us consider of it in the fear of God. And if we mind and seek the things of Christ as we ought to do, though our Enemies were more and greater then they are, and we fewer then we are, nevertheless we shall be victorious over them: As it was with the *Waldenses,* whilst they made Religion their business, and kept in with God, they prevailed wonderfully against those that waged War upon them.[53]

At one time eleven of them put to flight three hundred of their Enemies, & at another time five hundred of them destroyed five & twenty hundred of their Adversaries; and this is but according to what the Lord hath promised to his People as long as they are faithful unto that which is his and their interest.

6. *Give not way to desperate unbelieving thoughts:* say not there is no hope, the case is desperate: At first we too much despised the chastning of the Lord, let us not now faint when we are rebuked of him; we are apt to run into extreams. Are there not some that once thought this Calamity would be over-past in few dayes, who now are ready to say it will never be? well, do not think that God will utterly destroy *New-England* as yet. It was said of the Children of Israel of old, when they were in as degenerate a condition as we are in, yea and far worse, *the Lord was gracious to them, and had compassion on them, and had respect unto them, and would not destroy them, neither cast them from his presence as yet,* 2 King.13.23. what may come on this sinful Land at last I know not, nevertheless I am verily perswaded that utter destruction will not come *as yet*[.] For Jesus Christ hath by a wonderful hand of providence dispossessed Sathan who reigned in these dark corners of the Earth, in ages that are past, and hath taken possession of this Land for himself. Now, shall we think that Christ will suffer the Devil to drive him out of his possession again presently? The Lord hath a great Interest in this Land which he will not easily part with: There are many Churches of Christ here. In this Colony of *Mattachusets,* there are (or at least were when this War began) seven and forty Churches, and in *Plimouth* Colony there are twelve or thirteen

Churches: and in Connecticut Colony there are nineteen Churches, besides the three Churches in Long-Island: so that there are above fourscore Churches in *New-England.* Surely the Lord will not bring utter ruine upon them all as yet: And there are some of the first Generation (alas that there are so few of them) as yet surviving, now we may hope that God will not utterly consume all things in their dayes.

As a man that lived in *Luthers* time was wont to say, that he did not fear the ruine of *Germany* so long as *Luther* was alive, So neither doe I fear the utter ruine of *N-England,* so long as any of the first Generation who for the Gospels sake came into this Wilderness, are alive. Moreover though the body of the *second Generation* be wofully degenerate, nevertheless there are some of them (and through Grace many) that are eminently faithfull to the Lord Jesus and his interest, being of the same *Principles & Spirit,* that *their blessed Fathers* were of before them: we need not fear utter ruine in their dayes neither. Certainly if God intend to bring speedy destruction and desolation upon this whole land, he will find some way or other to remove such of his Servants as stand in the Gap to turn away his wrath from this people. Besides all this, the Children which have been born in *New-England,* are many of them the Posterity of those who have had an eminent Interest in God, yea the posterity of those who have been great sufferers for his name and Truth. Divines observe, that whereas in the *eight Beatitude* they that are persecuted are pronounced *blessed twice over,* it may intimate, that such shall be blessed not only in themselves, but in their *Posterity.* And if a due enquiry be made into that matter, I doubt not but that it will appear, that a special blessing hath attended the Children of those who have been *Martyrs* of Jesus: now the Children of *New-England* are many of them the posterity of such as have been eminent *Confessors,* and so in a degree Martyrs: If it should be said to a gracious Prince, behold here are Children, whose Fathers lost their Houses and Estates, and ventured their lives for your sake would he not shew peculiar favour unto them? Truly we may plead it as an Argument with the blessed God, and say before him, Lord as for the Children who have been born in *New-England,* their Fathers many of them ventured their lives into a wilderness for thy sake, they left their Fathers Houses and possessions in this world, out of respect to thy Kingdome, and therefore have thou compassion on them: *God will have compassion on them for his Covenant sake:*[54] And indeed the mercy which the Lord hath shewed in the midst of wrath, since the Sword has been drawn amongst us, argueth that he hath no mind to destroy us: what a favour of God was it that the Army was not cut off at the *Fort fight?* and that they perished not with cold when they were abroad day and night in the Snow, in the depth of Winter, and that God preserved them from mortal Contagious Diseases, albeit a Souldier fell sick of the Small Pox as he was going to the Army, yet none else took the Infection of that Disease. And whereas that terrible Disease, was in an *Ordinary* here in the midst of *Boston,* at the same time, yet only one therein was sick and dyed, and then the Lord was intreated to stay his hand; these are signs that God hath yet a favour for us. It is also a wonder of mercy that the Indians have done no more mischief, how easily might they have swallowed up *Plimouth Colony* long ago, and most of the Towns in the other Colonies, had not our God restrained them? Moreover, the Providence of God is to be admired, in that no more lives have been cut off. In some of those Towns which are desolated, not many lives have perished, I cannot learn that at the writing hereof, there are many above six hundred among the English who have been slain by the Enemy since this *War* began, whereas we might have expected that above so many thousand should have lost their lives, though the War had not continued so long as it hath. The Lord then sheweth, that his design, in bringing this Calamity on us, is not to destroy us, but to humble us, and reform us, and to do us good in the latter end. Wherefore although I am not without sad apprehensions, that Desolation will come upon the body of the present Generation in *New-England,* if not by this, then by some other Judgement ere long (if Repentance prevent it not) nevertheless *a Remnant shall escape:* That Scripture is like to be verified in *New-England,* even that *Zeph.*3.12,13. *I will also leave in the midst of thee an afflicted and poor people: and they shall trust in the Name of the Lord. The remnant of Israel shall not do iniquity nor speak lyes, neither shall a deceitful tongue be found in their mouth, for they shall feed, and lye down, and none shall make them afraid.* And as for the Enemy which is risen up against us, fear them not, the Lord our God will bring them down, who can do it, though we know not how to do it. It may be the Lord *slayeth them not* wholly and at once, but gradually, *lest his People should forget his mercy* towards them, *Psal.*59.11. yea I do believe, that if the Lord had not had a righteous designe utterly to destroy those of the *Heathen Nations* who have refused and horribly contemned the Gospel, they had not been permitted to do what they have done, that so they might bring swift destruction upon themselves, God may bring us Low, but he will not make a full end of us; as he will with our Adversaries, who are implacably set against his name and interest witness that Scripture, *Jer.*46,28-*Fear thou not O my servant Jacob, and be not dismayed O Israel, for behold I will save thee from afar off, and thy seed, for I am with thee, and I will make a full end of all the Nations whither I have driven thee, but I will not make a full end of thee, but correct thee in measure, yet will I not leave thee wholly unpunished.* And that Scripture, *Psal.*79.6,7. *Pour out thy wrath upon the Heathen that have not known thee, and upon the Kingdomes that have not called upon thy Name, for they have devoured Jacob, and laid waste his dwelling place,* yea and that Scripture, *Isai.*41.12. *They that War against thee shall be as nothing, and as a thing of nought.* Let us not then be faithless but believing. There hath been much Prayer made before the Lord on our behalf, and now we hear that the Churches in *Europe* joyn with us in earnest cryes to Heaven, certainly those Prayers and tears will come pouring down at last in streams of blood, and fire, and vengeance upon the Heathen: the vengeance of the Lord, the vengeance of his Temple is not far off. The Lord hath a controversie with the Heathen, and therefore he hath suffered them (in a degree) to pull down his Temple, that so they might pull down vengeance upon themselves for ever, God hath wayes to bring them down that we cannot think of: he can soon mingle a perverse Spirit amongst them, and cause them to destroy one another, he that did sometimes set the *Egyptians against the Egyptians* can set the *Indians* against the *Indians,* & who knoweth but that the Lord may do *as in the day of Midian?* And it may be God will send the destroying Angel amongst them. It is noted in the *Memorials of New-England*[55] (p.23,27.) that a little before the *English* came hither, the *Indians* were greatly wasted by Wars one with another, also the Plague was amongst them, and after that the small Pox, so as that the twentieth person was scarce left alive when the English arrived here, and they saw multitudes of skulls lying above ground, whereby they perceived that the living of them were not able to bury the dead. God is the same still, and will do for us as he did for our Fathers, only *he waits to be gracious,* he waits to see when we shall be fit for such mercy. It was said to the Church in *Thyatira, he that overcometh shall have power over the Nations, and as the vessels of a Potter shall they be broken to Shivers,* Rev.2.26. if the Lord Jesus help us to *overcome* the special corruptions and temptations whereby we have been carried away from God, those Nations who have risen up against us, shall be broken into shivers like a Potters Vessel, which all the World can never make whole again. I have been credibly informed, that a little before the beginning of this *War,* an *Indian Squaw* at *Nosset,* being with Child, the Child was heard crying three weeks before it was born into the World, whether dismal things to come upon them, might not be intimated by that Prodigy, I know not. And of late the Lord hath appeared more for us, and more against our Adversaries, then at the beginning of this War, so as that there seemeth to be a beginning of revenges upon the Enemy.

7. *When God hath perfected our deliverance, let us endeavour to be and doe better then ever heretofore.* If the Lord speak peace unto us, let us no more return unto folly. Let us sin no more lest a worse thing come unto us. It is an awfull word which *Ezra* spake, when the Lords people of old were delivered from their heathen enemies, *should we again break thy Commandments, wouldst not thou be angry with us till thou hadst consumed us, so that there should be no remnant nor escaping?*[56] So if people in *New-England* should again forsake God and his Ordinances out of respect to the world, what may we think would be the effect thereof at last? If the Lord restore peace unto this Land, and withall give us to possess the Lands of our enemies, it is to be feared that people will be apt to do as formerly, even to seek great things for themselves, with the neglect of the Kingdome of God, or with only a *secondary* respect thereto. That great Light of *New-England,* then whom no man was more instrumental in laying the foundation both of our civil and ecclesiastical constitution, blessed Mr. *Cotton,* did in his time observe and testify against such a spirit of worldliness and Apostacy, even in those dayes prevailing in this Country; wherefore in his Sermon on the third Vial pag. *ult* he thus expresseth himself.[57] "Sit

down no where without good Ministers, if it be possible, and sure possible it is, else Christians may resolve to tarry where they are, as Ezra tarried by the river Ahava, in the *8th.* of Ezra 15. till he had got some Levites to go with them, that they might go and make a comfortable work of it that they might not leave the ordinances behind them, and yet there were some there before, whither they went. It is true some may go and make a beginning, but yet never make a beginning but where you may come and partake of the waters of Gods house every Lords day, and let them that cannot so travel, let them continue where they are, and drink of the waters of eternal life, rather then run such hazards. You have seen when some have made a beginning without Ministers, they have staid three or four years before they have got any help, and when they have got them, they have had much adoe to settle, they have been suddenly unsetled, though they have not gone rashly about it, but with good advice: but for want of this, their not taking these Rivers and Fountains with them, they have been at a loss, and therfore in such a case let it be the wisdome of sincere hearted Christians, that come from old England for liberty and purity of the Ordinances, not to leave them now for fresh Meadows and Fountains, and for want of planting-ground and the like, it will not be suitable to those ends for which you left your native Country.["] Thus Mr. *Cotton.* Let there then be no more Plantations erected in New England, where people professing Christianity shall live like Indians, without any solemn invocation on the name of God, and altogether without instituted Worship. What a sad thing is it to consider, that there are many Children, born in New-England, who although they are come to adult age, never heard of the Lords-Supper, nor did ever see a child baptized in their lives? I am perswaded that one reason why the faithfull, holy God hath let loose the heathen upon us, is that so this disease might be cured. And wo to this land if it be not so. Yea and when the Lord shall have accomplished our Salvation, we ought to doe some singular thing tending to the honour of his name, as a sincere testimony of our gratitude towards him who hath by his own arm saved us. I have read concerning the States of *Holland,* that when they were miraculously delivered from the *Spaniards* great Army, to shew their thankfullness, they erected a *Colledge* at *Leyden,* & indowed it with goodly priviledges, and many famous lights have there been there, for whom the world hath had cause to bless God; *Poliander, Junius, Scaliger, Heinsius*[58] did sometime belong to that University. And what can be thought of amongst us, which will have a greater tendency to the Glory of God and good of the Souls of men then to take effectual care about that matter? That *Academical Learning,* (and with it Religion) may not fail in succeeding Generations. We find in Scripture, that whilst the first Generation of the children of Israel, who came out of Egypt lived, religion was upheld. Yea and whilst the Heads of the second Generation continued. But when *Joshuah* and *Eleazer* (the leaders of that Generation) slept with their Fathers, sad degeneracy and misery soon overwhelmed the rising Generation.[59] The Lord awaken us to do our utmost to prevent the like in New-England, but there will be no preventing of it, if due care be not taken, that there may be meet and able Instruments by whom the truth and Religion may be maintained and propagated. The *Centuriators*[60] and other Historians have noted that the Apostles and primitive Christians were greatly sollicitous in that thing. And so we see our Fathers of the first Generation in New-England have been[:] therefore did they erect a *Colledge* at *Cambridge,* which in their dayes was signally owned and blessed by the Lord, and what a dark miserable Land had New-England been before this day, had it not been for the Blessing of God upon that Society? most of the churches being supplyed with Teachers who have there been educated. Should *Academical Learning* fall in this land, it would be one of the saddest Omens that could be. Ignorance and Barbarisme would overspread the face of succeeding Generations; darkness shall then cover the earth, and gross darkness the people. *Papists* are wont to reflect upon *Protestants,* as if they were nor duly carefull in erecting and encouraging *Seminaries of Learning and Religion,* The most learned *Voetius,* was able to reply, that whereas there are no less then ten Provinces in Popish *Belgium,* there are but two Universityes therein, whenas although there are but seven Provinces in reformed *Belgium,* there are no less then five Universityes, and one Academical School, besides other illustrious Schools.[61] It will be a great mercy and happiness to Posterity, and we shall have wherewith to answer Adversaryes, if after this *War* more encouragement be given respecting the *Colledge* and other Schools of Learning. and if ever God shall give us the lands of our enemies, I cannot think how they can be disposed of better, or more to Gods Glory, and publick advantage, then in such a way and towards such an end as hath been expressed. And what a wonderfull providence will it be, if Barbarians should occasion the promotion of *good Literature.*?[62]

8. *In the last place let me assume the boldness to speak to any in other parts of the world, into whose hands this may come.* Let not those that bear us ill-will say in their hearts *Aha* so would we have it. Will not the Lord remember the children of Edom, who in the day of Jerusalems Calamity said *rase it, rase it to the foundation thereof?* Psal.137.7. And say unto the Ammonites hear the word of the Lord God, thus saith the Lord God, because thou saidst *Aha* against my Sanctuary when it was profaned, and against the land of Israel when it was desolate, and against the house of Judah when they went into Captivity, behold therefore I will stretch forth my hand upon thee, and will cause thee to perish, Ezek.25.3.7. Neither let the world be offended at these things that have hapned to *New-England,* as though neither we nor our Fathers were built upon right Foundations of Truth, because of this misery which our sins (and back slidings which are many) have brought upon us. It is famously known, that those ancient and orthodox Christians, the *Albigenses and Waldenses,* no less then ten hundred thousand were slain by barbarous and bloody Enemies, even Heathenish Idolatrous Papists; & when the Bishop of *Tolosse* endeavoured therupon to perswade them that they had not a righteous cause before them, they replyed, it is written in the *Book of Revelation,* concerning the Beast, that *unto him was given Power to make War against the Saints, and to overcome them,*[63] and therefore, notwithstanding the success which you have had you may be the Beast, and we may be the Saints of Christ. Nor is it any sign that these poor *New-English Churches* do not profess the Truth and way of Christ because such a Judgment hath overtaken us; therefore let no one make that use of it; but rather be awakened to take warning thereby to *prepare for Troubles;* for if this be done to *Immanuels Land,*[64] what may other Lands expect ere long? Are not the things that have hapned to *New-England* a Sign that the wine-cup of divine fury shall be given to all the Nations? and they shall drink, and be moved, and be mad, because of the sword which the Lord will send amongst them. In which respect

I pitty and marvel at the folly of those who are removing out of the Country, lest they should meet with trouble. To what ends is it for you? It is as if a man did flee from a Lion, and a Bear met him, or went into the house and leaned his hand on the wall, and a Serpent bit him. Shall not the day of the Lord be darkness & not light? even very dark, & no brightness in it[.][65] The time is come that Judgement must begin at the House of God, and if it first begin at us, what shall the end be of them that obey not the Gospel of God? verily I am perswaded, that the Calamity which is come upon *New-England,* is a solemn warning from Heaven, that dismal things are hastening upon the *English Nation,* and not only so, but indeed upon the whole World, that it will not be long before that Scripture be fulfilled, *Zeph.*3.8. where the Lord speaketh, saying. *My determination is to gather the Nations, that I may assemble the Kingdomes to pour upon them mine Indignation, even all my fierce anger, for all the Earth shall be devoured with the fire of my jealousie.* However, certain it is, that the most terrible changes are coming upon the Earth that ever were known since the world began. There are indeed glorious times not far off, *glorious things are spoken of thee, O thou Citty of God.*[66] After the destruction of *Rome* the Conversion of the Jews; and the fulness of the Gentiles shall come in (which things I know and am perswaded by the Lord Jesus, that they are nearer then some imagine for) peace and prosperity shall run down like a River, and like a mighty Stream, the whole World throughout, *the Nations shall learn War no more,* but a little before that, there shall be distress of Nations with great perplexity, mens hearts failing them for fear, and for looking after those things.[67] The powers of Heaven shall be shaken, the Sun shall be turned into darkness, the Moon into blood, and the Stars of Heaven shall loose their shining, Alas who shall live when God doth these things? *There shall be such a time of trouble as never was since there was a nation even to that same time,* Dan.12.1.

And as for those who in this or that place do in sincerity call upon the name of our Lord Jesus Christ, their Lord and ours, be intreated to *remember New-England,* in all your solemn addresses before the Throne of Grace, pitty and pray for us, who knoweth but the Lord may be gracious to the *remnant of Joseph,* through the help of your Prayers, yea, we know that God hath begun to answer your Prayers for us already: And therefore you who as yet have escaped the Sword, go away, stand not still, remember the Lord afar off, and let *Jerusalem* come into your minds. yea let *New-England* come into your minds, who spreadeth forth her hands, and shall there be none to comfort her, at this time when the Lord hath afflicted her in the day of his fierce anger? poor *New-England* cryeth unto you (as sometimes sorrowful *Job* unto his Friends) *have pitty on me, O ye my Friends, have pitty upon me, for the hand of the Lord hath touched me.*[68]

---

FINIS

---

## NOTES

1. Mather's references are to the Book of Judges, 6 (Gideon), 8:17 (Succoth and Penuel) and 11 (Jephthah).

2. Proud.

3. Refers to Bacon's Rebellion in Virginia (1676) and to the earthquake in the Barbadoes, West Indies, which is seen by Mather as an anticipation of the Apocalypse.

4. Thus even for Mather, the friendliness of Praying Indians is seen as unstable, given the congenital insolence of Indians and the greed of whites.

5. Isaiah, 21:11–12. The concluding words are particularly appropriate: "if ye will inquire, inquire ye: return, come." The pious listener intent on learning will take in this as the context, and feel himself called to return to his "first love."

6. Note this extensive quotation from Jeremiah, and the numerous other citations from that prophet. See Mather, *Brief History,* n. 1, above.

7. Jeremiah, 6:8 and 8:7.

8. Isaiah, 23:5. The report concerning Tyre was that it would be "laid waste, so that there is no house, no entering in." This was a warning to Israel of the punishment due for its degeneration since the days of the Patriarchs.

9. Ezekiel, 21:9–10. This prophecy was directed against Jerusalem itself, for its failings. Hence New-England, godliest of commonwealths, was to consider itself warned.

10. Hosea, 9:13.

11. Deuteronomy, 28:41. This and numerous other afflictions will come "if thou wilt not harken unto the voice of the Lord thy God" (28:15).

12. Amos, 4:10.

13. Jeremiah, 34:20; and, in almost the same words, 19:7. The formula occurs frequently throughout this book.

14. Deuteronomy, 32:21. This chapter consists of a song of Moses, written after the revelation that after the Patriarch's death, the people would go whoring after strange gods. Mather and other writers on the war refer to this chapter frequently. "Them that are not a people" is an interesting phrase in this context: it echoes early conceptions of the Indians such as those of William Bradford, who speaks of the New World as "unpeopled." The phrase implied that the Indians were not organized as a civil society: that they had, in effect, no laws or religion. That such a notion could be entertained of a people that manifestly had both suggests the depth of colonial ethnocentricity.

15. Revelation 6:1–8. This refers to the Four Horsemen of the Apocalypse. Mather once again is trying to correlate current events with the figures of Revelation in order to determine the imminence of mankind to final judgment.

16. Although the point seems legalistic, to a population of theological precisians it was a matter of some significance. If the war was a "trial," then the passing of it might suggest that atonement for sins had been accomplished. Mather insists that "correction" of departures from sanctified ways is yet to be accomplished, and that the war is merely a warning of the penalty that will follow failure of reformation.

17. 2 Samuel, 21:1. Another instance of Mather's attempt at what might be called scientific theology. David first consults the ordinary course of nature to explain the drought; and when that norm is exceeded, attributes it to the Lord. It is also interesting to note that the sin for which Israel was being punished in that instance was Saul's murder of the Gibeonites—a heathen tribe which had converted to the God of Israel. This parallels the situation of the Praying Indians, for whom Mather was much concerned. See note 43, below.

18. In forming the polity of the primitive church, the apostles divided the functions of the ministry: while they themselves specialized in preaching and serving the priestly function in the eucharist, service at the tables of the congregation (during the communion feast) was delegated to the seven deacons. This division paralleled the priest/Levite distinction of the Old Testament, to which Mather also refers. In the "Cambridge Platform" which defined the polity of the Congregational Puritan churches, an analogous division was preserved. While the teaching and ministering functions (including presiding at the Eucharist or Lord's Table) was reserved to the minister or teacher of the congregation, the deacons were entrusted with the functions of administration. Specifically, they were to serve the minister's table, by seeing to it that

the congregation provided adequately for the minister's needs. This is Mather's concern here: he believes that New England congregations have not been providing adequate support for their ministers, in the form of salary and other necessaries of life; nor have they provided sufficient facilities for the education of their ministry. These concerns of the "Second Table" are regarded as being equal in importance with those of the "First Table"—ill-treatment of ministers by deacons and congregation is likened to ill-serving of the Lord and the Lord's Table. Williston Walker, ed., "The Cambridge Synod and Platform," in *The Creeds and Platforms of Congregationalism*, pp. 210–13.

19. That is, it is not the doctrines of the Fathers that are the cause of God's displeasure with New England (as the Quaker and Anglican critics allege), but rather, the sins of the younger generation.

20. This contrast is interesting as a formulation of the Puritan conception of ministry. In Scriptural times the role of minister was prophetic, and the minister had direct access to divine revelation. In the latter days, the minister has access to God only through written records of divine revelations and providential interventions in the past; and his role is that of teacher and scholar. The text is Jeremiah, 6:17.

21. See note 14, above. The heathen are those who lack instituted worship, and the forms of civil organization. In this instance, the unconverted English (of the frontier districts especially) are seen as declining toward heathenism. Note also Mather's method of reasoning by metaphoric association: because heathens are the instruments of punishment, therefore it is heathenism in the English that is to be punished. Mary Rowlandson sees her captivity among the Indians in similar terms: see below, p. 308.

22. Leviticus 26 is rich in "tests" of Mather's interpretation of the war. If the Israelites will keep God's commandments, their land will be fruitful, the people healthy, five of them should triumph over a hundred enemies, and so forth. Failing to keep the commandments, they would be punished by pestilence, wastage of land, and military defeat, even by inferior numbers and fighters. All these calamities have come to pass on New England, as the *Brief History* attempts to show: the conclusion is inevitable that New England has sinned, and must reform.

23. Note that God is seen metaphorically in the figure of Tamurlaine, the Mongol conqueror—a pagan and non-European. This suits Mather's thesis that the heathen Indians have been the medium of divine revelation and warning. The "black flag" signifies "no quarter"—no prisoners will be taken, all will be exterminated. The white/red/black imagery is also used in the vision of the horses in the Apocalypse, cited by Mather earlier, p. 171, above.

24. Isaiah 3:16–26. Again Mather uses his texts to "test" reality by the biblical standard: if the figures of the prophecy are seen to have been realized, it follows that the prophet is correct in analyzing the people's fault and in his prescription of a remedy.

25. Nehemiah, 13:10–11.

26. John Davenport (1597–1670) was a Puritan minister of generally conservative tendencies, particularly on matters affecting church government. He was relatively late in breaking with the Church of England (1632), although he was an associate of the first incorporators of the Massachusetts Bay Company. He came to New England in 1638, where he took the orthodox position in the Antinomian controversy. As minister of a church in New Haven, he resisted that colony's union with Hartford; and he was also an opponent of the Half-Way Covenant (a position he shared with Mather). At the end of his life he was accused of having stretched a point of Congregational law in order to leave his church in New Haven for a higher-paying post with a church in Boston. The citation is an apology for such actions. Mather approved both the rationale, and in general the theological orientation of Davenport himself.

27. Isaiah, 9:19.

28. Thomas Shepard, *The Sound Believer* . . . (London, 1645). Shepard (1605–1649) was a leading figure in the first generation of New England ministers and magistrates.

29. Flavius Josephus, *The Jewish Wars,* is the probable source.

30. Genesis, 13:10–11. To Lot the plain of Jordan seemed "*even* as the garden of the Lord"—a phrase evocative of the promotional literature written to stimulate emigration to America. For Mather, these secular persuasions are morally suspect and politically dangerous, since they would tend to the dilution of the population of New England by worldly men, and distract the Puritans themselves with the pursuit of better lands beyond the frontier. Abraham illustrates the proper motivation for colonization in the previous chapter (12:1): he obeys a direct commandment of God, never considering his own convenience.

31. The "freemen" were the electors or full citizens of the colony: residents who had the right to vote for the magistrates. Before the Revolution of 1689, this right was restricted to church members, which is to say only to those who had had approved conversion experiences. In 1634, the class of freemen was expanded, and a new "Freeman's Oath" (a kind of loyalty oath) devised, to enable the political opponents of Governor Winthrop to replace him. Although this new arrangement expanded the franchise somewhat, it fell well short of political democracy; and the oath was designed to bind the newly enfranchised most firmly to conservative policy, as a way of further checking the potential for disorder in even so limited a liberalization. The oath is given in John G. Palfrey, *The History of New England,* vol. I, pp. 377–78. The portion of most direct relevance to Mather's concern is the last part of the oath, which states: "Moreover, I do solemnly bind myself, in the sight of God, that, when I shall be called to give my voice touching any such matter of this state, wherein freemen are to deal, I will give my vote and suffrage as I shall judge in mine own conscience may best conduce and tend to the public weal of the body, without respect of persons, or favor

of any man." Mather asserts that in fact the freemen have consulted not their consciences (which in Mather's view could not be so perverted as to disagree with his) but their political and economic advantage.

32. Numbers, 16:3. Korah and his sons rebelled against Moses and Aaron, asserting that "all the congregation are holy." Hence Koraism is radical egalitarianism in religious matters, especially Antinomianism.

33. See note 21, above; and also Benjamin Tompson, *New Englands Crisis*, p. 218, below.

34. 2 Samuel, 2:14. Abner commanded troops loyal to the House of Saul against King David; his frivolous giving of permission for the young men to "play" led to his defeat.

35. Genesis, 9:22.

36. Zephaniah, 1:8. "And it shall come to pass in the day of the Lord's sacrifice, that I will punish the princes, and the king's children, and all such as are clothed with strange apparel." Mather is about to embark on an attack on fashionable clothing. See also Tompson, *New Englands Crisis*, p. 216, below.

37. Athanasius was the bishop of Alexandria, 293–373—a commanding figure in the early church. He was the chief opponent of the Arian heresy and the emperors who supported or countenanced it, hence, a champion of orthodoxy against both kings and Christian enthusiasts.

38. Malachi, 3:3. The Levites were servants of the Temple, below the priestly rank, and hence equivalents for the ministers and magistrates of the latter days.

39. John Norton, *Three Choice and Profitable Sermons* . . . (Boston, 1664). Norton was also a eulogist of Mather's father-in-law and revered teacher, John Cotton.

40. Psalms, 81:15.

41. Numbers, 16:41. This was the response of Israel to Moses' and Aaron's suppression of the rebellion of the sons of Korah (see note 32, above). Mather is here defending ministers and magistrates against the accusation that their mistaken policies, not God's will, provoked and prolonged the war.

42. David Pareus, a German Reformed theologian, 1548–1622. A strict Calvinist, author of numerous polemical and theological works, including a series of commentaries (published between 1605 and 1618), from which the quotation is probably drawn.

43. Gibeon was a Canaanitish kingdom that allied itself with Israel and may have converted to the worship of Jehovah. In this case, the Gibeonites are comparable to the Praying Indians. See note 17, above.

44. Deuteronomy, 21:8. In context, this is given as a general law for the government of Israel. The reference to "Chelmsford" concerns the attack of a Praying Indian village by a mob of whites, in which a child was killed, in the fall of 1675.

45. Matthew, 8:11. Since only those who believe in Jesus Christ are to be saved, converts from the Gentiles of east and west may sit with the Jewish Patriarchs, while the descendants of the Patriarchs are cast

down. The passage has relevance for the Half-Way Covenant controversy, as well as for the rhetorical defense of the Praying Indians against their Christian calumniators.

46. Nonconformists: the original non-Separating Puritans who opposed the form of worship and polity of the Church of England; in context, Congregationalists are meant.

47. Presbyterians and Brownists represent other major wings of Puritanism, opposed to Congregationalism. Presbyterians imposed a hierarchy above the congregational organization; the followers of Robert Browne (among whom were the Pilgrims of Plymouth Colony) believed in the necessity of separating completely from the Church of England, and hence were called Separatists. The more conservative Puritans of Massachusetts were Congregationalists who opposed Presbyterian polity in favor of congregational independence, but preferred to reform and reorganize the Church of England rather than to separate from it. All three shared a Calvinistic theology. In America, Plymouth (and to a degree Rhode Island) exemplified the Brownist tendency, while Connecticut seemed to some to have taken a quasi-Presbyterian direction under Thomas Hooker.

48. Jonathan Mitchell, *Nehemiah on the Wall* . . . (Boston, 1671). Mitchell was to the second generation of American Puritans what Cotton and Shepard were to the first: a paramount intellectual leader in religious and civil affairs. He was Increase Mather's tutor, but unlike his pupil was favorable to the Half-Way Covenant at the start. His (and Mather's) remarks are intended to check the alteration of the government by those seeking to expand the franchise to Half-Way and nonmembers of the churches.

49. "Who is now among the blessed." The last word should be "*αγιοις*," and the accent on the first word should be "O."

50. I.e., the colonial charter, the original compact of government and the license to exist of its civic order. The patent had been challenged on these and other grounds several times before, and was under present scrutiny by the royal commissioners.

51. Page 102 in this edition.

52. Acts, 16:9.

53. The Waldensians were a heretical sect that flourished in France in the twelfth and thirteenth centuries, and were repressed and destroyed by the Inquisition. Survivors of the sect were associated with Luther and the German Protestants. Like the Albigensians, they represented an early (Mather implies a "premature") eruption of the spirit of the Reformation.

54. This passage alludes directly to the Half-Way Covenant controversy. Mather seems to be arguing that God ought, in reason, to be merciful to the children of those who have been *both* confessors and martyrs for his truth. It follows, by the logic of his assumptions, that if it is reasonable for God to show such compassion, he will *probably* do so (although if he refuses to do so he would violate no law, since the cov-

enant cannot bind him). However, Mather does not go the whole way toward the Half-Way Covenant: he notes that the present "children" are the descendents of those who were martyrs as well as confessors—if the next generation are the sons of confessors only, compassion may be less probable; and he leaves open the exact nature of divine compassion—while he seems to acquiesce in the opening of church membership on a compassionate basis, his words can also be read as implying a belief that God will show his compassion by permitting the children to have genuine conversion experiences. This ambiguity defines Mather's position accurately: he was willing to accommodate to the political necessity of the Half-Way Covenant, so long as the letter of doctrine remained unchanged.

55. [George Mourt (or Morton)], *A Relation . . . of the Beginning and Proceedings of the English Plantation Setled at Plimoth in New England . . .* (London, 1622).

56. Ezra, 9:14.

57. John Cotton, *The Powring Out of the Seven Vialls . . .*: see Mather, *Brief History*, n. 11, above.

58. These are Dutch and German Calvinist theologians: Johannes Poliander (Johann Gramann or Graumann), 1487–1541; Franciscus Junius (Francois du Jon), 1545–1602; and Joseph Justus Scaliger (de la Svala), 1540–1609.

59. Joshua, 24:33.

60. The Centuriators of Magdeburg were the authors of a church history down to 1400, divided by centuries, and published as the *Historia Ecclesiae Christi* in 1559–74.

61. For Voetius see Mather, *Brief History*, n. 14, above.

62. An interesting proposal, anticipating the later use of public lands for land-grant colleges under the Homestead Act (1862).

63. Saint Louis, Bishop of Toulouse, ordered the Crusade against the Albigensians and Waldensians, for which he was sainted. The quotation is from Revelation, 13:7.

64. Isaiah, 8:8, prophesies the conquest of "thy land, O Immanuel" by the Syrians, as punishment for the backsliding of Israel. Israel is Immanuel's land, the land of Christ who is called Immanuel or God-with-us, and Mather equates New England with this land for the purpose of warning less holy districts (especially England)—if such plagues are visited on the chosen, what may the unregenerate expect? In this way he rhetorically inverts the accusation that the war had been a special punishment for New England's doctrinal perversities.

65. Amos, 5:20. Mather also fears, and here rebukes, the flight of "faint-hearted" colonists back to England.

66. Psalms, 87:3.

67. Leviticus, 21:25. Mather suggests that the war and its associated providences are signs of an imminent Second Coming.

68. Job, 19:21.

TWO

# *BENJAMIN TOMPSON*
## First American Epic Poet

BENJAMIN TOMPSON is something of an anomaly among the chroniclers of King Philip's War. For one thing, although he and his family were intimately acquainted with the powerful Mather family of the infant Massachusetts Bay Colony and though his father, the Reverend William Tompson, was a minister, Benjamin Tompson spent his life primarily as a schoolteacher and, later, as a physician. For another, Tompson was a native-born American and in fact never visited England. His biographer and the editor of his poems, Howard J. Hall, sees this as the most significant fact of Tompson's biography and attributes to it the claim that Tompson's—in contrast to his contemporaries'—is the first truly native voice in American poetry.

This point can of course easily be overemphasized, yet in general it is a good one. One does not sense in Tompson's verse the longing for another life left behind, as one does, say, in the verse of his somewhat older contemporary, Anne Bradstreet; nor does one sense in Tompson's work, as one does quite often in the Mathers', the feeling of exile, of weeping by the waters of Babylon while remembering Zion. Though Tompson, in company with his Puritan fellows, may well have his eyes firmly fastened on his eternal reward, and though he may also think of himself as a wayfaring stranger in a world of woe, still New England is the only part of this world he knows, and one senses, as one senses in the later poetry of Emily Dickinson, how deeply drawn he is toward it.

A great poet, or for that matter even a passably good one, Tompson is not, even by the most charitable definition of poetry.

Yet however inept the particulars of his verse may be, one feels that Tompson is in control—of his historical material at least, if not always of his poetic form. One senses his possession of a dry humor and a gentle irony which give him some perspective on the life surrounding him; in a word, one develops a certain respect for the quality of his mind as it is revealed in his verse, for a trait that might simply be called "balance."

Tompson deserves all the more respect for his balanced and measured sensibility since his life was by no stretch of the imagination an easy one. He was born in 1642 in that part of the town of Braintree, Massachusetts, which is presently Quincy. His father, the Reverend William Tompson, was a minister who had come to Massachusetts with his family in 1636 or 1637. Reverend Tompson was a close friend of Richard Mather, whom he had known in England and whose friendship was important in awarding Tompson the pastorate of Braintree in 1639. This was an important pastorate at the time. It had been the site of the infamous Mount Wollaston colony, Thomas Morton's short-lived attempt to reestablish the merry England of old in the gray and godly Commonwealth of Massachusetts—a colony which a scandalized band of the faithful saints had summarily destroyed. More recently, Braintree had again been purged, this time of the so-called Antinomian heresy, by the banishment of the Reverend John Wheelwright, the brother-in-law of Anne Hutchinson. The Reverend William Tompson was apparently chosen as the pastor of Braintree because of his "zeal," as one contemporary put it; yet this zealousness was not an unmixed blessing, as it developed in his later years into severe melancholia and insanity. His son Benjamin cared for him until his death in 1666.

Benjamin's mother had died when he was an infant, and he had been raised by two of his father's Braintree parishioners, Mr. and Mrs. Thomas Blanchard. When Benjamin was a youth, the Blanchards moved to Charlestown taking him with them. They provided also for his education, sending him to Harvard College, from which he graduated in 1662. That the Blanchard family assumed responsibility both for Benjamin's upbringing and for his education speaks volumes for the straitened circumstances of the Tompson family. For most of his life Benjamin Tompson was to remain only one step ahead of abject poverty. Though never actually destitute, neither was he ever to be in comfortable financial circumstances.

Unlike most of his Harvard classmates, Tompson did not enter the ministry. Instead, he held a number of positions as schoolmaster—of the prestigious Boston Latin school (where Cotton Mather was his most illustrious pupil); of the Charlestown school; of the common school at Braintree; and of the Roxbury Latin School. In 1667 Tompson married Susanna Kirtland, who died in 1693. They had eight children, most of whom settled in Roxbury, Massachusetts, where Benjamin spent his last years. His son Philip was a doctor of medicine there, and in later life Benjamin Tompson also practiced medicine. Although this may seem somewhat odd to us, it was by no means unusual in seventeenth-century Massachusetts where formal training was not thought to be an absolutely necessary preparation for a medical career. The minister-poet Michael Wigglesworth and the Reverend Cotton Mather, to mention only two of many, were also highly thought of as physicians in the infant Massachusetts Bay Colony.

Tompson died in Roxbury in 1714. It is possible to read his own epitaph, which he had composed in 1713, as a statement of bitter disillusion with the world and all its works, and yet even this epitaph is conventional enough in terms of seventeenth-century graveyard verse. Because we know so little about Tompson's life, except for a few meager external details, it is tempting to impute a Byronic sensibility to him, to search for unknown and unnamable sorrows that must, we assume, have overflowed spontaneously into his verse. Yet an unprejudiced look at Tompson's poetry gives quite a different impression. Instead of a Byronic laughter, virtually a substitute for weeping at the infinite sadness of things, we sense the presence of a balanced and cheerful optimism that has surveyed God's world and found it good. Part of this optimism may be unintentional and may reflect Tompson's attempt to write poetry according to the canons of what he considered sophisticated contemporary taste. *New England's Crisis* is, in contemporary parlance, a poem of "wit": that is, roughly, a poem in which the intellectual play with words and concepts is highly prized for its own sake. To the seventeenth century, wit did not necessarily equal humor; yet, as Tompson's example makes clear, it is extremely difficult to write wittily in a totally serious manner. Indeed, when we fault *New England's Crisis* on esthetic grounds, it is probably because we wish Tompson had been more consistent in his approach to his subject. Since he never seems quite certain whether he is writing a heroic epic or a mock-heroic burlesque, we in turn are uncertain whether to take him seriously.

It is perhaps misleading to use the term *epic* at all when speaking of so slight a work as *New England's Crisis,* and it is doubtful whether Tompson himself would have referred to his creation in this fashion. He would probably have called his poem a "narrative," or, more likely, a "historical" poem, by which he would have meant a poem whose subject matter was historical rather than fanciful. Yet the problem of nomenclature is more than a merely verbal quibble; it gets to the heart of what we instinctively feel—whatever we ultimately decide to call *New England's Crisis*—to be its great weakness. Tompson himself would not have seen any great significance in the distinction between "history" and "epic," and it is precisely here that the sensitive reader of any era—his own included—will quarrel with his treatment of the events of King Philip's War. For Tompson's historical imagination is limited, and as a result his interpretation of events seems pat and superficial.

It is worth remarking that all the epic models upon which Tompson might have patterned *New England's Crisis* are far more ambiguous in their analysis of history than he is. The paradoxical nature of the world of events upon which Mary Rowlandson was to insist in her own account of King Philip's War is far more epic in spirit than is the straightforward narration of the "facts" which satisfies Tompson. For epics are profoundly doubtful in many ways, not only of the ultimate desirability of particular epic virtues but also of the providential scheme which Tompson discovers so clearly written in history.

It is certainly possible to argue, to take a clear example, that in the Trojan War the nice guys finished last; and indeed throughout classical antiquity and the Christian Middle Ages there was a considerable tradition of what we would today call "revisionist" history pointing out that Homer told the story wrong. Moreover, the Trojan defeat was accomplished through guile and deceit rather than by manly force of arms; the subtle strategem of the Trojan Horse (suggested by the "wily" Odysseus, who, it will be remembered, thought the whole war a fool's errand and tried unsuccessfully to avoid his military obligations by feigning madness) seems, when one stops to think of it, a metaphor which might more appropriately be applied to King

Philip's people than to the Puritan soldiers to whom Tompson relates it.

Virgil is probably more significant as a direct source of *New England's Tears* than is Homer, for a number of reasons. First, Virgil, because of an ambiguous passage in his *Georgics*, was widely esteemed as a pagan prophet of Christianity. Second, the *Aeneid* was often interpreted not only as a story of the founding of the Roman *imperium* (which it clearly was), but also as an allegory of the progress of the soul toward salvation, almost a pagan *Pilgrim's Progress*. And was the story of Aeneas not one of striking relevance to the saints of New England? Had Aeneas not fled the ruins of Troy to establish a greater kingdom in Rome, a kingdom which he had finally to wrest from its prior possessors by force of arms? Most important of all, did Virgil not tell his readers that Aeneas was *pius* (pious), and that his *pietas* (piety) was the source of his ultimate triumph over the forces of adversity?

Yet again the story is not this simple. Some would say that Aeneas—in the most famous romantic episode in the epic—had treated Dido, the Queen of Carthage, rather shabbily and that when he later met her shade in Hades she had behaved quite properly in turning her back on him and stalking away. Even in its own terms, the historic world of epic poetry is far more ambiguous and paradoxical than Tompson sees.

It is intriguing to speculate whether Tompson knew the greatest of the Puritan epics, *Paradise Lost*, published in 1667. If he did, he learned little from it; for *Paradise Lost* is based upon the greatest of all paradoxes, what St. Augustine had called the "fortunate" fall of Adam that had allowed for the redemption of mankind through the mediation of Christ. It is almost certain that Mary Rowlandson did not know Milton, and it is clear beyond doubt that, even if she did, his work had little direct influence on her. Yet in her obsession with the question of how good is brought from evil, she and Milton share in a great Puritan concern from which Tompson seems far removed. His definition of epic is unconsciously that of the typical Hollywood "epic" war movie: how our side won. He would not have understood Pogo's famous remark that "we have met the enemy and they are us."

Yet for all its admitted flaws, Tompson's poetry, with its humor and good nature, is not totally derivative. It reflects more to its author's credit than would a mere slavish following of poetic conventions only half understood. It is worth noting that Tompson, as a schoolmaster and a physician, was far more concerned professionally than were his ministerial colleagues with the affairs of this world. To teachers and doctors alike, life often seems more of a mixed bag than it does to ministers. God's grand design is not easily discovered in the anomalous world of snowball fights and toothaches. So Tompson sensibly reminds us that although King Philip may be a red devil and a fiend incarnate, he is also something of a buffoon, and that the saints, for all their admitted virtue, are more waspish than one might at first imagine.

## A NOTE ON THE TEXT

*New England's Crisis* was anonymously published "by a well-wisher to his country" in Boston in 1676 and apparently never reprinted. Only one complete copy of the first edition exists, in the Henry E. Huntington Library in California. Howard Judson Hall edited all Tompson's poems in a limited edition (Boston, 1924), and the present text is based on Hall's edition. *New England's Crisis* was probably composed during the spring of 1676 and was originally designed to conclude before the "Supplement" containing the histories of Marlboro, Providence, Seekonk, and Chelmsford. The final portion of the printed work concerning the fortification at Boston built by women was added still later, while the volume was in the press. A supplementary work, *New England's Tears,* published in London in 1676, was apparently originally designed as a continuation of *New England's Crisis.* Both *New England's Crisis* and *New England's Tears* deal in large part with the same historic material, and much of *New England's Tears* consists of reprinted portions of the earlier volume. *New England's Tears* has not been included in the present edition.

Editorial policy in preparing the present text has been conservative. Spelling has been modernized unless modernization would have changed the meter of Tompson's verse. Tompson's often shaky grammar has been left as is.

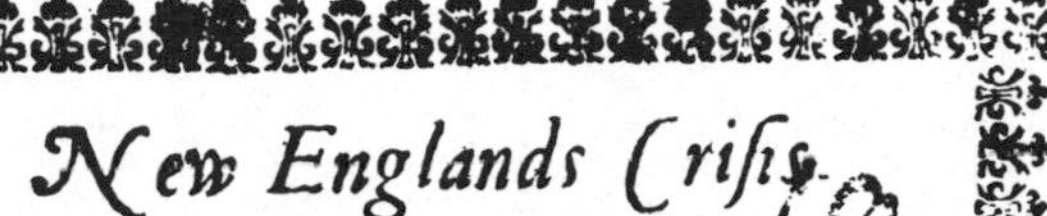

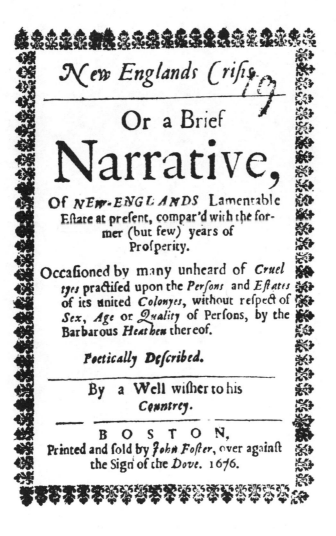

# *New Englands Crisis.*

## Or a Brief
# Narrative,

Of *NEW-ENGLANDS* Lamentable Estate at present, compar'd with the former (but few) years of Prosperity.

Occasioned by many unheard of *Cruel tyes* practised upon the *Persons* and *Estates* of its united *Colonyes*, without respect of *Sex*, *Age* or *Quality* of Persons, by the Barbarous *Heathen* thereof.

***Poetically Described.***

---

By a Well wisher to his *Countrey*.

---

B O S T O N,
Printed and sold by *John Foster*, over against the Sign of the *Dove*. 1676.

## *TO THE READER*

Courteous Reader:
I never thought this babe of my weak fantasy worthy of an imprimatur; but being an abortive, it was begged in these perplexing times to be cherished by the charity of others. If its lineaments please not the reader better than the writer, I shall be glad to see it pressed to death: but if it displease not many and satisfy any, it's to me a glorious reward, who am more willing than able to any service to my country and friend.

Farewell

# NEW ENGLAND'S CRISIS

## The Prologue

The times wherein old Pompion[1] was a saint,
When men fared hardly yet without complaint
On vilest cates;[2] the dainty Indian maize
Was eat with clamshells out of wooden trays
Under thatched huts without the cry of rent,
And the best sauce to every dish, content.
When flesh was food, & hairy skins made coats,
And men as well as birds had chirping notes.
When simnels[3] were accounted noble blood
Among the tribes of common herbage food.
Of Ceres' bounty formed was many a knack
Enough to fill *Poor Robin's Almanac.*[4]
These golden times (too fortunate to hold)
Were quickly signed away for love of gold.
'Twas then among the bushes, not the street
If one in place did an inferior meet,
"Good morrow, brother, is there ought you want?
Take freely of me, what I have you ha'n't."
Plain Tom and Dick would pass as current now,

As ever since "Your servant, Sir," and bow.
Deep-skirted doublets, puritanic capes
Which now would render men like upright apes,
Was comelier wear our wiser fathers thought
Than the cast[5] fashions from all Europe brought.
'Twas in those days an honest grace would hold
Til an hot pudding grew at heart a cold.[6]
And men had better stomachs to religion
Than I to capon, turkey cock, or pigeon.
When honest sisters met to pray not prate[7]
About their own and not their neighbors' state.
During plain dealing's reign, that worthy stud
Of th'ancient planters race before the flood.
These times were good, merchants cared not a rush
For other fare than jonakin[8] and mush.
Although men fared and lodged very hard
Yet innocence was better than a guard.
'Twas long before spiders & worms had drawn
Their dungy[9] webs or hid with cheating lawn
New England's beauties, which still seemed to me
Illustrious in their own simplicity.
'Twas ere the neighboring virgin land had broke
The hogsheads of her worse than hellish smoke.[10]
'Twas ere the islands sent their presents in,
Which but to use was counted next to sin.
'Twas ere a barge had made so rich a freight
As chocolate, dust gold, and bitts of eight.[11]
Ere wines from France and Muscovado[12] too
Without the which the drink will scarcely do,
From western isles, ere fruits and delicacies,
Did rot maids' teeth & spoil their handsome faces.
Or ere these times did chance the noise of war
Was from our towns and hearts removed far.
No bugbear comets in the crystal air
To drive our Christian planters to despair.
No sooner pagan malice peeped forth
But valor snibbed[13] it; then were men of worth
Who by their prayers slew thousands angel-like,
Their weapons are unseen with which they strike.
Then had the churches rest, as yet the coals

Were covered up in most contentious souls.
Freeness in judgment, union in affection,
Dear love, sound truth, they were our grand protection.
These were the twins which in our counsels sate,
These gave prognostics of our future fate,
If these be longer lived our hopes increase,
These wars will usher in a longer peace:
But if New England's love die in its youth
The grave will open next for blessed truth.
This theme is out of date, the peaceful hours
When castles needed not but pleasant bowers.[14]
Not ink, but blood and tears now serve the turn
To draw the figure of New England's urn.
New England's hour of passion is at hand,
No power except divine can it withstand;
Scarce hath her glass of fifty years run out,
But her old prosperous steeds turn heads about,
Tracking themselves back to their poor beginnings,
To fear and fare upon their fruits of sinnings:
So that the mirror of the Christian world
Lies burnt to heaps in part, her streamers furled.
Grief reigns, joys flee and dismal fears surprise,
Not dastard spirits only but the wise.
Thus have the fairest hopes deceived the eye
Of the big swollen expectant standing by.
Thus the proud ship after a little turn
Sinks into Neptune's arms to find its urn.
Thus hath the heir to many thousands born
Been in an instant from the mother torn.
Even thus thine infant cheeks begin to pale,
And thy supporters through great losses fail.
This is the prologue to thy future woe,
The epilogue no mortal yet can know.

## New England's Crisis

In seventy-five the critic of our years
Commenced our war with Philip and his peers.
Whether the sun in Leo had inspired
A feverish heat, and pagan spirits fired?

Whether some Romish agent hatched the plot?
Or whether they themselves? appeareth not.
Whether our infant thrivings did invite?
Or whether to our lands pretended right?
Is hard to say; but Indian spirits need
No grounds but lust to make a Christian bleed.
And here methinks I see this greasy lout[15]
With all his pagan slaves coiled round about,
Assuming all the majesty his throne
Of rotten stump, or of the rugged stone
Could yield; casting some bacon-rind-like looks,
Enough to fright a student from his books,
Thus treat his peers, & next to them his commons,
Kenneled together all without a summons.[16]
"My friends, our fathers were not half so wise
As we ourselves who see with younger eyes.
They sell our land to Englishmen who teach
Our nation all so fast to pray and preach:
Of all our country they enjoy the best,
And quickly they intend to have the rest.
This no wunnegin, so big matchit law,[17]
Which our old fathers' fathers never saw.
These English make and we must keep them too,
Which is too hard for them or us to do,
We drink we so big whipped, but English they
Go sneep, no more, or else a little pay.[18]
Me meddle squaw me hanged, our fathers kept
What squaws they would, whether they waked or slept.
Now if you'll fight I'll get you English coats,
And wine to drink out of their captains' throats.
The richest merchants' houses shall be ours,
We'll lie no more on mats or dwell in bowers.
We'll have their silken wives take they our squaws,
They shall be whipped by virtue of our laws.
If ere we strike 'tis now before they swell
To greater swarms than we know how to quell.
This my resolve, let neighboring sachems know,
And everyone that hath club, gun, or bow."
This was assented to, and for a close
He stroked his smutty beard and cursed his foes.

This counsel lightning-like their tribes invade,
And something like a muster's quickly made,
A ragged regiment, a naked swarm,
Whom hopes of booty doth with courage arm,
Set forth with bloody hearts, the first they meet
Of men or beasts they butcher at their feet.
They round our skirts, they pare, they fleece, they kill,
And to our bordering towns do what they will.
Poor hovels (better far than Caesar's court
In the experience of the meaner sort)
Receive from them their doom next execution,
By flames reduced to horror and confusion:
Here might be seen the smoking funeral piles
Of wildred towns[19] pitched distant many miles.
Here might be seen the infant from the breast
Snatched by a pagan hand to lasting rest:
The mother, Rachel-like, shrieks out "My child."
She wrings her hands and raves as she were wild.
The brutish wolves suppress her anxious moan
By cruelties more deadly of their own.
Will she or nill the chastest turtle must
Taste of the pangs of their unbridled lust.[20]
From farms to farms, from towns to towns they post,
They strip, they bind, they ravish, flay, and roast.
The beasts which want their master's crib to know,
Over the ashes of their shelters low.
What the inexorable flames do spare
More cruel heathen lug away for fare.
These tidings ebbing from the outward parts
Makes tradesmen cast aside their wonted arts
And study arms: the craving merchants plot
Not to augment but keep what they have got.
And every soul which hath but common sense
Thinks it the time to make a just defense.
Alarums everywhere resound in streets,
From West sad tidings with the Eastern meets.
Our common fathers in their counsels close
A martial treaty with the pagan foes.
All answers center here that fire and sword
Must make their sachem universal lord.

This arms the English with a resolution
To give the vaporing scab[21] a retribution.
Heavens they consult by prayer, the best design
A furious foe to quell or undermine.
Resolved that from the Massachusetts bands
Be pressed on service some Herculean hands
And certainly he well deserved a jerk
That slipped the collar from so good a work.
Some volunteers, some by compulsion go
To range the hideous forest for a foe.
The tender mother now's all bowels grown,
Clings to her son as if they'd melt in one.
Wives clasp about their husbands as the vine
Hugs the fair elm, while tears burst out like wine.
The new-sprung love in many a virgin heart
Swells to a mountain when the lovers part.
Nephews and kindred turn all springs of tears,
Their hearts are so surprised with panic fears.
But doleful shrieks of captives summon forth
Our walking castles, men of noted worth,
Made all of life, each captain was a Mars,
His name too strong to stand on waterish verse:
Due praise I leave to some poetic hand
Whose pen and wits are better at command.
Methinks I see the Trojan horse burst ope,
And such rush forth as might with giants cope:
These first the natives' treachery felt, too fierce
For any but eyewitness to rehearse.
Yet sundry times in places where they came
Upon the Indian skins they carved their name.
The trees stood sentinels and bullets flew
From every bush (a shelter for their crew).
Hence came our wounds and deaths from every side
While skulking enemies squat undescried,
That every stump shot like a musketeer,
And bows with arrows every tree did bear.
The swamps were courts of guard, thither retired
The straggling blue-coats[22] when their guns were fired,
In dark meanders, and these winding groves,
Where bears & panthers with their monarch moves

These far more cruel slyly hidden lay,
Expecting Englishmen to move that way.
One party lets them in, the other greets
Them with the next thing to their winding-sheets;
Most fall, the rest thus startled back return,
And from their bypassed foes receive an urn.
Here fell a captain, to be named with tears,
Who for his courage left not many peers,
With many more who scarce a number left
To tell how treacherously they were bereft.
This flushed the pagan courage, now they think
The victory theirs, not lacking meat or drink.
The ranging wolves find here and there a prey,
And having filled their paunch they run away
By their hosts' light, the thanks which they return
Is to lead captives and their taverns burn.
Many whose thrift had stored for after use
Sustain their wicked plunder and abuse.
Poor people spying an unwonted light,
Fearing a martyrdom, in sudden fright
Leap to the door to fly, but all in vain,
They are surrounded with a pagan train;
Their first salute is death, which if they shun
Some are condemned the gauntelet[23] to run;
Death would a mercy prove to such as those
Who feel the rigor of such hellish foes.
Posts daily on their Pegasean steeds
Bring sad reports of worse than Nero's deeds,
Such brutish murders as would paper stain
Not to be heard in a Domitian's reign.[24]
The field which nature hid is common laid,
And mothers' bodies ripped for lack of aid.
The secret cabinets which nature meant
To hide her masterpiece is open rent,
The half-formed infant there receives a death
Before it sees the light or draws its breath,
Many hot welcomes from the natives' arms
Hid in their skulking holes many alarms
Our brethren had, and weary weary trants,[25]
Sometimes in melting heats and pinching wants:

Sometimes the clouds with sympathizing tears
Ready to burst discharged about their ears:
Sometimes on craggy hills, anon in bogs
And miry swamps better befitting hogs,
And after tedious marches little boast
Is to be heard of stewed or baked or roast,
Their beds are hurdles,[26] open house they keep
Through shady boughs the stars upon them peep,
Their crystal drink drawn from the mother's breast
Disposes not to mirth but sleep and rest.
Thus many days and weeks, some months run out
To find and quell the vagabonding rout,
Who like enchanted castles fair appear,
But all is vanished if you come but near,
Just so we might the pagan archers track
With towns and merchandise upon their back;
And thousands in the south who settled down
To all the points and winds are quickly blown.
At many meetings of their fleeting crew,
From whom like hail arrows and bullets flew;
The English courage with whole swarms dispute,
Hundreds they hack in pieces in pursuit.
*Sed haud impune,*[27] English sides do feel
As well as tawny skins the lead and steel
And some such gallant sparks by bullets fell,
As might have cursed the powder back to hell:
Had only swords these skirmishes decided
All pagan skulls had been long since divided.
The lingering war outlives the summer sun,
Who hence departs hoping it might be done,
Ere his return at Spring: but, ah! he'll find
The sword still drawn, men of unchanged mind.
Cold winter now nibbles at hands and toes
And shrewdly pinches both our friends and foes.
Fierce Boreas whips the pagan tribe together
Advising them to fit for foes and weather:
The axe which late had tasted Christian blood
Now sets its steely teeth to feast on wood.
The forests suffer now, by weight constrained
To kiss the earth with soldiers lately brained.

The lofty oaks and ash do wag the head
To see so many of their neighbors dead;
Their fallen carcasses are carried thence
To stand our enemies in their defense.
Their myrmidons enclosed with clefts of trees
Are busy like the ants or nimble bees:
And first they limber poles fix in the ground,
In figure of the heavens convex: all round
They draw their arras-mats[28] and skins of beasts
And under these the elves to make their nests.
Rome took more time to grow than twice six hours,
But half that time will serve for Indian bowers.
A city shall be reared in one day's space
As shall an hundred Englishmen out-face.
Canonicus'[29] precincts there swarms unite,
Rather to keep a winter guard than fight.
A dern[30] and dismal swamp some scout had found
Whose bosom was a spot of rising ground
Hedged up with mighty oaks, maples, and ashes,
Nursed up with springs, quick bogs & miry plashes,[31]
A place which nature coined on very nonce
For tigers not for men to be a sconce.[32]
'Twas here these monsters, shaped and faced like men,
Took up their rendezvous and brumal[33] den,
Deeming the depth of snow, hail, frost, and ice
Would make our infantry more tame and wise
Than by forsaking beds and loving wives,
Merely for Indian skins to hazard lives:
These hopes had something calmed the boiling passion
Of this incorrigible warlike nation.
During this short parenthesis of peace
Our forces found, but left him not at ease.
Here English valor most illustrious shone,
Finding their numbers ten times ten to one.
A shower of leaden hail our captains feel
Which made the bravest blades among us reel.
Like to some anthill newly spurned abroad,
Where each takes heels and bears away his load:
Instead of plate and jewels, Indian trays
With baskets up they snatch and run their ways.

Sundry the flames arrest and some the blade,
By bullets heaps on heaps of Indians laid.
The flames like lightning in their narrow streets
Dart in the face of everyone it meets.
Here might be heard an hideous Indian cry,
Of wounded ones who in the wigwams fry.
Had we been cannibals here might we feast
On brave Westphalia gammons ready dressed.[34]
The tawny hue is Ethiopic made
Of such on whom Vulcan his clutches laid.
Their fate was sudden, our advantage great
To give them once for all a grand defeat;
But tedious travel had so cramped our toes
It was too hard a task to chase the foes.
Distinctness in the numbers of the slain,
Or the account of pagans which remain
Are both uncertain, losses of our own
Are too too sadly felt, too sadly known.
War digs a common grave for friends and foes,
Captains in with the common soldier throws.
Six of our leaders in the first assault
Crave readmission to their mother's vault
Who had they fell in ancient Homer's days
Had been enrolled with hecatombs of praise.
As clouds dispersed, the natives' troops divide,
And like the streams along the thickets glide.
Some breathing time we had, & short God knows
But new alarums from recruited foes
Bounce at our ears, the mounting clouds of smoke
From martyred towns the heavens for aid invoke:
Churches, barns, houses with most ponderous things
Made volatile fly o'er the land with wings.
Hundreds of cattle now they sacrifice
For airy spirits up to gormandize;
And to the Moloch[35] of their hellish guts,
Which craves the flesh in gross, their ale in butts.
Lancaster, Medfield, Mendon, wildred[36] Groton,
With many villages by me not thought on
Die in their youth by fire that useful foe,
Which this grand cheat the world will overflow.

The wandering priest to everyone he meets
Preaches his church's funeral in the streets.
Sheep from their fold are frighted, keepers too
Put to their trumps[37] not knowing what to do.
This monster war hath hatched a beauteous dove
In dogged hearts, of most unfeigned love,
Fraternal love the livery of a saint
Being come in fashion though by sad constraint,
Which if it thrive and prosper with us long
Will make New England forty thousand strong.
    But off the table hand,[38] let this suffice
    As the abridgment of our miseries.
    If mildew, famine, sword, and fired towns,
    If slaughter, captivating, deaths, and wounds,
    If daily whippings once reform our ways,
    These all will issue in our Father's praise;
    If otherwise, the sword must never rest
    Till all New England's glory it divest.

## A Supplement

What means this silence of Harvardine quills
While Mars triumphant thunders on our hills.
Have pagan priests their eloquence confined
To no man's use but the mysterious mind?
Have pow-wows[39] charmed that art which was so rife
To crouch to every Don[40] that lost his life?
But now whole towns and churches fire and die
Without the pity of an elegy.
Nay rather should my quills were they all swords
Wear to the hilts in some lamenting words.
I dare not style them poetry but truth,
The dwindling products of my crazy youth.
If these essays shall raise some quainter pens
'Twill to the writer make a rich amends.

## Marlboro's Fate

When London's fatal bills were blown abroad
And few but specters travelled on the road,

Not towns but men in the black bill enrolled
Were in gazettes by typographers sold:[41]
But our gazettes without erratas must
Report the plague of towns reduced to dust:
And fevers formerly to tenants sent
Arrest the timbers of the tenement.
Ere the late ruins of old Groton's cold,
Of Marlboro's peracute[42] disease we're told.
The feet of such who neighboring dwellings urned
Unto her ashes, not her doors returned.
And what remained of tears as yet unspent
Are to its final gasps a tribute lent.
If painter overtrack my pen let him
An olive color mix, these elves to trim;
Of such an hue let many thousand thieves
Be drawn like scarecrows clad with oaken leaves,
Exhausted of their verdant life and blown
From place to place without an home to own.
Draw devils like themselves, upon their cheeks
The banks for grease and mud, a place for leeks.
Whose locks, Medusa's snakes, do ropes resemble,
And ghostly looks would make Achilles tremble.
Limn them besmeared with Christian blood & oiled
With fat out of white human bodies boiled.
Draw them with clubs like mauls & full of stains,
Like Vulcan's anvilling New England's brains.
Let round be gloomy forests with cragged rocks
Where like to castles they may hide their flocks,
Till opportunity their cautious friend
shall jog[43] them fiery worship to attend.
Show them like serpents in an avious[44] path
Seeking to sow the firebrands of their wrath.
Most like Aeneas in his cloak of mist,
Who undiscovered move wheree'er they list
Cupid they tell us hath two sorts of darts,
One sharp and one obtuse, one causing wounds,
One piercing deep the other dull rebounds,
But we feel none but such as drill our hearts.[45]
From Indian sheaves which to their shoulders cling,
Upon the word they quickly feel the string.

Let earth be made a screen to hide our woe
From heaven's monarch and his lady's too;
And lest our jealousy think they partake,
For the red stage with clouds a curtain make.
Let dogs be gagged and every quickening sound
Be charmed to silence, here and there all round
The town to suffer, from a thousand holes
Let crawl these fiends with brands and fired poles,
Paint here the house & there the barn on fire,
With holocausts ascending in a spire.
Here granaries, yonder the churches smoke
Which vengeance on the actors doth invoke.
Let Morpheus with his leaden keys have bound
In featherbeds some, some upon the ground,
That none may burst his drowsy shackles till
The brutish pagans have obtained their will,
And Vulcan files them off; then Zeuxis[46] paint
The frenzy glances of the sinking saint.
Draw there the pastor for his bible crying,
The soldier for his sword, the glutton frying
With streams of glory fat, the thin-jawed miser,
"Oh had I given this I had been wiser."
Let here the mother seem a statue turned
At the sad object of her bowels burned.
Let the unstable weakling in belief
Be mounting Asshur's horses[47] for relief.
Let the half convert seem suspended twixt
The dens of darkness, and the planets fixed,
Ready to quit his hold, and yet hold fast
By the great Atlas of the heavens vast.
Paint papists muttering o'er their apish beads
Whom the blind follow while the blind man leads.
Let Ataxy[48] be mounted on a throne
Imposing her commands on everyone,
A many-headed monster without eyes
To see the ways which want to make men wise.
Give her a thousand tongues with wings and hands
To be ubiquitary[49] in commands,
But let the concave of her skull appear
Clean washed and empty quite of all but fear,

One she bids flee, another stay, a third
She bids betake him to his rusty sword,
This to his treasure, th'other to his knees,
Some counsels she to fry and some to freeze,
These to the garrison, those to the road,
Some to run empty, some to take their load:
Thus while confusion most men's hearts divide
Fire doth their small exchequer soon decide.
Thus all things seeming ope or secret foes,
An infant may grow old before a close,
But yet my hopes abide in perfect strength.[50]

## The Town Called Providence
## Its Fate

Why muse we thus to see the wheels run cross
Since Providence itself sustains a loss:
And yet should Providence forget to watch
I fear the enemy would all dispatch;
Celestial lights would soon forget their line,
The wandering planets would forget to shine,
The stars run all out of their common spheres,
And quickly fall together by the ears:
Kingdoms would jostle out their kings and set
The poor mechanic up whom next they met,
Or rather would whole kingdoms with the world
Into a chaos their first egg be hurled.
There's none this providence of the most high
Who can survive and write its elegy.
But of a solitary town I write,
A place of darkness yet receiving light
From pagan hands a miscellaneous nest
Of error's hectors,[51] where they sought a rest
Out of the reach of laws but not of God,
Since they have felt the smart of common rod.
'Twas much I thought they did escape so long,
Who gospel truth so manifestly wrong:
For one Lot's sake perhaps,[52] or else I think
Justice did at greatest offenders wink
But now the shot is paid, I hope the dross
Will be cashiered in this common loss.

Houses with substance feel uplifting wings,
The earth remains, the last of human things:
But know the dismal day draws near wherein
The fire shall earth itself dissolve and sin.

## Seekonk Plain Engagement

On our Pharsalian Plains, comprising space
For Caesar's host brave Pompey to outface,[53]
An handful of our men are walled round
With Indian swarms; anon their pieces sound
A madrigal like heaven's artillery
Lightning and thunderbolts their bullets fly.
Here's hosts to handfuls, of a few they leave
Fewer to tell how many they bereave.
Foolhardy fortitude it had been sure
Fierce storms of shot and arrows to endure
Without all hopes of some requital to
So numerous and pestilent a foe.
Some musing a retreat and thence to run,
Have in an instant all their business done,
They sink and all their sorrows' ponderous weight
Down at their feet they cast and tumble straight.
Such who outlived the fate of others fly
Into the Irish bogs of misery.
Such who might die like men like beasts do range
Uncertain whither for a better change,
These natives hunt and chase with currish mind,
And plague with cruelties such as they find.
    When shall this shower of blood be over? When?
    Quickly we pray, oh, Lord! say thou "Amen."

## Seekonk or Rehoboth's Fate

I once conjectured that those tigers hard
To reverend Newman's bones would have regard,[54]
But were all saints they met 'twere all one case,
They have no reverence to an angel's face:
But where they fix their griping lion's paws
They rend without remorse or heed to laws.
Rehoboth here in common English, Rest,[55]

They ransack, Newman's relics to molest.
Here all the town is made a public stage
Whereon these Nimrods act their monstrous rage.
All cruelties which paper stained before
Are acted to the life here o'er and o'er.

## Chelmsford's Fate

Ere famous Winthrop's bones are laid to rest[55]
The pagans Chelmsford with sad flames arrest,
Making an artificial day of night
By that plantation's formidable light.
Here's midnight shrieks and soul-amazing moans,
Enough to melt the very marble stones:
Firebrands and bullets, darts and deaths and wounds
Confusive[57] outcries everywhere resounds:
The natives shooting with the mixed cries,
With all the cruelties the foes devise
Might fill a volume, but I leave a space
For mercies still successive in their place
Not doubting but the foes have done their worst,
And shall by heaven suddenly be cursed.
Let this dear Lord the sad conclusion be
Of poor New England's dismal tragedy.
Let not the glory of thy former work
Blasphemed be by pagan, Jew, or Turk:
But in its funeral ashes write thy name
So fair all nations may expound the same:
Out of her ashes let a Phoenix rise
That may outshine the first and be more wise.

B. Tompson

## On a Fortification At Boston Begun by Women Dux Femina Facti[58]

A grand attempt some Amazonian dames
Contrive whereby to glorify their names,
A ruff for Boston neck of mud and turf,
Reaching from side to side from surf to surf,

Their nimble hands spin up like Christmas pies,
Their pastry by degrees on high doth rise.
The wheel at home counts it an holiday,
Since while the mistress worketh it may play.
A tribe of female hands, but manly hearts
Forsake at home their pastry-crust and tarts
To knead the dirt, the samplers down they hurl,
Their undulating silks they closely furl.
The pickaxe one as a commandress holds,
While t'other at her awkness[59] gently scolds.
One puffs and sweats, the other mutters why
Can't you promove[60] your work so fast as I?
Some dig, some delve, and others' hands do feel
The little wagon's weight with single wheel.[61]
And lest some fainting fits the weak surprise,
They want no sack[62] nor cakes, they are more wise.
These brave essays draw forth male stronger hands
More like to daubers[63] than to martial bands:
These do the work, and sturdy bulwarks raise,
But the beginners well deserve the praise.

## NOTES

1. Pumpkin.

2. Delicacies.

3. Biscuits

4. A popular almanac. Benjamin Franklin puns on the title in his own later *Poor Richard's Almanac.*

5. An archaic usage of the word, as something formed in a mold. The sense is "imitated," "slavishly copied."

6. That is, an "honest" grace before meals would last so long that a hot pudding would turn cold.

7. Gossip.

8. Johnny-cake, a cake made of corn meal.

9. Dirty.

10. The reference is obscure, but is probably to demon rum.

11. "Pieces of eight" were Spanish dollars, equal to eight reals. They were the most common coin in the infant colonies.

12. Muscovado is the sugar residue remaining after making molasses.

13. Removed.

14. That is, when we in New England did not need castles, but only pleasant bowers.

15. An unflattering reference to King Philip.

16. The following twenty-four lines supposedly represent King Philip's speech to his subjects.

17. In other words, this is not fair. Tompson attempts to ridicule Philip by insinuating he is an illiterate fool.

18. That is, the English pay nothing at all, or only a little. The syntax is intentionally obscure. Tompson is ridiculing what he considers Philip's foolish pomposity.

19. Towns in the "wilder-ness."

20. To us this is unintentionally comic; to Tompson it was poetic. Turtle means turtle-dove, a metaphor for "maiden."

21. King Philip. The use of the term is similar to the modern "scab labor."

22. Servants and wards of charity wore blue coats; hence, a term of contempt.

23. Gauntlet.

24. In popular historiography Nero was the archetypical evil Roman emperor. Domitian in contrast was a symbol of the just ruler.

25. Cunning tricks.

26. Piles of sticks woven together.

27. "But not unpunished."

28. Tapestries, in the sense of woven cloth hangings.

29. The Indian Canonchet. This Latinized (and inexact) form of his name is common among the chroniclers of the time.

30. Hidden.

31. Pools.

32. These two lines are best rendered as "A place which nature made for the purpose of sheltering tigers, not men."

33. Wintry.

34. Then as now Westphalian hams were synonymous with luxurious dining.

35. A Phoenician god, used here as a symbol of bestiality.

36. Distant, far off, in the "wilder-ness."

37. Left to their own expedients. We would say "on their own hook."

38. Probably a parenthetical remark meaning roughly "On the face of things," that is, "Let this be the moral." Tompson, however, was not a minister, and this phrase may betray a regrettable familiarity with one or more games of cards in which the declarer, by "tabling" his cards, may show his ability to claim all the tricks without actually playing out the hand.

39. Shamans, sorcerers.

40. Harvard "Dons," that is, professors.

41. A reference to years when the plague was epidemic in London

(notably 1664–1665, which Tompson may specifically have in mind) and lists of the dead were printed daily. Tompson compares the list of plague victims to the list of devastated New England towns.

42. Critical, in the sense of almost terminal. A medical term.

43. Nudge, i.e., urge.

44. Bird-like, that is, "flying."

45. So the text. Perhaps this line should come before the two preceding lines.

46. A Greek painter, famed in classical antiquity for his lifelike canvases. He is used here as a metaphor for the most graphic possible art.

47. Asshur, the Assyrian god of war, traditionally depicted with horses.

48. Ataxia, the goddess of disorder.

49. Ubiquitous, i.e., everywhere.

50. So the text. Apparently a line has been lost.

51. Braggarts. Note Tompson's unflattering opinion of the Colony of Rhode Island.

52. That is, there may be one just man who lives, like Lot, in the Sodom of Providence.

53. The Pharsalian Plains were the site of the decisive battle between Caesar and Pompey when Caesar gained control of the Roman republic in 48 B.C.

54. The Reverend Samuel Newman, founder of the town of Rehoboth.

55. Tompson renders the Hebrew "Rehoboth" as "Rest."

56. Governor Winthrop, who died during the course of the war.

57. Confusing.

58. The woman became the leader.

59. Awk[ward]ness.

60. Move.

61. This cunning metaphor prefigures a wheelbarrow.

62. An excellent white wine.

63. Wasps, who "daub" their nests with mud.

THREE

# *THOMAS WHEELER*
## The Christian Hero

THE essential point of the histories of Hubbard and Mather was their insistence that the war was meant to teach men their dependence on the will of almighty God. They took care to attribute each success or failure of English arms to divine will rather than to human agency. Yet there were deeds of heroism performed during the war that might well have created in their doers (and in any audience reading of them) that sense of egotistical pride and spiritual complacency that Mather so feared for the slayers of King Philip. Their preferred model for the account of a personal adventure was the captivity narrative, in which the protagonist is passive under first the scourge and later the grace of God. Not until long after the war did any narrative appear in which the deeds of an individual would be treated as having determined the course of events. Yet the reality of the war demanded that some account be taken of human heroism. The chief example of such an account is Thomas Wheeler's account of the siege of Brookfield.

Wheeler's brief narrative is full of stirring incidents, including a daring horseback rescue of the wounded protagonist by his wounded son. Yet he manages to keep within the bounds of orthodox historiography by ascribing all success to the providence of God. This is not simply a matter of occasional ejaculations of thankfulness. The whole account is framed as the introduction to a sermon that addresses the question of how we ought to go about remembering and expressing our thankfulness to God for his special mercies to us in times of peril. The narrative occupies fourteen-odd pages, the sermon thirty-two, which suggests the proportionate weight to be given to heroism and theology.

In his prefatory address to "The Christian Reader," Wheeler is at pains to state that he is not setting his adventure before the public in a boastful way. Instead, he is testifying to his and his company's gratitude for God's "providential" deliverance of them from destruction, in order that they and their children may have a permanent record of how the Lord deals with people. Perhaps the most characteristic concern of the preface is Wheeler's repeated justifications of the act of writing history at all. He seems to be arguing with an invisible interrogater, who questions the whole notion of recording human events in its deepest premises as an action akin to making an idolatrous image. It seems to placate this interrogator when Wheeler can cite scriptural injunctions to record the doings of the Lord for posterity. This is not the history of Thomas Wheeler's doings, but of the doings of the Lord with Thomas Wheeler. The only justification of writing an account of victorious battle is "that God may have the Glory of it." That Wheeler's concern is not the consequence of personal style is evidenced by Bulkeley's sermon, which argues at interminable length the doctrinal justification for the recording of historical events. For the Puritans, the achievement of a truly religious consciousness required a total revaluation of all the "givens" of personal, social, and cultural life. The basic premises of each item of behavior, each social role, each intellectual discipline had to be examined in the New Light.

The Battle of Brookfield was hardly more than a skirmish in the larger pattern of the war. Yet larger battles, like the Swamp Fight, or Turner's Battle at the falls of the Connecticut did not receive detailed treatment in a separate book. In part, this is the result of circumstance—a smaller battle is more easily comprehended by a single participant and can therefore be more coherently and completely recounted than a larger action. But the publication of Brookfield and the neglect of the Swamp Fight also typifies the Puritan scale of values in writing history and in comprehending the events they lived. At Brookfield the actions of providence can be more clearly perceived precisely because the scale of action is small and the focus on the few participants intensive. Since the purpose of writing history is to trace the workings of providence and since the Indian war and a single individual's experience of Grace are both equally significant aspects of the cosmic warfare of God and Satan, therefore an account of Brookfield is as significant as an account of the Swamp Fight. The last paragraph of Wheeler's preface gives a clear picture of this scale of values: the Brookfield adventure is a providential action, just like those providences that appear in the special favor shown to particular individuals in the larger battles, during the epidemic, and in the Indian raids. All of these alike deserve recording because "*it Concerns to do as we were then* Exhorted *to do, even* seriously to observe what God hath done *about them, and for them Carefully* to Return that Praise, Love and Obedience *which he expects from them.*"

Although the focus of the narrative on the actions of a few individual soldiers throws individual heroism into sharper relief than do the histories of Hubbard and Mather, comparison of Wheeler's narrative with that of Benjamin Church shows the difference between the Puritan and the heroic world view of later times.

Little is known of Wheeler's life beyond the facts contained in the narrative, which is itself so circumstantial as to require little explication.

# A Thankefull REMEMBRANCE OF GODS MERCY To several Persons at Quabaug or BROOKFIELD:

Partly in a Collection of Providences about them, and Gracious Appearances for them: And partly in a Sermon Preached By *Mr.* EDWARD BULKLEY, Pastor of the Church of Christ at *Concord*, upon a day of Thanksgiving, kept by divers for their Wonderfull Deliverance there.

Published by Capt. *THOMAS WHEELER.*

Psal. 107. 8. *Oh that men would Praise the Lord for his Goodness, and his Wonderfull Works to the Children of men.*

Psal. 111. 2. *The Works of the LORD are great, sought out of all those that Love him.*

*CAMBRIDGE*,
Printed and Sold by *Samuel Green* 1676.

## *THE PREFACE*

Christian Reader–

*I Purposing to Publish this ensuing narrative of Gods Providence towards,* Capt. Hutchinson & myself & others, & the *Sermon** preached on the occasion hereafter expressed: do Judge it exp[e]dient to give you a little further Account of matters, occasioning the going of *Captain Hutchinson* & my *self* to *Quabaug:* and also of the *Motives* inducing me to the Publication of both to the world:

*Philip* the Sachem of the *Wampanogs,* lying about *Mount-hope,* having done some Acts of *Hostility* against *Plimouth Colony* by murdering men, burning Houses and killing Cattel: the said *Colony* was necessitated to warr with him in their own defence: The *Massachusetts* and *Connecticut Colonies* being Confederate with them, and discerning the Justness of the Warr on their part: divers were sent forth of each *Colony* both Troopers and foot Souldiers to help our Brethren of that *Colony* against the said *Sachem.* The *Honoured Council* of the *Massachusets* did also send *Captain Hutchinson* with a Guard to the *Narroganset Sachems* and *Sagamores;* who were not farr from the said *Philip:* to see whether they intended to continue their peace with us, or to joyne with the *Wampanogs* against us: They promised to continue their peace with us, which they gave further hopes that they would do by sending over more of their *Sachems* to our *Council* where they also promised to remain Faithful Friends to us.[1] Our much Honoured *Governour* and *Council,* being desirous as farr as it might be to prevent shedding of blood, and the strengthening of the Enemy by others joyning with them, did also send *Ephraim Curtis* of *Sudbury* and others to several other *Sachems* in, and about the *Nipmuck* Country to the same purpose, they also promised Faithful Friendship to the *English* (though they afterwards proved wretchedly perfidious) and set a time wherein they would come to *Boston* further to engage themselves for the Councils satisfaction, but they came not at the time appointed: The *Council* sent the said *Ephraim Curtis* again to know the Reason thereof.[2] They again promised to come, but did not. The *Honoured Council* being willing to use all means to pre-

* Not included in this anthology.

vent a Warr with them if it might be, and their Assistance of *Philip,* and the rest then in Arms against us: sent *Captain Hutchinson* thither also to Treat with them in order to the Preservation of peace between us and them, they also appointed my self to Assist him with part of my *Troop,* which accordingly I did attend: We discerned by the *Indians* deserting the places of their Abode that they were afraid of us: and therefore the better to effect our business in a peacable way, and prevent Hostility on either side before we marched all to them, we sent three *English men,* and one *Indian* (all four, being men Familiarly acquainted with many of the *Indians*) to let them understand that we only desired a Treaty in Reference to the Preservation of Peace with them, and that we intended no hurt at all to them: but the Issue thereof was as in the *Narrative* is expressed. *Wherein the Providences of God towards us in his wayes about us were so Remarkable, in our sore Exercises, and gracious Deliverances that they ought never to be forgotten by us, but kept in Remembrance all our dayes: the Lord* hath made his wonderful works to be remembered, *saith the* Psalmist, *and he would have his* People to tell them to their Children, that they might also declare them to their Children,[3] And therefore for the help of our memories and the preventing of mistakes in Reports, and the *Advantage of our own Relations and others better Acquaintance with the manner of Gods dealings with us,* I have endeavoured the drawing up of this Following Declaration of what befell us in our *March* to, and at *Brookfield,* and our Returne homewards: I not at first intending that it should by my means be brought to *publick view:* but several persons having seen it, (though not altogether so large as now it is) they perswaded me, and urged it as a *Duty Incumbent* on me, (the Lord having taken away *Captain Hutchinson,* who might have performed it in a better manner) to put it forth in print, that many may thereby be provoked *to give God the glory of his great works in our Salvation, and that others may make use of his dealings with us to learn to trust and Rely upon him in the sorest straits, and may be encouraged to wait patiently for Deliverance in the greatest danger that may befall them: for greater danger of* Loss of Life *cannot well be with an* Escape, *then that of ours.* For from *Monday* about *Ten of the Clock* in the morning till *nine on Wednesday night, all hope that we should be saved (as Acts 27.20)* was in the Eye of Reason taken away, and we were in continual Expectation of Death, but yet even then we were not without some hopes *in the Lord our God to whom the Issues of Death belong:* who was pleased to *know our Souls in Adversity, to hear our Cries, and to save us for his mercy sake,*[4] as in the *Narrative* more fully appears, which goodness of God that it may be the better remembred by us, and others incited the more *to magnify God with us,* (as *David calls upon others to do for Gods mercy to him,* Psal 34.3.) *and also quickned to put their trust on God all their dayes:*[5] I have Adventured to publish this *Narration,* intreating your *Candid Acceptance* thereof, and overlooking all the defects and weaknesses therein: As for the *Sermon* added thereto, the occasion thereof was this. *When the Lord of his free and abundant mercy had sent* Deliverance *to us by* Honoured Majors [*sic*] Willards *coming to us, and our Enemies departing thereupon, and we had rest from them, I in the morning called together my Company both the wounded and the Rest who were weary with their hard Service, and much watching, and propounded this to them; whether though God had taken away divers from us, & others of us were sore wounded, yet in regard so many of us had our Lives* given us for a Prey, *& also that God had made us Instrumental to save so many Souls alive of the* Town dwellers, [(] *who would probably have been all or most of them destroyed, had not God carried us thither:) whether I say God did not Call for a* Solemn day of Thanksgiving *from us, when we should have Opportunity: They Rejoycing at the motion very readily Assented to it, and promised that those of us whom God should be pleased to Carry home would attend it in due Season: and when some others* with my self and Son, *were in some good measure recovered of our wounds: I Requested* Mr. *Bulkely to help us in the work of the day intended to be kept by us. He being of a ready Spirit to the utmost of his Strength to forward any good duty that God calls for, he also Judging it to be of very great Concernment, although the Country was in very great distress, our* Deliverance *being so* Remarkable, he did joynt with us therein on *October 21. 75.* and then preached what is here published, which we finding so seasonable to the *occasion and beneficial to ourselves.* I further Requested him that for the help of our memories, and our better Improvement of what was then delivered to us, as also for the *benefit* and *Edification* of others, he would give me a *Coppy* of it, and suffer me to *publish it:* which though for a time he delayed to do, yet hath at length given given me a *Coppy* with power to do as I shall think best, therein permitting it to be added to the aforesaid *Narrative.* I hope it may be profitable to many of Gods people, to whose view it may come, & I know that there be many in this *Country at this day* for whome it may be very *seasonable,* who having with our selves received *great mercies in Preservations and Deliverances in these Evil and Troublesome Times, in the* Naragansit Expedition, *and at other times, and in other places where they have been in very great danger, and in* hazard *of the loss of life, and all they had, as also having been* healed *of sore and* dangerous wounds: *been brought home safely to their* dear Relations, *or have had their* Relations Returned *to them, whom they feared they should not have seen again, and have had their* Habitations *and* Estates preserved *when near to Ruine; and others not farr from them were consumed: All whom, with all others whom God hath vouchsaved any special* mercy *to in* Recovery out of great sicknesses *or otherwise, it Concerns to do as we were then* Exhorted *to do, even* seriously to observe what God hath done *about them, and for them and Carefully to* Return that Praise, Love and Obedience *which he expects from them: I Crave your Prayers for the blessing of God to accompany both his Works and his Word to us for our Everlasting good.*

*Tho. Wheeler.*

# A TRUE NARRATIVE

*Of the Lords Providences in various dispensations towards Captain Edward Hutchinson of Boston and my self, and those that went with us into the Nipmuck Country, and also to Quabaug, alias Brookfield: The said Captain Hutchinson having a Commission from the Honoured Council of this Colony to Treat with several Sachems in those parts in order to the publick peace, and my self being also ordered for the said Council to accompany him with part of my Troop for Security from any danger that might be from the Indians: and to Assist him in the Transaction of matters committed to him.*

The said *Captain Hutchinson, and my self* with about twenty men or more marched from *Cambridge* to *Sudbury, July 28. 75.* and from thence into the *Nipmuck Country,* and finding that the *Indians* had deserted their Towns, and we having gone until we came within *twenty miles of New Norwitch,* on *July 31.* (only we saw two *Indians* having an Horse with them, whom we would have spoke with, but they fled from us and left their Horse, which we took) we then thought it not expedient to march any further that way, but set our march for *Brookfield,* whither we came on the Lords day about Noon. From thence the same day (being *August 1.*) we understanding that the *Indians* were about *Ten Miles Northwest* from us, we sent out *four men* to acquaint the *Indians* that we were not come to harm them, but our business was only to *deliver a Message* from our Honoured *Governour and Council* to them, and to receive their *Answer,* we desiring to come to a Treaty of Peace with them, (though they had for several days fled from us) they having before professed *Friendship,* and promised *Fidelity* to the *English.* When the Messengers came to them; they made an *Alarm,* and gathered together about an *hundred and Fifty* fighting men as near as they could judge; The young men amongst them were *stout* in their *Speeches,* and *surly* in their *Carriage;* But at length three of the *chief Sachems* promised to meet us on the next morning about *eight of the Clock* upon a plain within three miles of *Brookfield,* with which Answer the Messengers returned to us. Whereupon though their Speeches and Carriage did much discourage divers of our Company, yet we conceived that we had a cleer Call to go to meet them at the place whither they had promised to come. Accordingly we with our men accompanied with *three of the Principal Inhabitants* of that Town marched to the plain appointed; but the *Treacherous Heathen* intending mischief (if they could have opportunity) came not to the said place, and so failed our hopes of speaking with them there. Whereupon the said *Captain Hutchinson and my self* with the rest of our *Company* Considered what was best to be done, whether we should go any further towards them, or Return, divers of us apprehending much danger in Case we did proceed, because the *Indians* kept not promise there with us: But the *three men* who belonged to *Brookfield* were so strongly perswaded of their Freedome from any ill intentions towards us, (as upon other grounds, so especially because the greatest part of those *Indians* belonged to *David* one of their *chief Sachems,* who was taken to be great Friend to the *English:*) That the said *Captain Hutchinson* (who was principally Intrusted with the matter of Treaty with them) was thereby encouraged to proceed and march forward towards a *Swampe* where the *Indians* then were. When we came near the said *Swampe,* the way was so very bad that we could march only in a single File, there being a very *Rocky Hill* on the right hand, and a *thick Swampe* on the left. In which there were many of those *cruel blood-thirsty Heathen,* who there way-laid us, waiting an opportunity to cut us off; there being also *much brush* on the side of the said *Hill,* where they lay in *Ambush* to surprize us. When we had marched there about *sixty or seventy Rods,* the said *perfidious Indians* sent out their shot upon us as a *showre of haile,* they being (as was supposed) about *two hundred men* or more. We seeing ourselves so beset, and not having room to fight, Endeavoured to *fly* for the safety of our lives. In which *Flight* we were in no small danger to be all Cut off, there being a very *miry Swamp* before us into which we could not enter with our horses to go forwards, and there being no safety in retreating the way we came, because many of our Enemies, who lay behind the *Bushes,* and had let us pass by them quietly; when others had shot, they came out, and *stopt our way back:* so that we were forced as we could to get up the *steep and Rocky Hill:* But the greater our danger was, the greater was *Gods mercy in the pres-*

*ervation of so many of us from sudden destruction.* My self being gone up part of the Hill without any hurt, and perceiving some of my men to be fallen by the Enemies shot: I wheeled about upon the *Indians*, not calling on my men who were left to Accompany me, which they in all probability would have done had they known of my Return upon the Enemy. They firing violently out of the *Swamp*, and from behind the bushes on the Hill side *wounded me sorely, and shot my Horse* under me, so that he *Faultring* and *Falling*, I was forced to leave him, divers of the *Indians* being then but a *few Rods distant* from me, My Son *Thomas Wheeler* flying with the rest of the Company missed me amongst them, and fearing that I was either slain, or much endangered returned towards the *Swampe* again, though he had then received a dangerous wound in the *Reins*;[7] where he saw me in the danger aforesaid: Whereupon he endeavoured to *Rescue me*, shewing himself therein a *loving and dutiful Son*, he adventuring himself into great peril of his Life to help me in that distress, there being many of the Enemies about him. My Son set me on his own horse, and so escaped a while on Foot himself until he Caught an Horse whose Rider was slain, on which he mounted, and so through *Gods great mercy we both escaped:* But in this Attempt for my deliverance he received another dangerous wound by their shot in his left Arm. There were then slain to our great grief eight men *viz. Zechariah Philips* of *Boston, Timothy Farlow* of *Billericay*,[8] *Edward Coleborn* of *Chelmsford, Samuel Smedly* of *Concord, Sydrach Hopgood* of *Sudbury, Serjeant Eyres, Serjeant Prichard,* and *Corporal Coy* the Inhabitants of *Brookfield* aforesaid; It being the good pleasure of God, that they should all there fall by their hands, of whose good Intentions they were so Confident, and whom they so little mistrusted. There were also then five persons wounded, *viz. Captain Hutchinson, my self,* and my Son *Thomas* as aforesaid, *Corporal French* of *Billericay*, who having killed an *Indian* was (as he was taking up his gun) shot, and part of one of his *Thumbs taken off;* and also dangerously wounded through the *Body* near the *Shoulder*, the fifth was *John Waldoe* of *Chelmsford*, who was not so dangerously wounded as the rest; They also then killed *five* of our horses, and wounded some more, which soon died after they came to *Brookfield*. Upon this sudden and unexpected blow given us (wherein we desire to look higher then man the Instrument) we returned to the Town as fast as the badness of the way, and the weakness of our wounded men would permit, we being then Ten Miles from it. All the while we were going we durst not stay to *stanch* the *bleeding* of our *wounded men,* for fear the Enemy should have surprized us again, which they attempted to do, and had in probability done, but that we perceiving which way they went, wheeled off to the other hand, and so by *Gods good Providence towards us,* they missed us, and we all came readily upon, and safely to the Town, though none of us knew the way to it, those of the place being slain as aforesaid, and we avoiding any thick woods and riding in open places to prevent danger by them.[9] Being got to the Town we speedily betook our selves to one of the *largest and strongest houses* therein, where we fortified our selves in the best manner we could in such *straits of Time,* and there resolved to *keep Garrison,* though we were but few, and meanly fitted to make Resistance against so many Enemies. The News of the *Indians Treacherous dealing* with us, and the loss of so many of our Company thereby, did so *amaze the Inhabitants of the Town,* that they being informed thereof by us presently left their houses, divers of them carrying very little away with them, they being afraid of the *Indians* sudden coming upon them: and so came to the house we were entred into, very meanly provided of Cloathing, or furnished with Provisions.

I perceiving my self to be disenabled for the discharge of the duties of my place by reason of the wound I had received, and apprehending that the Enemy would soon come to spoyle the Town, and Assault us in the house, I appointed *Simon Davis* of *Concord, James Richardson,* and *John Fiske* of *Chelmsford* to manage Affairs for our Safety with those few men whom God hath left us, and were fit for any Service, and the Inhabitants of the said Town; who did well and Commendably perform the duties of the Trust committed to them with much Courage and Resolution through the Assistance of our gracious God who did not leave us in our low and distressed state, but did mercifully appear for us in our greatest need, as in the Sequel will clearly be manifested. Within two hours after our coming to the said house, or less, the said *Captain Hutchinson* and *my self* posted away *Ephraim Curtis* of *Sudbury,* and *Henry Young* of *Concord* to go to the *Honoured Council* at *Boston* to give them an Account of the Lords dealings with us, and our present Condition. When they came to the further end of the Town they saw the Enemy *Rifling of houses* which the Inhabitants had forsaken. The Post fired upon them, and immediately returned to us again, they discerning no safety in going forward, and being desirous to inform us of the *Enemies Actings,* that we might the more prepare for a *sudden Assault* by them. Which indeed presently followed, for as soon as the said *Post* was come back to us, the *Barbarous Heathen* pressed upon us in the house with great violence, *sending in their Shot* amongst us like haile through the walls, and shouting as if they would have *swallowed us up alive;* but our good God wrought wonderfully for us, so that there was but one man wounded within the house, *vis.* the said *Henry Young* who looking out at a garret window that Evening was *mortally wounded* by a Shot, of which wound he died within two dayes after. There was the same day another man slain, but not in the house, a Son of *Serjeant Prichards* adventuring out of the house wherein we were, to his Fathers house not far from it, to fetch more goods out of it, was Caught by those Cruel Enemies as they were coming towards us, who cut off his head, kicking it about like a *Foot-ball,* and then putting it upon a *Pole,* they set it up, before the *door* of his *Fathers house* in our sight.

The night following the said blow, they did *roar against* us like so many *wild Bulls,* sending in their Shot amongst us till towards the *Moon rising,* which was about *three of the Clock;* at which time they *Attempted to fire our house* by Hay and other Combustible matter which they brought to one Corner of the house, and set it on fire. Whereupon some of our Company were necessitated to expose themselves to very great danger to put it out: *Simon Davis* one of the three appointed by my self as *Captain,* to supply my place by Reason of my wounds as aforesaid, he being of a lively Spirit encouraged the Souldiers within the house to *fire upon the Indians;* and also those that Adventured out to put out the Fire (which began to rage and kindle upon the house side) with these and the like words, That *God is with us, and fights for us, and will deliver us* out of the hands of these Heathen; which Expressions of his the *Indians* hearing, they *shouted and scoffed* saying: now see how *your God delivers you,* or *will deliver you,* sending in many shots whilst our men were putting out the Fire.[10] But the Lord of Hosts wrought very graciously for us, in preserving our Bodies both within and without the house from their *shot,* and our house from being *consumed by Fire,* we had but *two men* wounded in that Attempt of theirs, but we apprehended that we killed divers of our Enemies. I being desirous to hasten Intelligence to the *Honoured Council* of our present *great distress,* we being so remote from *any succour,* (It being between *sixty* and *seventy* miles from us to *Boston,* where the *Council* useth to sit) and fearing our *Ammunition* would not last long to withstand them, if they continued so to Assault us, I spake to *Ephraim Curtis* to adventure forth again on that Service, and to Attempt it on Foot, as the way wherein there was most hope of getting away undiscovered; He *readily Assented,* and accordingly went out, but there were so many *Indians* every where thereabouts, that he could not pass, without apparent *hazard of Life,* so he came back again, yet towards morning the said *Ephraim* adventured forth the *third time,* and was fain to *creep on his hands and knees* for some space of ground, that he might not be discerned by the Enemy, who waited to prevent our sending if they could have hindred it. But through *Gods* mercy he escaped their hands, and got safely to *Marlborough,* though very much spent, and ready to faint by Reason of want of sleep before he went from us, and his sore travel *night and day* in that *hot Season* till he got thither, from whence he went to *Boston*[;] yet before the said *Ephraim* got to *Marlborough,* there was Intelligence brought thither of the burning of some houses, and killing some Cattel at *Quabaug* by some who were going to *Connecticut,* but they seeing what was done at the End of the Town, and hearing several guns shot off further within the Town, they durst proceed no further, but Immediately returned to *Marlborough,* though they then knew not what had befallen *Captain Hutchinson and my self, and Company,* nor of our being there [;] but that timely Intelligence they gave before *Ephraim Curtis* his coming to *Marlborough,* occasioned the Honoured *Major Willards* turning his *March* towards *Quabaug* for our Relief, who were in no small danger every hour of being destroyed; the said Major being when he had that Intelligence upon his *March* another way as he was Ordered by the *Honoured Council,* as is afterwards more fully expressed.

The next day being *August 3d,* they continued *shooting* & *shouting,* & proceeded in their *former wickedness blaspheming the Name of the Lord,* and *reproaching* us *his Afflicted Servants,* scoffing at our *prayers* as they were sending in their shot upon all quarters of the house And many of them went to the Towns *meeting house* (which was within *twenty Rods* of the house in which we were) who mocked saying, *Come and pray,* & *sing Psalms,* & in Contempt made an hideous noise *somewhat resembling singing.* But we to our power did endeavour our own defence, sending our shot amongst them the Lord giving us Courage to resist them, & preserving us from the destruction they sought to bring upon us. On the Evening following we saw our Enemies Carrying several of their *dead* or *wounded men* on their *Backs,* who proceeded that night to send in their shot as they had done the night before, & also still shouted as if the day had been certainly theirs, and they should without fail have prevailed against us which they might have the more hopes of in regard that we *discerned the coming of new Companies to them* to Assist and strengthen them, and the unlikelihood of any coming to our help. They also used several *Stratagems to Fire us,* namely by *wild fire* in *Cotton* and *Linnen Rags* with *Brimstone* in them, which Rags they tyed to the *Piles of their Arrows* sharp for the purpose, and shot them to the Roof of our house, after they had *set them on Fire,* which would have much endangered the burning thereof, had we not used means by cutting *holes through the Roof,* and otherwise, to beat the said *Arrows* down, and God being pleased to prosper our Indeavours therein. They carryed more *Combustible matter* as *Flax* and *Hay* to the sides of the house, & set it on fire, & then *stocked apace* towards the door of the house, either to prevent our going forth to quench the Fire, as we had done before, or to *kill our men* in their Attempt to go forth; or else to *break into the house by the door;* whereupon we were forced to break down the *wall* of the house against the *Fire* to *put it out:* They also shot a *Ball of wild Fire* into the *garret* of the *house* which fell amongst a great heap of *Flax or Tow* therein; which one of our Souldiers through Gods good Providence soon *espyed,* & having *water ready* presently quenched it; and so we were preserved by the *keeper of Israel,* both our *Bodies from their shot,* which they sent thick against us, and the *house from being consumed to Ashes,* although we were but weak to defend our selves, we being not above *twenty and six men* with those of that small Town, who were able for any Service, and our Enemies as I Judged them about (if not above) *three hundred,* I speak of the least, for many there present did guess them to be *four or five hundred.* It is the more to be observed that so little hurt should be done by the Enemies shot, it commonly piercing the walls of the house, and flying amongst the People, and there being in the house *fifty women and Children* besides the men before mentioned. But abroad in the yard one *Thomas Wilson* of that Town being sent to fetch water for our help in further need, (that which we had being spent in putting out the Fire) was shot by the Enemy in the *upper jaw,* and in the neck, the anguish of which wound was such at the first that he cried out with a *great noise,* by Reason whereof the *Indians* hearing him *rejoyced and triumphed at it;* But his wound was healed in a short time, praised be God.

On *Wednesday August the 4th.* the *Indians* Fortifyed themselves at the *meeting house,* and the *Barne* belonging to our house, which they Fortified both at the *great doors,* and at *both Ends* with *Posts, Rails, Boards, and Hay* to save themselves from our shot. They also devised other *Stratagems* to fire our house on the night following, namely, they took a *Cart,* and filled it with *Flax, Hay and Candlewood,* and other *Combustible matter,* and set up *Planks* fastened to the Cart to save themselves from the danger of our shot. Another Invention they had to make the more sure work in burning the house. They got many *Poles* of a Considerable length and bigness, and *spliced them together* at the Ends one of another, and made a Carriage of them about *Fourteen Rods long,* setting the Poles in two Rows with peils laid cross over them at the Front End, and dividing the said Poles about *three foot* asunder, and in the said *Front* of this their Carriage they set a *Barrel,* having made an *hole* through both Heads, and put an *Axle-Tree* through them, to which they fastened the said *Poles,* and under every joynt of the Poles where they were spliced, they set up a *pair of Truckle wheeles* to bear up the said Carriages, and they *loaded the Front* or fore-end thereof with matter *fit for firing,* as *Hay,* and *Flaxe,* and *Chips,* &c. Two of these Instruments they prepared, that they might Convey *Fire to the house,* with the more safety to themselves, they standing at such a distance from our shot, whilst they wheeled them to the house: great store of *Arrows* they had also prepared to shoot fire upon the house that night; which we found after they were gone, they having left them there.[11] But the Lord who is a *present help in Times of trouble,* and is pleased to make his *peoples Extremity his opportunity,* did graciously prevent them of Effecting what they hoped they should have done by the aforesaid devices, partly by sending a *showre of Rain* in season, whereby the matter prepared being wett would not so easily take Fire as it otherwise would have done, and partly by *Aide coming to our help.* For our danger would have been very great that night, had not the *only wise God (blessed for ever)* been pleased to send to us about an hour within night the *Worshipful Major Willard* with *Captain Parker* of *Groaton,* and *Forty six men* more with *five Indians* to relieve us in the *Low Estate* into which we were brought; *our Eyes were unto him the holy one of Israel;* In him we desired *to place our Trust,* hoping that he would in the time of our *great need appear for our deliverance,* and Confound all their plots by which they thought themselves most sure to prevail against us; And God *who comforteth the Afflicted,* as he comforted the holy *Apostle Paul by the coming of* Titus *to him,*[12] so he greatly comforted us his distressed Servants both *Souldiers* and *Town Inhabitants* by the coming of the said *Honoured Major,* and those with him. In whose so soon coming to us the *good Providence of God* did *marveilously appear;* For the help that came to us by the *Honoured Councils* order (after the tydings they received by our Post sent to them) came not to us till *Saturday August 7.* in the afternoon, nor sooner could it well come in regard of their distance from us, *i. e.* if we had not had help before that time, we see not how we could have held out, the number of the *Indians* so encreasing, and they making so many Assaults upon us, that our Ammunition before that time would have been spent, and our selves disenabled for any Resistance, we being but few, and alwaies fain to stand upon our defence; that we had little time for *Refreshment of our selves either by Food or Sleep;* The said *Honoured Majors* coming to us so soon was thus occasioned; He had a *Commission* from the *Honoured Council* (of which himself was one) to look after some *Indians* to the *West-ward* of *Lancaster* and *Groaton,* (where he himself lived) and to secure them, and was upon his *March* towards them on the foresaid *wednesday* in the morning, *August 4th.* When Tydings coming to *Marlborough* by those that returned thither as they were going to *Connecticut,* concerning what they saw at

*Brookfield* as aforesaid, some of *Marlborough* knowing of the said *Majors* march from *Lancaster* that morning presently sent a *Post* to acquaint him with the Information they had received; The *Major* was gone before the *Post* came to *Lancaster;* but there was one speedily sent after him, who overtook him about *five or six miles* from the said Town; He being acquainted, that it was feared, that *Brookfield* (a small Town of about *fifteen or sixteen Families*) was either destroyed, or in great danger thereof, & conceiving it to require more speed to succour them (if they were not past help) then to proceed at present, as he before intended, and being also very desirous (if it were possible) to afford Relief to them, (he being then not above *Thirty Miles* from them) he Immediately *altered his Course* and *marched* with his *Company* towards us: and came to us about an *hour after it was dark* as above said; though he knew not then, neither of our being there, nor of what had befallen us at the *Swampe* and in the house those two days before.

The merciful Providence of God also appeared in preventing the danger that the *Honoured Major* and his *Company* might have been in, when they came near to us, for those *Beastly men* our *Enemies Skilful to destroy,* Indeavoured to prevent any help from coming to our Relief, and therefore sent down *Sentinels,* (some nearer and some further off) the furthest about *two miles* from us, who if they saw any coming from the *Bay* they might give notice by an *Alarm.* And there were about an *hundred* of them who for the most part kept at an house some little distance from us, by which if any help came from the said *Bay,* they must pass, and so they intended (as we conceive) having notice by their *Sentinels* of their approach to *way-lay them,* and if they could, to *cut them off* before they came to the house where we kept.

But as we probably guess, they were so intent and buisy in preparing their Instruments (as above said) for our destruction by Fire, that they were not at the house where they used to keep for the purpose aforesaid, and that they heard not their *Sentinels* when they *shot;* and so the *Majors* way was clear from danger till he came to our house. And that it was their purpose so to have fallen upon him, or any other coming to us at that house, is the more probable in that (as we have since had Intelligence from some of the *Indians* themselves) there were a party of them at *another place* who *let him pass by them* without the least hurt or Opposition, waiting for a *blow to be given* him at the said *house,* and then they themselves to fall upon them in the *Reare,* as they intended to have done with us at the *Swamp,* in Case we had *fled back* as is before expressed. The *Major* & *Company* were no sooner come to the house, and understood (though at first they knew not they were *English* who were in the house, but thought that they might be *Indians,* and therefore were ready to have shot at us, till we discerning they were *English* by the *Majors* speaking, I caused the *Trumpet to be sounded*) that the said *Captain Hutchinson, my self, and Company* with the *Towns Inhabitants* were there, but the *Indians* also discerned that there were some come to our Assistance, whereupon they spared not their shot, but poured it out on them; but through the Lords goodness, though they stood not farr asunder one from another, they *killed not one man,* wounded only *two* of his Company; and killed the *Majors Sons horse;* after that we within the house perceived the *Indians* shooting so at them, we hastened the *Major* and all his Company into the house as fast as we could, and their horses into a little yard before the house, where they wounded *five other horses* that night; After they were come into the house to us, the *Enemies* continued their shooting some Considerable time, so that we may well say, *had not the Lord been on our side when these Cruel Heathens rose up against us, they had then swallowed us up quick,* when their wrath was kindled against us. But *wherein they dealt proudly, the Lord was above them.*

When they saw their *divers designes unsuccessful,* and their hopes therin disappointed, they then fired the *house* & *barns* (wherein they had before kept to lye in wait to surprize any coming to us) that by the Light thereof they might the better direct their shot at us, but *no hurt* was done thereby *praised be the Lord.* And not long after they burnt the *Meeting house* wherein their Fortifications were, as also the *Barne* which belonged to our house, and so perceiving more strength come to our Assistance: they did as we suppose, *despair of effecting* any more mischief against us. And therefore the greatest part of them towards the breaking of the day *August the fifth* went away and left us, and we were quiet from any further molestations by them; and on that morning we went forth of the house without danger, and so daily afterward, only one man was wounded about two dayes after, as he went out to look after horses and some few of them *sculking* thereabouts. We cannot tell how many of them we killed in all that time, but one that afterwards was taken confessed that there were killed and wounded about *eighty men* or more: *Blessed be the Lord God of our Salvation* who kept us from being all a *prey to their Teeth.* But before they went away they *burnt all the Town* except the house we kept in, and another that was not then finished. They also made great spoyle of the Cattel belonging to the Inhabitants; and after our Entrance into the house, and during the time of our *Confinement* there, they either killed or drove away almost all the horses of our Company.

We Continued there both well and wounded towards a *Fortnight,* and *August the thirteenth Captain Hutchinson and my self* with the most of those that had escaped without hurt, and also some of the wounded came from thence; my Son *Thomas* and some other wounded men came not from thence, being not then able to endure Travel so farr as we were from the next Town, till about a *Fortnight* after. We came to *Marlborough* on *August the Fourteenth,* where *Captain Hutchinson* being not recovered of his wound before his coming from *Brookfield,* and overtyred with his *long Journy* by Reason of his weakness quickly after grew worse, and more dangerously ill, and on the *nineteen*th *day* of the said moneth dyed, and was there the day after buried, the Lord being pleased to deny him a return to his own habitation, and his near Relations at *Boston,* though he was come the greatest part of his Journy thitherward.[13] The Inhabitants of the *Town* also not long after, *men, women,* and *Children,* removed safely with what they had left to several places, either where they had lived before their planting or sitting down there; or where they had Relations to receive and entertain them. The Honoured *Major Willard* stayed at *Brookfield* some weeks after our coming away, there being several Companies of Souldiers sent up thither and to *Hadly* and the Towns thereabouts, which are about *Thirty Miles* from *Brookfield;* whither also the Major went for a time upon the Service of the Country in the present warr, and from whence there being need of his presence for the ordering of matters concerning his own *Regiment* and the safety of the *Towns* belonging to it, he through Gods goodness and mercy returned in safety and health to his house, and dear Relations at *Groaton.*

Thus I have Indeavoured to set down and declare both what the Lord did against us in the Loss of several persons Lifes, and the wounding of others, some of which wounds were very painful in dressing, and long ere they were healed, besides many dangers that we were in, and fears that we were exercised with; and also what great things he was pleased to do for us in frustrating their many Attempts, and vouchsafing such a Deliverance to us. The Lord *avenge the Blood that hath been shed* by these *Heathen* who *hate us without a Cause,* though he be most Righteous in all that hath befallen there, and in all other parts of the Country;[14] He help us to *humble our selves* before him, and with our *whole hearts to return to him,* and also to improve all his mercies which we still enjoy, that so his *anger may cease* towards us and he may be pleased either to make our Enemies at *peace with us,* or more, *destroy them* before us. I tarried at *Marlborough* with *Captain Hutchinson* until his death, and came home to *Concord August the 21.* (though not throughly recovered of my wound) and so did others that went with me. But since I am Reasonable well, though I have not the use of my hand and Arm as before: My Son *Thomas* though in great *hazard of Life* for some time after his return to Concord, yet is now very well Cured, and his strength well restored.! *Oh that we could praise the Lord for his great goodness towards us.* Praised be his Name, that though he took away some of us, yet was pleased to spare so many of us, and adde unto our dayes; He help us *whose Souls he hath delivered from Death, and Eyes from Tears, and Feet from falling to walk before him in the Land of the Living* till our great Change come,[15] and to *sanctifie his Name* in all *his wayes* about us, that both our Afflictions, and our mercies may quicken us to live more to his glory all our dayes.

## NOTES

Ms. Rebecca Stamelman assisted in editing the text.

1. Hutchinson's first mission to the Narragansetts was part of the "diplomatic offensive" that began on June 23, 1675.

2. Curtis's expedition was also part of the "diplomatic offensive"; like Hutchinson's, it was unsuccessful.

3. Psalms 78:6. The reason for God's commanding the retelling for the "generation to come the praises of the Lord, and his strength" is

"That they might set their hope in God, and not forget the works of God, but keep his commandments."

4. Chapter 27 of the Acts of the Apostles recounts the voyage of the imprisoned Paul to Italy, and verse 20 the storm which nearly overwhelmed their ship: "And when neither sun nor stars in many days appeared, and no small tempest lay on *us*, all hope that we should be saved was then taken away." The storm, like the Indian war, tests the faith of the "chosen people," whether Apostles or Visible Saints of New England. Interestingly, the chapter sounds the recurrent theme (in Puritan literature) of "captivity," suggesting a parallel between the besieged troopers and the heroine of the captivity tale.

5. Psalms 34:3: "O magnify the LORD with me, and let us exalt his name together." The Psalm recounts a time of trouble and humiliation for David, in which the humbled hero is enabled to bear his difficulties because of his abiding faith in God's promises and justice. God will uphold the righteous and cast down the wicked—a promise most appropriate to the imperiled colony. More to the point, in view of Wheeler's preoccupation with the theological character of the chronicler's role, the psalm declares that the Lord will "cut off the remembrance of them [that do evil] from the earth." Psalms 34:16.

6. Refers to the Swamp Fight of December 19, 1675.

7. "Reins" means "the kidneys, loins, or lower back regions."

8. Billerica, Mass.

9. Their escape was chiefly due to the fact that they possessed horses, while the Indians did not.

10. That the Indians should speak English and understand Christianity well enough to mock and (as they do later) parody it suggests that there were some Praying Indians, or some ex-Praying Indians, among the warriors. It is suggestive of the nature of cultural interaction in the colony that many of the Indians had learned English, while few English learned the native languages.

11. Note the military ingenuity of the Indians in adapting an alien technology—one moreover not designed for war—to their purposes.

12. 2 Corinthians 7:5–7. "For, when we were come into Macedonia, our flesh had no rest, but we were troubled on every side; without *were* fightings, within *were* fears. Nevertheless God, that comforteth those that are cast down, comforted us by the coming of Titus [Paul's brother]." Titus brought news of the Corinthian church's sorrow for having disagreed with Paul.

13. Note Wheeler's characteristically Puritan way of recounting an incident that is intended to evoke pity. The pathos of Hutchinson's death after coming so close to a "restoration" to his family—the captivity/restoration theme again—must be evoked without the implication that God's providence is in any way to be deprecated in this instance. Hence the odd, inverted way of stating the event—"the Lord being *pleased* to deny him, etc."

14. Again Wheeler is careful not to question the actions of the Lord. He asks the Lord to avenge his own; but his call for vengeance must not be construed as questioning in any way the propriety and justice of the Lord's having unleashed the Indians in the first place.

15. The "Great Change" is the ultimate transformation of the "justified" saint who, having undergone the first "Great Change" of religious conversion, now undergoes the final "Change" of death and transfiguration, leaving the world to appear in full saintly splendor among the elect in Heaven. For a study of the imagery of transformation, see Dickran and Ann Tashjian, *Memorials for Children of Change,* chapts. 1–2.

FOUR

## *SAMUEL NOWELL*
## Prophet of Preparedness

> I wish I could particularly give an immortal memory to all the brave men who signalized themselves in this action [the Swamp Fight]. But among them all, *O quam te memorem,* thou excellent SAMUEL NOWEL, never to be forgotten! This now *reverend,* and afterwards *worshipful* person, a chaplain to the army, was author to a good sermon preached unto the *artillery-company* of the *Massachusetts,* which he entitled *Abraham in Arms;* and at this fight there was no person more like a true son of *Abraham in arms,* or that with more courage and hazardly fought in the midst of a shower of bullets from the surrounding *Salvages.*[1]

Samuel Nowell, the militant divine thus praised by Cotton Mather in his *Magnalia Christi Americana,* was more than a military chaplain. He was a Puritan of the first generation born in America, the eldest surviving son of Increase Nowell, who had come over with Governor Winthrop in the *Arbella* in the first wave of the Great Migration of 1630. Nowell's partiality for America and the American-born generations (which as we have seen was not shared by those psychologically tied to the founding fathers) is expressed in the preface to his sermon, where he extols "this Country, where I drew my first breath." He graduated from Harvard in 1653 and was ordained as a minister, but he never had a settled congregation of his own. Rather, his abilities and inclinations led him into military and political life. After his service in King Philip's War as chaplain to Winslow's and Talcott's "Armies," he served the colony as a member of the Court of Assistants (the chief magistrates), and in 1685 was chosen as treasurer of Massachusetts Bay Colony. Deposed as treasurer by the royal commission that established the government of Sir Edmund Andros, he argued both privately and publicly for resistance to the royal authority. He was chosen to accompany Increase Mather to London to plead the colony's case against the new governor before the royal court, but Nowell died in London in September 1688.[2]

As one whose professional attributes united the characters of soldier, preacher, and magistrate, Nowell was a perfect choice to preach the annual sermon on the election of officers of the provincial artillery. This was a civic ritual of considerable importance, both from a political and from an ideological perspective. The military system of the colonies was a rather informal one. There was no standing army; rather, each town maintained a militia or "trained band," in which some proportion of the able-bodied males were required to serve. This militia constituted the colonies' chief defense against Indians and was an ultimate power to lean on in case of civil broils arising out of social or religious controversy (although watch and magistrates were usually sufficient for police purposes). Militia officers were elected, generally from among the better class of citizens—partly because of the universal Puritan conservatism in matters of social stratification, and partly because it required a certain amount of property for an officer to outfit himself properly with sword, sidearms, and perhaps a horse and uniform. Although the towns maintained small arsenals and magazines, most of the colonists (particularly in rural districts) possessed firearms for hunting and could bring their own weapons to a muster.[3]

Chief among the weapons possessed by the colonies and stored in the arsenals were the artillery pieces. They represented not only the most potent firearm—at least for the defense of fortified towns—but the most expensive single item in the colonial army, the most significant capital investment. Since they could not be cast in America, they had to be imported and hence were doubly dear. The arsenals that held the artillery and associated equipment had to be watched and kept watertight and well locked; moreover, the artillery were called upon for the firing of salutes even in time of peace. They required trained personnel for their use, as the gunners had to perform several specialized functions. Hence the artillery officers exercised the most important category of militia command in time of peace. Their military labors were the most visible and frequent, involved them most intensively with the training of men, and gave them care of the most valued weapons. In an Indian war, of course, their pieces were generally too cumbersome to be of much use and got left in town when the militia went skirmishing. Still, they represented (if only symbolically) the most permanent, visible, and elite division of the colonial military establishment.

Thus the annual election of their officers was an occasion for Puritan ministers to employ their best symbolism in pointing the parallels between the discipline of the soldier and the discipline of the Christian. Over the years, the artillery election sermon came to constitute a minor but coherent subgenre within the Puritan sermon literature.[4]

Nowell's *Abraham in Arms*, preached on June 3, 1678, provides a paradigmatic instance of the artillery election sermon, as well as offering an insight into the effects of the Indian war on Puritan ideology. The sermon was taken down by friends who heard Nowell preach it and published at their request. Nowell says in his preface "To the Reader" that he was unable to write it down himself "by reason of . . . an infirmity in my right hand, which God hath been pleased to exercise me with, almost wholly taking away the use of my hand." Perhaps from this cause, the published text has a number of typographical errors, and the divisions of the sermon by sections (Text, Doctrine, Reasons, Uses) and numbered paragraphs is imperfect. (Corrections and interpolations are indicated by [ ].) Still, the text follows closely the sermon form discussed earlier in the introduction to Increase Mather's history of the war. Nowell's "Text" is from Genesis, 14:14: "*And when Abram heard that his Brother was taken captive, he armed his trained Servants, born in his own house, three hundred and eighteen, and pursued them to Dan.*" The text is followed by an introductory interpretation of the text itself and of some associated passages, which formulates the "Doctrine" in the broadest terms. Nowell then follows the Puritan pattern of exfoliating layers of meaning from the divine Word, according to a typological system, in which the Old Testament text is made to prefigure the coming of Christ and the New Testament. In Nowell's sermon the priest Melchizedech who blesses Abraham's war, "was eminently a Type of Jesus Christ, . . . who is even a Priest after the order of Melchizedech."

Just as Old Testament stories can be made to divulge New Testament patterns, so the two Testaments—New superimposed on Old in a kind of double image—provide patterns for understanding the history of New England. Nowell uses this association of ideas in several ways: to evoke the community's sense of its spiritual connection to the chosen people of Israel, to justify the Puritans' engaging in warfare, and to argue for a linkage between spiritual reformation and the better practice of military discipline. Beyond these practical concerns, Nowell also looks to the "apocalyptic timetable" provided by typological analysis of the Book of Revelation. He uses phrases and symbols from that and other books to suggest that specific events in the war correlate with the symbolism in which the prophetic description of the Second Coming was couched. Thus the Indian war is made to point toward an approaching Armageddon, which Nowell sees as not far off.

He begins by noting that Abraham was highly commended in Scripture for teaching his people piety and for instructing them in military discipline. From this, we are "to see, / That the highest practice of Piety and practice of War, may agree well in one person." Indeed, "the Lord assumes the name to himself. The Lord is a Man of War." Abraham's piety and military discipline thus make him an analogue for Jehovah himself: he is not simply chieftain but patriarch, and the servants he arms are his own children. Since the Old Testament is simply the prophecy of the New, Nowell then makes a symbolic leap, calling Abraham a Christian: "It is the first exploit of a Christian Souldier being in arms, or of a religious Captain, with his Army of Religion and Arms joyned together." From this, Nowell moves immediately to draw the parallel between Abraham's war and New England's. He notes that the reason for Abraham's going to war was that his brother Lot was taken captive, that he armed his men himself, that all was in readiness for battle, and that Abraham's men were trained. He then tells us that Abraham's victory in battle was followed by the blessing of Melchizedech, representing Jesus Christ, and praises Abraham for his noble generosity in restoring the goods of the king of Sodom. Nowell then urges the parallel with New England: the Puritans took up arms to defend themselves and their allies and to rescue those the Indians had taken captive. Although he leaves the sequel for the conclusion, his audience would certainly have seen their present condition of peace with victory as proof of God's blessing.

Now Nowell buckles to his doctrine. Abraham was "eminent in his place," both for preparing his servants for war and for the Christian manner in which he carried it through. Nowell wants first to prove "that the Training of Souldiers to be fit for War, is a commendable practice, yea a Duty of great Consequence." He means this in the most pragmatic way and calls for frequent musters and military exercises and for the hardening of bodies to bear the rigors of warfare. But the spelling of "Souldiers" suggests the important linkage in Nowell's (and the Puritans') mind(s) between military and religious discipline. In the military form, commanders command, "souldiers" follow. As in the Christian community, the leaders are teachers as well as commanders and magistrates, instructing their charges in the military arts, and in the discipline of soldierly behavior. The commander's disciplining of the body is analogous to the minister's disciplining of the soul. Indeed, in a well-ordered army operated on Christian principles, communal discipline may be as a whole more perfect, since the power of the commander against heresy and backsliding in matters of discipline is more absolute than that of the civil ruler or cleric. Here Nowell and his audience could draw on the traditions of the Puritan Revolution in England, in which Cromwell's New Model Army—reorganized ideologically and politically around firmly Puritan principles and persons—triumphed over the forces of the king.

"There is such agreement between the Spiritual and temporal Warfare, that everything belonging to a Souldier, is made use of to resemble some Grace or Duty of a Christian." Twice Nowell reminds his audience that Christ praised the centurion who spoke of himself as "a man under authority" as well as of a giver of orders ("I say to one go and he goeth."), saying of him, "I have not found so great faith, no, not even in Israel." And he extends his military model to the analogous realms of the Church, civil state, and household by addressing as "types" of Abraham "Rulers, Governours and Parents," enjoining them to supplement the labor of military commanders in training their "Children" to endure "hardness" and be "expert for War."

Nowell's fondness for the analogy goes beyond the merely formal. His rhetoric becomes almost Jeremiad-like when he condemns "a strange piece of dotage befallen this crazy-headed Age [,] that men should not use the sword." Behind his doctrine is a sense of New England's place in history as the cutting edge of Christ's army in the eternal Manichean warfare of good and evil, Jehovah and Satan—a war paralleled by the struggle of pagan and Christian, Catholic and Protestant nations. But he reserves his historical and political analysis until he has made clear the biblical sources of his thesis. The commendability of military exercise is proved by the following "reasons." Firstly (as he has already said) the Lord calls himself a god of war and armies, exhibiting this function in several ways. He speaks of Himself as the giver of spirit and courage and the determiner of victory. Moreover, the Lord has commanded men to make weapons, given them "spirits to such a work," and taught them the skill of it. Here Nowell invokes the Puritan concept of the "calling"—the conception of human labor as both secular task and profession of faith—and connects it directly to the war ethic. The soldier's profession meets the requirements of Christian calling as defined by John Cotton, for the "quickening" of spirit sent by the Lord to his biblical soldiery is one of the crucial signs of the validity or "warrantability" of a calling. Nowell and Cotton cite the identical passage in support of this concept, Psalms 44:1.[6]

Since this is the "Reasons" section of the sermon, Nowell now moves to show that historical and natural phenomena, scientifically observed, confirm the biblical teaching—Natural Reason, rightly followed, must always confirm the findings of Revealed Truth. Thus we are told that the wisest and most prudent rulers, even of pagandom, prepared against the day of war, that this has been the common practice of nations, and that even the "irrational creatures, when sent by God in way of Judgment, act as if they were under Military Conduct"—as in the examples of the "armies" of locusts and other insects cited in Scripture.

Nowell's second point of doctrine is that the practice of military art is not merely praiseworthy but is enjoined as a duty. Indeed, he has already prepared for this conclusion, since he has linked warfare with Christian "calling." Here his argument again links scriptural revelation with practical wisdom. Self-defense is not merely permitted by the Bible, it is enjoined as a command, since God has made it the central principle of natural existence. Given this command, whatever is needful to achieve preservation of self and society is a duty implicit in the divine creation. Christ himself, says Nowell, said that *"he that hath not a Sword, let him sell his garment and buy one,"* for when the milennium approaches and the Second Coming nears, *"in the latter days there shall be Wars and Rumors of War."* In the struggles that presage Armageddon, man will have to defend himself and his God by the means provided in natural life, for though "God can work miracles, . . . when ordinary means may be had, he will not work miracles." Here Nowell was echoing the basic tenet of Puritan scientific thought, which—like the doctrine of free grace and the "calling"—urged the pious to examine and act within the normal processes of nature, never expecting to be aided by miraculous intervention. For Nowell, "our Military Strength is, under God, the appointed means, or in the ordinary way of Providence, is the proper and only means for our preservation; therefore it is a duty to encourage Souldiers." The "Uses" which Nowell would have his audience make of his doctrine chiefly concern the respecting of military men and the necessity of preparedness (equipment, training, etc.). Indeed *"they are to blame"* who shirk or slight their duty to prepare for war by hardening their bodies, perfecting their skills, and purchasing and maintaining their weapons in good order.

Here at the end of the sermon, Nowell expands his vision of the war to take in a larger struggle than the skirmish just concluded. The Indian war has been a warning. "God in his providence keeps some Nations and people unsubdued, as he did with Israel of old [:] he kept some people unsubdued on purpose to teach Israel War." The Indians' only purpose, their only justification within the divine schema, is to provide a testing ground or a crucible for Puritan martial spirit. Thanks to the presence of unsubdued Indians, succeeding generations of Puritans—who would not know the physical and spiritual hardships, the testing of the Puritan Revolution and Migration—might maintain the vigor and discipline of their forefathers. That the Indians might have some claim to the land does not occur to Nowell. Like Canaan, New England was granted to a chosen people by God's Will.

This hardening and disciplining of the latter generations by Indian warfare is essential if Christianity—represented by New England Puritanism—is to triumph in the larger struggle against paganism, Catholicism, Islam, and Satan. Armageddon still lies ahead. "The highest piece of Service that ever Souldiers were employed in is yet behind, [i.e., "to come"] and is commonly believed not to be very far off: the highest service that ever was done for the Lord Jesus Christ is yet behind, the destruction of *Gog and Magog,* so the enemies of the Church are called in Scripture; whether it be Pope or Turk, or whoever else meant, that shall oppose the advancement of the Kingdome of Christ." For Nowell, the advancement of Christ's kingdom has a worldly equivalent in the advancement of Protestantism in general and New England in particular. He points to the religious wars in Holland and Germany, and warns New England, "I apprehend we shall not live quiet long." The "Princes of note in *Europe*" have their eye upon the prosperity of the English colonies: France and Spain will soon be at war with England in a global struggle for colonial supremacy. "*Rome* will have no peace with you, and you ought to have no peace with it." Behind France and Spain is the power of the Catholic Church, which can strike through a restored Catholic monarch as well as through foreign enemies. Indeed, before the decade was out the colony (with Nowell as its agent) would be engaged in struggle with the governor sent by the Catholic James II.

Nowell's use of typological paradigms here is not simply a way of rhetorically ornamenting his political message. Despite his imprecision about whether the Pope or the Turk is Gog and Magog or who is the antitype of the Beast in the *Book of Revelation,* we are to take seriously his implication that the coming worldwide warfare will in fact mark one of the necessary stages in the scenario or timetable of the Apocalypse.

And always, never to be forgotten, the Indians remain unsubdued nations threatening the borders of the state. In this context, Nowell stresses the *racial* antipathy of Englishmen and Indians, by way of emphasizing the permanence and the fundamental character of the conflict (and thereby paralleling it with the struggle against Rome). He notes that "The Inhabitants of the land will not joyn or mix with us to make one Body," and contrasts this with the biblical efforts of Hamor and Sichem to make peace with Jacob by saying, *"Let us marry together and make one nation."* This, says Nowell, has always been the French policy, but he notes ironically that though the French "may think thereby to escape some scourge that hangs over them," yet it seems within God's providence that war between Indians and whites (Frenchmen included) is inevitable. Of course, the enmity cited by Nowell was at least as inherent in English as in Indian principles. In fact, it may have been more so, since the Indians had welcomed, whereas the English always designed to replace, the other race. Certainly, the prohibition against intermarriage was not an Indian principle. Rather, the English were fearful that the attractions of Indian marriage (and the consequent political and economic alliances to be made by individuals) might weaken the political as well as the moral fiber of their community, and they therefore placed severe penalties, including death, on the crime of intermarriage.

For Nowell, the justification of this racial separation and of the racial warfare that accompanies it lies in the divine ordering of nature. He sees the New World as torn between forces representing absolute dark and pure light, embodied in two nations of different blood and religion. Each nation strives to become the master of the world that is yet to be, to control the future of human history and religion. "Two Nations [are in] the womb and will be striving." Therefore, "we must either learn to defend ourselves, or resolve to be vassals." No reconciliation between the races can occur, no marriage, for "When God intended the Canaanites to be destroyed, he did forbid Israel to marry with them: they were to be thorns to them, and Israel was to root them out." One or the other must be destroyed or enslaved. This represents a radical shift from the policy of converting the Indians and from the typological interpretation of Eliot, who saw the Indians as the Lost Tribes of Israel, rather than as Canaanites (or Amalekites as Mather puts it).

Thus the need for "souldierly" virtues is paramount: self discipline, obedience to ministers and commanders, physical fitness, temperance, chastity. Yet "The sins of *New-England* increase," as is evidenced by heretical tendencies within the Church (see Nowell's rebuke of "Atheisme" as the basis of souldierly virtue), and by the negligence of rulers and citizens toward their military duties. Some shirk musters or are lax in the exercises; others "goe to the Tavern or Ale-house, and seldome away before Drunk, or well tipled. It is rare to find men we can call Drunkards, but there are abundance of Tiplers in *New-England.*" Here Nowell echoes the strictures of his master, Increase Mather, against the luxurious affectations of the backsliding younger generations.

Yet Nowell's condemnation of the people is never so thoroughgoing and unrelieved as Mather's—perhaps because Nowell is not so theoretical and doctrinal, but more practical in his acquaintance with men and affairs (especially military). Where Mather attributes all victory to prayer and sees humans as frail and degenerate, Nowell declares to ministers and magistrates,

> Through the goodness and favor of God, you have a people under you that have Spirit and Courage enough . . . to bless God for: there hath been rather an excess of Courage then defect or want of it; most of our losses have been occasioned meerly by it. . . . You have a People bred up in this Country, that have the heart of Lions . . . [Who] *mocks at fear, . . . is not afraid, neither turns . . . back from the Sword.* . . . I speak this because I have seen and heard something myself of the Courage of Souldiers, that hath been better and more refreshing then the greatest Daintyes or Feast could be.

The great strength of New England lies in the character and strength of the generations raised in this country—the younger generations, not only the revered ancient fathers. "They can endure hardness, that is another thing by way of encouragement to Rulers, that is a great mercy. A tender, softly effeminate People is a curse and a misery, when God is pleased to frame a people to be such." Yet the edge of this hardness must not be lost. Parents and rulers must train their children to hardness, for "You doe not know what hardness your Children may be called to."

Nowell's view of the role of New England in the world struggle against the allied forces of Antichrist is more an echo of the vision propounded by the Mathers and others than an original contribution. The interest in Nowell's treatment of the theme lies in his uniting—both in his character and in the rhetoric of his sermon—the attributes of minister and practical soldier, of purveyor of ideology and man of affairs. In his mouth the image of the Christian as Christ's "souldier" becomes more than cliche; he speaks out of experience and can exhibit scars to prove it. This gives his sermon some peculiar differences of emphasis when compared with the writings of Mather. He emphasizes the virtues and strengths of the American-born sons, where Mather extols only the virtues of the fading generation of European-born fathers, and he lays far more weight on the practical and physical side of "preparedness" than on the need for prayer which preoccupies Mather. Abraham's reputation for piety gets a single paragraph of extraordinary brevity on the first page of the sermon; all the rest, save for an occasional digression, concerns war in (and much of it for) the world.

Nowell sees the Indian war just concluded as merely a prelude to a larger struggle—in fact, as a providential "testing" of Puritan mettle and methods of war that could (if read aright) teach the Puritans how best to prepare for and conduct a larger war. Nowell is purposely vague about the character of the larger struggle he has in mind, allowing the reader or listener to associate it with a Matherian conception of the warfare of Christ and Antichrist. Yet, as T. H. Breen argues, there is reason to suppose that Nowell and his audience had a more immediate struggle in mind: the incipient struggle with the English Crown for control of the government and revenues of the Puritan colonies. Nowell's treatment of the subject is radical: in effect, he urges preparedness for military resistance to England in *Abraham in Arms*. This point was recognized by no less a personage than Edward Randolph, the royal commissioner to New England, who accused Nowell of "preaching up rebellion." In 1689 Nowell appeared as a true prophet when the Puritan coup overthrew Andros. But Nowell's position is interesting in other ways as well. As Breen points out, Nowell roots the justification for preparedness and war in the right of men to defend their property. Although he also sees the defense of religion as a central concern—thus making possible his alliance with Mather—he gives equal emphasis to the defense of property and legal rights. This shifts the ground of Puritan politics from the defense of religion to a defense of property sanctified by religion. Nowell's position is one small, important step in the cultural process that would secularize the Puritan ethic in the eighteenth century.[7]

In making his ideological point through the indirect and

symbolic speech of an Indian war sermon, Nowell also employs an interesting metaphorical association of the Indians and the home-English. (The "Two Nations" metaphor works equally well for the English–New English conflict.) The Indian war prefigures the coming struggle with England and the forces of Antichrist in the world at large; therefore the Indian is a "type" or symbol closely related to if not identical with the home-Englishman. This association of the primitive Indian and the metropolitan Englishman is one that became typical of American writing—particularly in the late eighteenth and early nineteenth centuries, when literary nationalists sought to locate the American character between the polarities represented by pagan savagery and corruptly sophisticated civilization. It is curious and appropriate that a militant nationalist like Nowell should make (however tentatively) the first gesture toward the articulation of this metaphor.

If Nowell's view of history as an eternal struggle between Christ and Antichrist ties him to the traditions of Puritan historiography, his nationalism and militarism look ahead to later phases of American development. His view of history as perpetual warfare between individuals and groups representing fundamentally opposed principles is carried on (in secularized form) in the rhetoric of manifest destiny, of the struggles over slavery before the Civil War, of the Social Darwinist view of class and social evolution, of White Man's Burden imperialism, and of the cold war. One hears constant echoes of Nowell-like formulations in the writings of Theodore Roosevelt—particularly in "The Strenuous Life," which agrees with Nowell's central thesis that the life of struggle and military discipline makes better men, soldiers, and Christians.[8] These echoes of phrase and coincidences of concern suggest the abiding strength of the colonial-Puritan world view in American culture, as well as serving to illustrate the particular debt of Roosevelt to the Calvinist tradition. Out of Mather's and Nowell's interpretation of the Indian wars emerges the conception of the "long twilight struggle" against dark races and darker ideologies, leading through jungle and suburb to an apocalyptic confrontation—a Last War which will end either in the triumph of righteousness (ourselves and our peculiar institutions) or in universal destruction. In such a world, to prepare for the coming of God and the coming of war are the same thing.

## NOTES

1. Cotton Mather, *Magnalia Christi Americana*, 2:492.

2. T. H. Breen, *The Character of the Good Ruler*, pp. 117–22; *Genealogical Dictionary of New England*, 3:295.

3. Douglas Edward Leach, *Flintlock and Tomahawk*, pp. 11–14, and chap. 6.

4. See, for example, Urian Oakes, "The Soveraign Efficacy of Divine Providence," in *The Puritans*, ed. Perry Miller and Thomas Johnson, pp. 350–67.

5. For a fuller discussion of typology, see pp. 58–60 above. Nowell's use of specific biblical texts to align the war with the apocalyptic timetable can be followed in the notes to *Abraham in Arms*, below.

6. Miller and Johnson, *The Puritans*, pp. 319–27.

7. Breen, *Character of the Good Ruler*, pp. 119–22; 145–46.

8. Theodore Roosevelt, "The Strenuous Life," in *The Works of Theodore Roosevelt*, 12: 3–22.

# Abraham *in Arms*;

OR

The first Religious

# GENERAL

WITH HIS

# ARMY

*Engaging in*

# A VVAR

*For which he had wisely prepared, and by which, not only an eminent*

# VICTORY

Was obtained, but

# A BLESSING

gained also.

Delivered in an *Artillery-Election-Sermon*, *June*, 3. 1678.

**By S. N.**

BOSTON;
Printed by *John Foster*, 1678.

## *TO THE READER*

*Friendly Reader,*

A Desire to gratifie my Friends, hath made [me], against my own Judgement, to consent to the Publication of these Notes, taken by one of the Auditors; to which I am not able to make that addition, by reason of my inability to write, through infirmity in my right hand, which God hath been pleased to exercise me with, almost wholly taking away the use of my hand: What is therefore made publick, is not mine own Notes, but agreeing in the substance with what was delivered: This Argument also prevailed with me to let this come forth, [:] I thought others more able, seeing this imperfect work to find acceptance with some, might thereby be provoked to Preach and Print something that might be more effectual to revive our Military Discipline, and the Spirit of Souldiery, which seems to be in its Wane, in an Age when never more need of it.

The Love I have for this Country, where I drew my first Breath, hath made me Run the Gauntlet by exposing this to the world,[1] hoping that they that fault it, will endeavour to mend it by some mean[s] or other, and to pray for the Author, who is a Friend to all of such a spirit,[2]

**Samuel Nowell.**

> Gen. 14. 14. *And when Abram heard that his Brother was taken captive, he armed his trained Servants, born in his own house, three hundred and eighteen, and pursued them to Dan.*

Our Father Abraham is highly commended in Scripture for two things with respect to his Family, besides his own Faith and Piety, that the Scripture gives account of: so we have his care with respect to his Family,

1. *To Teach them Piety.* Gen. 18–19. *I know Abraham* [,] *there is none like him in all the earth, he will command his Family, and his household in the wayes of the Lord.*

2. *We have his care to instruct them in Military Discipline,* appearing in these words, *he armed his trained Servants,* such as he had *Trained* up to be fit for such a piece of Service as God by

his providence called him to: His *Trained* or instructed Servants for such a service, prepared for it by instruction or by *Training,* which is our usual word for such an end. This labour and care of Abraham in this work is much commended, from his success in War, or his martial Exploit of which we have an account in this Chapter.[3] And that Abraham undertakes War, and successfully, and gets a Blessing by it, *Melchizedech's* Blessing in his return out of the Field: we see,

That the highest practice of Piety and practice of War, may agree well in one person. Religion and Arms may well be joyned together; they agree so well together, that the Lord assumes the name to himself, *The Lord is a Man of War, the Lord is his name.*[4] It is the first song that ever was penned to celebrate Gods praises, in that Song *God is magnified for this,* as if it were one of his highest and chiefest attributes, *The Lord is a man of War:* The Creation is overlooked, and the first piece of praise given to God is, *The Lord is a Man of War.* Exod. 15.1,2,3. *I will sing to the Lord, for he hath triumphed gloriously, the horse and his Rider hath he cast into the Sea, the Lord is a Man of War, the Lord is his name.*

In this Chapter[5] we have the first mention in sacred Story of any warlike exploit; not but that there had been war before, as is implyed in the beginning of the Chapter, the Kings of *Sodom* and *Gomorrah,* had served *Chedarlaomer* twelve years, in the thirteenth year they rebelled, in the fourteenth year, he with three other Kings makes War upon them, and he overcomes them and takes *Lot* Captive; and this is the first mention of any Battle fought, and as eminent an instance of valour in Abraham and his Army, as is in the whole Book of God; for though Gideon and three hundred men fought with a great Army, yet there was a great deal more Strategem on his part: his pitchers with lamps in them, being broken in the night, put a fright on the enemy; but Abraham fairly won his battel with dry blows.[6] It is the first exploit of a Christian Souldier being in arms, or of a religious Captain, with his army of Religion and arms joyned together, this account of Abrahams arming his own Servants.

In this piece of Story, four things are hinted,

1. The Occasion of Abrahams armining his Souldiers at this time; *When Abraham heard that his brother Lot was taken Captive.*

2. We have an account of the Generall of the Army in this undertaking of War, and that is *Abraham.*

3. We have an account of his Souldiers, 1. The number of them, *they were three hindred and eighteen.* 2. The Quality of them [,] they were *trained men,* they had their arms ready, and skil to make use of them: He [Abraham] presently takes arms, he had not arms to seek, nor men to learn how to make use of them; but every thing was ready, fit to pursue and overtake the enemy.

4. We have the success of it, with the consequents thereof: the success, he recovers his Brother Lot, beats the enemy, wins a compleat victory[,] takes all the Captives. The Consequents of it were.[:]

1. He gets a Blessing of *Melchizedech* for it. Melchizedech that was eminently a Type of Jesus Christ.[7] God did so far own and encourage Abraham in this undertaking that he would not let this action go without a special Blessing, to encourage Souldiers in a lawfull War. He hath the special blessing of Christ; it is more than if an Angel had done it. Melchizedech so eminently representing Jesus Christ, who is a Priest for ever after the order of Melchizedech.

2. His Restauration of the goods and persons to the King of Sodom, in which he shews as much of nobleness or gallantry of spirit, as in fighting with *Chedarlaomer.* The King of Sodom offers Abraham to take the goods, if he would restore the persons. No saith Abraham, I will not take the least from a thread to a shoe latchet, lest the King of Sodom should say, he hath made Abraham rich. It shews it was not for gain or advantage he had ventured his life, his spirit was above it. It was not any reward from men that he expected, but was contented with the blessing of God, that rich blessing which he got. It was a great piece of praise (but in a bad cause) of *Sisera's* [soldiers], that came to the waters of *Tanach* and fought, [that] they took no gain of money:[8] had it not been in a bad cause, it had been an high commendation of them[,] but it was in a wicked Cause, and so they lost the praise that otherwise had belonged to them. Those souldiers of Jesus Christ, that valued not their lives to the death, will shew themselves to be of that same spirit that Abram was, that will not so much look at gain, or reward of men, as the advancement of a good Cause.[9]

But to hint something to you from the words,

1. From the occasion of Abrahams taking up arms, *when Abram heard his brother Lot was taken Captive,* or his Nephew, he was his brothers son, it was for the rescue of his Kinsman. To take up arms for the defence of friennds and Allies is lawfull. To take up arms for such as are confederate with us, for united Colonies or Provinces from this example of Abraham and his confederate[s], that were engaged in a league, offensive and defensive; So *Anar, Eshcol* and *Mamre* were confederate with him. Though there be not an expression of such a league, yet there was a great friendship and relation between him and *Lot;* and through Abrams wisdome, they parted lovingly, though they did part and could not live together, therefore Abram engaged in a War for the rescue of *Lot* and his Family.[10]

1. Hence our late War was justifiable, though the Quarrel was firstly with our neighbours.[11]

2. Hence consequently, it is lawfull by war to defend what we lawfully obtained and come by, as our possessions, lands, and inheritance here, to which we have as fair a title as any ever had, since Israels title to Canaan. Theirs was not only a gift of Providence, but of Promise. Ours we can call only a gift of Providence, but yet such as we may lawfully defend. As Jephtah said to the Children of Ammon, *What Chemosh thy God gives thee to possess, wilt thou not possess it?*[12] So what God hath providentially given us, without injury to other, is that which we may lawfully defend.

There are commonly reckoned three causes of War,

1. For defence of our selves.

2. To recover what hath been taken away.

3. To punish for injuries done. But to pass by the occasions of the War; through the goodness of God we have peace. Abram armed his trained servants, or Souldiers, three hundred and eighteen: the number was small to encounter with four Kings such as they were[,] *Chedarlaomer* being supposed to be *Nimrod's* successour, and *Tubal* King of Nations, could not be a mean Prince, or have a small number of Souldiers, so that three hundred and eighteen men must in reason be but a very small handfull or number to encounter with such an Army, an Army heightend with success, flushed with victory over the five Kings of Sodom and Gomorrah, and those neighbouring cities. They had a great Army for number, in probability though it be not expressed, they

had an army that was heightened with success, their spirit & courage was [heightened] which makes men abundantly more considerable. Take men flushed with success[,] they will undertake any thing, though very hazardous. Here was but a little handfull to goe out against such an army. But what is it that a few men will not dare to doe, if the Cause, the Courage, the Conduct be but like that of Abram[?]

But to note some things from the words, *Abram armed his trained Servants:* Abram was eminent in his place,

1. For preparation before War, his servants were trained men.

2. For his carriage in the business and management of it, when he undertook it.

I shall speak chiefly to the first of these.

*Doctr.*[13] *That the Training of Souldiers to be fit for War, is a commendable practice, yea a Duty of Great Consequence, or not of the lowest rank,* or thus,

*Frequent Trainings for the instructing of men in military Discipline that they may be ready and expert for War, is a commendable practice, yea a Duty which God expecteth of all Gods Abrahams in their respective places*[:] that is, by Gods Abrahams in their respective places, I mean such as are meerly civil Rulers, to encourage such exercises by their authority and presence, when convenient. Such as are military officers, it is their duty actually to instruct men; such may be supposed to represent Abraham, and God doth expect it from them, that they should take care of this part, which *Abraham* acted so happily to so good end; And which is the consequent of this second Doctrine, It is the duty of those that would be accounted of Abrahams Family to learn of them, when God requires to teach them the use of their weapons, and order of War. If it be Abrahams duty to teach, it is the duty of Abrahams servants, [(] those that represent them[)] to learn of those God sets over them, the use of their weapons, and the order of War, that they may be expert for War. It is a commendation of a people or of souldiers to be expert for war, that which the Scripture frequently mentioneth, I shall look but to two places, 1 *Chron.* 12.33,35,36. in many verses of that Chapter, *Of Zebulun such as went forth to battle, expert for War, with all instruments of war, fifty thousand that could keep rank.* Here was *Training* up men to be expert and fit for War. And so in the following verse, *of the Danites, expert for War, twenty eight thousand, of Asher such as went forth to battle, expert in War, fourty thousand.* In that Song of Solomon, *Cant.* 3. 7,8. *Behold his bed which is Solomons, threescore valiant men are about it, of the valiant of Israel, they all hold swords, being expert in War. Every man hath his sword upon his thigh, because of fear in the night.*[14] It is an high Commendation of any people, when care is taken by Rulers, and people are willing to learn, and hearken to Rulers, that they may be instructed to be expert in war. It is a part of the general Calling, whereto God calls every man that is capable (not impotent[15] men nor children, but according to that time the Scripture reckoneth[,] from twenty years and upward [)] all that were ready to go forth to war. It is not a thing by the by, but that which men should make their business. It is a duty and praiseworthy piece of skill, to be *expert for war.* To be good souldiers is a matter of praise or honour, which made the Apostle use it in a spiritual sence, *therefore my Son endure hardness as a good souldier of Jesus Christ.* 2 Tim. 2.3.[16] It is a strange piece of dotage befallen this crazy-headed age, that men should not use the sword:[17] the best of men have done it, and it hath been reckoned among their most praiseworthy actions, that they have used the sword. Of some it is said, that *their hands did cleave to their swords* they were so much in the use of it[,] so happily for the advantage of the Church.[18] The Apostle to the *Hebrews Cap.* 11.33, 34[,] when he makes mention of the Worthyes, he mentioneth these two together, *Who through Faith subdued Kingdoms, wrought righteousness;* they two may well go together: that is reckoned one of the great works of their Faith; there is not anything wherein the glory of the Faith of many Believers did more shine forth, then in the use of it in War.[19] There is no higher occasion ordinary or outward, wherein we have a higher opportunity or use for Faith, & other Graces. A Souldier may be and should be an holy man, and the more fit he is for a Souldier. But that it is a duty of great Consequence, I shall speak to the Doctrine in these two parts.[20]

1. It is a commendable practice.

2. It is the duty of Gods Abrahams to have a care of this work to instruct Souldiers that they may be fit for War:

I. It is a commendable practice [;] that may appear in four or five things.

1. In that the Lord himself doth claim the honour of it: if it were not an honourable work, God would not challenge the honour of it, *He teacheth my hands to war, and my fingers to fight.*[21] Military skill is such a piece of divine wisdome, that the Lord will not loose the honour of it. If every good and perfect gift be from him [,] he doth challenge every good and perfect gift as from him, but peculiarly claims the honour of this gift, of giving Military skill: God is the Author of it, *The Lord is a Man of War, the Lord is his Name.* That the Lord doth claim the honour of it, I might shew you by induction of Particulars by instances. Every thing, every part that belongeth to a Souldier, God challengeth or claims as being from him, every thing that is honourable or praise-worthy,

1. The giving Spirit and Courage to men, of raising up the Spirits of men, that he claims as being from him. *Jer.* 51, [.]11. *Make bright the arrows, gather the shields: the Lord hath raised up the Spirits of the King of the Medes.*[22] He raiseth up mens spirits, when they are raised up for war; God hath a hand in it.

2. God challengeth this, he teacheth to make weapons of War and the use of them. God doth not only give spirits to such as work, but teacheth the framing and making of weapons, and hath a hand in the whetting and furbishing of them. He directeth the Smith to form or frame weapons for war, *Isai.* 54. 16, 17. to shew that he hath the ordering and the use of weapons. *Behold I have created the Smith that bloweth the coal in the fire, and that bringeth forth an instrument for his work. And I have created the Waster to destroy, and no weapon that is formed against thee shall prosper.*[23] God useth it as an Argument to encourage his people to trust in him, there is no weapon of War, but I do direct the making of it. He whets the sword, and furbisheth it to the battel. *If I whet my glitering sword, and my hand take hold on vengeance,* Deut. 32. 41.[24] He looks to the forming of the weapons, He teacheth men the ordering of the battel: God doth give that wisdome also to the Sons of men, he teacheth them by the order of his own Host, the Stars: But more especially he provideth a Captain for his own Host, *Josh.* 5.14. *It came to pass, when Joshua was by Jericho, he lift up his eyes and looked, and behold there stood a man over against him with a sword drawn in his hand; and Joshua went to him and said unto him, Art thou for us or our adversaries? And he said nay, but as Captain of the*

*Host of the Lord am I now come.*[25] It was an Angel appeared. When any Host of his is called forth the Lord doth take care, as he did for Israel, when he intended to possess them of Canaan he sent his Angel to goe along with them; for he came to be as Captain of the Lords Hosts. And therefore that good King encourageth the people, *the Lord is with us to fight our Battels.* He hath a hand in ordering the battel, 2 *Chron.* 32.8.[26] He appeareth eminently in the day of Battel, raising the spirits on the one side, and taking it [*sic* them] away from the other. *The Race is not to the swift, nor the Battle to the strong*[;] God over-rules it, gives it where he pleases, It is the Lord of Hosts that mustereth the Host of the Battle. *Isa.* 13.4,5. *The noise of a multitude in the mountains, like as the noise of a great people, a tumultuous noise of the Kingdoms of nations gathered together: the Lord of Host* [*s*] *mustereth the Host of the Battle, they come from a far country, from the end of heaven, even the Lord, and the weapons of his indignation.*[27] And therefore we have this as a frequent expression, *The Battle is the Lords,* & hath been used for encouragement by those that have been Commanders of the People of God, when in any eminent danger, *Be not afraid for the Battle is the Lords.* 1. *Sam.* 17.47. That the Battle is the Lords, appears by Gods turning the battle by such a small accident as he doth frequently: one stone directed right, casteth the day, as it was with the Philistines fighting against Israel. One arrow drawn at a venture smote the King of Israel between the joints of the harness, and that one stroke turns the day.[28] God covers the head in the day of Battle, God particularly saith in every thing, He hath a hand in it, in forming weapons, giving Skill, raising the Spirit. God hath a hand in it, and eminently in this, in *Covering the Head in the day of Battle.*[29] How neer doe the Bullets or instruments of death come [,] but God covers the head in the day of Battle: Therefore it is a commendable thing to teach and instruct men to be expert for War, because God hath so great a hand in it, and doth claim the honour of it.

2. The wisest of Rulers, and holiest of men, have been still carefull about this duty and work, in the seting of this part [of] making preparation for War, in Peace, and in order to it, instructing men in the use of weapons; the holyest, the best, and wisest of men have alwayes had a care about it. *David* made a Law, *he commanded them to teach Israel the use of the bow.* 2 Sam. 1.

18. By that weapon the Worthyes of Israel fell [,] Saul and Jonathan. David made a Law of it, to teach the use of that particular weapon, that had been so destructive to the Church of God. Abraham *Trains* his Servants, Jacob that was so eminent for holiness, was skilfull in the use of his sword & bow; he won a parcel of land by it, that he gave to Joseph, by Will at his death. *Gen.* 48. *ult.* [A]nd that he taught his children the use of it is apparent by the ill use of it, made by Simeon and Levi. He had both used it himself, was expert in the use of it, had won a considerable portion of the country by it, and had taught it to his children, It was apparent they were so ready at it.[30] Solomon, that wise man, though he enjoyed such peace in his dayes, that it is said, there was no adversary, nor evil occurrent, yet none made greater preparation for War then Solomon did: the Scripture speaks of it as his commendation, to make such preparation for war:[31] so that the holyest, and wisest of men have still had a care about this.

3. The common practice of Nations, in all ages, where the Rulers have been prudent, have had a care of this: and the Scripture brandeth those with infamy that have failed in it. The men of Laish were secure; in the Book of Judges, the Danites had not taken up their inheritance, they sent men to Laish *Judg.* 18.7. *Then the five men departed, and came* [*to*] *Laish and saw the people that were therein therein* [*sic*] [,] *how they dwelt carelessly after the manner of the Zidonians,* quiet and secure, & had no business with any man, they made no provision for war, promised themselves peace: these were a people fit for destruction it was reckoned their great folly and shame.[32] That that was a means to their destruction, we may be abundantly furnished from holy Writ, as well as humane Writing, with examples of the care, both of the people of Israel, and other nations, looking carefully after this matter. *The number of Israel, from twenty years old and upward, all that were able to goe forth to War:*[33] it implyes the Children of Israel with their Rulers, had regard to this to know who were capable to go forth to War. The number of Israel was still taken from their Muster Rolls; therefore it was committed to the military Officers still to take the number of the people, Joab the General and so the inferiour officers, were sent out to take the number of the people, and they were reckoned from twenty years old and upward, all that were able to go out to War.[34]

4. The irrational creatures, when sent by God in way of Judgment, act as if they were under Military Conduct, which shews that it is an advantagious thing to carry on a design. *Ioel* 2.7.[35] We read of the Caterpillars & the Locusts, & the Canker-worm, God would send them [as] a great Army, they should be like the noise of Chariots on the tops of mountains, like the noise of a flame of fire that devoureth stubble as a strong people set in battle array, they shall run like mighty men and climb the wall like men of war, and they shall march every one on his wayes, they shall not break their Rank. God doth by it commend military order to rational persons, when he tells us the irrational creatures sent by him in way of Judgment, to accomplish such designs as he by his Providence intendeth, when they shall march in this manner, it doth commend to us, that Order used in War; Military Discipline is greatly advantagious, in that God gives that instinct even to irrational creatures, when he makes use of them that they come in such a manner.

5. The field or Camp hath been famous for the accomplishment of all sorts of men; it hath ripened parts to that height, that it made many the wonders of the world in their Age.

II. It is not only a commendable practice, but it is a duty.

1. The Law of nature, which teacheth man self-preservation, requireth this as a means for that end. [W]hatsoever is needfull for our defence is a duty, it requires and enjoynes whatsoever is a means for that end; so that acquaintance with or the exercise of ourselves in the use of arms, or other parts of military exercise, may be enforced from that Commandment which requires men to use all means to preserve life, to defend themselves[.] [I]t were to no end to make a law requiring duty, if to our might we should not use the proper means for our own preservation[.] Let but a Prince never so great tread upon a worm, and it will turn; they have that instinct in them to defend themselves. There are our Rights both as Men, and as Christians, our civil Rights and Libertyes as Men and our religious Liberties and Rights as Christians; both which we are to defend with the sword, as far as we are able, or to commit ourselves to God in the way of duty in doing of it. There is such a thing as Liberty and Property given to us, both by the Laws of God & Men[;] when they are invaded, we may defend ourselves.[36] God hath not given great ones in the world that absolute power over men, to devour them at pleasure,

as great Fishes do the little ones; he hath set Rulers their bounds & by his Law hath determined peoples libertyes and property. He that rules over men must be just, that is should be so, ruling in the fear of God: therefore Kings are commanded to read the Book of the Law, because it is a boundary of their authority, as well as of the peoples liberty. *Naboths* Vineyard taken away by *Ahab* in that manner as it was, was revenged by God on *Ahab* and *Jezebel* too.[37] If we have that that is our Right and Due, it is not anothers being stronger can make our Right Null and void: therefore that Law that gives us a Right, requires attendance on the work of this day,[38] that is Martial exercise, in order to the defence of ourselves by Arms, when the providence of God puts us upon it.

2. God by his providence keeps some Nations and people unsubdued, as he did with Israel of old[:] he kept some people unsubdued on purpose to teach Israel War. So the Lord hath dealt with us by his Providence here in this wilderness, *these are the Nations which the Lord hath left to prove Israel by,* those that had not known the War of Canaan, only that the generations might know to teach them War. *Judg.* 3. 1,2. It was the duty of Israel therefore to learn, that they might be expert for war. So the Lord hath dealt with us, though he hath given us a good Country, yet not that full possession, but that there are some which our sad experience hath taught us, they have been left to teach us war, and therefore it is a duty to keep up such military exercises, as may make us expert for War.

3. Our Saviour Christs Command is an Argument that it is a Duty, *he that hath not a Sword, let him sell his garment and buy one.* Luk. 22.36.[39] which doth infer the learning, the use of it, or whatsoever is needfull to defend our selves in troublesome times. It is the duty and wisdome of any people to put themselves in such a posture as they may be fit to defend themselves: and our Saviours Command, shows also the use of a sword is as needfull as a garment [:] he that hath not a sword, let him sell his Garment and buy one. Also when our Saviour tells us *in the latter dayes there shall be Wars and Rumors of Wars,* more in these dayes than at other times,[40] it is to teach us that wisdome, that we may be found fitted and prepared to act our parts in our day. Millittary Skill ought to be taught & learned in the latter dayes more then at other times.

4. Our Military Strength is, under God, the appointed means, or in the ordinary way of Providence, is the proper and only means for our preservation; therefore it is a duty to encourage Souldiers. God can work miracles, but when ordinary means may be had, he will not work miracles.[41] When Israel came out of Egypt, God did take the Battle into his own hand. So frighted as they were with Egypts following of them in a better posture for War then they, so low as their spirits were brought by hard bondage, God did miraculously fight for them, and destroy Pharaoh; but when it is otherwise with the People of God, that they have time to furnish themselves, the Lord doth direct us to use them[42] and they are the only means of our preservation, they are the only walls and bulwarks of Gods Herititage [*sic*] here. Gods vineyard hath no other walls, but only our Souldiery, that and our Poverty. We have no walled towns, as they have in other places, our Forts and Castles are contemptible[.] We have not any bank of money to hire souldiers: our strength by Sea is small, & for firendship & favour in the world with any that should help us is not much, or our friends lye too far off to help us in time of need; so that we have nothing left us but only this, First that Hedge which God made about Job,[43] 2. As to means it is only that wall of Bones (as one calls it) better then a wall of Stones, our Souldiers, which, howsoever it may seem weak to some, yet as when God made the fear of Jacob and his Family fall on the Nations, not one of them durst rise up to disturb Jacob and his Family. The resolution that appear'd in Simeon and Levi, together with the fear of God, begat such an awe and dread of that little Family on the Country round about, they knew they were resolute men, and would sell their lives dear; this as a means had a great influence upon all round about, that none did dare pursue Jacob;[44] but this hath been our defence. Souldiers have been the Wall, the Strength, the Glory of this little Commonwealth; the name of our military Skill, our readiness & expertness in military exercises, is that for which we have been famed abroad in other countryes, both among the Dutch and French. What the Governour of *Manadus* saw in that little time when he was here, gave us no small credit in *Holland.*[45] What made the Indians live quietly by us so long? they had hatred to us many years before it broke out. What was the reason it did not break out? they saw we had skill, that Skill in Military Discipline which they understood not:

that was an awe and dread to them, and is at this day, that they dare not meet us on equal terms.[46]

*USE.* 1. *Hence it is no wayes unbecoming a Christian to learn to be a Souldier,* not only a Spiritual Souldier but in the true proper sence of the letter. To be a Souldier is a Credit, a praise and a glory, to be a good Souldier; it is so not only to men but to us as Christians, to have this added to us, to be good Souldiers. It was a part of Abrahams praise and glory that he acted the part of a Souldier so honourably, Nay it is a duty, not a piece of indifferency, but a point of Duty, a praiseworthy part, he that learns and acts his part honourably. There is such agreement between the Spiritual and temporal Warfare, that everything belonging to a Souldier, is made use of to resemble some Grace or Duty of a Christian, something belonging to a Christian. Nothing of what is outward, but what may be made some Spiritual and good use of: As Solomon saith, *I beheld the Vineyard of the Slothfull, & from thence I learned Instruction.*[47] There is nothing belonging to a Souldier but be sure some spiritual use may be made of it, all the parts of his Armour, every one doth exceedingly well set out some Grace or duty of a Christian, *put on the Armour of God,*[48] there he shews how every thing belonging to a Souldier did set forth something which a good man should learn and have. All his weapons[,] all his motions [and] policy in War are made use of to instruct a Christian in some act of Religion: the Church Militant is therefore compared to an Army with Banners, for Order and for terribleness *Cant.* 6.4, 10.[49] Again, John Baptist gives directions to Souldiers on their address to him to be content with their wages or hire: every one would know their duty, their instruction was to be content with their hire, the work was warrantable, and instruction is given, for the better ordering of it.[50]

*USE* II. *Hence they are to blame, that either wholly neglect, or slight over this work.* If this be so becoming a Christian, they are greatly to blame that do neglect it, or slight over it, do not make conscience of it, in endeavoring to fit themselves, or to teach others to be expert for War: what we have suffered by it, is a sufficient Argument to press this; some have their Arms to seek, when their houses, or the Towns are beset; others are so rusty they cannot be used: these are uncomely things, the want of Arms, or the unfitness of them for the work and service God calls to: It is a great evil to have them defective: Abrahams Souldiers were ready immediately on notice, they had not their arms to seek, Abraham was not to buy them, they were ready to pursue and follow the enemy; they were not to *Train* them, to learn to know their order and Rank, but were fitted and prepared being *Trained* before.

*USE.*III. *Of Exhortation to this Duty, that Abraham was so carefull about, the* Training *of his Servants:* under which,

1. I would propound some Considerations yet fourther to excite and stir up to it,

2. Some Directions: more particularly, 1. To such as represent Abraham, Rulers in the Commonwealth, both civil and military. 2. To such as Abrahams Servants inferiour Officers and Souldiers.

1. *Some Considerations as a means to excite and stir up to this duty to be fit for War.*

1. The highest piece for Service that ever Souldiers were employed in is yet behind,[51] and is commonly believed not to be very far off: the highest service that ever was done for the Lord Jesus Christ is yet behind, the destruction of *Gog and Magog,* so the enemies of the Church are called in Scripture; whether it be Pope or Turk, or whoever else is meant, that shall oppose the advancement of the Kingdome of Christ:[52] God doth intend his Son shall be known and proclaimed as *King of Nations,* as well as *King of Saints, he will take to him his great power and reign, and the Kingdomes of this world shall bcome the Kingdomes of our Lord & of his Christ* [;][53] the Lamb will have followers such as shall not love their lives to the death, he hath work to do in the world; and work that is even at the door is commonly believed[54] [;] and therefore we should be exhorted to be the Servants waiting for our Lord. *The Lord Jesus is not coming to send peace on the Earth, but the Sword;*[55] Reformation never went on yet without it; Look at it in *Germany* or *Holland,*[56] or where ever else there hath been any attempt first or last, there hath been something of a War for the defence of it, or for laying the Foundation [;] the Sword will be drawn upon Christs account, and therefore that consideration should stir us up to keep up this military Skill or Exercises, that we may be the better fitted for it.

2. Our own greatest tryals seem to me to be behind,[57] & that for several Reasons. I apprehend we shall not live quiet long, or

at least we have no Reason to promise ourselves that we shall, on these accounts.

1. There are none of the Princes of note in *Europe* that have any interest in *America,* but have long had their Espyals upon us, as I might easily demonstrate, but the reason of the thing it self is sufficient to convince us of this, [:] no Merchant but observeth anothers motions and actions, trading and advantage that he makes, no Husbandman but hath his eye on his Neighbour, to see how he profiteth by his labour and pains, that he may do the like; So it is in other things, no Plantation[58] goes on and thrives, but they that have neighbouring plantations are looking on it and observing it, our own dayly observation may be sufficient to make us believe this, there is not a small Island in *America,* but the Princes or States of *Europe* are striving for it, as we see the other day for *Tobago,* St. *Christophers,* &c.[59] If these be looked after what can we expect?

2. *Rome* will have no peace with you, and you ought to have no peace with it, and that *Rome's* Agents are abroad at work is plain, from that fire-light we have seen in the world, if the Beasts deadly wound should ever be healed, that we read of in *Rev.* 13 we are like to feel the Influence of it, if their Councels should happen to sway the world, it is a vain thing for us to promise ourselves peace.[60]

3. The sins of *New-England* increase, *iniquity doth abound, and the Love of many doth wax cold,*[61] and therefore trouble will be, usually the sword is one means, by which God punisheth this sin in his people, and therefore probably yet more of it.

4. The Inhabitants of the land will not joyn or mix with us to make one Body, which is the more likely they are preferred to be thorns in our sides. When *Hamor* and *Sichem* propounded a firm peace with Jacobs Family, they cry *Let us marry together and make one nation* or people: a Policy used by the *French* at this day, not far from us, they may think thereby to escape some scourge that hangs over them; the issue of which we must leave to God. When God intended the Canaanites to be destroyed, he did forbid Israel to marry with them: they were to be thorns to them, and Israel was to root them out in the conclusion:[62] therefore frequent trouble, we may probably and rationally reckon of, to meet with from the heathen. Two Nations are in the womb and will be striving. That is a second consideration, we must ei-

ther learn to defend ourselves, or resolve to be vassals.[63] It is a base spirit that of Issachar, a strong Ass couching between two burdens, he saw that rest was good, and the land was pleasant, and bowed his shoulders to bear, and became a Servant to tribute.[64] So servile are some, that they will pay tribute to heathens, rather than endure a little difficulty.[65] Low spirited men, let them have Issachars lot, that make his choice [.]

3. The World, however pride and lust dispose them to quarrel, yet are not disposed to breed up souldiers,[66] there is such abounding of intemperance, or debauching that doth wound mens Consciences, and in the day of danger and trouble will fly in their faces, wounded Consciences will be felt then, as it was in the case of Josephs brethren, when they were in distress, they cry, *we are verily guilty concerning our Brother:*[67] many humane stories might be mentioned for the confirmation of this. Take one. A Captain in the Low Countryes challenged Major General *Skippon,* the Lord *Veer* hearing of it, told them, to morrow I intend to assault such a Town, and then I shall see who will be the best Souldier: accordingly a breach being made in the Wall, this Bravado was commanded to enter, but would not, saying, I am not fit to dye.[68] Conscience will fly in mens faces, when they have eminent apprehensions of death. [A] man that did not know how to put on his Spur right, if an honest man, was wont to be accounted a fitter person to make a Souldier, then those that would cry *God damn me* at every word, that slight and despise Hell, and eternal Damnation. Intemperance, Luxury,[69] filthiness, and uncleaness in the world doth so debauch men, they are not like to breed up Souldiers for Christ, to do service for Christ, *he that striveth for Mastery must be temperate in all things.*[70] I will tell you how we breed up Souldiers, both in Old England and New, every Farmers Son, when he goes to Market-Town, must have money in his purse; and when he meets with his Companions, they goe to the Tavern or Ale-house, and seldome away before Drunk, or well tipled. It is rare to find men that we can call Drunkards, but there are abundance of Tiplers in *New-England.* This makes Youth effeminate and wanton, besides the injury to mens Consciences; this doth make men not so bold, *The Righteous are bold as a Lion.* Prov. 28.1.

It hath been a question whether Atheisme or Piety have made the better Souldiers? [L]ate experience as well as this of

*Abraham* doth teach us, that a well established Conscience, is better than a seared Conscience to fill a man with Courage[;] some fill themselves with drink, to make them forget the fear of death, but *David* that was a couragious Souldier, knew no way so fit to animate his spirit as to go to the promise of God; to encourage himself in God, fulness of Corn and wine cannot heighten and raise the spirits of men, so as assurance of the love of God. *Psal.* 4.6,7. Faith in the promises, is above all such means as the poor simple sinfull world useth. That Atheisme cannot do so much as a good Conscience, may appear from two Reasons.

1. Because an Atheist hath no assurance of a Reward, whereas a Believer hath. That should make a Believer more couragious, because he is sure of a Reward: when a man goes to the Battle it is uncertain whether he shall out-live the Battle, and also it is uncertain whether he shall have the victory; and if either of these happen, an Atheist hath no reward if he loose the day or loose his life: but a true Christian is assured of his Reward. He that doth what he doth, as service to God *we know our labour is not in vain* in the Lord, he must needs be the better spirited for his work.[71]

2. A true Christian is a gainer by Death; it is not so with an Atheist, *To me to dye is gain*, Phil. 1. 21.[72] Therefore saith Solomon, *the day of Death is better then the day of a mans Birth*, viz. to the Saints, because there is an end of all a mans sin and sorrow, and the beginning of his never ending Joy.[73] He that fighteth in the Faith of this, must needs out doe one that hath no such expectation: an Atheist reckoneth of nothing in the world to come, he can beleive for no reward in the world to come, that thinketh there is no God; He cannot be so adventurous in looking Death in the face, as he that knows he shall be a Gainer by Death. It is Hope that animateth all our work. The heathen that had not true peace of Conscience, yet had some sence of the natural Conscience excusing, and doe express it in a strange manner.[74] What is it such a man needs to fear? [I]t is not all the violent storms he can be in or the hazzard by them: not the cruelty of Tyrants, nor though the world should rush together. It is but an Heathen speech, but expresseth a strange apprehension they had of the benefit of peace of natural Conscience: they know not peace with God. A man that is whole and sound within, may better look Death in the Face, then any other, from any Consid-

eration[.] The Psalmist expresseth it in another manner, *Psal.* 112. 7. *He shall not be afraid of evil Tidings, his heart is fixed trusting to the Lord.*

2. To come to some *Directions.*

1. To such as represent Abraham, Rulers in the Commonwealth, both Civil and Military; God expecteth from you that you should act Abrahams part. 1. I would speak a few works of Encouragement to you. 2. By way of Direction. For *Encouragement.*

1. Through the goodness and favour of God, you have a people under you that have Spirit and Courage enough, that have a large share of that: a great blessing to this country, a mercy that we have all cause to bless God for: there hath rather been an excess of Courage then defect or want of it; most of our losses have been occasioned meerly by it.[75] You have men full of activity and Courage, forward enough, notwithstanding danger. You have a People bred up in this Country, that have the heart of Lions, I *Chron.* 12.8. Or Lion-like men. I *Chron.* 11.22.[76] What is said of the Horse, one may by way of similitude apply to men, *He mocks at fear, he is not afraid, neither turns he back from the sword.* Job. 39. 22–25. I speak this because I have seen and heard something myself of the Courage of Souldiers, that hath been better and more refreshing then the greatest Daintyes or Feast could be: to see the hearts of men raised in danger, rather than cast down with it. The spirits of men to be raised and heightned in danger, if we had the Mines of *Mexico* and *Peru,* it would not be such a mercy and blessing to the Country as this is.

2. They can endure hardness, that is another thing by way of encouragement to Rulers, that is a great mercy. A tender, softly, effeminate People is a curse and misery, when God is pleased to frame a people to be such. And by the way, I might encourage Rulers, Governours and Parents to train & bring up their Children in such manner that they may endure *Hardness.* Tho' Isaac was a great Prince, as the king of the Philistines acknowledged him, yet when he sent away Jacob, he sent not so much as a Servant with him; he took of the stones, & made a pillow of them; it was a hard pillow, had no feathers in it; but when he had the hardest night's lodging, he had the best night's rest. *He saw a Vision of a ladder reaching to heaven:* it was as comfortable a night as ever Jacob had.[77] Isaac was a Prince, acknowledged by the King of the Philistines, yet he brings up Jacob in such a manner,

that he should not complain of this hardness, to be sent out alone, to lye in the woods, & have nothing but a stone for his pillow, to have a piece of bread in his pocket, and water to drink, he did endure without murmuring and repining. It is probable his Father did not bring him up deliciously.

One leaving of *New-England,* did commend that to Parents. ["]You doe not know what hardness your Children may be called to.["][78]

By way of Advice, two or three words.

1. Require of all the exercise of *Trainings,* or attendance upon them: That Rulers should look unto[,] that they may have Souldiers ready for any Expedition. There are good Laws, but there needs a strictness in the execution of them.

2. Keep up martial Discipline: a Souldier is the worst of creatures that is not under Discipline, and such as are Commanders should look to that. You know the praise worthy example of the *Centurion, I say to one goe, and he goeth, and to another come, and he cometh.* Mat. 8.9.[79] Discipline is the life of the work. Captains are greatly to blame that are softly men, and do not hold their authority in the field. That which would be no fault, or might be winked at at home, should not be suffered in the Field.

3. Encourage your Horse, those exercises also. Foreign Princes know they can easily over-master you in Foot, but know not how to over-master you in Horse. They that have had an aking tooth at this place have been afraid of this; that have Foot-Souldiers enough at our backs, yet know not how to match us in Horse.[80]

4. Look with a favourable aspect upon, and afford your presence as much as may be, at such Meetings as are the work of this day. Encourage *Artillery-Trainings.* 1. It is a way and means to give encouragement to dilligent and expert Men, by giving them titles answerable to their activity and skill. In Grammar Schools, to be a Captain for a day, makes young Schollars strive at their Books. It is a way that affordeth opportunity to put honour and respect upon Men of activity, as their Diligence, Valour and activity calls for it. The Law of nature teacheth, that the virtuous Skil of any doth call for honour.[81] 2. It is a Nursery for Officers beyond our common Trainings or a better means to accomplish those that are Officers, *Artilery Meetings* consisting in a great

measure of such.[82] It is also a proper means for trying the Skill of Souldiers beyond what is at other times.

2. A few words to inferiour Officers and Souldiers, to such as represent Abrahams Servants, labour to be good Souldiers, and to that end, Fellow Souldiers, I would commend a few things, 1. Something to you as Christian Souldiers. 2. Something to you as Souldiers Literal, or men.

1. Something as Christian-Souldiers, only these two words,

1. Get Armour of proof *put on the whole Armour of God,* that is the way to make a good Souldier, to have his compleat Armour, Armour for his inward man; without there be a Guard to that, there will be a Failing: if the Conscience be wounded, or be not safe, if the *Breast-plate of Righteousness* be not on, if men have guilty Consciences, they will find and see the sad effects of it, when they come to be in danger, *Put on your spiritual Armour,* look to that *Breast-plate of Righteousness.*[83] I would commend the keeping of a good Conscience: with that Breast-plate a man may look Death in the Face. When the vitals are secured, a man that hath any Courage or Spirit will not vallue a scratch in the arm or leg. If a man have a good Brest-plate and large, sufficient to defend his life; and he that hath any spirit will venture his Limbs. Take care of your inward man therefore, as you would make good Souldiers. Look to your inward man, the Heart, that that be wel guarded and defended, that you have a good Brest-plate for the defence of that. Abraham first taught Piety: Engage God with you, and that would make a very coward fight. For a man to have his Conscience against him in the day of Battle, is a very sad thing, it frighteth a man far more than the enemy. *God is departed from me, and answereth me no more, and the Philistines are upon me:* That made the Philistines as bad as so many Devils to him.[84]

2. Be Temperate and endure hardness, do not live as if your great study were to please the flesh, one that is given to appetite will never credit the profession of a Souldier or himself.

2. A hint or two to you as Souldiers.

1. Be in subjection to [O]fficers, to those God sets over you: to dispute commands is unbecoming a Souldier, *I am a man under Authority, and say to one goe and he goes,* saith the *Centurion, Luk.* 7. [8].[85]

2. Goe to, or attend upon Trainings as those that do not

reckon it a Task, but account it your Recreation, and Priviledge, as those that have a mind to be expert in war. The Lord Jesus when he calls out any, they shall not be bunglers, it will not be long ere the Lord Jesus will call out Souldiers, those that he will use shall be expert for War, and therefore let us accustome ourselves to this work[;] that fatal blow at *Black-point* should make men love *Training;* the unreadiness they were in there, they were raw & undisciplined:[86] let us labour to be expert for War; to be like our General Iesus Christ. *The Lord is a Man of War.*

Lastly, look to your Arms, that becomes a Souldier to keep them fixed, and to be expert in the use of them, 2 *Sam.* 1. 18. according to that of David, *he commanded to teach them the use of the Bow.*[87]

---

FINIS.

---

# NOTES

1. Running the gauntlet was an ordeal suffered by some captives in which they were stripped naked and forced to run between two lines of Indians armed with cudgels or more deadly weapons. Humiliation in such an ordeal was certain, death likely if the beating was severe or if weapons were used. Nowell's use of the term invokes the readers' memory of his Indian-fighting past and plays humorously with the concept of the author as one who exposes himself or appears naked before a critical public.

2. That is, he hopes that those who find fault with the sermon for its style or theological argument will nonetheless try to mend the condition of military unpreparedness to which it is addressed.

3. Genesis, chapter 14, recounts the war between the king Chedorlaomer and his rebellious vassals, the kings of Sodom and Gomorrah (with some other cities). Abraham's brother Lot, a subject of the king of Sodom, was taken captive by Chedorlaomer's army and recaptured by Abraham, who mustered his armed servants and defeated Chedorlaomer's conquering army. Abraham took his booty to the camp of the king of Sodom, where he was blessed by Melchizedek (see note 8 below),

the king of Salem (later Jerusalem) and a "priest of the most high God." Content with this blessing of the Lord, Abraham refused to take any reward from the king of Sodom, "lest thou shouldest say, I have made Abram rich."

4. Exodus, 15:3.

5. "This Chapter" refers to Genesis, chapter 14 (the Abraham story), not to the chapter of Exodus cited just before.

6. Nowell here echoes the military doctrine of writers like Hubbard who characterized the Indian mode of forest warfare—which relied on ambushes and other strategems—as cowardly and devilish, and held that the whites should not abandon their regular order of fighting in the open simply to cope with such strategems.

7. Melchizedek's character is not as clearly defined as Nowell would have it: he is a Canaanitish priest-king, apparently a monotheist, but his deity is the Canaanite Elyon or the Phoenician Zidik.

8. Judges, 5:19.

9. Reference to the difficulties of recruiting soldiers during the worst period of the war; the government had to pay cash or land bounties to obtain sufficient soldiers, a practice that became traditional in military recruiting from the eighteenth through the beginning of the twentieth century. See Douglas Leach, *Flintlock and Tomahawk*, chap. 6.

10. Nowell is at great pains to justify the colonies' making war in concert after only one of their number was attacked. His care may seem excessive unless we remember that the colonies were, according to their organic charters, separate corporate entities: they shared interests both secular and religious and they shared a nationality, but they were not legally bound to support one another, and a royalist looking to the greater subjection of the colonies to the Crown might see in *any* confederation a clear threat—and might therefore want to claim that if the charters did not *require* confederation or unified military action, then they did not *permit* it. The legislative and executive acts which led to the confederation of the United Colonies were in a sense presumptive of power not explicitly granted by the Crown, and the application of the confederation's military force in war constituted a dramatic proof that the power so assumed would be exercised. The second part of the passage indicates that the union of the colonies was far from complete: Lot and Abram go their separate ways after the war, although they remained bound by a sentiment of unity in the face of external threat.

11. That is, the origin of the war was in a quarrel between Plymouth Colony ("our neighbours") and King Philip.

12. Judges 11:24. "Wilt thou not possess that which Chemosh thy God giveth thee to possess? So whomsoever the Lord our God shall drive out from before us, them will we possess." Chapter 11 recounts the victory of Jephthah over the Amorites. Jephthah held that it was legal for Israel to claim the land of the Amorites, refuting Amoritish critics

by saying that just as their God (Chemosh) had given them land, so now the Lord had given the land to Israel—the pagan god and law of conquest acting as precedent for the act of the scriptural deity. The whole of chapter 11 concerns the morality of taking land by conquest and planting one's people as a colony among the heathen. In 11:13–16, Jephthah answers Ammon in language appropriate to Puritans defending themselves against the accusation that they had stolen the Indian's land.

13. *Doctr.* means Doctrine: the second major rhetorical division in the sermon form (text, doctrine, reasons, uses).

14. Canticles frequently compares the "beloved" to an "army with banners" (6:10). Hugh Thomson Kerr (*The Interpreter's Bible*, vol. 4, p. 100) sees this recurrent metaphor as suggesting the "severity" of God's love and the love of God—an appropriate reading for a Puritan.

15. Impotent means debilitated or weak, not sexually impotent.

16. Nowell picks up the theme of "hardness" in his conclusion. The succeeding verse is also of interest and reinforces Nowell's equation of Puritan and soldierly virtues: 2 Tim. 2:4. "No man that warreth entangleth himself with the affairs of *this* life; that he may please him who hath chosen him a soldier." This is very close to the Puritan notion of the "calling," which saw the necessity for the saint to remain engaged in the world while heeding the injunction to "be not of it."

17. The Quakers are probably meant. As the dominant party in Rhode Island, the Quakers were political and religious opponents of consequence, whose reluctance to arm and fight before and during the war is here remembered. But Nowell may also be looking ahead to the looming conflict with England and the need for Puritan unity: as partisans of Rhode Island's claims, the Quakers would be a source of internal division; as pacifists, they would not aid should it come to armed conflict.

18. 2 Samuel, 23:10.

19. Nowell is not simply extending his earlier association of military and spiritual virtues (or "swords" and "faith"). He says that the "worthies" of Israel—prophets, judges and kings—fought for both spiritual or religious and secular or national objects, and that therefore it is as lawful for New England to defend its civil liberties as to defend its life or its religion. However, the verses themselves place a greater emphasis on the power of faith than on the power of the sword, which is nearly the reverse of what Nowell intends.

20. At this point the third or "Reasons" section of the sermon begins.

21. Psalms, 18:34. Challenge means claim.

22. Jer., 51:11. This chapter prophesies the destruction of Babylon by the Medes, which will avenge the subjection of Israel to Babylon. The situation parallels that of New England (Israel) and Old (Babylon), as Nowell sees it: the Crown seeks to oppress God's chosen people and their church, and the Lord promises his people vengeance and redemp-

tion. These passages relate closely to the timetable of the Apocalypse, when interpreted typologically: if Nowell's interpretation is valid, the imminence of Armageddon is indicated.

23. Isaiah, chapter 54, deals with the Lord's promises that Israel will be defended against its enemies and will rise to grandeur among the nations. Verses 2 and 3 are particularly apropos of Nowell's thesis about the meaning of the Indian war and the political struggle with England: "Enlarge the place of thy tent . . . For thou shalt break forth on the right hand and on the left; and thy seed shall inherit the Gentiles, and make the desolate cities to be inhabited."

24. Chapter 32 consists of a song of Moses on the theme of Israel's coming greatness as a nation, if the people will remember the goodness of the Lord in the days of the fathers and not run after strange gods. At the end of the chapter Moses is shown the Promised Land, which he will not enter but which is given to his people for their inheritance. The passage, in context, becomes a warning to Puritans to hold to their ancestors' course and a reminder that the "New-English Canaan" of the Gentiles is their promised portion.

25. Actually, Joshua, 5:13, 14.

26. Chronicles 32:8. "With us is the Lord our God to help us, and to fight our battles."

27. The chapter concerns the prophesied destruction of Babylon by the Medes.

28. The "stone directed right" is David's against Goliath; King Ahab was killed by the arrow "drawn at a venture" (1 Kings, 22:34).

29. Psalms, 140:7.

30. That Jacob taught his children the use of the sword is attested by the fact that it is said of Simeon and Levi that they made ill use of it—by implication, they had learned less well than their brothers. That he had taught it to his children is further attested by the fact that they were apparently "so ready at it" when fighting was demanded of them. Genesis 49:5–7 deals with Simeon and Levi.

31. 1 Kings, 4:26 and 10:26 may be meant.

32. The peoples referred to were despoiled by the tribe of Dan in the time when "there was no king in Israel"; the Danites had not yet come into the inheritance promised them as their portion in Israel. Hence the despoiling of the heathens of Laish parallels the seizure of Indian lands in the days before royal interference was felt in the New English Israel, the Puritan promised land.

33. The phrase is endlessly repeated in the Book of Numbers. Nowell's citation of the book is important to his argument for a military recruitment program linked to a census of able-bodied males, since it recounts the divine commandment to Moses and Aaron to number the people of Israel before embarking on the conquest of Canaan.

34. Here Nowell has begun to mix the language of New England military affairs (muster rolls, etc.) wtih biblical examples. He means to make the biblical example his model for a plan of recruitment. The ef-

fect of his proposals would have been a greater centralizing of authority in the colonial government, since the census could also be used to make taxation more efficient as well as increasing the rigor of the requirement of militia service. Nowell's plan looked toward a total reorganization of institutions and practices around the principle of military efficiency.

35. The prophecy of Joel concerns a vision of the Apocalypse, in which the coming of the Lord brings destruction and fear. The agent of divine judgment is a new nation, "strong, without number," "a great people and a strong; there hath not been ever the like," who devour the land with flame, leaving a wilderness; "The appearance of them is as the appearance of horses; and as horsemen, so shall they run." In an earlier verse, their coming is foreshadowed in the invasion of the crop-lands by the insects named also by Nowell in the rest of this passage. What Nowell has done is to confuse the invading "nation" with the "horses" they are said to resemble and the vermin that preceded their coming in order to show that irrational creatures use martial array when they are serving God's judgments. Joel, 1:4–6; 2:2–7.

36. Nowell's equation of civil and religious rights and his assertion that both are to be defended with the sword, represents the most militant Puritan stance against the encroachment of royal power. The "Prince" is of course the English king, Charles II. Note that Nowell grounds this part of his argument in analogies drawn from natural law—first seeing the natural order as a model for political action (in the example of the Prince and the worm), then contrasting the law of might in the animal kingdom with the law of limited government in the human, in the example of the fishes. However, the analogies should not obscure the fact that God, not some version of Natural Law, is the source of human rights for Nowell. See T. H. Breen, *The Character of the Good Ruler*, pp. 119–20.

37. The story of Ahab and Naboth is in 1 Kings 21. King Ahab desired Naboth's vineyard, and when Naboth refused to sell, Ahab's wife Jezebel used the royal seal to procure Naboth's death by stoning. Charles II is the "Ahab" in the controversy over taxation in New England, and in Naboth Nowell finds scriptural sanction for resistance to the king and protection of property.

38. That is, attendance to the officering, mustering, and training of the armed force of the colony.

39. Christ orders his disciples to get swords because he expects to be arrested by the priests and the Roman authority; Nowell, for his part, sees the coming war as involving an attack by the agents of Rome—either directly, via the Catholic French, or indirectly, via the crypto-Catholic Charles.

40. Matthew, 24:6, Mark, 13:7. These are signs of the coming of the Last Judgment, or of Armageddon (the last battle between good and evil); Nowell has the latter possibility in mind, certainly in a figurative way (the coming war will pit Protestant Puritan and Catholic in a final struggle for dominance) and possibly in a literal way.

41. A succinct statement of the basic assumption of Puritan science and historiography. See Miller and Johnson, eds., *The Puritans*, pp. 57–59, 729–33.

42. By "them" is meant "other or ordinary means," i.e., military art.

43. Job, 1:10. That "hedge" is to be removed by God so that Satan can test Job's faith by destroying his family and his prosperity. "Hast not thou made a hedge about him, and about his house, and about all that he hath on every side? . . . 11. But put forth thine hand now, and touch all that he hath, and he will curse thee to thy face." (10, 11). It is part of Nowell's argument that the "hedge" may soon be withdrawn from New England and the final trial of its faith be commenced.

44. Genesis, 34:25.

45. "*Manadus*" is probably "Manhattan" (Mannahatto)—either a corruption or Latinization of the name. The governor referred to may have been Peter Stuyvesant, who visited Boston in 1663 and 1664.

46. This runs counter to the thesis propounded by Increase Mather which was that the piety of the Puritan fathers had caused God to make the Indians afraid of them.

47. Proverbs, 24:30.

48. Ephesians, 6:11, 13.

49. The texts compare the "beloved" in the *Song of Solomon* to an "army with banners": the "Church Militant" is Nowell's extension of the symbolism.

50. Matthew, 8:9. This is also an implicit rebuke of those soldiers who would not enlist unless paid a bounty in land.

51. "Behind" in this instance means "hidden"; thus the sense of it is "yet to come" or "before."

52. Revelation, 20:8. The battle of Gog and Magog is a signal of the Second Coming. Nowell links "Pope and Turk" to the scriptural Gog and Magog and by implication couples Stuart England as well.

53. Matthew, 25:31–33; Rev., 2:26.

54. That is, the work of Armageddon is to begin soon. The Second Coming is imminent.

55. Matthew 10:34. The "sword" here is figurative, representing the sharp division to be made between those who have believed in Christ and those who have not when God makes his judgment.

56. The Reformation provoked religious wars in Germany and Holland in both the sixteenth and seventeenth centuries, especially the Thirty Years War of 1618–48.

57. As above, "ahead of us."

58. Plantation means colony.

59. These islands, like others in the West Indies, changed hands frequently during the wars and treaties of the seventeenth century. The British and French contested St. Christophers (St. Kitts); the English, French, Dutch, Spanish and others vied for Tobago.

60. Nowell leans heavily on interpreting Revelation for indications that the Second Coming is imminent. Chapter 13 tells of a blaspheming "beast" who was able to make successful "war with the saints, and to

overcome them" for a time, leading some into captivity; until God permits his destruction, and "He that leadeth into captivity shall go into captivity." This beast and his career correspond roughly to King Philip and his war, which was at first successful and yielded Christian captives, but ended in Philip's death and the enslavement of the Indians. A second beast then arises, who attacks (among other things) the economic and property rights of the saints: "And that no man might buy or sell, save he that had the mark, or the name of the beast, or the number of his name" (17). The second beast, of course, corresponds to England and the mercantile legislation.

61. Matthew, 24:12. Jesus speaks of the signs which will precede his Second Coming.

62. The prohibition against intermarriage with the Canaanites is in Joshua, 7:9 and also in Genesis 28:1, 6. The only alternatives for dealing with the Canaanites (and by analogy the Indians) were therefore either enslavement (Joshua, 17:3) or extermination.

63. Genesis, 25:23. "And the Lord said unto [Rebekah], Two nations are in thy womb, and two manner of people shall be separated from thy bowels; and *the one* people shall be stronger than *the other* people; and the elder shall serve the younger." The reference is to Jacob and Esau and the figure does double service for Nowell: as a metaphor of the struggle between New England and the Indians (holy Jacob and Esau the man of violence, the wanderer), in which the weaker people is enslaved by the stronger; and as an allusion to the struggle with England (the "elder" people), which will end by proving the superiority of New England (the "younger").

64. Genesis, 49:14. Issachar was condemned by Jacob because he consented to pay tribute; the condemnation would fit, according to Nowell, a New England that consented to be unjustly taxed by England.

65. Ostensibly the "heathens" are the Indians, whose neutrality or friendship the English had attempted to purchase with gifts, but "heathen" is an epithet equally suited to the non-Puritan English.

66. "Worldliness" does not produce soldiers or soldierly virtue.

67. Genesis, 42:21.

68. According to the *Dictionary of National Biography*, Sir Horace Vere (1565–1635) was an English soldier serving with the Dutch in the war of independence against Spain and France. Philip Skippon (d. 1660) served under Vere at Maastricht in 1629, but earned his greatest fame as a commander of Parliamentary (Puritan) troops in the English Civil War. He was also the author of three religious tracts, in which he refers to himself as "The Christian Centurion." Nowell's frequent references to the "centurion" who appears at the Crucifixion as a model of Christian character suggests an admiration of Skippon's writings (as does the citation of the anecdote) and his soldierly character. The anecdote also contrasts the aristocratic code of the duel with the bourgeois concept of soldierly virtue (service to the cause and the army rather than to personal fame or honor), to the advantage of the latter.

69. Lechery.

70. 1 Corinthians, 9:25; 2 Timothy, 2:5.

71. Isaiah, 65:23.

72. "For me to live *is* Christ, and to die *is* gain."

73. Ecclesiastes, 7:1.

74. The "natural conscience" of the heathen has not been infused with the knowledge of divine revelation or the power of grace. Their testimony to the desire for a good conscience is used in much the same way as the earlier analogies between the behavior of men and of the "unreasoning creatures"—as a way of bringing extrascriptural evidence to bolster revelation.

75. The most striking example would be the loss of officers in the Swamp Fight.

76. The "Lion-like men" of the first quote were David's soldiers, but the second quotation refers to the Moabites, David's enemies.

77. Genesis 28:10–17.

78. The source of the quotation is unknown.

79. Jesus then says of the centurion, "I have not found so great faith, no, not in Israel."

80. The "foot-soldiers" held at "our backs" probably are the French and Indians in Canada, although Nowell may have in mind some more general idea of an imminent war to be fought in Europe as well as in America. The cavalry had performed useful service in Philip's War in providing mobility for rescues of outlying garrisons (as at Brookfield) or sweeps of Indian territory (as in Major Savage's expedition on the upper Connecticut in 1676). However, cavalry was unsuited to forest warfare such as occupied New England for the next century and was too expensive to train and equip.

81. John Cotton's "Christian Calling" emphasizes that the service of a man in his calling is given to God and the rewards of men are not to be given great importance. (Miller and Johnson, eds. *The Puritans,* p. 322.)

82. The artillery trainings provided training for officers who would serve in other units; it was in effect a muster of officers (or one in which officers predominated) rather than a general muster.

83. Isaiah 59:17, Ephesians 6:14.

84. 1 Samuel, 28:15. Saul says these words to the spirit of Samuel, called up by the Witch of Endor; Samuel tells him that he will be defeated and his power will pass to David.

85. Same as Matthew 8:9, above.

86. Perhaps a reference to a skirmish with Indians in Maine, where hostilities persisted until 1678.

87. This commandment is interpolated before the beginning of David's lamentation for Saul and Jonathan, who had perished fighting against the "uncircumcised" Philistines.

FIVE

# *MARY ROWLANDSON*
## Captive Witness

"On the tenth of February 1675, came the Indians with great numbers upon Lancaster: Their first coming was about sun-rising; hearing the noise of some guns, we looked out; several houses were burning and the smoke ascending to heaven." So Mrs. Mary Rowlandson begins the first and probably the finest example of a uniquely American literary genre, the so-called captivity narrative: that is, the history of a white European—or later, an American—made captive by hostile Indians and of what transpired between his or (more generally) her capture and ultimate release.

The captivity narrative found immediate favor in both America and Europe. Mary Rowlandson's *Narrative,* for instance, went through numerous American and English editions during the course of the seventeenth and eighteenth centuries. Part of this interest in captivity narratives was of course historical; but even more, it has been suggested, the genre fulfilled a real literary need in an age and community to which novels were suspect. But captivity narratives, however historical in fact, are novelistic in effect; and indeed, subsequent to Mary Rowlandson, the historical content of these captivity narratives became more and more dilute, while the fanciful elements grew more and more pronounced, although the pretense of historical veracity was always maintained.

Although these narratives were usually rather brief and literarily slight, their influence should not be underestimated. Their popularity was great, their circulation large—not only among those who first invented them but throughout the eighteenth and into the nineteenth century as well. From the publication of Mary Rowlandson's narrative in 1682 until the publication of

Benjamin Church's narrative in 1716, captivity narratives were virtually the only form of personal narrative about the frontier approved for publication by the Puritan censors. These narratives formed the archetype of a kind of official mythology in which the colonial experience was symbolized by the peril of a white Christian woman in the Indian-haunted wilderness. According to *Golden Multitudes*, Frank L. Mott's study of best-sellers, of four narrative works that attained best-seller status between 1680 and 1720, three were captivity narratives. Not until the nineteenth century did a novel written by an American gain a similar degree of popularity, and as late as 1824, a captivity narrative could successfully compete with the novels of Cooper and Scott in the literary marketplace.[1]

Rowlandson's book is therefore to be taken not only as the creation of a Puritan myth, but as the starting point of a cultural myth affecting America as a whole. Gradually, "the captivity" became part of the basic vocabulary of American writers and historians, offering a symbolic key to the drama of American history: a white woman, symbolizing the values of Christianity and American civilization, is captured and threatened by a racial enemy and must be rescued by the grace of God (or, after the Puritan times, by an American hero). Captivity mythology is central to such works as Charles Brockden Brown's *Edgar Huntly* (1799), to Cooper's Leatherstocking Tales, and to the hundreds of pseudo-Coopers who published dime novels and "pulp" westerns from 1850 to the present.[2]

We know little more of Mary Rowlandson than what she tells us in her *Narrative*, and what little we do know is strangely unrevealing. She was born, probably in 1635 and probably in England, the daughter of John White, wealthiest of the original proprietors of the infant settlement of Lancaster, Massachusetts. About 1656 she married Joseph Rowlandson, the first minister of Lancaster. As his wife, she had a position of considerable prestige in the community and until the outbreak of hostilities twenty years later, she lived an uneventful life there. In the successful assault upon Lancaster on February 10, 1676, however, she and her three children were carried off by Indian attackers. Her husband, she tells us, was absent at the time, somewhere "in the Bay," that is, at or near Boston. Presumably the Reverend Rowlandson was petitioning the colonial officials for a garrison of troops to be stationed at Lancaster, whose exposed position had become all too evident after the first unsuccessful Indian raid on the town during the preceding August. In any event his absence was fortunate for himself, since the Indians killed the male defenders and took only women and children captive. Mary Rowlandson and her three children were taken prisoner, and the youngest child, who had been seriously wounded in the fighting, died shortly afterward. Rowlandson's Indian captors apparently realized the value of their prisoner and kept her with the notion of ransom in mind. On May 2 she was returned to her own people for the considerable sum of £20 in goods. Soon after her release, her two surviving children were also set free. Increase Mather saw in her deliverance a sign that God was at last consenting to harken to the prayers of his people, and the event has an important place in his history.

Lancaster had been utterly destroyed during the attack, and was not resettled until 1681. The Rowlandson family, after Mary's release, resided for a short while in Charlestown and Boston, but in 1677 moved to Wethersfield, Connecticut, where the Reverend Rowlandson had been called as minister and where he died the following year. His widow was awarded an annual pension of £30, but the Wethersfield town records do not indicate its ever having been paid. Presumably—although again documentary evidence is lacking—she died in 1678, shortly after her husband.

In one sense it is fortunate that we know so little about the external facts of Mary Rowlandson's life, for such lack of knowledge forces us back to the text of the *Narrative* itself for its interpretation. And this *Narrative* is a far more complex document than is generally realized. As a historical document reflecting shifts in Puritan ideas and values, Mary Rowlandson's book is extremely valuable.

Chief among the shifts she registers is the wartime change in Puritan attitudes toward the Indians. Prior to 1675 opinion at least among the ministry had held that the Indians were "heathens"; subsequently they became "savages." A "Praying Indian," according to Mary Rowlandson's eloquent witness, was no more than a hypocrite, totally enslaved still to his master Satan, the Prince of this World and the Father of Lies—and it should be remembered that she was by birth and by marriage part of the group that had previously most staunchly defended the enterprise of the "Apostle" Eliot in his attempts at converting the Indians to Christianity.

No human quality is easier, of course, than omniscience after the fact. It is simple enough for us to see, from the vantage point of three hundred years later, that the Indians were not the devilish savages into which contemporary opinion—reacting, admittedly, to the stresses of war—transformed them and that the colonists were not entirely the godly saints they thought themselves to be. The conflict between the two parties, it is evident enough now, was not primarily a moral struggle of good against evil which the Puritans interpreted it to be, but a far more basic difference in attitude toward life itself. The Puritans were dedicated entirely to an idea of progress by which, to adapt Kipling, "lesser breeds without the law" would be raised up from their savagery and included in the godly commonwealth of Christian men. The Puritans could scarcely be expected to sympathize with the unaccountable tenacity with which America's Indian inhabitants clung to their old ways. The Indians evinced what seemed from the Puritan point of view an inexplicable fondness for their traditional values and an equally inexplicable resistance to those ways in which good Christian men—again, the Apostle Eliot is a convenient but by no means unique example—endeavored to lead them. Although they would not have used the term, the events of the war forced the Puritans to the reluctant belief that the heathens were "invincible" in their "ignorance," and hence would have to be dealt with summarily. And here is where Mary Rowlandson's limited and fallible account of the Indian wars becomes a uniquely human and touching document, both as a record of incredible fortitude under hardship in which the inner life is as carefully observed as the outer and as an account of the Indians that couples genuine human sympathy with a hatred almost unimaginable to one who has not gone through her experiences.

Ostensibly, as the original title tells us, the subject of that work we have come to know as the *Narrative of the Captivity and Restoration of Mrs. Mary Rowlandson* is in fact *The Sovereignty and Goodness of God, together with the Faithfulness of His Promises Displayed,* and it is certainly true that few Puritan texts hold so uncompromisingly as this *Narrative* to a demonstration of the ostensible moral they set themselves. Yet it has been insufficiently noticed that the Providence to which Mary Rowlandson directs the reader is a peculiarly Puritan one, the paradoxical expression of a paradoxical faith; it is not a simple naive statement that God is in his heaven and that all must therefore be right with the world.

Most commentators on American intellectual history begin with an acknowledgment that Puritanism is (in style, at least) a highly Manichean religion, one in which the powers of evil are seen as almost equal to the powers of good. Although the whole world may show forth the sovereignty and goodness of God, these powers are quite often shown by inversion, and quite often as well they are not indicated through a statement of how benevolent this world is, but of how malevolent it can be. Mary Rowlandson's *Narrative,* in short, often argues the sovereignty and goodness of God through a peculiarly tough-minded Puritan variant of the traditional argument from design, a descendant not of Paley's simple-mindedly optimistic notion that when one sees a watch he infers a watchmaker but of the more sophisticated ontological proof of the existence of God: that God exists because I can conceive of him. For Mary Rowlandson, quite simply, the fact that this world is so bad is the most convincing possible proof that somewhere there must be a better one.

Consequently, Mary Rowlandson's faith, as shown in her *Narrative,* is itself as dualistic as the Calvinism that brought it forth. The ultimate paradox is simple, easy enough to demonstrate albeit hard to explain: God is in control of all his creation, but for his own good reasons he has allowed his saints to exist in a world which, at least from their finite point of view, is at times an evil one. Stated this way the argument is old and commonplace, one of the timeworn justifications for a problem with which religious thinkers have wrestled since the dawn of time, that of a benevolent God who nonetheless permits evil in his creation. But few, at least within an orthodox Christian tradition, have been so uncompromising in their dualism as Mary Rowlandson.

Doubling this basic paradox in Mary Rowlandson's Puritan thought is another, less philosophically basic to Calvinism but more operative as a specific value in the *Narrative.* This is the notion of a "special providence," an idea ultimately derived from the Old Testament notion of the Israelites as a chosen people, a group with whom God has made an individual covenant. According to this idea, which depends upon a somewhat simplistic reading of the Old Testament as moral history, God made a special covenant with his chosen people, by which he would guarantee their welfare if they did not fall from his ways. The various misfortunes of the Hebrews, then, were inflicted upon them as a chastisement by a just if impatient God to punish them for straying from his commandments. According to the Puritan reading of the Old Testament, God had finally lost faith in the Hebrews as his chosen people and had chosen the Puritans in their stead, but the notion of the chosen people itself, protected by a just God from misfortune, survives intact, even though the specific identity of these chosen people has been changed. Yet this view is itself heavily qualified: if, as Christ reminds us, God marks the sparrow's fall, clearly his providence is general as well as special and larger than the protection of a small group of his saints. For his own wise ends, God sometimes chooses to chastise his own, even if in order to do so he must also sustain his enemies.

In the *Narrative* this paradoxical view of the quality and direction of God's providence is most clearly seen in the ambiguous role of Mary Rowlandson's Indian captors. She specifically raises the question in her discussion, during the "twentieth remove," of five "remarkable passages of providence" in which God had specifically protected his enemies at the expense of the general welfare of his saints. Here the term "remarkable" clearly becomes synonymous with "paradoxical," and the paradox is very simply that God has reserved his special care not for his saints but for his enemies.

Nor is this the only example of Rowlandson's ambiguous treatment of her captors. The observant reader will notice first off that, her protestations to the contrary, her treatment as a prisoner was not particularly harsh. The hardships she suffered were common to the whole party, Indians and captives alike. Perhaps, as some commentators have suggested, her captors realized that she would prove to be a valuable commodity for exchange; more to the point, however, is the fact—which the reader must look carefully to distinguish—that the Indians themselves were by no means living off the fat of the land. Indeed, on one level at least, the *Narrative* may be read as an account of the hardships to which the *Indians* had been reduced by the inroads of the English upon their supplies.

In any event, during the course of the *Narrative* Rowlandson's rhetorical treatment of the Indians as devilish instruments of Satan becomes more and more conventional and pro forma. Although she never admits as much, her awareness that her captors, whatever their ultimate purpose in the providential scheme of things may be, are not personally especially malevolent, becomes increasingly evident. And this brings us to one final consideration of the implications of this paradoxical *Narrative,* the not-so-obvious point that it is in many ways a psychological text as well as a theological or historic document.

Mary Rowlandson is tantalizingly silent about her reunion with her husband. We may only speculate upon their conversations after her return from captivity and her final remove to Boston. The ostensible "moral" to her story, and the one upon which we may be certain their speculations partially dwelt, is summed up in the various biblical captivities and restorations to which she refers her readers in her Preface and at various points in the body of the *Narrative;* and yet we may hope that her curious mind did not rest on only this obvious and simple moral. For there is another dimension to her *Narrative* than the moral one, a dimension that explains as well as any other single factor both the power of this particular book and the popularity, among serious readers, of the whole genre of Indian captivities. This dimension is, for lack of a more precise term, an internal, psychological one.

The modern reader, unused to the rhetoric of theological argumentation, may well find the temptation overwhelming to reduce Rowlandson's *Narrative* to a historical account issuing in a conventional ethical moral; for from the vantage point of the mid-twentieth century the reductive equation of a religious text with an ethical one seems so self-evident as to be almost axiomatic. The modern reader, far more than Rowlandson or her contemporaries, is inclined to assume without thinking that a religious treatise finally comes down to an implied moral, included in it somewhere, of "thou shalt not." More than Mary Rowlandson's, the modern reader's interpretation of the Bible reduces that book to an expanded paraphrase of the Decalogue.

Yet Mary Rowlandson and her husband may well have begun their own speculations from a different point of view, one summed up perhaps best by the prophet Amos, whom she mentions twice in the body of her *Narrative:* "Woe to them that are at ease in Zion." For the power of Rowlandson's *Narrative,* leaving aside for the moment its ethical and historical significance, lies in its study of the emotional effects of what she calls "affliction" rather than in whatever philosophical reflections may be drawn from her own particular misfortunes. From this point of view her *Narrative* conforms to an ancient and powerful literary archetype, the story of a person who is placed in a position of comfort and affluence and who then has everything stripped away.

For the Puritans, this story had special significance. Complacency of spirit was the great enemy of Puritan religiosity: to experience the crisis of conversion, the soul had to be in a state of grave anxiety about its chances of salvation. Under the persecutions of the Anglicans or the hardships of the early emigration and settlement, such a keyed-up psychology was more easily maintained than it could be in 1675 when persecutions had ended and the circumstances of American life were growing more easy and homelike. Out of a resulting complacency could arise such movements as the Half-Way Covenant or the still more latitudinarian Brattle Street Church; under such complacency the teaching of children and servants, the missionary work to the Indians, the care and maintenance of the ministry would all decay, and with them the discipline of a true Bible Commonwealth. If Rowlandson's captivity was therefore a punishment for complacency or slothfulness in religion, it could serve as a symbolic rebuke to a backsliding Puritan community. This in fact was the use made of captivity materials by the ministry. After the war, they were often made the occasions of revival sermons and were published as appendices to sermons calling for the renewal of the covenant by new conversions.

That Rowlandson was herself aware of this dimension to her *Narrative* is evident enough from the fact that a great many of her religious references and allusions are drawn from the Book of Job, the classic biblical statement of this archetypal theme. Job, who is described in the biblical account as God's good servant is mysteriously afflicted by all kinds of misfortunes in order to test the depth of his faith. Though sorely tempted to curse God and die, Job remains true to him and is at last restored to his former state. Significantly, Job is surrounded by various "comforters" (the term *Job's comforter* has come to mean someone who gives false help on the basis of superficial understanding) who try to rationalize God's treatment of Job on the assumption that he must have done something to arouse God's anger, an act of which he is himself unaware. God, however, when called upon to explain his actions, speaks to Job from a whirlwind and propounds to him a set of paradoxes, nonc of which Job can answer; the point is that God's ways are beyond the understanding of man and that man must accept God's will without question. God's justice is beyond the powers of man's interpretation. That God is just, then, becomes a statement of faith rather than of reason.

This "moral" to the Book of Job has left many thinkers unhappy, and some—Melville in *Moby-Dick* being the classic example—have taken bitter exception to it; but the central issue of the Book of Job, the statement of the uncertainty of the world itself, is a notion from which few who, with Mary Rowlandson, have experienced affliction would recoil. Moreover, if—in terms of the Book of Job—God's ways are by their very nature beyond the powers of human interpretation, then their rational explication becomes ultimately futile, as Mary Rowlandson's five examples of "remarkable passages of providence" make eloquently clear. Of more importance than the moral is the psychological study of the behavior of man in the throes of affliction. And in my opinion this explains the remarkable power of Mary Rowlandson's *Narrative*.

Basically, then, this book is an examination of the price of survival, of what one must learn and of the compromises one must make merely to stay alive. Behind all Rowlandson's moralizing stands an eloquent testimony to the value of life itself as something ultimately precious and worth preserving. The question of how one survives under affliction is one to which Mary Rowlandson devotes many pages, some eloquently descriptive of the shrifts to which she was reduced by a world suddenly and inexplicably gone mad. But behind this question stands another, never directly confronted, of why one should take the trouble. In short, is life worth it? The answer, for Mary Rowlandson, is yes.

Yet, as her *Narrative* soberly reminds us, this life itself, valuable as it may be, is to be purchased only at great cost. Mary Rowlandson discovered that the "value," as it were, of her life was £20 in goods. Still, this was not the total reckoning: the greatest expense proved to be an internal one, and the ransom Mary Rowlandson finally paid was the sacrifice of that ease in Zion of which the prophet Amos spoke. "I can remember the time," she tells us soberly at the end of her *Narrative*, "when I used to sleep quietly without workings in my thoughts, whole nights together, but now it is other ways with me." Her experiences have marked and altered her, given her a vision that alienates her from her restored family. She is perhaps experiencing what a post-Holocaust world would call "the guilt of the survivor," but she herself experiences this in her own Puritan terms. She feels that she has seen through the veil that covers the face of God, like Melville's Pip, and the vision has made her not insane, but possessed of a sanity that makes the real world hollow, empty of meaning, vain, a spider's web held out of nothingness by the mere will of an angry God.

To the basic humanity of her vision she brings a language steeped in the Bible and in Puritan mythology. Both the structure of the narrative and its recurrent images tie it to the common heritage of the Puritan audience. The structure of her adventure is essentially that of the conversion experience, that most central of Puritan rituals, and its imagery links the individual adventure to larger myths of collective experience, particularly the myth of the Apocalypse and the experience of emigration with its attendant traumas. Thus, the narrative lends itself to interpretation in the favored Puritan mode of "exfoliation," of revealing microcosms that imply macrocosms.[3]

Imagery and allusions extend the reference of the basic structure. As a captive, Rowlandson experienced starvation, but in her narrative fact is transmuted into symbol, boiled horses' feet and parched corn becoming almost sacramental in function. When the Indians take her, their waste of food symbolizes their wasting the opportunity of grace afforded by the presence of the Christians among them. Her past and present misuse of "food," temporal and spiritual, is symbolized in the vile stuff she not only has to eat but actually finds "savoury" (even when it is filched from fellow captives). It is as if she has been made to partake of a Black Eucharist, like the supposed cannibal sacraments that the "possessed" spoke of during the Salem witchcraft hysteria. When through the grace of God she is both rescued and saved, she declares that though she despaired of ever again having "bread" (either of wheat or symbolic wafer), "now we are fed with the finest of Wheat and, as I may say, with honey out of the rock." Or, as she says elsewhere, God has made "meat out of the eater," converting the Indians who would have devoured the Puritans into "food"—for thought, at least.

The attack of the Indians and the dividing of the Rowlandson family by the raiders contain echoes of Wigglesworth's extremely popular poetic account of the Last Judgment, *The Day of Doom* (Boston, 1662). Like the Last Judgment, the captivity begins with the breaking of the familial circle. In Wigglesworth it is Christ who makes the division, separating families according to judgment. The Christian is forbidden to pity the damned, for "such compassion is out of fashion." Therefore:

The tender Mother will own no other of all her numerous brood
But such as stand at Christ's right hand acquitted through His blood.
The pious Father had now much rather his graceless Son should lie
In Hell with Devils, for all his evils burning eternally.[4]

Rowlandson is not quite up to Wigglesworth's standard: she mourns her children left in the wilderness and her murdered kindred. Yet in the end she accepts their fates with resignation, and she praises God for giving her strength to bear her losses.

The theme of the breaking of the family has historical significance as well. It became the central metaphor in orthodox Puritan literature for any rupturing of the social compact by dissident religionists, political opponents of the Puritan regime, or backsliding children. But in the captivity narratives it also served to acknowledge and exorcise the spiritual malaise of the "emigration trauma": the feeling that the Puritans themselves might have broken the familial claim of English law and English kinship by coming to America. Thomas Shepard, defending New England from critics who thought the settlers should return to England, justified the emigration by reference to "a strange poise of spirit the Lord hath laid upon many of our hearts," to go "against so many perswasions of friends," forsaking "our accommodations and comforts, . . . [forsaking] our dearest relations, Parents, brethren, Sisters, Christian friends . . . and all this to go to a wildernesse."[5] In Mrs. Rowlandson's *Narrative,* the will of God that the family be broken and the salvation-seeker removed into a wilderness is clear beyond question, and if there is guilt associated with the seeker's departure, there is also atonement provided in the *Narrative* itself. Thus, myth resolves into credible imagery what to logic is paradox or contradiction.

## NOTES

1. Frank Luther Mott, *Golden Multitudes,* p. 303. R. W. G. Vail, *Voice of the Old Frontier,* lists works about the frontier published before 1800.

2. Roy Harvey Pearce, "The Significances of the Captivity Narrative," *American Literature* 19:1 (March 1949), pp. 1–20; Richard Slotkin, *Regeneration through Violence,* chaps. 4–5, pp. 257–59, 326–30, 384–93, 440–59, 518–38.

3. Slotkin, *Regeneration through Violence,* chap. 4.

4. Michael Wigglesworth, "The Day of Doom," reprinted in *Colonial American Writing,* ed. Roy Harvey Pearce, pp. 233–34, 248, 289–90.

5. Thomas Shepard, "A Defense of the Answer," in *The Puritans,* ed. Perry Miller and Thomas H. Johnson, p. 121.

### A NOTE ON THE TEXT

The text of Mary Rowlandson's *Narrative* provides a number of problems for the editor, especially if, in the interest of establishing a wider audience for the book, he wishes above all to preserve its readability. Although Mary Rowlandson's vigorous prose can in all probability survive almost any amount of well-meant editorial meddling, the establishment with reasonable confidence of what she actually wrote is by no means either easy or certain. No copy of the first edition of the *Narrative,* published in 1682, exists. All subsequent editions therefore ultimately depend upon the text of the second edition of 1682, printed by Samuel Green in Cambridge, Massachusetts. His claim on the title page that this is "the second addition corrected and amended" is not immediately reassuring, and indeed this edition, however carefully emended it may be, is still filled with errors, most of little consequence but some of considerable magnitude. No manuscript of the *Narrative* is known; and, to add to the difficulty of establishing a reasonably authoritative text, the *Narrative* was published posthumously, although presumably it had seen private circulation in manuscript before publication in book form.

The reasons for publication of the *Narrative*, are mysterious. A good conjecture is that interest in Lancaster, destroyed in 1676 and only recently (1681) resettled, led to the resurrection of the manuscript, which had presumably languished, half-forgotten, since Mary Rowlandson's death.

Even the exact dates of composition of the *Narrative* are obscure. The only hint the text gives us is that the Rowlandsons lived in Boston for "about three quarters of a year" after Mary Rowlandson's release. If this statement is accurate, the *Narrative* could not have been completed before February 1677. A reasonable although unverifiable time for the composition of the *Narrative*, then, is early in 1677, probably shortly after the Rowlandson family moved to Wethersfield. The *Narrative* was almost certainly written before 1678, since nowhere in it does Rowlandson mention the death of her husband in that year. Another plausible conjecture, which cannot at this late date be substantiated, is that the *Narrative* was written for the instruction and edification of the Reverend Rowlandson's Wethersfield parishioners, presumably (on the basis of the rather ambiguous statements in Mary Rowlandson's Preface) at their request.

In any case, the text of the second edition, although authoritative, cannot be considered sacrosanct. But, lacking any other text of any authority whatever, the editor must fall back on his own presumably better judgment in attempting to emend the *Narrative*. My own editorial policy has been conservative. Mary Rowlandson's sometimes erratic spelling has been both regularized and modernized, and obvious compositors' errors in the text have been silently corrected. Punctuation, however, has generally been left alone—being changed only in those few cases when it was evidently corrupt—on the theory that the readability of the *Narrative* is not significantly improved by heavy-handed attempts to make its punctuation conform to twentieth-century ideas of correctness. Explanatory notes have been added, which are intended to clear up doubtful points only in interpretation of the text. They are not meant to serve as running commentary upon the history of King Philip's War. Long discursive footnotes have generally been avoided.

I am much indebted to Charles H. Lincoln's earlier edition of the *Narrative* (in *Narratives of the Indian Wars, 1675–1699*, pp. 107–67), from which I have on occasion adapted a note and to which I refer the reader interested in further study.

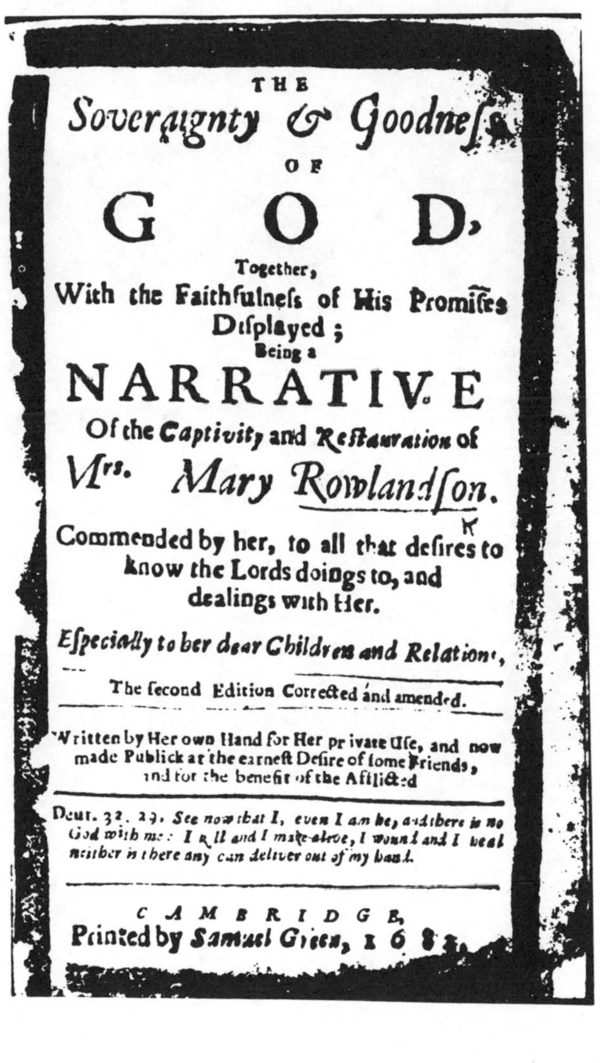
THE
Soveraignty & Goodness
OF
GOD,
Together,
With the Faithfulness of His Promises
Displayed;
Being a
NARRATIVE
Of the Captivity and Restauration of
Mrs. Mary Rowlandson.
Commended by her, to all that desires to
know the Lords doings to, and
dealings with Her.
Especially to her dear Children and Relations,
The second Edition Corrected and amended.
Written by Her own Hand for Her private Use, and now
made Publick at the earnest Desire of some Friends,
and for the benefit of the Afflicted
Deut. 32. 29. See now that I, even I am he, and there is no
God with me: I kill and I make alive, I wound and I heal
neither is there any can deliver out of my hand.
CAMBRIDGE,
Printed by Samuel Green, 1 6 8 2.

The Sovereignty and Goodness of God, together with the Faithfulness of His Promises Displayed; Being a Narrative of the Captivity and Restoration of Mrs. Mary Rowlandson. Commended by her to all that Desire to Know the Lord's Doings to, and Dealings with Her. Especially to Her Dear Children and Relations.

---

Written by Her Own Hand for Her Private Use, and Now Made Public at the Earnest Desire of Some Friends, and for the Benefit of the Afflicted.

---

Deut. 32.29. *See Now that I, Even I am He, and There Is No God with Me; I Kill and I Make Alive, I Wound and I Heal, Neither Is There Any Can Deliver Out of My Hand.*

## *THE PREFACE TO THE READER*

It was on Tuesday, Feb. 1, 1675,[1] in the afternoon, when the Narragansetts' quarters (in or toward the Nipmuck country, whither they are now retired for fear of the English army lying in their own country) were the second time beaten up, by the forces of the united colonies, who thereupon soon betook themselves to flight, and were all the next day pursued by the English, some overtaken and destroyed. But on Thursday, Feb. 3rd, the English having now been six days on their march, from their headquarters, at Wickford, in the Narragansett country, toward, and after the enemy, and provision grown exceeding short, insomuch that they were fain to kill some horses for the supply, especially of their Indian friends, they were necessitated to consider what was best to be done. And about noon (having hitherto followed the chase as hard as they might) a council was called, and though some few were of another mind, yet it was concluded by far the greater part of the council of war, that the army should desist the pursuit, and retire: the forces of Plymouth and the Bay to the next town of the Bay, and Connecticut forces to their own next towns; which determination was immediately put in execution. The consequence whereof, as it was not difficult to be foreseen by those that knew the causeless enmity of these barbarians, against the English, and the malicious and revengeful spirit of these heathen: so it soon proved dismal.

The Narragansetts were now driven quite from their own country, and all their provisions there hoarded up, to which they durst not at present return, and being so numerous as they were, soon devoured those to whom they went, whereby both the one and other were now reduced to extreme straits, and so necessitated to take the first and best opportunity for supply, and very glad, no doubt, of such an opportunity as this, to provide for themselves, and make spoil of the English at once;[2] and seeing themselves thus discharged of their pursuers, and a little refreshed after their flight, the very next week upon Thursday, Feb. 10th, they fell with mighty force and fury upon Lancaster: which small town, remote from aid of others, and not being garrisoned as it might, the army being now come in, and as the time indeed required[3] (the design of the Indians against that place being known to the English some time before) was not able to make effectual resistance: but notwithstanding utmost endeavor of the inhabitants, most of the buildings were turned into ashes; many people (men, women and children) slain, and others captivated. The most solemn and remarkable part of this tragedy, may that justly be reputed, which fell upon the family of that reverend servant of God, Mr. Joseph Rowlandson, the faithful pastor of Christ in that place, who being gone down to the council of the Massachusetts to seek aid for the defense of the place, at his return found the town in flames, or smoke, his own house being set on fire by the enemy, through the disadvantage of a defective fortification, and all in it consumed: his precious yokefellow, and dear children, wounded and captivated (as the issue evidenced, and following narrative declares) by these cruel and barbarous savages. A sad catastrophe! Thus all things come alike to all: none knows either love or hatred by all that is before him. It is no new thing for God's precious ones to drink as deep as others, of the cup of common calamity: take just Lot (yet captivated) for instance beside others.[4] But it is not my business to dilate on these things, but only in few words introductively to preface to the following script, which is a narrative of the wonderfully awful, wise, holy, powerful, and gracious providence of God, towards that worthy and precious gentlewoman, the dear consort of the said Reverend Mr. Rowlandson, and her children with her, as in casting of her into such a waterless pit, so in preserving, supporting, and carrying through so many such extreme hazards, unspeakable difficulties and disconsolateness, and at last delivering her out of them all, and her surviving children also. It was a strange and amazing dispensation, that the Lord should so afflict His precious servant, and handmaid. It was as strange, if not more, that He should so bear up the spirits of His servant under such bereavements and of His handmaid under such captivity, travels and hardships (much too hard for flesh and blood) as he did, and at length deliver and restore. But He was their saviour, who hath said, *When thou passest through the waters, I will be with thee, and through the rivers, they shall not overflow thee: When thou walkest through the fire thou shalt not be burnt, nor shall the flame kindle upon thee,* Isaiah 43. 2 and again, *He woundeth and his hands make whole. He shall deliver thee in six troubles, yea in seven there shall no evil touch thee. In famine he shall redeem thee from death, and in war from the power of the sword.* Job 5. 18–20. Methinks this dispensation doth bear some resemblance to those of Joseph, David and Daniel; yea, and of the three children too, the stories whereof do represent us with the excellent textures of divine providence, curious pieces of divine work: and truly so doth this, and therefore not to be forgotten, but worthy to be exhibited to, and viewed, and pondered by all, that disdain not to consider the operation of His hands.[5]

The works of the Lord (not only of creation, but of providence also, especially those that do more peculiarly concern His dear ones, that are as the apple of His eye, as the signet upon His hand, the delight of His eyes, and the object of His tenderest care) are great, sought out of all those that have pleasure therein. And of these verily this is none of the least.

This narrative was penned by the gentlewoman herself, to be to her a memorandum of God's dealing with her, that she might never forget, but remember the same, and the several circumstances thereof, all the days of her life. A pious scope which deserves both commendation and imitation. Some friends having obtained a sight of it, could not but be so much affected with the many passages of working providence discovered therein, as to judge it worthy of public view, and altogether unmeet that such works of God should be hid from present and future generations: and therefore though this gentlewoman's modesty would not thrust it into the press, yet her gratitude unto God made her not hardly persuadable to let it pass, that God might have his due glory, and others benefit by it as well as herself. I hope by this time none will cast any reflection upon this gentlewoman, on the score of this publication of her affliction and deliverance. If any should, doubtless they may be reckoned with the nine lepers, of whom it is said, *Were there not ten cleansed, where are the nine?*[6] but one returning to give God thanks. Let such further know that this was a dispensation of public note, and of universal concernment, and so much the more, by how much the nearer this gentlewoman stood related to that faithful servant of God, whose capacity and employment was public in the house of God, and his name on that account of a very sweet savor in the churches of Christ. Who is there of a true Christian spirit, that did not look upon himself much concerned in this bereavement, this captivity in the time thereof, and in this deliverance when it came, yea more than in many others; and how many are there, to whom so concerned, it will doubtless be a very acceptable thing to see the way of God with this gentlewoman in the aforesaid dispensation, thus laid out and portrayed before their eyes.

To conclude: whatever any coy fantasies may deem, yet it highly concerns those that have so deeply tasted, how good the Lord is, to enquire with David, *What shall I render to the Lord for all his benefits to me.* Psalms 116. 12. He thinks nothing too great; yea, being sensible of his own disproportion to the due praises of God he calls in help. *Oh, magnify the Lord with me, let us exalt his name together,* Psalms 34. 3.[7] And it is but reason, that our praises should hold proportion with our prayers: and that as many hath helped together by prayer for the obtaining of His mercy, so praises should be returned by many on this behalf; and forasmuch as not the general but particular knowledge of things make deepest impression upon the affections, this narrative particularizing the several passages of this providence will not a little conduce thereunto. And therefore holy David in order to the attainment of that end, accounts himself concerned to declare what God has done for his soul, Psalms 66.16. *Come and hear, all ye that fear God, and I will declare what God hath done for my soul, i.e.* for his life, see verses 9, 10. *He holdeth our soul in life, and suffers not our feet to be moved, for thou our God hast proved us, thou hast tried us, as silver is tried.* Life mercies, are heart-affecting mercies, of great impression and force, to enlarge pious hearts, in the praises of God, so that such know not how but to talk of God's acts, and to speak of and publish His wonderful works. Deep troubles, when the waters come in unto thy soul, are wont to produce vows: vows must be paid. It is better not vow, than vow and not to pay.[8] I may say, that as none knows what it is to fight and pursue such an enemy as this, but they that have fought and pursued them: so none can imagine what it is to be captivated, and enslaved to such atheistical, proud, wild, cruel, barbarous, brutish (in one word) diabolical creatures as these, the worst of the heathen; nor what difficulties, hardships, hazards, sorrows, anxieties and perplexities do unavoidably wait upon such a condition, but those that have tried it. No serious spirit then (especially knowing anything of this gentlewoman's piety) can imagine but that the vows of God are upon her. Excuse her then if she come thus into public, to pay those vows, come and hear what she hath to say.

I am confident that no friend of divine providence will ever repent his time and pains spent in reading over these sheets, but will judge them worth perusing again and again.

Here reader, you may see an instance of the sovereignty of God, who doth what He will with His own as well as others; and who may say to Him, What dost Thou? Here you may see an instance of the faith and patience of the saints, under the most heart-sinking trials; here you may see, the promises are breasts full of consolation, when all the world besides is empty, and gives nothing but sorrow. That God is indeed the supreme Lord of the world, ruling the most unruly, weakening the most cruel and savage, granting His people mercy in the sight of the unmerciful, curbing the lusts of the most filthy, holding the hands of the violent, delivering the prey from the mighty, and gathering together the outcasts of Israel. Once and again you have heard, but here you may see, that power belongeth unto God; that our God is the God of salvation, and to Him belong the issues from death. That our God is in the heavens, and doth whatever pleases Him. Here you have Samson's riddle exemplified, and that great promise, Romans 8. 28, verified, *Out of the eater comes forth meat, and sweetness out of the strong;* The worst of evils working together for the best good.[9] How evident is it that the Lord hath made this gentlewoman a gainer by all this affliction, that she can say, 'tis good for her yea better that she hath been, than that she should not have been thus afflicted.

Oh how doth God shine forth in such things as these!

Reader, if thou gettest no good by such a declaration as this, the fault must needs be thine own. Read therefore, peruse, ponder, and from hence lay by something from the experience of another against thine own turn comes, that so thou also through patience and consolation of the scripture mayest have hope.

TER AMICAM[10]

## A NARRATIVE OF THE CAPTIVITY AND RESTORATION OF MRS. MARY ROWLANDSON

On the tenth of February 1675,[11] came the Indians with great numbers upon Lancaster: Their first coming was about sun-rising; hearing the noise of some guns, we looked out; several houses were burning, and the smoke ascending to heaven. There were five persons taken in one house, the father, and the mother and a sucking child, they knocked on the head; the other two they took and carried away alive. There were two others, who being out of their garrison upon some occasion were set upon; one was knocked on the head, the other escaped: another there was who running along was shot and wounded, and fell down; he begged of them his life, promising them money (as they told me) but they would not hearken to him but knocked him in the head, and stripped him naked, and split open his bowels. Another seeing many of the Indians about his barn, ventured and went out, but was quickly shot down. There were three others belonging to the same garrison who were killed; the Indians getting up upon the roof of the barn, had advantage to shoot down upon them over their fortification. Thus these murderous wretches went on, burning, and destroying before them.

At length they came and beset our own house, and quickly it was the dolefullest day that ever mine eyes saw. The house stood upon the edge of a hill; some of the Indians got behind the hill, others into the barn, and others behind any thing that could shelter them; from all which places they shot against the house, so that the bullets seemed to fly like hail; and quickly they wounded one man among us, then another, and then a third. About two hours (according to my observation, in that amazing time) they had been about the house before they prevailed to fire it (which they did with flax and hemp, which they brought out of the barn, and there being no defense about the house, only two flankers[12] at two opposite corners and one of them not finished) they fired it once and one ventured out and quenched it, but they quickly fired again, and that took. Now is the dreadful hour come, that I have often heard of (in time of war, as it was the case of others) but now mine eyes see it. Some in our house were fighting for their lives, others wallowing in their blood, the house on fire over our heads, and the bloody heathen ready to knock us on the head, if we stirred out. Now might we hear mothers and children crying out for themselves, and one another, Lord, What shall we do? Then I took my children (and one of my sisters, hers) to go forth and leave the house: but as soon as we came to the door and appeared, the Indians shot so thick that the bullets rattled against the house, as if one had taken an handful of stones and threw them, so that we were fain to give back. We had six stout dogs belonging to our garrison, but none of them would stir, though another time, if any Indian had come to the door, they were ready to fly upon him and tear him down. The Lord hereby would make us the more to acknowledge his hand, and to see that our help is always in him. But out we must go, the fire increasing, and coming along behind us, roaring, and the Indians gaping before us with their guns, spears and hatchets to devour us. No sooner were we out of the house, but my brother-in-law (being before wounded, in defending the house, in or near the throat) fell down dead whereat the Indians scornfully shouted, and holloed, and were presently upon him, stripping off his clothes, the bullets flying thick, one went through my side, and the same (as would seem) through the bowels and hand of my dear child in my arms. One of my elder sister's children, named William, had then his leg broken, which the Indians perceiving, they knocked him on the head. Thus were we butchered by those merciless heathen, standing amazed, with the blood running down to our heels. My eldest sister being yet in the house, and seeing those woeful sights, the infidels haling mothers one way, and children another, and some wallowing in their blood: and her elder son telling her that her son William was dead, and myself was wounded, she said, And, Lord, let me die with them; which was no sooner said, but she was struck with a bullet, and fell down dead over the threshold. I hope she is reaping the fruit of her good labors, being faithful to the service of God in her place. In her younger years she lay under much trouble upon spiritual accounts, till it pleased God to make that precious scripture take hold of her heart, 2 Corinthians 12. 9. *And he said unto me, my grace is sufficient for thee.* More than twenty years after I have heard her tell how sweet and comfortable that place was to her. But to return: the Indians laid hold of us, pulling me one way, and the Children another, and said,

Come go along with us; I told them they would kill me: they answered, If I were willing to go along with them, they would not hurt me.

Oh the doleful sight that now was to behold at this house! *Come, behold the works of the Lord, what desolations he has made in the earth.*[13] Of thirty-seven persons who were in this one house, none escaped either present death, or a bitter captivity, save only one, who might say as he, Job 1. 15, *And I only am escaped alone to tell the news.* There were twelve killed, some shot, some stabbed with their spears, some knocked down with their hatchets. When we are in prosperity, oh the little that we think of such dreadful sights, and to see our dear friends, and relations lie bleeding out their heart's blood upon the ground. There was one who was chopped into the head with a hatchet, and stripped naked, and yet was crawling up and down. It is a solemn sight to see so many Christians lying in their blood, some here, and some there, like a company of sheep torn by wolves. All of them stripped naked by a company of hell-hounds, roaring, singing, ranting and insulting, as if they would have torn our very hearts out; yet the Lord by his almighty power preserved a number of us from death, for there were twenty-four of us taken alive and carried captive.

I had often before this said, that if the Indians should come, I should choose rather to be killed by them than be taken alive but when it came to the trial my mind changed; their glittering weapons so daunted my spirit, that I chose rather to go along with those (as I may say) ravenous beasts, than that moment to end my days; and that I may the better declare what happened to me during that grievous captivity, I shall particularly speak of the several removes we had up and down the wilderness.

### *The First Remove*[14]

Now away we must go with those barbarous creatures, with our bodies wounded and bleeding, and our hearts no less than our bodies. About a mile we went that night, up upon a hill within sight of the town, where they intended to lodge. There was hard by a vacant house (deserted by the English before, for fear of the Indians). I asked them whether I might not lodge in the house that night to which they answered, What will you love English men still? This was the dolefullest night that ever my eyes saw. Oh the roaring, and singing and dancing, and yelling of those black creatures in the night, which made the place a lively resemblance of hell. And as miserable was the waste that was there made, of horses, cattle, sheep, swine, calves, lambs, roasting pigs, and fowl (which they had plundered in the town) some roasting, some lying and burning, and some boiling to feed our merciless enemies; who were joyful enough though we were disconsolate. To add to the dolefulness of the former day, and the dismalness of the present night: my thoughts ran upon my losses and sad bereaved condition. All was gone, my husband gone (at least separated from me, he being in the Bay;[15] and to add to my grief, the Indians told me they would kill him as he came homeward) my children gone, my relations and friends gone, our house and home and all our comforts within doors, and without, all was gone (except my life) and I knew not but the next moment that might go too. There remained nothing to me but one poor wounded babe, and it seemed at present worse than death that it was in such a pitiful condition, bespeaking compassion, and I had no refreshing for it, nor suitable things to revive it. Little do many think what is the savageness and brutishness of this barbarous enemy, aye even those that seem to profess more than others among them,[16] when the English have fallen into their hands.

Those seven that were killed at Lancaster the summer before upon a Sabbath day, and the one that was afterward killed upon a week day, were slain and mangled in a barbarous manner, by One-eyed John, and Marlborough's praying Indians, which Captain Mosely brought to Boston, as the Indians told me.

### *The Second Remove*

But now, the next morning, I must turn my back upon the town, and travel with them into the vast and desolate wilderness, I knew not whither. It is not my tongue, or pen can express the sorrows of my heart, and bitterness of my spirit, that I had at this departure: but God was with me, in a wonderful manner, carrying me along, and bearing up my spirit, that it did not quite fail. One of the Indians carried my poor wounded babe upon a horse, it went moaning all along, I shall die, I shall die. I went on foot after it, with sorrow that cannot be expressed. At length I took it off the horse, and carried it in my arms till my strength failed, and I fell down with it: Then they set me upon a horse with my wounded child in my lap, and there being no furniture[17] upon the horse's back, as we were going down a steep hill, we both fell over the horse's head, at which they like inhuman creatures laughed, and rejoiced to see it, though I thought we should there have ended our days, as overcome with so many difficulties. But the Lord renewed my strength still, and carried me along, that I might see more of his power; yea, so much that I could never have thought of, had I not experienced it.

After this it quickly began to snow, and when night came on, they stopped: and now down I must sit in the snow, by a little fire, and a few boughs behind me, with my sick child in my lap; and calling much for water, being now (through the wound) fallen into a violent fever. My own wound also growing so stiff, that I could scarce sit down or rise up; yet so it must be, that I must sit all this cold winter night upon the cold snowy ground, with my sick child in my arms, looking that every hour would be the last of its life; and having no Christian friend near me, either to comfort or help me. Oh, I may see the wonderful power of God, that my spirit did not utterly sink under my affliction: still the Lord upheld me with his gracious and merciful spirit, and we were both alive to see the light of the next morning.

### *The Third Remove*

The morning being come, they prepared to go on their way. One of the Indians got up upon a horse, and they set me up behind him, with my poor sick babe in my lap. A very wearisome and tedious day I had of it; what with my own wound, and my child's being so exceeding sick, and in a lamentable condition with her wound. It may be easily judged what a poor feeble condition we were in, there being not the least crumb of refreshing[18] that came within either of our mouths, from Wednesday night to Saturday night, except only a little cold water. This day in the afternoon, about an hour by sun, we came to the place where they intended, *viz.* an Indian town called Wenimesset, northward of Quabaug. When we were come, Oh the number of pagans (now merciless enemies) that there came about me, that I may say as

David, Psalms 27. 13, *I had fainted, unless I had believed,* etc.[19] The next day was the Sabbath: I then remembered how careless I had been of God's holy time, how many Sabbaths I had lost and misspent, and how evilly I had walked in God's sight; which lay so close unto my spirit, that it was easy for me to see how righteous it was with God to cut off the thread of my life, and cast me out of his presence forever. Yet the Lord still showed mercy to me, and upheld me; and as he wounded me with one hand, so he healed me with the other. This day there came to me one Robert Pepper (a man belonging to Roxbury) who was taken in Captain Beers his fight, and had been now a considerable time with the Indians; and up with them almost as far as Albany, to see King Philip, as he told me, and was now very lately come into these parts. Hearing, I say, that I was in this Indian town, he obtained leave to come and see me. He told me, he himself was wounded in the leg at Captain Beers his fight; and was not able some time to go, but as they carried him, and as he took oaken leaves and laid to his wound, and through the blessing of God he was able to travel again. Then I took oaken leaves and laid to my side, and with the blessing of God it cured me also; yet before the cure was wrought, I may say, as it is in Psalms 38. 5–6. *My wounds stink and are corrupt, I am bowed down greatly, I go mourning all the day long.* I sat much alone with a poor wounded child in my lap, which moaned night and day, having nothing to revive the body, or cheer the spirits of her, but instead of that, sometimes one Indian would come and tell me in one hour, that your master will knock your child in the head, and then a second, and then a third, your master will quickly knock your child in the head.

This was the comfort I had from them, miserable comforters are ye all, as he said.[20] Thus nine days I sat upon my knees, with my babe in my lap, till my flesh was raw again; my child being even ready to depart this sorrowful world, they bade me carry it out to another wigwam (I suppose because they would not be troubled with such spectacles) whither I went with a very heavy heart, and down I sat with the picture of death in my lap. About two hours in the night, my sweet babe like a lamb departed this life, on Feb. 18, 1675, it being about six years, and five months old. It was nine days from the first wounding, in this miserable condition, without any refreshing of one nature or other, except a little cold water. I cannot, but take notice, how at another time I could not bear to be in the room where any dead person was, but now the case is changed; I must and could lie down by my dead babe, side by side all the night after. I have thought since of the wonderful goodness of God to me, in preserving me in the use of my reason and senses, in that distressed time, that I did not use wicked and violent means to end my own miserable life. In the morning, when they understood that my child was dead they sent for me home to my master's wigwam: (by my master in this writing, must be understood Quinnapin, who was a sagamore,[21] and married King Philip's wife's sister; not that he first took me, but I was sold to him by another Narragansett Indian, who took me when first I came out of the garrison). I went to take up my dead child in my arms to carry it with me, but they bid me let it alone: there was no resisting, but go I must and leave it. When I had been at my master's wigwam, I took the first opportunity I could get, to go look after my dead child: when I came I asked them what they had done with it? Then they told me it was upon the hill: then they went and showed me where it was, where I saw the ground was newly digged, and there they told me they had buried it: there I left that child in the wilderness, and must commit it, and myself also in this wilderness condition, to Him who is above all. God having taken away this dear child, I went to see my daughter Mary, who was at this same Indian town, at a wigwam not very far off, though we had little liberty or opportunity to see one another. She was about ten years old, and taken from the door at first by a Praying Indian and afterward sold for a gun. When I came in sight, she would fall a-weeping; at which they were provoked, and would not let me come near her, but bade me begone; which was a heart-cutting word to me. I had one child dead, another in the wilderness, I knew not where, the third they would not let me come near to: *Me* (as he said) *have ye bereaved of my children, Joseph is not, and Simeon is not, and ye will take Benjamin also, all these things are against me.*[22] I could not sit still in this condition, but kept walking from place to another. And as I was going along, my heart was even overwhelmed with the thoughts of my condition, and that I should have children, and a nation which I knew not ruled over them. Whereupon I earnestly entreated the Lord, that He would consider my low estate, and show me a token for good, and if it were

His blessed will, some sign and hope of some relief. And indeed quickly the Lord answered, in some measure, my poor prayers: for as I was going up and down mourning and lamenting my condition, my son came to me, and asked me how I did; I had not seen him before, since the destruction of the town, and I knew not where he was, till I was informed by himself, that he was amongst a smaller parcel of Indians, whose place was about six miles off; with tears in his eyes, he asked me whether his sister Sarah was dead; and told me he had seen his sister Mary; and prayed me, that I would not be troubled in reference to himself. The occasion of his coming to see me at this time, was this: there was, as I said, about six miles from us, a small plantation of Indians, where it seems he had been during his captivity: and at this time, there were some forces of the Indians gathered out of our company, and some also from them (among whom was my son's master) to go to assault and burn Medfield: In this time of the absence of his master, his dame brought him to see me. I took this to be some gracious answer to my earnest and unfeigned desire. The next day, *viz.* to this, the Indians returned from Medfield, all the company, for those that belonged to the other small company, came through the town that now we were at. But before they came to us, Oh! the outrageous roaring and whooping that there was: They began their din about a mile before they came to us. By their noise and whooping they signified how many they had destroyed (which was at that time twenty-three). Those that were with us at home, were gathered together as soon as they heard the whooping, and every time that the other went over their number, these at home gave a shout, that the very earth rung again: and thus they continued till those that had been upon the expedition were come up to the Sagamore's wigwam; and then, Oh, the hideous insulting and triumphing that there was over some Englishmen's scalps that they had taken (as their manner is) and brought with them. I cannot but take notice of the wonderful mercy of God to me in those afflictions, in sending me a Bible. One of the Indians that came from Medfield fight, had brought some plunder, came to me, and asked me, if I would have a Bible, he had got one in his basket. I was glad of it, and asked him, whether he thought the Indians would let me read? He answered, Yes: So I took the Bible, and in that melancholy time, it came into my mind to read first the

28th Chapter of Deuteronomy, which I did, and when I had read it, my dark heart wrought on this manner, That there was no mercy for me, that the blessings were gone, and the curses come in their room, and that I had lost my opportunity. But the Lord helped me still to go on reading till I came to Chapter 30 the seven first verses, where I found, there was mercy promised again, if we would return to him by repentance; and though we were scattered from one end of the earth to the other, yet the Lord would gather us together, and turn all those curses upon our enemies. I do not desire to live to forget this scripture, and what comfort it was to me.[23]

Now the Indians began to talk of removing from this place, some one way, and some another. There were now besides myself nine English captives in this place (all of them children, except one woman). I got an opportunity to go and take my leave of them; they being to go one way, and I another, I asked them whether they were earnest with God for deliverance, they told me, they did as they were able, and it was some comfort to me, that the Lord stirred up children to look to Him. The woman *viz.* Goodwife Joslin told me, she should never see me again, and that she could find in her heart to run away; I wished her not to run away by any means, for we were near thirty miles from any English town, and she very big with child, and had but one week to reckon; and another child in her arms, two years old, and bad rivers there were to go over, and we were feeble, with our poor and coarse entertainment. I had my Bible with me, I pulled it out, and asked her whether she would read; we opened the Bible and lighted on Psalm 27, in which Psalm we especially took notice of that, *ver. ult., Wait on the Lord, Be of good courage, and he shall strengthen thine heart, wait I say on the Lord.*[24]

### *The Fourth Remove*

And now I must part with that little company I had. Here I parted from my daughter Mary (whom I never saw again till I saw her in Dorchester, returned from captivity), and from four little cousins and neighbors, some of which I never saw afterward: the Lord only knows the end of them. Amongst them also was that poor woman before mentioned, who came to a sad end, as some of the company told me in my travel: she having much grief upon her spirit, about her miserable condition, being so near her time, she would be often asking the Indians to let her go home; they not being willing to that, and yet vexed with her importunity, gathered a great company together about her, and stripped her naked, and set her in the midst of them; and when they had sung and danced about her (in their hellish manner) as long as they pleased, they knocked her on head, and the child in her arms with her: when they had done that, they made a fire and put them both into it, and told the other children that were with them, that if they attempted to go home, they would serve them in like manner: the children said, she did not shed one tear, but prayed all the while. But to return to my own journey; we travelled about half a day or little more, and came to a desolate place in the wilderness, where there were no wigwams or inhabitants before; we came about the middle of the afternoon to this place, cold and wet, and snowy, and hungry, and weary, and no refreshing, for man, but the cold ground to sit on, and our poor Indian cheer.

Heart-aching thoughts here I had about my poor children, who were scattered up and down among the wild beasts of the forest: my head was light and dizzy (either through hunger or hard lodging, or trouble or all together) my knees feeble, my body raw by sitting double night and day, that I cannot express to man the affliction that lay upon my spirit, but the Lord helped me at that time to express it to himself. I opened my Bible to read, and the Lord brought that precious scripture to me, Jeremiah 31. 16. *Thus saith the Lord, refrain thy voice from weeping, and thine eyes from tears, for thy work shall be rewarded, and they shall come again from the land of the enemy.* This was a sweet cordial to me, when I was ready to faint, many and many a time have I sat down, and wept sweetly over this scripture. At this place we continued about four days.

### *The Fifth Remove*

The occasion (as I thought) of their moving at this time, was, the English army, it being near and following them: for they went, as if they had gone for their lives, for some considerable way, and then they made a stop, and chose some of their stoutest men, and sent them back to hold the English army in play whilst the rest escaped: and then, like Jehu, they marched on furiously, with their old, and with their young:[25] some carried their old decrepit mothers, some carried one, and some another. Four of them carried a great Indian upon a bier; but going through a thick wood with him, they were hindered, and could make no haste; whereupon they took him upon their backs, and carried him, one at a time, till they came to Baquag River. Upon a Friday, a little after noon we came to this river. When all the company was come up, and were gathered together, I thought to count the number of them, but they were so many, and being somewhat in motion, it was beyond my skill. In this travel, because of my wound, I was somewhat favored in my load; I carried only my knitting work and two quarts of parched meal: being very faint I asked my mistress to give me one spoonful of the meal, but she would not give me a taste. They quickly fell to cutting dry trees, to make rafts to carry them over the river: and soon my turn came to go over: by the advantage of some brush which they had laid upon the raft to sit upon, I did not wet my foot (which many of themselves at the other end were mid-leg deep) which cannot but be acknowledged as a favor of God to my weakened body, it being a very cold time. I was not before acquainted with such kind of doings or dangers. *When thou passeth through the waters I will be with thee, and through the rivers they shall not overflow thee,* Isaiah 43. 2. A certain number of us got over the river that night, but it was the night after the Sabbath before all the company was got over. On the Saturday they boiled an old horse's leg which they had got, and so we drank of the broth, as soon as they thought it was ready, and when it was almost all gone, they filled it up again.

The first week of my being among them, I hardly ate anything; the second week, I found my stomach grow very faint for want of something; and yet it was very hard to get down their filthy trash: but the third week, though I could think how formerly my stomach would turn against this or that, and I could starve and die before I could eat such things, yet they were sweet and savory to my taste. I was at this time knitting a pair of white cotton stockings for my mistress; and had not yet wrought upon a Sabbath day; when the Sabbath came they bade me go to work; I told them it was the Sabbath day, and desired them to let me rest, and told them I would do as much more tomorrow; to which they answered me, they would break my face. And here I cannot but take notice of the strange providence of God in preserving the heathen: they were many hundreds, old and young, some sick, and some lame, many had papooses at their backs, the greatest number at this time with us, were squaws, and they travelled with all they had, bag and baggage, and yet they got over this river aforesaid; and on Monday they set their wigwams on fire, and away they went: on that very day came the English army after them to this river, and saw the smoke of their wigwams, and yet this river put a stop to them. God did not give them courage or activity to go over after us; we were not ready for so great a mercy as victory and deliverance; if we had been, God would have found out a way for the English to have passed this river, as well as for the Indians with their squaws and children, and all their luggage. *Oh, that my people had hearkened to me, and Israel had walked in my ways, I should soon have subdued their enemies, and turned my hand against their adversaries,* Psalms 81: 13–14.

### *The Sixth Remove*

On Monday (as I said) they set their wigwams on fire, and went away. It was a cold morning, and before us there was a great brook with ice on it; some waded through it, up to the knees and higher, but others went till they came to a beaver dam, and I amongst them, where through the good providence of God, I did not wet my foot. I went along that day mourning and lamenting, leaving farther my own country, and travelling into the vast and howling wilderness, and I understood something of Lot's wife's temptation, when she looked back:[26] we came that day to a great swamp, by the side of which we took up our lodging that night. When I came to the brow of the hill, that looked toward the swamp, I thought we had been come to a great Indian town (though there were none but our own company). The Indians were as thick as the trees: it seemed as if there had been a thousand hatchets going at once: if one looked before one, there was nothing but Indians, and behind one, nothing but Indians, and so on either hand, I myself in the midst, and no Christian soul near me, and yet how hath the Lord preserved me in safety! Oh the experience that I have had of the goodness of God, to me and mine!

### *The Seventh Remove*

After a restless and hungry night there, we had a wearisome time of it the next day. The swamp by which we lay, was, as it were, a deep dungeon, and an exceeding high and steep hill before it. Before I got to the top of the hill, I thought my heart and legs, and all would have broken, and failed me. What through faintness, and soreness of body, it was a grievous day of travel to me. As we went along, I saw a place where English cattle had been: that was comfort to me, such as it was: quickly after that we came to an English path, which so took with me, that I thought I could have freely lain down and died. That day, a little after noon, we came to Squakeag, where the Indians quickly spread themselves over the deserted English fields, gleaning what they could find; some picked up ears of wheat that were crickled[27] down, some found ears of Indian corn, some found ground nuts,[28] and others sheaves of wheat that were frozen together in the shock, and went to threshing of them out. Myself got two ears of Indian corn, and whilst I did but turn my back, one of them was stolen from me, which much troubled me. There came an Indian to them at that time, with a basket of horse liver. I asked him to give me a piece: What, says he, can you eat horse liver? I told him, I would try, if he would give a piece, which he did, and I laid it on the coals to roast; but before it was half ready they got half of it away from me, so that I was fain to take the rest and eat it as it was, with the blood about my mouth, and yet a savory bit it was to me: *for to the hungry soul, every bitter thing is sweet.*[29] A solemn sight methought it was, to see fields of wheat and Indian corn forsaken and spoiled: and the remainders of them to be food for our merciless enemies. That night we had a mess of wheat for our supper.

### *The Eighth Remove*

On the morrow morning we must go over the river, *i. e.* Connecticut,[30] to meet with King Philip; two canoes full, they had carried over, the next turn I myself was to go; but as my foot was upon the canoe to step in, there was a sudden outcry among them, and I must step back; and instead of going over the river, I must go four or five miles up the river farther northward. Some of the Indians ran one way, and some another. The cause of this rout was, as I thought, their espying some English scouts, who were thereabout. In this travel up the river, about noon the company made a stop, and sat down; some to eat, and others to rest them. As I sat amongst them, musing of things past, my son Joseph unexpectedly came to me: we asked of each other's welfare, bemoaning our doleful condition, and the change that had come upon us. We had husband and father, and children, and sisters, and friends, and relations, and house, and home, and many comforts of this life: but now we may say, as Job, *Naked came I out of my mother's womb, and naked shall I return: the Lord gave, and the Lord hath taken away, blessed be the name of the Lord.*[31] I asked him whether he would read; he told me, he earnestly desired it. I gave him my Bible, and he lighted upon that comfortable scripture, Psalm 118. 17–18. *I shall not die but live, and declare the works of the Lord: the Lord hath chastened me sore, yet he hath not given me over to death.* Look here, mother (says he), did you read this? And here I may take occasion to mention one principal ground of my setting forth these lines: even as the psalmist says, To declare the works of the Lord, and His wonderful power in carrying us along, preserving us in the wilderness, while under the enemy's hand, and returning of us in safety again, and His goodness in bringing to my hand so many comfortable and suitable scriptures in my distress. But to return, we travelled on till night; and in the morning, we must go over the river to Philip's crew. When I was in the canoe, I could not but be amazed at the numerous crew of pagans that were on the bank on the other side. When I came ashore, they gathered all about me, I sitting alone in the midst: I observed they asked one another questions, and laughed, and rejoiced over their gains and victories. Then my heart began to fail: and I fell a-weeping which was the first time to my remembrance, that I wept before them. Although I had met with so much affliction, and my heart was many times ready to break, yet could I not shed one tear in their sight: but rather had been all this while in a maze, and like one astonished: but now I may say as, Psalm 137. 1. *By the rivers of Babylon, there we sat down: yea, we wept when we remembered Zion.* There one of them asked me, why I wept, I could hardly tell what to say: yet I answered, they would kill me: No, said he, none will hurt you. Then came one of them and gave me two spoonfuls of meal to comfort me, and another gave me half a pint of peas; which was more worth than many bushels at another time. Then I went to see King Philip, he bade me come in and sit down, and asked me whether I would smoke (a usual compliment nowadays amongst saints and sinners) but this no way suited me. For though I had formerly used tobacco, yet I had left it ever since I was first taken. It seems to be a bait, the devil lays to make men lose their precious time: I remember with shame, how formerly, when I had taken two or three pipes, I was presently ready for another, such a bewitching thing it is: but I thank God, he has now given me power over it; surely there are many who may be better employed than to lie sucking a stinking tobacco pipe.

Now the Indians gather their forces to go against Northampton: overnight one went about yelling and hooting to give notice of the design. Whereupon they fell to boiling of ground nuts, and parching of corn (as many as had it) for their provision: and in the morning away they went. During my abode in this place, Philip spake to me to make a shirt for his boy, which I did, for which he gave me a shilling: I offered the money to my master, but he bade me keep it: and with it I bought a piece of horse flesh. Afterwards he asked me to make a cap for his boy, for which he invited me to dinner. I went, and he gave me a pancake, about as big as two fingers; it was made of parched wheat, beaten, and fried in bear's grease, but I thought I never tasted pleasanter meat in my life. There was a squaw who spake to me to make a shirt for her sannup,[32] for which she gave me a piece of bear. Another asked me to knit a pair of stockings, for which she gave me a quart of peas: I boiled my peas and bear together, and invited my master and mistress to dinner, but the proud gossip, because I served them both in one dish, would eat nothing, except one bit that he gave her upon the point of his knife.[33] Hearing that my son was come to this place, I went to see him, and found him lying flat upon the ground: I asked him how he could sleep so? He answered me, that he was not asleep, but at prayer; and lay so, that they might not observe what he was doing. I pray God he may remember these things now he is returned in safety. At this place (the sun now getting higher) what with the beams and heat of the sun, and the smoke of the wigwams, I thought I should have been blind. I could scarce discern one wigwam from another. There was here one Mary Thurston of Medfield, who seeing how it was with me, lent me a hat to wear: but as soon as I was gone, the squaw (who owned that Mary Thurston) came running after me, and got it away again. Here was the squaw that gave me one spoonful of meal. I put it in my pocket to keep it safe: yet notwithstanding somebody stole it, but put five Indian corns in the room of it: which corns were the greatest provisions I had in my travel for one day.

The Indians returning from Northampton, brought with them some horses, and sheep, and other things which they had taken: I desired them, that they would carry me to Albany, upon one of those horses, and sell me for powder: for so they had sometimes discoursed. I was utterly hopeless of getting home on foot, the way that I came. I could hardly bear to think of the many weary steps I had taken, to come to this place.

### *The Ninth Remove*

But instead of going either to Albany or homeward, we must go five miles up the river, and then go over it. Here we abode a while. Here lived a sorry Indian, who spoke to me to make him a shirt. When I had done it, he would pay me nothing. But he living by the riverside, where I often went to fetch water, I would often be putting of him in mind, and calling for my pay: at last he told me if I would make another shirt, for a papoose not yet born, he would give me a knife, which he did when I had done it. I carried the knife in, and my master asked me to give it him, and I was not a little glad that I had anything that they would accept of, and be pleased with. When we were at this place, my master's maid came home, she had been gone three weeks into the Narragansett country, to fetch corn, where they had stored up some in the ground: she brought home about a peck and a half of corn. This was about the time that their great captain, Naananto, was killed in the Narragansett country. My son being now about a mile from me, I asked liberty to go and see him, they bade me go, and away I went: but quickly lost myself, travelling over hills and through swamps, and could not find the way to him. And I cannot but admire at the wonderful power and goodness of God to me, in that, though I was gone from home, and met with all sorts of Indians, and those I had no knowledge of, and there being no Christian soul near me; yet not one of them offered the least imaginable miscarriage to me. I turned homeward again, and met with my master, he showed me the way to my son: when I came to him I found him not well: and withall he had a boil on his side, which much troubled him: we bemoaned[34] one another a while, as the Lord helped us, and then I returned again. When I was returned, I found myself as unsatisfied as I was before. I went up and down mourning and lamenting: and my spirit was ready to sink, with the thoughts of my poor children: my son was ill, and I could not but think of his mournful looks, and no Christian friend was near him, to do any office of love for him, either for soul or body. And my poor girl, I knew not where she was, nor whether she was sick, or well, or alive, or dead. I repaired under these thoughts to my Bible (my great comfort in that time) and that scripture came to my hand, *Cast thy burden upon the Lord, and He shall sustain thee*, Psalms 55. 22.

But I was fain to go and look after something to satisfy my hunger, and going among the wigwams, I went into one, and there found a squaw who showed herself very kind to me, and gave me a piece of bear. I put it into my pocket, and came home, but could not find an opportunity to broil it, for fear they would get it from me, and there it lay all that day and night in my stinking pocket. In the morning I went to the same squaw, who had a kettle of ground nuts boiling: I asked her to let me boil my piece of bear in her kettle, which she did, and gave me some ground nuts to eat with it: and I cannot but think how pleasant it was to me. I have sometimes seen bear baked very handsomely among the English, and some like it, but the thought that it was bear, made me tremble: but now that was savory to me that one would think was enough to turn the stomach of a brute creature.

One bitter cold day, I could find no room to sit down before the fire: I went out, and could not tell what to do, but I went into another wigwam, where they were also sitting around the fire, but the squaw laid a skin for me, and bade me sit down, and gave me some ground nuts, and bade me come again: and told me they would buy me, if they were able, and yet these were strangers to me that I never saw before.

### *The Tenth Remove*

That day a small part of the company removed about three-quarters of a mile, intending further the next day. When they came to the place where they intended to lodge, and had pitched their wigwams, being hungry I went again back to the place we were before at, to get something to eat: being encouraged by the squaw's kindness, who bade me come again; when I was there, there came an Indian to look after me, who when he had found me, kicked me all along: I went home and found venison roasting that night, but they would not give me one bit of it. Sometimes I met with favor, and sometimes with nothing but frowns.

### *The Eleventh Remove*

The next day in the morning they took their travel, intending a day's journey up the river. I took my load at my back, and quickly we came to wade over the river: and passed over tiresome and wearisome hills. One hill was so steep that I was fain to creep up upon my knees, and to hold by the twigs and bushes to keep myself from falling backward. My head also was so light, that I usually reeled as I went; but I hope all these wearisome steps that I have taken, are but a forewarning to me of the heavenly rest. *I know, O Lord, that thy judgments are right, and that thou in faithfulness hast afflicted me,* Psalm 119. 75.

### *The Twelfth Remove*

It was upon a Sabbath day morning, that they prepared for their travel. This morning I asked my master whether he would sell me to my husband; he answered me Nux,[35] which did much rejoice my spirit. My mistress, before we went, was gone to the burial of a papoose, and returning, she found me sitting and reading in my Bible; she snatched it hastily out of my hand, and threw it out of doors; I ran out and caught it up, and put it into my pocket, and never let her see it afterward. Then they packed up their things to be gone, and gave me my load: I complained it was too heavy, whereupon she gave me a slap in the face, and bade me go; I lifted up my heart to God, hoping the redemption was not far off: and the rather because their insolence grew worse and worse.

But the thoughts of my going homeward (for so we bent our course) much cheered my spirit, and made my burden seem light, and almost nothing at all. But (to my amazement and great perplexity) the scale was soon turned: for when we had gone a little way, on a sudden my mistress gives out, she would go no further, but turn back again, and said, I must go back again with her, and she called her sannup, and would have had him gone back also, but he would not, but said, he would go on, and come to us again in three days. My spirit was upon this, I confess, very impatient, and almost outrageous. I thought I could as well have died as went back: I cannot declare the trouble that I was in about it; but yet back again I must go. As soon as I had an opportunity, I took my Bible to read, and that quieting scripture came to my hand, Psalms 46. 10. *Be still, and know that I am God.* Which stilled my spirit for the present: but a sore time of trial, I concluded, I had to go through. My master being gone, who seemed to me the best friend that I had of an Indian, both in cold and hunger, and quickly so it proved. Down I sat, with my heart as full as it could hold, and yet so hungry that I could not sit neither: but going out to see what I could find, and walking among the trees, I found six acorns, and two chestnuts, which were some refreshment to me. Towards night I gathered me some sticks for my own comfort, that I might not lie a-cold: but when we came to lie down they bade me go out, and lie somewhere else, for they had company (they said) come in more than their own: I told them, I could not tell where to go, they bade me go look; I told them, if I went to another wigwam they would be angry, and send me home again. Then one of the company drew his sword, and told me he would run me through if I did not go presently. Then was I fain to stoop to this rude fellow, and to go out in the night, I knew not whither. Mine eyes have seen that fellow afterwards walking up and down Boston, under the appearance of a friendly Indian, and several others of the like cut. I went to one wigwam, and they told me they had no room. Then I went to another, and they said the same; at last an old Indian bade me come to him, and his squaw gave me some ground nuts; she gave me also something to lay under my head, and a good fire we had: and through the good providence of God, I had a comfortable lodging that night. In the morning, another Indian bade me come at night, and he would give me six ground nuts, which I did. We were at this place and time about two miles from Connecticut river. We went in the morning to gather ground nuts, to the river, and went back again that night. I went with a good load at my back (for they when they went, though but a little way, would carry all their trumpery with them). I told them the skin was off my back, but I had no other comforting answer from them than this, That it would be no matter if my head were off too.

### *The Thirteenth Remove*

Instead of going toward the Bay, which was that I desired, I must go with them five or six miles down the river into a mighty thicket of brush: where we abode almost a fortnight. Here one asked me to make a shirt for her papoose, for which she gave me a mess of broth, which was thickened with meal made of the bark of a tree, and to make it the better, she had put into it about a handful of peas, and a few roasted ground nuts. I had not seen my son a pretty while, and here was an Indian of whom I made inquiry after him, and asked him when he saw him: he answered me, that such a time his master roasted him, and that himself did eat a piece of him, as big as his two fingers, and that he was very good meat: but the Lord upheld my spirit, under this discouragement; and I considered their horrible addictedness to lying, and that there is not one of them that makes the least conscience of speaking of truth. In this place, on a cold night, as I lay by the fire, I removed a stick that kept the heat from me, a squaw moved it down again, at which I looked up, and she threw a handful of ashes in my eyes: I thought I should have been quite blinded, and have never seen more: but lying down, the water run out of my eyes, and carried the dirt with it, that by the morning, I recovered my sight again. Yet upon this, and the like occasions, I hope it is not too much to say with Job, *Have pity upon me, have pity upon me, O ye my friends, for the hand of the Lord has touched me.*[36] And here I cannot but remember how many times sitting in their wigwams, and musing on things past,

I should suddenly leap up and run out, as if I had been at home, forgetting where I was, and what my condition was: but when I was without, and saw nothing but wilderness, and woods, and a company of barbarous heathens, my mind quickly returned to me, which made me think of that, spoken concerning Samson, who said, *I will go out and shake myself as at other times, but he wist not that the Lord was departed from him.*[37] About this time I began to think that all my hopes of restoration would come to nothing. I thought of the English army, and hoped for their coming, and being taken by them, but that failed. I hoped to be carried to Albany, as the Indians had discoursed before, but that failed also. I thought of being sold to my husband, as my master spake, but instead of that, my master himself was gone, and I left behind, so that my spirit was now quite ready to sink. I asked them to let me go out and pick up some sticks, that I might get alone, and pour out my heart unto the Lord. Then also I took my Bible to read, but I found no comfort here neither, which many times I was wont to find: so easy a thing it is with God to dry up the streams of scripture comfort from us. Yet I can say, that in all my sorrows and afflictions, God did not leave me to have my impatience work towards himself, as if his ways were unrighteous. But I knew that he laid upon me less than I deserved. Afterward, before this doleful time ended with me, I was turning the leaves of my Bible, and the Lord brought to me some scriptures, which did a little revive me, as that Isaiah 55. 8, *For my thoughts are not your thoughts, neither are your ways my ways, saith the Lord.* And also that, Psalms 37. 5, *Commit thy way unto the Lord, trust also in him, and he shall bring it to pass.* About this time they came yelping from Hadley, where they had killed three Englishmen, and brought one captive with them, *viz.* Thomas Read. They all gathered about the poor man, asking him many questions. I desired also to go and see him; and when I came, he was crying bitterly, supposing they would quickly kill him. Whereupon I asked one of them, whether they intended to kill him; he answered me, they would not: he being a little cheered with that, I asked him about the welfare of my husband, he told me he saw him such a time in the Bay, and he was well, but very melancholy. By which I certainly understood (though I suspected it before) that whatsoever the Indians told me respecting him was vanity and lies. Some of them told me, he was dead, and they had killed him: some said he was married again, and that the governor wished him to marry; and told him he should have his choice, and that all persuaded I was dead. So like were these barbarous creatures to him who was a liar from the beginning.

As I was sitting once in the wigwam here, Philip's maid came in with the child in her arms, and asked me to give her a piece of my apron, to make a flap for it. I told her I would not: then my mistress bade me give it, but still I said no: the maid told me if I would not give her a piece, she would tear a piece off it: I told her I would tear her coat then, with that my mistress rises up, and takes up a stick big enough to have killed me, and struck at me with it, but I stepped out, and she struck the stick into the mat of the wigwam. But while she was pulling of it out, I ran to the maid and gave her all my apron, and so that storm went over.

Hearing that my son was come to this place, I went to see him, and told him his father was well, but very melancholy: he told me he was as much grieved for his father as for himself; I wondered at his speech, for I thought I had enough upon my spirit in reference to myself, to make me mindless of my husband and everyone else: they being safe among their friends. He told me also, that a while before, his master (together with other Indians) were going to the French for powder; but by the way the Mohawks met with them, and killed four of their company which made the rest turn back again, for which I desired that myself and he may bless the Lord; for it might have been worse with him, had he been sold to the French, than it proved to be in his remaining with the Indians.

I went to see an English youth in this place, one John Gilbert of Springfield. I found him lying without doors, upon the ground; I asked him how he did? He told me he was very sick of a flux, with eating so much blood: they had turned him out of the wigwam, and with him an Indian papoose, almost dead (whose parents had been killed), in a bitter cold day, without fire or clothes: the young-man himself had nothing on, but his shirt and waistcoat. This sight was enough to melt a heart of flint. There they lay quivering in the cold, the youth round like a dog; the papoose stretched out, with his eyes and nose and mouth full of dirt, and yet alive, and groaning. I advised John to go and get to some fire: he told me he could not stand, but I persuaded him still, lest he should lie there and die: and with much ado I got him to a fire, and went myself home. As soon as I was got home, his master's daughter came after me, to know what I had done with the Englishman, I told her I had got him to a fire in such a place. Now had I need to pray Paul's prayer, 2 Thessalonians 3. 2. *That we may be delivered from unreasonable and wicked men.* For her satisfaction I went along with her, and brought her to him; but before I got homc again, it was noised about, that I was running away and getting the English youth, along with me; that as soon as I came in, they began to rant and domineer: asking me where I had been, and what I had been doing? and saying they would knock him on the head: I told them, I had been seeing the English youth, and that I would not run away, they told me I lied, and taking up a hatchet, they came to me, and said they would knock me down if I stirred out again; and so confined me to the wigwam. Now may I say with David, 2 Samuel 24. 14, *I am in a great strait.* If I keep in, I must die with hunger, and if I go out, I must be knocked in head. This distressed condition held that day, and half the next; and then the Lord remembered me, whose mercies are great. Then came an Indian to me with a pair of stockings that were too big for him, and he would have me ravel them out, and knit them fit for him. I showed myself willing, and bade him ask my mistress if I might go along with him a little way; she said yes, I might, but I was not a little refreshed with that news, that I had my liberty again. Then I went along with him, and he gave me some roasted ground nuts, which did again revive my feeble stomach.

Being got out of her sight, I had time and liberty again to look into my Bible: which was my guide by day, and my pillow by night. Now that comfortable scripture presented itself to me, Isaiah 54. 7. *For a small moment have I forsaken thee, but with great mercies will I gather thee.* Thus the Lord carried me along from one time to another, and made good to me this precious promise, and many others. Then my son came to see me, and I asked his master to let him stay a while with me, that I might comb his head, and look over him, for he was almost overcome with lice. He told me, when I had done, that he was very hungry, but I had nothing to relieve him; but bid him go into the wigwams as he went along, and see if he could get anything among them. Which he did, and it seems tarried a little too long;

for his master was angry with him, and beat him, and then sold him. Then he came running to tell me he had a new master, and that he had given him some ground nuts already. Then I went along with him to his new master who told me he loved him: and he should not want. So his master carried him away, and I never saw him afterward, till I saw him at Pascataqua in Portsmouth.

That night they bade me go out of the wigwam again: my mistress's papoose was sick, and it died that night, and there was one benefit in it, that there was more room. I went to a wigwam, and they bade me come in, and gave me a skin to lie upon, and a mess of venison and ground nuts, which was a choice dish among them. On the morrow they buried the papoose, and afterward, both morning and evening, there came a company to mourn and howl with her: though I confess, I could not much condole with them. Many sorrowful days I had in this place: often getting alone; *like a crane, or a swallow, so did I chatter: I did mourn as a dove, mine eyes ail with looking upward. Oh, Lord, I am oppressed; undertake for me,* Isaiah 38. 14. I could tell the Lord as Hezekiah, verse 3. *Remember now O Lord, I beseech thee, how I have walked before thee in truth.*[38] Now had I time to examine all my ways: my conscience did not accuse me of unrighteousness toward one or other: yet I saw how in my walk with God I had been a careless creature. As David said, *Against thee, thee only have I sinned:* and I might say with the poor publican, *God be merciful unto me a sinner.*[39] On the Sabbath days, I could look upon the sun and think how people were going to the house of God, to have their souls refreshed; and then home, and their bodies also: but I was destitute of both; and might say as the poor prodigal, *he would fain have filled his belly with the husks that the swine did eat, and no man gave unto him,* Luke 15. 16. For I must say with him, *Father I have sinned against heaven, and in thy sight,* verse 21.[40] I remembered how on the night before and after the Sabbath, when my family was about me, and relations and neighbors with us, we could pray and sing, and then refresh our bodies with the good creatures of God; and then have a comfortable bed to lie down on: but instead of all this, I had only a little swill for the body, and then like a swine, must lie down on the ground. I cannot express to man the sorrow that lay upon my spirit, the Lord knows it. Yet that comfortable scripture would often come to my mind,

*For a small moment have I forsaken thee, but with great mercies will I gather thee.*

### *The Fourteenth Remove*

Now must we pack up and be gone from this thicket, bending our course toward the Bay towns, I having nothing to eat by the way this day, but a few crumbs of cake, that an Indian gave my girl the same day we were taken. She gave it me, and I put it in my pocket; there it lay, till it was so moldy (for want of good baking) that one could not tell what it was made of; it fell all to crumbs, and grew so dry and hard, that it was like little flints; and this refreshed me many times, when I was ready to faint. It was in my thoughts when I put it into my mouth, that if ever I returned, I would tell the world what a blessing the Lord gave to such mean food. As we went along, they killed a deer, with a young one in her, they gave me a piece of the fawn, and it was so young and tender, that one might eat the bones as well as the flesh, and yet I thought it very good. When night came on we sat down; it rained, but they quickly got up a bark wigwam, where I lay dry that night. I looked out in the morning, and many of them had lain in the rain all night, I saw by their reeking. Thus the Lord dealt mercifully with me many times, and I fared better than many of them. In the morning they took the blood of the deer, and put it into the paunch, and so boiled it; I could eat nothing of that, though they ate it sweetly. And yet they were so nice[41] in other things, that when I had fetched water, and had put the dish I dipped the water with, into the kettle of water which I brought, they would say, they would knock me down: for they said, it was a sluttish trick.

### *The Fifteenth Remove*

We went on our travel. I having got one handful of ground nuts, for my support that day, they gave me my load, and I went on cheerfully (with the thoughts of going homeward) having my burden more on my back than my spirit: we came to Baquag river again that day, near which we abode a few days. Sometimes one of them would give me a pipe, another a little tobacco, another a little salt: which I would change for a little victuals. I cannot but think what a wolfish appetite persons have in a starving condition: for many times when they gave me that which was hot, I was so greedy, that I should burn my mouth, that it would trouble me hours after, and yet I should quickly do the same again. And after I was thoroughly hungry, I was never again satisfied. For though sometimes it fell out, that I got enough, and did eat till I could eat no more, yet I was as unsatisfied as I was when I began. And now could I see that scripture verified (there being many scriptures which we do not take notice of, or understand till we are afflicted) Micah 6. 14. *Thou shalt eat and not be satisfied.* Now I might see more than ever before, the miseries that sin hath brought upon us: many times I should be ready to run out against the heathen, but the scripture would quiet me again, Amos 3. 6, *Shall there be evil in the city, and the Lord hath not done it?* The Lord help me to make a right improvement of His word, and that I might learn that great lesson, Micah 6. 8–9. *He hath showed thee (O Man) what is good, and what doth the Lord require of thee, but to do justly, and love mercy, and walk humbly with thy God? Hear ye the rod, and who hath appointed it.*

### *The Sixteenth Remove*

We began this remove with wading over Baquag river: the water was up to the knees, and the stream very swift, and so cold that I thought it would have cut me in sunder. I was so weak and feeble, that I reeled as I went along, and thought there I must end my days at last, after my bearing and getting through so many difficulties; the Indians stood laughing to see me staggering along: but in my distress the Lord gave me experience of the truth, and goodness of that promise, Isaiah 43. 2. *When thou passest through the waters, I will be with thee, and through the rivers, they shall not overflow thee.* Then I sat down to put on my stockings and shoes, with the tears running down mine eyes, and many sorrowful thoughts in my heart, but I got up to go along with them. Quickly there came up to us an Indian, who informed them, that I must go to Wachusett to my master, for there was a letter come from the Council to the Sagamores, about redeeming the captives, and that there would be another in fourteen days, and that I must be there ready. My heart was so heavy before that I could scarce speak or go in the path; and yet now so light, that I could run. My strength seemed to come again, and recruit my feeble knees, and aching heart: yet it pleased them to go but one mile that night, and there we stayed two days. In that time came a company of Indians to us, near thirty, all on horseback. My heart skipped within me, thinking they had been Englishmen at the first sight of them, for they were dressed in English apparel, with hats, white neckcloths, and sashes about their waists, and ribbons upon their shoulders: but when they came near, there was a vast difference between the lovely faces of Christians, and the foul looks of these heathens, which much damped my spirit again.

### *The Seventeenth Remove*

A comfortable remove it was to me, because of my hopes. They gave me a pack, and along we went cheerfully; but quickly my will proved more than my strength; having little or no refreshing my strength failed me, and my spirits were almost quite gone. Now may I say with David, Psalm 109. 22–24. *I am poor and needy, and my heart is wounded within me. I am gone like the shadow when it declineth: I am tossed up and down like the locust; my knees are weak through fasting, and my flesh faileth of fatness.* At night we came to an Indian town, and the Indians sat down by a wigwam discoursing, but I was almost spent, and could scarce speak. I laid down my load, and went into the wigwam, and there sat an Indian boiling of horse's feet (they being wont to eat the flesh first, and when the feet were old and dried, and they had nothing else, they would cut off the feet and use them). I asked him to give me a little of his broth, or water they were boiling in; he took a dish, and gave me one spoonful of samp, and bid me take as much of the broth as I would. Then I put some of the hot water to the samp, and drank it up, and my spirit came again. He gave me also a piece of the ruff or ridding of the small guts, and I broiled it on the coals;[42] and now may I say with Jonathan, *See, I pray you, how mine eyes have been enlightened, because I tasted a little of this honey,* 1 Samuel. 14. 29. Now is my spirit revived again; though means be never so inconsiderable, yet if the Lord bestow his blessing upon them, they shall refresh both soul and body.

### *The Eighteenth Remove*

We took up our packs and along we went, but a wearisome day I had of it. As we went along I saw an Englishman stripped naked, and lying dead upon the ground, but knew not who it was. Then we came to another Indian town, where we stayed all night. In this town there were four English children, captives; and one of them my own sister's. I went to see how she did, and she was well, considering her captive condition. I would have tarried that night with her, but they that owned her would not suffer it. Then I went into another wigwam, where they were boiling corn and beans, which was a lovely sight to see, but I could not get a taste thereof. Then I went to another wigwam, where there were two of the English children; the squaw was boiling horse's feet, then she cut me off a little piece, and gave one of the English children a piece also. Being very hungry I had quickly eaten up mine, but the child could not bite it, it was so tough and sinewy, but lay sucking, gnawing, chewing and slobbering of it in the mouth and hand, then I took it of the child, and ate it myself, and savory it was to my taste. Then I may say as Job, 6. 7. *The things that my soul refused to touch, are as my sorrowful meat.* Thus the Lord made that pleasant refreshing, which another time would have been an abomination. Then I went home to my mistress's wigwam; and they told me I disgraced my master with begging, and if I did so any more, they would knock me in the head: I told them, they had as good knock me in the head as starve me to death.

### *The Nineteenth Remove*

They said, when we went out, that we must travel to Wachusett this day. But a bitter weary day I had of it, travelling now three days together, without resting any day between. At last, after many weary steps, I saw Wachusett hills, but many miles off. Then we came to a great swamp, through which we travelled, up to the knees in mud and water, which was heavy going to one tired before. Being almost spent, I thought I should have sunk down at last, and never gotten out; but I may say, as in Psalm 94. 18, *When my foot slipped, thy mercy, O Lord, held me up.* Going along, having indeed my life, but little spirit, Philip, who was in the company, came up and took me by the hand, and said, Two weeks more and you shall be mistress again. I asked him, if he spake true? He answered, Yes, and quickly you shall come to your master again; who had been gone from us three weeks. After many weary steps we came to Wachusett, where he was: and glad I was to see him. He asked me, When I washed me? I told him not this month, then he fetched me some water himself, and bid me wash, and gave me the glass to see how I looked; and bid his squaw give me something to eat: so she gave me a mess of beans and meat, and a little ground nut cake. I was wonderfully revived with this favor showed me, Psalm 106. 46, *He made them also to be pitied, of all those that carried them captives.*

My master had three squaws, living sometimes with one, and sometimes with another one, this old squaw, at whose wigwam I was, and with whom my master had been those three weeks. Another was Weetamoo, with whom I had lived and served all this while: a severe and proud dame she was, bestowing every day in dressing herself neat as much time as any of the gentry of the land: powdering her hair, and painting her face, going with necklaces, with jewels in her ears, and bracelets upon her hands: when she had dressed herself, her work was to make girdles of wampum and beads. The third squaw was a younger one, by whom he had two papooses. By that time I was refreshed by the old squaw, with whom my master was, Weetamoo's maid came to call me home, at which I fell a-weeping. Then the old squaw told me, to encourage me, that if I wanted victuals, I should come to her, and that I should lie there in her wigwam. Then I went with the maid, and quickly came again and lodged there. The squaw laid a mat under me, and a good rug over me; the first time I had any such kindness showed me. I understood that Weetamoo thought, that if she should let me go and serve with the old squaw, she would be in danger to lose, not only my service, but the redemption pay also. And I was not a little glad to hear this; being by it raised in my hopes,[43] that in God's due time there would be an end of this sorrowful hour. Then in came an Indian, and asked me to knit him three pair of stockings, for which I had a hat, and a silk handkerchief. Then another asked me to make her a shift, for which she gave me an apron.

Then came Tom and Peter,[44] with the second letter from the Council, about the captives. Though they were Indians, I got them by the hand, and burst out into tears; my heart was so full that I could not speak to them; but recovering myself, I asked them how my husband did, and all my friends and acquaintance: They said, They are all very well, but melancholy. They brought me two biscuits, and a pound of tobacco. The tobacco I quickly gave away; when it was all gone, one asked me to give him a pipe of tobacco, I told him it was all gone; then began he to rant and threaten. I told him when my husband came I would give him some: Hang him rogue (says he) I will knock out his brains, if he comes here. And then again, in the same breath they would say, That if there should come an hundred without guns, they would do them no hurt. So unstable and like madmen they were. So that fearing the worst, I durst not send to my husband, though there were some thoughts of his coming to redeem and fetch me, not knowing what might follow. For there was little more trust to them than to the master they served.[45] When the letter was come, the sagamores met to consult about the captives, and called me to them to enquire how much my husband would give to redeem me. When I came I sat down among them, as I was wont to do, as their manner is: then they bade me stand up, and said, they were the General Court.[46] They bid me speak what I thought he would give. Now knowing that all we had was destroyed by the Indians, I was in a great strait: I thought if I should speak of but a little, it would be slighted, and hinder the matter; if of a great sum, I knew not where it would be procured: yet at a venture, I said twenty pounds, yet desired them to take less; but they would not hear of that, but sent that message to Boston, that for twenty pounds I should be redeemed. It was a Praying Indian that wrote their letter for them. There was another Praying Indian, who told me, that he had a brother, that would not eat horse; his conscience was so tender and scrupulous (though as large as hell, for the destruction of poor Christians). Then he said, he read that scripture to him, 2 Kings, 6. 25. *There was a famine in Samaria, and behold they besieged it, until an ass's head was sold for fourscore pieces of silver, and the fourth part of a kab of dove's dung, for five pieces of silver.* He expounded this place to his brother, and showed him that it was lawful to eat that in a famine which is not at another time. And now, says he, he will eat horse with any Indian of them all. There was another Praying Indian, who when he had done all the mischief that he could, betrayed his own father into the English hands, thereby to purchase his own life. Another Praying Indian was at Sudbury fight, though, as he deserved, he was afterward hanged for it. There was another Praying Indian, so wicked and cruel, as to wear a string about his neck, strung with Christians' fingers. Another Praying Indian, when they went to Sudbury fight, went with them, and his squaw also with him, with her papoose at her back: before they went to that fight, they got a company together to powwow; the manner was as followeth. There was one that kneeled upon a deerskin, with the company round him in a ring who kneeled, and striking upon the ground with their hands, and with sticks, and muttering or humming with their mouths; beside him who kneeled in the ring, there also stood one with a gun in his hand: then he on the deerskin made a speech, and all manifested assent to it: and so they did many times together. Then they bade him with the gun go out of the ring, which he did, but when he was out, they called him in again; but he seemed to make a stand, then they called the more earnestly, till he returned again: then they all sang. Then they gave him two guns, in either hand one: and so he on the deerskin began again; and at the end of every sentence in his speaking, they all assented, humming or muttering with their mouths, and striking upon the ground with their hands. Then they bade him with the two guns go out of the ring again; which he did, a little way. Then they called him in again, but he made a stand; so they called him with greater earnestness; but he stood reeling and wavering as if he knew not whither he should stand or fall, or which way to go. Then they called him with exceeding great vehemency, all of them, one and another: after a little while he turned in, staggering as he went, with his arms stretched out, in either hand a gun. As soon as he came in, they all sang and rejoiced exceedingly a while. And then he upon the deerskin, made another speech unto which they all assented in a rejoicing manner: and so they ended their business, and forthwith went to Sudbury-fight. To my thinking they went without any scruple, but that they should prosper, and gain the victory. And they went out not so rejoicing, but they came home with as great a victory. For they said they had killed two captains, and almost an hundred men. One Englishman they brought along with them: and he said, it was too true, for they had made sad work at Sudbury, as indeed it proved. Yet they came home without that rejoicing and triumphing over their victory, which they were wont to show at other times, but rather like dogs (as they say) which have lost their ears. Yet I could not perceive that it was for their own loss of men: they said, they had not lost above five or six: and I missed none, except in one wigwam.[47] When they went, they acted as if the devil had told them that they should gain the victory: and now they acted, as if the devil had told them they should have a fall. Whether it were so or no, I cannot tell, but so it proved, for quickly they began to fall, and so held on that summer, till they came to utter ruin. They came home on a Sabbath day, and the powwow that kneeled upon the deerskin[48] came home (I may say, without abuse) as black as the devil. When my master came home, he came to me and bid me make a shirt for his papoose, of a holland-laced pillowbeer.[49] About that time there came an Indian to me and bid me come to his wigwam, at night, and he would give me some pork and ground nuts. Which I did, and as I was eating, another Indian said to me, he seems to be your good friend, but he killed two Englishmen at Sudbury, and there lie their clothes behind you: I looked behind me, and there I saw bloody clothes, with bullet holes in them; yet the Lord suffered not this wretch to do me any hurt; yea, instead of that, he many times refreshed me: five or six times did he and his squaw refresh my feeble carcass. If I went to their wigwam at any time, they would always give me something, and yet they were strangers that I never saw before. Another squaw gave me a piece of fresh pork, and a little salt with it, and lent me her pan to fry it in; and I cannot but remember what a sweet, pleasant and delightful relish that bit had to me, to this day. So little do we prize common mercies when we have them to the full.

### *The Twentieth Remove*

It was their usual manner to remove, when they had done any mischief, lest they should be found out: and so they did at this time. We went about three or four miles, and there they built a great wigwam, big enough to hold an hundred Indians, which they did in preparation to a great day of dancing. They would say now amongst themselves, that the governor would be so angry for his loss at Sudbury, that he would send no more about the captives, which made me grieve and tremble. My sister being not far from the place where we now were, and hearing that I was here, desired her master to let her come and see me, and he was willing to it, and would go with her: but she being ready before him, told him she would go before, and was come within a mile or two of the place; then he overtook her, and began to rant as if he had been mad; and made her go back again in the rain; so that I never saw her till I saw her in Charlestown. But the Lord requited many of their ill doings, for this Indian her master, was hanged after at Boston. The Indians now began to come from all quarters, against their merry dancing day. Among some of them came one Goodwife Kettle: I told her my heart was so heavy that it was ready to break: so is mine too, said she, but yet said, I hope we shall hear some good news shortly. I could hear how earnestly my sister desired to see me, and I as earnestly desired to see her: and yet neither of us could get an opportunity. My daughter was also now about a mile off, and I had not seen her in nine or ten weeks, as I had not seen my sister since our first taking. I earnestly desired them to let me go and see them: yea, I entreated, begged, and persuaded them, but to let me see my daughter; and yet so hard-hearted were they, that they would not suffer it. They made use of their tyrannical power whilst they had it: but through the Lord's wonderful mercy, their time was now but short.

On a Sabbath day, the sun being about an hour high in the afternoon, came Mr. John Hoar (the Council permitting him, and his own forward[50] spirit inclining him) together with the two forementioned Indians, Tom and Peter, with their third letter from the Council. When they came near, I was abroad: though I saw them not, they presently called me in, and bade me sit down and not stir. Then they caught up their guns, and away they ran, as if an enemy had been at hand; and the guns went off apace. I manifested some great trouble, and they asked me what was the matter? I told them, I thought they had killed the Englishman (for they had in the meantime informed me that an Englishman was come), they said, No; they shot over his horse, and under, and before his horse; and they pushed him this way and that way, at their pleasure, showing what they could do: then they let them come to their wigwams. I begged of them to let me see the Englishman, but they would not. But there was I fain to sit their pleasure. When they had talked their fill with him, they suffered me to go to him. We asked each other of our welfare, and how my husband did, and all my friends? He told me they were all well, and would be glad to see me. Amongst other things which my husband sent me, there came a pound of tobacco: which I sold for nine shillings in money: for many of the Indians for want of tobacco, smoked hemlock, and ground ivy. It was a great mistake in any, who thought I sent for tobacco: for through the favor of God, that desire was overcome. I now asked them, whether I should go home with Mr. Hoar? They answered No, one and another of them: and it being night, we lay down with that answer; in the morning, Mr. Hoar invited the sagamores to dinner; but when we went to get it ready, we found that they had stolen the greatest part of the provision Mr. Hoar had brought, out of his bags, in the night. And we may see the wonderful power of God, in that one passage, in that when there was such a great number of the Indians together, and so greedy of a little good food; and no English there, but Mr. Hoar and myself: that there they did not knock us in the head, and take what we had: there being not only some provision, but also trading cloth, a part of the twenty pounds agreed upon: but instead of doing us any mischief, they seemed to be ashamed of the fact, and said, it were some matchit Indian[51] that did it. Oh that we could believe that there is nothing too hard for God! God showed his power over the heathen in this, as he did over the hungry lions when Daniel was cast into the den. Mr. Hoar called them betime to dinner, but they ate very little, they being so busy in dressing themselves, and getting ready for their dance: which was carried on by eight of them, four men and four squaws; my master and mistress being two. He was dressed in his holland shirt, with great laces sewed at the tail of it, he had his silver buttons, his white stockings, his garters were hung round with shillings, and he had girdles of wampum upon his head and shoulders. She had a kersey coat, and covered with girdles of wampum from the loins upward: her arms from her elbows to her hands were covered with bracelets; there were handfuls of necklaces about her neck, and several sorts of jewels in her ears. She had fine red stockings, and white shoes, her hair powdered and face painted red, that was always before black. And all the dancers were after the same manner. There were two other singing and knocking on a kettle for their music. They kept hopping up and down one after another, with a kettle of water in the midst, standing warm upon some embers, to drink of when they were dry. They held on till it was almost night, throwing out wampum to the standers-by. At night I asked them again, if I should go home? They all as one said No, except my husband would come for me. When we were lain down, my master went out of the wigwam, and by and by sent in an Indian called James the Printer, who told Mr. Hoar, that my master would let me go home tomorrow, if he would [let] him have one pint of liquors. Then Mr. Hoar called his own Indians, Tom and Peter, and bid them go and see whether he would promise before them three: and if he would, he should have it; which he did, and he had it. Then Philip smelling the business called me to him, and asked me what I would give him, to tell me some good news, and speak a good word for me. I told him, I could not tell what to give him, I would anything I had, and asked him what he would have? He said, two coats and twenty shillings in money, and half a bushel of seed corn, and some tobacco. I thanked him for his love: but I knew the good news as well as the crafty fox. My master after he had had his drink, quickly came ranting into the wigwam again, and called for Mr. Hoar, drinking to him, and saying, He was a good man: and then again he would say, Hang him, rogue: being almost drunk, he would drink to him, and yet presently say he should be hanged. Then he called for me. I trembled to hear him, yet I was fain to go to him, and he drank to me, showing no incivility. He was the first Indian I saw drunk all the while that I was amongst them. At last his squaw ran out, and he after her, around the wigwam, with his money jingling at his knees: but she escaped him: but having an old squaw he ran to her: and so through the Lord's mercy, we were no more troubled that night. Yet I had not a comfortable night's rest: for I think I can say, I did not sleep for three nights together. The night before the letter came from the council, I could not rest, I was so full of fears and troubles, God many times leaving us most in the dark, when deliverance is nearest: yea, at this time I could not rest night nor day. The next night I was overjoyed, Mr. Hoar being come, and that with such good tidings. The third night I was even swallowed up with the thoughts of things, *viz.* that ever I should go home again; and that I must go, leaving my children behind me in the wilderness; so that sleep was now almost departed from my eyes.

On Tuesday morning they called their General Court (as they call it) to consult and determine, whether I should go home or no: and they all as one man did seemingly consent to it, that I should go home; except Philip, who would not come among them.

But before I go any further, I would take leave to mention a few remarkable passages of providence, which I took special notice of in my afflicted time.

1. Of the fair opportunity lost in the long march, a little after the fort fight, when our English army was so numerous, and in pursuit of the enemy, and so near as to take several and destroy them: and the enemy in such distress for food, that our men might track them by their rooting in the earth for ground nuts, whilst they were flying for their lives. I say, that then our army should want provision, and be forced to leave their pursuit and return homeward:[52] and the very next week the enemy came upon our town, like bears bereft of their whelps, or so many ravenous wolves, rending us and our lambs to death. But what shall I say? God seemed to leave His people to themselves, and order all things for His own holy ends. *Shall there be evil in the city and the Lord hath not done it? They are not grieved for the affliction of Joseph, therefore shall they go captive, with the first that go captive.*[53] It is the Lord's doing, and it should be marvelous in our eyes.

2. I cannot but remember how the Indians derided the slowness, and dullness of the English army, in its setting out. For after the desolations at Lancaster and Medfield, as I went along with them, they asked me when I thought the English army would come after them? I told them I could not tell: It may be they will come in May, said they. Thus did they scoff at us, as if the English would be a quarter of a year getting ready.

3. Which also I have hinted before, when the English army with new supplies were sent forth to pursue after the enemy, and they understanding it, fled before them till they came to Baquag river, where they forthwith went over safely: that that river should be impassable to the English. I can but admire to see the

wonderful providence of God in preserving the heathen for further affliction to our poor country. They could go in great numbers over, but the English must stop: God had an overruling hand in all those things.

4. It was thought, if their corn were cut down, they would starve and die with hunger: and all their corn that could be found, was destroyed, and they driven from that little they had in store, into the woods in the midst of winter; and yet how to admiration did the Lord preserve them for his Holy ends, and the destruction of many still amongst the English! Strangely did the Lord provide for them; that I did not see (all the time I was among them) one man, woman, or child, die with hunger.

Though many times they would eat that, that a hog or a dog would hardly touch; yet by that God strengthened them to be a scourge to His people.

The chief and commonest food was ground nuts: they ate also nuts and acorns, artichokes, lily roots, ground beans,[54] and several other weeds and roots, that I know not.

They would pick up old bones, and cut them to pieces at the joints, and if they were full of worms and maggots, they would scald them over the fire to make the vermin come out, and then boil them, and drink up the liquor, and then beat the great ends of them in a mortar, and so eat them. They would eat horse's guts, and ears, and all sorts of wild birds which they could catch: also bear, venison, beaver, tortoise, frogs, squirrels, dogs, skunks, rattlesnakes; yea, the very bark of trees; besides all sorts of creatures, and provision which they plundered from the English. I can but stand in admiration to see the wonderful power of God, in providing for such a vast number of our enemies in the wilderness, where there was nothing to be seen, but from hand to mouth. Many times in a morning, the generality of them would eat up all they had, and yet have some further supply against what they wanted. It is said, Psalm 81. 13–14. *Oh, that my people had hearkened to me, and Israel had walked in my ways, I should soon have subdued their enemies, and turned my hand against their adversaries.* But now our perverse and evil carriages in the sight of the Lord, have so offended Him, that instead of turning His hand against them, the Lord feeds and nourishes them up to be a scourge to the whole land.

5. Another thing that I would observe is, the strange provi-

dence of God, in turning things about when the Indians were at the highest, and the English at the lowest. I was with the enemy eleven weeks and five days, and not one week passed without the fury of the enemy, and some desolation by fire and sword upon one place or other. They mourned (with their black faces) for their own losses, yet triumphed and rejoiced in their inhuman, and many times devilish cruelty to the English. They would boast much of their victories; saying, that in two hours time they had destroyed such a captain, and his company at such a place; and such a captain and his company, in such a place; and such a captain and his company in such a place: and boast how many towns they had destroyed, and then scoff, and say, They had done them a good turn, to send them to heaven so soon. Again, they would say, This summer that they would knock all the rogues in the head, or drive them into the sea, or make them fly the country: thinking surely, Agag-like, *The bitterness of death is past.*[55] Now the heathen begin to think all is their own, and the poor Christians' hopes to fail (as to man) and now their eyes are more to God, and their hearts sigh heavenward: and to say in good earnest, *Help Lord, or we perish:*[56] When the Lord had brought His people to this, that they saw no help in anything but Himself: then He takes the quarrel into His own hand: and though they had made a pit, in their own imaginations, as deep as hell for the Christians that summer, yet the Lord hurled themselves into it. And the Lord had not so many ways before to preserve them, but now He hath as many to destroy them.

But to return again to my going home, where we may see a remarkable change of providence: at first they were all against it, except my husband would come for me; but afterwards they assented to it, and seemed much to rejoice in it; some asked me to send them some bread, others some tobacco, others shaking me by the hand, offering me a hood and scarf to ride in; not one moving hand or tongue against it. Thus hath the Lord answered my poor desire, and the many earnest requests of others put up unto God for me. In my travels an Indian came to me, and told me, if I were willing, he and his squaw would run away, and go home along with me: I told him No: I was not willing to run away, but desired to wait God's time, that I might go home quietly, and without fear. And now God hath granted me my desire. O the wonderful power of God that I have seen, and the experience that I have had: I have been in the midst of those roaring lions, and savage bears, that feared neither God, nor man, nor the devil, by night and day, alone and in company: sleeping all sorts together, and yet not one of them ever offered me the least abuse of unchastity to me, in word or action. Though some are ready to say, I speak it for my own credit; but I speak it in the presence of God, and to His glory. God's power is as great now, and as sufficient to save, as when he preserved Daniel in the lions' den; or the three children in the fiery furnace. I may well say as his Psalm 136. 1, *Oh give thanks unto the Lord for He is good, for His mercy endureth forever.* Let the redeemed of the Lord say so, whom He hath redeemed from the hand of the enemy, especially that I should come away in the midst of so many hundreds of enemies quietly and peaceably, and not a dog moving his tongue. So I took my leave of them, and in coming along my heart melted into tears, more than all the while I was with them, and I was almost swallowed up with the thoughts that ever I should go home again. About the sun going down, Mr. Hoar, and myself, and the two Indians came to Lancaster, and a solemn sight it was to me. There had I lived many comfortable years amongst my relations and neighbors, and now not one Christian to be seen, nor one house left standing. We went on to a farm house that was yet standing, where we lay all night: and a comfortable lodging we had, though nothing but straw to lie on. The Lord preserved us in safety that night, and raised us up again in the morning, and carried us along, that before noon, we came to Concord. Now was I full of joy, and yet not without sorrow: joy to see such a lovely sight, so many Christians together, and some of them my neighbors: there I met with my brother, and my brother-in-law, who asked me, if I knew where his wife was? Poor heart! He had helped to bury her, and knew it not; she being shot down by the house was partly burnt: so that those who were at Boston at the desolation of the town, and came back afterward, and buried the dead, did not know her. Yet I was not without sorrow, to think how many were looking and longing, and my own children amongst the rest, to enjoy that deliverance that I had now received, and I did not know whether ever I should see them again. Being recruited with food and raiment we went to Boston that day, where I met with my dear husband, but the thoughts of our dear children, one being dead, and the other we could not tell where, abated our comfort each to other. I was not before so much hemmed in with the merciless and cruel heathen, but now as much with pitiful, tender-hearted and compassionate Christians. In that poor, and distressed, and beggarly condition I was received in, I was kindly entertained in several houses: so much love I received from several (some of whom I knew, and others I knew not) that I am not capable to declare it. But the Lord knows them all by name: the Lord reward them sevenfold into their bosoms of His spirituals, for their temporals! The twenty pounds the price of my redemption was raised by some Boston gentlemen, and Mrs. Usher, whose bounty and religious charity, I would not forget to make mention of. Then Mr. Thomas Shepard of Charlestown received us into his house, where we continued eleven weeks; and a father and mother they were to us. And many more tender-hearted friends we met with in that place. We were now in the midst of love, yet not without much and frequent heaviness of heart for our poor children, and other relations, who were still in affliction. The week following, after my coming in, the governor and Council sent forth to the Indians again; and that not without success; for they brought in my sister, and goodwife Kettle: their not knowing where our children were, was a sore trial to us still, and yet we were not without secret hopes that we should see them again. That which was dead lay heavier upon my spirit, than those which were alive and amongst the heathen; thinking how it suffered with its wounds, and I was in no way able to relieve it; and how it was buried by the heathen in the wilderness from among all Christians. We were hurried up and down in our thoughts, sometimes we should hear a report that they were gone this way, and sometimes that; and that they were come in, in this place or that: we kept enquiring and listening to hear concerning them, but no certain news as yet. About this time the Council had ordered a day of public thanksgiving: though I thought I had still cause of mourning, and being unsettled in our minds, we thought we would ride toward the eastward, to see if we could hear anything concerning our children. And as we were riding along (God is the wise disposer of all things) between Ipswich and Rowley we met with Mr. William Hubbard, who told us that our son Joseph was come in to Major Waldron's, and another with him, which was my sister's son. I asked him how he knew it? He said, the Major himself told him so. So along we went till we came to Newbury; and their minister being absent, they desired my husband to preach the thanksgiving for them. But he was not willing to stay there that night, but would go over to Salisbury, to hear further, and come again in the morning; which he did, and preached there that day. At night, when he had done, one came and told him that his daughter was come in at Providence: here was mercy on both hands: now hath God fulfilled that precious scripture which was such a comfort to me in my distressed condition. When my heart was ready to sink into the earth (my children being gone I could not tell whither) and my knees trembled under me, and I was walking through the valley of the shadow of death: then the Lord brought, and now has fulfilled that reviving word unto me: *Thus saith the Lord, Refrain thy voice from weeping, and thine eyes from tears, for thy work shall be rewarded, saith the Lord, and they shall come again from the land of the enemy.*[57] Now we were between them, the one on the east, and the other on the west: our son being nearest, we went to him first, to Portsmouth, where we met with him, and with the major also: who told us he had done what he could, but could not redeem him under seven pounds; which the good people thereabouts were pleased to pay. The Lord reward the major, and all the rest, though unknown to me, for their labor of love. My sister's son was redeemed for four pounds, which the Council gave order for the payment of. Having now received one of our children, we hastened toward the other; going back through Newbury, my husband preached there on the Sabbath day: for which they rewarded him many-fold.

On Monday we came to Charlestown, where we heard that the governor of Rhode Island had sent over for our daughter, to take care of her, being now within his jurisdiction: which should not pass without our acknowledgments. But she being nearer Rehoboth than Rhode Island, Mr. Newman went over, and took care of her, and brought her to his own house. And the goodness of God was admirable to us in our low estate, in that he raised up passionate[58] friends on every side to us, when we had nothing to recompense any for their love. The Indians were now gone that way, that it was apprehended dangerous to go to her: but the carts which carried provision to the English army, being guarded, brought her with them to Dorchester, where we received her safe: blessed be the Lord for it, for great is His power, and He can do whatsoever seemeth Him good. Her coming in was after this manner: she was travelling one day with the Indians, with her basket at her back; the company of Indians were got before her, and gone out of sight, all except one squaw; she followed the squaw till night, and then both of them lay down, having nothing over them but the heavens, and under them but the earth. Thus she travelled three days together, not knowing whither she was going: having nothing to eat or drink but water, and green hurtleberries. At last they came into Providence, where she was kindly entertained by several of that town. The Indians often said, that I should never have her under twenty pounds: but now the Lord hath brought her in upon free-cost,[59] and given her to me the second time. The Lord make us a blessing indeed, each to others. Now have I seen that scripture also fulfilled, Deuteronomy 30. 4, 7. *If any of thine be driven out to the outmost parts of heaven, from thence will the Lord thy God gather thee, and from thence will he fetch thee. And the Lord thy God will put all these curses upon thine enemies, and on them which hate thee, which persecuted thee.* Thus hath the Lord brought me and mine out of that horrible pit, and hath set us in the midst of tender-hearted and compassionate Christians. It is the desire of my soul, that we may walk worthy of the mercies received, and which we are receiving.

Our family being now gathered together (those of us that were living) the South Church in Boston hired an house for us: then we removed from Mr. Shepard's, those cordial friends, and went to Boston, where we continued about three-quarters of a year: still the Lord went along with us, and provided graciously for us. I thought it somewhat strange to set up housekeeping with bare walls; but as Solomon says, *Money answers all things;*[60] and that we had through the benevolence of Christian friends, some in this town, and some in that, and others: and some from England, that in a little time we might look, and see the house furnished with love. The Lord hath been exceeding good to us in our low estate, in that when we had neither house nor home, nor other necessaries, the Lord so moved the hearts of these and those towards us, that we wanted neither food, nor raiment for ourselves or ours, Proverbs 18. 24. *There is a friend which sticketh closer than a brother.* And how many such friends have we found, and are now living amongst? And truly such a friend have we found him to be unto us, in whose house we lived, *viz.* Mr. James Whitecomb, a friend unto us near hand, and afar off.

I can remember the time, when I used to sleep quietly without workings in my thoughts, whole nights together, but now it is other ways with me. When all are fast about me, and no eye open, but His who ever waketh, my thoughts are upon things past, upon the awful dispensation of the Lord towards us; upon His wonderful power and might, in carrying of us through so many difficulties, in returning us in safety, and suffering none to hurt us. I remember in the night season, how the other day I was in the midst of thousands of enemies, and nothing but death before me: it is then hard work to persuade myself, that ever I should be satisfied with bread again. But now we are fed with the finest of the wheat, and, as I may say, with honey out of the rock: instead of the husk, we have the fatted calf:[61] the thoughts of these things in the particulars of them, and of the love and goodness of God towards us, make it true of me, what David said of himself, Psalms 6. 6. *I watered my couch with my tears.* Oh! the wonderful power of God that mine eyes have seen, affording matter enough for my thoughts to run in, that when others are sleeping mine are weeping.

I have seen the extreme vanity of this world: one hour I have been in health, and wealth, wanting nothing: but the next hour in sickness and wounds, and death, having nothing but sorrow and affliction.

Before I knew what affliction meant, I was ready sometimes to wish for it. When I lived in prosperity, having the comforts of the world about me, my relations by me, my heart cheerful, and taking little care for anything; and yet seeing many, whom I preferred before myself, under many trials and afflictions, in sickness, weakness, poverty, losses, crosses, and cares of the world, I should be sometimes jealous lest I should not have my portion in this life, and that scripture would come to my mind, Hebrews 12. 6. *For whom the Lord loveth he chasteneth, and scourgeth every son whom he receiveth.* But now I see the Lord had his time to scourge and chasten me. The portion of some is to have their afflictions by drops, now one drop and then another; but the dregs of the cup, the wine of astonishment, like a sweeping rain that leaveth no food, did the Lord prepare to be my portion. Affliction

I wanted, and affliction I had, full measure (I thought) pressed down and running over; yet I see, when God calls a person to anything, and through never so many difficulties, yet He is fully able to carry them through and make them see, and say they have been gainers thereby. And I hope I can say in some measure, as David did, *It is good for me that I have been afflicted.*[62] The Lord hath showed me the vanity of these outward things. That they are the vanity of vanities, and vexation of spirit; that they are but a shadow, a blast, a bubble, and our whole dependence must be upon Him. If trouble from smaller matters begin to arise in me, I have something at hand to check myself with, and say, why am I troubled? It was but the other day that if I had had the world, I would have given it for my freedom, or to have been a servant to a Christian. I have learned to look beyond present and smaller troubles, and to be quieted under them, as Moses said, Exodus 14. 13. *Stand still and see the salvation of the Lord.*[63]

---

FINIS

---

# NOTES

1. Actually, 1676. Until the eighteenth century the new year was generally reckoned as beginning on March 25, the traditional date of birth of the Virgin Mary. Dates preceding March 25 are conventionally noted in both years as, in this case, 1675/6.

2. The syntax of this sentence is confusing, although the meaning is clear enough: the Narragansetts, cut off from their food supply, chose to revenge themselves upon the English by attacking the settlements in order to replenish their stores.

3. That is, the unsettled times required that Lancaster be garrisoned. Previous requests to the authorities of the Massachusetts Bay colony for an adequate military garrison at Lancaster had been ignored.

4. For the captivity and restoration of Lot, see Genesis 14.

5. Joseph, sold by his jealous brothers to the Ishmaelites, was even-

tually made ruler of Egypt (Genesis 37–41); David, forced into exile by Saul, after numerous tribulations finally became King of Judah and later of all Israel (1 Samuel 18; 2 Samuel 5); Daniel, of course, was thrown by King Darius into a den of lions from which he was providentially delivered by the Lord, who sealed the lions' mouths (Daniel 6); the "three children," Shadrach, Meshach, and Abednego, were delivered by an angel of the Lord from the fiery furnace into which they had been cast by King Nebuchadnezzar (Daniel 3).

6. Of ten lepers cleansed by Christ, only one gave thanks to the Lord (Luke 17: 11–19). The convoluted syntax of the next sentence is hard to follow, though the meaning is clear enough. The author of the Preface—who may or may not be Mary Rowlandson herself—defends Mary Rowlandson from the charge of immodesty by pointing out first that her captivity and restoration were well-known events "of universal concernment"; the more so because she was the wife of a prominent minister. I have emended the corrupt punctuation of the original text to make the meaning clearer.

7. The reader is expected to recall the following verse as well: *I sought the Lord, and he heard me, and delivered me from all my fears.*

8. A close paraphrase of Ecclesiastes 5:5.

9. This passage is confusing, whether because of a corrupt text or the author's elliptical style is impossible to ascertain at this late date. The quotation is Samson's riddle (Judges 14:14), not, as it appears, Romans 8:28 *(And we know that all things work together for good to them that love God, to them who are the called according to his purpose).* The author uses the answer to Samson's riddle—that honey miraculously came from a dead lion—to exemplify the great promise that all apparent evil ultimately works for good.

10. Roughly, "thy three-fold friend." Correctly, *ter amica.*

11. 1675/6.

12. Flankers are projecting fortifications that enable defenders of a building to keep attackers from reaching the walls.

13. Psalms 46:8.

14. Mary Rowlandson's successive "removes" may be traced by using the map following page 45.

15. That is "Massachusetts Bay"—at, or near, Boston.

16. That is, those Christianized Indians who were most vehement in their professions of faith. Mrs. Rowlandson characteristically has little use for these "praying Indians" whom, like "One-eyed John" below, she consistently dismisses as hypocrites.

17. That is, no saddle.

18. That is, refreshment.

19. *I had fainted, unless I had believed to see the goodness of the Lord in the land of the living.*

20. This is Job's reproof to his comforters, Job 16:2.

21. That is, a chief.

22. The lament of Jacob for his children, Genesis 42:36.

23. Chapters 28 and 29 of Deuteronomy detail the blessings for obedience and the curses for disobedience to God. Chapter 30: 1–7, promises restoration from captivity and destruction of the enemy.

24. The last verse, Psalms, 27:14.

25. Jehu was a proverbial figure for fast marching and driving. See 2 Kings 9:20.

26. Lot's wife was turned into a pillar of salt for looking backward with longing toward Sodom, Genesis 19:26.

27. That is, trampled.

28. The edible tubers of the American wild bean, a climbing plant.

29. Proverbs 27:7.

30. The Connecticut River.

31. Job 1:21.

32. That is, her husband.

33. "Gossip" is used in the archaic sense of "fellow," almost equivalent to modern "hussy." The meaning of the sentence is apparently that her mistress would not eat because Mary Rowlandson had served both *people* from one dish, not that she had served both *foodstuffs* from the same dish.

34. That is, commiserated with.

35. Yes.

36. Job 19:21.

37. Judges 16:20. The point of this passage seems to be that Mary Rowlandson was reminded that, like Samson, she too was a captive among the Philistines.

38. Isaiah 38:3.

39. For David's confession, see Psalms 51:4. The parable of the pharisee and the publican is in Luke 18:10–14.

40. The parable of the Prodigal Son may be found in Luke 15.

41. That is, particular or fastidious.

42. Rowlandson's dinner consisted of samp—coarse meal made of Indian corn—to which she added water to make porridge; and the outside of the lining of the small intestine (presumably of the horse mentioned earlier) which she broiled over the coals.

43. That is, "for it raised my hopes."

44. Two Christian Indians who were conducting the ransom negotiations.

45. The master they served was of course the Devil, the father of lies. See John 8:44.

46. That is, the General Assembly of Massachusetts Bay.

47. At "Sudbury fight," April 18, 1676, the Indians ambushed and killed two captains and some thirty men. Rowlandson seems unaware that the powwow she has just described was a council of war at which the decision was made to attack the English. The Indians' lack of enthusiasm upon returning was in fact due to their own losses. The statistical notion of victory—over thirty enemy dead (not, as Rowlandson errone-

ously reports, nearly one hundred) at the cost of only five or six of one's own troops—was foreign to the Indian concept of successful warfare, the ideal of which was that a victory should be won at no cost to one's own side.

48. That is, the Indian who had kneeled upon the deerskin at the powwow.

49. Pillowcase.

50. Adventuresome.

51. Bad Indian.

52. The elliptical syntax is confusing. Rowlandson means that it was a remarkable passage of providence for the army to have turned homeward with victory in its grasp.

53. Amos 3:6; 6:6–7.

54. Another variety of ground nut.

55. 1 Samuel 15:32. The point is that Samuel later killed Agag, King of the Amalekites.

56. Matthew 8:25; Luke 8:24. The allusion is to Christ's stilling the tempest on the Sea of Galilee, the point being that the Christians are in such terrible straits that they have no hope but in God himself.

57. Jeremiah 31:16.

58. Compassionate.

59. A feudal term. Compare modern English slang "home free."

60. Ecclesiastes 10:19.

61. The allusion is to the parable of the Prodigal Son, Luke 15:11–32.

62. Psalms 119:71.

63. Rowlandson expects us to recall the continuation of this verse: *for the Egyptians whom you have seen today, ye shall see them again no more forever.*

SIX

# *BENJAMIN CHURCH*
## King of the Wild Frontier

On August 12, 1676, King Philip was hunted down by a party of white rangers and non–Praying Indian allies under the command of Captain Benjamin Church of Plymouth Colony. "Our *Lebbeus,*" as Cotton Mather called him, was the preeminent hero of the war on the English side. His rangers accounted for Philip and most of his lieutenants, and with them upwards of a thousand followers. Church himself was personally responsible for converting numerous Indians to the English cause—some of them on the field of battle itself.

Indeed, so striking were Church's accomplishments that the orthodox Mather felt constrained to remind his readers that the will of God and the power of Puritan society were, after all, the true determinants of historical movements—since otherwise the reader might conceive an exaggerated sense of the power of individuals to shape events. Therefore, although "some of his achievements were truly so magnanimous and extraordinary, that my reader will suspect me to be transcribing the silly old *romances,* where the *knights* do conquer so many *giants,*" Mather reminds his readers that "there were many other commanders whom if we should measure by conduct rather than by success, the fame of Captain Church ought by no means to bring an eclipse upon theirs."

As Church's fame must be limited by the context of the total effort of the Puritan society, so his power to achieve is circumscribed by the will of God. Mather suggests this by playing on Church's name to bring his adventures within the comprehension of an allegorical reading of events: "captain *Church;* whose very *name,* now, might suggest unto the miserable salvages, *what,* they must be undone by fighting against; and whose *lot* it was to be employ'd by the providence of heaven at the time and place of the *catastrophe*, now waiting for a generation ripe for desolation."[1]

Church's fame derived in part from the character of his exploits. Although other English commanders fought bigger battles, their victories were always attended with heavy losses and hence were never as clear-cut as Church's forays. Moreover, they commanded and served within English "armies," while Church led small parties of men, the majority of whom might be Indians. Thus, Church's victories seemed more clearly the work of a single identifiable figure; and when he became the conqueror of Philip himself, in something close to a man-to-man confrontation, his preeminence was assured. When one adds the fortunate coincidence of his name with Cotton Mather's taste for allegorical punning, his celebrity seems to have been inevitable.

But Church's fame and his influence on American mythology derive in larger measure from the very popular account of his exploits that he published in 1716 as *Entertaining Passages Relating to Philip's War* . . . . Other Puritan commanders like Talcott and Turner and Winslow may have fought the big battles that broke the Indians' strength, but they never had their careers set before the public in the form of heroic and "entertaining" narrative. Encased in Puritan histories and in the logic of Calvinist antiheroism, their reputations withered when the decline of Calvinism left the histories of Hubbard and the Mathers as food for antiquarians. In contrast, Church's part in the war was thrown into high relief by his own book; therefore, his stature continued to grow as time passed, until finally he became a model or prototype of the frontier hero of American literary myth.

Church was born at Plymouth in 1639 and learned from his father the family trade of carpentry. As a skilled craftsman whose trade was much in demand, Richard Church moved quite frequently during Benjamin's youth, taking up and then selling a number of farms and houses in different parts of the colony.[2] This restless shifting to better one's condition—by seeking markets for one's skill or by selling land at a profit to aftercomers—was typical of frontier communities and became remarkably so in the nineteenth century. In the Jacksonian period, Johnson Jones Hooper's archetypal frontier rogue, Simon Suggs, had as his motto: "IT IS GOOD TO BE SHIFTY IN A NEW COUNTRY." In

Church's early career one sees the roots of such a philosophy. Mobility and pragmatic flexibility rather than "knowing one's place" and "sticking to one's last" were to be valued by one whose ambition was to rise in the world—particularly when the world one had to rise in was a wilderness, divided between Indians and Puritans and strewn with complexly intertwined opportunities and pitfalls.

Benjamin Church was one of those against whom Increase Mather inveighed in his attack on those who have "foresaken Churches, and Ordinances, and all for land and elbow-room." Religion and instituted worship seem to have been less important to him than his restless pursuit of landed wealth, since his moving about kept him from joining any congregation until he was well advanced in age. Not that he was opposed to religion as such—his family worshipped together and Church himself would expound Scripture at table. Membership in a congregation was simply not a high-priority concern. By 1674 he had left carpentry and the tradesman's life for good and at the same time gone (temporarily at least) beyond the bounds of both organized worship and organized settlement, planting himself on "Sogkonate," the present Little Compton, Rhode Island, where, as he boasted in his narrative, he was the sole white settler.

Although this boast is a significant indicator of Church's sense of values and his orientation toward the frontier, it would not do to press the analogy to nineteenth-century frontiersmen too far. The later pioneer immersed himself and his family in a deep woods or distant prairie, often with major rivers and mountain ranges intervening between him and his original home. Church's wanderings were on a smaller scale and he was never very far away from the larger towns and the sea. Nautical terms like "pilot" come more naturally to him than "guide" or "scout," and he speaks of Indians "tacking about" in battle. Natty Bumppo, who in some ways resembles Church, is wholly a creature of the land and woods; Church still has the smack of salt water.

Church's connection to his society—despite his psychological and physical departures from it—was close in other ways. He was part of a fairly considerable combination of speculators concerned with developing the land along the Rhode Island–Plymouth border. His relationships with the other investors, who were prominent men in both colonies, were personally close, which suggests that his status and fortunes were on the rise even before the war made him a hero. These friendships also served to make Church a useful go-between for the Plymouth and Rhode Island governments during the war. But his role in the partnership was that of chief pioneer and Indian diplomatist, rather than financier.

His position in Sogkonate was sustained by his friendship with the "Squaw Sachem" of the local Indians, a woman named Awashonks. Rumor and romantic legend suggest that she was Church's mistress and that his gaining and holding his plantation was a by-product of their affair.[3] Church had married Alice Southworth in 1671 but had not brought his wife to the Sogkonate plantation at the time of the outbreak of King Philip's War. Therefore, such an affair would not have been impossible. What is evident from Church's own narrative is a genuine friendship between the two. Awashonks warned Church of the war's onset, and Church writes of her with a kind of humorous affection. Church's friendship with Awashonks gave him an early role in the war as a would-be peacemaker, attempting to hold Awashonks in friendship to the English against Philip's threats and blandishments; he was also able to send timely warning to the authorities of Philip's planned onset. Later in the war, this friendship would enable Church finally to detach Awashonks from Philip and employ her warriors to track and kill the chieftain.

More important than the fact of the friendship itself is what its acknowledged existence implies about Church's character. If he was not what nineteenth-century dime novel parlance would call a "squaw man," he was at least a man not deterred by religious or racial antipathy from forming close ties with Indians. His friendships with Indians were personal: he approached them as one desiring to live on equal terms among them, neither as missionary nor, initially, as conqueror. He did share some of the Puritan prejudice toward the Indians: he could, for example, speak of the Indians' beheading English corpses and putting their heads up on poles as evidence of their "barbarism," while rarely seeing the identical practice of the English as anything more than regrettable (and then only when he had some personal feeling for the Indian involved). But on the whole, Church presents himself as one who genuinely likes Indians both collectively and—what is more significant—individually. Indian friends figure prominently in his book, which makes it virtually unique in the period. His efforts to protect peaceful or Praying Indians from persecution by white bigots contrasts sharply with the practice of the colonies' other great Indian fighter, Captain Samuel Mosely.

His openness to human relationships with Indians made Church capable of learning from them. It was this quality that made him successful in partisan warfare. Unlike the regular soldiery, Church learned from Indians how to fight Indians, and since he also knew how to recognize and evoke the humanity of the Indians, he was able to bring personal influence to bear in diplomacy and in recruiting Indians to fight against King Philip. One of the thematic structures that gives his narrative coherence is the recounting of his progressive initiation by Indians into the arts of Indian warfare—an initiation that culminated in his receiving the most profound of accolades from an enemy chief.

Church's tenuous connection with the settlements and their governments prevented an early recognition of his special competence as an Indian fighter–diplomat. His advice was often ignored or actually spurned by commanders of the regular colonial militia, either because of intercolonial jealousies or because Church lacked social position and high official military rank. His intimacy with Indians may actually have made his advice suspect until events proved his wisdom. Church's friends, after all, were unconverted pagans. Other "Indian-lovers" like Oliver Guggins and John Eliot came in danger of mob violence at this time for their sympathetic defense of the Praying Indians. And Hubbard's history condemns English attempts to fight like Indians as a likely source both of defeat and of spiritual degeneracy.[4] Church's exploits are therefore punctuated by correspondence reflecting a running feud with Puritan authorities, both over matters of policy and over the niggardly bounties and payments made for Church's captures and general military-diplomatic services. Even in victory, he did not receive as much recognition as he felt he deserved.

However, the war was the foundation of Church's prosperity and reputation. Although he had opposed the policy of enslaving captured Indians and confiscating excessive amounts of Indian lands (on grounds that need discussion later), he profited directly from the land seizures and held both Indians and Negroes as permanent or temporary slaves. In the later wars against the French and Indians in Nova Scotia, Church led several raiding parties, on one of which he incontinently had some French prisoners "knocked in the head." The resulting controversy with the colonial authorities exacerbated his perennial discontent with officialdom's failure to appreciate his services, and he retired in disgust (and under something of a cloud) in 1705.

No picture or engraving of Church survives, but in his later years at least he grew immensely fat, a natural consequence of his prosperity coupled with the *joie de vivre* that is reflected in his account of his adventures. His self-indulgence did not, however, impair his vigor: he chased the French and Indians as heartily as ever, although he had to be lifted over downed trees by two Indian sergeants who ran by his side. He seems to have been rather choleric and impetuous, especially in his later campaigns and in his relationships with the authorities, but these qualities were offset by a sense of humor that enabled him to laugh at his own foibles as well as at those of his enemies.

Church's account of his adventures did not appear until forty years after King Philip's War. The delay may be attributed to his continuing activity in his own and the colony's affairs, but the preferences of Puritan censors and literary fashion-setters probably played a role as well. The orthodox view of the Indian war was that it had served as a warning from Jehovah to a perverse generation who had departed from the piety and obedience of their fathers to pursue worldly comfort in the wilderness. Cotton Mather's account of Church's final battle with Philip reveals the essence of this view: noting that Alderman (one of Church's Indians) and not a white man killed Philip, Mather rejoices in the providence of God, for "indeed, if any *Englishman* might have had the honour of *killing* him, he must have had a good measure of *grace* to have repressed the *vanity of mind* whereto he would have had some temptations." [5] During and just after the war itself a similar spirit prevailed, as the sermon-histories of Increase Mather and William Hubbard and the captivity narrative of Mrs. Rowlandson reveal. It is in the context of these authorized sermon-histories and captivity narratives as well as the context of Church's clouded departure from active service, that we must see the composition of his book.

## *Entertaining Passages Relating to Philip's War* ...

The book was written by Church's son Thomas, who evidently worked from his father's diary or "minute-book" and his official correspondence.[6] The colloquial flavor of much of the narrative is interrupted periodically by passages in a more formal style, which suggests that the actual composition involved a collaboration between the "Old Souldier" and his somewhat less salty son. Ten years after the event, Church's anger against those who had criticized his last expedition was still warm:

> ... after he came home: for all his great Expences, Fategues & Hardships ... He received of his Excellency *Fifteen Pounds* as an earnest Peny towards Raising of Volunteers; and when he came to receive his Debenture for his Colonels Pay, there was 2 *s* 4 *d.* due him; and as for his Captains Pay, & Man *Jack* he has never received any thing as yet. Also after he came home some ill minded Persons did their endeavour to have taken away his Life, for that there was some of the French Enemy Kill'd this Expedition: but his Excellency the Governour ... saw cause to Clear him, and gave him Thanks for his good Service done.[7]

Clearly one of his motives for writing was to clear his reputation and to remind people that, while his last expeditions may have been unproductive, he had done some few things for the colony in times past. His critics he regards as a niggardly lot of armchair soldiers whose finicky moral scruples are ridiculous in the view of one who has actually taken the field. The purpose of war is to kill the enemy, and to try Church for murder as a result of such killings is to carry moral principle to an absurd conclusion.

Criticism and grudging rewards of this sort were something Church had met with before, and in putting his memories in order he seems to have had in mind not only his immediate opponents but also those who had thwarted and frustrated and nearly killed him in the old days. His response to his critics thus extends itself into a response to those Puritan leaders who misunderstood and so misdirected the Indian war in 1675–1677, and to those historians whose accounts of the war had simply written justifications of the earlier misunderstanding and incompetence into the permanent record.

Still, Church is not an infallible or unbiased reporter. Built into the structure of his personal narrative, and into the character of the man himself, is a strain of egocentricity, perhaps of egomania: the important battles are the ones in which Church is involved, and only when Church is allowed to succeed does the war move toward an end. Church, no less than Mather, is an apologist—though the subject, manner, and purposes of his apology differ radically from Mather's. Church's ideological difference emerges immediately in the title of his narrative and his rationale for presenting it to the public. He calls the work *Entertaining Passages,* presenting it as something to amuse and excite the reader, rather than as a didactic moral fable intended for the instruction of the pious. Where the protagonists of Puritan personal narratives had constantly to efface themselves as characters and authors, ascribing both the power of action and the responsibility for appearing in print to God and his commandments, Church means for the reader to be taken with the hero of his account—himself.

In the first half of Church's narrative he recounts the process of his initiation into the arts of Indian warfare. As his skill develops, he begins to develop a distinctive personal style, a personal code of morality, and a characteristic point of view. The war evokes his character and develops it in unexpected ways. What captivity does for Mary Rowlandson, battle does for Church. Both are variants of the "conversion experience," but the modes and ultimate direction of the two conversions differ radically. Whereas Rowlandson's experience carries her beyond worldliness to a sense of the vanity of the world and of dependence on the power and authority of the biblical God, Church's experience teaches him to rely on the world for necessary knowledge, and on his own skill and wisdom and courage for protection. Church is aware of the difference between his outlook and that of orthodox Puritanism. He plays up the differences by counterpointing anecdotes that reflect his own growing skill and success in warfare with caustic references to the wartime policies of the Puritan governments and their favored officers and to the postwar historical *apologia* of Hubbard and the Mathers. As the narrative traces Church's movement deeper into the Indians' world, it also reflects what appears as a growing critical distance between himself and the Puritan elite. At the end he stands at a point of balance, accepting accolades both from Indians and from the Puritan government.

The character of the hero who emerges from this initiation is founded on a pragmatic approach to both temporal affairs and moral question, as well as on a code of self-reliance, buttressed by a quality that can be described as "heroic ease." Church is at home in an environment of wilderness and warfare that is clearly alien and threatening to his fellows. This is reflected in his ability to adjust to the forest and learn from the Indians, but it is best conveyed, in literary terms, by Church's use of humor. Rather than parade before the reader as a model of piety and prowess, he exhibits himself in some ridiculous moments: wrestling with a naked Indian so greasy that he keeps slipping through Church's hands, playing a practical joke on one of his fellow ambassadors to the Indians, a Mr. Howland, throwing a temper tantrum when his raw troops flee from the fire of Indians whose shooting is so poor that they fire at Church and only manage to hit one of the runaways. This ability to laugh at himself and to mix laughter with derring-do makes Church seem more of a hero than Mather's symbolical "Lebbeus." It suggests that here is a man with human limitations, who yet behaves like a hero, a man so courageous that he can laugh at others and at himself, even in the heat of action.

Much of Church's humor is directed at official policy and historiography. If his self-mockery ultimately enhances heroism by humanizing it, his sarcasm about official Puritanism is ultimately denigrating and deflationary. He consistently punctures the moralizing inflation of trivial incidents into scenarios of "temptation and resistance"—compare his handling of the "tobacco question" with Mary Rowlandson on the same theme. But irony is more than a surface feature here; it is part and parcel of a fundamental divergence from Puritan war policies and from Puritan literary and theological principles.

Church rejects the providential and theocentric model of historical causation in favor of the pragmatic and heroic model. Puritan histories structure narrative around the archetype of the History of Redemption; Church structures his history of the war around the narrative of his personal success story. A comparison of Church's self-portrayal with Cotton Mather's portrait of him (quoted at the beginning of this essay) highlights these distinctions. Mather puns on Church's name to inflate and allegorize his victory; Church eschews allegory, declares his intention is simply to entertain, and deflates his own heroism to human proportions. Mather sees Church's success as the result of providential coincidences; Church is at pains to tell how much skill and effort the hunt required. Mather asserts that Church's fame ought not "eclipse" that of other commanders, because good "conduct" is of equal value, morally, with success itself. For Church, success is the only measure, and he heaps ridicule on those commanders (and their apologists) whose adherence to traditional but inappropriate doctrines or practices led to failure.

As writer and soldier Church asserts the primacy of the values and powers of men of affairs against those of the distant custodians of moral doctrine and political authority. Where Mather includes incidents in his history that offer ground for moral lessons or typological explication, Church's narrative adheres to incidents that advance the story of the hero's success and bear empirically on the final victory.

Church's departures from Puritan principles are reflected in literary form in the narrative. But these literary contrasts derive from real disagreements about war policies. In Church's view, the Puritan leadership's irrational fear of the Indian and the wilderness led to incompetence and poltroonery in the field as well as in diplomacy. In the early part of the war, Church served under a succession of regular commanders who exhibited a spectrum of qualities from cowardice to ineffectuality. Convinced by religious mythology that the woods were the abode of sinister forces and the Indians very demons, such commanders could construe no order in the landscapes they confronted. Of the enemy any sort of treachery might be expected, and ambushes were to be feared at every moment. Capture by the Indians was not to be thought on, since an enemy so alien in blood and character might be capable of committing inconceivable barbarities. Even brave men could be led into absurd behavior by such attitudes. On an early pursuit of Philip, Church and some Plymouth militia under Captain Henchman chased the Indians into a swamp. Although the swamps and forests of Rhode Island were Philip's native element, the Plymouth troops determined to lay siege to the swamp by building a fort at one end of it—as if Philip had but the one exit and so would stay put. Church says that he spoke of the move with "contempt." "And to speak the truth, it must be said, That as they gain'd not that Field, by their Sword, nor their Bow; so 'twas rather their fear than their courage, that oblig'd them to set up the marks of their Conquest." Not content with rebuking the commanders, Church then alludes sarcastically to the chronicles of Increase and Cotton Mather and William Hubbard, ridiculing those who "pleased themselves [to] fancy a mighty conquest."

The motives behind such errors are suggested quite clearly in Hubbard's account:

> Capt. *Henchman* and the *Plimouth* forces kept a diligent Eye upon the Enemy, but were not willing to run into the Mire and Dirt after them in a Dark Swamp, being taught by Experience how dangerous it is to fight in such dismal Woods, when their Eyes would be muffled with the Leaves, and their Arms pinioned with the thick Boughs of the Trees, as their Feet were continually shackled with the Roots spreading every Way in those boggy Woods. It is ill fighting with a beast in his own Den. They resolved therefore to starve them out of the Swamp. . . . To that End they began to build a Fort, as it were to beleaguer the Enemy.[8]

The recurrent images of the forest are those of captivity: "muffled," "pinioned," "shackled." For Church, to hunt the beast in his own den was not a shackling but a liberating experience, giving scope to his growing prowess and expertise. The "dismal" landscape had no terrors for one who had sought a wilderness to live in, and the denizen of the woods, the Indian, held no irrational terrors for one who knew him as neighbor and friend as well as enemy.

According to the narrative, it was Church's ability to relate to and learn from the Indians that set him on the path to heroic fulfillment. From his initial diplomatic effort to gain Awashonks's allegiance to his final mopping up of Indian resistance, Church dealt with Indians on terms of personal intimacy. When the English forces met with reverses in several ambushes, Church asked his Indian scouts what the English were doing wrong and reformed his military practice to suit their recommendations. By exhibiting courage and skill in battle and by proving trustworthy in his treatment of surrendering Indians, he was able to recruit Indians for the English, sometimes on the battlefield itself. His approach, he says, was to "clap them on the back, and tell them, *Come, come you look wild and surly, and mutter, but that signifies nothing, these my best souldiers were a little while ago as you are now; but by that time you have been but one day with me, you'l love me too, and be as brisk as any of them.* And it prov'd so." However, before we celebrate Church's humanity, we should note in qualification that he did not object to slavery or to Indian-killing as such. Only when those practices were conducted in such a way as to hamper the achievement of victory did he disparage them. Pragmatism, not moral scruple, made Church relatively more humane than his commanders—that and his ability to see *some* Indians as human beings.

The first phase of his initiation into forest warfare ended with the Swamp Fight of 1675. Just as the battle was crucial to the course of the war, it was a crisis and turning point in the narrative of the war's self-appointed hero. The colonial forces, having marched in dead of winter to surprise Canonchet's village, became lost and wandered in the dismal and treacherous swamp. Coming upon the village by surprise, they attacked and suffered severe losses until, thanks to a flank attack by Church, they were able to storm the Indian palisades. What followed was a seventeenth-century My Lai—the troops, driven beyond endurance by the hardship and anxiety of the march and by the punishment inflicted in battle, ran amok, killing the wounded men, women, and children indiscriminately, firing the camp, burning the Indians alive or dead in their huts. In their histories, Cotton Mather and William Hubbard exulted that here the Indians were properly "Berbikew'd" and "fried with their Mitchin." According to his own account, Church—alone among the officers—tried to get General Winslow to stop the massacre, but Winslow allowed himself to be bullied by junior officers. A doctor even threatened the wounded Church that if he did not desist the doctor would allow him to "bleed to Death like a Dog before he would endeavour to stench his blood." Church's motives are typical of the man: a mixture of human concern, disgust at the irrational fears of the town-bred soldiers, and pragmatism: the soldiers were destroying the only food and shelter in the area, thus making inevitable a greater than necessary loss from wounds, starvation, and exposure on the return march. In addition, Church believed that if the English had preserved and held the village, the Narragansetts would have been forced to surrender in order to avoid starvation. The commanders, however, ignored Church, with the result that the surviving Indians fled to strengthen Philip, and the colonial army suffered such losses from exposure and lack of food that the striking force of the colony was immobilized. Church, wounded and disgusted, nearly resigned his commission.

At this low point, the narrative takes its upward turn. Church receives permission to conduct negotiations with Awashonks's Sogkonates, and to form a company of white rangers and friendly Indians to fight Philip in Church's chosen manner. Now the character created in the early episodes enters a sustained narrative of the final pursuit and killing of the Indian chiefs. In the ministerial histories, this concluding phase of the war was seen as a series of providential events, answering the prayers of the faithful and revealing the character of the divine Overlord of New England. Church first negotiates the enlistment of Awashonks's people in the hunt for Philip: for Increase Mather, this proves that God answers the prayers of the saints, for "How often have we prayed that the Lord would take away Spirit and Courage from [the Enemy] and cause those Haters of the Lord to submit.... In this Thing also the Lord hath had Respect to our Requests ... e.g., ... the Squaw-Sachim of Saconit, with above an hundred Indians submitted themselves to Mercy"[9] With Awashonks's people to aid him, Church pursues the "beast" into his "den," driving Philip from refuge to refuge, capturing each time some of his trusted followers and finally his wife and son as well. For Hubbard, this event provides the kind of symmetrical justice that characterizes Jehovah: the great captor of English women and children is himself made to feel "the Sence and experimental Feeling of the captivity of his Children, loss of his Friends, slaughter of his Subjects, bereavment of all Family Relations, and being stript of all outward Comforts, before his own Life should be taken away." At the end,

> *Philip*, like a Salvage and wild Beast, having been hunted by the English Forces through the Woods ... at last was driven

> to his own Den, . . . which proved but a Prison to keep him fast, till the Messengers of Death came by Divine Permission to execute Vengeance upon him.[10]

With the "imprisonment," captivity and killing of the great beast-king, divine vengeance is fulfilled. Symmetry is completed, evil is exorcized, and the climax of the war and of the history is achieved.

In Church's narrative these events have a different texture and structure, and move toward a different end. For Church, the final hunting of the king is not an exorcism but the final stage of his initiation into the life of the wilderness. It is not the death of Philip that climaxes the hunt, but the capture of a subchief named Annawon—a figure whom Church regards as being the true embodiment of Indian resistance to the English and the real war leader of the Wampanoags, his true stature being invisible to historians bemused by their own symbolism. Church does not kill Annawon—that is left for the Puritan magistrates to perform—but the two warriors exchange highly symbolic honors and very human reminiscences.

The long hunt begins when Church meets, by chance, some Sogkonates, and arranges for a conference with Awashonks. To this conference he comes alone, bringing gifts of tobacco and a calabash of rum. To allay Awashonks's fears that the rum may be poisoned, Church takes a mouthful from his calabash by way of demonstration, then pours rum on his hand and "supps" it with obvious relish, finally "took the Shell and drank to her again, and drank a good Swig which indeed was no more than he needed." The Indians and Church then get tipsy on treaty rum and strike their bargain. Mather and his prayers and fasts enter into it not at all; given the prevalence of Matherian writing on the war the omission is palpable.

The pursuit of Philip, and later of Annawon, is long and wearing. By its end, Church is virtually the only white man in a company of Indians, none of whom is a Christian and all of whom were fighting against the English a year before. With these troops, Church first captures Philip's family, then ambushes and kills the chief himself. For Church this moment is not the climax of the tale, and his deflation of the event—the climax of every previous account—is (in that context) quite drastic. Church sees the dead Philip as a "great, doleful, naked, dirty beast"; by implication he is also a coward, since he is shot fleeing the field while Annawon cries "Fight! Fight!" in a great booming voice. The Indian who shoots Philip, far from being bloated with that sense of self-importance that Cotton Mather feared for, passes the event off with a vulgarism, boasting that though Philip was a big man in life, "he would now chop his Ass for him." After expressing annoyance at the niggardly bounty paid for Philip's head, Church returns to his real business, the pursuit of Annawon.

In a manner that has since become formulaic in western stories and films, Church—with only a handful of his battlefield "converts"—approaches the camp of Annawon and over one hundred warriors. Crawling and hiding, Church reaches the center of the camp where Annawon and his son are asleep, knocks the son senseless, and seizes the old chief. The son's outcry rouses the camp, but Church bluffs them into submission by threatening them with his surrounding "army." Then, to distract the Indians while his men disarm them, Church declares, "I am come to sup with you," and accepts a meal of "cow-beef" and green corn. To demonstrate his absolute confidence, he then lies down beside Annawon to "sleep" for the rest of the night.

In the darkness Annawon crawls away to the bushes. Church first thinks he has gone to relieve himself "so as not to offend me with the stink"; then as time passes, he begins to suspect treachery. But Annawon returns with a bundle, and the climactic moment of Church's initiation, his long "hunting of the beast," is reached:

> The Moon now shining bright, he [Church] saw him at a distance coming with something in his hands, and coming up to Capt. *Church*, he fell upon his knees before him, and offered him what he had bro't . . . . *"Great Captain, you have killed* Philip, and conquered his Country for I believe, I and my company *are the last that War against the* English, so suppose the War is ended by your means; and therefore these things belong *unto you."* Then opening his pack, he pull'd out *Philips* belt, curiously wrought with *Wompom,* being Nine inches broad wrought with black and white *Wompom,* in various figures, and flowers, and pictures of many birds and beasts. This, when hanged upon Capt. *Churches* shoulders, reach'd his ancles. And another belt of *Wompom* he presented him with, wrought after the former manner, which

> *Philip* was wont to put upon his head . . . and another small belt with Star upon the end of it, . . . edged with red hair, which Annawon said he got in the Muhhogs country.

These were "*Philips* Royalties, which he was wont to adorn himself with when he sat in State."

Thus Church, who has just been rewarded in a grudging and ungenerous way by his own superiors, receives from the hand of his great enemy the royalties of the Indian king, including a belt adorned with red scalps (presumably taken from white men, since the "Muhhogs" were not rich in redheads). For the Indian, exchanges between men are never simply economic or political, but always concern gods and powers in men and in the land. The exchange of land for gifts or cash or the rendering of tribute to a battle-victor therefore involves "spiritual and supernatural interplay" rather than being an exchange of objects of only intrinsic value. The "Wompom"—whether received or given as payment for goods or land, or as tribute—"was to them a symbol over which they transferred their good will and spiritual power over forces dormant in the land, clearing away the poison that might have been engendered by the inequality of value in the transfer" or (as in this case) by the killing done in the war. Annawon had lost his king, his land, and most of his tribe: he may have known he would lose his life as well. His gesture to Church is meant by him to transfer his own people's "power over [spiritual] forces dormant in the land" to a proven worthy successor. The King of the Woods has died, and his slayer is crowned in his place.[11]

Only an Indian would have been capable of such a gesture, and only a man attuned to the Indian world view could have accepted such a gift as Church does. The two warriors then spend the night swapping war yarns, and—as with Awashonks—a genuine affection seems to develop between the two. When Annawon, despite Church's promise, is executed, Church later sees "to his grief" the head of Annawon displayed on a pole in Plymouth town. This act was "so hateful to Mr. *Church*, that he opposed it, to the loss of the good will and respects of some that before were his good friends." (In Hubbard's account, of course, the conversation between the two men is characterized as a "confession" of crimes.)

Church's crowning as "King of the Wild Frontier" completes

the narrative of initiation and the heroic hunt-quest. But for Church, the triumph gained in the long hunt cannot be carried over to his peacetime occupations. As the slayer of Philip he will be celebrated only by men who have no true comprehension of the means and character of his victory. Annawon appreciates Church at his true worth, but the very deeds that earn that appreciation lead directly to Annawon's death and the withering away of both the Indian and the wilderness. Like Cooper's Natty Bumppo, it is Church's tragedy that the process by which he creates or transforms his character and becomes a hero ultimately destroys the conditions within which that heroic character had meaning and function. He becomes a hero by engaging in an intimate combat with Indians and destroying their power, but when the Indian vanishes, the hero's profession is obsolete, heroism's context becomes invisible in all save memory, and his most appreciative audience perishes. In more mundane terms, Church is a king to Annawon. But to the colonial authorities he will remain simply "Captain" or, much later, "Colonel" Church—a somewhat bristly old war dog. Church's appreciation of these circumstances is registered in the narrative's conclusion, and in his characteristic manner, he ends with a joke. On his last expedition he catches an Indian named "Conscience," evidently a former Christian Indian who had joined the "hostiles." "*Conscience*, said the Captain (smiling) then the War is over, for that was what they were searching for, it being much wanting." Thus Church, with a grin, concisely parodies the ministerial "myth" of the war, in which the actual struggles are less important than the quest for salvation.

## *Literary Significance of Church's Book*

Church and his book exercised both a direct and an indirect influence on later writers, and it is rather difficult to disentangle the two. The book was popular enough in the eighteenth century to be considered a standard source for anyone attempting to exploit—in fiction or popular history—the materials of the colonial wars. Certainly Church is the pattern for later frontier heroes—Major Robert Rogers of the rangers, Daniel Boone, Cooper's fictional Leatherstocking. In part this is simply the consequence of the colonies' deeper penetration of the wilderness and their growing sense of national identity.

The core of Church's narrative is the structuring archetype of the initiation—in this case, the story of the Englishman's acculturation, through battle, to the American environment and its native culture. The problems arising from acculturation were central to the cultural life of the colonies. In the early days, Puritans agonized over their relationship to their home country: Were they permanent exiles or would they return to regenerate old England? Was America to be a permanent home or a temporary way station in the Pilgrims' progress toward salvation? As succeeding generations of Puritans acculturated to New England, adopting ways that seemed "Indian-like" (or at least un-English) to earlier generations, the fear of acculturation was symbolized as the "degeneration" of civilized men into savages and dramatized in the captivity of helpless white women by fiendish savages. Church's narrative belatedly spoke for the Americanized Puritan whose concern lay chiefly with the development of the land and his own fortunes, who would not stay within prescribed social or physical bounds, and who was willing to enter the wilderness and adapt to it in order to fulfill his desires—even if this meant becoming closer in spirit or life-style to the Indians.

Although resistance to such tendencies by colonial and, later, national authorities would remain a factor in American politics and literature, the tendency of American society was all in Church's direction. By the time of the Revolution, the Indian would be used by American writers as a symbol of American identity, a primitive type of virtues that were distinctly national. American writers prided themselves that their people could fight like Indians, as well as like redcoats—that they combined the best of a dual heritage. As in Church's narrative, this appreciation of and partial identification with the Indian is the result of warfare with the Indians, and thus the symbolic acceptance of the Indian coexists, as it does in Church's narrative, with the celebration of the wars of annihilation and displacement waged against the Indians.

In the literary works of writers like Cooper, this paradox is the source of rich and poignant ironies. Leatherstocking's success as a warrior helps to annihilate the Indians and wilderness which are the bases of his preferred life-style and the preconditions of his heroism. In politics, ironies shifted toward hypocrisies, as in the assertion of ex–Indian fighters like Andrew Jackson that their policy of Indian removal was based on a sympathy for the primitive red man acquired in the intimacies of frontier warfare. Still, the idea that Indian fighters have the finest appreciation of Indian character remained a staple of Indian-policy rhetoric, at least till the end of the nineteenth century.[12]

The increasing popularity of the initiation structure in later American literature and the resemblance of later heroes (like Daniel Boone and Leatherstocking) to Benjamin Church should not be attributed to the power of Church's narrative itself, but rather to the persistence of frontier conditions and the recurrence of acculturative situations in later American history. Writers working with similar problems and materials tend to arrive at similar solutions independently of one another. Such may also be the case with the persistence of Church's peculiar type of "heroic humor." The colloquial language, the elaborate practical joking, the poking of fun at dudes and highfalutin authorities are characteristics of the classic American humorists of the nineteenth-century writers of the Southwest "school," like Johnson Jones Hooper. The Davy Crockett of literature is certainly a hero in the Churchian mode, combining as he does deflationary humor and self-parody with deeds of genuine bravery.[13]

Cooper's Leatherstocking owes a good deal to Church, as well as to later chroniclers like the various biographers of Daniel Boone. Cooper certainly knew Church's book after 1829, since he used it as a source for his Philip's-war novel, *The Wept of Wish-Ton-Wish.* It seems likely that he would have come across the narrative still earlier, since he read widely in histories and reminiscences of the colonial Indian Wars. Church's narrative was several times reprinted in Boston by Samuel G. Drake between 1825 and 1829, so its availability is not at issue. The conception of Leatherstocking as a mediating figure binding the Indian world to the white represents a development of the "acculturating" character of Church. Leatherstocking is a Benjamin Church frozen at the moment of his crowning by Annawon, perpetually balanced between worlds, ultimately choosing neither. His characterization likewise reflects something of Church's personal style: the colloquial speech, the quirky humor, the outbursts of old-soldier crustiness, the implicit mockery of sophistication and of those who think that their social authority is more valuable than genuine expertise in a real wilderness. Church's affectionate portrayals of Indians, his depiction of genuine friendship for particular Indians like Awashonks and Annawon, may also have something to do with Cooper's depiction of the relationships between Leatherstocking and his Indian companions. While other colonial writers, like John Eliot, show sympathy for Indians as a group (e.g., "poor heathens"), Church is the only writer between John Smith (1624) and Alexander Henry (1809) who details personal friendships.[14]

Church's influence on American literary myth is partly attested by direct and indirect allusions to his work by writers like Cooper, Irving, Thoreau, Parkman, and Melville. But perhaps more significant is the fact that the narrative transcended the category of historical document and became part of a cultural tradition, a given in the vocabulary of myths and references used by writers. A suggestive instance of the operation of this kind of influence occurs in Melville's *Moby-Dick,* where Ishmael, in defending the "reasonableness" of the events he will recount, compares the hunting out of particular whales with Church's chase of Philip and Annawon:

> New Zealand Jack and Don Miguel, after at various times creating great havoc among the boats of different vessels, were finally gone in quest of, systematically hunted out, chased and killed by valiant whaling captains, who heaved up their anchors with that express object as much in view, as in setting out through the Narragansett Woods, Captain Butler of old had it in his mind to capture that notorious murderous savage Annawon, the headmost warrior of the Indian King Philip.

Melville has obviously mixed up Captain Church with a hero of the Revolutionary War, Colonal William Butler, who had similarly pursued a particular chief in 1778.[15] Unless one assumes that the confusion is, for some obscure reason, deliberate, it seems clear that Melville's memory has conflated two hero tales out of his past reading, much as a later writer might attribute an adventure of Daniel Boone to Kit Carson or an exploit of Sam Spade to Philip Marlowe. Church's narrative is not the sort of historical source Melville might keep for reference; but the story is a part of his memory, in which the name of the hero is obscured but the character of the adventure precisely recalled. It is as a figure in popular mythological tradition, rather than as documentary source, that Church can be understood as the ancestor of Boone and Bumppo and Crockett.

## NOTES

1. *Magnalia Christi Americana,* 2: 497, 499.

2. Henry Martyn Dexter, "Introduction" and footnotes *passim, The History of King Philip's War* by Thomas [and Benjamin] Church; Douglas Edward Leach, *Flintlock and Tomahawk,* pp. 34–35, 51–55, 63–65,130–34, 208–10, 216–20, 228–40; Richard Slotkin. *Regeneration through Violence,* chap. 6.

3. Marion Vuilleumeir, *Indians of Olde Cape Cod,* pp. 35–41.

4. Leach, *Flintlock and Tomahawk,* p. 93; William Hubbard, *A Narrative of the Troubles,* p. 38.

5. *Magnalia Christi Americana,* 2: 499.

6. For a discussion of the question of authorship, see Slotkin, *Regeneration through Violence,* p. 577n.

7. [Benjamin and] Thomas Church, *Entertaining Passages Relating to Philip's War,* p. 120.

8. Hubbard, *A Narrative of the Troubles,* p. 87.

9. *Historical Discourse Concerning the Prevalency of Prayer,* pp. 256–57.

10. Hubbard, *A Narrative of the Troubles,* pp. 263, 265.

11. Slotkin, *Regeneration through Violence,* pp. 170–77.

12. See Michael P. Rogin, *Fathers and Children: Andrew Jackson and the Subjugation of the American Indian,* for a full discussion of this paradox as it operated in the personal and political mythology of Jackson; see also Thomas C. Leonard, "Red, White and the Army Blue: Empathy and Anger in the American West," *American Quarterly,* 26:2 (May, 1974), pp. 176–91, for a discussion of the phenomenon in the later nineteenth century.

13. Slotkin, *Regeneration through Violence,* pp. 165–68.

14. Ibid., chaps. 10, 13.

15. Herman Melville, *Moby-Dick,* p. 177. If Melville was referring to any historical document, Cotton Mather's history of King Philip's War in the *Magnalia* is a likely candidate. In recounting Church's killing of

Philip, Mather says that "God sent 'em the head of a leviathan for a *thanksgiving-feast*" (*Magnalia Christi Americana*, 2:499); and the crippled fin of Moby Dick is echoed in the crippled hand of Philip which was also cut off and displayed after his death. The motive of vengeance and metaphysical passion that spurs Ahab's hunt chimes nicely with Mather's interpretation of the war—he speaks of Church as engaged in "exterminating the rabid animals," and sees the war as a struggle of cosmic principles that foreshadows the Apocalypse, when the saved will feast on the leviathan. Such an interpretation of the war and such a response to Indian (or leviathan) character was of course antithetical to Church, as it is ultimately to Ishmael. Just after his reference to Church, Melville warns the reader against interpreting his book the way Ahab interprets his whale, as a "hideous and intolerable allegory"—and this, of course, is perfectly consonant with Church's response to Mather's rendering of King Philip's War.

## A NOTE ON THE TEXT

Editions of this narrative are:

C[hurch], T[homas]. *Entertaining Passages Relating to Philip's War* . . . . Boston: Printed by B. Green, 1716.

Church, Thomas. *The Entertaining History of King Philip's War*. . . . Newport, Rhode Island: Reprinted by Solomon Southwick, 1771.

Church, Thomas. *The History of King Philip's War* . . . , edited by Samuel G. Drake. Boston: [?], 1825. Second edition, Boston: J.H.A. Frost, [1827]. Boston: Wiat, 1827. Exeter, N.H.: J. & B. Williams, 1829. Boston: Milo, Mower & Co., 1829. Third edition, Boston: 1825 [?]. Exeter. [?], 1836; 1839; 1840; 1841.

Church, Thomas. *The History of King Philip's War*. Edited by Henry Martyn Dexter. Boston: John Kimball Wiggin, 1865.

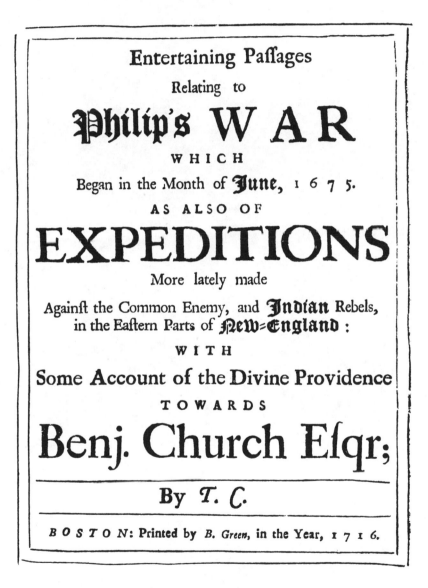

# Entertaining Passages
Relating to
# Philip's WAR
WHICH
Began in the Month of June, 1675.
AS ALSO OF
# EXPEDITIONS
More lately made
Against the Common Enemy, and Indian Rebels, in the Eastern Parts of New-England:
WITH
Some Account of the Divine Providence
TOWARDS
# Benj. Church Esqr;

By *T. C.*

*BOSTON*: Printed by *B. Green*, in the Year, 1716.

## *TO THE READER*

*The subject of this following Narrative offering it self to your friendly Perusal; relates to the Former and Later Wars of* New-England, *which I myself was not a little concerned in: For in the Year,* 1675. *that unhappy and bloody* Indian *War broke out in* Plymouth *Colony, where I was then building, and beginning a Plantation, at a Place called by the* Indians Sekonit; *and since by the* English, Little Compton. *I was the first* English Man *that built upon that Neck, which was full of* Indians. *My head and hands were full about Settling a New Plantation, where nothing was brought to; no preparation of Dwelling House, or Out-Housing or Fencing made. Horses and Cattel were to be provided, Ground to be clear'd, and broken up; and the uttermost Caution to be used, to keep my self free from offending my* Indian *Neighbours all round about me: While I was thus busily Employed, and all my Time and Strength laid out in this Laborious Undertaking; I Received a Commission from the Government to engage in their Defence. And with my Commission I receiv'd another heart inclining me to put forth my Strength in Military Service. And through the Grace of* GOD *I was Spirited for that work, and Direction in it was renewed to me day by day. And altho' many of the Actions that I was concerned in, were very Difficult and Dangerous; yet my self and those that went with me Voluntarily in the Service, had our Lives for the most part, wonderfully preserved, by the over-ruling Hand of the Almighty, from first to last; which doth aloud bespeak our Praises: And to declare His Wonderful Works, is our Indispensible Duty. I was ever very sensible of my own Littleness and Unfitness, to be imployed in such Great Services; but calling to mind that* GOD *is* STRONG, *I Endeavoured to put all my Confidence in Him, and by His Almighty Power was carried through every difficult Action: and my desire is that His Name may have the Praise.*

*It was ever my Intent having laid my self under a Solemn promise, that the many and Repeated Favours of* GOD *to my self, and those with me in the Service, might be published for Generations to come. And now my great Age requiring my Dismission from Service: in the Militia, and to put off my Armour; I am willing that the great and Glorious works of Almighty* GOD, *to us Children of Men, should appear to the World; and having my Minutes by me; my Son has taken the care and pains to Collect from them the Insuing Narrative of many passage relating to the Former and Later Wars, which I have had the perusal of, and find nothing a-miss, as to the Truth of it; and with as little Reflection upon any particular person as might be, either alive or dead.*

*And seeing every particle of historical Truth is precious; I hope the Reader will pass a favourable Censure upon an Old Souldier, telling of the many Ran-Counters he has had, and yet is come off alive. It is a pleasure to Remember what a great Number of Families in this and the Neighbouring Provinces in* New-England *did during the War, enjoy a great measure of Liberty and Peace by the hazardous* Stations *and* Marches *of those Engaged in Military Exercises, who were a Wall unto them on this side and on that side.*[1] *I desire Prayers that I may be enabled Well to accomplish my Spiritual Warfare, and that I may be more than Conquerour through* JESUS CHRIST *loving of me.*

BENJAMIN CHURCH.

ENTERTAINING PASSAGES
Relating to
Philip's WAR which began in the Year, 1675.
With the Proceedings of
BENJ. CHURCH ESQR;

In the year 1674, Mr. *Benjamin Church* of *Duxbury* being providentially at *Plymouth* in the time of the Court, fell into acquaintance with Capt. *John Almy* of *Rhode-Island.* Capt. *Almy* with great importunity invited him to ride with him, and view that part of *Plymouth* Colony that lay next to *Rhode-Island,* known then by their Indian Names of *Pocasset* & *Sogkonate.* Among other arguments to perswade him, he told him, the Soil was very rich, and the Situation pleasant. Perswades him by all means, to purchase of the Company some of the Court grant rights. He accepted his invitation, views the Country, & was pleased with it; makes a purchase, settled a Farm, found the Gentlemen of the Island very Civil & obliging. And being himself a Person of uncommon Activity and Industry, he soon erected two buildings upon his Farm, and gain'd a good acquaintance with the Natives; got much into their favour, and was in a little time in great esteem among them.[1]

The next Spring advancing,[2] while Mr. *Church* was diligently Settling his new Farm, stocking, leasing & disposing of his Affairs, and had a fine prospect of doing no small things; and hoping that his good success would be inviting unto other good Men to become his Neighbours; Behold! the rumour of a War between the *English* and the Natives gave check to his projects. People began to be very jealous of the *Indians,* and indeed they had no small reason to suspect that they had form'd a design of War upon the *English.* Mr. *Church* had it daily suggested to him that the Indians were plotting a bloody design. That *Philip* the great *Mount-hope* Sachem was Leader therein: and so it prov'd, he was sending his Messengers to all the Neighbouring Sachems, to ingage them in a Confederacy with him in the War.

Among the rest he sent Six Men to *Awashonks* Squaw, Sachem of the *Sogkonate* Indians, to engage her in his Interests: *Awashonks* so far listened unto them as to call her Subjects together, to make a great Dance, which is the custom of that Nation when they advise about Momentous Affairs. But what does *Awashonks* do, but sends away two of her Men that well understood the *English* Language (*Sassamon*[4] and *George* by Name) to invite Mr. *Church* to the Dance. Mr. *Church* upon the Invitation, immediately takes with him *Charles Hazelton* his Tennants Son, who well understood the *Indian* Language, and rid down to the Place appointed: Where they found hundreds of *Indians* gathered together from all Parts of her Dominion.[5] *Awashonks* her self in a foaming Sweat was leading the Dance. But she was no sooner sensible of Mr. *Churches* arrival, but she broke off, sat down, calls her Nobles round her, orders Mr. *Church* to be invited into her presence. Complements being past, and each one taking Seats. She told him, King *Philip* had sent Six Men of his with two of her People that had been over at *Mount-hope,* to draw her into a confederacy with him in a War with the *English.* Desiring him to give her his advice in the case, and to tell her the Truth whether the *Umpame*[6] Men (as *Philip* had told her) were gathering a great Army to invade *Philips* Country. He assured her he would tell her the Truth, and give her his best advice. Then he told her twas but a few days since he came from *Plymouth,* and the *English* were then making no Preparations for War; That he was in Company with the Principal Gentlemen of the Government, who had no Discourse at all about War; and he believ'd no tho'ts about it. He ask'd her whether she tho't he would have brought up his Goods to Settle in that Place, if he apprehended an entering into War with so near a Neighbour. She seem'd to be some-what convinc'd by his talk, and said she believ'd he spoke the Truth.

Then she called for the *Mount-hope* Men: Who made a formidable appearance, with their Faces Painted, and their Hair Trim'd up in Comb-fashion, with their Powder-horns, and Shot-bags at their backs; which among that Nation is the posture and figure of preparedness for War. She told Mr. *Church,* these were the Persons that had brought her the Report of the *English* preparation for War: And then told them what Mr. *Church* had said in answer to it.

Upon this began a warm talk among the Indians, but 'twas soon quash'd, and *Awashonks* proceeded to tell Mr. *Church* that *Philips* Message to her was that unless she would forth-with enter into a confederacy with him in a War against the *English,* he would send his Men over privately, to kill the *English* Cattel, and burn their Houses on that side the River, which would provoke the *English* to fall upon her, whom they would without doubt suppose the author of the Mischief. Mr. Church told her he was sorry to see so threatning an aspect of Affairs; and steping to the *Mount-hope,* he felt of their bags, and finding them filled with Bullets, ask'd them what those Bullets were for: They scoffingly reply'd to shoot *Pigeons* with.

Then Mr. *Church* turn'd to *Awashonks,* and told her if *Philip* were resolv'd to make War, her best way would be to knock those Six *Mount-hopes* on the head, and shelter herself under the Protection of the *English;* upon which the *Mount-hopes* were for the present Dumb. But those two of *Awashonks* Men who had been at *Mount-hope* express'd themselves in a furious manner against his advice. And *Little Eyes* one of the Queens Council joyn'd with them, and urged Mr. *Church* to go aside with him among the bushes that he might have some private Discourse with him, which other Indians immediately forbid being sensible of his ill design: but the Indians began to side and grow very warm. Mr. *Church* with undaunted Courage told the *Mount-hopes* they were bloody wretches, and thirsted after the blood of their *English* Neighbours, who had never injur'd them, but had always abounded in their kindness to them. That for his own part, tho' he desired nothing more than Peace, yet if nothing but War would satisfie them, he believed he should prove a sharp thorne in their sides; Bid the Company observe those Men that were of such bloody dispositions, whether Providence would suffer them to Live to see the event of the War, which others more Peaceably disposed might do.

Then he told *Awashonks* he thought it might be most advisable for her to send to the Governour of *Plymouth,* and shelter her self, and People under his Protection. She lik'd his advice, and desired him to go on her behalf to the *Plymouth* Government, which he consented to: And at parting advised her what ever she did, not to desert the *English* Interest, to joyn with her Neighbours in a Rebellion which would certainly prove fatal to her. [He mov'd none of his Goods from his House that there might not be the least umbrage from such an Action.][7] She thank'd him for his advice, and sent two of her Men to guard him to his House; which when they came there, urged him to take care to secure his Goods, which he refused for the reasons before mentioned. But desired the *Indians* that if what they feared should happen, they would take care of what he left, and directed them to a Place in the woods where they should dispose them; which they faithfully observed.[8]

He took his leave of his guard, and bid them tell their Mistress, if she continued steady in her dependence on the *English,* and kept within her own limits of *Sogkonate,* he would see her again quickly; and then hastned away to *Pocasset,* where he met with *Peter Nunnuit,* the Husband of the Queen of *Pocasset,* who was just then come over in a Canoo from *Mount-hope.*[9] *Peter* told him that there would certainly be War; for *Philip* had held a Dance of several Weeks continuance, and had entertain'd the Young Men from all Parts of the Country: And added that *Philip* expected to be sent for to *Plymouth* to be examined about *Sasamons* death, who was Murder'd at *Assawomset*-Ponds; knowing himself guilty of contriving that Murder. The same Peter told him that he saw Mr. *James Brown* of *Swanzey* and Mr. *Samuel Gorton*[10] who was an Interpreter, and two other Men who brought a Letter from the Governour of *Plymouth* to *Philip.* He observ'd to him further, that the Young Men were very eager to begin the War, and would fain have kill'd Mr. *Brown,* but *Philip* prevented it; telling them that his Father had charged him to shew kindness to Mr. *Brown.* In short, *Philip* was forc'd to promise them that on the next Lords-Day when the *English* were gone to Meeting they should rifle their Houses, and from that time forward kill their Cattel.[11]

*Peter* desir'd Mr. *Church* to go and see his Wife, who was but up the hill; he went and found but few of her People with her. She said they were all gone, against her Will to the Dances; and she much fear'd there would be a War. Mr. *Church* advis'd her to go to the Island and secure her self and those that were with her; and send to the Governour of *Plymouth* who she knew was her friend; and so left her, resolving to hasten to *Plymouth* and wait on the Governour: and he was so expeditious that he was with the Governour early next Morning, tho' he waited on some of the Magistrates by the way, who were of the Council of War, and also met him at the Governours. He gave them an account of his observations and discoveries, which confirmed their former intelligences, and hastned their preparation for Defence.

*Philip* according to his promise to his People, permitted them to March out of the Neck on the next Lords-Day, when they plundred the nearest Houses that the Inhabitants had deserted; but as yet offer'd no violence to the People, at least none were killed.[12] However the alarm was given by their Numbers, and hostile Equipage, and by the Prey they made of what they could find in the forsaken Houses.

An express came the same day[13] to the Governour, who immediately gave orders to the Captains of the Towns to March the greatest Part of their Companies, and to randezvous at *Taunton*, on *Monday* Night, where Major *Bradford* was to receive them, and dispose them under Capt. (now made Major) *Cutworth*[14] of *Situate*. The Governour desired Mr. Church to give them his Company, and use his interest in their behalf with the Gentlemen of *Rhode-Island*. He comply'd with it, and they March'd the next day. Major *Bradford* desired Mr. *Church* with a commanded party consisting of *English* and some *Friend-Indians*, to March in the Front at some distance from the Main body. Their orders were to keep so far before, as not be in sight of the Army. And so they did, for by the way, they killed a Deer instead, roasted, and eat the most of him before the Army came up with them. But the *Plymouth* Forces soon arriv'd at *Swanzey*, and were posted at Major *Browns* and Mr. *Miles's* Garrisons chiefly; and were there soon joyned with those that came from *Massachusetts*, who had entred into a Confederacy with their *Plymouth* Brethren, against the Perfidious Heathen.[15]

The Enemy who began their Hostilities with plundring and destroying Cattel, did not long content themselves with that game. They thirsted for *English* blood, and they soon broached it; killing two Men in the way not far from Mr. *Miles's* Garrison. And soon after, eight more at *Mattapoiset:* Upon whose bodies they exercised more than brutish barbarities; beheading, dismembring and mangling them, and exposing them in the most inhumane manner, which gash'd and ghostly objects struck a damp on all beholders.[16]

The Enemy flush'd with these exploits, grew yet bolder, and skulking every where in the bushes, shot at all Passengers, and kill'd many that ventured abroad. They came so near as to shoot down two Sentinels at Mr. *Miles's* Garrison, under the very Noses of most of our Forces. These provocations drew out the resentments of some of Capt. *Prentices* Troop, who desired they might have liberty to go out and seek the Enemy in their own quarters. Quarter Masters *Gill & Belcher* commanded the Parties drawn out, who earnestly desired Mr. *Churches* company: They provided him a Horse and Furniture (his own being out of the way) he readily comply'd with their desires, and was soon Mounted.[17]

This party were no sooner over *Miles's* Bridge, but were fired on by an Ambuscado of about a dozen *Indians*, as they were afterwards discovered to be. When they drew off, the Pilot[18] was Mortally wounded, Mr. *Belcher* received a shot in his knee, and his Horse was kill'd under him, Mr. *Gill* was struck with a Musket-ball on the side of his belly; but being clad with a buff Coat[19] and some thickness of Paper under it, it never broke his skin. The Troopers were surprized to see both their Commanders wounded, and wheel'd off. But Mr. *Church* perswaded, at length storm'd and stampt, and told them 'twas a shame to run, and leave a wounded Man there to become a Prey to the barbarous Enemy. For the Pilot yet sat his Horse, tho' so maz'd with the Shot, as not to have sense to guide him. Mr. *Gill* seconded him, and offer'd, tho' much disenabled, to assist in bringing him off. Mr. *Church* asked a Stranger who gave them his company in that action, if he would go with him and fetch off the wounded Man: He readily consented, they with Mr. *Gill* went, but the wounded Man fainted and fell off his Horse before they came to him; but Mr. *Church* and the Stranger dismounted, took up the Man dead, and laid him before Mr. *Gill* on his Horse. Mr. *Church* told the other two, if they would take care of the dead Man, he would go and fetch his Horse back, which was going off the Cassey[20] toward the Enemy; but before he got over the Cassey he saw the Enemy run to the right into the Neck. He brought back the Horse, and call'd earnestly and repeatedly to the Army to come over & fight the Enemy; and while he stood calling & perswading, the skulking Enemy return'd to their old stand, and all discharged their Guns at him at one clap, tho' every shot miss'd him; yet one of the Army on the other side of the river received one of the balls in his foot. Mr. *Church* now began (no succour coming to him) to think it time to retreat: Saying, *The Lord have Mercy on us*, if such a handful of Indians shall thus dare such an Army!

Upon this 'twas immediately resolv'd, and orders were given to March down into the Neck,[21] and having passed the Bridge, and Cassey, the direction was to extend both wings, which being not well headed, by those that remain'd in the Center, some of them mistook their Friends for their Enemies, and made a fire upon them in the right wing, and wounded that noble Heroick Youth Ensign *Savage* in the thigh; but it happily prov'd but a flesh wound. They Marched[22] until they came to the narrow of the Neck, at a Place called *Krekkamuit,* where they took down the heads of Eight *English* Men that were kill'd at the head of *Metapoiset*-Neck, and set upon Polls, after the barbarous manner of those Salvages.[23] There *Philip* had staved all his Drums, and conveyed all his Canoo's to the East-side of *Metapoiset*-River. Hence it was concluded by those that were acquainted with the Motions of those People, that they had quitted the Neck. Mr. *Church* told 'em that *Philip* was doubtless gone over to *Pocasset* side, to ingage those Indians in Rebellion with him: which they soon found to be true. The Enemy were not really beaten out of *Mount-hope* Neck, tho' 'twas true they fled from thence; yet it was before any pursu'd them. 'Twas but to strengthen themselves, and to gain a more advantagious Post. However, some and not a few pleased themselves with the fancy of a Mighty Conquest.[24]

A grand Council was held, and a Resolve past, to build a Fort there to maintain the first ground they had gain'd, by the Indians leaving it to them. And to speak the Truth, it must be said, That as they gain'd not that Field by their Sword, nor their Bow; so 'twas rather their fear than their courage, that oblig'd them to set up the marks of their Conquest.[25] Mr. *Church* look'd upon it, and talk'd of it with contempt, and urged hard the pursuing the Enemy on *Pocasset* side, and with the greater earnestness, because of his promise made to *Awashonks,* before mentioned. The Council adjourned themselves from *Mount-hope* to *Rehoboth,* where Mr. Treasurer *Southworth*[26] being weary of his charge of Commissary General, (Provision being scarce & difficult to be obtained, for the Army, that now lay still to Cover the People from no body, while they were building a Fort for nothing) retired, and the Power & Trouble of that Post was left with Mr. *Church,* who still urged the Commanding Officers to move over to *Pocasset* side to pursue the Enemy and kill *Philip,* which would in his opinion be more probable to keep possession of the Neck, than to tarry to build a Fort. He was still restless on that side of the River, and the rather because of his promise to the *Squaw Sachem* of *Sogkonate.* And Capt. *Fuller* also urged the same, until at length there came further order concerning the Fort. And with all, an order for Capt. *Fuller* with Six files to cross the River to the side so much insisted on, and to try if he could get Speech with any of the *Pocasset* or *Sogkonate* Indians, and that Mr. *Church* should go his Second. Upon the Captains receiving his orders, he ask'd Mr. Church whither he was willing to engage in this interprize: To whom 'twas indeed too agreeable to be declined; tho' he thought the enterprize was hazardous enough, for them to have more Men assign'd them. Capt. *Fuller* told him that for his own part he was grown Ancient and heavy, he feared the travel and fatigue would be too much for him. But Mr. Church urged him, and told him, he would chearfully excuse him, his hardship and travel, and take that part to himself, if he might but go; for he had rather do any thing in the World than stay there to build the Fort.

Then they drew out the Number assigned them and March'd the same Night to the Ferry, and were transported to *Rhode-Island,* from hence the next Night they got a passage over to *Pocasset*-side in *Rhode-Island* Boats, and concluded there to dispose themselves in two Ambuscado's before day, hoping to surprize some of the Enemy by their falling into one or other of their Ambusments. But Capt. *Fullers* party being troubled with the Epidemical plague of lust after Tobacco, must needs strike fire to Smoke it; and thereby discovered themselves to a party of the Enemy coming up to them, who immediately fled with great preciptation.[27]

This Ambuscado drew off about break of day, perceiving they were discover'd, the other continued in their Post until the time assigned them, and the light and heat of the Sun rendred their Station both insignificant and troublesome, and then return'd, unto the place of Randezvous, where they were acquainted with the other parties disappointment, and the occasion of it. Mr. *Church* calls for the breakfast he had ordered to be brought over in the Boat: but the Man that had the charge of it confessed that he was a-sleep when the Boats-men called him, and in haste came away and never thought of it. It happened that

Mr. *Church* had a few Cakes of Rusk in His Pocket, that Madam *Cranston* (the Governour of *Rhode-Island's* Lady)[28] gave him, when he came off the Island, which he divided among the Company, which was all the Provisions they had.

Mr. *Church* after their slender breakfast proposed to Capt. *Fuller,* That he would March in quest of the Enemy, with such of the Company as would be willing to March with him; which he complyed with, tho' with a great deal of scruple, because of his small Number, & the extream hazard he foresaw must attend them.[29]

But some of the Company had reflected upon Mr. *Church,* that notwithstanding his talk on the other side of the River, he had not shewn them any *Indians* since they came over. Which now mov'd him to tell them, That if it was their desire to see *Indians,* he believ'd he should now soon shew them what they should say was enough.

The Number allow'd him soon drew off to him, which could not be a many, because their whole Company consisted of no more than Thirty Six. They mov'd towards *Sogkonate,* until they came to the brook that runs into *Nunnaquohqut* Neck, where they discovered a fresh and plain Track, which they concluded to be from the great Pine Swamp about a Mile from the Road that leads to *Sogkonet.* Now says Mr. *Church* to his Men, If we follow this Track no doubt but we shall soon see *Indians* enough; they express'd their willingness to follow the Track, and mov'd in it, but had not gone far before one of them narrowly escaped being bit with a *Rattle-snake:* And the Woods that the Track lead them through was haunted much with those Snakes, which the little Company seem'd more to be afraid of than the black Serpents[30] they were in quest of, and therefore bent their course another way; to a Place where they thought it probable to find some of the Enemy. Had they kept the Track to the Pine Swamp they had been certain of meeting *Indians* enough; but not so certain that any of them should have return'd to give account how many.

Now they pass'd down into *Punkatees* Neck; and in their March discovered a large Wigwam full of *Indian* Truck, which the Souldiers were for loading themselves with; until Mr. *Church* forbid it; telling them they might expect soon to have their hands full, and business without caring for Plunder. Then crossing the head of the Creek into the Neck, they again discovered fresh Indian Tracks, very lately pass'd before them into the Neck. They then got privately and undiscovered, unto the Fence of Capt. *Almy's* Pease field, and divided into two Parties, Mr. *Church* keeping the one Party with himself sent the other with *Lake* that was acquainted with the ground on the other side. Two *Indians* were soon discovered coming out of the Pease field towards them: When Mr. *Church* & those that were with him concealed themselves from them, by falling flat on the ground; but the other division not using the same caution were seen by the Enemy, which occasioned them to run; which when Mr. *Church* perceiv'd, he shew'd himself to them, and call'd, telling them he desired but to speak with them, and would not hurt them. But they run, and *Church* pursued. The *Indians* clim'd over a Fence and one of them facing about discharged his Piece, but without effect on the *English:* One of the *English* Souldiers ran up to the Fence and fir'd upon him that had discharged his Piece; and they concluded by the yelling they heard that the *Indian* was wounded; but the *Indians* soon got into the thickets, whence they saw them no more for the present.

Mr. *Church* then Marching over a plain piece of Ground where the Woods were very thick on one side; order'd his little Company to March at double distance, to make as big a show (if they should be discovered) as might be. But before they saw any body, they were Saluted with a Volly of fifty or sixty Guns; some Bullets came very surprizingly near Mr. *Church,* who starting, look'd behind him, to see what was become of his Men, expecting to have seen half of them dead, but seeing them all upon their Leggs and briskly firing at the Smokes of the Enemies Guns, (for that was all that was then to be seen) *He Bless'd God, and called to his Men not to discharge all their Guns at once, lest the Enemy should take the advantage of such an opportunity to run upon them with their Hatches.*[31]

Their next Motion was immediately into the Pease field. When they came to the Fence Mr. *Church* bid as many as had not discharg'd their Guns; to clap under the Fence, and lye close, while the other at some distance in the Field stood to charge; hoping that if the Enemy should creep to the Fence to gain a shot at those that were charging their Guns, they might be surprized by those that lay under the Fence. But casting his Eyes to the side of the Hill above them, the hill seem'd to move, being covered over with *Indians,* with their bright Guns glittering in the Sun, and running in a circumference with a design to surround them.

Seeing such Multitudes surrounding him and his little Company; it put him upon thinking what was become of the Boats that were ordered to attend him: And looking up, he spy'd them a shore at *Sandy-point* on the Island side of the River, with a number of Horse and Foot by them, and wondred what should be the occasion; until he was afterwards informed, That the Boats had been over that Morning from the Island and had landed a Party of Men at *Fogland,* that were design'd in *Punkatees* Neck to fetch off some Cattel and Horses, but were Ambuscado'd, and many of them wounded by the Enemy.

Now our Gentlemans Courage and Conduct were both put to the Test, he incourages his Men; and orders some to run and take a Wall to shelter before the Enemy gain'd it. Twas time for them now to think of escaping if they knew which way. Mr. *Church* orders his Men to strip to their white Shirts, that the *Islanders* might discover them to be English Men; & then orders Three Guns to be fired distinct, hoping it might be observ'd by their friends on the opposite shore. The Men that were ordered to take the Wall being very hungry, stop'd a while among the Pease to gather a few; being about four Rod from the Wall; the Enemy from behind it hail'd them with a Shower of Bullets; but soon all but one came tumbling over an old hedge down the bank where Mr. *Church* and the rest were, and told him that his Brother *B. Southworth,* who was the Man that was missing, was kill'd, that they saw him fall; and so they did indeed see him fall, but 'twas without a Shot, and lay no longer than till he had opportunity to clap a Bullet into one of the Enemies Forehead, and then came running to his Company. The meanness[32] of the *English's* Powder was now their greatest misfortune; when they were immediately upon this beset with Multitudes of *Indians,* who possessed themselves of every Rock, Stump, Tree, or Fence that was in sight, firing upon them without ceasing; while they had no other shelter but a small bank & bit of water Fence. And yet to add to the disadvantage of this little handful of distressed Men; The *Indians* also possessed themselves of the Ruines of a Stone-house that overlook'd them, and of the black Rocks to the Southward of them; so that now they had no way to prevent lying quite open to some, or other of the Enemy, but to heap up Stones before them, as they did, and still bravely and wonderfully defended themselves, against all the numbers of the Enemy. At length came over one of the Boats from the Island Shore, but the Enemy ply'd their Shot so warmly to her as made her keep at some distance; Mr. *Church* desired them to send their Canoo a-shore to fetch them on board; but no perswasions, nor arguments could prevail with them to bring their Canoo to shore. Which some of Mr. *Churches* Men perceiving, began to cry out, *For God's sake to take them off, for their Ammunition was spent,* &c. Mr. *Church* being sensible of the danger of the Enemies hearing their Complaints, and being made acquainted with the weakness and scantiness of their Ammunition, fiercely called to the Boats-master, and bid either send his Canoo a-shore, or else begone presently, or he would fire upon him.

Away goes the Boat and leaves them still to shift for themselves. But then another difficulty arose; the Enemy seeing the Boat leave them, were reanimated & fired thicker & faster than ever; Upon which some of the Men that were lightest of foot, began to talk of attempting an escape by flight: until Mr. *Church* sollidly convinc'd them of the impracticableness of it; and incouraged them yet, told them, *That he had observ'd so much of the remarkable and wonderful Providence of God hitherto preserving them, that incouraged him to believe with much confidence that God would yet preserve them; that not a hair of their head should fall to the ground; bid them be Patient, Couragious and Prudently sparing of their Ammunition, and he made no doubt but they should come well off yet,* &c. until his little Army, again resolve one and all to stay with, and stick by him. One of them by Mr. *Churches* order was pitching a flat Stone up an end before him in the Sand, when a Bullet from the Enemy with a full force stroke the Stone while he was pitching it an end; which put the poor fellow to a miserable start, till Mr. *Church* call'd upon him to observe, *How God directed the Bullets that the Enemy could not hit him when in the same place, yet could hit the Stone as it was erected.*

While they were thus making the best defence they could against their numerous Enemies that made the Woods ring with their constant yelling and shouting: And Night coming on, some body told Mr. *Church*, they spy'd a Sloop up the River as far as

*Gold-Island,* that seemed to be coming down towards them: He look'd up and told them *Succour was now coming, for he believ'd it was Capt.* Golding, *whom he knew to be a Man for business; and would certainly fetch them off, if he came:* the Wind being fair, the Vessel was soon with them; and Capt. *Golding* it was. Mr. *Church* (as soon as they came to Speak one with another) desired him *to come to Anchor at such a distance from the Shore that he might veer out his Cable and ride afloat, and let slip his Canoo that it might drive ashore;* which directions Capt. *Golding* observ'd; but the Enemy gave him such a warm Salute, that his Sails, Colour, and Stern were full of Bullet holes.

The Canoo came ashore, but was so small that she would not bare above two Men at a time; and when two were got aboard, they turn'd her loose to drive ashore for two more: and the Sloops company kept the *Indians* in play the while. But when at last it came to Mr. *Churches* turn to go aboard, he had left his Hat and Cutlash at the Well where he went to drink, when he first came down; he told his Company, *He would never go off and leave his Hat and Cutlash for the* Indians; *they should never have that to reflect upon him.* Tho' he was much disswaded from it, yet he would go fetch them. He put all the Powder he had left into his Gun (and a poor charge it was) and went presenting his Gun at the Enemy, until he took up what he went for; at his return he discharged his Gun at the Enemy to bid them farewel, for that time; but had not Powder enough to carry the Bullet half way to them.

Two Bullets from the Enemy st[r]uck the Canoo as he went on Board, one grazed the hair of his Head a little before; another struck in a small Stake that stood right against the middle of his Breast.

Now this Gentleman with his Army, making in all 20 Men, himself, and his Pilot being numbred with them, got all safe aboard after Six hours ingagement with 300 *Indians*; whose Number we were told afterwards by some of themselves. *A deliverance which that good Gentleman often mentions to the Glory of God, and His Protecting Providence.* The next day meeting with the rest of their little Company whom he had left at *Pocasset,* (that had also a small skirmish with the *Indians,* and had two Men Wounded) they return'd to the *Mount-hope* Garrison; which Mr. *Church* us'd to call the loosing [losing] Fort. Mr. *Church* then returning to the Island to seek Provision for the Army, meets with *Alderman,* a noted *Indian* that was just come over from the *Squaw Sachem's* Cape of *Pocasset,*[33] having deserted from her, and had brought over his Family: Who gave him an account of the State of the *Indians,* and where each of the *Sagamores* head quarters were. Mr. *Church* then discours'd with some who knew the Spot well where the *Indians* said *Weetamores* head quarters were, and offered their Service to Pilot him. With this News he hastned to the *Mount-hope* Garrison. The Army express'd their readiness to imbrace such an opportunity.[34]

All the ablest Souldiers were now immediately drawn off equip'd & dispatch'd upon this design, under the Command of a certain Officer:[35] and having March'd about two Miles, *viz.* until they came to the Cove that lyes *S. W.* from the Mount, where orders was given for an halt. The Commander in Chief told them he thought it proper to take advice before he went any further; called Mr. *Church* and the Pilot, and ask'd them, *How they knew that* Philip *and all his Men were not by that time got to* Weetamores *Camp; or that all her own Men were not by that time return'd to her again?* With many more frightful questions. Mr. *Church* told him, *they had acquainted him with as much as they knew, and that for his part he could discover nothing that need to discourage them from Proceeding, that he thought it so practicable, that he with the Pilot would willingly lead the way to the Spot and hazard the brunt.* But the Chief Commander insisted on this, *That the Enemies number were so great, and he did not know what numbers more might be added unto them by that time: And his Company so small, that he could not think it practicable to attack them.* Added moreover, *That if he was sure of killing all the Enemy, and knew that he must lose the Life of one of his Men in the action, he would not attempt it.* Pray Sir, then (Reply'd Mr. *Church*) *Please to lead your Company to yonder Windmill on* Rhode-Island, *and there they will be out of danger of being kill'd by the Enemy, and we shall have less trouble to supply them with Provisions.* But return he would, and did, unto the Garrison until more strength came to them: And a Sloop to transport them to the Fall River, in order to visit *Weetamores* Camp. Mr. *Church,* one *Baxter* and Capt. *Hunter* an Indian,[36] profer'd to go out on the discovery on the left Wing; which was accepted; they had not March'd above a quarter of a Mile before they started Three of the Enemy. Capt. *Hunter* wounded one of them in his knee, whom when he came up he discovered to be his near kinsman; the Captive desired favour for his *Squaw,* if she should fall into their hands, but ask'd none for himself, excepting the liberty of taking a Whiff of Tobacco, and while he was taking his Whiff, his kinsman with one blow of his Hatchet dispatch'd him. Proceeding to *Weetamores* Camp, they were discover'd by one of the Enemy, who ran in and gave Information; upon which a lusty Young Fellow left his Meat upon his Spit, running hastily out told his companions, *he would kill an English man before he eat his dinner:* but fail'd of his design, being no sooner out but shot down. The Enemies fires, and what shelter they had was by the Edge of a thick Cedar Swamp, into which on this Alarm they betook themselves; and the English as nimbly pursued; but were soon commanded back by their Chieftain after they were come within hearing of the Crys of their Women, and Children, and so ended that Exploit. But returning to their Sloop the Enemy pursued them and wounded two of their Men. The next day return'd to the *Mount-hope* Garrison.[37]

Soon after this, was *Philips* head Quarters visited by some other *English* Forces; but *Philip* and his gang had the very fortune to escape that *Weetamore* and hers (but now mentioned) had: they took into a Swamp and their pursuers were commanded back.[38] After this *Dartmouths* distresses required Succour, great Part of the Town being laid desolate, and many of the Inhabitants kill'd;[39] the most of *Plymouth* Forces were order'd thither: And coming to *Russels* Garrison at *Poneganset,* they met with a Number of the Enemy that had surrendred themselves Prisoners on terms promised by Capt. *Eels* of the Garrison; and *Ralph Earl* that perswaded them (by a friend *Indian* he had employed) to come in. And had their promises to the *Indians* been kept, and the *Indians* farely treated, 'tis probable that most if not all the *Indians* in those Parts, had soon followed the Example of those that had now surrendred themselves; which would have been a good step towards finishing the War. But in spite of all that Capt. *Eels, Church,* or *Earl* could say, argue, plead, or beg, some body else that had more Power in their hands improv'd it; and without any regard to the promises made them on their surrendring themselves they were carry'd away to *Plymouth,* there sold, and transported out of the Country; being about Eight-score

Persons. An action so hateful to Mr. *Church,* that he oppos'd it to the loss of the good Will and Respects of some that before were his good Friends.[40] But while these things were acting at *Dartmouth, Philip* made his escape, leaving his Country, fled over *Taunton*-River, and *Rehoboth*-Plain, and *Petuxet*-River, where Capt. *Edmunds* of *Providence* made some spoil upon; and had probably done more, but was prevented by the coming up of a Superiour Officer, that put him by.[41] And now another Fort was built at *Pocasset,* that prov'd as troublesome and chargeable as that at *Mount-hope;* and the remainder of the Summer was improv'd in providing for the Forts and Forces there maintained, while our Enemies were fled, some hundreds of Miles into the Country, near as far as *Albany.* And now strong Suspicions began to arise of the *Narraganset Indians,* that they were ill affected, and designed mischief; and so the event soon discovered The next Winter they began their Hostilities, upon the *English.*[42] The United Colonies then agreed to send an Army to suppress them: Governour *Winslow*[43] to command the Army. He undertaking the Expedition, invited Mr. *Church* to command a Company in the Expedition;, which he declin'd, craving excuse from taking Commission, he promised to wait upon him as a *Reformado*[44] thro' the Expedition. Having rid with the General to *Boston,* and from thence to *Rehoboth.* Upon the Generals request he went thence the nearest way over the Ferries, with Major *Smith* to his Garrison in the *Narraganset Country,* to prepare and provide for the coming of General *Winslow;* who March'd round thro' the Country with his Army proposing by Night to surprize *Pumham* (a certain *Narraganset* Sachem) and his Town; but being aware of the approach of our Army made their escape into the desarts. But Mr. *Church* meeting with fair Winds arriv'd safe at the Major's Garrison in the evening.[45] And soon began to inquire after the Enemies Resorts, Wigwams or Sleeping Places; and having gain'd some intelligence, he proposed to the *Eldriges,* and some other brisk hands, that he met with, to attempt the Surprizing of some of the Enemy to make a Present of to the General, when he should arrive: which might advantage his design; being brisk blades, they readily comply'd with the motion, and were soon upon their March. The Night was very cold, but bless'd with the *Moon;* before the day broke they effected their exploit, and by the rising of the Sun arrived at the Major's Garrison, where they met the General and presented him with Eighteen of the Enemy, they had Captiv'd.[46] The General pleas'd with the exploit, gave them thanks, particularly to Mr. *Church,* the mover and chief actor of the business; and sending two of them (likely Boys) a present to *Boston;* smiling on Mr. *Church,* told him, *That he made no doubt but his Faculty would supply them with* Indian Boys *enough before the War was ended.*

Their next move was to a Swamp which the Indians had Fortifyed with a Fort.[47] Mr. *Church* rid in the Generals guard when the bloudy ingagement began; but being impatient of being out of the heat of the action, importunately beg'd leave of the General that he might run down to the assistance of his friends, the General yielded to his request, provided he could rally some hands to go with him. Thirty Men immediately drew out and followed him: They entred the Swamp and passed over the Log that was the passage into the Fort, where they saw many Men and several Valiant Captains lye slain: Mr. *Church* spying Capt. *Gardner* of *Salem* amidst the Wigwams in the East end of the Fort, made towards him, but on a sudden, while they were looking each other in the Face, Capt. *Gardner* settled down, Mr. *Church* step'd to him and seeing the blood run down his cheek, lifted up his Cap, and calling him by his Name; he look'd up in his Face, but spoke not a Word being Mortally Shot thro' the head; and observing his Wound, Mr. *Church* found the ball entred his head on the side that was next the Upland, where the *English* entred the Swamp. Upon which, having ordered some care to be taken of the Captain, he dispatch'd information to the General that the best and forwardest of his Army that hazarded their lives to enter the Fort, upon the muzzle of the Enemies Guns, were Shot in their backs and kill'd by them that lay behind. Mr. *Church* with his small Company hasten'd out of the Fort (that the English were now possessed of) to get a Shot at the *Indians* that were in the Swamp, & kept firing upon them. He soon met with a broad bloody track, where the Enemy had fled with their Wounded men; following hard in the tract, he soon spy'd one of the Enemy, who clap'd his Gun across his breast, made towards Mr. *Church* and beckned[48] to him with his hand; Mr. *Church* immediately commanded no Man to hurt him, hoping by him to have gain'd some intelligence of the Enemy, that might be of advantage; but it unhappily fell out that a Fellow that had lag'd behind coming up, shot down the *Indian,* to Mr. *Church's* great grief and disappointment. But immediately they heard a great shout of the Enemy, which seem'd to be behind them, or between them and the Fort; and discover'd them running from tree to tree to gain advantages of firing upon the *English* that were in the Fort. Mr. *Churches* great difficulty now was how to discover himself to his Friends in the Fort, using several inventions, till at length gain'd an opportunity to call to, and inform a Serjeant in the Fort, that he was there, and might be exposed to their Shots, unless they observ'd it. By this time he discovered a number of the Enemy almost within Shot of him, making towards the Fort; Mr. *Church* and his Company were favoured by a heap of brush that was between them and the Enemy, and prevented their being discover'd to them. Mr. *Church* had given his Men their particular orders for firing upon the Enemy; and as they were rising up to make their Shot, the afore-mentioned Serjeant in the Fort called out to them, *for God's sake not to fire, for he believed they were some of their* Friend Indians; they clap'd down again, but were soon sensible of the Serjeants mistake. The Enemy got to the top of the Tree, the body whereof the Serjeant stood upon, and there clap'd down out of sight of the Fort, but all this while never discovered Mr. *Church,* who observed them to keep gathering unto that Place, until there seem'd to be a formidable black heap of them. *Now brave boys* (said Mr. *Church* to his Men) *if we mind our hits, we may have a brave Shot, and let our sign for firing on them, be their rising up to fire into the Fort.* It was not long before the *Indians* rising up as one body, designing to pour a Volley into the Fort. When our *Church* nimbly started up and gave them such a round Volley, and unexpected clap on their backs, that they who escaped with their Lives, were so surprized, that they scampered, they knew not whether themselves; about a dozen of them ran right over the Log into the Fort, and took into a sort of a Hovel that was build with Poles, after the manner of a corn crib. Mr. *Church's* Men having their Catteridges[49] fix'd, were soon ready to obey his order, which was immediately to charge and run on upon the Hovel, and over-set it, calling as he run on to some that were in the Fort to assist him in over-setting of it; they no sooner came to Face the Enemies shelter, but Mr. *Church* discover'd that one of them had found a hole to point his Gun through, right at him; but however incouraged his Company, and ran right on, till he was struck with Three Bullets, one in his Thigh, which [bullet] was near half of it cut off as it glanced on the joynt of the Hip-bone; another thro' the gatherings of his Breeches and Draws, with a small flesh Wound; a third pierced his Pocket, and wounded a pair of Mittins, that he had borrowed of Capt. *Prentice;* being wrap'd up together had the misfortune of having many holes cut thro' them with one Bullet; But however he made shift to keep on his Legs, and nimbly discharged his Gun at them that wounded him: being disinabled now to go a step his Men would have carried him off, but he forbid their touching of him, until they had perfected their project of over-setting the Enemies shelter; bid them run, *for now, the Indians had no Guns charged.* While he was urging them to run on, the *Indians* began to shoot Arrows, and with one pierc'd thro' the Arm of an *English* Man that had hold of Mr. *Churches* Arm to support him. The *English,* in short, were discourag'd, and drew back. And by this time the *English People* in the Fort had began to set fire to the *Wigwams & Houses* in the Fort, which Mr. *Church* laboured hard to prevent; they told him, *They had orders from the General to burn them;* he beg'd them to forbear until he had discours'd the General; and hastning to him, *he beg'd to spare the Wigwams &c. in the Fort from fire,* told him, *The Wigwams were Musket-proof, being all lin'd with Baskets and Tubbs of Grain, and other Provisions, sufficient to supply the whole Army until the Spring of the Year; and every wounded Man might have a good warm House to lodge in, which other-ways would necessarily perish with the Storms and Cold. And moreover, that the Army had no other Provision to trust unto or depend upon; that he knew that* Plymouth *Forces had not so much as one Biscake left, for he had seen their last dealt out,*[50] &c. The General advising a few Words with the Gentlemen that were about him, Mov'd towards the Fort, designing to ride in himself, and bring in the whole Army. But just as he was entering the Swamp, one of his Captains[51] meet him, and asked him *Whither he was going?* He told him into the Fort; the Captain laid hold of his Horse, and told him, *His Life was worth an hundred of theirs, and he should not expose himself.* The General told him, *That he supposed the brunt was over, and that Mr.* Church *had inform'd him that the Fort was taken,* &c. *And as the case was circumstanced he was of the Mind, that it was most practicable for him, and his Army to shelter themselves in the Fort.* The Captain in a great heat, reply'd, *that Church ly'd;* and told the General, *That if he mov'd another step towards the Fort he would shoot his Horse under him.* Then brusled[52] up another Gentleman, a certain Doctor,[53] and opposs'd Mr. *Church's* advice, and said, *If it were comply'd with, it would kill more Men than the Enemy had killed; for* (said he) *by to Morrow the wounded Men will be so stiff that there will be no moving of them:* And looking upon Mr. *Church,* and seeing the blood flowing a pace from his Wounds, told him, *That if he gave such advice as that was, he should bleed to Death like a Dog before they would endeavour to stench his blood.* Though after they had prevailed against his advice, they were sufficiently kind to him. And burning up all the Houses and Provisions in the Fort; the Army return'd the same Night in the Storm and Cold: And I Suppose every one that is acquainted with the circumstances of that Nights March, deeply laments the miseries that attended them, especially the wounded & dying Men. But it mercifully came to pass that Capt. *Andrew Belcher* arrived at Mr. *Smiths* that very Night from *Boston,* with a Vessel loaden with Provisions for the Army, who must otherwise have perish'd for want. Some of the Enemy that were then in the Fort have since inform'd us, that near a third of the *Indians* belonging to all that *Narraganset Country* were killed by the *English,* and by the Cold that Night, that they fled out of their Fort so hastily that they carried nothing with them: that if the *English* had kept in the Fort, the *Indians* had certainly been necessitated, either to surrender themselves to them, or to have perished by Hunger, and the severity of the Season. Some time after this Fort-fight a certain *Sogkonate Indian* hearing Mr. Church relate the manner of his being wounded, told him, *That he did not know but he himself was the* Indian *that wounded him, for that he was one of that company of* Indians *that Mr.* Church *made a Shot upon when they were rising up to make a Shot into the Fort; they were in number about* 60 *or* 70, *that just then came down from* Pumhams *Town, and never before then fired a Gun against the* English; *that when Mr.* Church *fired upon them he killed* 14 *dead in the Spot, and wounded a greater number than he killed, many of which dyed afterwards with their wounds, in the Cold and Storm the following Night.*

Mr. *Church* was mov'd with other wounded men over to *Rhode Island,* where in about a Months time he was in some good measure recovered of his Wounds, and the Fever that attended them. And then went over to the General to take his leave of him, with a design to return home.

But the Generals great importunity again perswaded him, to accompany him in a long March, into the *Nipmuck* Country, tho' he had then Tents[54] in his Wounds, and so Lame as not able to Mount his Horse without two Mens assistance.

In this March[55] the first thing remarkable was, they came to an *Indian* Town, where there were many *Wigwams* in sight, but an Icy Swamp lying between them and the *Wigwams,* prevented their running at once upon it as they intended: there was much firing upon each side before they pass'd the Swamp. But at length the Enemy all fled, and a certain *Moohegan* that was a friend *Indian,* pursued and seiz'd one of the Enemy, that had a small wound in his Leg, and brought him before the General, where he was examined. Some were for torturing of him to bring him to a more ample confession, of what he knew concerning his Country-men. Mr. *Church* verily believing he had been ingenious in his confession, interceeded and prevailed for his escaping torture. But the Army being bound forward in their March, and the *Indians* wound somewhat disinabling him for Travelling, 'twas concluded he should be knock'd on the Head: Accordingly he was brought before a great fire, and the *Moohegan* that took him was allowed, as he desired, to be the Executioner. Mr. *Church* taking no delight in the Sport,[56] fram'd an arrant at some distance among the baggage Horses, and when he had got some Ten Rods, or thereabouts from the fire, the Executioner fetching a blow with his Hatchet at the head of the Prisoner, he being aware of the blow, dodged his aside, and the Executioner missing his stroke the Hatchet flew out of his hand, and had like to have done execution where 'twas not designed. The Prisoner upon his narrow escape broke from them that held him, and notwithstanding his Wound made use of his Legs, and hap'd to run right upon Mr. *Church,* who laid hold on him, and a close skuffle they had, but the *Indian* having no Clothes on slip'd from him, and ran again, and Mr. *Church* pursued the *Indian,* altho' being Lame, there was no great odds in the Race, until the *Indian* stumbled and fell, and they closed again, skuffled and fought pretty smartly, until the *Indian* by the advantage of his nakedness slip'd from his hold again, and set out on his third Race, with Mr. *Church* close at his heels, endeavouring to lay hold on the hair of his Head, which was all the hold could be taken of him; and running thro' a Swamp that was covered with hollow Ice, it made so loud a noise that Mr. *Church* expected (but in vain) that some of his English friends would follow the noise, and come to his assistance. But the *Indian* hap'd to run a-thwart a mighty Tree that lay fallen near breast-high, where he stop'd, and cry'd out a loud for help; but Mr. *Church* being soon upon him again, the Indian seized him fast by the hair of his Head, and endeavouring by twisting to break his Neck; but tho' Mr. *Churches* wounds had some what weakned him, and the *Indian* a stout fellow, yet he held him well in play, and twisted the *Indians* Neck as well, and took the advantage of many opportunities, while they hung by each others hair gave him notorious bunts in the face with his head. But in the heat of this skuffle they heard the Ice break with some bodies coming a-pace to them, which when they heard, *Church* concluded there was help for one or other of them, but was doubtful which of them must now receive the fatal stroke; anon some body comes up to them, who prov'd to be the Indian that had first taken the Prisoner. Without speaking a word, he felt them out (for twas so dark he could not distinguish them by sight) the one being clothed, and the other naked, he felt where Mr. *Churches* hands were fastned in the Netops[57] hair, and with one blow settled his Hatchet in between them, and ended the strife. He then spoke to Mr. Church and hugg'd him in his Arms, and thank'd him abundantly for catching his Prisoner; and cut off the head of his Victim, and carried it to the Camp, and giving an account to the rest of the friend Indians in the Camp, how Mr. *Church* had seized his Prisoner, &c they all joyn'd a mighty shout.

Proceeding in this March, they had the success of killing many of the Enemy: until at length their Provision failing, they return'd home.

King *Philip* (as was before hinted) was fled to a Place called *Scattacook* between *York* and *Albany,* where the *Moohags* made a descent upon him and killed many of his Men, which moved him from thence.

His next kennelling Place was at the falls of Connecticut River, where sometime after Capt. *Turner* found him, came upon him by Night, kill'd him a great many Men, and frighted many more into the River, that were hurl'd down the falls and drowned.[58]

*Philip* got over the River, and on the back side of the *Wetuset-hills*[59] meets with all the Remnants of the *Narraganset* and *Nipmuck Indians,* that were there gathered together, and became very numerous; and made their descent on *Sudbury,* and the Adjacent Parts of the Country, where they met with and swallowed up Valiant Capt. *Wadsworth* and his Company, and many other doleful desolations, in those Parts.[60] The News whereof coming to *Plymouth,* and they expecting probably the Enemy would soon return again into their Colony: The Council of War were called together;[61] and Mr. *Church* was sent for to them, being observed by the whole Colony to be a Person extraordinarily qualify'd for and adapted to the Affairs of War. Twas proposed in Council that least the Enemy in their return should fall on *Rehoboth,* or some other of their Out-Towns, a Company consisting of 60 or 70 Men should be sent in to those Parts; and Mr. *Church* invited to take the Command of them. He told them, *That if the Enemy returned into that Colony again, they might reasonably expect that they would come very numerous; and that if he should take the Command of Men, he should not lye in any Town or Garrison with them, but would lye in the Woods as the Enemy did: And that to send out such small Companies against such Multitudes of the Enemy that were now Mustered together, would be but to deliver so many Men into their hands, to be destroyed, as the Worthy Capt.* Wadsworth *and his Company were.* His advice upon the whole was That if they sent out any Forces, to send not less than 300 Souldiers; and that the other Colonies should be ask'd to sent out their *Quota's* also; adding, *That if they intended to make an end of the War, by subduing the Enemy, they must make a business of the War, as the Enemy did; and that for his own part, he had wholly laid aside all his own private business and concerns, ever since the War broke out.* He told them, *That if they would send forth such Forces as he should direct to, he would go with them for Six weeks March, which was long enough for Men to be kept in the Woods at once; and if they might be sure of Liberty to return in such a space, Men would go out chearfully. And he would engage* 150 *of the best Souldiers should immediately List Voluntarily to go with him, if they would please to add* 50 *more; and* 100 *of the Friend Indians; and with such an Army he made no doubt but he might do good Service; but on other terms he did not incline to be concern'd.*

Their reply was, That they were already in debt, and so big an Army would bring such charge upon them, that they should never be able to pay. And as for sending out *Indians*, they thought it no wayes advisable, and in short, none of his advice practicable.

Now Mr. *Churches* consort, and his then only Son were till this time remaining at *Duxborough*, and his fearing their safety there (unless the War were more vigorously ingaged in) resolved to move to *Rhode-Island;* tho' it was much opposed both by the Government, and by Relations. But at length, the Governour considering that he might be no less Serviceable by being on that side of the Colony, gave his permit, and wish'd he had Twenty more as good Men to send with him.[62]

Then preparing for his Removal, he went with his small Family to *Plymouth* to take leave of their Friends; where they met with his Wives Parents, who much perswaded that She might be left at Mr. *Clarks* Garrison, (which they supposed to be a mighty safe Place) or at least that She might be there until her soon expected lying-inn was over (being near her time.) Mr. *Church* no ways inclining to venture her any longer in those Parts, and no arguments prevailing with him, he resolutely set out for *Taunton,* and many of their Friends accompanyed them. There they found Capt. *Peirce,* with a commanded Party, who offered Mr. *Church* to send a Relation of his with some others to guard him to *Rhode-Island.* But Mr. *Church* thank'd him for his Respectful offer, but for some good reasons refus'd to accept it. In short, they got safe to Capt. *John Almy's* house upon *Rhode-Island,* where they met with friends and good entertainment. But by the way, let me not forget this remarkable Providence. *viz.* That within Twenty-four hours or there abouts, after their arrival at *Rhode-Island,* Mr. *Clarks* Garrison that Mr. *Church* was so much importuned to leave his Wife and Child at, was destroyed by the Enemy.[63]

Mr. *Church* being at present disinabled from any particular Service in the War, began to think of some other employ; but he no sooner took a tool to cut a small stick, but he cut off the top of his Fore finger, and the next to it, half off; upon which he smillingly said, That he thought he was out of his way to leave the War; and resolved he would to War again. Accordingly his Second Son being born on the 12th of *May* and his Wife & Son like to do well, Mr. *Church* imbraces the opportunity of a passage in a sloop bound to *Barnstable;* who landed him at *Sogkonesset,* from whence he rid to *Plymouth;* arrived there on the first Tuesday in *June:* The General Court then sitting, welcom'd him, told him they were glad to see him Alive. He reply'd, He was glad to see them Alive, for he had seen so many fires and smokes towards their side of the Country since he left them, that he could scarce eat or sleep with any comfort, for fear they had been all destroyed. For all Travelling was stop'd, and no News had passed for a long time together. He gave them account, that the *Indians* had made horrid desolations at *Providence, Warwick, Petuxit,* and all over the *Narraganset* Country, & that they prevailed daily against the *English* on that side of the Country. Told them he long'd to hear what Methods they design'd in the War. They told him, They were particularly glad that Providence had brought him there at that juncture: For they had concluded the very next day to send out an Army of 200 Men, two third *English,* and one third Indians, in some measure agreeable to his former proposal; expecting *Boston,* and *Connecticut* to joyn with their *Quota's.* In short, It was so concluded. And that Mr. *Church* should return to the *Island,* and see what he could Muster there, of those that had mov'd from *Swanzey, Dartmouth,* &c. So returning the same way he came; when he came to *Sogkonesset,* he had a sham put upon him, about a Boat he had bought to go home in; and was forced to hire two of the friend Indians to paddle him in a Canoo from *Elișabeths* to *Rhode-Island.*

It fell out that as they were in their Voyage passing by *Sogkonate-point,* some of the Enemy were upon the Rocks a fishing; he bid the *Indians* that managed the Canoo to paddle so near to the Rocks as that he might call to those *Indians;* told them, That he had a great mind ever since the War broke out to speak with some of the *Sogkonate Indians,* and that they were their Relations, and therefore they need not fear their hurting of them. And he added, *That he had a mighty conceit that if he could gain a fair Opportunity to discourse them, that he could draw them off from* Philip, *for he knew they never heartily loved him.* The

Enemy hollowed and made signs for the Canoo to come to them: But when they approach'd them they skulked and hid in the clifts of the Rocks; then Mr. *Church* ordered the Canoo to be paddled off again, least if he came too near they should fire upon him. Then the *Indians appearing again, beckn'd and call'd in the Indian* Language and bid them come a-shore, they wanted to speak with them. The Indians in the Canoo answered them again; but they on the Rocks told them, That the surff made such a noise against the Rocks they could not hear any thing they said. Then Mr. *Church* by signs with his hands, gave to understand That he would have two of them go down upon the point of the beach (a place where a Man might see who was near him) accordingly two of them ran a-long the beach, and met him there; without their Arms, excepting that one of them had a Lance in his hand; they urged Mr. *Church* to come a-shore for they had a great desire to have some discourse with him; He told them, if he that had his weapon in his hand would carry it up some distance upon the beach and leave it, he would come a-shore and discourse them: He did so, and Mr. Church went a-shore, halled up his Canoo, ordered one of his *Indians* to stay by it, and the other to walk above on the beach, as a Sentinel to see that the Coasts were clear. And when Mr. *Church* came up to the *Indians,* one of them happened to be honest *George* one of the two that *Awashonks* formerly sent to call him to her Dance, and was so careful to guard him back to his House again; the last *Sogkonate Indian* he spoke with before the War broke out; he spoke *English* very well. Mr. *Church* asked him where *Awashonks* was? he told him in a Swamp about three Miles off. Mr. *Church* again asked him, What it was he wanted that he hollowed and called him a-shore? he answered, That he took him for *Church* as soon as he heard his Voice in the Canoo, and that he was very glad to see him alive, and he believed his Mistriss would be as glad to see him, and speak with him; he told him further, That he believed she was not fond of maintaining a War with the *English;* and that she had left *Philip,* and did not intend to return to him any more; he was mighty earnest with Mr. *Church* to tarry there while he would run and call her: but he told him no; for he did not know but the *Indians* would come down and kill him before he could get back again; he said, if *Mount-hope* or *Pocasset Indians* could catch him, he believed they would knock him on the head: But all *Sogkonate Indians* knew him very well, and he believed would none of them hurt him. In short, Mr. *Church* refused then to tarry, but promised that he would come over again, and speak with *Awashonks,* and some other *Indians* that he had a mind to talk with.

Accordingly he appointed him to notifie *Awashonks,* her Son *Peter,* their Chief Captain, and one *Nompash* (an *Indian* that Mr. *Church* had formerly a particular respect for) to meet him two dayes after, at a Rock at the lower end of Capt. *Richmonds* Farm; which was a very noted place; and if that day should prove Stormy, or Windy, they were to expect him the next moderate day. Mr. *Church* telling *George,* that he would have him come with the Persons mentioned, and no more. They giving each other their hand upon it parted, and Mr. *Church* went home,[64] and the next Morning to *New-port,* and informed the Government what had passed between him and the *Sogkonate Indians.* And desired their permit for him and *Daniel Wilcock,* (a Man that well understood the *Indian* Language) to go over to them. They told him, They thought he was mad, after such Service as he had done, and such dangers that he escaped, now to throw away his Life, for the Rogues would as certainly kill him, as ever he went over; and utterly refused to grant his permit, or to be willing that he should run the risque.

Mr. *Church* told them, *That it had ever been in his thoughts since the War broke out, that if he could discourse the* Sogkonate Indians, *he could draw them off from* Philip, and *employ them against him; but could, till now, never have an Opportunity to speak with any of them, and was very lothe to lose it,* &c. At length, they told him, If he would go, it should be only with the two Indians that came with him; but they would give him no permit under their hands. He took his leave of them, Resolving to prosecute his design; they told him they were sorry to see him so Resolute, nor if he went did they ever expect to see his face again.

He bought a Bottle of Rhum, and a small role of Tobacco, to carry with him, and returned to his Family. The next Morning, being the day appointed for the Meeting, he prepared two light Canoo's for the design, and his own Man, with the two *Indians* for his company. He used such arguments with his tender, and now almost broken hearted Wife, from the experience of former preservations, and the prospect of the great service he might do, might it please God to succeed his design, &c. that he obtained her consent to his attempt; and committing her, his Babes and himself to Heavens protection. He set out, they had from the Shore about a League to paddle; drawing near the place they saw the *Indians* setting on the bank, waiting for their coming. Mr. *Church* sent one of the *Indians* a-shore in one of the Canoo's to see whither it were the same *Indians* whom he had appointed to meet him, and no more; and if so to stay a-shore and send George to fetch him. Accordingly *George* came and fetch'd Mr. *Church* a-shore while the other Canoo play'd off to see the event, and to carry tydings if the *Indians* should prove false.

Mr. *Church* ask'd *George* whether *Awashonks* and the other *Indians* he appointed to meet him were there? He answered they were. He then ask'd him, If there were no more than they whom he appointed to be there? To which he would give him no direct answer. However he went a-shore, where he was no sooner landed, but *Awashonks* and the rest that he had appointed to meet him there, rose up and came down to meet him; and each of them successively gave him their hands, and expressed themselves glad to see him, and gave him thanks for exposing himself to visit them. They walk'd together about a Gun-shot from the water to a convenient place to sit down. Where at once a-rose up a great body of *Indians*, who had lain hid in the grass, (that was as high as a Mans waste) and gathered round them, till they had clos'd them in; being all arm'd with Guns, Spears, Hatchets, &c. with their hair trim'd and faces painted, in their Warlike appearance. It was doubtless some-what surprizing to our Gentleman at first, but without any visible discovery of it, after a small silent pause on each side, He spoke to *Awashonks*, and told her, *That* George *had inform'd him that she had a desire to see him, and discourse about making Peace with the* English. She answered, *Yes.* Then said Mr. *Church, It is customary when People meet to treat of Peace to lay aside their Arms, and not to appear in such Hostile form as your People do:* desired of her that if they might talk about Peace, which he desired they might, *Her men might lay aside their Arms, and appear more treatable.* Upon which there began a considerable noise and murmur among them in their own Language. Till *Awashonks* ask'd him, What Arms they should lay down, and where? He (perceiving the *Indians* look'd very surly, and much displeased) Replied, *Only their Guns at some small distance, for formality sake.* Upon which with one consent they laid aside their Guns, and came and sat down.

Mr. *Church* pulled out his Callebash[66] and asked *Awashonks, Whether she had lived so long at* Wetuset, *as to forget to drink* Occapechees;[67] and drinking to her, he perceived that she watch'd him very diligently, to see (as he thought) whether he swallowed any of the Rhum; he offered her the Shell, but she desired him to drink again first, He then told her, *There was no poison in it,* and pouring some into the Palm of his hand, sup'd it up, and took the Shell and drank to her again, and drank a good Swig which indeed was no more than he needed. Then they all standing up, he said to *Awashonks, You wont drink for fear there should be poison in it:* And then handed it to a little ill look'd fellow, who catched it readily enough, and as greedily would have swallowed the Liquor when he had it at his mouth: But Mr. *Church* catch'd him by the throat and took it from him, asking him, *Whether he intended to swallow Shell and all?* And then handed it to *Awashonks,* she ventured to take a good hearty dram, and pass'd it among her Attendants.

The Shell being emptied, he pulled out his Tobacco, and having distributed it, they began to talk.

*Awashonks* demanded of him, the Reason why he had not (agreeable to his promise when she saw him last) been down at *Sogkonate* before now; Saying that probably if he had come then according to his promise, they had never joyned with *Philip* against the *English.*

He told her he was prevented by the Wars breaking out so suddenly. And yet, he was afterwards coming down, & came as far as *Punkateese,* where a great many *Indians* set upon him, and fought him a whole afternoon, tho' he did not come prepared to fight, had but Nineteen Men with him, whose chief design was to gain an Opportunity to discourse some *Sogkonate Indians.*[68] Upon this there at once arose a mighty Murmur, confused noise, & talk among the fierce look'd Creatures, and all rising up in a hubbub; and a great surly look'd fellow took up his *Tomhog,* or wooden *Cutlash,* to kill Mr. *Church,* but some others prevented him.

The Interpreter asked Mr. *Church,* if he understood what it was that the great fellow (they had hold of) said? He answered him, *No.* Why, said the Interpreter, He says, you killed his Brother at *Punkateese,* and therefore he thirsts for your blood. Mr. *Church* bid the Interpreter tell him that his Brother began first: That if he had kept at *Sogkonate* according to his desire and order, he should not have hurt him.

Then the chief Captain[69] commanded *Silence,* and told them, That they should talk no more about old things, &c. and quell'd the tumult, so that they sat down again, and began upon a discourse of making Peace with the *English.* Mr. *Church* ask'd them, *What Proposals they would make, and on what terms they would break their League with* Philip? Desiring them to make some Proposals that he might carry to his Master's, telling them that it was not in his Power to conclude a Peace with them, but that he knew that if their Proposals were reasonable, the Government would not be unreasonable and that he would use his Interest in the Government for them. And to encourage them to proceed, put them in mind that the *Pequots* once made War with the *English* and that after they subjected themselves to the *English,* the *English* became their Protectors and defended them against other Nations that would otherwise have destroyed them, &c. After some further discourse, and debate, he brought them at length to consent that if the Government of *Plymouth* would firmly ingage to them, *That they, and all of them, and their Wives and Children, should have their Lives spared, and none of them transported out of the Country, they would subject themselve to them, and serve them in what they were able.*

Then Mr. *Church* told them, That he was well satisfyed the Government of *Plymouth* would readily concur with what they proposed, and would sign their Articles: And complementing them upon it, how pleased he was with the thoughts of their return, and of the former friendship that had been between them, &c.

The chief Captain rose up, and expressed the great value and respect he had for Mr. *Church;* and bowing to him said, *Sir, If you'l please to accept of me and my men, and will head us, we'l fight for you, and will help you to* Philips *head before Indian Corn be ripe.* And when he had ended, they all express'd their consent to what he said, and told Mr. Church they loved him, and were willing to go with him and fight for him, as long as the *English* had one Enemy left in the Country.

Mr. *Church* assured them, That if they proved as good as their word, they should find him their's and their Children's fast friend. And (by the way) the friendship is maintain'd between them to this day.[70]

Then he proposed unto them, that they should choose five men to go straight with him to *Plymouth:* They told him, No; they would not choose, but he should take which five he pleased: some complements passed about it, at length it was agreed, They should choose Three, and he Two. Then he agreed, with that he would go back to the Island that Night, and would come to them the next Morning, and go thro' the Woods to *Plymouth.* But they afterwards objected, That this travelling thro' the Woods would not be safe for him; the Enemy might meet with them, and kill him, and then they should lose their friend, and the whole design ruined beside. And therefore proposed, That he should come in an English Vessel, and they would meet him and come on board at *Sogkonate-point,* and Sail from thence to *Sandwich:* which in fine, was concluded upon.

So Mr. *Church* promising to come as soon as he could possibly obtain a Vessel, and then they parted. He returned to the Island, and was at great pains and charge to get a Vessel, but with unaccountable disappointments; sometimes by the falseness, and sometimes by the faint-heartedness of Men that he bargained with, and something by Wind and Weather, *&c.*

Until at length Mr. *Anthony Low* put into the Harbour with a loaden Vessel bound to the Westward, and being made acquainted with Mr. *Churches* case, told him, *That he had so much kindness for him, and was so pleased with the business that he was ingaged in, that he would run the venture of his Vessel & Cargo, to wait upon him.* Accordingly, next Morning they set Sail with a Wind that soon brought them to *Sogkonate-point;* but coming there they met with a contrary wind, and a great swelling Sea.

The *Indians* were there waiting upon the Rocks, but had nothing but a miserable broken Canoo to get aboard in. Yet *Peter Awashonks* ventured off in it, and with a great deal of difficulty and danger got aboard. And by this time it began to Rain and Blow exceedingly, and forced them away up the Sound; and then went away thro' *Bristol* Ferry, round the Island to *New-port,* carrying *Peter* with them.

Then Mr. *Church* dismiss'd Mr. *Low,* and told him, *That inasmuch as Providence oppos'd his going by Water, and he expected that the Army would be up in a few days, and probably if he should be gone at that juncture, it might ruine the whole design; would therefore yield his Voyage.*

Then he writ the account of his transactions with the *Indians,* and drew up the Proposals, and Articles of Peace, and dispatch'd Peter with them to *Plymouth;* that his Honour the Governour if he saw cause might sign them.

*Peter* was set over to *Sogkonate* on the Lords day Morning, with orders to take those men that were chosen to go down, or some of them at least with him.[71] The time being expired that was appointed for the *English* Army to come, there was great looking for them. Mr. *Church* on the Monday Morning (partly to divert himself after his fategue, and partly to listen for the Army) Rid out with his Wife and some of his friends to *Portsmouth,* under a pretence of Cherrying; but came home without any News from the Army: But by Midnight, or sooner, he was roused with an Express from Maj. *Bradford,* who was arrived with the Army at *Pocasset.* To whom he forth-with repaired, and informed him of the whole of his proceedings, with the *Sogkonate Indians.* With the Majors consent and advice, he returned again next Morning to the Island, in order to go over that way to *Awashonks,* to inform her that the Army was arrived, *&c.*[72] Accordingly from *Sachueeset-Neck,* he went in a Canoo to *Sogkonate;* told her Maj. *Bradford* was arrived at *Pocasset,* with a great Army, whom he had inform'd of all his proceedings with her. That if she would be advised and observe order she nor her People need not to fear being hurt by them. Told her, She should call all her People down into the Neck, least if they should be found straggling about, mischief might light on them. That on the Morrow they would come down and receive her, and give her further orders. She promised to get as many of her People together as possibly she could. Desiring Mr. *Church* to consider that it would be difficult for to get them together at such short warning. Mr. *Church* returned to the Island, and to the Army the same Night: The next Morning the whole Army Marched towards *Sogkonate* as far as *Punkateese;* and Mr. Church with a few Men went down to *Sogkonate* to call *Awashonks,* and her People to come up to the English Camp; as he was going down, they met with a *Pocasset Indian,* who had killed a Cow and got a Quarter of her on his back, and her Tongue in his Pocket; who gave them an account, That he came from *Pocasset* two days since in company with his Mother and several other *Indians* now hid in a Swamp above *Nomquid;* disarming of him, he sent him by two Men to Maj. *Bradford,* and proceeded to *Sogkonate;* they saw several *Indians* by the way skulking about, but let them pass. Arriving at *Awashonks* Camp, told her, *He was come to invite her and her people up to* Punkateese, *where Maj.* Bradford *now was with the* Plymouth *Army, expecting her and her Subjects to receive orders, until further order could be had from the Government.* She complyed, and soon sent out orders for such of her Subjects as were not with her, immediately to come in; and by Twelve a Clock of the next day,[73] she with most of her Number appear'd before the English Camp at *Punkateese.* Mr. *Church* tender'd the Major to Serve under his Commission, provided the Indians might be accepted with him, to fight the Enemy. The Major told him, *his Orders were to improve him, if he pleased, but as for the* Indians, *he would not be concerned with them.* And presently gave forth orders for *Awashonks,* and all her Subjects both Men, Women and Children to repair to *Sandwich,* and to be there upon Peril, in Six days. *Awashonks* and her chiefs gather'd round Mr. *Church,* (where he was walk'd off from the rest) expressed themselves concerned that they could not be confided in, nor improv'd. He told them, *'twas best to obey Orders; and that if he could not accompany them to* Sandwich, *it should not be above a Week before he would meet them there; That he was confident the Governour would Commission him to improve them.* The Major hastened to send them away with *Jack Havens,* (an *Indian* who had never been in the Wars) in the Front with a flag of Truce in his hand. They being gone, Mr. *Church,* by the help of his Man *Toby* (the *Indian* whom he had taken Prisoner, as he was going down to *Sogkonate*) took said *Toby's* Mother, & those that were with her, Prisoners. Next Morning the whole Army moved back to *Pocasset.* This *Toby* informed them that there were a great many *Indians* gone down to *Wepoiset* to eat Clams (other Provisions being very scarce with them;) that *Philip* himself was expected within 3 or 4 dayes at the same Place: being asked, *What Indians they were?* He answered, Some *Weetemores Indians,* some *Mount-hope In-*

*dians,* some *Narraganset Indians,* and some other Upland *Indians,* in all about 300. The Rhode-Island Boats by the Majors order meeting them at *Pocasset,* they were soon imbark'd, it being just in the dusk of the Evening, they could plainly discover the Enemies fires at the Place the *Indian* directed to; and the Army concluded no other but they were bound directly thither, until they came to the North End of the Island, and heard the word of Command for the Boats to bare away. Mr. *Church* was very fond of having this probable opportunity of surprizing that whole Company of *Indians* imbraced: But Orders, 'twas said, must be obeyed, which was to go to *Mount-hope,* and there to fight *Philip.* This with some other good opportunities of doing spoil upon the Enemy, being unhappily miss'd. Mr. *Church* obtain'd the Majors Consent to meet the *Sogkonate Indians,* according to his promise. He was offer'd a Guard to *Plymouth,* but chose to go with one Man only, who was a good Pilot. About Sun-set he with *Sabin* his Pilot mounted their Horses at *Rehoboth,* where the Army now was, and by two Hours by Sun next Morning arrived safe at *Plymouth:*[74] And by that time they had refreshed themselves, the Governour and Treasurer came to Town.[75] Mr. *Church* giving them a short account of the affairs of the Army, &c. His Honour was pleased to give him thanks for the good and great Service he had done at *Sogkonate,* told him, *He had confirmed all that he promised* Awashonks, *and had sent the* Indian *back again that brought his Letter.* He asked his Honour, *Whether he had any thing later from* Awashonks? He told him he had not. Where upon he gave his Honour account of the Majors orders relating to her and hers, and what discourse had passed *pro & con* about them; and that he had promised to meet them, and that he had incouraged them, that he thought he might obtain of his Honour a Commission to lead them forth to fight *Philip.* His Honour smilingly told him, *That he should not want Commission if he would accept it, nor yet good English men enough to make up good Army.* But in short, he told his Honour the time was expired that he had appointed to meet the *Sogkonates* at *Sandwich.* The Governour asked him, when he would go? He told him that afternoon, by his Honours leave. The Governour ask'd him, How many Men he would have with him? He answered Not above half a dozen, with an order to take more at *Sandwich,* if he saw cause; and Horses provided. He no sooner moved it, but had his number of Men tendering to go with him, among which was Mr. *Jabez Howland,* and *Nathanael Southworth;* they went to *Sandwich* that Night; where Mr. *Church* (with need enough) took a Nap of Sleep. The next Morning with about 16 or 18 Men proceeded as far as *Agawam,* where they had great expectation of meeting the *Indians,* but met them not; his Men being discouraged about half of them returned; only half a dozen stuck by him, & promised so to do until they should meet with the *Indians.* When they came to *Sippicin River,* Mr. *Howland* began to tyre, upon which Mr. *Church* left him, and two more, for a Reserve at the River, that if he should meet with Enemies and be forced back, they might be ready to assist them in getting over the River. Proceeding in their March, they crossed another River, and opened a great Bay, where they might see many Miles along shore, where were Sands and Flats; and hearing a great noise below them towards the Sea. They dismounted their Horses, left them and crep'd among the bushes, until they came near the bank, and saw a vast company of *Indians,* of all Ages and Sexs, some on Horse-back running races, some at Foot-ball, some catching Eels & Flat-fish in the water, some Clamming, &c. but which way with safety to find out what *Indians* they were, they were at a loss. But at length, retiring into a thicket. Mr. *Church* hallow'd to them; they soon answered him, and a couple of smart young Fellows, well mounted, came upon a full Career to see who it might be that call'd, and came just upon Mr. Church before they discovered him; but when they perceived themselves so near *English* Men, and Arm'd, were much surprized, and tack'd short about to run as fast back as they came forward, until one of the Men in the bushes call'd to them, and told them his Name was *Church,* and need not fear his hurting of them. Upon which, after a small pause, they turned about their Horses, and came up to him; one of them that could speak English, Mr. *Church* took aside and examin'd, who inform'd him, That the *Indians* below were *Awashonks,* and her company, and that *Jack Havens* was among them; whom Mr. Church immediately sent for to come to him, and order'd the Messenger to inform *Awashonks* that he was come to meet her; *Jack Havens* soon came, and by that time Mr. *Church* had ask'd him a few Questions, and had been satisfyed by him, That it was *Awashonks,* and her company that were below, and that *Jack* had been kindly treated by them; a company of *Indians* all Mounted on Horse-back, and well Arm'd came riding up to Mr. Church, but treated him with all dew respects. He then order'd *Jack* to go tell *Awashonks,* that he designed to Sup with her in the Evening, and to lodge in her Camp that Night. Then taking some of the *Indians* with him, he went back to the River to take care of Mr. *Howland:* Mr. *Church* being a Mind to try what Mettal he was made of, imparted his notion to the *Indians* that were with him, & gave them directions how to act their parts; when he came pretty near the Place, he and his *English* Men pretendedly fled, firing on their retreat towards the *Indians* that pursued them, and they firing as fast after them. Mr. *Howland* being upon his guard, hearing the Guns, and by & by seeing the motion both of the *English* and *Indians,* concluded his friends were distressed, was soon on the full Career on Horseback to meet them, until he perceiving their laughing mistrusted the Truth. As soon as Mr. *Church* had given him the News, they hasted away to *Awashonks.* Upon their arrival, they were immediately conducted to a shelter, open on one side, whither *Awashonks* and her chiefs soon came & paid their Respects: and the Multitudes gave shouts as made the heavens to ring. It being now about Sun-setting, or near the dusk of the Evening; The Netops came running from all quarters loaden with the tops of dry Pines, & the like combustible matter making a huge pile thereof, near Mr. *Churches* shelter, on the open side thereof: but by this time Supper was brought in, in three dishes, *viz.* a curious young Bass, in one dish, Eels & Flat-fish in a second, and Shell-fish in a third, but neither Bread nor Salt to be seen at Table. But by that time Supper was over, the mighty pile of Pine Knots and Tops, *&c.* was fired, and all the *Indians* great and small gathered in a ring round it. *Awashonks* with the oldest of her People Men and Women mix'd, kneeling down made the first ring next the fire, and all the lusty, stout Men standing up made the next; and then all the Rabble in a confused Crew surrounded on the out-side. Then the Chief Captain step'd in between the rings and the fire, with a Spear in one hand and an Hatchet in the other danced round the fire, and began to fight with it, making mention of all the several Nations & Companies of *Indians* in the Country that were Enemies to the English; & at naming of every particular Tribe of *Indians,* he would draw out & fight a new fire brand, & at his finishing his fight with each particular fire brand, would bow to him and thank him; and when he had named all the several Nations and Tribes, and fought them all he stuck down his Spear and Hatchet, and came out; and another stept in and acted over the same dance, with more fury, if possible, than the first; and when about half a dozen of their chiefs had thus acted their parts, The Captain of the Guard stept up to Mr. *Church* and told him, *They were making Souldiers for him, and what they had been doing was all one Swearing of them, and having in that manner ingaged all the lusty stout men. Awashonks* & her chiefs came to Mr. *Church;* and told him, *That now they were all ingaged to fight for the* English, *and he might call forth all, or any of them at any time as he saw occasion to fight the Enemy;* and presented him with a very fine Firelock. Mr. *Church* accepts their offer, drew out a number of them, and set out next Morning before day for *Plymouth,* where they arrived safe the same day.

The Governour being informed of it, came early to Town next Morning; and by that time he had *English* Men enough to make up a good Company, when joyned with Mr. *Churches* Indians, that offered their Voluntary Service to go under his Command in quest of the Enemy. The Governour then gave him a Commission, which is as follows,[76]

> *Captain* Benjamin Church, *you are hereby Nominated, Ordered, Commission'd, and Impowred to raise a Company of Volunteers of about 200 Men,* English *and* Indians; *the English not exceeding the number of 60, of which Company, or so many of them as you can obtain, or shall see cause at present to improve, you are to take the command and conduct, and to lead them forth now and hereafter, at such time and unto such places within this Colony, or else where, within the confederate Colonies, as you shall think fit; to discover, pursue, fight, surprize, destroy, or subdue our* Indian *Enemies, or any part or parties of them that by the Providence of God you may meet with; or them or any of them by treaty and composition to receive to mercy, you see reason (provided they be not Murderous Rogues, or such as have been principal Actors in those Villanies:) And for as much as your Company may be uncertain, and the Persons often changed, You are also hereby impowred with advice of your Company to chuse and Commissionate a Lieutenant,*

*and to establish Serjeants, and Corporals as you see cause: And you herein improving your best judgment and discretion and utmost ability, faithfully to Serve the Interest of God, His Majesty's Interest, and the Interest of the Colony; and carefully governing your said Company at home and abroad: these shall be unto you full and ample Commission, Warrant and Discharge. Given under the Publick Seal, this 24th Day of* July, *1676.*

*Per* Jos. Winslow, *GOV.*

Receiving Commission, he Marched the same Night into the Woods, got to *Middleberry* before day, and as soon as the light appeared, took into the Woods and Swampy thickets, towards a place where they had some reason to expect to meet with a parcel of *Narraganset Indians,* with some others that belonged to *Mount-hope:* Coming near to where they expected them, Capt. *Church's* Indian Scout discovered the Enemy, and well observing their fires, and postures, Returned with the intelligence to their Captain, who gave such directions for the surrounding of them, as had the direct effect; surprizing them from every side so unexpectedly, that they were all taken, not so much as one escaped. And upon a strict examination, they gave intelligence of another parcel of the Enemy, at a Place called *Munponset-Pond* Capt. *Church* hastning with his Prisoners, thro' the Woods to *Plymouth,* disposed of them all, excepting only one *Jeffery,* who proving very ingenious & faithful to him, in informing where other parcels of the *Indians* harboured Capt. *Church* promised him, that if he continued to be faithful to him, he should not be Sold out of the Country, but should be his waiting man, to take care of his Horse, *&c.* and accordingly he Served him faithfully as long as he lived.[77]

But Capt. *Church* was forth-with sent out again; and the Terms for his incouragement being concluded on: *viz. That the Country should find them Ammunition* & *Provision;* & *have half the Prisoners, & Arms, they took: The Captain and his English Souldiers to have the other half of the Prisoners, and Arms: and the Indian Souldiers the loose Plunder.* Poor incouragement! But after some time it was mended.

They soon Captivated the *Munponsets,* and brought in, not one escaping. This stroke he held several Weeks, never returning empty handed. When he wanted intelligence of their Kennelling

Places, he would March to some place likely to meet with some travellers or ramblers, and scattering his Company, would lye close; and seldom lay above a day or two, at the most, before some of them would fall into their hands: Whom he would compel to inform, where their Company was; and so by his method of secret and sudden surprizes took great Numbers of them Prisoners.

The Government observing his extraordinary courage and conduct, and the success from Heaven added to it, saw cause to inlarge his Commission; gave him power to raise, and dismiss his Forces, as he should see occasion; to Commissionate Officers under him, and to March as far as he should see cause, within the limits of the three United Colonies: to receive to mercy, give quarter, or not; excepting some particular & noted Murderers: *viz. Philip* and all that were at the destroying of Mr. *Clark's* Garrison, and some few others.[78]

Major *Bradford* being now at Taunton with his Army, and wanting Provisions; some Carts were ordered from Plymouth for their supply, and Capt. *Church* to guard them. But he obtaining other guards for the Carts, as far as *Middleborough,* ran before with a small Company, hoping to meet with some of the Enemy, appointing the Carts and their guards to meet them at *Nemascut* about an hour after the Suns rising next Morning: he arrived there about the breaking of the day-light, discovered a company of the Enemy; but his time was too short to wait for gaining advantage; and therefore ran right in upon them, Surprized and Captivated about 16 of them: who upon examination, inform'd, That *Tispaquin,* a very famous Captain among the Enemy was at *Assawompset,* with a numerous Company.[79]

But the Carts must now be guarded, and the opportunity of visiting *Tispaquin* must now be laid aside: The Carts are to be faithfully guarded, lest *Tispaquin* should attack them.

Coming towards Taunton, Capt. *Church* taking two Men with him, made all speed to the Town; and coming to the River side, he hollow'd, and inquiring of them that came to the River, for Maj. *Bradford,* or his Captains; he was inform'd, they were in the Town, at the Tavern. He told them of the Carts that were coming, that he had the cumber of guarding of them; which had already prevented his improving opportunities of doing Service. Pray'd therefore that a guard might be sent over to receive the Carts, that he might be at Liberty; refusing all invitations and perswasions, to go over to the Tavern to visit the Major; he at length obtain'd a guard to receive the Carts; by whom also he sent his Prisoners to be convey'd with the Carts to *Plymouth*, directing them not to return by the way they came, but by *Bridgwater*.

Hastening back he purposed to Camp that Night at *Assawompset* Neck. But as soon as they came to the River that runs into the great Pond thro' the thick Swamp at the entering of the Neck; the Enemy fired upon them, but hurt not a Man. Capt. *Churches* Indians ran right into the Swamp and fired upon them, but it being in the dusk of the Evening, the Enemy made their escape in the thickets: The Captain then moving about a Mile into the Neck, took advantage of a small Valley to feed his Horses; some held the Horses by the Bridles, the rest on the guard look'd sharp out for the Enemy, within hearing on every side, and some very near; but in the dead of the Night, the Enemy being out of hearing, or still, Capt. *Church* moved out of the Neck. (not the same way he came in, least he should be Ambuscado'd) toward *Cushnet*, where all the Houses were burnt; and crossing *Cushnet* River being extreamly fategued, with two Nights and one Days ramble without Rest or Sleep; and observing good forage for their Horses, the Captain concluded upon baiting, and taking a Nap. Setting Six Men to watch the passage of the River, two to watch at a time, while the other slept, & so to take their turns; while the rest of the Company went into a thicket to Sleep under the guard of two Sentinels more. But the whole Company being very drowsy, soon forgot their danger, and were fast a-sleep, Sentinels, and all. The Captain first awakes, looks up, and judges he had slept four Hours, which being longer than he designed, immediately rouses his Company, and sends away a file to see what were become of the watch at the passage of the River, but they no sooner opened the River in sight, but they discovered a company of the Enemy viewing of their tracts, where they came into the Neck; Capt. *Church* and those with him soon dispers'd into the brush on each side of the way, while the file sent, got undiscovered to the passage of the River, and found their watch all fast a sleep; but these Tidings thoroughly awakened the whole Company. But the Enemy giving them no present disturbance, they examined their Snapsacks, and taking a little refreshment, the Captain orders one party to guard the

Horses, and the other to Scout, who soon met with a Track, and following of it, they were bro't to a small company of *Indians*, who proved to be *Little Eyes*, and his Family, and near Relations, who were of *Sogkonate*, but had forsaken their Country men; upon their making Peace with the *English*. Some of Capt. *Churches* Indians asked him, *If he did not know that Fellow?* Told him. *This is the Rogue that would have killed you at* Awashonks *Dance;* and signified to him that now he had an opportunity to be revenged on him. But the Captain told them, *It was not English-mans fashion to seek revenge; and that he should have the same quarter the rest had.* Moving to the River side, they found an old Canoo, with which the Captain ordered *Little Eyes* and his company to be carryed over to an Island; Telling him, *he would leave him on that Island until he returned; and lest the English should light on them, and kill them, he would leave his cousin* Light-foot *(whom the English knew to be their Friend) to be his guard. Little Eyes* expressed himself very thankful to the Captain.[80] He leaving his orders with *Light-foot*, returns to the Rivers side towards *Poneganset*, to *Russels* Orchard, coming near the Orchard they clap'd into a thicket and there lodg'd the rest of the Night without any Fire; and upon the morning light appearing, moves towards the Orchard, discovers some of the Enemy, who had been there the day before, and had beat down all the Apples, and carryed them away; discovered also where they had lodg'd that Night, and saw the ground where they set their baskets bloody, being as they supposed and as it was afterwards discovered to be with the flesh of Swine, *&c.* which they had killed that day: They had lain under the Fences without any fires; and seem'd by the marks they left behind them to be very numerous, perceived also by the dew on the grass that they had not been long gone; and therefore mov'd a-pace in pursuit of them. Travelling three Miles, or more, they came into the Country Road, where the track parted, one parcel steered towards the West end of the great Cedar Swamp, and the other to the East end. The Captain halted and told his *Indian Souldiers, That they had heard as well as he, what some Men had said at* Plymouth *about them,* &c. *That now was a good opportunity for each party to prove themselves: The Track being divided they should follow one, and the English the other, being equal in number.* The *Indians* declined the Motion, and were not willing to move any where without him; said, *they should not think themselves safe without him.* But the Captain insisting upon it, they submitted; he gave the *Indians* their choice to follow which track they pleased; they replyed, *They were light and able to Travel, therefore if he pleased they would take the West Track.* And appointing the Ruins of *John Cooks* House at *Cushnet* for the place to meet at; each Company set out briskly to try their Fortunes. Capt. *Church* with his *English* Souldiers followed their Track until they came near entring a miery Swamp, when the Capt. heard a Whistle in the Rear, (which was a note for a halt) looking behind him, he saw *William Fobes* start out of the Company and made towards him, who hasten'd to meet him as fast as he could; *Fobes* told him they had discovered abundance of *Indians,* and if he pleased to go a few steps back he might see them himself: he did so, and saw them a-cross the Swamp, observing them, he perceived they were gathering of *Hurtle-Berries,* and that they had no apprehensions of their being so near them; The Captain supposed them to be chiefly Women, and therefore calling one Mr. *Dillano,* who was acquainted with the ground, and the Indian Language, and another named Mr. *Barns;* with these two Men he takes right thro' the Swamp as fast as he could, and orders the rest to hasten after them. Capt. *Church* with *Dillano* & *Barns* having good Horses, spur'd on and were soon among the Thickest of the *Indians,* and out of sight of their own Men: Among the Enemy was an *Indian* Woman (who with her Husband had been drove off from *Rhode-Island*) notwithstanding they had an House upon Mr. *Sanford's* Land, and had planted an Orchard before the War; yet the Inhabitants would not be satisfyed till they were sent off; and Capt. *Church* with his Family, living then at the said *Sanfords,* came acquainted with them, who thought it very hard to turn off such old, quiet People: but in the end it prov'd a Providence & an advantage to him and his Family, as you may see afterwards. This *Indian* Woman knew Capt. *Church,* and as soon as she saw him, held up both her hands and came running towards him, crying aloud, *Church, Church, Church.* Capt. *Church* bid her stop the rest of the *Indians,* and tell them, *The way to save their Lives was not to run, but yield themselves Prisoners, and he would not kill them;* so with her help, and *Dillano's,* who could call to them in their own Language, many of them stop'd and surrendred themselves; others scampering and casting away their baskets, &c. betook themselves to the thickets, but Capt. *Church* being on Horse-back soon came up with them, and laid hold on a Gun that was in the hand of one of the foremost of the company, pull'd it from him, and told him he must go back. And when he had turned them, he began to look about him to see where he was, and what was become of his Company, hoping they might be all as well imploy'd as himself, but could find none but *Dillano,* who was very busy gathering up Prisoners; the Captain drove his that hc had stop'd to the rest, inquiring of *Dillano* for their Company, but could have no news of them. But moving back picked up now and then a skulking Prisoner by the way. When they came near the place where they first started the *Indians,* they discover'd their Company standing in a body together, and had taken some few Prisoners; when they saw their Captain, they hastened to meet him: They told him they found it difficult getting thro' the Swamp, and neither seeing nor hearing any thing of him, they concluded the Enemy had kill'd him, and were at a great loss what to do. Having brought their Prisoners together they found they had taken and kill'd 66 of the Enemy. Capt. *Church* then ask'd the old Squaw, *What company they belonged unto?* She said, They belonged part to *Philip,* and part to *Qunnappin* and the *Narraganset-Sachem,* discovered also upon her declaration that both *Philip* and *Qunnappin* were about two Miles off in the great Cedar Swamp; he enquired of her, *What company they had with them?* She answered, *Abundance of Indians: The Swamp,* she said, *was full of Indians from one end unto the other, that were settled there, that there were near an* 100 *men came from the Swamp with them, and left them upon that plain to gather Hurtle-berry's, and promised to call them as they came back out of* Sconticut-Neck, *whither they went to kill Cattel and Horses for Provisions for the company.* She perceiving Capt. *Church* move towards the Neck, told him, *If they went that way they would all be kill'd.* He ask'd her, *Whereabout they cross'd the River?* She pointed to the upper passing place. Upon which Capt. Church passed over so low down as he thought it not probable they should meet with his Track in their return; and hastened towards the Island, where he left *Little Eyes,* with *Light-foot.* Finding a convenient place by the River side for the Securing their Prisoners, Capt. *Church,* and Mr. *Dil-*

*lano* went down to see what was become of Capt. *Light-foot,* and the Prisoners left in his charge. *Light-foot* seeing and knowing them, soon came over with his broken Canoo; and inform'd them, *That he had seen that day about* 100 *Men of the Enemy go down into* Sconticut Neck, *and that they were now returning again:* Upon which they three ran down immediately to a Meadow where *Light-foot* said the *Indians* had passed; where they not only saw their Tracks, but also them: Where-upon they lay close until the Enemy came into the said Meadow, and the foremost sat down his load and halted, until all the company came up, and then took up their loads & march'd again the same way that they came down into the Neck, which was the nearest way unto their Camp; had they gone the other way along the River, they could not have missed Capt. *Churches* Track, which, would doubtless have expos'd them to the loss of their Prisoners, if not of their lives. But as soon as the Coast was clear of them, the Captain sends his *Light-foot* to fetch his Prisoners from the Island, while he and Mr. *Dillano* returns to the company, sent part of them to conduct *Light-foot* & his company to the aforesaid Meadow, where Capt. *Church* and his company met them; crossing the Enemies Track they made all hast, until they got over *Mattapoiset-river,* near about four Miles beyond the ruines of *Cooks* House, where he appointed to meet his *Indian* company, whither he sent *Dillano,* with two more to meet them; ordering them, that if the *Indians* were not arrived, to wait for them. Accordingly, finding no *Indians* there, they waited until late in the Night, when they arrived with their booty. They dispatch'd a Post to their Captain to give him an account of their Success; but the day broke before they came to him: And when they had compared Successes, they very remarkably found that the number that each Company had taken and slain, was equal. The *Indians* had kill'd 3 of the Enemy, and taken 63 Prisoners, as the *English* had done before them, both *English* and *Indians* were surpriz'd at this remarkable Providence, and were both parties rejoycing at it; being both before afraid of what might have been the event of the unequal Success of the parties.[81] But the *Indians* had the fortune to take more Arms than the *English.* They told the Captain, *That they had missed a brave Opportunity by parting; They* came upon a great Town of the Enemy, viz *Capt.* Tyasks *company, (Tyasks* was the next man to *Philip) They fired upon the*

*Enemy before they were discovered, and ran upon them with a shout; the Men ran and left their Wives and Children, and many of them their Guns: They took* Tyasks *Wife and Son, and tho't that if their Captain & the English company had been with them they might have taken some hundreds of them: And now they determined not to part any more.*

That Night *Philip* sent (as afterwards they found out) a great Army to way-lay Capt. *Church* at the entring on of *Assawompset* Neck, expecting he would have returned the same way he went in; but that was never his method to return the same way that he came; & at this time going another way he escaped falling into the hands of his Enemies. The next day they went home by *Scipican,* and got well with their Prisoners to *Plymouth.*[82]

He soon went out again; and this stroke he drove many Weeks; and when he took any number of Prisoners, he would pick out some that he took a fancy to, and would tell them, *He took a particular fancy to them, and had chose them for himself to make Souldiers of; and if any would behave themselves well, he would do well by them, and they should be his men and not Sold out of the Country.* If he perceived they look'd surly, and his *Indian* Souldiers call'd them treacherous Dogs, as some of them would sometimes do, all the notice he would take of it, would only be to clap them on the back, and tell them, *Come, come, you look wild and surly, and mutter, but that signifies nothing, these my best Souldiers were a little while a go as wild and surly as you are now; by that time you have been but one day along with me, you'l love me too, and be as brisk as any of them.* And it prov'd so. For there was none of them but (after they had been a little while with him, and see his behaviour, and how chearful and successful his Men were) would be as ready to Pilot him to any place where the *Indians* dwelt or haunted (tho' their own Fathers or nearest Relations should be among them) or to fight for him, as any of his own Men.

Capt. *Church* was in two particulars much advantaged by the great *English* Army that was now abroad. One was, that they drove the Enemy down to that part of the Country, *viz.* to the Eastward of *Taunton* River by which means his business was nearer home. The other was that when ever he fell on with a push upon any body of the Enemy (were they never so many) they fled expecting the great Army. And his manner of Marching thro' the Woods was such, as if he were discovered, they appeared to be more than they were. For he always Marched at a wide distance one from another, partly for their safety: and this was an *Indian* custom, to March thin and scatter.[83] Capt. *Church* inquired of some of the *Indians* that were become his Souldiers, *How they got such advantage often of the English in their Marches thro' the Woods?* They told him, That the *Indians* gain'd great advantage of the *English* by two things; The *Indians* always took care in their Marches and Fights, not to come too thick together. But the *English* always kept in a heap together, that it was as easy to hit them as to hit an House. The other was, that if at any time they discovered a company of *English* Souldiers in the Woods, they knew that there was all, for the *English* never scattered; but the *Indians* always divided and scattered.

Capt. *Church* now at *Plymouth,* something or other happen'd that kept him at home a few days, until a Post came to *Marshfield* on the Lords day Morning, informing the Governour that a great Army of *Indians* were discovered, who it was supposed were designing to get over the River towards *Taunton* or *Bridgwater,* to Attack those Towns that lay on that side the River.[84] The Governour hastned to *Plymouth,* raised what Men he could by the way, came to *Plymouth* in the beginning of the forenoon Exercise; sent for Capt. *Church* out of the Meetinghouse, gave him the News, and desired him immediately to Rally what of his Company he could; and what Men he had raised should joyn them. The Captain bestirs himself, but found no Bread in the Store-house, and so was forc'd to run from House to House to get House-hold Bread for their March; but this nor any thing else prevented his Marching by the beginning of the afternoon Exercise;[85] Marching with what Men were ready, he took with him the Post that came from *Bridgwater* to Pilot him to the Place, where he tho't he might meet with the Enemy. In the Evening they heard a smart firing at a distance from them, but it being near Night, and the firing but of short continuance, they miss'd the place and went into *Bridgwater* Town. It seems, the occasion of the firing, was, That *Philip* finding that Capt. *Church* made that side of the Country too hot for him, design'd to return to the other side of the Country that he came last from. And coming to *Taunton* River with his company, they fell'd a great Tree a-cross the River for a Bridge to pass over on; and just as *Philips* old Uncle *Akkompoin*, and some other of his chiefs were passing over the Tree, some brisk *Bridgwater* Lads, had Ambush'd them, fired upon them, and killed the old man, and several others, which put a stop to their coming over the River that Night.

Next Morning[86] Capt. *Church* moved very early with his Company which was increased by many of *Bridgwater* that listed under him for that Expedition, and by their Piloting, he soon came very still, to the top of the Great Tree which the Enemy had fallen a-cross the River; and the Captain spy'd an Indian sitting upon the stump of it on the other side of the River; and he clap'd his Gun up, and had doubtless dispatch'd him, but that one of his own *Indians* called hastily to him, Not to fire, for he believed it was one of his own men; upon which the *Indian* upon the stump look'd about, and Capt. *Churches Indian* seeing his face perceived his mistake, for he knew him to be *Philip;* clap'd up his Gun and fired, but it was too late, for *Philip* immediately threw himself off the stump, leap'd down a bank on the side of the River, and made his escape. Capt. *Church* as soon as possible got over the River, and scattered in quest of *Philip*, and his company; but the Enemy scattered and fled every way; but he pick'd up a considerable many of their Women and Children, among which was *Philip's* Wife, and Son of about Nine Years Old. Discovering a considerable new Track along the River, and examining the Prisoners, found that it was *Qunnappin* and the *Narragansets*, that were drawing off from those parts towards the *Narraganset* Country, he inquired of the Prisoners, *Whither* Philip *were gone in the same Track?* they told him, *They did not know, for he fled in a great fright when the first* English *Gun was fired, and they had none of them seen or heard anything of him since.* Capt. *Church* left part of his Company there to secure the Prisoners they got, and to pick up what more they could find; and with the rest of his company hasted in the Track of the Enemy to over-take them, if it might be, before they got over the River, and ran some Miles along the River until he came unto a place where the *Indians* had waded over; and he with his Company waded over after them up to the Arm pits; being almost as wet before with Sweat as the River could make them: Following about a Mile further, and not overtaking them, and the Captain being under a necessity to return that Night to the Army, came to an halt, told his Company, *he must return to his other men.* His

*Indians* Souldiers moved for leave to pursue the Enemy (tho' he return'd;) said, *The* Narragansets *were great Rogues, and they wanted to be revenged on them for killing some of their Relations;* named, *Tokkamons* (*Awashonks* Brother) and some others. Capt. *Church* bad them go & prosper, and made *Light-foot* their chief, and gave him the title of Captain, *Bid them go and quit themselves like men.* And away they scampered like so many Horses. Next Morning[87] early they returned to their Captain, and informed him, *That they had come up with the Enemy, and kill'd several of them, and brought him Thirteen of them Prisoners;* were mighty proud of their Exploit, and rejoyced much at the opportunity of avenging themselves. Capt. *Church* sent the Prisoners to *Bridgwater,* and sent out his Scouts to see what Enemies or Tracks they could, discovering some small Tracks, he follows them, found where the Enemy had kindled some fires, and roasted some flesh, *&c.* but had put out their fires and were gone. The Captain followed them by the Track, putting his *Indians* in the Front; some of which were such as he had newly taken from the Enemy, and added to his Company. Gave them order to March softly, and upon hearing a whistle in the Rear to sit down, till further order. Or upon discovery of any of the Enemy to stop, for his design was, if he could, discover where the Enemy were, not to fall upon them (unless necessitated to do it) until next Morning. The *Indians* in the Front came up with many Women and Children, and others that were faint and tired, and so not able to keep up with the Company; these gave them an account that *Philip* with a great number of the Enemy were a little before. Capt. *Churches Indians* told the others, *They were their Prisoners, but if they would submit to order and be still no one should hurt them:* They being their old acquaintance, they were easily perswaded to conform. A little before Sun-set there was a halt in the Front until the Captain came up, and they told him, *They discovered the Enemy:* he order'd them, to dog them, and watch their motion till it was dark. But *Philip* soon came to a stop, and fell to breaking and chopping Wood, to make fires: and a great noise they made. Capt. *Church* draws his company up into a ring, and sat down in the Swamp without any noise or fire: The *Indian* Prisoners were much surprized to see the *English* Souldiers; but the Captain told them, *If they would be quiet and not make any disturbance or noise, they should meet with civil* *treatment, but if they made any disturbance, or offered to run, or make their escape, he would immediately kill them all;* so they were very submissive & obsequious. When the day broke,[88] Capt. *Church* told his Prisoners, *That his Expedition was such at this time that he could not afford them any guard:* Told them, *They would find it to be their interest to attend the orders he was now about to give them; which was, That when the fight was over, which they now expected; or as soon as the firing ceased, they must follow the Tracks of his Company and come to them.* (An *Indian* is next to a blood-hound to follow a Track.) He said to them, *It would be in vain for them to think of disobedience, or to gain any thing by it, for he had taken and killed a great many of the Indian Rebels, and should in a little time kill and take all the rest,* &c. By this time it began to be so light, as the time that he usually chose to make his on-set. He moved sending two Souldiers before to try if they could privately discover the Enemies postures. But very unhappily it fell out, that the very same time *Philip* had sent two of his as a Scout upon his own Track, to see if none dog'd them; who spy'd the two *Indian* men, and turn'd short about, and fled with all speed to their Camp: and Capt. *Church* pursued as fast as he could; the two *Indians* set a yelling and howling, and made the most hideous noise they could invent, soon gave the Alarm to *Philip* & his Camp; who all fled at the first tydings, left their Kittles boiling & Meat roasting upon their wooden Spits, & run into a swamp with no other Breakfast, then what Capt. *Church* afterwards treated them with. Capt. *Church* pursuing, sent Mr. *Isaac Howland* with a party on one side of the Swamp, while himself with the rest ran on the other side, agreeing to run on each side, until they met on the further end: placing some men in secure Stands at that end of the Swamp where *Philip* entered, concluding that if they headed him and beat him back, that he would take back in his own Track. Capt. *Church* and Mr. *Howland* soon met at the further end of the Swamp (it not being a great one) where they met with a great number of the Enemy, well armed, coming out of the Swamp. But on sight of the *English* they seemed very much surprized & track'd short. Capt. *Church* called hastily to them, and said, *If they fired one Gun they were all dead men; for he would have them know that he had them hem'd in, with a force sufficient to command them; but if they peaceably surrender'd they should have good quarter,* &c. They seeing both *Indians* and *English* come so thick upon them, were so surprized that many of them stood still and let the *English* come and take the Guns out of their hands, when they were both charged and cock'd. Many both Men, Women and Children of the Enemy were imprisoned at this time; while *Philip, Tispaquin, Totoson,* &c. concluded that the *English* would pursue them upon their Tracks, so were way-laying[89] their Tracks at the first end of the Swamp, hoping thereby to gain a shot upon Capt. *Church* who was now better imploy'd in taking his Prisoners & running them into a Valley, in form something shap'd like a Punch-bole, and appointing a guard of two files trible[90] armed with Guns taken from the Enemy. But *Philip* having waited all this while in vain, now moves on after the rest of his company to see what was become of them. And by this time Capt. *Church* was got into the Swamp ready to meet him; and as it happen'd made the first discovery, clapt behind a Tree until *Philips* company came pretty near, and then fired upon them, kill'd many of them, and a close skirmish followed. Upon this *Philip* having grounds sufficient to suspect the event of his company that went before them, fled back upon his own Track; and coming to the place where the Ambush lay, they fired on each other, and one *Lucus* of *Plymouth,* not being so careful as he might have been about his Stand, was kill'd by the *Indians.* In this Swamp skirmish Capt. *Church* with his two men which always ran by his side as his guard, met with three of the Enemy, two of which surrendred themselves, and the Captains guard seized them, but the other being a great stout surly fellow, with his two locks ty'd up with red, and a great Rattle-snake skin hanging to the back part of his head, (whom Capt. *Church* concluded to be *Totoson*) ran from them into the Swamp Capt. *Church* in person pursued him close, till coming pretty near up with him, presented his Gun between his Shoulders, but it missing fire, the *Indian* perceiving it, turn'd and presented at Capt. *Church,* and missing fire also; their Guns taking wet with the Fog, and Dew of the Morning; but the *Indian* turning short for another run, his foot trip'd in a small grapevine, and he fell flat on his face; Capt. Church was by this time up with him, and struck the Muzzle of his Gun an inch and half into the back part of his head, which dispatch'd him without another blow. But Capt. *Church* looking behind him saw *Totoson* the Indian whom he tho't he had kill'd, come flying at him like a dragon: But this happened to be fair in sight of the guard that were set to keep the Prisoners, who spying *Totoson,* and others that were following of him, in the very seasonable juncture made a shot upon them, and rescued their Captain; tho' he was in no small danger from his friends bullets, for some of them came so near him that he tho't he felt the wind of them. The skirmish being over, they gathered their Prisoners together, and found the number that they had killed and taken was 173 (the Prisoners which they took over Night included) who after the skirmish came to them, as they were ordered.

Now having no Provisions, but what they took from the Enemy, they hastened to *Bridgwater,* sending an express before to provide for them, their Company being now very numerous. The Gentlemen of *Bridgwater* met Capt. *Church* with great expression of honour and thanks, and received him and his Army with all due respect and kind treatment.

Capt. *Church* drove his Prisoners that Night into *Bridgwater* Pound, and set his *Indian* Souldiers to guard them. They being well treated with Victuals and drink, they had a merry Night; and the Prisoners laugh'd as loud as the Souldiers, not being so treated a long time before.

Some of the *Indians* now said to Capt. *Church, Sir, You have now made* Philip *ready to dye, for you have made him as poor, and miserable as he us'd to make the* English; *for you have now killed or taken all his Relations. That they believed he would now soon have his head, and that this bout had almost broke his heart.*

The next day Capt. *Church* moved and arrived with all his Prisoners safe at *Plymouth.*[91] The great *English* Army were now at *Taunton,* and Maj. *Talcot* with the *Connecticut* Forces being in these parts of the Country, did considerable spoil upon the Enemy.

Now Capt. *Church* being arrived at *Plymouth,* received thanks from the Government for his good Service, *&c.* many of his Souldiers were disbanded; and he tho't to rest himself a while, being much fategued and his health impared, by excessive heats and colds, and wading thro' Rivers, *&c.* But it was not long before he was call'd upon to Rally, upon advice that some of the Enemy were discovered in *Dartmouth* woods.[92] He took his *In-*

*dians*, and as many *English* Volunteers as presented to go with him, and scattering into small parcels. Mr. *Jabez Howland* (who was now, and often his Lieutenant and a worthy good Souldiers [sic]) had the fortune to discover and imprison a parcel of the Enemy. In the Evening they met together at an appointed place, and by examining the Prisoners they gain'd intelligence of *Totosons* haunt; and being brisk in the Morning, they soon gain'd an advantage of *Totosons* company, tho' he himself with his Son of about Eight Years old made their escape, and one old Squaw with them, to *Agawom* his own Country. But *Sam Barrow*, as noted a Rogue as any among the Enemy, fell into the hands of the *English*, at this time. Capt. *Church* told him, *That because of his inhumane Murders and Barbarities, the Court had allow'd him no quarter, but was to be forthwith put to Death, and therefore he was to prepare for it. Barrow* reply'd, *That the Sentence of Death against him was just, and that indeed he was ashamed to live any longer, and desired no more favour than to Smoke a Whiff of Tobacco before his Execution.* When he had taken a few Whiffs, he said, *He was ready;* upon which one of Capt. *Churches Indians* sunk his Hatchet into his Brains. The famous *Totoson* arriving at *Agawom*, his Son which was the last which was left of his Family (Capt. *Church* having destroyed all the rest) fell sick: The wretch reflecting upon the miserable condition he had bro't himself into, his heart became as a stone within him, and he dy'd. The old Squaw flung a few leaves and brush over him, and came into *Sandwich*, and gave this account of his death, and offered to shew them where she left his body; but never had the opportunity for she immediately fell sick and dy'd also.

Capt. *Church* being now at *Plymouth* again weary and worn, would have gone home to his Wife and Family, but the Government being Solicitous to ingage him in the Service until *Philip* was slain, and promising him satisfaction and redress for some mistreatment that he had met with: He fixes for another Expedition; he had soon Volunteers enough to make up the Company he desired and Marched thro' the Woods, until he came to *Pocasset.*[93] And not seeing nor hearing of any of the Enemy, they went over the Ferry to *Rhode-Island* to refresh themselves. The Captain with about half a dozen in his company took Horse & rid about eight Miles down the *Island*, to Mr. *Sanfords* where he had left his Wife; who no sooner saw him but fainted with the surprize; and by that time she was a little revived, they spy'd two Horse men coming a great pace. Capt. *Church* told his company that those men (by their riding) came with Tydings. When they came up they prov'd to be Maj. *Sanford* and Capt. *Golding;* who immediately ask'd Capt. *Church, What he would give to hear some News of* Philip? He reply'd, *That was what he wanted.* They told him, *They had rid hard with some hopes of overtaking of him, and were now come on purpose to inform him, That there was just now Tydings from* Mount-hope; *An* Indian *came down from thence (where* Phillips *Camp now was) on to* Sand point *over against* Trips, *and hollow'd, and made signs to be fetch'd over; and being fetch'd over, he reported, That he was fled from* Philip, *who* (said he) *has kill'd my Brother just before I came away, for giving some advice that displeased him.* And said, *he was fled for fear of meeting with the same his Brother had met with.* Told them also, *That* Philip *was now in* Mount-hope *Neck.* Capt. *Church* thank'd them for their good News, and said, he hop'd by to Morrow Morning to have the Rogues head. The Horses that he and his company came on standing at the door, (for they had not been unsaddled) his Wife must content her self with a short visit, when such game was a-head; they immediately Mounted, set Spurs to their Horses, and away. The two Gentlemen that bro't him the Tydings, told him, *They would gladly wait upon him to see the event of this Expedition.* He thank'd them, and told them, he should be as fond of their company as any Mens; and (in short) they went with him. And they were soon as [at] *Trips* Ferry (with Capt. *Churches* company) where the deserter was; who was a fellow of good sense, and told his story handsomely: he offered Capt. *Church* to Pilot him to *Philip,* and to help to kill him, that he might revenge his Brothers death. Told him, That *Philip* was now upon a little spot of Upland that was in the South end of the miery Swamp just at the foot of the Mount, which was a spot of ground that Capt. *Church* was well acquainted with, By that time they were got over the Ferry, and came near the ground half the Night was spent,[95] the Capt. commands a halt, and bringing the company together, he asked Maj *Sanford* & Capt. *Goldings* advice, what method was best to take in making the on-set, but they declining giving any advice, telling him, *That his great Experience & Suc-*

*cess forbid their taking upon them to give advice.* Then Capt. *Church* offered Capt. *Golding*, that he should have the honour (if he would please to accept of it) to beat up *Philips* headquarters.[94] He accepted the offer and had his alotted number drawn out to him, and the Pilot. Capt. *Churches* instructions to him were to be very careful in his approach to the Enemy, and be sure not to shew himself until by day light they might see and discern their own men from the Enemy. Told him also, That his custom in the like cases was to creep with his company on their bellies, until they came as near as they could; and that as soon as the Enemy discovered them they would cry out; and that was the word for his Men to fire and fall on. Directed him when the Enemy should start and take into the Swamp, they should pursue with speed, every man shouting and making what noise they could; for he would give orders to his Ambuscade to fire on any that should come silently. Capt. *Church* knowing it was *Philips* custom to be foremost in the flight, went down to the Swamp and gave Capt. *Williams* of *Situate* the command of the right wing of the Ambush, and placed an *English-man* and an *Indian* together behind such shelters of Trees, *&c.* that he could find, and took care to place them at such distance as none might pass undiscovered between them, charg'd 'em to be careful of themselves, and of hurting their friends: And to fire at any that should come silently thro' the Swamp: But it being some-what further thro' the Swamp than he was aware of, he wanted men to make up his Ambuscade; having placed what men he had, he took Maj. *Sanford* by the hand, said, *Sir, I have so placed them that 'tis scarce possible* Philip *should escape them.* The same moment a Shot whistled over their heads and then the noise of a Gun towards *Philips* Camp. Capt. *Church* at first tho't it might be some Gun fired by accident: but before he could speak a whole Volley followed, which was earlier than he expected. One of *Philips* gang going forth to ease himself, when he had done, look'd round him, & Capt. *Golding* thought the *Indian* looked right at him (tho' probably 'twas but his conceit) so fired at him, and upon his firing, the whole company that were with him fired upon the Enemies shelter, before the *Indians* had time to rise from their sleep, and so over-shot them. But their shelter was open on that side next the Swamp, built so on purpose for the convenience of flight on occasion. They were soon in the Swamp and *Philip* the foremost, who starting at the first Gun threw his Petunk[96] and Powder horn over his head, catch'd up his Gun and ran as fast as he could scamper, without any more clothes than his small breeches and stockings, and ran directly upon two of Capt. *Churches* Ambush; they let him come fair within shot, and the *English* mans Gun missing fire, he bid the *Indian* fire away, and he did so to purpose, sent one Musket Bullet thro' his heart, and another not above two inches from it; he fell upon his face in the Mud & Water with his Gun under him. By this time the Enemy perceived they were way laid on the east side of the Swamp, tack'd short about. One of the Enemy who seem'd to be a great surly old fellow, hollow'd with a loud voice, & often called out, *iootash, iootash,* Capt. *Church* called to his *Indian Peter* and ask'd him, *Who that was that called so?* He answered, It was old *Annowon Philips* great Captain, calling on his Souldiers to stand to it and fight stoutly. Now the Enemy finding that place of the *Swamp* which was not Ambush'd, many of them made their escape in the *English* Tracks. The Man that had shot down *Philip,* ran with all speed to Capt. *Church,* and informed him of his exploit, who commanded him to be Silent about it, & let no man more know it, until they had drove the *Swamp* clean; but when they had drove the *Swamp* thro' & found the Enemy had escaped, or at least the most of them; and the Sun now up, and so the dew gone, that they could not so easily Track them, the whole Company met together at the place where the Enemies Night shelter was; and then Capt. *Church* gave them the news of *Philips* death; upon which the whole Army gave Three loud *Huzza's.* Capt. *Church* ordered his body to be pull'd out of the mire on to the Upland, so some of Capt. *Churches Indians* took hold of him by his Stockings, and some by his small Breeches, (being otherwise naked) and drew him thro' the Mud unto the Upland, and a doleful, great, naked, dirty beast, he look'd like. Capt. *Church* then said, *That for asmuch as he had caused many an* English mans *body to lye unburied and rot above groud, that not one of his bones should be buried.* And calling his old *Indian* Executioner, bid him behead and quarter him.[97] Accordingly, he came with his Hatchet and stood over him, but before he struck he made a small Speech directing it to *Philip;* and said, *He had been a very great Man, and had made many a man afraid of him, but so big as he was he would now chop his Ass for him;* and so went to work, and did as he was ordered. *Philip* having one very remarkable hand being much scarr'd, occasioned by the splitting of a Pistol in it formerly. Capt. *Church* gave the head and that hand to *Alderman,* the Indian who shot him, to show to such Gentlemen as would bestow gratuities upon him; and accordingly he got many a Peny by it. This being on the last day of the Week, the Captain with his Company returned to the Island, tarryed there until Tuesday; and then went off and ranged thro' all the Woods to *Plymouth,* and received their *Premium,* which was *Thirty Shillings per* head, for the Enemies which they had killed or taken, instead of all Wages; and *Philips* head went at the same price. Methinks it's scanty reward and poor incouragement; tho' it was better than what had been some time before. For this March they received *Four Shillings* and *Six Pence* a Man, which was all the Reward they had, except the honour of killing *Philip.* This was in the latter end of *August,* 1676.[98]

Capt. Church had been but a little while at *Plymouth,* before a Post from *Rehoboth* came to inform the Government, that old *Annawon, Philips* chief Captain was with his company ranging about their Woods, & was very offensive & pernicious to *Rehoboth* & *Swansey.* Capt. *Church* was immediately sent for again, & treated with to ingage one Expedition more; he told them, *Their incouragement was so poor he feared his Souldiers would be dull about going again:* But being a hearty friend to the cause, he Rally's again, goes to Mr. *Jabesh Howland* his old Lieutenant, and some of his Souldiers, that us'd to go out with him; told them how the case was circumstanced, and that he had intelligence of old *Annawon's* walk, & haunt, and wanted hands to hunt him; they did not want much intreating; but told him, *They would go with him, as long as there was an* Indian *left in the Woods.* He moved & ranged thro' the Woods to *Pocasset.*[99] It being the latter end of the Week, he proposed to go on to *Rhode-Island,* and rest until Monday. But early on the Lords day Morning, there came a Post to inform the Captain, That early the same Morning a canoo with several *Indians* in it passed from *Prudence Island* to *Poppasquash* Neck. Capt. *Church* tho't if he could possibly surprize them, he might probably gain some intelligence of more game; therefore he made all possible speed after them: the Ferry-boat being out of the way he made use of Canoo's: But by that time they had made two fraights, and had got over the Captain, and about 15 or 16 of his *Indians*, the Wind sprung up with such violence that Canoo's could no more pass. The Capt. seeing it was impossible for any more of his Souldiers to come to him, he told his *Indians, If they were willing to go with him, he would go to* Poppasquash, *and see if they could catch some of those Enemy* Indians. They were willing to go, but were sorry they had no *English* Souldiers; so they March'd thro' the thickets that they might not be discovered, until they came unto the Salt Meadow, to the Northward of *Bristol* Town, that now is. Then they heard a Gun, the Capt. look'd about, not knowing but it might be some of his own company in the rear; so halting till they all came up, he found 'twas none of his own Company that fired. Now tho' he had but a few Men, was minded to send some of them out on a Scout. He moved it to Capt. *Lightfoot* to go with three more on a Scout; he said he was willing provided the Captains man *Nathanael* (which was an *Indian* that they had lately taken) might be one of them, because he was well acquainted with the Neck, and coming lately from among them, knew how to call them. The Capt. bid him choose his three companions, and go; and if they came a-cross any of the Enemy not to kill them if they could possibly take them alive; that they might gain intelligence concerning *Annawon*. The Capt. with the rest of his company moved out a little way further toward *Poppasquash*, before they heard another Gun, which seemed to be the same way with the other, but further off. But they made no halt until they came unto the narrow of *Poppasquash* Neck; where Capt. *Church* left three men more, to watch if any should come out of the Neck, and to inform the Scout when they returned which way he was gone. He parted the remainder of his company, half on one side of the Neck, and the other with himself went on the other side of the Neck, until they met; and meeting neither with *Indians* nor Canoo's returned big with expectations of Tydings by their Scout: But when they came back to the three men at the narrow of the Neck, they told their Captain the Scout was not returned, had heard nor seen any thing of them, this fill'd them with tho'ts what should become of them; by that time they had sat down & waited an hour longer, it was very dark, and they despaired of their returning to them. Some of the *Indians* told their Captain, *They feared his new man* Nathanael *had met with his old* Mount-hope *friends, and was turned*

*Rogue.* They concluded to make no fires that Night, (and indeed they had not great need of any) for they had no Victuals to cook, had not so much as a morsel of Bread with them. They took up their lodging scattering, that if possibly their Scout should come in the Night, and whistle (which was their sign) some or other of them might hear them. They had a very solitary, hungry Night; and as soon as the day broke they drew off thro' the brush to a hill without the Neck, and looking about them they espy'd one *Indian* man come running somewhat towards them, the Captain ordered one man to step out of the brush and show himself. Upon which the *Indian* ran right to him, and who should it be but Capt. *Lightfoot*, to their great joy. Capt. *Church* ask'd him, *What News?* He answered, *Good News, they were all well and had catch'd Ten* Indians, *and that they guarded them all Night in one of the Flankers of the old* English *Garrison; that their Prisoners were part of* Annawons *company, and that they had left their Families in a Swamp above* Mattapoiset Neck. And as they were Marching towards the old Garrison *Lightfoot* gave Capt. *Church* a particular account of their Exploit. *viz. That presently after they left him, they heard another Gun, which seem'd to be towards the* Indian *burying place, & moving that way, they discovered two of the Enemy fleeing of an Horse. The Scout clapping into the brush,* Nathanael *bid them sit down, and he would presently call all the* Indians *thereabout unto him. They hid, and he went a little distance back from them and sat up his note & howled like a Wolf: One of the two immediately left his Horse & came running to see who was there; but* Nathanael *howling lower and lower drew him in between those that lay in wait for him, who seized him;* Nathanael *continuing the same note, the other left the Horse also following his mate, & met with the same. When they caught these two they examined them apart, and found them to agree in their Story, that there were Eight more of them come down into the Neck to get Provisions, and had agreed to meet at the burying place that evening. These two being some of* Nathanaels *old acquaintance, he had great influence upon them, and with his inticing Story, (telling what a brave Captain he had, how bravely he lived since he had been with him, & how much they might better their condition by turning to him,* &c.*) perswaded, and ingaged them to be on his side, which indeed now began to be the better side of the hedge.*

*They waited but a little while before they espy'd the rest of theirs coming up to the burying place, and* Nathanael *soon howl'd them in as he had done their mates before.* When Capt. *Church* came to the Garrison, he met his Lieutenant and the rest of his Company; and then making up good fires they fell to roasting their Horse-beaf, enough to last them the whole day, but had not a morsal of Bread; tho' Salt they had which they always carryed in their Pockets, which at this time was very acceptable to them. Their next motion was towards the place where the Prisoners told them they had left their Women and Children, and surprized them all, and some others that were newly come to them. And upon examination they held to one Story, that it was hard to tell where to find *Annawon,* for he never roosted twice in a place. Now a certain *Indian* Souldier that Capt. *Church* had gain'd over to be on his side, pray'd that he might have liberty to go and fetch in his Father, who he said was about four Miles from that place, in a *Swamp* with no other than one Young *Squaw;* Capt. *Church* inclined to go with him, thinking it might be in his way to gain some intelligence of *Annawon;* and so taking one *English* Man and a few *Indians* with him leaving the rest there, he went with his new Souldier to look his Father; when he came to the *Swamp,* he bid the Indian go see if he could find his Father: he was no sooner gone but Capt. *Church* discover'd a Track coming down out of the Woods, upon which he and his little company lay close some on one side of the Track & some on the other. They heard the *Indian* Souldier make a howling for his Father; and at length some body answered him, but while they were listening, they thought they heard some body coming towards them, presently saw an old man coming up with a Gun on his Shoulder, and a young Woman following of him, in the Track which they lay by: They let them come up between them, and then started up and laid hold on them both. Capt. *Church* immediately examined them a part, telling them, *What they must trust too if they told false Stories:* He ask'd the young Woman, *What company they came last from?* She said, *from Capt.* Annawons. He asked her, *How many were in company with him when she left him?* She said, 50 *or* 60. He ask'd her, *How many Miles it was to the place where she left him?* She said, *She did not understand Miles, but he was up in* Squannaconk *Swamp? The old man who had been one of Philips* Council, upon examination, gave exactly the same account. Capt. *Church* ask'd him, *If they could get there that Night?* He said, *If they went presently and travelled stoutly, they might get there by Sun set.* He ask'd, *Whither he was going?* He answered, *That* Annawon *had sent him down to look for some* Indians, *that were gone down into* Mount-hope *Neck to kill Provisions:* Capt. *Church* let him know that those *Indians* were all his Prisoners. By this time came the *Indian* Souldier & brought his Father and one *Indian* more. The Captain was now in great straight of mind what to do next he had a mind to give *Annawon* a visit, now knew where to find him, but his company was very small, but half a dozen men beside himself, and was under a necessity to send somebody back to acquaint his Lieutenant & company with his proceedings. However he asked his small company that were with him, *Whither they would willingly go with him and give* Annawon *a visit?* They told him, *They were always ready to obey his commands,* &c. But withal told him, *That they knew this Capt.* Annawon *was a great Souldier; that he had been a valiant Captain under* Asuhmequn, Philips *Father,*[100] *and that he had been* Philips *Chieftain all this War; a very subtle man, and of great resolution, and had often said, that he would never be taken alive by the* English; *and moreover they knew that the men that were with him were resolute fellows, some of* Philips *chief Souldiers; and therefore feared whether it was practicable to make an attempt upon him with so small a handful of assistants as now were before him.* Told him further, *That it would be a pitty that after all the Great Things he had done, he should throw away his Life at last,* &c. Upon which he replyed, That he doubted not *Annawon* was a subtle & valiant Man: that he had a long time but in vain sought for him, and never till now could find his quarters; and he was very loth to miss of the opportunity; and doubt not but that if they would chearfully go with him, the same Almighty Providence that had hitherto protected and befriended them would do so still, *&c.* Upon this with one consent they said, *They would go.* Capt. *Church* then turned to one *Cook* of *Plymouth,* (the only *English* Man then with him) and ask'd him, *What he thought of it?* Who replyed, *Sir, I am never afraid of going any where when you are with me.* Then Capt. *Church* asked the old *Indian,* if he could carry his Horse with him? (for he conveyed a Horse thus far with him:) He reply'd that it was impossible for an Horse to pass the

Swamps. Therefore he sent away his new *Indian* Souldier with his Father and the Captains Horse to his Lieutenant, and orders for him to move to *Taunton* with the Prisoners, to secure them there, and to come out in the Morning in the *Rehoboth* Road, in which he might expect to meet him, if he were alive and had success. The Captain then asked the old fellow, if he would Pilot him unto *Annawon?* He answered, that he having given him his life he was obliged to serve him. He bid him move on then; and they followed: The old man would out-travel them, so far sometimes that they were almost out of sight; looking over his Shoulder and seeing them behind, he would halt. Just as the Sun was setting, the old man made a full stop and sat down, the company coming up also sat down, being all weary. Capt. *Church* asked, *What News?* He answered, That about that time in the Evening Capt. *Annawon,* sent out his Scouts to see if the Coast were clear, and as soon as it began to grow dark the Scouts return. And then (said he) we may move again securely. When it began to grow dark the old man stood up again, Capt. *Church* asked him, if he would take a Gun and fight for him? He bowed very low and pray'd him not to impose such a thing upon him, as to fight against Capt. *Annawon* his old friend. But sayes he, I will go along with you, and be helpful to you, and will lay hands on any man that shall offer to hurt you. It being now pretty dark they moved close together; anon they heard a noise, the Captain stay'd the old man with his hand, and asked his own men what noise they thought it might be? they concluded it to be the pounding of a Mortar. The old man had given Capt. *Church* a description of the Place where *Annowon* now lay, and of the Difficulty of getting at him: being sensible that they were pretty near them, with two of his *Indians* he creeps to the edge of the Rocks, from whence he could see their Camps; he saw three companies of *Indians* at a little distance from each other, being easy to be discovered by the light of their fires. He saw also the great *Annawon* and his company, who had formed his Camp or Kennelling place by falling a Tree under the side of the great clefts of Rocks, and sitting a row of birch bushes up against it, where he himself, and his Son, and some of his chiefs had taken up their lodging, and made great fires without them, and had their Pots and Kittles boiling, and Spits roasting. Their Arms also he discovered, all set together in a place fitted for the purpose standing up an end against a stick lodged in two crotches, and a Mat placed over them, to keep them from the wet or dew. The old *Annawons* feet and his Sons head were so near the Arms as almost to touch them: But the Rocks were so steep that it was impossible to get down, but as they lowered themselves by the bows, and the bushes that grew in the cracks of the Rock. Capt. *Church* creeping back again to the old man, asked him If there was no possibility of getting at them some other way? He answered, no, That he and all that belonged to *Annawon* were ordered to come that way, and none could come any other way without difficulty or danger of being shot. Capt. *Church* then ordered the old man and his daughter to go down fore-most with their baskets at their backs, that when *Annawon* saw them with their baskets he should not mistrust the intregue; Capt. *Church* and his handful of Souldiers crept down also under the shadow of these two and their baskets, and the Captain himself crept close behind the old man, with his Hatchet in his hand, and step'd over the young mans head to the Arms, the young *Annawon* discovering of him, whip'd his blanket over his head and shrunk up in a heap: The old Capt. *Annawon* started up on his breech, and cryed out *Howoh,*[101] and despairing of escape throw himself back again, and lay silent until Capt. *Church* had secured all the Arms, *&c.* And having secured that company, he sent his *Indian* Souldiers to the other fires & companies, giving them instructions, what to do and say. Accordingly, they went into the midst of them: When they discovered themselves who they were, told them that their Capt. *Annawon* was taken, and it would be best for them quietly and peaceably to surrender themselves, which would procure good quarter for them: Otherwise if they should pretend to resist or make their escape, it would be in vain, and they could expect no other but that Capt. *Church* with his great Army,[102] who had now entrap'd them, would cut them to pieces: told them also if they would submit themselves, and deliver up all their Arms unto them, and keep every man his place until it was day; they would assure them that their Capt. *Church* who had been so kind to themselves when they surrendred to him, should be as kind unto them. Now they being old acquaintance, and many of them Relations did much the readier give heed to what they said, and complyed & surrendred up their Arms unto them, both their Guns and Hatchets, *&c.* and were forthwith carryed to Capt. *Church.* Things being so far settled, Capt. *Church* asked *Annawon,* What he had for Supper, for (said he) I am come to Sup with you. *Taubut*[103] (said *Annowon*) with a big voice; and looking about upon his Women, bid them hasten and get Capt. *Church* and his company some Supper; then turned to Capt. *Church* and asked him, Whether he would eat Cow-beaf or Horse beaf, The Captain told him Cow-beaf would be most acceptable: It was soon got ready, and pulling his little bag of Salt out of his Pocket, which was all the Provision he brought with him; this season'd his Cow-beaf so that with it and the dry'd green corn, which the old Squaw was pounding in the Mortar, while they were sliding down the Rocks, he made a very hearty Supper. And this pounding in the Mortar proved lucky for Capt. *Churches* getting down the Rocks, for when the old Squaw pounded they moved, and when she ceased to turn the corn, they ceased creeping, the noise of the Mortar prevented the Enemies hearing their creeping: and the corn being now dressed supplyed the want of Bread, and gave a fine relish with the Cow-beaf. Supper being over, Capt. *Church* sent two of his men to inform the other companies that he had killed *Philip,* and had taken their friends in *Mount-hope* Neck, but had spared their lives, and that he had subdued now all the Enemy (he supposed) excepting this company of *Annawons,* and now if they would be orderly and keep their places until Morning, they should have good quarter, and that he would carry them to *Taunton,* where they might see their friends again, *&c.* The Messengers return'd, that the *Indians* yielded to his proposals. Capt. *Church* tho't it was now time for him to take a Nap, having had no sleep in two days and one night before; told his men that if they would let him sleep two hours, they should sleep all the rest of the night. He lay'd himself down and endeavoured to sleep, but all disposition to sleep departed from him. After he had lain a little while he looked up to see how his Watch managed, but found them all fast a-sleep. Now Capt. *Church* had told Capt. *Annawons* company as he had ordered his *Indians* to tell the others, that their lives should all be spared, excepting Capt. *Annawons,* and it was not in his power to promise him his life, but he must carry him to his Masters at *Plymouth,* and he would intreat them for his life. Now when Capt. *Church* found not only his own men, but all the *Indians* fast a-sleep, *Annowon* only excepted, whom he perceived was as broad awake as himself; and so they lay looking one upon the other perhaps an hour; Capt. *Church* said nothing to him, for he could not speak *English;* at length *Annawon* raised himself up, cast off his blanket, and with no more clothes than his small breeches, walked a little way back from the company: Capt. *Church* tho't no other but that he had occasion to ease himself, and so walked to some distance rather than offend him with the stink: but by and by he was gone out of sight and hearing; and then Capt. *Church* began to suspect some ill design in him, and got all the Guns close to him, and crouded himself close under young *Annawon,* that if he should any where get a Gun he should not make a shot at him without indangering his Son; lying very still a while waiting for the event: at length, he heard some body coming the same way that *Annawon* went. The Moon now shining bright, he saw him at a distance coming with something in his hands, and coming up to Capt. *Church,* he fell upon his knees before him, and offer'd him what he had bro't, and speaking in plain *English,* said *Great Captain, you have killed* Philip, *and conquered his Country, for I believe, that I & my company are the last that War against the* English, *so suppose the War is ended by your means; and therefore these things belong unto you.* Then opening his pack, he pull'd out *Philips* belt curiously wrought with *Wompom,* being Nine inches broad, wrought with black and white *Wompom,* in various figures and flowers, and pictures of many birds and beasts.[104] This when hung upon Capt. *Churches* shoulders it reach'd his ancles. And another belt of *Wompom* he presented him with, wrought after the former manner, which *Philip* was wont to put upon his head; it had two flags on the back part which hung down on his back: and another small belt with a Star upon the end of it, which he used to hang on his breast; and they were all edg'd with red hair, which *Annawon* said they got in the Muhhogs[105] Country. Then he pulled out two horns of glazed Powder, and a red cloth Blanket: He told Capt. *Church,* these were *Philips* Royalties which he was wont to adorn himself with when he sat in State.[106] That he tho't himself happy that he had an opportunity to present them to Capt. *Church,* who had won them, *&c* spent the remainder of the night in discourse; and gave an account of what mighty success he had formerly in Wars against many Nations of *Indians,* when served *Asuhmequin, Philips* Father, *&c.* In the Morning as soon as it was light, the Captain March'd with his Prisoners out of that *Swampy* Country towards *Taunton,* met his Lieutenant and Company, about four Miles out of Town, who expressed a great deal of joy to see him again, and said, 'twas more than ever he expected. They went into *Taunton,* were civily and kindly treated by the Inhabitants, refreshed and rested themselves that night. Early next Morning, the Captain took old *Annawon,* and half a dozen of his *Indian* Souldiers, and his own man, and went to *Rhode-Island,* sending the rest of his Company and his Prisoners by his Lieutenant to *Plymouth.* Tarrying two or three days upon the Island, he then went to *Plymouth,* and carryed his Wife and his two Children with him.

Capt. *Church* had been but a little while at *Plymouth,* before he was informed of a parcel of *Indians,* that haunted the Woods between *Plymouth* and *Sippican,* that did great damage to the *English* in killing their Cattel, Horses, and Swine; and the Captain was soon in pursuit of them: Went out from *Plymouth* the next Monday in the afternoon; next Morning early they discovered a Track; the Captain sent two *Indians* on the Track to see what they could discover, while he and his Company followed gently after, but the two *Indians* soon returned with Tydings that they had discovered the Enemy sitting round their fires, in a thick place of brush. When they came pretty near the place, the Captain ordered every man to creep as he did; and surround them by creeping as near as they could, till they should be discovered, and then to run on upon them and take them alive, if possible, (for their Prisoners were their pay:) They did so, took every one that was at the fires, not one escaping. Upon examination they agreed in their Story, that they belonged to *Tispaquin,* who was gone with *John Bump,* and one more, to *Agawom* and *Sippican* to kill Horses, and were not expected back in two or three days. This same *Tispaquin* had been a great Captain, and the Indians reported that he was such a great *Pouwau,*[107] that no bullet could enter him, *&c.* Capt. *Church* said, He would not have him killed, for there was a War broke out in the Eastern Part of the Country, and he would have him saved to go with them to fight the *Eastern Indians.* Agreeably he left two old Squaws of the Prisoners, and bid them tarry there until their Capt. *Tispaquin* returned, and to tell him, that *Church* had been there, and had taken his Wife, Children, and company, and carryed them down to *Plymouth;* and would spare all their lives, and his too, if he would come down to them and bring the other two that were with him, and they should be his Souldiers, *&c.* Capt. *Church* then returned to *Plymouth,* leaving the old Squaws well provided for, and Bisket for *Tispaquin* when he returned: Telling his Souldiers, that he doubted not but he had laid a Trap that would take him. Capt. *Church* two days after went to *Boston;* (the Commissioners[108] then sitting) and waited upon the Honourable Governour *Leverett,* who then lay Sick; who requested of Capt. *Church* to give him some account of the War; who readily obliged his Honour therein, to his great Satisfaction, as he was pleased to express himself; taking him by the hand, and telling him, if it pleased God he lived, he would make it a brace of a hundred pounds advantage to him out of the *Massachusetts* Colony, and would endeavour the rest of the Colonies should do Proportionably; but he dyed within a Fortnight after, and so nothing was done of that nature.[109] The same day *Tispaquin* came in and those that were with him, but when Capt. *Church* return'd from *Boston,* he found to his grief that the heads of *Annawon, Tispaquin, &c.* cut off, which were the last of *Philips* friends. The General Court of *Plymouth* then sitting sent for Capt. *Church* who waited upon them accordingly, and received their Thanks for his good Service, which they Unanimously Voted, which was all that Capt. *Church* had for his aforesaid Service.

Afterwards in the Year 1676, in the Month of *January*[110] Capt. *Church* received a Commission from Governour *Winslow,* to Scoure the Woods of some of the lurking Enemy, which they were well informed were there. Which Commission is as follows:

> *Being well informed that there are certain parties of our* Indian *Enemies, (remains of the People, or Allies of* Philip, *late Sachem of* Mount-hope, *our Mortal Enemy) that are still lurking in the Woods near some of our Plantations, that go on to disturb the Peace of His Majesty's Subjects in this & the Neighbouring Colonies, by their frequent Robberies, and other Insolences. Capt.* Benjamin Church *is therefore hereby Nominated, Ordered, and Commissioned, and Impowred to raise a Company of Volunteers consisting of* English *and* Indians; *so many as he shall judge necessary to improve in the*

*present Expedition, and can obtain; And of them to take the Command, and Conduct, and to lead them forth unto such place or places within this or the Neighbouring Colonies, as he shall think fit, and as the Providence of God, and his Intelligence may lead him; To Discover, Pursue, Fight, Surprize, Destroy, and Subdue our said* Indian *Enemy, or any party or parties of them, that by the Providence of God they may meet with; Or them, or any of them to receive to Mercy, if he see cause (provided they be not Murderous Rogues, or such as have been principal Actors in those Vilanies.) And for the Prosecution of this design, liberty is hereby granted to the said Capt.* Church, *and others, to Arm and set out such of our friendly* Indians, *as he is willing to Entertain. And for asmuch as all these our Enemies that have been taken, or at any time may be taken by our Forces, have by our Courts and Councils, been rendered lawful Captives of War, and condemned to perpetual Servitude; this Council do also determine and hereby declare, That all such Prisoners as by the blessing of God the said Captain and Company, or any of them shall take, together with their Arms, and other Plunder, shall be their own, and to be distributed amongst themselves, according to such agreement as they may be at one with another: And it shall be lawful, and is hereby warrantable for him and them to make Sale of such Prisoners as their perpetual Slaves; or otherwise to retain and keep them as they think meet, (they bring such as the Law allows to be kept:) Finally, the said Capt.* Church *herein improving his best judgment and discretion, and utmost ability, faithfully to Serve the Interest of God, his Majesties Interest, and the Interest of the Colony; and carefully governing his said Company at home and abroad; these shall be unto him full and ample Commission, Warrant and Discharge. Given under the Publick Seal,* January *15th. 1676.*

*Per* Josiah Winslow, *GOV.*

Accordingly Capt. *Church* accompanied with several Gentlemen and others went out, and took divers parties of *Indians;* and in one of which Parties there was a certain old man whom Capt. *Church* seem'd to take particular notice of, and asking him where he belonged, who told him to *Swanzey;* the Captain ask'd his name, who replyed; his name was *Conscience; Conscience* said the Captain (smiling) then the War is over, for that was what they were searching for, it being much wanting; and then returned the said *Conscience* to his Post again at *Swanzey*, to a certain person the said *Indian* desired to be Sold to, and so return'd home.

## NOTES

Ms. Rebecca Stamelman assisted in editing the text.

1. A formulaic allusion to a common Bible phrase, which Increase Mather uses as well. Note that it is Church and his troops, not the Almighty, who constitute the "wall."

2. According to Henry Martyn Dexter, editor of the 1865 edition of Church's narrative, the Proprietors' Records show that Church bought the land unseen and later decided to remove there. Henry Martyn Dexter, ed., *The History of King Philip's War,* p. 3. (Hereafter cited as *HMD.*)

3. April 1675—shortly after Sassamon's murder. All dates are New Style.

4. Not to be confused with John Sassamon, the supposed spy murdered by Philip's men.

5. Church's visit to Awashonks, June 14–16, 1675. Unless otherwise specified, all data on chronology are taken from Dexter's notes, and from Douglas Edward Leach, *Flintlock and Tomahawk.*

6. Indian name for Plymouth colony.

7. Brackets in original.

8. Church's diplomatic skill and friendship with Awashonks would be crucial in ending the war. Note that his proposed device for forcing Awashonks to move toward the English (i.e., by murdering Philip's ambassadors) parallels Philip's own device for creating a *casus belli* by having his men raid Awashonks's neighbors. Church learns from his enemies as well as his friends.

9. Petonowowet or Petan-a-nuet was the man's Indian name; the "Queen of Pocasset" is Weetamoo. The widow of Philip's brother and predecessor Alexander (Wamsutta), she married "Peter Nunuit" and fought as Philip's ally while her second husband helped the English. *HMD,* pp. 11–12. Unless otherwise specified, all information on Indian customs, productions, and language is taken from Dexter.

10. This was the same Gorton who figured prominently in the early religious strife between Massachusetts and the heterodox religionists of Rhode Island and who led a dissident faction within the Rhode Island colony against the rule of Roger Williams.

11. According to Church, Philip seems less a conspirator than a leader reluctantly driven to war by the proverbial "Hot-blooded young braves." This goes against the accounts of Increase Mather (pp. 86–88) and William Hubbard which Leach accepts.

12. June 20, 1675.

13. Actually the following day, June 21.

14. Also spelled "Cudworth."

15. The Plymouth army marched on June 21 and arrived on June 22 or 23; the Massachusetts contingent arrived on June 28, 1675.

16. This happened on June 23 or 24, 1675.

17. June 28, 1675.

18. Pilot means guide. Note that Church uses terminology drawn from seafaring to describe events and characters in forest warfare—a reminder of how little penetration of the wilderness had been accomplished even by the most forward of pioneers.

19. A military coat made of "buffalo" or bull hide, which served as light armor for protection against distant shots and sword cuts. *HMD*, p. 21.

20. Causeway.

21. The next day, June 29, 1675.

22. June 30, 1675.

23. Church later condemns the English for their murder of Annawon and display of his head, but in general does not find the English "barbaric" when they display the heads and/or hands of executed Indians.

24. Compare the accounts of Increase Mather (p. 90), Hubbard, *History of the Indian Wars,* 1:87, or Cotton Mather, *Magnalia Christi Americana,* p. 562, all of whom paint this campaign and the building of the fort as a victory and even as a masterpiece of military sagacity. Leach (p. 70) agrees with Church that this adoption of the defensive was a great blunder.

25. Psalms 44:3. "For they got not the land in possession by their own sword, neither did their own arm save them: but thy right hand, and thine arm, and the light of thy countenance, because thou hadst a favor unto them." Church's omissions from the quotation alter the sense from a praise of God for giving victory to an ironic condemnation of human folly, vanity and perhaps cowardice.

26. Southworth was Church's father-in-law; the lucrative post of commissary seems to have been in the Southworth family's gift. See *HMD*, pp. 25–26.

27. They left the fort on July 7, and divided in two groups which operated separately under Captains Fuller and Church. They frightened off the Indians on July 8, 1675. *HMD*, p. 27, unscrambles the chronology.

28. Cranston was deputy governor in 1672–1673 and 1676–1678, and was later governor. *HMD*, pp. 28–29.

29. The breakfast and the "Pease-field Fight" that followed took place on July 8, the same day as the tobacco-smoking incident.

30. One of the few deeply derogatory epithets applied to Indians in Church's narrative.

31. Hatchets.

32. "Church seems here to use the word 'meanness' as equivalent to scantiness—with reference to the quantity rather than the quality." *HMD*, p. 35.

33. Alderman was the Indian who later killed King Philip. He has just come from the cape where the Squaw Sachem of Pocasset (Weetamoo) lived.

34. This decision and the abortive expedition which followed took place on July 9 and 10, 1675.

35. Church suppresses the name as is usual when he is about to accuse someone of poltroonery; the official record is also silent on the man's identity. *HMD*, p. 41.

36. A Christian Nipmuck Indian, captain of a company of Praying Indians officially enrolled as militia on July 6, 1675. *HMD*, p. 43.

37. This scout or raid took place between July 11 and 14, 1675.

38. The expedition started on July 15, and discovered Philip's camp on July 19, 1675.

39. Some time in the last half of July, 1675. *HMD*, p. 44.

40. Another example of Church's approach to Indian diplomacy which contrasts sharply with the line taken by Mather and Hubbard.

41. Philip escaped from Pocasset Swamp on July 29, and was attacked at Nipsachuck by the pursuing forces under Captain Henchman (Edmunds's "Superiour Officer") on July 31, 1675. Henchman was the builder of the useless fort earlier condemned by Church, who sees himself as sharing Edmunds' plight of subordination to incompetent and interfering commanders. Henchman was a supporter of the Reverend John Eliot, and a moderate on questions of Indian policy.

42. The Narragansett crisis developed in several stages: early fears of their hostility were allayed by a military-diplomatic expedition in July 1675. In September the sachems were again called to a conference at Wickford, R.I., and in October—suspicions of their intentions rising again—they were compelled to sign another treaty at Boston. The colonists apparently placed no faith in this arrangement since they began preparations for an attack on the Narragansetts almost immediately after the treaty was signed.

43. Josiah Winslow, governor of Plymouth and a close friend of Church.

44. Reformado means a volunteer officer serving while his own company is disbanded or inactivated for reforming and recruiting; as such he has no authority to command specific troops, but serves as a kind of irregular staff officer.

45. December 11, 1675.

46. Ca. December 12, 1675.

47. The army marched on December 18, 1675, discovered the In-

dians and fought the Swamp Fight on the 19th, and returned to base on the 20th.

48. Beckoned.

49. Cartridges.

50. In fact, the army's lack of provisions would immobilize it for two months and cause its disbandment after the futile "hungry march" of February 1675.

51. Captain Samuel Moseley, a veteran Indian-fighter like Church, but also a rabid Indian-hater noted for his hostility to and ill-treatment of Praying Indians. *HMD*, p. 58; Leach, *Flintlock and Tomahawk*, pp. 148, 150, 153, 162.

52. Bustled.

53. Again Church suppresses the name of a person he censures. *HMD*, p. 58, suggests either Dr. John Clark or Dr. Matthew Fuller.

54. Tents means lint or cotton cylinders inserted in a wound to keep it open for drainage or probing; movement with tented wounds would be rather painful even if the wounds were superficial.

55. The "Hungry March," January 27–February 5, 1676.

56. At the time of the book's publication, Church was in retirement and under something of a cloud for executing French prisoners taken in Maine; he may be using this incident to establish his character as a man usually tender toward his prisoners.

57. Originally *netop* signified "friend" in the language of the New England Indians; whites came to use it as the equivalent of "mister" or "fellow." *HMD*, p. 64.

58. May 19, 1676.

59. Wachusett Mountain, near which the hostile Nipmucks gathered.

60. April 21, 1676. Church has reversed the chronological order of the two last-cited events and the one that follows.

61. Several meetings of the council are confused here, all of which took place *before* the Sudbury and Connecticut-Falls battles. Church's testimony and advice was probably given at the February 29 meeting, despite his assertion that he was informed at the meeting of Wadsworth's defeat (below). *HMD*, pp. 66–67.

62. This action is interesting for two reasons: it illustrates Church's confidence in his own judgment, since he is in effect moving his family closer to the active seat of the war (although to a far more defensible position), and it suggests the depth of discouragement that the colonists had reached, since the Plymouth Council of War, fearing the abandonment of the frontier settlements by frightened settlers, passed a law requiring all potential refugees to obtain official permission before changing their residence. (February 29, 1676). The grant of permission to Church and the governor's remarks to him suggest Church's favored position with Winslow, and perhaps also constitute a kind of apology for what must have seemed, in context, a questionable act. *HMD*, p. 69.

63. March 12, 1676.

64. To his temporary residence at Almy's plantation, on Aquidneck Island.

65. Wilcox.

66. Drinking gourd.

67. Wetuset means Wachusett Mountain, Philip's base in the late summer and fall, 1675, and again in March-May, 1676. Occapechees means "strong drink," rum or whiskey.

68. Refers to Church's battle at the Almy's pease-field, July 8, 1675; he risks arousing their anger at their loss of men and of face, but reminds them of his courage and skill in defeating them with a few men.

69. Probably the chief referred to earlier as "Peter," son of Awashonks and the war leader of her people.

70. 1715–16. An epidemic in 1750 destroyed the remnants of Awashonks's people; by 1803 not more than ten were left, and by the Civil War not one. *HMD*, p. 85.

71. June 25, 1676.

72. June 28, 1676.

73. June 30, 1676.

74. July 6–7, 1676.

75. Governor Josiah Winslow and Treasurer Constant Southworth, Church's father-in-law.

76. This is not the first commission Church received after his return, but is a copy of the much larger commission issued ten days later which granted him larger powers.

77. *HMD*, p. 103, suggests July 10–11, 1676, as possible dates.

78. This is the larger commission of July 24, 1676, erroneously inserted above.

79. July 20–27, 1676, are approximate dates for this and the subsequent expedition.

80. Lightfoot, later styled "Captain," was Church's friend and accompanied him on his Canadian expedition of 1689.

81. If the Indians did less well than the English, Church suggests, their loyalty would have been suspect and English hopes of alliance thwarted; if they had done better, jealousy might have resulted. Given the state of colonial attitudes toward the Indians, there were very few ways for an Indian to do "right" and many ways of doing "wrong."

82. Probably July 27, 1676.

83. Church's insistence on fighting in the Indian manner ran against the views of the Puritan civil and religious establishment, which seems to have agreed with their historian, William Hubbard, that fighting like Indians was both tactically and morally reprehensible. Hubbard, *History of the Indian Wars,* 1:38. These techniques were later codified by Major Robert Rogers of the Rangers (1755–1764), by Thomas Hutchins (in an appendix to Provost William Smith's *Historical Account of the Expedition . . .* [1765]), and by James Smith in his autobiography (1799) and his *A Treatise, On the Mode and Manner of Indian War . . .* (1812). The debate

between the "scouts" and the "regulars," the guerrilla or commando concept and the conventional concept of infantry training and tactics, has been central to American military policymaking from the Indian-fighting era down to the day of the Green Berets.

84. July 30, 1676.

85. E.g., at the time afternoon services would have begun.

86. August 1, 1676.

87. August 2, 1676.

88. August 3, 1676.

89. E.g., lying in ambush along the trail, which Church is presumed to be following.

90. Triple.

91. August 4, 1676.

92. August 7, 1676.

93. August 11, 1676.

94. It was now early morning on August 12, 1676.

95. That is, to act as "beaters" might on a hunt, attacking one side of the camp to drive the "game" into Church's ambush on the other side.

96. A sling-pouch.

97. The punishment for treason included "quartering"; since Philip was officially considered a rebel or traitor, the punishment was deemed appropriate.

98. Actually August 12, 1676.

99. September 6 or 7, 1676. The dates of this expedition are "one of the most perplexing" problems in establishing the chronology of the war. *HMD,* p. 154, suggests that Church departed on the 6th or 7th, and captured Annawon on September 11. Dexter agrees with Hubbard that the capture of Tispaquin *preceded* that of Annawon.

100. More generally known as Massasoit.

101. "Who is that?"

102. I.e., five English and twenty Indians, something less than half Annawon's number.

103. "It is well," or "I am glad."

104. *Wompom (wampum),* plural *wompompeag* (occasionally called "*peak*" by the English). The name referred specifically to objects worked with white clamshell beads, but later came to refer to any beaded object, especially belts.

105. Mohawks. The red hair is probably that of an Englishman or Dutchman.

106. Afterward sent to the King by Governor Winslow, and later lost. *HMD,* p. 174.

107. "*Pouwau,*" *pauaw,* pow-wow: an Indian shaman, priest, or medicine-man.

108. Of the United Colonies.

109. This is entirely incorrect. Leverett died in March 1679. Either Church's memory is at fault or he wants to emphasize the point that officialdom has always rewarded him scantily for great services.

110. In the Old Style calendar, the month of January 1676 came *after* November and December, since the year began on March 25. The date of this expedition in New Style would be January 15, 1677.

# *BIBLIOGRAPHY*


Andrews, Charles M., ed. *Narratives of the Insurrections, 1675–1690.* Original Narratives of Early American History Series. New York: Barnes and Noble, 1943.

Barthes, Roland. *Mythologies.* Selected and translated by Annette Lavers. New York: Hill and Wang, 1972.

Bercovitch, Sacvan. *The Puritan Origins of the American Self.* New Haven: Yale University Press, 1975.

——, ed. *Typology and Early American Literature.* Amherst: University of Massachusetts Press, 1972.

Bradford, William. *Of Plymouth Plantation.* Edited by Samuel Eliot Morison. New York: Modern Library, 1967.

Breen, Timothy. *The Character of the Good Ruler: Puritan Political Ideas in New England, 1630–1730.* New York: W. W. Norton and Company, Inc., 1970.

Brown, Charles Brockden. *Edgar Huntly: Or, Memoirs of a Sleepwalker.* Edited by David Lee Brown. New York: Macmillan Company, 1928.

Burr, George Lincoln, ed. *Narratives of the Witchcraft Cases: 1648–1706.* Original Narratives of Early American History Series. New York: Barnes and Noble, 1968.

Carroll, Peter N. *Puritanism and the Wilderness: The Intellectual Significance of the New England Frontier, 1629–1700.* New York: Columbia University Press, 1969.

C[hurch], [Benjamin and] T[homas]. *Entertaining Passages Relating to Philip's War, Which Began in the Month of June, 1675: As Also of Expeditions More Lately Made Against the Common Enemy, and Indian Rebels, in the Eastern Parts of New-England; with Some Account of the Divine Providence Towards Benj. Church Esqr.* Boston: B. Green, 1716.

Church, [Benjamin and] Thomas. *The History of King Philip's War, Commonly Called the Great Indian War, of 1675 and 1676: Also of the French and Indian Wars at the Eastward, in 1689, 1690, 1692, and 1704. . . .* Edited and with an appendix by Samuel G. Drake. Exeter, N. H.: J. and B. Williams, 1829.

Church, Benjamin [and Thomas]. *The History of King Philip's War.* Edited, with an introduction by Henry Martyn Dexter. Reprinted from the Newport, 1772 edition. Boston: John Kimball Wiggin, 1865.

Cooper, James Fenimore. *The Wept of Wish-Ton-Wish.* Introduction by Richard Beale Davis. Facsimile of the revised edition, published as *The Borderers: or, The Wept of Wish-Ton-Wish (1833).* Columbus, Ohio: Charles E. Merrill Publishing Company, 1970.

Cotton, John. *The Powring Out of the Seven Vials: or an Exposition, of the 16. Chapter of the Revelation, with an Application of it to Our Times . . .* London: [?], 1642.

Eliot, John. A *Late and Further Manifestation of the Progress of the Gospel amongst the Indians in New-England. Declaring Their Constant Love and Zeal to the Truth: With a Readiness to Give Accompt of their Faith and Hope; as of Their Desires in Church to be Partakers of the Ordinances of Christ. Being a Narrative of the Examinations of the Indians, About Their Knowledge in Religion, by the Elders of the Churches.* Reprinted from the London, 1655 edition. Collections of the Massachusetts Historical Society, 3d series, 4 (1834): 261–87.

Eliot, John, and Mayhew, Thomas. *Tears of Repentance: Or, A Further Narrative of the Progress of the Gospel amongst the Indians in New-England: Setting Forth not Only Their Present State and Condition, but Sundry Confessions of Sin by Diverse of the Said Indians, Wrought Upon by the Saving Power of the Gospel; Together with the Manifestation of Their Faith and Hope in Jesus Christ, and the Work of Grace Upon Their Hearts.* Reprinted from the London, 1653 edition. Collections of the Massachusetts Historical Society, 3d series, 4 (1834): 197–260.

Geertz, Clifford. "Ideology as Cultural System," in David Apter, ed., *Ideology and Discontent.* New York: Free Press, 1964. Pp. 47–76.

Hall, David D., ed. *The Antinomian Controversy, 1636–1638: A Documentary History.* Middletown: Wesleyan University Press, 1968.

——. *The Faithful Shepherd: A History of the New England Ministry in the Seventeenth Century.* Chapel Hill: University of North Carolina Press, 1971.

Henry, Alexander. *Travels and Adventures in Canada and the Indian Territories Between the Years 1760 and 1776.* New York: I. Riley, 1809.

Hill, Christopher. *Antichrist in Seventeenth-Century England.* London: Oxford University Press, 1971.

Hollister, G. H. *Mount Hope; or, Philip, King of the Wampanoags: An Historical Romance.* New York: Harper and Brothers, 1851.

Hubbard, William. *The History of the Indian Wars in New-England from the First Settlement to the Termination of the War with King Philip in 1677.* Edited by Samuel G. Drake. 2 vols. Roxbury, Mass.: W. Elliot Woodward, 1815. Reprint of Hubbard, *A Narrative of the Troubles with the Indians in New-England . . . .* Boston: John Foster, 1677.

Hunt, George T. *Wars of the Iroquois: A Study of Intertribal Trade Relations.* Madison: University of Wisconsin Press, 1940.

——.*The Interpreter's Bible.* 12 vols. New York: Abingdon-Cokesbury Press, 1953.

[Irving, Washington]. *The Sketch-Book of Geoffrey Crayon, Gentn.* Author's revised edition. Philadelphia: David McKay, Publisher, 1895.

Jennings, Francis. *The Invasion of America: Indians, Colonialism, and the Cant of Conquest.* Chapel Hill: University of North Carolina Press, 1976.

Leach, Douglas Edward. *Flintlock and Tomahawk: New England in King Philip's War.* New York: Macmillan, 1958.

Leonard, Thomas. "Red, White and the Army Blue: Empathy and Anger in the American West," *American Quarterly* 26 (2) (May 1974): 176–191.

Lincoln, Charles Henry, ed. *Narratives of the Indian Wars: 1675–1699.* Original Narratives of Early American History Series. New York: Barnes and Noble, 1966.

Lockridge, Kenneth. *Literacy in Colonial New England: An Enquiry into the Social Context of Literacy in the Early Modern West.* New York: W. W. Norton and Company, 1974.

Maclear, J. F. "New England and the Fifth Monarchy: The Quest for the Millennium in Early American Literature," *William and Mary Quarterly* 32 (1966):223–60.

Malone, Patrick M. "Changing Military Technology among the Indians of Southern New England, 1600–1677." *American Quarterly* 25 (1) (March 1973): 48–63.

Mather, Cotton. *Magnalia Christi Americana: Or, The Ecclesiastical History of New-England, from its First Planting in the Year 1620, unto the Year of Our Lord, 1698.* 2 vols. Hartford: Silas Andrus, 1820.

——. *The Short History of New-England: A Recapitulation of Wonderful Passages which have Occurr'd, First in the Protections, and then in the Afflictions, of New-England; with a Representation of Certain Matters Calling for the Singular Attention of the Country; Made at Boston-lecture, in the Audience of the Great and General Assembly of the Province of Massachusetts-Bay, June 7, 1694.* Boston: Printed by B. Green for Samuel Phillips, 1694.

Mather, Increase. *A Brief History of the Warr with the Indians in New-England, (From June 24, 1675. when the First Englishman was Murdered by the Indians, to August 12, 1676. when Philip, alias Metacomet, the Principal Author and Beginner of the Warr, was Slain): Wherein the Grounds, Beginning, and Progress of the Warr, Is Summarily Expressed; Together with a Serious Exhortation to the Inhabitants of the Land.* Boston: John Foster, 1676.

——. *A Dissertation Concerning the Future Conversion of the Jewish Nation* . . . . London: R. Tookey for Nath. Hillier, 1709.

——. *An Earnest Exhortation to the Inhabitants of New-England: To Hearken to the Voice of God in his Late and Present Dispensations, as Ever They Desire to Scape Another Judgement, Seven Times Greater Then Any Thing Which Yet Hath Been.* Boston: John Foster, 1676.

——. *A Relation of the Troubles Which Have Hapned in New-England, by Reason of the Indians There, from the Year 1614 to the Year 1675: Wherein the Frequent Conspiracyes of the Indians to Cutt Off the English, and the Wonderfull Providence of God, in Disappointing Their Devices, Is Declared; Together with an Historical Discourse Concerning the Prevalency of Prayer: Shewing that New-Englands Late Deliverance from the Rage of the Heathen is an Eminent Answer to Prayer.* Boston: John Foster, 1677.

Melville, Herman. *Moby-Dick.* Edited by Harrison Hayford and Hershel Parker. Norton Critical Editions. New York: W. W. Norton and Co., 1967.

Miller, Perry. *Errand into the Wilderness.* New York: Harper and Row, 1964.

——. *The New England Mind: From Colony to Province.* Cambridge: Harvard University Press, 1953.

——. *The New England Mind: The Seventeenth Century.* Cambridge: Harvard University Press, 1954.

Miller, Perry, and Thomas H. Johnson, eds. *The Puritans.* Rev. Ed. 2 vols. New York: Harper and Row, 1963.

Mitchel, Jonathan. *Nehemiah on the Wall in Troublesome Times* . . . . Cambridge, Mass.: S. G[reen] and M. J[ohnson], 1671.

Morgan, Edmund S. *The Puritan Family: Religion and Domestic Rela-*

*tions in Seventeenth-Century New England.* Rev. ed. New York: Harper and Row, 1966.

Morison, Samuel Eliot. *Builders of the Bay Colony.* London: Oxford University Press, 1930.

Mott, Frank Luther. *Golden Multitudes: The Story of Best-Sellers in the United States.* New York: Macmillan, 1947.

[Mourt (or Morton), George, ed.]. *A Relation or Journall of the Beginning and Proceedings of the English Plantation Setled at Plimouth in New England . . .* London: John Bellamie, 1622.

Norton, John. *Three Choice and Profitable Sermons upon Severall Texts of Scripture. . . .* Cambridge, Mass.: S[amuel] G[reen] and M[armaduke] J[ohnson] for Hezekiah Usher, 1664.

Nowell, Samuel, *Abraham in Arms: Or, the First Religious General with His Army Engaging in a War for which He Had Wisely Prepared, and by which, Not Only an Eminent Victory was Obtained, but a Blessing Gained also; Delivered in an Artillery-Election-Sermon, June 3, 1678.* Boston: John Foster, 1678.

Palfry, John Gorham. *The History of New England.* 5 vols. Boston: Little, Brown and Co., 1858–92.

Pearce, Roy Harvey. "The Significances of the Captivity Narrative." *American Literature* 19 (1) (March 1949): 1–20.

Plumstead, A. W., ed. *The Wall and the Garden: Selected Massachusetts Election Sermons, 1670–1775.* Minneapolis: University of Minnesota Press, 1968.

Pope, Robert G. *The Half-Way Covenant: Church Membership in Puritan New England.* Princeton: Princeton University Press, 1969.

Rogers, Robert. *Journals of Major Robert Rogers: Reprinted from the Original Edition of 1765.* Edited by Howard H. Peckham. American Experience Series. New York: Corinth Books, 1961.

Rogin, Michael Paul. *Fathers and Children: Andrew Jackson and the Subjugation of the American Indian.* New York: Alfred A. Knopf, 1975.

Roosevelt, Theodore. *The Strenuous Life: The Works of Theodore Roosevelt.* Volume 12. New York: P. F. Collier and Son, 1900.

Rowlandson, Mary. *The Soveraignty and Goodness of God, Together with the Faithfulness of His Promises Displayed: Being a Narrative of the Captivity and Restauration of Mrs. Mary Rowlandson; Commended by Her, to All that Desires to Know the Lords Doings to, and Dealings with Her; Especially to her Dear Children and Relations . . . Written by Her Own Hand for Her Private Use, and Now Made Publick at the Earnest Desire of Some Friends, and for the Benefit of the Afflicted.* 2d ed., corrected and amended. Cambridge, Mass.: Samuel Green, 1682.

Sedgwick, Catherine Maria. *Hope Leslie: Or, Early Times in the Massachusetts.* New York: Harper and Brothers, 1842.

Shepard, Thomas. *The Sound Beleever. Or, a Treatise of Evangelicall Conversion. . . .* London: [?], 1645.

Silverman, Kenneth, ed. *Colonial American Poetry.* New York: Hafner, 1968.

Slotkin, Richard. *Regeneration through Violence: The Mythology of the American Frontier, 1600–1860.* Middletown: Wesleyan University Press, 1973.

Smith, James. *An Account of the Remarkable Occurences in the Life and Travels of Col. James Smith, During His Captivity with the Indians, in the Years 1755, '56, '57, '58, and '59: with an Appendix of Illustrative Notes.* Edited by William M. Darlington and Robert Clarke. Ohio Valley Historical Series, No. 5. Cincinnati: Robert Clarke and Company, 1870. A reprint of Smith's *Account of the Remarkable Occurrences* . . . (1799) and his *Treatise, on the Mode and Manner of Indian War* . . . (1812).

[Smith, William (Provost) ]. *Historical Account of Bouquet's Expedition Against the Ohio Indians, in 1764.* Edited by Francis Parkman. Ohio Valley Historical Series, No. 1. Cincinnati: Robert Clarke and Company, 1868.

Tashjian, Dickran and Ann. *Memorials for Children of Change: The Art of Early New England Stonecarving.* Middletown: Wesleyan University Press, 1974.

Tawney, Richard H. *Religion and the Rise of Capitalism: A Historical Study.* New York: Harcourt, Brace, and World, 1926.

[Tompson, Benjamin]. *New-Englands Crisis: Or a Brief Narrative, of New-Englands Lamentable Estate at Present, Compar'd with her Former (but Few) Years of Prosperity; Occasioned by Many Unheard-of Crueltyes Practised upon the Persons and Estates of its United Colonyes, without Respect of Sex, Age, or Quality of Persons, by the Barbarous Heathen Thereof; Poetically Described.* Boston: John Foster, 1676.

——. *New-Englands Tears for Her Present Miseries: Or, A Late and True Narration of the Calamities of New-England Since April Last Past, with an Account of the Battel between the English and Indians upon Seaconck Plain and of the Indians Burning and Destroying of Marlbury, Rehoboth, Chelmsford, Sudbury, and Providence; with the Death of Antononies the Grand Indian Sachem; and with an Elegy on the Death of John Winthrop Esq.; Late Governour of Connecticut, and a Fellow of the Royal Society.* Boston: John Foster, 1676.

Vaughan, Alden T. *The New England Frontier: Puritans and Indians, 1620–1675.* Boston: Little, Brown and Co., 1965.

Vuilleumier, Marion. *Indians on Olde Cape Cod.* Taunton, Mass.: W. W. Sullwold, Publishers, [1970].

Walker, Williston, ed. *The Creeds and Platforms of Congregationalism.* Boston: Pilgrim Press, 1960.

Walzer, Michael. *The Revolution of the Saints: A Study in the Origins of Radical Politics.* Cambridge: Harvard University Press, 1965.

Washburn, Willcomb L. *The Governor and the Rebel: A History of Bacon's Rebellion in Virginia.* Chapel Hill: University of North Carolina Press, 1957.

Watkins, Owen. *The Puritan Experience: Studies in Spiritual Autobiography.* [New York]: Schocken Books, 1972.

Weber, Max. *The Protestant Ethic and the Spirit of Capitalism.* Translated by Talcott Parsons. Foreword by R. H. Tawney. New York: Charles Scribner's Sons, 1948.

[Wharton, Edward]. *New-Englands Present Sufferings, Under Their Cruel Neighbouring Indians: Represented in Two Letters, Lately Written from Boston to London.* London: [B. Clark], 1675.

Wheeler, Thomas. *A Thankfull Remembrance of Gods Mercy to Several Persons at Quabaug or Brookfield: Partly in a Collection of Providences about Them, and Gracious Appearances for Them; and Partly in a Sermon Preached by Mr. Edward Bulkley, Pastor of the Church of Christ at Concord, upon a Day of Thanksgiving, Kept by Divers for Their Wonderfull Deliverance There.* Cambridge: Samuel Green, 1676.

White, Hayden. *Metahistory: The Historical Imagination in Nineteenth Century Europe.* Baltimore: Johns Hopkins University Press, 1973.

Ziff, Larzer. *The Career of John Cotton: Puritanism and the American Experience.* Princeton: Princeton University Press, 1962.

# INDEX